I0225045

Al-Kafi

Volume 2 of 8

English Translation

Al-Kafi

Volume 2 of 8
('Usul al-Kafi)

English Translation

Second Edition

Compiled by
Thiqatu al-Islam, Abu Ja'far Muhammad
ibn Ya'qub al-Kulayni

Translated by
Muhammad Sarwar

Published by
The Islamic Seminary Inc.
www.theislamicseminary.org

The Islamic Seminary Inc., New York
© 2015 by The Islamic Seminary Inc.
All rights reserved
Second Edition 2015
Printed in the United States of America.

ISBN: 978-0-9914308-8-8

Al-Kafi, Volume 2 of 8. English Translation – 2nd ed.
Rabi' al-Awwal 1436
January 2015

Terms of Use:

By using/reading this book, you agree to the following
conditions/stipulations which, upon being set, are obligatory
to abide by according to the Fatwas of all Maraj'i.

It is expressly forbidden to reproduce, copy, duplicate, scan
or photograph any part or parts of this book, for any reason
whatsoever, regardless if it is done on paper or electronically,
or any other form.

Furthermore, this book is copyright protected by the Islamic
Seminary Inc. under U.S. and International copyright laws, all
rights reserved.

These measures are an effort to preserve the translation from
being altered as has been the unfortunate case in past
publications.

Note to Readers

Dear respected readers, please note the following:

The English translation of this volume from Kitab al-Kafi is now, by the will of Allah, in your hands. It was only because of the beauty of the words of Ahl al-Bayt *'Alayhim al-Salam* that made it all possible. The magnitude of this project had become quite large and complex due to two language texts and it was sometimes difficult to handle.

All comments, suggestions and corrections will be very much appreciated. In fact it will be your participation in the good cause and rewarding in the sight of Allah, most Majestic, most Glorious. Please e-mail your comments, suggestions or corrections to: info@theislamicseminary.org.

With thanks,

The Islamic Seminary
www.theislamicseminary.org

Contents

Part One: The Book of Belief and Disbelief

Part Two: The Book of Prayers

Part Three: Book of the Excellence of the Holy Quran

Part Four: The Book of Social Manners

An Outline of the Number of Volumes, Sections and Sub-divisions of Kitab al-Kafi

Part 1 - Al-'Usul (Principles)

Volume 1

This part of the book consists of *Ahadith* on the principles of beliefs and it is called 'Usul (principles) in *al-Kafi.*

The sections or chapters in volume 1 are as follows:

1. The Book of Intelligence and Ignorance (*Kitab al-'Aql wa al-Jahl*)
2. The Book of the Excellence of Knowledge (*Kitabu Fad al-'Ilm*)
3. The Book on Oneness of Allah (*Kitab al-Tawhid*)
4. The Book about the people who possess Divine Authority (*Kitab al-Hujja*)

Volume 2

Sections or Chapters in Volume 2:

5. The Book on Belief and Disbelief (*Kitab al-'Iman wa al-Kufr*)
6. The Book on Prayers (*Kitab al-Du'a'*)
7. The Book on the Excellence of the Holy Quran (*Kitabu Fadl al-Quran*)
8. The Book of Social Discipline (*Kitab al-'Ishra*)

PART 2 - Al-*Furu'* (Branches)

Volumes 3-7

This part consists of *Ahadith* on Islamic practical laws such as:

The acts of worship (*'Ibadat*)

Business transactions (*mu'amalat*)

Judicial laws (*al-Qada'*)

Furu' al-Kafi (volume 3 – 7): The rules of conduct, the practical laws of the Islamic system, consists of the following:

9. The Book of Laws of Cleanliness (*Kitab al-Tahara*)
10. The Book of Laws of Menstruation (*Kitab al-Hayd*)
11. The Book of Laws about the dying people and their burials (*Kitab al-Jana'iz*)
12. The Book of Laws of Prayer (*Kitab al-Salat*)
13. The Book of Laws of Charities, Taxes (*Kitab al-Zakat*)
14. The Book of Laws of Fasting (*Kitab al-Siyam*)

PART 3 - Al-Rawdah (Garden of Flowers (Hadith))

Volume 8

This part consists of miscellaneous *Ahadith* of both the *'Usul* and *Furu'* of *al-Kafi*. The topics are not arranged and organized as in the other volumes. The chapters are not in alphabetical order of *Ahadith* or narrators.

This volume comprises about six hundred *Hadith* on various topics and is a treasure of knowledge of the matters of belief, spiritual discipline, interpretations of many verses of the Holy Quran, accounts of the noble manners of the Holy Prophet and infallible members of his family and information about the system of this and the next life.

In the Name of Allah, the Beneficient, the Merciful

Part One:
The Book of Belief and Disbelief

Chapter 1 (a) - The Clay from Which the Believers and Unbelievers Are Made

H 1438, Ch. 1a, h 1

Ali ibn Ibrahim has narrated from his father from Hammad ibn 'Isa from Rib'i ibn 'Abd Allah from a man from Ali ibn al-Husayn, *'Alayhi al-Salam*, who has said the following:

"Allah, the Majestic, the Glorious, created the prophets from the clay of 'Illiyiyyn (paradise), both their bodies and souls. He made the hearts of the believers from such clay and He made their bodies from a world lower than that world. He created the unbelievers, both their bodies and souls from the clay of Sijjin (fire). He thus mixed the two clays. For this reason children of unbelievers become believers and vice versa. For this reason the believers get afflicted with evil and unbelievers receive good things. Thus, the hearts of the believers incline to that from which they are created and the hearts of the unbelievers incline to that from which they are created."

H 1439, Ch. 1a, h 2

Muhammad ibn Yahya has narrated from Muhammad ibn al-Hassan from al-Nadr ibn Shu'ayb from 'Abd al-Ghaffar al-Jaziyy from abu 'Abd Allah, *'Alayhi al-Salam*, who has said the following:

"Allah, the Majestic, the Glorious, created the believers from the clay of paradise. He created the unbelievers from the clay of fire. He then said, 'When Allah, the Majestic, the Glorious, decides to grant good to one of His servants, He purifies his spirit and body. Whenever he hears any good thing he recognizes it. Whenever he hears any bad things he dislikes them.' I (the narrator) then heard him saying, 'The clays are of three kinds: (a) one is the clay of the prophets from which the believers are also created, except that the prophets are made of the superior kind of clay. The prophets are the roots and the believers are the branches and for this reason they are more excellent than the believers. The believers are created from a stickier kind of clay. Thus Allah, the Majestic, the Glorious will not keep them apart from their followers.' The Imam than said, 'The clay of those who insult ('A'immah) are from a black clay that smells foul. The weak ones are made from soil. The believers do not change their faith nor do evil doers (those who insult 'A'immah, *'Alayhim al-Salam*) do so and Allah has a definite goal behind it.'"

H 1440, Ch. 1a, h 3

Ali ibn Ibrahim has narrated from his father from ibn Mahbub from Salih ibn Sahl who has said that I asked abu abu 'Abd Allah, *'Alayhi al-Salam*, the following:

"May Allah keep my soul of service to you, from what kind of material has Allah, the Majestic, the Glorious, created the clay of the believers? He then replied, 'He has created them with the clay from which the prophets were made. Thus, they never become unclean.'"

H 1441, Ch. 1a, h 4

Muhammad ibn Yahya and others have narrated from Ahmad ibn Muhammad ibn Khalaf from abu Nahshal who has said that Muhammad ibn 'Isma'il narrated from abu Hamza al-Thumali who has the following:

"I heard abu Ja'far, *'Alayhi al-Salam*, saying, 'Allah, the Majestic, the Glorious, created us from the top most of paradise. He made the hearts of our followers from that which He had created us. He created their bodies from that which is below, thus, their hearts incline to us; they are made from what He had made us.' He then recited this verse of the Holy Quran. 'However, the records of the deeds of the virtuous ones will certainly be in Illiyin (83:18). Would that you had known what Illiyin is! (19). It is a comprehensively written Book (of records) (20). The ones nearest to Allah will bring it to the public (83:21).' He then said, 'Allah has created our enemies from Sijjin (the fire) and He has created the hearts of their followers from what He had created them. He created the bodies of their followers (followers of our enemies) from other matters. Thus, their hearts (the hearts of the followers of our enemies) incline to them (to our enemies) because they are created from what they (our enemies) are created.' Then he recited this verse of the Holy Quran: 'Let them know that the records of the sinners' deeds are in Sijin (83:7). Would that you had known what Sijin is! (8). It is a comprehensively written Book (of records) (9). Woe, on that day, to those who have rejected Allah's revelations (10) and those who have rejected the Day of Judgment (83:11).'"

H 1442, Ch. 1a, h 5

A number of our people have narrated from Sahl ibn Ziyad, who has narrated from more than one person from al-Husayn ibn al-Hassan. All of the above have narrated from Muhammad ibn 'Uwarma from Muhammad ibn Ali from 'Isma'il ibn Yasar from 'Uthman ibn Yusuf who has said that, reported to him 'Abd Allah ibn Kaysan, from abu 'Abd Allah, *'Alayhi al-Salam*, who has said the following:

"Once I said to the Imam, 'May Allah keep my soul in service for your cause, I am your servant, abu 'Abd Allah ibn Kaysan.' The Imam said, 'I know your genealogy. However, I do not know you (so well).' I said, 'I was born in the mountains and grew up in the land of Persia. I associate with people in business and other occasions. I, thus, associate with a man and find his appearance very good, to be of good manners and more trustworthy. When I investigate I find him to be one of your enemies. I also associate with another man who has bad manners, is less trustworthy and hot tempered. I then investigate and find him to be of your supporters and followers. Why is it so?'

"He (the Imam) said, 'O ibn Kaysan, Allah, the Majestic, the Glorious, took a clay from paradise and also from fire and then mixed them together. Then He separated this from that and that from this. The good appearances, good manners and trustworthiness that you find in them (our enemies) is because of the touch of the clay from paradise but they will return to that from which they are made. The deceitfulness, bad manners and hot-temperament that you find in them (our supporters and followers) is because of the touch of the clay from fire, however, they will return to that from which they were made.'"

H 1443, Ch. 1a, h 6

Muhammad ibn Yahya has narrated from Ahmad ibn Muhammad from Muhammad ibn Khalid from Salih ibn Sahl who has said the following:

"I asked abu 'Abd Allah, 'Are the believers made from the clay from which the prophets were made?' He said, 'Yes, that is correct.'"

H 1444, Ch. 1a, h 7

Ali ibn Muhammad has narrated from Salih ibn abu Hammad from al-Husayn ibn Yazid from al-Hassan ibn Ali ibn abu Hamza from Ibrahim from abu 'Abd Allah, *'Alayhi al-Salam*, who has said the following:

"When Allah, the Majestic, the Glorious, willed to create Adam He sent Jibril in the first hours of the Friday. He picked up with his right hand a handful. His hand had in its reach from the seventh heavens to the heaven above earth. From each of the heavens he picked up a handful. He also picked up another handful from the seventh earth of the above-most and to the farthest seventh earth. Allah, the Majestic, the Glorious, then commanded His word to hold the first handful in his right and the other in his left. The clay then was cleaved into two. It was scattered from earth and from the heavens and then said to the clay in his right hand, 'From you will be the messengers, the prophets, their successors, the truthful ones, the believers, those who will achieve salvation and those whom I will to have honors.' It then became necessary for them to be as He said them to be. He then said to that which was on his left, 'From you will be the tyrants, the polytheists, the unbelievers, the devils and those whom I will to humiliate and be of the wicked ones.' It then became necessary for them to become what He said them to become. Thereafter the two clays mixed together as Allah, the Majestic, the Glorious, has said, 'Allah makes the seed and the nuts to cleave apart.' (6:95) The seed is the clay of the believers upon which Allah has placed His love. The nuts are the clay of the unbelievers that are far from all good. It is called nuts (al-Nawa') because it is far away from all good and from Him. Allah, the Majestic, the Glorious, has said, 'He (Allah) brings forth the living from the dead and the dead from the living.' (6:95) The living are the believers who come out from the unbelievers and the dead who come out of the living are the unbelievers who are from the believers. The living are the believers and the dead are the unbelievers. This is because of the words of Allah, 'Are those whom We brought to life after their being dead . . .' (6:122) Their death was the mixing of their clay with the clay of the unbelievers and his coming to life was when Allah, the Majestic, the Glorious, caused separation between them through His word. In this way Allah, the Majestic, the Glorious, takes the believers at birth out to light from darkness after their entering therein and He takes the unbelievers out of the light to darkness after their entering into the light as it is said in the words of Allah, the Majestic the Glorious, 'So that he can give warning to those who are of the living and the word about the unbelievers truly come to pass.'" (36:70)

Chapter 1 (b) - The Clay from Which the Believers and Unbelievers Are Made (Additional)

H 1445, Ch. 1b, h 1

Abu Ali al-Ash'ari and Muhammad ibn Yahya have narrated from Muhammad ibn 'Isma'il from Ali ibn al-Hakam from Aban ibn 'Uthman from Zurara from abu Ja'far, 'Alayhi al-Salam, who has said the following:

"Had people known how the beginning of the creation was, no one would have disagreed with another person. Allah, the Majestic, the Glorious, before creating the creatures said, 'Be a sweet water so I create from you My paradise and people who obey My commands. Be very salty water; from you I create My fire and those who disobey Me.' He then commanded them to mix and from this the believers give birth to unbelievers and the unbelievers give birth to the believers. Then He took a clay from the surface of the earth and kneaded it very strongly whereby they (children of Adam) appeared as particles crawling about. He then said to the people of the right hand, 'To paradise (you go) in peace.' To the people of the left hand He said, 'To the fire (you go) and I am not concerned.' He then commanded a fire that began to blaze and He said to the people of the left hand, 'Enter therein.' They then were frightened thereby. He then said to the people of the right hand, 'Enter the fire.' They then entered therein and He said, 'O fire be cool and peaceful.' The fire became cool and peaceful. The people of the left hand then said, 'O Lord forgive us and reduce our burden.' The Lord said, 'I have reduced it for you. Enter.' They went but were afraid of it. It was there that obedience and disobedience came to take place. Thus, these will not be able to become of those and they will not be able to become of these.'"

H 1446, Ch. 1b, h 2

Ali ibn Ibrahim has narrated from his father from ibn abu 'Umayr from ibn 'Udhayna from Zurara who has said the following:

"Once a man asked abu Ja'far, 'Alayhi al-Salam, about the words of Allah, the Majestic the Glorious, 'When your Lord took from the back of the children of Adam their offspring and told them to bear testimony to the words of Allah, "Am I not your Lord," they all said, "Yes, You are our Lord. . . ."'" (7:172)

"He (the Imam), while his father, 'Alayhi al-Salam, was listening, said, 'My father narrated to me that Allah, the Majestic, the Glorious, took a handful of clay, from which He created Adam. He poured upon it sweet water from Euphrates and left it for forty mornings. Then He poured upon it very salty water and left it for forty mornings. When the clay fermented He then kneaded it strongly and they (children of Adam) appeared as particles from his right and left sides. He ordered all of them to enter the fire. The people of the right hand entered it and it became cool and peaceful for them but the people of the left hand refused to enter.'"

H 1447, Ch. 1b, h 3

Ali ibn Ibrahim has narrated from his father from Ahmad ibn Muhammad ibn abu Nasr from Aban ibn 'Uthman from Muhammad ibn Ali al-Halabi from abu 'Abd Allah, 'Alayhi al-Salam, who has said the following:

"When Allah, the Majestic, the Glorious, willed to create Adam He sent water on the clay. He then took a handful and kneaded it and then divided it in two parts with His hands then scattered them and they began to move. He then started a fire for them and commanded the people of the left hand to enter therein. They went near but were afraid of it and they did not enter therein. He then commanded the people of the right hand to enter in the fire. They went and entered into it and Allah, the Majestic, the Glorious, commanded the fire to become cool and peaceful for them. When the people of the left hand observed it they said, 'Our Lord, forgive us.' He forgave them and said to them, 'Enter into the fire.' They went but did not enter therein. He then changed them to clay and He created Adam therefrom. Abu 'Abd Allah, 'Alayhi al-Salam, then said, 'Those will never be able to become these and they will never be able to become of those.' He, 'Alayhi al-Salam, then said, 'They saw the Messenger of Allah, 'Alayhi al-Salam, to be the first to enter that fire. For this reason is the words of Allah, the Majestic, the Glorious, '(Muhammad), Say, "Had the Beneficent had a son then I would have been the first to worship."'" (43: 81)

Chapter 1 (c) - The Clay from Which the Believers and Unbelievers are Made (Additional)

H 1448, Ch. 1c, h 1
Muhammad ibn Yahya has narrated from Ahmad ibn Muhammad from Ali ibn al-Hakam from Dawud al-'Ijli from Zurara from Humran from abu Ja'far, 'Alayhi al-Salam, who has said the following:
"Abu Ja'far, 'Alayhi al-Salam, has said, 'As Allah, the Most Holy the Most High, created the creation, He created sweet water and a very salty water and then mixed the two together. Then He took a (kind of) clay from the surface of the earth and kneaded it intensely. He then said to the people of the right, as they crawled about like particles, "To paradise (you go) in peace." He then said to the people of the left hand, "To the fire (you go) and I am not concerned." Then He asked, "Am I not your Lord?" They all said, "Yes, You are our Lord we testify." Allah said, "I make you to witness this) so that on the Day of Judgment you will not say, 'We were unaware of this.'" (7:172)

'Then He made the prophets to form the covenant. He asked them, "Am I not your Lord and is not this Muhammad, My messenger and is not this Ali, the commander of the believers?" They said, "Yes, it is just as You said." This established their prophethood. He then made the 'Ulu al-'Azm messengers to testify and acknowledge this fact: "I am your Lord, Muhammad is My messenger, Ali is the commander of the believers and his successors, 'Alayhim al-Salam, after him are people who possess My Authority and are the reservoir of My knowledge. That al-Mahdi, 'Alayhi al-Salam, is one whom I will make to lend support to My religion. Through him I will establish My kingdom on earth and make My enemies to face justice for their crimes. Through him I will make them to worship Me willingly or otherwise." The prophets altogether said, "Yes, Lord we testify to these facts and bear witness." Adam did not refuse and did not affirm (verbally) the fact about al-Mahdi, 'Alayhi al-Salam, so he was not included in the group of five 'Ulu al-'Azm messengers of Allah. Adam did not have the resolve to affirm the facts about al-Mahdi, *'Alayhi al-Salam.* Allah, the Majestic, the Glorious, has said in the Holy Quran, "We had made a covenant with Adam before but he forgot all about it and we did not find in him a firm resolve." (20:115) He said that it was so but he ignored it. He then created a fire that blazed and told the people of the left hand to enter in the fire. They were afraid thereby. He said to the people of the right hand, "Enter in the fire." They entered in the fire and it was cool and peaceful to them. The people of the left hand then said, "Lord, forgive us and reduce our sins." The Lord said, "I have forgiven you but you must go in the fire." They were afraid. Thus, with this the obedience, authority and disobedience came to take place.'"

H 1449, Ch. 1c, h 2

Muhammad ibn Yahya has narrated from Ahmad ibn Muhammad and Ali ibn Ibrahim has narrated from his father from al-Hassan ibn Mahbub from Hisham ibn Salim from Habib al-Sajistani who has said the following:

"I heard abu Ja'far, *'Alayhi al-Salam,* saying, 'There was a time when Allah, the Majestic, the Glorious, took the descendents of Adam from his back to establish a covenant with them to testify that He is their Lord and to believe in the prophethood of all the prophets. The first among the prophets whose prophethood Allah wanted them to accept through a covenant was Muhammad ibn 'Abd Allah, *'Alayhi al-Salam.* Allah, the Majestic, the Glorious, then said to Adam, "Look (to find) what you can see."

'The Imam then said, "Adam then looked and saw his descendents appearing as small particles that filled the sky. Adam then said, 'Lord, how huge in number my descendents are! For what purpose have You created them and for what reason did You make them to establish a covenant with You?'" Allah, the Majestic, the Glorious, replied, "So that they worship Me and do not consider anything else as My equal and so that they believe in My messengers and follow them (for guidance)." Adam then asked, "Lord, why is it that I see certain ones of the particles are greater, others have a great deal of lights, yet others among them have very little light and still others among them have no lights at all?" Allah, the Majestic, the Glorious, replied, "Thus, I have created them to place them to test in every condition that they will live." Adam then asked, "My Lord, will You grant me permission to speak so I may express myself?" Allah, the Majestic the Glorious said, "Speak up; your spirit is from My spirit but your nature is different from My being." Adam then asked, "Lord, had You created them all just like each other, by the same measure, the same nature, of likewise design, of the same color, of equal life span, of equal amount of means of living they would not act against each other. No jealousy, animosity and differences would exist among them over anything." Allah, the Majestic, the Glorious, said, "O Adam, through My spirit you just spoke and due to the weakness of your nature you made an effort to give an opinion about that of which you have no knowledge. I Am the Creator of the world. I knowingly have created each one different from the others and through My Own way I will make My commands to take effect and they will continue existing through My plans and measures. There will be no changes in My creation. I have created the Jinn and human beings only to worship Me. I have created

6

paradise for those who obey and worship Me and follow My messengers. I have no regrets in what I have done. I have created the fire for those who disbelieve, disobey Me and do not follow My messengers and I have no regrets in it. I have created you and your descendents not because I ever need you or your descendents in anyway or form. I have created you and created them to test you and test them to see which ones among you do good deeds in the worldly life before your deaths. For this reason I have created the world and the life thereafter, life, death, obedience, disobedience, paradise and the fire. This is how I willed in My measure and plan. Through My all-pervasive knowledge in them I have placed differences in their forms, bodies, colors, lifespan, means of living, obedience and disobedience. I, thus, have made certain ones of them to be unfortunate or very fortunate. Certain ones among them will have eyesight or be blind, others among them will be of short size or tall ones, beautiful or otherwise, knowledgeable or ignorant, wealthy or poor, obedient or disobedient, of good health or suffering from illness, of defective bodies or free of bodily defects. In this way those of perfect bodies will look at the defective ones and thank Me for the perfect body that I have given them and those with defective bodies will look at the perfect ones and will pray to Me and ask Me to grant them good health and exercise patience when and in the way I test them. Thus, I will grant them good rewards. The wealthy ones after looking to the poor ones will thank Me and appreciate My favors. When the poor ones look to the wealthy ones they pray to Me and ask Me favors. It is as such so that the believers will look to the unbelievers and thank Me for the guidance that I have granted them. For such reasons I have created them. I test them in ease and in hardships and in good health that I grant them and in the matters with which I test them, in the matters of what I grant them and in the matters that I refuse them. I am Allah, the powerful King. It is all up to Me to allow all of My measures and plans to take form or change them as I wish to the time that I wish. I may change the sequel of the timing of my measures and plans and allow, that which comes first to come last and vice versa. I am Allah, and I execute whatever I will. I am not questioned for whatever I do but I question My creatures about their deeds."'"

H 1450, Ch. 1c, h 3

Muhammad ibn Yahya has narrated from Muhammad ibn al-Husayn from Muhammad ibn 'Isma'il from Salih ibn 'Aqaba from 'Abd Allah ibn Muhammad al-Ju'fi and 'Aqaba together from abu Ja'far, 'Alayhi al-Salam, who has said the following:

"Allah, the Majestic, the Glorious, created the creation. He created His most beloved ones from that which He loved most. What was most beloved to Him was the fact that he created His most beloved ones from the clay of paradise. He created those whom He hated most from that which he hated most. What was most hated to Him was the fact that he created from the clay of the fire and then sent them to the shadows. I asked him, 'What are the shadows?' He replied, 'Have you not seen your own shadow in a sunny day that looks like a thing but is nothing? Allah then raised from them the prophets who called them to believe in Allah, the Majestic, the Glorious, as mentioned in His, words, "When you ask them who has created them they will say, 'Allah." (31:25) He then called them to express their belief in the prophets. Some expressed their belief as such and others among them

7

did not do so. He then called them to express their (Wala') belief and support to us (Ahl al-Bayt). I swear by Allah, those whom He loved expressed their belief that we were the people who possess Divine Authority and only those whom He hated refused to express such beliefs as it is said in the following verse of the Holy Quran. "They do not express faith in what they before had refused to have faith in."' (7:101) Abu Ja'far, *'Alayhi al-Salam*, then said, 'Rejection (to have faith in us) was then.'"

Chapter 2 - The Messenger of Allah, *'Alayhi al-Salam*, Was the First to Respond to the Call of Allah, the Majestic, the Glorious, and Testify That He is the Lord

H 1451, Ch. 1c, h 1

Muhammad ibn Yahya has narrated from Ahmad ibn Muhammad from al-Hassan ibn Mahbub from Salih ibn Sahl fro abu 'Abd Allah, *'Alayhi al-Salam*, who has said the following:

"Certain persons of Quraysh asked, 'O messenger of Allah, by what means have you surpassed the prophets in excellence while you are the last and final one among them to come (with Divine message)?' He replied, 'I was the first among them to express my belief in my Lord and the first one to answer the call when Allah made a covenant with the prophets. He asked them to bear testimony against their ownselves that they have answered, affirmatively to Allah's Question, "Am I not your Lord?" I was the first among the prophets to say, "Yes, O Lord, You are the Lord." By expressing and affirming my belief in Allah, the Majestic, the Glorious, as the first one I surpassed them in excellence.'"

H 1452, Ch. 1c, h 2

Ahmad ibn Muhammad has narrated from Muhammad ibn Khalid from certain persons of our people from 'Abd Allah ibn Sinan who has said the following:

"Once I said to abu 'Abd Allah, *'Alayhi al-Salam*, 'May Allah keep my soul in service for your cause, I find certain persons of our people who seem light-minded and very temperamental and this extremely saddens me. On the other hand I find certain persons of those who do not accept our belief seem to (have very good Simt) be very dignified.' The Imam said, 'Do not call it Simt because Simt means straight path. Call it Dignified appearance because Allah, the Majestic, the Glorious, has said, "They have marks of the effects of frequent prostration on their faces,"' (48:29). I (the narrator) then said, 'I see them to be of good appearance and of dignity and this makes me very sad.' The Imam said, 'Do not feel sad for what you see of light-mindedness and temperamental conditions of your people and the good appearance of those who do not accept your belief. When Allah, the Most Holy, the Most High, willed to create Adam, He created those two kinds of clay. He then divided them into two portions. To the people of the right hand He said, "Be a creature by My permission." They became creatures that looked like small particles running around. He then said to the people of the left hand, "Be a creature by My permission." They became a creature as small particles that crawled. He then started a fire for them and said to them, "Enter therein by My permission." The first one who entered therein was Muhammad, *'Alayhi al-Salam*, followed by the 'Ulu al-'Azm messengers, their successors and their followers. He then said to the people of the left hand, "Enter therein by My permission." They said, "Our Lord, have you created us just to burn?" They disobeyed. He then said to the people of the right hand, "Come out from the fire by My permission" and the fire had caused no injuries to any of them and had left no marks on any one of them. When the people of the left hand saw this they said, "Our Lord, we see our people have come out safe and sound from the fire. Lord, forgive us and command us to enter the fire." The Lord said, "I Have forgiven you, now you must enter the fire." They went near the fire but when they felt the heat of the fire they turned back and said, "Our Lord, we are not able to endure the fire burning us and they disobeyed." He commanded those ones three times to enter into the fire but every time they disobeyed and turned back. He commanded the others three times, each time they obeyed and came out of the fire. He then said to them, "Be a clay by My permission." He then created Adam therefrom.' The Imam then said, 'Whoever is of those will never become of these (people of the right hand) and whoever is from these will never become of those ones (people of the left hand). When you find your people as light-minded ones and it causes sadness to you it is because of their mix with people of the left hand. The good appearance and dignity that you find in those who do not accept your belief is because of their mix with the people of the right hand.'"

H 1453, Ch. 1c, h 3
Muhammad ibn Yahya has narrated from Muhammad ibn al-Husayn from Ali ibn 'Isma'il from Muhammad ibn 'Isma'il from Sa'dan ibn Muslim from Salih ibn Sahl from abu 'Abd Allah, *'Alayhi al-Salam*, who has said the following:
"The messenger of Allah was asked, 'By what means have you surpassed other descendents of Adam?' He said, 'I was the first one to affirm my faith in my Lord. Allah established a covenant with the prophets and made them to bear testimony against their own souls when the Lord asked, "Am I not your Lord." They all said, "Yes, You are the Lord." I was the first one to answer that question positively.'"

Chapter 3 - How They Answered While They Were as Small Particles

H 1454, Ch. 3, h 1
Ali ibn Ibrahim has narrated from his father from ibn abu 'Umayr from certain persons of our people from abu Basir who has said the following:
"Once I asked abu 'Abd Allah, *'Alayhi al-Salam*, 'How did they answer when they (offspring of Adam) were small particles?' The Imam said, 'Allah placed in them the ability to answer Him when He questioned them at the time of establishing a covenant with them.'"

Chapter 4 - Creation of the Creatures with Belief in Oneness of Allah in Their Nature

H 1455, Ch. 4, h 1
Ali ibn Ibrahim has narrated from his father from ibn abu 'Umayr from Hisham ibn Salim from abu 'Abd Allah, *'Alayhi al-Salam*, who has said the following:

"I asked (the Imam) about the words of Allah, '. . . the invention of Allah (had a certain) nature with which He created all people. . . .' (30:30) The Imam, *'Alayhi al-Salam*, said, 'It (invention, Fitrat) refers to belief in Oneness of Allah (belief in Allah only is placed in their nature).'"

H 1456, Ch. 4, h 2

Ali ibn Ibrahim has narrated from his father from Muhammad ibn 'Isa from Yunus from 'Abd Allah ibn Sinan from abu 'Abd Allah, *'Alayhi al-Salam*, who has said the following:

"I asked him about the words of Allah, the Majestic, the Glorious, 'The invention of Allah (had a certain) nature with which He created all people. . . .' (30:30) What is that creation (and nature)? The Imam said, 'It is al-Islam. Allah created them with such nature at the time He made a covenant with them to believe in Oneness of Allah as He asked them all, "Am I not your Lord?" when all the believers and the unbelievers were there.'"

H 1457, Ch. 4, h 3

Muhammad ibn Yahya has narrated from Ahmad ibn Muhammad from ibn Mahbub from Ali ibn Ri'ab from Zurara who has said the following:

"Once I asked abu 'Abd Allah, *'Alayhi al-Salam*, about the words of Allah, the Majestic, the Glorious, '. . . the creation (and invention) of Allah (had a certain) nature with which He created all people. . . .' (30:30) The Imam said, 'He created them and placed belief in Oneness of Allah in the nature of every one of them.'"

H 1458, Ch. 4, h 4

Ali ibn Ibrahim has narrated from his father from ibn abu 'Umayr from 'Udhayna from Zurara from abu Ja'far, *'Alayhi al-Salam*, who has said the following:

"I asked him, *'Alayhi al-Salam*, about the words of Allah, the Majestic, the Glorious, 'They are humble before Allah and they do not consider anything as partners of Allah.' The Imam said, 'Humbleness comes from the nature with which Allah has created all people and there is no change in the creation of Allah.' The Imam also said, 'He created them with the ability to know Him.' Zurara has said, 'I then asked him about the words of Allah, the Majestic, the Glorious: "(Consider), when your Lord took from the backs of the children of Adam all of their offspring. He asked them to bear a testimony. (Testimony to the fact that) when He asked them all, 'Am I not your Lord?' They all said, 'Yes, You are our Lord.'" (7:172) The Imam said, "This happened when Allah took all descendents of Adam - who were to be born to the Day of Judgment - out from his back. They all came out in the form of small particles. He then introduced and showed Himself to them. Had this not happened no one could know his Lord." The Imam said, "The Messenger of Allah has said, 'Every newborn is born with the nature (to believe in Allah).' It means (He created them) with knowledge that Allah, the Majestic, the Glorious, is his/her Creator and so is His words, 'When you ask them, "Who has created the heavens and the earth?" They will certainly say, 'Allah has created them.'""" (31:25)

Ali ibn Ibrahim has narrated from his father from ibn Faddal from abu Jamila from Muhammad al-Halabi from abu 'Abd Allah, *'Alayhi al-Salam*, who has said the following:

"About the words of Allah, the Majestic, the Glorious, '. . . the creation of Allah (had a certain) nature with which He created all people. . . .' (30:30), the Imam said, 'He has created them with belief in Oneness of Allah in their nature.'"

Chapter 5 - Believers as Offspring of Unbelievers

H 1459, Ch. 5, h 1

Al-Husayn ibn Muhammad has narrated from Mu'alla ibn Muhammad from al-Hassan ibn Ali al-Washsha' from Ali ibn Maysara who has said the following:

"Abu 'Abd Allah, *'Alayhi al-Salam*, has said, 'The seed for a believer may exist in the back of a pagan and no evil affects it until it is transferred into the womb of a pagan woman wherein no evil affects it also. It is not affected even after birth and up to the time the person is considered responsible for his/her deeds.'"

H 1460, Ch. 5, h 2

Ali ibn Ibrahim has narrated from his father from ibn abu 'Umayr from Ali ibn Yaqtin from abu al-Hassan Musa, *'Alayhi al-Salam*, who has said the following:

"Once I said to the Imam, 'I am afraid of the prayer of abu 'Abd Allah, *'Alayhi al-Salam*, against Yaqtin and his offspring.' The Imam said, 'O abu al-Hassan, it is not as you think. A believer in the back of an unbeliever is like a small piece of stone in a brick. Rain can wash away the brick but it never harms the solid piece of stone.'"

Chapter 6 - When Allah, the Majestic, the Glorious, Wills to Create a Believer (In certain manuscripts it says, "The Way Allah Creates the Believer")

H 1461, Ch. 6, h 1

Muhammad ibn Yahya has narrated from Ahmad ibn Muhammad from ibn Faddal from Ibrahim ibn Muslim al-Hulwani from abu Isma'il al-Sayqal al-Razi from abu 'Abd Allah, *'Alayhi al-Salam*, who has said the following:

"In paradise there is a tree called al-Muzn. When Allah wants to create a believer He makes a drop to drip from it. It then falls on vegetable or fruit that either a believer or unbeliever then consumes for food but Allah, the Most Majestic, the Most Glorious, brings out a believer from his back."

Chapter 7 - The Coloring (Referred to in the Holy Quran) is Islam

H 1462, Ch. 7, h 1

Ali ibn Ibrahim has narrated from his father and Muhammad ibn Yahya from Ahmad ibn Muhammad all from ibn Mahbub from 'Abd Allah ibn Sinan from abu 'Abd Allah, *'Alayhi al-Salam*, who has said the following:

"About the words of Allah, the Majestic, the Glorious, '. . . It is the coloring of Allah. Who has a better color than Allah's color?' (2:138), abu 'Abd Allah, *'Alayhi al-Salam*, said, 'Color is a reference to this belief.' The Imam also said, 'It (color) stands for al-Islam.' In the words of Allah, the Majestic, the Glorious, '. . . He has established a firm hold onto the strong ring'. . . (2:256), he said, 'It (the strong ring) is a reference to the faith and belief in Allah, Who is One and has no partners.'"

H 1463, Ch. 7, h 2

A number of our people have narrated from Sahl ibn Ziyad from Ahmad ibn Muhammad ibn abu Nasr from Dawud ibn Sarhan from 'Abd Allah ibn Farqad from Humran from abu 'Abd Allah, *'Alayhi al-Salam*, who has said the following:

"About the words of Allah, the Majestic, the Glorious: '. . . it is the coloring of Allah. Who has a better color than Allah's color?' (2:138), the Imam said, 'It stands for al-Islam, the religion.'"

H 1464, Ch. 7, h 3

Hamid ibn Ziyad has narrated from al-Hassan ibn Muhammad ibn Sama'a from more than one persons from Aban from Muhammad ibn Muslim from one of them, *'Alayhi al-Salam*, who has said the following:

"About the words of Allah, the Majestic, the Glorious, '. . . it is the coloring of Allah. Who has a better color than Allah's color?' (2:138), the Imam said, 'Color stands for al-Islam, the religion.' He, about the words of Allah, the Majestic, the Glorious, also said, 'Whoever then rejects the Devil and establishes belief in Allah he, thus, has established his grasp securely with the strong ring,' it (strong ring) means belief.'"

Chapter 8 - Serenity is Belief

H 1465, Ch. 8, h 1

Muhammad ibn Yahya has narrated from Ahmad ibn Muhammad ibn 'Isa from Ali ibn al-Hakam from abu Hamza from abu Ja'far, *'Alayhi al-Salam*, who has said the following:

"Once I asked abu Ja'far, *'Alayhi al-Salam*, about the words of Allah, the Majestic, the Glorious, 'He sent down serenity into the hearts of the believers. . . .' (48:4) The Imam said, 'It (serenity) is belief.' I (the narrator) then asked him about the words of Allah, the Majestic, the Glorious, 'He supported them with a spirit from Him. . . .' (58:22) The Imam said, 'It (spirit) is belief.'"

H 1466, Ch. 8, h 2

It is narrated from the above narrator from Ahmad from Safwan from Aban from Fudayl who has said the following:

"I asked abu 'Abd Allah, *'Alayhi al-Salam*, about the words of Allah, 'These are those into whose hearts belief is written. . . .' (58:22), do they have any say in what is written into their hearts? The Imam said, 'No, they do not have any say in it.'"

H 1467, Ch. 8, h 3

A number of our people have narrated from Ahmad ibn Muhammad ibn Khalid from ibn Mahbub from al-'Ala' from Muhammad ibn Muslim from abu Ja'far, *'Alayhi al-Salam*, who has said the following:

"Abu Ja'far, *'Alayhi al-Salam*, has said, 'Serenity (al-Sakinah) is belief."

H 1468, Ch. 8, h 4

Ali ibn Ibrahim has narrated from his father from ibn abu 'Umayr from Hafs ibn al-Bakhtari and Hisham ibn Salim and people other than the two from abu 'Abd Allah, *'Alayhi al-Salam*, who has said the following:

"About the words of Allah, the Majestic, the Glorious, 'It is He who has sent serenity (al-Sakinah) into the hearts of the believers,' (48:4) the Imam said, 'It (serenity) is belief.'"

H 1469, Ch. 8, h 5

Ali ibn Ibrahim has narrated from Muhammad ibn 'Isa ibn 'Ubayd from Yunus from Jamil who has said the following:

"Once I asked abu 'Abd Allah, *'Alayhi al-Salam*, about the words of Allah, the Majestic, the Glorious, 'It is He who has sent serenity (al-Sakinah) into the hearts of the believers.' (48:4) The Imam said, 'It (serenity) is belief.' I then asked about, ' . . . and supported them with a spirit from Him. . . .' (58:22) The Imam said, 'It (spirit) is belief.' I asked him about the words of Allah, 'He made them to accompany piousness. . . .' (48:26) The Imam said, 'It (piousness) is belief.'"

Chapter 9 - Purely Sincere

H 1470, Ch. 9, h 1

Ali ibn Ibrahim has narrated from Muhammad ibn 'Isa from Yunus from 'Abd Allah ibn Maskan from abu 'Abd Allah, *'Alayhi al-Salam*, who has said the following:

"About the words of Allah, the Majestic, the Glorious, '. . . humble and submitted.' (3:67), the Imam said, 'It (humble and submitted) is one purely sincere who has not worshipped any idols.'"

H 1471, Ch. 9, h 2

A number of our people have narrated from Ahmad ibn abu 'Abd Allah from his father in a Marfu' manner from abu Ja'far, *'Alayhi al-Salam*, who has said the following:

"The Messenger of Allah, *'Alayhi al-Salam*, has said, 'O people, what there is, is Allah and Satan, Truth and falsehood, guidance and straying, wisdom and error, present and future, the consequences, the good deeds and evil deeds. Good deeds are for Allah and evil deeds are for Satan, may Allah condemn him.'"

H 1472, Ch. 9, h 3

A number of our people have narrated from Sahl ibn Ziyad from Ali ibn Asbat from abu al-Hassan al-Rada, *'Alayhi al-Salam*, who has said the following:

"Amir al Mu'minin, *'Alayhi al-Salam*, has said, 'Paradise is for those who maintain sincerity in worshipping Allah and in prayer to Him. Whatever they see does not occupy their heart. Whatever they hear does not make them forget to speak of Allah and they do not feel depressed because of what is given to others.'"

H 1473, Ch. 9, h 4

Ali ibn Ibrahim has narrated from his father from al-Qasim ibn Muhammad from al-Minqari from Sufyan ibn 'Uyayna from abu 'Abd Allah, *'Alayhi al-Salam*, who has said the following:

"About the words of Allah, the Most Majestic, the Most Holy, 'So that He may try you to see who among you is best in good deeds. . . .' (67:2), the Imam said, 'He has not meant thereby the quantity of deeds. He thereby has meant the most correct ones in deeds. Correctness comes only from overwhelming respect for

13

Allah, true intention and goodness.' He then said, 'It comes from continuity of the good deeds. In fact, maintaining continuity until deeds reach purity is more difficult than performing the deed itself. It is the intention that forms the deed.' The Imam then recited the words of Allah, the Most Majestic, the Most Holy, 'Say (O Muhammad), "Everyone acts according to his way," (17:84) it (way) means according to his intentions.'"

H 1474, Ch. 9, h 5
It is reported through the same chain of narrators that he said:
"Once I asked abu 'Abd Allah, *'Alayhi al-Salam*, about the words of Allah, the Most Majestic, the Most Holy, 'Except those who would come to Allah with safe and protected hearts. . . .' (26:89) The Imam said, 'A safe and protected heart is such a heart that goes in the presence of his Lord while there is nothing in it besides his Lord. He then said that every heart in which there is polytheism or doubt, such a heart is a failing heart. They (pious people) have chosen to restrict themselves from worldly matters so that their hearts are reserved for the matters of the life hereafter only.'"

H 1475, Ch. 9, h 6
It is reported through the same chain of narrators from Sufyan ibn 'Uyayna from al-Sindy from abu Ja'far, *'Alayhi al-Salam*, who has said the following:
"Abu Ja'far, *'Alayhi al-Salam*, has said, 'If a servant maintains pure belief in Allah, the Most Majestic, the Most Holy, for forty days, Allah, the Most Majestic, the Most Holy, purifies his heart in this world and shows him his illnesses and the cure for them (illnesses).' Also he, *'Alayhi al-Salam*, said, 'Whenever a servant of Allah speaks of Him in a beautiful way for forty days Allah, the Most Majestic, the Most Holy, purifies his heart in this world and shows him his illnesses and the cure for such illnesses. He then establishes wisdom in his heart and will make his tongue to speak wisdom.' The Imam then recited this verse of the Holy Quran, 'Those who took the calf as their Lord will face anger and humiliation from their Lord in the worldly life and thus, We recompense those who forge lies.' (7:157)

"The Imam said, 'You should note that all those who forge lies are but despicable persons. So also is one who forges lies against Allah, the Most Majestic, the Most Holy, His messenger and his Ahl al-Bayt, *'Alayhim al-Salam*. Such person is nothing but a despicable one.'"

Chapter 9 (a) - On the Shari'a (System of Laws)

H 1476, Ch. 9a, h 1
Ali ibn Ibrahim has narrated from his father from Ahmad ibn Muhammad ibn abu Nasr. And a number of our people from Ahmad ibn Muhammad ibn Khalid from Ibrahim ibn Muhammad al-Thaqafi from Muhammad ibn Marwan all of them have narrated from Aban ibn 'Uthman from those whom he has mentioned from abu 'Abd Allah, *'Alayhi al-Salam*, who has said the following:
"Allah, the Most Blessed, the Most High, granted to Muhammad, *'Alayhi al-Salam*, the system of laws of Noah, Abraham, Moses and Jesus, peace be upon them. The laws consisted of belief in monotheism, purity of such belief, the negation of all associates of Allah and the culture, that it is free and clean of

14

idolatry, that it is easy to follow and that it does not allow total abandonment of the worldly life or total indulgence in it. He has made lawful in such a system of laws all that is good and clean and has made unlawful all that is filthy. Through such system He has removed all hardships and obstacles that were imposed on them (people). He then made it necessary for them, in such system of laws, to perform prayers, pay the charity (Zakat), complete the Fasting, and perform Hajj. And that they must fulfill their duty in the matters of virtue and vices (ask others to perform their duties and not to commit sins). And that they must follow the rules of lawful and unlawful matters, the rules of inheritance, penalties and compensations for losses and the obligations and the duty of Jihad (defending the faith) in the way of Allah. He has made Wuzu an additional obligation. He has granted him (the Holy Prophet), *'Alayhi al-Salam*, distinction through the following revelations: the first Chapter of the Holy Quran and the last verses of Chapter Two of the Holy Quran as well as the detailed Chapters from Chapter 47 to the end of the Holy Quran. He made lawful for Prophet Muhammad, *'Alayhi al-Salam*, the spoils of war and the land given to him without resistance. He supported him by giving him an awesome personality, made for him the earth to use in performing prostration before the Lord and to use it to clean himself. He was sent to all human beings, black and white, and to all Jinns. He granted him authority to receive taxes. He helped him to capture the pagans and then set them free on being ransomed. Then he imposed on him such duties that were not imposed on the prophets before. He sent down to him from heaven an unsheathed sword. He was told, 'Fight for the cause of Allah and do not hold anyone responsible besides your ownself.'" (4:84)

H 1477, Ch. 9a, h 2

A number of our people have narrated from Ahmad ibn Muhammad ibn Khalid from 'Uthman ibn 'Isa from Sama'a ibn Mahran who has reported the following:

"Once I asked abu 'Abd Allah, *'Alayhi al-Salam*, about the words of Allah, the Most Majestic, the Most Holy, 'Exercise patience as the messengers who possessed determination had exercised patience. . . . '(46:35) The Imam said, 'They were Noah, Abraham, Moses, Jesus and Muhammad, *'Alayhi al-Salam*.' I then asked, 'How did they become messengers who possessed great determination?' The Imam replied, 'It was because Noah had received a book from Allah and a system of laws and those who came after Noah, they followed his book and his system of laws until Abraham came with books and firm determination. He left the book of Noah aside but not out of rejection. Thereafter every prophet followed the system of laws of Abraham and his books (al-Suhuf) until Moses came with the Torah, his system of laws and with firm determination. He left the books (al-Suhuf) aside. Every prophet thereafter followed the Torah and the system of laws of Moses until Jesus came with the Gospel and firm determination. He left aside the system of laws of Moses. Every prophet thereafter followed the system of laws of Jesus until Prophet Muhammad, *'Alayhi al-Salam*, came. He brought the Holy Quran and his system of laws (the Shari'a). All that is lawful in his system of laws will remain lawful until the Day of Judgment and all that is unlawful in his system of laws will remain unlawful until the Day of

Judgment. This is how the messengers who possessed firm determination have been.'"

Chapter 10 - The Fundamentals of Islam

H 1478, Ch. 10, h 1

Al-Husayn ibn Muhammad al-Ash'ari narrated to me from Mu'alla ibn Muhammad al-Ziyadi from Hassan ibn Ali al-Washsha' who has said that narrated to us Aban ibn 'Uthman from Fudayl from abu Hamza from abu Ja'far, *'Alayhi al-Salam*, who has said the following:

"Abu Ja'far, *'Alayhi al-Salam*, has said, 'Islam is based on five principles. It is based on Prayer, Charity (al-Zakat), Fasting, Hajj and al-Wilayah (Divine Authority of 'A'immah). The call to none of the other principles has been so emphatic as it has been to al-Wilayah.'"

H 1479, Ch. 10, h 2

Ali ibn Ibrahim has narrated from Muhammad ibn 'Isa from Yunus ibn 'Abd al-Rahman from 'Ajlan ibn Salih who has said the following:

"I requested abu 'Abd Allah, *'Alayhi al-Salam*, 'Teach me, please, the principles of beliefs. The Imam said, 'They are: to testify and affirm that there is no one who deserves to be worshipped except Allah, to testify and affirm that Muhammad is the Messenger of Allah and to affirm that whatever he has taught is from Allah. (It is of the principles of beliefs) to affirm and accept that there is prayer five times every day. (It is of the principles of beliefs) to pay Zakat (charity), to fast in the month of Ramadan and to perform Hajj of the House (of Allah). (It is of the principles of beliefs) to love those who love us ('A'immah from the family of the Messenger of Allah), to disown our enemies and to become part of the group of the truthful ones. (All such issues are of principles and obligatory matters).'"

H 1480, Ch. 10, h 3

Abu Ali al-Ash'ari has narrated from al-Hassan ibn Ali al-Kufi from 'Abbas ibn 'Amir from Aban ibn 'Uthman from Fudayl ibn Yasar from abu Ja'far, *'Alayhi al-Salam*, who has said the following:

"Abu Ja'far, *'Alayhi al-Salam*, has said, 'Islam is based on five principles. They are: Prayer, al-Zakat (charity) fasting, Hajj and al-Wilayah. The call to none of the other principles has been so emphatic as it has been to al-Wilayah. People accepted the other four but they left aside this [al-Wilayah].'"

H 1481, Ch. 10, h 4

Muhammad ibn Yahya has narrated from Ahmad ibn Muhammad ibn 'Isa from al-Husayn ibn Sa'id from al-'Arzami from his father from abu 'Abd Allah, *'Alayhi al-Salam*, who has said the following:

"Abu 'Abd Allah, *'Alayhi al-Salam*, has said, 'The tripod of Islam consists of prayer, al-Zakat (charity) and al-Wilayah. No one of these can be considered correct without the other two."

H 1482, Ch. 10, h 5

Ali ibn Ibrahim has narrated from his father and 'Abd Allah ibn al-Salt all of them from Hammad ibn 'Isa from Hariz ibn 'Abd Allah from Zurara from abu Ja'far, *'Alayhi al-Salam*, who has said the following:

"Abu Ja'far, *'Alayhi al-Salam*, has said, 'Islam is based on five issues. It is based on prayer, charity (al-Zakat), Hajj, Fasting and al-Wilayah.' Zurara has said, 'I then asked the Imam, "Which of these is more important than the others?"' The Imam said, 'Al-Wilayah is more important. It is the key to the others. The person who possesses Divine Authority is the guide to the other principles.' I then asked, 'Which is the next important?' The Imam said, 'Thereafter is prayer. The Messenger of Allah has said, "Prayer is the pillar of your religion."' I then asked, 'Which is the next important among them?' The Imam said, 'Al-Zakat is the one thereafter. Allah has mentioned it next to prayer but He has mentioned prayer first. The Messenger of Allah has said, "Al-Zakat removes sins."' I then asked, 'Which one is important thereafter?' The Imam said, 'Hajj is important thereafter. Allah, the Most Majestic, the Most Holy, has said, "It is a duty of the people to Allah to perform Hajj of the House if they are capable to do so. Whoever rejects it should know that Allah does not need anyone in the world." (3:97) The messenger of Allah has said, "Performing Hajj that is accepted is more virtuous than twenty Rak'at optional prayer. Whoever walks around the House seven times and performs the two Rak'at prayers thereafter properly Allah will grant him cover." He (The Messenger of Allah) did say on the ninth of the month of Dil Hajj and on the tenth of the month of Dil Hajj in Muzdalifa (a place in Makka), what he wanted to say.' I then asked, 'Which one is important thereafter?' The Imam said, 'It is fasting.'

"I then asked, 'Why is fasting the last of all in importance?' The Imam said, 'The Messenger of Allah has said, "Fasting is a shield against the fire."' The narrator has said that the Imam said, 'The best of all things is that for which, if you miss, you do not find an alternative accept going back to achieve it. Prayer, al-Wilayah and Hajj are not of matters replaceable with their own kind. On the other hand if fasting is missed on a journey one has the choice to fast on other days as remedy, or compensate for the sin with expiation and no fasting is necessary as a remedy. In the cases of the other four issues there is no alternative for them.' The narrator has said that the Imam then said, 'The topmost, the peak of the issue, the key and the door to it and the pleasure of the Beneficent (Lord) is to obey the Imam properly after knowing him clearly. Allah, the Most Majestic, the Most Holy, says, "Whoever obeys the Messenger he has obeyed Allah and whoever turns away from such obedience then you should know that We have not sent you to guard them." (4:80)

'Without recognizing the Divine Authority of the Imam, the deputy of Allah, no one has the right to receive any reward from Allah, the Most Majestic, the Most Holy. This is true even though in his lifetime he may stand up in worship the whole night, fast during the day, give all his belongings in charity and perform Hajj every year. So also it is if he does not acknowledge the Divine Authority of his Imam with which all of one's deeds can take place with the guidance of the Imam. Wiothout al-Wilayah, one is not considered of the people of belief.' Thereafter the Imam said, 'Allah will admit, those of them who do good deeds into paradise through His extra mercy.'"

H 1483, Ch. 10, h 6

Muhammad ibn Yahya has narrated from Ahmad ibn Muhammad from Safwan ibn Yahya from 'Isa ibn al-Sariyy abu al-Yasa' who has said the following:

"Once I said to abu 'Abd Allah, *'Alayhi al-Salam*, 'Teach me, please, the basic principles of Islam that are necessary for everyone to know to his limits of understanding, and if he fails to learn them to the necessary levels his religion is destroyed and Allah does not accept his deeds. What is the limit of learning about the deeds with which someone's religion can take proper shape and Allah may accept his deeds? What are the limits and degrees of the permissible level of ignorance and lack of knowledge of certain aspects of these principles?'

"The Imam said, 'The matters necessary to learn are to testify that no one deserves to be worshipped except Allah, that Muhammad, *'Alayhi al-Salam*, is the Messenger of Allah, that whatever he has brought from Allah is the truth and to affirm that paying Zakat (charity) is a right. (Of such necessary matters is) to affirm al-Wilayah (Divine Authority of 'A'immah) that Allah, the Most Majestic, the Most Holy, has made obligatory upon the other people to obey and acknowledge the Divine Authority of certain members of the family of Prophet Muhammad, *'Alayhi al-Salam*.' I (the narrator) then asked the Imam, 'Is al-Wilayah of an exclusive nature?' The Imam said, 'Yes, Allah, the Most Majestic, the Most Holy, has said, "O believers, obey Allah, obey the Messenger and those among you who possess Divine Authority." (4:59) The Merssenger of Allah has said, "Whoever dies without knowing who the Imam of his time is, he is considered as a person dying in the time of ignorance (as an unbeliever)." There was the Messenger of Allah and there was Ali, *'Alayhi al-Salam*, but others said there was Mu'awiyah. Then there was al-Hassan, *'Alayhi al-Salam*, and then there was al-Husayn, *'Alayhi al-Salam*. Others said that there were Yazid ibn Mu'awiyah and Husayn ibn Ali. They were not equals and certainly they were not equals, meaning thereby Ali, al-Hassan and al-Husayn with Mu'awiyah and his son Yazid.' He has said that the Imam remained calm for a while and then said, 'Do you want me to tell you additional facts?' Hakam ibn al-'A'War said, 'Yes, may Allah keep my soul in service to your cause.' The Imam said, 'Then there was Ali ibn al-Husayn, *'Alayhi al-Salam*, then there was Muhammad ibn Ali, abu Ja'far. The Shi'a before abu Ja'far did not know the rules of Hajj, the lawful matters and the unlawful matters until there was abu Ja'far, *'Alayhi al-Salam*. He opened it (system of religion) for them and explained to them the rules of their Hajj, the lawful and unlawful matters. People began to realize that they needed him very much while before they would ask other people for what they needed. This is how the facts are. The earth does not remain without an Imam and one who dies without knowing, who his Imam is, he is as though he was of the people of the dark ages of ignorance. The time when you need al-Wilayah most urgently is the time when your soul reaches here (pointing to his throat) and the world is cut off from you and then you say, 'I have certainly been on the good side of the affairs, (a supporter of al-Wilayah).'"

Abu Ali al-Ash'ari has narrated from Muhammad ibn 'Abd al-Jabbar from Safwan from 'Isa ibn al-Sariyy abu al-Yasa' from abu 'Abd Allah, *'Alayhi al-Salam*, a similar Hadith.

H 1484, Ch. 10, h 7

A number of our people have narrated from Sahl ibn Ziyad from Ahmad ibn Muhammad ibn abu Nasr from Muthanna al-Hannat from 'Abd Allah 'Ajlan from abu Ja'far, *'Alayhi al-Salam*, who has said the following:

"Abu Ja'far, *'Alayhi al-Salam*, has said, 'Islam is based on five principles. They are al-Wilayah, (accepting the Divine Authority of 'A'immah), the prayer, al-Zakat (charity), fasting in the month of Ramadan and al-Hajj.'"

H 1485, Ch. 10, h 8

Ali ibn Ibrahim has narrated from Salih ibn al-Sindy from Ja'far ibn Bashir from Aban from Fudayl from abu Ja'far, *'Alayhi al-Salam*, who has said the following:

"Abu Ja'far, *'Alayhi al-Salam*, has said, 'Islam is based on five principles: The prayer, al-Zakat (charity), fasting, al-Hajj and al-Wilayah. The call to no one of the other principles has been so emphatic as it was for al-Wilayah on the day of al-Ghadir (name of a place between Makka and Madina.)'"

H 1486, Ch. 10, h 9

Ali ibn Ibrahim has narrated from Muhammad ibn 'Isa from Yunus from Hammad ibn 'Uthman from 'Isa al-Sariyy who has said the following:

"Once I asked abu 'Abd Allah, *'Alayhi al-Salam*, to teach me the principles of Islam in such a way that on holding to them my deeds can take pure and correct form and thereafter the ignorance of whatever I am ignorant of cannot harm me. The Imam said, 'Of the principles of Islam are to testify and acknowledge that no one deserves to be worshipped except Allah, and that Muhammad, *'Alayhi al-Salam*, is the Messenger of Allah. Of such principles is to affirm and acknowledge that whatever he has brought is from Allah, to pay al-Zakat (charity) is a right and that al-Wilayah which Allah, the Most Majestic, the Most Holy, has commanded to accept and acknowledge is al-Wilayah (Divine Authority) of Ahl al-Bayt of Muhammad, *'Alayhi al-Salam*. The Messenger of Allah has said, "Whoever dies while he does not know who his Imam is, he is considered as one who has died in the darkness of ignorance." Allah, the Most Majestic, the Most Holy, has said, "Obey Allah, obey the Messenger of Allah and the persons among you who possess Divine Authority." (4:59). Imam Ali was there (possessed Divine Authority) and after him were Imam Hassan, Imam Husayn and Ali ibn al-Husayn and after them was Muhammad ibn Ali, *'Alayhim al-Salam*, successively and thus it will continue. The land will not take an ideal shape without an Imam. Whoever dies while he does not know who his Imam is, he is considered as one who has died in the darkness of ignorance. What everyone of you will need very urgently when his soul will reach here (pointing to his chest) is to know him (the Imam) so that he can say it is certain that I have been holding to a genuinely good matter.'"

H 1487, Ch. 10, h 10

It is narrated from him (Ali ibn Ibrahim) from abu al-Jarud who has said the following:

"Once I asked abu Ja'far, *'Alayhi al-Salam*, 'Do you know, O child of the Messenger of Allah that I love you (Ahl al-Bayt), that I have disassociated myself from other people to associate with you only and that I support you (Ahl al-Bayt)?' The Imam said, 'Yes, I know it.' I then said, 'I ask you to answer my question; my eyes are restricted, I walk very little and I am not able to visit you except every now and then.' The Imam said, 'What is your question?' I then said, 'What is the religion by which you obey Allah, the Most Majestic, the Most Holy, and the religion that your Ahl al-Bayt follow so that I will also obey Allah, the Most Majestic, the Most Holy, by the rules of your religion?' The Imam said, 'Although your introduction was brief, your question is a great question. By Allah, I will certainly teach you my religion and the religion of my ancestors by the rules of which we worship Allah, the Most Majestic, the Most Holy. It is to testify that no one deserves to be worshipped except Allah, that Muhammad, *'Alayhi al-Salam*, is the Messenger of Allah, and that whatever (message) he has brought is from Allah. That it is obligatory to love and support those who support and love us (Ahl al-Bayt) and disassociate from our enemies. That it is obligatory to obey our commands, cherish the hope for the coming of the one from us who will rise with Divine Authority and to strive hard (Ijtihad) for progress in the matters of religion and live a life of piety, wara' (stay away from sins).'"

H 1488, Ch. 10, h 11

Ali ibn Ibrahim has narrated from Salih ibn al-Sindy from Ja'far ibn al-Bashir from Ali ibn abu Hamza from abu Basir who has said the following:

"Once I heard abu Basir asking abu 'Abd Allah, *'Alayhi al-Salam*, 'May Allah keep my soul in service for your cause, teach me the religion that Allah, the Most Majestic, the Most Holy, has made obligatory for people to follow. Teach me the religion of which they must not remain ignorant and besides which no other religion is accepted. What is this religion?' The Imam said, 'Repeat your question.' He repeated his question. The Imam said, 'It (such religion) is to testify that no one else deserves to be worshipped except Allah, that Muhammad, *'Alayhi al-Salam*, is the Messenger of Allah, and that it is obligatory to perform prayer, pay al-Zakat (charity), perform Hajj of the House if one has the ability and fast in the month of Ramadan.' Then he remained silent for a little while and said twice, "Al-Wilayah." He then said, 'This is what Allah has made obligatory upon His servants. The Lord on the Day of Judgment will not sk His servants why you have not done more than what I had made obligatory upon you. However, if someone does more good deeds Allah will grant him additional rewards. The Messenger of Allah has set up noble and beautiful traditions and it is very good for the people to practice them all.'"

H 1489, Ch. 10, h 12

Al-Husayn ibn Muhammad has narrated from Mu'alla ibn Muhammad from Muhammad ibn Jumhur from Fadalah ibn Ayyub from abu Zayd al-Hallal from 'Abd al-Hamid ibn abu al-'Ala' al-Azdi who has said the following:

"I heard abu 'Abd Allah, *'Alayhi al-Salam*, saying, 'Allah, the Most Majestic, the Most Holy, has made five things obligatory upon His creatures. He has given them permission in four but in one of them He has not given permission.'"

H 1490, Ch. 10, h 13

It is narrated from him (narrator of the Hadith above) from Mu'alla ibn Muhammad from al-Washsha' from Aban from Isma'il al-Ja'fi who has said the following:

"Once a man came to abu Ja'far, *'Alayhi al-Salam*. He had a book with him. Abu Ja'far said, 'This is the book of a polemicist who wants to learn a religion that if followed ones deeds are accepted.' The man said, 'May the blessings of Allah be with you, this is exactly what I want.' Abu Ja'far, *'Alayhi al-Salam*, said, 'Such religion is to testify that no one deserves to be worshipped except Allah, Who has no partners. That Muhammad, *'Alayhi al-Salam*, is His servant and Messenger. And that you affirm and acknowledge that whatever he has brought is from Allah. That one has love (in his heart) for us, Ahl al-Bayt, and disassociates himself from our enemies, obeys our commands, maintains piety and humbleness in life and has hope in the rise from us of one with the Divine Authority. For us there is a government and he will establish it when Allah wills.'"

H 1491, Ch. 10, h 14

Ali ibn Ibrahim has narrated from his father and abu Ali al-Ash'ari from Muhammad ibn 'Abd al-Jabbar all of them from Safwan from 'Amr ibn Harith who has said the following:

"Once I went to see abu 'Abd Allah, *'Alayhi al-Salam*, and he was in the house of his brother, 'Abd Allah ibn Muhammad, and I said, 'May Allah keep my soul in service for your cause, what has brought you to this house?' 'Seeking privacy,' said the Imam. I said, 'May Allah keep my soul in service for your cause, can I state before you my religion?' The Imam said, 'Yes, you may do so.' I then said, 'I follow a religion (that requires me) to obey Allah and testify that no one else deserves to be worshipped except Allah Who has no partners. That Muhammad, *'Alayhi al-Salam*, is His servant and messenger, that the Hour (of reckoning) will certainly come, that Allah will bring all people from their graves, that it is obligatory to pray, pay Zakat (charity), fast in the month of Ramadan and perform Hajj of the House. I affirm and acknowledge the Divine Authority of Ali ibn abu Talib after the Messenger of Allah, the Divine Authority of al-Hassan, al-Husayn, the Divine Authority of Ali ibn al-Husayn, the Divine Authority of Muhammad ibn Ali and your Divine Authority after him (your father), *'Alayhim al-Salam*. You are my Imam. With such beliefs I live and with them I will die and such is my religion before Allah.' The Imam said, 'Such, O 'Amr, I swear by Allah, is the religion of Allah and the religion of my ancestors and such is the religion that I follow to obey Allah in private and in public. Maintain piety before Allah and hold your tongue except from good and do not say, "I have guided myself." In fact, Allah has guided you. Give thanks to Allah, the Most Majestic, the Most Holy, for the favor that He has done to you. Do not be of those who on their moving forward are hit in the eyes or when moving backwards are hit from the back. Do not allow people ride on your shoulders for if you do so they cause injury to your shoulders.'"

H 1492, Ch. 10, h 15

Muhammad ibn Yahya has narrated from Ahmad ibn Muhammad from Ali ibn al-Ni'man from ibn Maskan from Sulayman ibn Khalid from abu Ja'far *'Alayhi al-Salam*, who has said the following:

"Do you want me to teach you the root of Islam, its branch and its peak? I said, 'Yes, may Allah take my soul in service for your cause.' The Imam said, 'Its root is prayer, its branch is al-Zakat (charity) and its peak is Jihad (the hard work in defense and preaching of the belief).' The Imam then said, 'If you want I can teach you about the gates to all good.' I said, 'Yes, please, May Allah keep my soul in service for your cause, do so.'

"The Imam said, 'Fasting is a shield against fire, charity removes sins and of the gates to good is to stand up (for worship) during the night to speak of Allah.' He then read (the words of Allah) 'They do not allow their sides to rest in bed (but they stand up at night to pray to Allah).'" (32:16)

Chapter 11 - Islam is to Spare Lives (and to Keep the Trust) but Reward Comes from Belief

H 1493, Ch. 11, h 1
Ali ibn Ibrahim has narrated from his father from ibn abu 'Umayr from al-Hakam ibn Ayman from al-Qasim al-Sayrafi associate of al-Mufaddal who has said the following:
"I heard abu 'Abd Allah, *'Alayhi al-Salam*, saying, 'Islam is to spare lives, protect the trust and make the marriage lawful, but reward comes from faith and belief.'"

H 1494, Ch. 11, h 2
Ali has narrated from his father from ibn abu 'Umayr from al-'Ala' from Muhammad ibn Muslim from one of them (the two Imams), *'Alayhi al-Salam*, who has said the following:
"Faith or belief is to affirm and act accordingly. Islam is just an affirmation."

H 1495, Ch. 11, h 3
Ali ibn Ibrahim has narrated from his father from Muhammad ibn 'Isa from Yunus from Jamil ibn Darraj who has said the following:
"I asked abu 'Abd Allah, *'Alayhi al-Salam*, about the words of Allah, the Most Majestic, the Most Holy, 'The Arabs have said, "We have established belief." Say, "You have not established belief but say, 'We have accepted Islam.' Belief has not yet entered your hearts."' (49:14) The Imam said, 'You must note that belief is something other than Islam'"

H 1496, Ch. 11, h 4
Muhammad ibn Yahya has narrated from Ahmad ibn Muhammad from Ali ibn al-Hakam from Sufyan ibn al-Simt who has said the following:
"Once a man asked abu 'Abd Allah, *'Alayhi al-Salam*, 'What is the difference between Islam and belief?' The Imam then did not answer. Again he asked and the Imam did not answer. They then met each other on the road while the man was about to leave. Abu 'Abd Allah, *'Alayhi al-Salam*, said, 'It seems as if you are about to leave.' He said, 'Yes, I am about to leave.' The Imam then said, 'Come home for a meeting.' He met the Imam and asked him about Islam and belief and about the difference between the two. The Imam said, 'Islam is what people have publicly accepted, such as that no one deserves to be worshipped except Allah, Who has no partners. That Muhammad, *'Alayhi al-Salam*, is His servant and His Messenger, that it is obligatory to perform prayer, pay al-Zakat (charity), to perform Hajj of the House and fast in the month of Ramadan. This is Islam.' The Imam (also) said, 'Belief is recognition of this issue (that the Imam

possesses Divine Authority). In such a condition, if one affirms the other principles of Islam but does not recognize this issue (that the Imam possesses Divine Authority) he is a Muslim but is lost.'"

H 1497, Ch. 11, h 5
Al-Husayn ibn Muhammad has narrated from Mu'alla ibn Muhammad and a number of our people from Ahmad ibn Muhammad all of them from al-Washsha' from Aban from abu Basir who has said the following:

"I heard Abu Ja'far, *'Alayhi al-Salam*, saying, 'The Arabs have said, "We have established belief." Say, "You have not established belief but say, 'We have accepted Islam.' Belief has not yet entered your hearts." (49:14) Whoever thinks that they (Arabs) had belief, his thoughts are false and whoever thinks that they had not accepted Islam, he has lied.'"

H 1498, Ch. 11, h 6
Ahmad ibn Muhammad has narrated from al-Husayn ibn Sa'id from Hakam ibn Ayman from Qasim associate of al-Mufaddal who has said that he heard abu 'Abd Allah, *'Alayhi al-Salam*, say the following:

"Abu 'Abd Allah, *'Alayhi al-Salam*, has said, 'Islam is to protect life, return the trust and make marriages lawful. Reward, however, comes from belief.'"

Chapter 12 - Belief is Inclusive of Islam but Islam is Not Inclusive of Belief

H 1499, Ch. 12, h 1
Muhammad ibn Yahya has narrated Ahmad ibn Muhammad from al-Hassan ibn Mahbub from Jamil ibn Salih from Sama'a who has said the following:

"I requested abu 'Abd Allah, *'Alayhi al-Salam*, 'Teach me about Islam and belief. Are they different?' He said, 'Belief is inclusive of Islam but Islam is not inclusive of belief.' I then asked, 'Please describe them to me.' He said, 'Islam is to testify that no one deserves to be worshipped except Allah and to affirm the truthfulness of the Messenger of Allah. With it lives are protected, marriages and inheritance become lawful and a group of people acknowledge this much. Belief is guidance and that which forms in the heart of the qualities of Islam and that which takes form from its practice. Belief is a degree higher than Islam. Belief is inclusive of Islam in appearance but Islam is not inclusive of belief esoterically even though they may both apply to words and in description.'"

H 1500, Ch. 12, h 2
Ali ibn Ibrahim has narrated from Muhammad ibn 'Isa from Yunus ibn 'Abd al-Rahman from Musa ibn Bakr from Fudayl ibn Yasar from abu 'Abd Allah, *'Alayhi al-Salam*, who has said the following:

"Belief is inclusive of Islam but Islam is not inclusive of belief."

H 1501, Ch. 12, h 3
Ali has narrated from his father from ibn abu 'Umayr from Jamil ibn Darraj from Fudayl ibn Yasar who has said the following:

"I heard abu 'Abd Allah, *'Alayhi al-Salam*, saying, 'Belief is inclusive of Islam but Islam is not inclusive of it. Belief is what sits in the heart and Islam is that which legalizes marriages and inheritance and protects lives. Belief is inclusive of Islam but Islam is not inclusive of belief.'"

H 1502, Ch. 12, h 4

A number of our people have narrated from Ahmad ibn Muhammad ibn Khalid from al-Hassan ibn Mahbub from abu al-Sabah al-Kinani who has said the following:

"I asked abu 'Abd Allah, *'Alayhi al-Salam,* 'Which is better, belief or Islam? Certain people say Islam is better than belief.' The Imam said, 'Belief is higher than Islam.' I then said, 'Help me understand it.' He said, 'What do you say if one commits, purposely, an act of heresy in Masjid al-Haram (Sacred Mosque)?' I said, 'He should be made to suffer severe pains.' The Imam responded, 'You said the right thing. What if one commits such a thing, purposely, inside the Ka'ba?' I said, 'He must be put to death.' The Imam responded, 'You said the right thing again. Do you note that Ka'ba is better than the Sacred Mosque? The Ka'ba is inclusive of the Mosque (in excellence) but the Mosque is not inclusive of the Ka'ba in this respect. In the same way belief is inclusive of Islam but Islam is not inclusive of belief.'"

H 1503, Ch. 12, h 5

A number of our people have narrated from Sahl ibn Ziyad and Muhammad ibn Yahya from Ahmad ibn Muhammad all of them from ibn Mahbub from Ali ibn Ri'ab from Humran ibn A'yun who has said the following:

"I heard from Abu Ja'far, *'Alayhi al-Salam,* saying, 'Belief is what settles down in the heart and takes it to Allah, the Most Majestic, the Most Holy. One's deeds testify to (its existence), (deeds) that come in the form of obedience to Allah and submission to His command. Islam is what appears through one's words or deeds and that is what a group of people of all the sects live by. Through Islam lives are protected, inheritance is settled thereby, marriages become lawful and they have the prayer, al-Zakat (charity), the fasting and al-Hajj in common. This takes them out of rejection of belief and they are ascribed to belief. Islam is not inclusive of belief while belief is inclusive of Islam, but words and deeds are common among them. Just as the case of Holy Ka'ba is in the Sacred Mosque but the Sacred Mosque is not in the Holy Ka'ba so is belief that is inclusive of Islam but Islam is not inclusive of belief. Allah, the Most Majestic, the Most Holy, has said, "The Arabs have said, 'We have established belief.' Say, "You have not established belief but say, 'We have accepted Islam.' Belief has not yet entered your hearts.'" (49:14) Therefore, the words of Allah, the Most Majestic, the Most Holy, are the most truthful ones.' I then said, 'Does a believer have any distinction over a Muslim in terms of excellence, rules and judicial matters and so forth?' He said, 'No, they both in this matter walk the same path. However, a believer has distinction over a Muslim in the form of deeds through which he seeks nearness to Allah, the Most Majestic, the Most Holy.' I said, 'Does Allah, the Most Majestic, the Most Holy, not say, "Whoever does a good deed for him the reward will be tenfold. . . ." (6:160) You just stated that they both accept the obligations of the prayer, al-Zakat (charity), the fasting and al-Hajj.' He (the Imam) said, 'Has Allah, the Most Majestic, the Most Holy, not said, ". . . He will add to his reward many additions." (2:245) Believers are the ones to whose good deeds Allah, the Most Majestic, the Most Holy, increases seventy times. Thus is the distinction of the believer. Allah increases to his (believer's) good deeds, proportionate to the degree of the correctness of his belief, many additions. Allah does good to the believer as He wishes.' I said, 'Is it not that whoever enters in Islam has entered belief?' He said, 'No, but he is ascribed to belief and has come out of rejection, and I will give you an example that will help understand the distinction of belief over Islam. Consider, if you see a person in the Sacred Mosque, do you testify that you have seen him in the Holy Ka'ba?' I said, 'No, that is not permissible for me.' He said, 'If you see a person in the Holy Ka'ba will you testify that he has entered the Sacred Mosque?' I said, 'Yes, I will do so.' He asked, 'Why do you do so?' I said, 'He cannot reach the Holy Ka'aba without entering first the Sacred Mosque.' He said, 'You said the right thing and you did well.' He then said, 'Thus, are Islam and belief.'"

Chapter 13 - Another Chapter on the Same Issue That Islam is Before Belief

H 1504, Ch. 13, h 1
Ali ibn Ibrahim has narrated from 'Abbas ibn al-Ma'ruf from 'Abd al-Rahman ibn abu Najaran from Hammad ibn 'Uthman from 'Abd al-Rahim al-Qusayr who has said the following:
"Abd al-Malik ibn A'yan and I wrote to abu 'Abd Allah, *'Alayhi al-Salam*, asking him, 'What is belief?' He then wrote to us. 'You, may Allah grant you favors, have asked about belief. Belief is affirmation, with the tongue, that is established in the heart and by the deeds of the body. Beliefs are from each other. Belief is a house. So also, Islam is a house. Rejection (of Islam) is a house. Sometimes a servant (of Allah) is a Muslim before he becomes a believer but he cannot become a believer before becoming a Muslim. Therefore, Islam is before belief and it shares belief. Whenever a servant (of Allah) commits one of the major sins or one of the minor sins that Allah, the Most Majestic, the Most Holy, has prohibited he is out of belief and belief falls off of him but the name 'Muslim' still applies to him. When he repents and asks forgiveness he returns to the house of belief. Nothing takes him out to rejection but rejection of what is lawful, such as saying to what is lawful, 'It is unlawful' or saying lawful to what is unlawful and living thereby (such attitude) as a religion. In such a case one is out of Islam and belief and is in rejection. It is like one's entering the Sacred Mosque then the Holy Ka'ba wherein he invents an act of heresy. He then is taken out of the Holy Ka'ba and the Sacred precinct and is decapitated and that turns him to hell (for his act of defiant and treachery).'"

H 1505, Ch. 13, h 2
A number of our people have narrated from Ahmad ibn Muhammad from 'Uthman ibn 'Isa from Sama'a ibn Mihran who has said the following:
"I asked the Imam about belief and Islam, inquiring, 'Is there a difference between Islam and belief?' The Imam said, 'I can give an example.' I said, 'Please do so.' He said, 'The case of belief and Islam is like the Holy Ka'ba and the Sacred precinct. One may have entered the Sacred precinct but not the Holy Ka'ba. One cannot enter the Holy Ka'ba before entering the Sacred precinct. One may become a Muslim but he may not yet be a believer. However, one cannot become a

believer before becoming a Muslim.' I (the narrator) then asked, 'Can one go out of belief to anything?' He said, 'Yes.' I asked, 'What then does one become?' He said, 'One may go out to Islam or rejection (disbelief).' He then said, 'If a man enters the Holy Ka'ba and his urine comes out he is taken out of the Holy Ka'ba but he will not be taken out of the Sacred precinct. He washes his cloth and purifies and then he is not stopped from entering the Holy Ka'ba. However, if a man enters the Holy Ka'ba and urinates therein out of animosity he is taken out of the Holy Ka'ba and the Sacred Mosque and is decapitated.'"

Chapter 14

H 1506, Ch. 14, h 1

Ali ibn Muhammad has narrated from certain persons of his people from Adam ibn Ishaq from 'Abd al-Razzaq from ibn Mihran from al-Husayn ibn Maymun from Muhammad ibn Salim from abu Ja'far, *'Alayhi al-Salam*, who has said the following:

"Abu Ja'far, *'Alayhi al-Salam*, has said, 'Certain people have spoken from this Holy Quran without knowledge. It is because Allah, the Most Holy, the Most High, has said, "It is Allah Who has revealed the Book to you in which certain verses are clear statements (that accept no interpretation), and these are the fundamental ideas of the Book, while other verses may have several possibilities. Those whose hearts are perverse follow the unclear statements in pursuit of their own mischievous goals by interpreting them in a way that will suit their own purpose. No one knows its true interpretations except Allah, and those who have a firm grounding in knowledge say, 'We believe in it. All its verses are from our Lord.' No one can grasp this fact except the people of reason." (3:7)

'The suspended verses are of the unclear ones and the verses whose meaning can clearly be understood are of the suspending ones. Allah, the Most Majestic, the Most Holy, sent Prophet Noah to his people who said to them, "Worship Allah, have fear of Him and obey me" (71:3). He then called them to Allah alone to worship Him only and not to take any partners for Him. Thereafter He sent the prophets until (their coming ended with) Muhammad, *'Alayhi al-Salam*. He invited people to worship Allah only and not to take partners for Him. And He said, "He has plainly clarified the religion which is revealed to you and that which Noah, Abraham, Moses, and Jesus were commanded to follow (He has explained it) so that you may remain steadfast and united in your religion. What you call the pagans to is extremely grave for them. Allah attracts (to the religion) whomever He wants and guides to it whoever turns to Him with repentance." (42:13)

'He sent the prophets to their people with the testimony that stated, "No one deserves to be worshipped except Allah and that whatever every one (of the prophets) has brought is from Allah." Those who sincerely accepted the faith and died with what they had accepted, Allah, through this will, admit them in paradise. Allah is not unjust to His servants, and Allah will not punish a servant unless he intensely sins such as committing murder or the sins for which Allah has made it clear that perpetrators thereof go to hell. When the believers of the people of each prophet followed them He gave them a system of laws and guidance. Al-Shari'a is a system, a path and tradition. Allah said to Prophet Muhammad, "(Muhammad), We have sent revelations to you just as were sent to Noah and the prophets who lived after him . . ." (4:163). Allah commanded every prophet to follow the path and the tradition. Of the traditions that Allah, the Most Majestic, the Most Holy, commanded Moses to follow was al-Sabbath. Those who observed its greatness and did not violate it out of respect for Allah, Allah admitted them to paradise. Those who violated its sanctity and considered lawful what Allah had made unlawful and prohibited, Allah, the Most Majestic, the Most Holy, sent them to hellfire for their making fishing lawful. They captured fish and ate them on Sabbath. Allah showed anger toward them even though they had not taken anyone as partners of the Beneficent or doubted the truth of what Moses had brought. Allah, the Most Majestic, the Most Holy, has said, "You certainly knew about those among you who were transgressors on the Sabbath. We commanded them, 'Become detested apes . . .'" (2:65) Then Allah sent Jesus with the testimony that said, "No one deserves to be worshipped except Allah and all that he (Jesus) had brought was from Allah." He made for them a system of law and a path. He abolished the Sabbath for which they, before, were commanded to pay respect and the ways and traditions that Moses had brought. Whoever did not follow Jesus, Allah sent them to fire, although all that the prophets had said was that no one must be considered as a partner of Allah. Then He sent Prophet Muhammad and for the ten years that he lived in Makka everyone who testified to the fact that "No one deserves to be worshipped except Allah, and that Muhammad is His messenger" Allah admitted him to paradise just because of his affirmation. It was belief and affirmation. Allah did not punish anyone of those who died following Muhammad in that matter except those who took partners for the Beneficent. Evidence of this is what Allah, the Most Majestic, the Most Holy, has revealed in Chapter 17 in Makka). "Your Lord has ordained that you must not worship anything other than Him and that you must be kind to your parents . . . He is Well-aware and watches over His servants." (17:30)

'It (besides belief in Allah) is discipline, advice and education. It (law) is a light prohibition and there is no warning about it and there is no warning against violating what is prohibited. He has revealed prohibitions of certain matters without warning (for issues less serious than disbelief) saying:

"Do not kill your children for fear of poverty. We will give sustenance to all of you. To kill them is certainly a great sin. (17:31)

"Do not even approach adultery. It is indecent and an evil act. (17:32)

"Do not kill a respectable soul without a just cause. If anyone is wrongfully killed, We have given the heirs of that person the right (to demand satisfaction or to forgive). He must not exceed the law in having vengeance; law shall also assist his victim. (17:33)

"Do not get close to the property of the orphans (unless it is for a good reason) until they are mature and strong. Keep your promise; you will be questioned about it. (17:34)

"While weighing, use proper measurements in the exchange of your property. This is fair and will be better in the end. (17:35)

"Do not follow what you do not know; the ears, eyes, and hearts will all be held responsible for their deeds. (17:36)

"Do not walk proudly on the earth; your feet cannot tear apart the earth nor are you as tall as the mountains (17:37). All such things are sins and detestable in the sight of your Lord. (17:38)

"(Muhammad), these are words of wisdom, which your Lord has revealed to you. Do not consider anything equal to Allah lest you be thrown into hell, despised, and driven away from Allah's mercy." (17:39)

'(About more serious issues) Allah has also said, "By the night when it covers the day. (92:1) I have warned you about the fierce blazing fire (14) in which no one will suffer forever (15) except the wicked ones who have rejected the (Truth) and have turned away from it." (92:16)

'This (the wicked) is a pagan and in Chapter 84 Allah has said, "But as for those whose Book of Records will be given behind their backs, (84:10) they will say, 'Woe to us!' (11). They will suffer the heat of hellfire (12). They lived among their people joyfully (13) and had thought that they would never be brought back to life again." (84:14)

'This (one rejecting the Day of Judgment) is a pagan and in Chapter 67 Allah has said, "Whenever a group is thrown into it (hell), its keepers will ask them, 'Did no one come to warn you? (67:8)

"They will say, 'Yes, someone did come to warn us, but we rejected him saying, "Allah has revealed nothing. You are in great error."' (67:9)

'These are pagans and in Chapter 56 Allah has said, "If he is of those who have rejected the Truth and have gone astray, (56:92) the dwelling (for him) will be (in) boiling water (93) and the heat of hellfire." (94)

'These also are pagans. In Chapter 69 Allah has said, "However, one who will receive the book of the records of his deeds in his left hand will say, 'I wish that this record was never given to me (69:25) and that I never known what my records contained. (26) Would that death had taken me away for good. (27) My wealth has been of no benefit to me (28) . . . he did not believe in Allah, the Great . . .' (69:33)

'This also is a pagan, and in Chapter 26 Allah has said, ". . . hell will be left open for the rebellious ones (26:91) who will be asked, 'What did you worship (26:92) besides Allah? Will the idols help you? Can they help themselves? (26:93). The idol worshippers, the idols, the rebellious ones, (26:94) and the army of Satan will all be thrown headlong into hell.'" (26:95) The army of Satan and his descendents are of the devils (Shayatin)

'Allah's words, "Only the sinful ones made us go astray," (26:99) refers to pagans whom they had followed in their pagan manners and they were of the people of Prophet Muhammad, *'Alayhi al-Salam*, of whom no one was a Jew or a Christian. Evidence of this is the words of Allah, the Most Majestic, the Most Holy, in Chapter 38 verse 12, "The people of Noah then rejected our messengers." "The dwellers of the forest also rejected the Messengers." (26:176) "The people of Lot rejected the Messengers." (26:160)

'Among them there is no one of the Jews who considered 'Uzayr as the son of Allah or of the Christians who considered Jesus as the son of Allah. Allah will send (such) Jews and Christians to fire as well as those who had acted similarly. It comes from their own word, "Only the sinful ones made us go astray," (26:99) they invited us to their ways.

'Evidence of this (more serious sins) is the words of Allah, the Most Majestic, the Most Holy, about them on their being brought together in fire, "The last group will accuse the first saying, 'Lord, they made us go astray. Therefore, double their torment in the Fire . . .'" (7:38) They will condemn and accuse each other. They argue in the hope of winning but there will be no winning, trial or acceptance of excuses and there will be no way to safety. Such verses and similar other ones were revealed in Makka. Allah does not send to fire anyone except the pagans.

'When Allah granted Muhammad permission to leave Makka for Madina he spoke of Islam having five principles:

'To testify that no one deserves to be worshipped except Allah, that Muhammad is His servant and His messenger, that performing the prayer, paying al-Zakat (charity), Hajj of the House and fasting in the month of Ramadan are obligatory. That Allah sent to him judicial rules, and the rules for the distribution of inheritance, and informed him of the sins for which Allah has made it obligatory to punish in fire those who commit such sins. About the murder He has revealed, "The punishment for one who purposely slays a believer will be to live in hellfire forever. Allah is angry with him and has condemned him. He has prepared for him a great torment." (4:93)

'Allah does not condemn the believers. Allah, the Most Majestic, the Most Holy, has said, "Allah has condemned the unbelievers and prepared for them a burning torment (33:64) wherein they will live forever without being able to find any guardian or helper." (33:65)

'Committing murder does not come from His wish; His anger and condemnation apply to the murderer by sending him to fire. In the book he (murderer) is condemned. About the properties of the orphans that are consumed unjustly He has said, "Those who wrongfully consume the property of orphans are, in fact, consuming fire in their bellies and they will suffer the blazing fire." (4:10)

'On the Day of Judgment, those who consume such properties unjustly will come when fire will be blazing in their bellies so much so that it will come out of their mouth. All the people in the gathering will learn that they are wrongful consumer of orphan's properties.

'About measurement for transactions He has said, "Wayl, a place in hell, is for those who do not maintain proper measurement." (83:2) He has not said that Wayl is for any kinds of people other than those whom He has called to be of those who reject the faith. Allah, the Most Majestic, the Most Holy, has said, "Wayl' is for those who reject faith and belief. The unbelievers shall face a woeful condition on the great Day (of Judgment)." (19:37)

'About the covenant Allah has said: "Those who sell their covenant with Allah and their promises for a small price will have no share in the life hereafter. Allah on the Day of Judgment will not speak to them nor will He look at them nor will He purify them. They will face a painful torment." (3:77)

'If someone will have no share on the Day of Judgment then by what means would he enter paradise?

'The following was revealed in Madina. "No one should marry a (male) fornicator except a (female) fornicator or a pagan woman. No one should marry a (female) fornicator except a (male) fornicator or a pagan man. Such (marriage) is unlawful to the believers." (24:3)

'Allah has not called a male or female fornicator a believer. People of knowledge do not doubt what the Messenger of Allah has said to them: "At the time of committing fornication a male or female is not a believer, a thief, male or female is not a believer at the time of committing theft and if one does commit theft one is devoid of belief. It is like a shirt removed from one's body." The following verse of the Quran was revealed in Madina: "Those who accuse married women of committing adultery, but are not able to prove their accusation by producing four witness, must be flogged eighty lashes. Never accept their testimony thereafter; they are sinful, (24:4) except that of those who afterwards repent and reform themselves; Allah is All-forgiving and All-merciful." (24:5)

'Allah has not called an accuser a believer. Allah, the Most Majestic, the Most Holy, has said, "Is a believer equal to an evildoer? They are not equal at all." (32:18)

'Allah had made him a hypocrite. As Allah, the Most Majestic, the Most Holy, has said, "The hypocrites indeed are evildoers." (9:67)

'Allah, the Most Majestic, the Most Holy, has made them of the friends of Satan as He has said, ". . . except Iblis. He was a Jinn and he sinned against the command of his Lord. . . ." (18:50)

'Allah called him 'condemned' in his words, "Those who slander the unaware but chaste and believing women (of committing unlawful carnal relations) are condemned in this life and in the life hereafter. They will suffer a great punishment (24:23) on the day when their tongues, hands and feet will testify to what they have done." (24:24)

'Parts of the body do not testify against a believer. They testify against those who have become subject to punishment. However, the believers will receive the book of their account in their right hand as Allah, the Most Majestic, the Most Holy, has said, ". . . those whose records of deeds are given to their right hands will read the book and the least wrong will not be done to them." (17:71)

'Chapter 24 was revealed after Chapter 4. There is evidence for this in what Allah, the Most Majestic, the Most Holy, sent down to him (Muhammad) in Chapter 4 as follows:

"Agaisnt those of your women who commit fornication, let four (Muslim) witness testify to their act. If there is sufficient testimony, confine them to their homes until they die, or until Allah provides a way for their freedom." (4:15)

'The path is what Allah, the Most Majestic, the Most Holy, has said, "This is a Chapter which We have revealed to you and made obligatory for you to following its guidance. We have revealed clear verses in it so that perhaps you may take heed. (24:1)

"Flog the (female) fornicator and the (male) fornicator with a hundred lashes each. Let there be no reluctance in enforcing the laws of Allah, if you have faith in Allah and the Day of Judgment. Let it take place in the presence of a group of believers."'" (24:2)

H 1507, Ch. 14, h 2

Muhammad ibn Yahya has narrated from Ahmad ibn Muhammad from Muhammad ibn Isma'il from Muhammad ibn Fudayl from abu al-Sabbah al-Kinani from abu Ja'far, *'Alayhi al-Salam*, who has said the following:

"Amir al-Mu'minin (Ali ibn abu Talib) was asked, 'Is one who testifies that no one deserves to be worshipped except Allah and that Muhammad is the Messenger of Allah, a believer?' The Imam said, 'Wherefore, then, are the obligations toward Allah?'

"I (the narrator) heard the Imam saying, 'Ali, *'Alayhi al-Salam*, would say, "Had belief been just 'asserted words' nothing about fasting, prayer, lawful and unlawful matters would have been needed to come down (from heaven)."' He has said, 'I reported to abu Ja'far, *'Alayhi al-Salam*, "We know a people who say that upon saying, 'No one deserves to be worshipped except Allah and Muhammad is the Messenger of Allah,' one becomes a believer." The Imam said, 'Is it then that (there is no need) to apply any judicial rules to them, like the rules about theft? Allah, the Most Majestic, the Most Holy, has not created any creature more honorable to Allah, the Most Majestic, the Most Holy, than a believer. The angels serve the believers; they are near Allah, that paradise is for the believers; that spouses with large black eyes are for the believers.' He then said, 'Do they, who reject the obligations, know that they are unbelievers?'"

H 1508, Ch. 14, h 3
Ali ibn Ibrahim has narrated from Muhammad ibn 'Isa from Yunus from Salam al-Ju'fiy who has said the following:
"Once I asked abu 'Aabd Allah, *'Alayhi al-Salam*, about belief. He said, 'Belief is whereby Allah is obeyed and (with it) one does not commit sins.'"

Chapter 15 - Belief Spreads in all Parts of the Body

H 1509, Ch. 15, h 1
Ali ibn Ibrahim has narrated from his father from Bakr ibn Salih from al-Qasim ibn Burayd who has said that narrated to us abu 'Amr al-Zubayri who has said the following:
"I said to abu 'Abd Allah, *'Alayhi al-Salam*, 'O scholar, tell me which deed is more virtuous before Allah?' He said, 'It is the deed without which Allah does not accept any (deed).' I asked, 'What is such a thing?' He said, 'Belief in Allah besides whom no one deserves to be worshipped. It (belief) is the highest in degree among the deeds, the most valuable among them and the topmost among them in (matters of) reward.' I then said, 'Please, tell me then about belief, is it deeds or it is words without deeds?'

"He said, 'All of belief is deeds and certain parts of such deeds are words. Allah has made it obligatory as is explained in His book. Its light is clear, its evidence well established. The (Holy) book testifies to it for one, and calls one to it.' I (the narrator) then asked, 'May Allah keep my soul in service for your cause, explain it to me so I may understand.' He (the Imam) said, 'Belief is of degrees, conditions, levels and stages. Of belief there is that which is perfect and complete in perfection. Of belief there is that which is defective and the defect is clear. Of belief there is that which is heavier on the perfection side.' I then asked, 'Does belief become perfect, decrease and increase?' He said, 'Yes, it does.' I then asked, 'How does it happen?' He said, 'It is because Allah, the Most Blessed, the Most High, has written belief for each part of the body of the children of Adam and has divided and distributed it among them. There is no part of thier body but that has a guard of belief different from such guard assigned to other parts. Of such part is one's heart, with which one understands and reasons to comprehend, and it is the commander of his body. It oversees the body and without its opinion no part moves to act. Of the parts of the body are one's eyes with which one sees and his ears with which one listens. There are one's hands with which one works, one's legs with which one walks, one's sexual organs from which comes carnal desires, one's tongue with which one speaks and one's head on which there is one's face. For each of these parts a different guard of belief is assigned. It is all due to what Allah, Most Blessed is Whose name, has written, to which His Holy book speaks and testifies.

'For each of these parts a different obligation is written. The obligation of the heart is different from the obligation of the ears. What is made obligatory for the ears is different from the obligation of the eyes and what is made obligatory for the eyes is different from what is made obligatory for the tongue. What is made obligatory for the tongue is different from what is made obligatory for the hands and what is made obligatory for the hands is different from what is made obligatory for the legs. The obligation of the legs is different from the obligations of the sexual organs. What is obligatory for the sexual organs is different from the obligation of the face.

'What is made obligatory for the heart of belief is affirmation, recognition and the formation of belief, consent and submission to the fact that no one deserves to be worshipped except Allah Who is One and has no partner. He is the One and only. He has not taken any companion and children. That Muhammad is His servant and messenger, he and his family being *'Alayhim al-Salam*, and to affirm that whatever he has brought is from Allah, be it about a prophet or a book. That is what Allah has made obligatory for the heart; the task of affirmation and recognition, which is its deed. This is stated in the words of Allah, the Most Majestic, the Most Holy, ". . . but his heart is confident about his faith. However, those whose breasts have become open to disbelief will be subject to the wrath of Allah and will suffer a great torment." (16:106)

'Allah has said, ". . . Remembrance (speaking) of Allah certainly brings comfort to all hearts." (13:28)

'Allah has said, ". . . They only say that they believe but, in fact, they have no faith in their hearts. . . ." (5:41)

'Allah has said, "Allah will call you to account for all that you may reveal from your souls and all that you may conceal. Allah will forgive or punish whoever He wants. . . ." (2:284)

'These are what Allah, the Most Majestic, the Most Holy, has made obligatory on the hearts of affirmation and recognition, and these are its deeds and this is the head of the belief.

'On the tongue Allah has made it obligatory to speak and express what the heart has established and has confirmed as Allah, the Most Blessed, the Most High, has said, " . . . that they should speak righteous words to people . . ." (2:83)

'Allah has said, "Tell them, we believe in Allah and in what is revealed to us and to you. Our Lord and your Lord are one. We have submitted ourselves to His will." (29:46)

33

'This is what Allah has made obligatory for the tongue and this is its deed. He has made it obligatory for the ears to keep it clean from what is unlawful to listen to, and to keep away from things that Allah, the Most Majestic, the Most Holy, has prohibited to listen to attentively; it angers Allah, the Most Majestic, the Most Holy. And in this regard He has said, "Allah has told you (believers) in the Book that when you hear people disbelieving and mocking Allah's revelations, do not sit with them unless they change the subject . . ." (4:140)

'Allah, the Most Majestic, the Most Holy, then has made an exception for the case of forgetfulness, 'If Satan causes you to forget this, do not sit with the unjust people when you recall." (6:68)

'Allah has also said, "(Muhammad), give the glad news to those of My servants who listen to the words and follow only the best ones. Tell them that they are those whom Allah has guided. They are the people of understanding." (39:18)

'Allah, the Most Majestic, the Most Holy, has said, "Triumphant indeed are the believers, (23:1) who are submissive to Allah in their prayers, (23:2) who avoid impious talks (23:3) and pay al-Zakat (charity)." (23:4)

'Allah has said, "When they hear impious words, they ignore them, saying, 'We shall be responsible for our deeds and you will be responsible for yours. . . .'" (28:55)

'Allah has said, ". . . when they come across something impious, they pass it by nobly." (25:72)

'This is what Allah has made obligatory for the ears in relation to belief; that they must not listen to what is unlawful to listen to, and such matters are of its deeds, which is of belief. He has made it obligatory for the eyes not to look at things He has made unlawful to look at and to stay away from what Allah has prohibited of the things that are not lawful for them. Such things are of their deeds and of belief.

'Allah, the Most Blessed, the Most High, has said, "(Muhammad), tell the believing men to cast down their eyes and guard their carnal desires." (24:30)

'Allah has prohibited looking at the privacy of one's brother and to keep one's privacy protected from the onlookers. Allah has said, ". . .Tell the believing woman to cast down their eyes, guard their chastity (private parts)." (24:31)

'They must find protection against being looked upon and keep away from looking at their sisters (private parts). The Imam said that everywhere in the Holy Quran where protection of private parts is mentioned it is a reference to fornication except this verse which is a reference to looking.

'Allah has spoken about the obligations of the heart, tongue, ears and eyes in another verse also: "You did not (think to) hide your deeds from your ears, eyes and skin and you felt that Allah would not know all that you had been doing." (41:22)

'Skin is reference to private parts and thighs. Allah has said, "Do not follow what you do not know; the ears, eyes, and hearts will all be held responsible for their deeds." (17:36)

'This is what Allah has made obligatory for the eyes; to cast down away from what Allah, the Most Majestic, the Most Holy, has prohibited. This is their deed and it is of belief. Allah has made it obligatory for the hands not to move to what He has prohibited, instead move to what Allah, the Most Majestic, the Most Holy, has commanded to move to such as charity, good relation with relatives and striving for the cause of Allah and cleansing for prayer.

'Allah has said, "Believers, when you are about to pray, wash your face and your hands along with the elbows and wipe your head and your feet to the ankles. . . ." (5:6)

'Allah has said, "If you encounter the unbelievers in a battle, strike-off their heads. Take them as captives when they are defeated. Then you may set them free as a favor to them, with or without a ransom, when the battle is over. . . ." (47:4)

'This is what Allah has made obligatory for the hands; striking is their task. Allah has made it obligatory for the legs not to walk to what is made unlawful and in disobedience to Allah. He has made it obligatory for them to walk to what makes Allah, the Most Majestic, the Most Holy, happy. Allah has said, "Do not walk proudly on the earth; your feet cannot tear apart the earth nor are you as tall as the mountains." (17:37) "Do not walk around inflated with pride; be moderate in your walking and your talking. The most unpleasant sound is the braying of donkeys." (31:19)

'About the testifying of the hands and legs against their ownselves and their master for their disregard of the commands of Allah, the Most Majestic, the Most Holy, and the obligation upon them, Allah has said: ". . . this Day, We seal their mouths and their hands will speak to Us and their feet will testify to what they had achieved." (36:65)

'This also is what Allah has made obligatory for the hands and the legs and this is their deed and it is of belief. Allah has made it obligatory for the face to prostrate before Him in the days and nights in the times of the prayers. Allah has said, "Believers, worship your Lord, bow down and prostrate yourselves before Him and do virtuous deeds so that perhaps you will have everlasting happiness." (22:77)

'This is an obligation that involves the face, hands and legs. In another passage He has said, 'All the parts of the body to be placed on the ground during prostration belong to Allah. Do not prostrate before anyone other than Him. . . ." (72:18) It was in regards to the obligations upon the parts of the body in the form of purification for prayer that Allah, the Most Majestic, the Most Holy, made His prophet to change facing the Holy House in Palestine to facing al-Ka'ba. Allah, the Most Majestic, the Most Holy, revealed this: "Allah did not want to make your previous belief (prayers) worthless; Allah is Compassionate and All-Merciful to people." (2:143) He has called prayer 'Belief.' Therefore, whoever meets Allah, the Most Majestic, the Most Holy, perfecting his belief is of the people of paradise. Whoever cheats in any of the obligations or violates the commands of Allah, the Most Majestic, the Most Holy, will meet Allah, the Most Majestic, the Most Holy, with a defective belief.'

"I then asked the Imam, 'I now understand perfect and defective belief. Where does the increase in belief come from?' The Imam said, 'Consider the words of Allah, the Most Majestic, the Most Holy, "When a Chapter (of the Quran) is revealed, certain people ask others, 'Whose belief among you people has received strength from this (revelation)?' It (the revelation) certainly strengthens the belief of the believers and they consider it to be glad news. (9:124) But to those whose hearts are sick, it adds more filth to their hearts and they die as unbelievers." (9:125) Allah has said, ". . .We tell you this story for a genuine purpose. They were young people who believed in their Lord and We gave them further guidance." (18:13)

'Had belief been the same and without any difference in defects and in perfections no one of them would have had any distinction over the others and the favors would have been equal to all. People had been all equal and excellence would become void. However, with perfection in belief believers enter paradise. By increase in belief the believers excel in degrees before Allah and for the defect in belief the extremists go in fire.'"

H 1510, Ch. 15, h 2

A number of our people have narrated from Ahmad ibn Muhammad ibn Khalid from his father. And Muhammad ibn Yahya has narrated from Ahmad ibn Muhammad ibn 'Isa all have narrated from al-Barqi from al-Nadr ibn Suwayd from Yahya ibn 'Imran al-Halabi from 'Ubayd Allah ibn al-Hassan from al-Hassan ibn Harun who has said the following:

"Once abu 'Abd Allah, *'Alayhi al-Salam,* said to me, 'It is of certainty that the ears, eyes and heart will all be questioned.'(17:36) He said, 'The ears will be questioned about what they have heard, the eyes will be questioned about what they have looked upon and the heart will be questioned about what it has established as belief.'"

H 1511, Ch. 15, h 3

Abu Ali al-Ash'ari has narrated from Muhammad ibn 'Abd al-Jabbar from Safwan or one other than him from al-'Ala' from Muhammad ibn Muslim who has said the following:

"Once I asked abu 'Abd Allah, *'Alayhi al-Salam,* about belief. He said, 'It is to testify that no one deserves to be worshipped except Allah, Muhammad, *'Alayhi al-Salam,* is the Messenger of Allah and to affirm that whatever he (Muhammad) brought is from Allah. That which is established in the hearts through acknowledgement of such facts is belief.' I then asked, 'Is it not that the testimony is a deed?' He said, 'Yes, it is a deed.' I then asked, 'Is the deed of belief?' He said, 'Yes, belief does not shape up without deed. The deed is from belief and belief cannot stand firmly without deed.'"

H 1512, Ch. 15, h 4

A number of our people have narrated from Ahmad ibn Muhammad ibn Khalid from 'Uthman ibn 'Isa from 'Abd Allah ibn Muskan from certain individuals of his people who has said the following:

"I asked abu 'Abd Allah, *'Alayhi al-Salam*, 'What is Islam?' He said, 'It is the name of the religion of Allah. It was the religion of Allah before you were as you are now and after you it will be there. Whoever professes the religion of Allah, is a Muslim. Whoever does what Allah, the Most Majestic, the Most Holy, has commanded, is a believer.'"

H 1513, Ch. 15, h 5

From him from his father from al-Nadr ibn Suwayd from Yahya ibn 'Imran al-Halabi from Ayyub ibn al-Hurr from abu Basir who has said the following:

"I was in the presence of abu Ja'far, *'Alayhi al-Salam*, when Salam said, 'Khaythamah ibn abu Khaythamah narrates to us from you that you were asked about Islam and you said, 'Islam is this: Whoever faces our Qibla (direction of Makka), testifies to our testament of belief, practices our practice, is a friend of our friend and an enemy of our enemies, he is a Muslim.' The Imam said, 'Khaythamah has told the truth.' I then said, 'He had asked you about belief and you said, 'It is belief in Allah, to acknowledge the book of Allah and not to disobey Allah.' He said, 'Khaythamah has told the truth.'"

H 1514, Ch. 15, h 6

Muhammad ibn Yahya has narrated from Ahmad ibn Muhammad ibn 'Isa from ibn abu 'Umayr from Jamil ibn Darraj who has said the following:

"I asked abu 'Abd Allah, *'Alayhi al-Salam*, about belief. He said, 'It is to testify that no one deserves to be worshipped except Allah and that Muhammad, *'Alayhi al-Salam*, is the Messenger of Allah.' I asked, 'Is it not a deed?' He said, 'Yes, it is a deed.' I then asked, 'Is deed of belief?' He said, 'One's belief does not take any root without deed and deed is from belief.'"

H 1515, Ch. 15, h 7

Certain individuals of our people have narrated from Ali ibn 'Abbas from Ali ibn Maysir from Hammad ibn al Nusaybi who has said the following:

"A man asked the scholar, *'Alayhi al-Salam*, 'O scholar, tell me which deed is more virtuous before Allah?' He said, 'It is the deed without which Allah does not accept any deed.' He asked, 'What is such thing?' He said, 'It is belief in Allah (besides Whom no one deserves to be worshipped). It (belief) is the highest in degree among the deeds, the most valuable among them (in virtue) and the topmost among them in reward.' The man then said, 'Please, tell me then about belief. Is it deeds or it is words without deeds?'

"The Imam said, 'All of belief is deeds and parts of such deeds are words. Allah has made it obligatory as is explained in His book. Its light is clear, its evidence well established. The (Holy) book testifies to it for one, and calls one thereto.' I (the narrator) then asked, 'Explain it to me so I may understand.' He (the Imam) said, 'Belief is of degrees, conditions, levels and stages. Of belief there is that which is perfect and complete in perfection. Of belief there is that which is defective and the defect is clear. Of belief there is that which is heavier on the perfection side.' The man then asked, 'Does belief become perfect, decrease and increase?' He said, 'Yes, it does.' The man then asked, 'How does it happen?' He said, 'It is because Allah, the Most Blessed, the Most High, has written belief for each part of the body of the children of Adam and has divided and distributed it among them. There is no part of the parts but that has a guard of belief that is different from such guard as is assigned to other parts. Of such part is one's heart with which one understands and rationalizes to comprehend, and he is the commander of one's body. It oversees the body and without its opinion no part moves to act. Of the parts of the body are one's hands with which one works, one's legs with which one walks, one's sexual organs from which come carnal desires, one's tongue with which one speaks of the book and testfies thereby, one's eyes with which one sees and one's ears with which one listens.

'For each of these parts a different obligation is written. The obligation of the heart is different from the obligation of the tongue. What is made obligatory for the tongue is different from the obligation of the eyes and what is made obligatory for the eyes is different from what is made obligatory for the ears. What is made obligatory for the ears is different from what is made obligatory for the hands and what is made obligatory for the hands is different from what is made obligatory for the legs. The obligation of the legs is different from the obligations of the sexual organs. What is obligatory for the sexual organs is different from the obligation of the face.

'What is made obligatory for the heart of belief is affirmation, recognition and formation of belief, consent and submission to the fact that no one deserves to be worshipped except Allah Who is One and has no partner. He is the One and only Who deserves to be worshipped. He has not taken any companion and children. Muhammad, *'Alayhi al-Salam*, is His servant and messenger.'"

H 1516, Ch. 15, h 8

Muhammad ibn al-Hassan has narrated from certain individuals of our people from al-Ash'ath ibn Muhammad from Muhammad ibn Hafs ibn Kharija who has said the following:

"I heard abu 'Abd Allah, *'Alayhi al-Salam*, saying - when a man asked him about the words of al-Murji'a, a religious sect, about rejection (disbelief) and belief -, 'They argue against us and say, "Just as to us one who disbelieves is a rejecter of belief, so also is he in the sight of Allah. The same applies to a believer. We find a believer that when he affirms his belief he is a believer in the sight of Allah." He, *'Alayhi al-Salam*, said, "Glory belongs to Allah. How can these two be equal? Rejection of belief is an affirmation and confession of a servant, and thereafter he is not required to present any witness to prove his case. (On the other hand) belief is a claim, which is not accepted without the testimony of a witness. Witness to prove his case is his deed and intention. If they (deed and intention) agree, a servant is a believer in the sight of Allah. Rejection of belief exists in all the three things; word, deed and intention and rules of law apply to both word and deed. In of favor many persons believers testify to prove them to be believers and the rules of law applicable to believers are applied to them, but in the sight of Allah they are rejecters of belief. In certain conditions one's applying rules of law, applicable to believers, to such unbelievers is also correct according to the apparent condition of his deed and words."""

Chapter 16 - Advancement in Belief

H 1517, Ch. 16, h 1

Ali ibn Ibrahim has narrated from his father from Bakr ibn Salih from al-Qasim ibn Burayd who has said that abu 'Amr al-Zubayri who has said the following:

"I asked abu 'Abd Allah, *'Alayhi al-Salam*, 'Are there degrees and stages of belief in which the believers may excel in the sight of Allah?' He said, 'Yes, there are.' I then said, 'Explain to me, please, may Allah grant you favors, so I can understand.' The Imam said, 'Allah has set a contest among the believers like the contest set for horses. He then has given degrees of excellence for those who excel to win. For each contestant there He has set a level and everyone receives (a reward) exactly to the degree he has achieved. Those left behind do not go ahead of those who have advanced forward and have excelled others. Such was the case of the people who lived in the earliest period of the history of this nation and those who lived later. Had there been no distinction for those advanced in belief over those behind, the last of this nation could catch up with those of the earliest times of this nation. This certainly happens if those advancing in belief are given no distinction over those slow in their progress for belief.

'In fact, by the degrees of belief Allah has given preference to the advancing ones, and due to slow progress in (matters of) belief Allah has left back those with shortcomings in belief. We find that of the believers of the later (generations) there are those who have many more (good) deeds than those of the earlier (generations), more prayer, fasting, Hajj al-Zakat (charity), hard work (Jihad) for the cause of Allah. Were it not for advancing being considered reason for distinction among the believers in the sight of Allah, those of later (generations) would have had superiority over those earlier, due to more deeds. However, Allah, the Most Majestic, the Most Holy, abstains from allowing the last, in degrees of belief, to reach the first and forward ones. It amounts to forwarding those whom Allah has made to be the last, and throwing back those whom Allah has made to be forward.

'I then said, "Tell me about Allah's call on the believers to advance in belief." The Imam said, 'It is in the words of Allah, the Most Majestic, the Most Holy, "Compete with one another to achieve forgiveness from your Lord and to reach paradise, which is as vast as the heavens and the earth, and is prepared for those who believe in Allah and His Messenger. . . ." (58:21) Allah has said, "(The foremost ones) will be the nearest ones to Allah." (56:11) Allah has said, "Allah is well pleased with the foremost ones of those who left their homes for the cause of Allah, those who helped them after their arrival in Medina and those who nobly followed these two groups. . . ." (9:100)

'He (Allah) has begun with the first immigrants according to the degree of their advancing. He then has spoken of the Ansars (first Muslims of Madina) and thirdly He has spoken of the second generation who followed them in good deeds. He has placed each group according to their degrees and stages in the sight of Allah. Thereafter Allah, the Most Majestic, the Most Holy, has mentioned the degrees of His friends (messengers) of whom there are those who excel over the others. Allah, the Most Majestic, the Most Holy, has said, "We gave certain ones of Our Messengers preference over others. To others of them Allah spoke and He raised the rank of a number of them. . . ." (2:253)

'Allah has said, "We have given preference to certain prophets over others and We gave the psalms to David." (17:55) Allah has said, "Consider how We have given preference to certain people above others, yet the life to come has more honor and respect." (17:21) Allah has said, "People are of various grades in the sight of Allah. . . ." (3:163) Allah has said, "He (Allah) will reward everyone according to his merits." (11:3) Allah has said, "To those who have believed in Allah, left their homes and fought for His cause with their possessions and in person, Allah will grant high ranks and success." (9:20)

'Allah has said, "He will grant greater reward to those who strive for His cause than to those who stay home (for no reason). (4:95) Allah will grant to those who strive, high ranks, forgiveness and mercy. . . ." (4:96) Allah has said, "Those who spend for the cause of Allah and fight before victory will have higher positions than those who spend for the cause of Allah and fight after victory. . . ." (57:10) Allah has said, "Allah will raise the position of the believers and of those who have received knowledge. Allah is Well-aware of what you do." (58:11)

'Allah has said, ". . . they did not experience any hardships of thirst, fatigue or hunger in their struggle for the cause of Allah, nor has any of their traveling enraged the disbelievers, and they did not receive any injury from enemies for which Allah did not record for them a virtuous deed. . . ." (9:120) Allah has said, "You will receive a good reward from Allah for all your good works. . . ." (2:110) Allah has said, "Whoever has done an atom's weight of good (99:7) will see it, and whoever has done an atom's weight of evil will also see it." (99:8)

'Such are the stages and degrees of belief in the sight of Allah, the Most Majestic, the Most Holy.'"

Chapter 17 (a) - Degrees of Belief

H 1518, Ch. 17a, h 1

A number of our people have narrated from Ahmad ibn abu 'Abd Allah from al-Hassan ibn Mahbub from 'Ammar ibn abu al-Ahwas from abu 'Abd Allah, *'Alayhi al-Salam*, who has said the following:

"Abu 'Abd Allah, *'Alayhi al-Salam*, has said, 'Allah, the Most Majestic, the Most Holy, made belief in seven shares: virtue, truthfulness, certainty, compliance, loyalty, knowledge and forbearance. He then distributed it among the people. Whoever received all seven shares is perfect and heavy. He has given to certain people one share or two or three and so on up to seven.' The Imam then said, 'Do not expect two shares from those who have been given one share or three from those who have received two shares lest you overburden them, and so on up to seven,' he added."

H 1519, Ch. 17a, h 2

Abu Ali al-Ash'ari has narrated from Muhammad ibn 'Abd al-Jabbar from Muhammad ibn Yahya from Ahmad ibn Muhammad ibn 'Isa all from ibn Faddal from al-Hassan ibn al-Jahm from abu al-Yaqzan from Ya'qub ibn al-Dahhak from a man of our people, Sarraj who was a servant of abu 'Abd Allah, 'Alayhi al-Salam, has said the following:

" Abu 'Abd Allah, 'Alayhi al-Salam, once sent me with a group of his followers for an errand and at that time he was in Hirah (a place near Kufa, Iraq). We left for it and returned depressed. My bed was in al-Ha'ir (a comfortable private quarter). I went there in an upset condition and threw myself thereat. At this time abu 'Abd Allah, 'Alayhi al-Salam, came in saying, 'We have come to see you,' or he said, 'We have come to you.' I then sat up straight and he sat in the middle of my bed and asked me about the errand for which he had sent me. I reported to him and he thanked Allah. Thereafter, a mention of certain people came up and I said, 'May Allah keep my soul in service for your cause, we disassociate from these people; they do not say what we say.' The Imam then said, 'If they love and support us, but do not say what you say, do you (still) disassociate from them?' I then said, 'Yes, we do so.'

"The Imam said, 'It is just like this ('A'immah's case). We have what you do not have. Should we disassociate from you?' I then said, 'No, may Allah keep my soul in service for your cause.' The Imam said, 'It is just like this (the case of Allah). With Him there is what we do not have. Do you think we should give it up?'

"I then said, 'No, may Allah keep my soul in service for your cause. We should not do so.' The Imam said, 'Be friends with them and do not disassociate from them. Among the Muslims there are those who have only one share, those who have two shares, three shares, four shares, five shares, six shares and those who have seven shares. It is not proper for those who have one share to blame those who have two shares, or those who have two shares to blame those who have three shares, those who have three shares to blame those who have four shares, those who have four shares to blame those who have five shares, those who have five shares to blame those who have six shares and those who have six shares to blame those who have seven shares. I will give an example:

"A man had a Christian neighbor to whom he preached Islam attractively and the neighbor accepted. It was early next morning when he knocked at his (convert's) door. He said, 'Who is it?' He (the preacher) said, 'I am so and so.' 'What do you want?' the (convert) said. 'Make Wuzu, dress up in your two cloths and join us for prayer,' said the preacher. The new convert then made Wuzu, dressed up in his two pieces of cloth and joined him. They performed prayers a great deal. Then they prayed the morning-prayer, then waited until it was light. The convert got up to go home and the man asked him, 'Where are you going? The day is short. The time left to noontime is very little.' The new convert sat down with him until noontime and they prayed the noontime prayer. Then he said that there is very little time to afternoon prayer. He prevented the new convert from going home until they said the afternoon prayer. He then wanted to go home but he (the preacher) said, 'It is the last part of the day and is less than the beginning of it.' So he (the preacher) stopped him until they performed the prayer at sunset. Then the new convert wanted to go home, he (the preacher) said, 'Only one more prayer is left.' He then waited until they performed the late evening prayer and then they departed each other. Next early morning he (the preacher) went and knocked at the door of the new convert. He (the new convert) asked, 'Who is it?' He (the preacher) said, 'I am so and so.' He (the new convert) asked, 'What do you want?' He (the preacher) said, 'Make Wuzu, dress up in your two pieces of cloth and join us for prayer.' He (the Christian man) said, 'Find other persons for this religion who have more free time. I am a poor person with a family to feed.'

"Abu 'Abd Allah, *'Alayhi al-Salam*, then said, 'He (the preacher) took him (Christian) into a thing in such a way that it took him (the new convert) out of it. Or that the Imam said, 'Took him in like this and forced him out like that.'"

Chapter 17 (b) - Degrees of Belief (Additional)

H 1520, Ch. 17b, h 1
Ahmad ibn Muhammad has narrated from al-Hassan ibn Musa from Ahmad ibn 'Umar from Yahya ibn Aban from Shihab who has said the following:
"I heard abu 'Abd Allah, *'Alayhi al-Salam*, saying, 'Had the people known how Allah, the Most Blessed, the Most High, has created this creation no one would blame others.' I then said, 'May Allah grant you well being, how is that?' The Imam said, 'Allah, the Most Blessed, the Most High, created parts numbering ninety-four parts. He then made them into tenths; thus, He made one part into ten parts. He then distributed them among the creatures. In one man He placed one tenth, in another person He placed two tenths until there came a man in whom He place a whole part. In another He placed one part and one tenth, in another person one part and two tenths and in another one part and three tenths up to a man in whom He placed two whole parts and so on up to the highest one in whom He placed ninety-four whole parts. Therefore, one in whom only one tenth of a part is placed cannot be like the one in whom two tenths are placed. The one in whom two tenths of a part are placed cannot be like the one in whom three tenths are placed. So also the owner of one part cannot be like the owner of two whole parts. Had the people known that Allah, the Majestic, the Glorious, has created them in this way no one would have blamed the others.'"

H 1521, Ch. 17b, h 2
Muhammad ibn Yahya has narrated from Muhammad ibn Ahmad from certain individuals of his people from al-Hassan from Ali ibn abu 'Uthman from Muhammad ibn 'Uthman from Muhammad ibn Hammad al-Khazzaz from 'Abd al-'Aziz al-Qaratisi who has said the following:
"Once abu 'Abd Allah, *'Alayhi al-Salam*, said, 'O 'Abd al-'Aziz, belief is of ten stages like the steps of a ladder. To climb, one uses it one step after the other one by one. One who possesses two degrees of belief should never say to one who

possesses only one degree that he does not have enough belief and so on up to the tenth degree or stage. One who is higher should not throw back the one below because the one above you may also fall. If you see one below, you should help him climb up higher gently and do not burden him with what he cannot lift up; he may break down and if one breaks down a believer, he will be held responsible for compensation to him.'"

H 1522, Ch. 17b, h 3
Muhammad ibn Yahya has narrated from Ahmad ibn Muhammad ibn 'Isa from Muhammad ibn Sinan from ibn Muskan from Sadir who has said the following:

"Abu Ja'far, *'Alayhi al-Salam*, said to me,'Believers are of various positions in connection with belief. There are those who have one degree of belief, others have two degrees, still others may have three or four, five, six or seven degrees of belief. If you expect two degrees of belief from one who has only one degree of belief he is not able to bear it, or expect three degrees of belief from the one who has only two degrees of it he also is not able to bear it. The one who may have three cannot bear four degrees of belief, the one who has four degrees of belief is not able to bear five degrees of belief. One who has only five degrees of belief is not able to bear six degrees of belief and one who has six degrees of belief is not able to bear seven degrees of belief. This is how the degrees of belief are.'"

H 1523, Ch. 17b, h 4
It is narrated from him (Muhammad ibn Yahya) from Ali ibn al-Hakam from Muhammad ibn Sinan from al-Sabah ibn Siyabah from abu 'Abd Allah, *'Alayhi al-Salam*, who has said the following:

"What is this disavowing and disassociation of yours? There are those of you who renounce the others. Among the believers there are those who are better than others. Among them there are those who pray more, and others are of sharp insight. Such are the degrees of belief."

Chapter 18 - Description of Islam

H 1524, Ch. 18, h 1
A number of our people have narrated from Ahmad ibn Muhammad ibn Khalid from certain individuals of our people in a marfu' manner from Amir al-Mu'minin (Ali ibn abu Talib) who has said the following:

"I will describe Islam in a way that no one could have done before or would do after me except just as my description: 'Islam is submission and submission is certainty. Certainty is affirmation (and confirmation). Affirmation is professing. Professing is action. Action and deeds are completion and remittance. A believer does not take his religion from his own personal opinion. It comes from his Lord and he accepts it. A believer finds his certainty in his deeds. An unbeliever finds his rejection in his deeds. I swear by the One in whose hands is my soul, they did not recognize their goal. Take a lesson from the case of the filthy deeds of the unbelievers and the hypocrites.'"

H 1525, Ch. 18, h 2
It is narrated from him from his father from 'Abd Allah ibn al-Qasim from Mudrik ibn 'Abd al-Rahman from abu 'Abd Allah, *'Alayhi al-Salam*, who has said the following:

"The Messenger of Allah has said, 'Islam is bare. Its dress is bashfulness, dignity is its ornament, virtuous deeds are its kindness and strict following of law is its support. Everything has a foundation. The foundation of Islam is loving us, Ahl al-Bayt.'"

H 1526, Ch. 18, h 3

Ali ibn Ibrahim has narrated from his father from Ali ibn Ma'bad from 'Abd Allah ibn al-Qasim from Murik ibn 'Abd al-Rahman from abu 'Abd Allah, *'Alayhi al-Salam*, a similar Hadith.

H 1527, Ch. 18, h 4

A number of our people have narrated from Ahmad ibn Muhammad from 'Abd al-'Azim from 'Abd Allah al-Hassani from Abu Ja'far al-Thani, *'Alayhi al-Salam*, from his father from his grandfather, *'Alayhi al-Salam*, who has said the following:

"Amir al-Mu'minin (Ali ibn abu Talib), *'Alayhi al-Salam*, has said that the Messenger of Allah said, 'Allah created Islam and made for it a backyard and front-yard, a light, a fortress and supporter. Its backyard and front-yard are the Holy Quran. Wisdom is its light. Lawfulness is its fortress. My Ahl al-Bayt (my family), our Shi'a (followers) and I are its supporters. You must love my Ahl al-Bayt (members of my family), their followers (Shi'a) and their supporters. When I was taken to heaven above the earth, Gibril introduced me to its inhabitants. Allah entrusted the love for me, my Ahl al-Bayt and their followers (Shi'a) to the hearts of the angels. It is with them in trust until the Day of Judgment. Then I was brought to earth and he introduced me to the inhabitants of earth. Allah entrusted the love for me, my Ahl al-Bayt and their followers (Shi'a) to the hearts of the believers of my people. They will keep my trust and the trust of my Ahl al-Bayt until the Day of Judgment. One must know that if a man of my people would worship Allah, the Most Majestic, the Most Holy, all the time of his life and then would meet Allah, the Most Majestic, the Most Holy, while hating my Ahl al-Bayt and my followers (Shi'a) Allah will not open his chest for anything but in hypocrisy.'"

Chapter 19 - Qualities of a Believer

H 1528, Ch. 19, h 1

Muhammad ibn Yahya has narrated from Ahmad ibn Muhammad ibn 'Isa from al-Hassan ibn Mahbub from Jamil ibn Salih from 'Abd al-Malik ibn Ghalib from abu 'Abd Allah, *'Alayhi al-Salam*, who has said the following:

"A believer should have eight qualities. He is dignified in turbulent times. He is patient in afflicting conditions. He is thankful in prosperous life. He is content with what Allah has granted him. He does not do injustice to the enemies. He does not overburden friends. His own body is tired due to his efforts and people are comfortable with him. Knowledge is a friend of the believer, forbearance is his secretary, reason is the commander-in-chief of his army, kindness is his brother and virtuous deed is his father."

H 1529, Ch. 19, h 2

Ali ibn Ibrahim has narrated from his father from al-Nawfali form al-Sakuni from abu 'Abd Allah from his father, *'Alayhi al-Salam*, who has said the following:

"Amir al-Mu'minin (Ali ibn abu Talib), *'Alayhi al-Salam*, has said, 'Belief has four corner (stones): They are trust in Allah, having Allah as the person in charge of one's affairs, to agree with the decision of Allah and to submit to the command of Allah, the Most Majestic, the Most Holy.'"

H 1530, Ch. 19, h 3

A number of our people have narrated from Ahmad ibn Muhammad ibn Khalid from his father from those whom he has mentioned from Muhammad ibn 'Abd al-Rahman ibn abu Layla from his father from abu 'Abd Allah, *'Alayhi al-Salam*, who has said the following:

"You will not become virtuous until you learn, you will not learn until you affirm and you will not affirm until you accept four Chapters, the first of which will be of no benefit without the last one. People of three Chapters have strayed far away. Allah, the Most Blessed, the Most High, does not accept anything but virtuous deeds and Allah does not accept (anything) without loyalty in keeping up with one's stipulations and covenants. Whoever fulfils his stipulations toward Allah and completes whatever is in one's covenant, he will find (the reward that is) with Him and He will fulfill His promise. Allah, the Most Majestic, the Most Holy, has informed the people of the ways of guidance and has established for it the lighthouse. He has informed them how to behave, saying, 'I am All-forgiving to the righteously striving believers who repent and follow the right guidance.' (20:82) Allah has also said, 'Allah accepts only the offerings of the pious ones.' (5:27)

"Whoever maintains piety before Allah, the Most Majestic, the Most Holy, in the matter of His commands he will come in the presence of Allah, the Most Majestic, the Most Holy, as a believer in whatever Muhammad, *'Alayhi al-Salam*, has brought from Him. How remote, far away and lost are the people who have died before achieving guidance, and had thought that they were believers. They had considered things as partners of Allah without knowing what they had done. Whoever comes to a house through its door finds proper guidance, and whoever looks for a way other than the door has chosen a condemned path. Allah has joined obedience to His Messenger with obedience to those who possess Divine Authority and the obedience to His Messenger with obedience to His own commands. Therefore, whoever does not obey the people who possess Divine Authority, they have not obeyed Allah and His Messenger and it (obedience to people who possess Divine Authority) is the affirmation of what has come from Allah. Dress up (in piety) before every Mosque. Find the houses through the doors to them, the houses for which Allah has granted permission to be raised high, wherein people speak of Him. He has informed you that in these houses there are men who do not become distracted because of trade and business from speaking of Allah, the Most Majestic, the Most Holy, from prayer and paying al-Zakat (charity). These men fear the Day wherein the hearts and eyes undergo turbulent conditions. Allah chose and purified the messengers for His command, then He purified and chose them (people who possess Divine Authority) who are confirmed in His warnings. Allah has said, 'No nation who lived before was left without a Warner. . . .' (35:25)

"Lost are those who remained ignorant and guided are those who thought and understood. Allah, the Most Majestic, the Most Holy, has said, 'It is not their seeing ability that is blind but it is their hearts which are in their chests.' (22:46)

"How can one who does not think find guidance? How can one who has not received warnings think? Follow the Messenger of Allah, affirm whatever has come from Allah, follow the marks of guidance; they are the signs of trust and piety. You must know that if a man rejects Jesus Christ and acknowledges all the other messengers of Allah, he is not a believer. Find the way through finding the lighthouse and look for the marks from behind the curtains. Strive to perfect the affairs of your religion and believe in Allah your Lord.'"

H 1531, Ch. 19, h 4
It is narrated from him from his father from Sulayman al-Ja'fary from abu al-Hassan al-Rida from his father, *'Alayhi al-Salam*, who has said the following:
"A people came to the Messenger of Allah during one of the armed expeditions and he asked who are these people? They said, 'Believers, O Messenger of Allah.' He then asked, 'What is the degree of your belief?' They replied, 'It is patience in hardships, thankfulness in prosperous life and agreement with the decision of Allah.' The Messenger of Allah then said, 'These are forbearing and knowledgeable people. Their understanding is almost to the degree of the prophets. If you really are what you say you are, do not build what you will not use for dwelling, do not accumulate what you will not eat and be pious before Allah to whom you will return.'"

Chapter 20

H 1532, Ch. 20, h 1
Ali ibn Ibrahim has narrated from his father from Muhammad ibn Yahya from Ahmad ibn Muhammad ibn 'Isa and a number of our people have narrated from Ahmad ibn Muhammad ibn Khalid all from al-Hassan ibn Mahbub from Ya'qub al-Sarraj from Jabir from Abu Ja'far, *'Alayhi al-Salam*, and through various chain of narrators from Asbagh ibn Nubatah who has said the following:
"Amir al-Mu'minin (Ali ibn abu Talib), *'Alayhi al-Salam*, once addressed us at his home or - that he said - in the castle, and we were all gathered. He (may Allah's favors be with him) issued a written order that was read to people. Others have narrated that ibn al-Kawwa asked Amir al-Mu'minin (Ali ibn abu Talib), *'Alayhi al-Salam*, to describe Islam, belief, rejection and hypocrisy. He then said, '(First I express my thanks to and praise of Allah), thereafter (I must say that) Allah, the Most Blessed, the Most High, established Islam and made its paths clear for the people coming in Islam. He gave strength to its corners against the enemies. He made it (to be a source of) dignity for those who love it, peace for those who enter therein, guidance for those who follow it, beauty for those who glorify it, protection for those who accept it, a stronghold for those who seek security, a rope for those who like to hold on to it, solid proof for those who speak from it, light for those who search for brightness, a rescuer for those who cry for help, a witness for those who fight for it, success for those who argue by the facts therein, knowledge for those who imbibe it, good report for those who narrate it, judgment for those who take it as the source of decrees, forbearance for those who

46

experience it, a dress for those who contemplate on it, understanding for those who find good points in it, certainty for those who reason with it, insight for those who make a decision, a sign for those who take it as landmark, a good lesson for those who look for good lessons, salvation for those who affirm it, serenity for those who reform, success for those who come close to it, confidence for those who trust it, ease for those who make it the factor-in-charge of thier affairs, advancement for those who do it well, goodness for those who come to it fast, a shield for those who bear patience, dressing for those who observe piety, a supporter for those who take it as a guide, a cave of protection for those who seek safety, peace and comfort for those who accept it, hope for those who believe it and self-sufficiency for those who are content. That is the truth. Its path is guidance, its narratives are honorable and its description is goodness. Its system is clear, its lighthouse shines, its lamp is clean and bright, its aims are high, its training is easy and its advancing is a great deal. Its advancing is quick and its disciplining painful. Its assets are sufficient and its staff honorable. Belief is its system, virtuous deeds are its lighthouse, laws and understanding are the sources of its light, the world is its arena and death is its end, the hereafter its reward, paradise its finish line, hell its resentment, piety its supplies and people of good deeds its soldiers. Through belief good deeds are found, with good deeds good understanding is achieved and with good understanding fear for death is felt and with death the world ends. With the world one reaches the Day of Judgment. On the Day of Judgment paradise is bedecked. Paradise is (the cause of) regret for people of hell. Hell is a good lesson for the pious people and piety is the foundation of belief."

Chapter 21 - Description of Belief

H 1533, Ch. 21, h 1

Through the same chain of narrators as the above Hadith it is narrated from ibn Mahbub from Ya'qub al-Sarraj from Jabir from abu Ja'far, *'Alayhi al-Salam*, who has said the following:

"Amir al-Mu'minin (Ali ibn abu Talib), *'Alayhi al-Salam*, was asked about belief and he said, 'Allah, the Most Majestic, the Most Holy, made belief upon four pillars:

'Patience, Certainty, Justice and Jihad (hard work for the cause of Allah).

'The Patience therein has four branches: nostalgia, fear, restraint and vigilance. One who has a longing for paradise forgets the worldly desires. One who has fear of hell abstains from unlawful things. One who exercises restraint in worldly matters the worldly hardships become easier for him, and one who is vigilant of death hastens to good deeds.

'The Certainty therein is also of four branches. They consist of sharp understanding, proper application of wisdom, recognizing good lessons and knowledge of the traditions of the people of the past. One who possesses sharp understanding recognizes the matters of wisdom. One who applies wisdom properly recognizes the good lessons, and one who recognizes the good lessons recognizes the traditions, and one who recognizes traditions is like the one who has lived with the people of the past and has found proper and firm guidance. He has seen who found salvation and by what means they found. He has also seen those who were destroyed and things that destroyed them. Allah destroys only those who disobey Him and grants salvation for ones obedience to His commands.

'The Justice therein is also of four branches. It is a matter of deep understanding, a huge body of knowledge, the bloom of wisdom and the garden of forbearance. One who has deep understanding has the ability to interpret all knowledge. One who has a huge body of knowledge knows the ways of wisdom, and one who is forbearing is not an extremist in his decrees and lives among the people with a good name.

'The Jihad (hard work for the cause of Allah) therein, is also of four branches. They consist of helping others to perform their duties and to stay away from that which is prohibited, to speak the truth whenever needed and to shun sins and sinners. One who helps others to perform their duties has supported the believer. One who helps stop others from sinning has humiliated the hypocrites and has thwarted their wicked plans. One who speaks the truth at the right time, his is the winning side. One who shuns the sinners has used anger for Allah. One who becomes angry for Allah, Allah becomes angry for him. Such is belief, its pillars and branches.'''

Chapter 22 - Superiority of Belief over Islam and Certainty over Belief

H 1534, Ch. 22, h 1
Abu Ali al-Ash'ari has narrated from Muhammad ibn Salim from Ahmad ibn al-Nadr from 'Amr ibn Shamir from Jabir from abu 'Abd Allah, *'Alayhi al-Salam*, who has said the following:

"Abu 'Abd Allah, *'Alayhi al-Salam*, once said, 'O brother from Ju'f (name of his tribe) belief is superior to Islam and certainty is superior to belief. Nothing there is dearer than certainty."

H 1535, Ch. 22, h 2
A number of our people have narrated from Sahl ibn Ziyad and al-Husayn ibn Muhammad from Mu'alla ibn Muhammad all from al-Washsha' who has said the following:

"I heard abu Al-Hassan, *'Alayhi al-Salam*, saying, 'Belief is above Islam by one degree. Piety is above belief by one degree. Certainty is above piety by one degree. Nothing is distributed so little among people as certainty is.'"

H 1536, Ch. 22, h 3
Muhammad ibn Yahya has narrated from Ahmad ibn Muhammad ibn 'Isa from Al-Hassan ibn Mahbub from Ali ibn Ri'ab from Humran ibn 'A'Yun who has said the following:

"I heard abu Ja'far, *'Alayhi al-Salam*, saying, 'Allah has given superiority to belief over Islam by one degree just as He has given superiority to al-Ka'ba over the Sacred Mosque.'"

H 1537, Ch. 22, h 4

A number of our people have narrated from Ahmad ibn Muhammad ibn Khalid from Harun ibn al-Jahm or others from 'Amr ibn Aban ibn al-Kalbi from 'Abd al-Hamid al-Wasiti from abu Basir who has said the following:

"Once abu 'Abd Allah, *'Alayhi al-Salam,* said to me, 'O abu Muhammad, Islam is a high status.' I said, 'Yes, indeed it is.' The Imam said, 'Belief is above Islam by one degree.' I said, 'Yes, it is.' The Imam said, 'Piety is above belief by one degree.' I said, 'Yes, it is.' The Imam said, 'Certainty is above piety by one degree.' I said, 'Yes, it is.' The Imam said, 'Nothing is given to people as little as certainty is. What you are holding to is very little of Islam. Pay attention not to lose it.'"

H 1538, Ch. 22, h 5

Ali ibn Ibrahim has narrated from Muhammad ibn 'Isa from Yunus who has said the following:

"I asked abu al-Hassan al-Rida, *'Alayhi al-Salam,* about belief and Islam and he said, abu Ja'far, *'Alayhi al-Salam,* has said the following: 'There is Islam. Belief is one degree higher above Islam, and piety is one degree higher above belief. Certainty is by one degree higher above piety and nothing is distributed among people so little as certainty is.' I then said, 'What then is certainty?' The Imam said, 'It is trust in Allah, submission to Allah, accepting the decision of Allah and allowing Allah to be the person in charge of one's affairs.' I then said, 'What then is the interpretation of that?' The Imam said, 'This is how abu Ja'far, *'Alayhi al-Salam,* said it is.'"

H 1539, Ch. 22, h 6

Muhammad ibn Yahya has narrated from Ahmad ibn Muhammad ibn 'Isa from Ahmad ibn Muhammad ibn abu Nasr from al-Rida, *'Alayhi al-Salam,* who has said the following:

"Belief is one degree higher than Islam. Piety is one degree higher than belief. Certainty is one degree higher above piety. Nothing is distributed among people so little as certainty is."

Chapter 23 - The Essence of Belief and Certainty

H 1540, Ch. 23, h 1

A number of our people have narrated from Ahmad ibn Muhammad ibn Khalid from Muhammad ibn Isma'il from Dazi' from Muhammad ibn 'Azafir from his father from abu Ja'far, *'Alayhi al-Salam,* who has said the following:

"During one of the journeys of the Messenger of Allah a group of people who were riding came to meet him. They said, 'Salute to you O Messenger of Allah.' He asked, 'Who are you?' They replied, 'We are believers, O Messenger of Allah.' He then asked, 'What is the essence of your belief?' They replied, 'It is to agree with the decision of Allah, allow Him be the person in charge of one's affairs and submit to the command of Allah.' The Messenger of Allah said, 'They are scholars and people of wisdom who for their wisdom can almost be prophets. If what you say is true then do not build that which you do not use as dwelling, do not accumulate what you do not eat and be pious before Allah to whom you will return.'"

H 1541, Ch. 23, h 2

Muhammad ibn Yahya has narrated from Ahmad ibn Muhammad ibn 'Isa and Ali ibn Ibrahim has narrated from his father all from ibn Mahbub from abu Muhammad al-Wabishi and Ibrahim ibn Mehzam from Ishaq ibn 'Ammar who has said the following:

"I heard abu 'Abd Allah, *Alayhi al-Salam*, saying, 'Once the Messenger of Allah after leading the morningprayer for the people looked at a young man in the Mosque whose head hung down. He looked pale and slim and his eyes sunk into his head. The Messenger of Allah asked, 'O so and so, how is your morning?' He (the young man) replied, 'This morning, I, O Messenger of Allah, am in a condition of certainty. The messenger of Allah admired him for his words and he said, 'For everything there is an essence. What is the essence of your certainty?' The young man said, 'My certainty, O Messenger of Allah, is that which has made me depressed. It has kept me awake all night and to endure thirst during the day. My soul is withdrawn from the world and the things in it, so much so, as if I am looking at the Throne of my Lord that is established to call everyone to Judgment, all creatures are resurrected and I am among them. It is as if I am looking at the people of paradise who enjoy therein being introduced to each other while leaning against raised couches. It is also as if I am looking at the people of hell wherein they suffer and cry for help. Right now, it is as if I hear the roaring of the fire. It is striking against my ears.' The Messenger of Allah said to his companions, 'This is a servant of Allah whose heart He has brightened up with belief.' He (the Messenger of Allah) said to him (the young man), 'Keep up with what you are in (condition of your belief).' The young man said, 'Pray to Allah for me, O Messenger of Allah, to grant me martyrdom (while working hard in support of your cause) along with you.' The Messenger of Allah prayed for him. Not very long thereafter he joined the prophet in an armed expedition and he was the tenth man to become a martyr.'"

H 1542, Ch. 23, h 3

Muhammad ibn Yahya has narrated from Ahmad ibn Muhammad from Muhammad ibn Sinan from 'Abd Allah ibn Muskan from abu Basir from abu 'Abd Allah, *Alayhi al-Salam*, who has said the following:

"The Messenger of Allah once met Harithah ibn Malik al-Nu'man al-Ansari and asked him, 'How are you, O Harithah ibn Malik?' He replied, 'O Messenger of Allah, I am a believer in a real sense.' The Messenger of Allah then asked, 'Everything has a reality and essence. What are the reality and essence of your words?'

"He replied, 'O Messenger of Allah, my soul has withdrawn from this world; it has kept me awake all night and to endure thirst in the middle of the day. It is as if I am looking to the Throne of my Lord that is established to bring all people to account. It is as if I am looking at the people of paradise who are visiting each other and I hear the barking of the people of hell therefrom.' The Messenger of Allah, then said, 'He is a servant whose heart is brightened (by the command of) Allah. You have reached (true) understanding, remain steadfast.' He then asked, 'O Messenger of Allah, pray to Allah for me to grant me martyrdom (while working hard to support your cause) along with you.' The Messenger of Allah prayed, 'O Allah, grant him martyrdom.' Within very few days thereafter, he (the messenger of Allah) dispatched a group of people for an armed expedition and Harithah was among them. He (Harithah) fought the enemy and did away with eight or nine people before he became a martyr.

"In the narration of al-Qasim from his father from abu Basir it is said that Harithah was martyred in the army of Ja'far ibn abu Talib after the martyrdom of nine people."

H 1543, Ch. 23, h 4
Ali ibn Ibrahim has narrated from his father from al-Nawfali from al-Sakuni from abu 'Abd Allah, *'Alayhi al-Salam*, who has said the following:
"Amir al-Mu'minin (Ali ibn abu Talib), *'Alayhi al-Salam*, has said, 'Over every truth there certainly is a reality and over every correct issue there is light.'"

Chapter 24 - Contemplation (Thinking)

H 1544, Ch. 24, h 1
Ali ibn Ibrahim has narrated from his father from al-Nawfali from al-Sakuni from abu 'Abd Allah, *'Alayhi al-Salam*, who has said the following:
"Amir al-Mu'minin (Ali ibn abu Talib), *'Alayhi al-Salam*, has said, 'Awaken your heart by thinking. Keep your side off the bed at night (meaning stand up for nightly prayers) and be pious before your Lord, Allah.'"

H 1545, Ch. 24, h 2
Ali ibn Ibrahim has narrated from his father from certain individuals of his people from Aban from al-Hassan al-Sayqal who has said the following:
"Once I asked abu 'Abd Allah, *'Alayhi al-Salam*, about what people's narration, 'Thinking for one hour is better than worshipping a whole night,' how should they think? The Imam said, 'They pass by the ruins of dwellings or a building and ask, "Where are your inhabitants? Where are your builders? Why do you not speak?"'"

H 1546, Ch. 24, h 3
A number of our people have narrated from Ahmad ibn Muhammad ibn Khalid from Ahmad ibn Muhammad ibn abu Nasr from certain individuals of his people from abu 'Abd Allah, *'Alayhi al-Salam*, who has said the following:
"Abu 'Abd Allah, *'Alayhi al-Salam*, has said, 'The most virtuous form of worship is thinking about Allah very often and about His power.'"

H 1547, Ch. 24, h 4
Muhammad ibn Yahya has narrated from Ahmad ibn Muhammad ibn 'Isa from Mu'ammar ibn Khallad who has said the following:
"I heard abu al-Hassan al-Rida, *'Alayhi al-Salam*, saying, 'A great deal of prayer and fasting only are not (everything in) worship. Worship is only in thinking about the affairs of Allah, the Most Majestic, the Most Holy.'"

H 1548, Ch. 24, h 5
Muhammad ibn Yahya has narrated from Ahmad ibn Muhammad from Isma'il ibn Sahl from Hammad from Rib'I who has said the following:

"Abu 'Abd Allah, *'Alayhi al-Salam*, has said that Amir al-Mu'minin (Ali ibn abu Talib), *'Alayhi al-Salam*, has said, 'Thinking leads to virtue and to acting virtuously.'"

Chapter 25 - The Noble Qualities (of Man)

H 1549, Ch. 25, h 1
Muhammad ibn Yahya has narrated from Ahmad ibn Muhammad ibn 'Isa from al-Hatham ibn abu Masruq from Yazid ibn Ishaq Sha'ar from al-Husayn ibn al-'Atiyah from abu 'Abd Allah, *'Alayhi al-Salam*, who has said the following:

"Abu 'Abd Allah, *'Alayhi al-Salam*, has said, 'Noble (human) qualities are ten. If you can establish all of them so be it. Such qualities may be found in a man but may not be found in his children. They may be found in the children but not in the father. At times they are found in a slave person but not in a free one.' It was asked, 'What are these noble qualities?' The Imam said they are: 'Losing all hope in the true sense for receiving help from anyone other than Allah, truthfulness of tongue, returning the trust (safely), maintaining good relations with relatives, entertaining guests, feeding the needy, making up for favors in a proper corresponding manner, keeping up with one's responsibilities toward the neighbors and with one's companion, and the head of such qualities is bashfulness.'"

H 1550, Ch. 25, h 2
A number of our people have narrated from Ahmad ibn Muhammad ibn Khalid from 'Uthman ibn 'Isa from 'Abd Allah ibn Muskan from abu 'Abd Allah, *'Alayhi al-Salam*, who has said the following:

"Allah, the Most Majestic, the Most Holy, chose His messengers for noble moral (human) qualities. You must test yourselves. If you find the noble qualities in you then be thankful to Allah and understand that it is of goodness. If you do not find them in you, then pray to Allah to grant them to you and show Him that you are interested in having them. The narrator has said that the Imam counted the noble qualities up to ten: They consist of Certainty, Contentment, Patience, Thankfulness, Forbearance, Good Moral Behavior, Generosity, Dignity, Bravery and Kindness.

"Certain narrators have listed other qualities after the above-mentioned ones and have added to them Truthfulness and Keeping Trust."

H 1551, Ch. 25, h 3
It is narrated from him from Bakr ibn Salih from Ja'far ibn Muhammad al-Hashimi from Isma'il 'Abbad who has said that perhaps he has heard it from Isma'il from 'Abd Allah ibn Bukayr from abu 'Abd Allah, *'Alayhi al-Salam*, who has said the following:

"We certainly love a person of reason, of good understanding, who has good knowledge and understanding of the law, who is forbearing, who is kind, who bears patience, who is truthful and who is loyal. Allah, the Most Majestic, the Most Holy, has chosen the prophets for noble moral (human) qualities. Whoever has them (noble qualities) should be thankful to Allah. Whoever does not have them he must pray humbly to Allah, the Most Majestic, the Most Holy, and request Him to grant them to him. "I (the narrator) then said, 'May Allah keep my soul in service for your cause, what are the noble qualities?'

"The Imam said, 'They consist of restraint from indulging in worldly matters, to be content, to bear patience, to be thankful, to be forbearing, to be bashful, to be generous, to have dignity, to be virtuous, to be truthful in one's words and to be trustworthy.'"

H 1552, Ch. 25, h 4

Muhammad ibn Yahya has narrated from Ahmad ibn Muhammad ibn 'Isa from al-Hassan ibn Mahbub from certain individuals of his people from abu 'Abd Allah, *'Alayhi al-Salam*, who has said the following:

"Allah, the Most Majestic, the Most Holy, has chosen Islam to be your religion. Keep good company with your religion by means of exercising generosity and good moral behavior."

H 1553, Ch. 25, h 5

Ali ibn Ibrahim has narrated from his father from al-Nawfali from al-Sakuni from abu 'Abd Allah, *'Alayhi al-Salam*, who has said the following:

"Amir al-Mu'minin (Ali ibn abu Talib) has said, 'Belief has four pillars. They consist of agreeing with the decision of Allah, trusting Allah, choosing Allah to be the person in charge of all affairs and submission to the command of Allah.'"

H 1554, Ch. 25, h 6

Al-Husayn ibn Muhammad has narrated from Mu'alla ibn Muhammad from al-Hassan ibn Ali from 'Abd Allah ibn Sinan from a man from Banu Hashim who has said the following:

"If four things are found in a person his Islam is perfect, even though he may be filled with sins from his top to his toes it will not harm him. They consist of Truthfulness, Bashfulness, Good Moral Behavior and Thankfulness."

H 1555, Ch. 25, h 7

A number of our people have narrated from Sahl ibn Ziyad and Ali ibn Ibrahim has narrated from his father all from ibn Mahbub from ibn Ri'ab from abu Hamza from Jabir ibn 'Abd Allah who has said the following:

"The Messenger of Allah, *'Alayhi al-Salam*, once said, 'Do you want me to tell you about the best men among you?' We said, 'Yes, O, Messenger of Allah, do so.' He said, 'The best men among you are the pious, clean, of forgiving hands, clean on both ends (tongue and genitals) who is kind to his parents and does not leave out his dependents to (trouble) others.'"

Chapter 26 - Excellence of Certainty

H 1556, Ch. 26, h 1

Al-Husayn ibn Muhammad has narrated from Mu'alla ibn Muhammad from al-Hassan ibn Ali al-Washsha' from al-Muthanna ibn al-Walid from abu Basir from abu 'Abd Allah, *'Alayhi al-Salam*, who has said the following:

"Abu 'Abd Allah, *'Alayhi al-Salam*, once said, 'There is nothing without a limit.' I (the narrator) then asked, 'May Allah keep my soul in service for your cause, what is the limit of trust?' The Imam said, 'It is certainty.' I then asked, 'What is the limit of certainty?' The Imam said, 'It is when, with having Allah on your side, you do not fear anything.'"

H 1557, Ch. 26, h 2

It is narrated from him from Mu'alla from al-Hassan ibn Ali al-Washsha' from 'Abd Allah ibn Sinan from abu 'Abd Allah, *'Alayhi al-Salam*, and Muhammad ibn Yahya from Ahmad ibn Muhammad from ibn Mahbub from abu Wallad al-Hannat and 'Abd Allah ibn Sinan from abu 'Abd Allah, *'Alayhi al-Salam*, who has said the following:

"Abu 'Abd Allah, *'Alayhi al-Salam*, once said, 'It is due to a Muslim's correctness of certainty that he does not make people happy to anger Allah and does not blame them for what (of belongings) Allah has not given him. The share of sustenance is something that is not driven by the greed of the greedy ones and is not pushed back due to the dislike of those who dislike. Even if one of you may run away from his share of sustenance just as one runs away from death, still his share of sustenance reaches him just as death one day will reach him.' He then said, 'Allah through His justice and fairness has placed in certainty spirit and comfort and agreement with the decision of Allah. He has placed anxiety and sadness in doubts and anger.'"

H 1558, Ch. 26, h 3

Ibn Mahbub has narrated from Hisham ibn Salim who has said the following:

"I heard abu 'Abd Allah, *'Alayhi al-Salam*, saying, 'The little but continuous deed with certainty is far better in the sight of Allah than a great deal of deeds without certainty.'"

H 1559, Ch. 26, h 4

Al-Husayn ibn Muhammad has narrated from Mu'alla ibn Muhammad from al-Washsha' from Aban from Zurara from abu 'Abd Allah, *'Alayhi al-Salam*, who has said the following:

"Amir al-Mu'minin (Ali ibn abu Talib), *'Alayhi al-Salam*, once said from the pulpit, 'No one among you can ever sense the taste of belief until he comes to know that whatever has happened right could not have happened wrong and whatever has happened wrong could not have happened right.'"

H 1560, Ch. 26, h 5

Ali ibn Ibrahim has narrated from his father from ibn abu 'Umayr from Zayd al-Shahham from abu 'Abd Allah, *'Alayhi al-Salam*, who has said the following:

"Once, Amir al-Mu'minin (Ali ibn abu Talib), *'Alayhi al-Salam*, during his court session, had sat leaning against a wall that was bent. Certain people asked him not to sit near the defective wall. Amir al-Mu'minin (Ali ibn abu Talib), *'Alayhi al-Salam*, said, 'This is like a man's guarding his death,' (Imam's expression shows such guarding is useless). When the Imam moved away, the wall crumbled. The Imam said, 'Amir al-Mu'minin (Ali ibn abu Talib), *'Alayhi al-Salam*, would often do such and similar things and that was because of certainty.'"

H 1561, Ch. 26, h 6

A number of our people have narrated from Ahmad ibn Muhammad ibn Khalid from Ahmad ibn Muhammad ibn abu Nasr from Safwan al-Jammal who has said the following:

"Once I asked abu 'Abd Allah, *'Alayhi al-Salam*, about the words of Allah, the Most Majestic, the Most Holy: 'The tumbling wall belonged to two orphans in the town whose father has been a righteous person. Underneath the wall there was a treasure that belonged to them. . . .' (18:82)

"The Imam said, 'It is a fact that the treasure did not consist of gold and silver. It consisted of four words: "No one deserves to be worshipped except I (Allah). Whoever has realized with certainty that death is inevitable has enough reason not to laugh for a year. Whoever has realized with certainty that accountability on the Day of Judgment is true has enough reason for his heart not to rest in ease. Whoever has realized with certainty that Allah does everything with strict measurements has enough reason not to fear anyone except Allah.""""

H 1562, Ch. 26, h 7

It is narrated from him (narrator of the Hadith above) from Ali ibn al-Hakam from Safwan al-Jammal from abu 'Abd Allah, *'Alayhi al-Salam*, who has said the following:

"Amir al-Mu'minin (Ali ibn abu Talib), *'Alayhi al-Salam*, has said, 'A servant of Allah cannot sense the taste of belief until he comes to know that whatever has happened to him right could not have happened wrong and whatever has happened to him wrong could not have happened right. The one who can harm or benefit others is only Allah, the Most Majestic, the Most Holy.'"

H 1563, Ch. 26, h 8

Muhammad ibn Yahya has narrated from Ahmad ibn Muhammad ibn 'Isa from al-Washsha' from 'Abd ibn Sinan from abu Hamza from Sa'id ibn Qays al-Hamadani who has said the following:

"One day during a war I looked on a man who was wearing two pieces of garment on him. I moved my horse nearer to him and I found him to be Amir al-Mu'minin (Ali ibn abu Talib), *'Alayhi al-Salam*, and I said, 'O Amir al-Mu'minin, is this a place (to be in with just two pieces of garment and no coats of arms)?' The Imam said, 'Yes, O Sa'id ibn al-Qays. For every servant of Allah there is a guard from Allah and a protecting angel to see that he will not fall off of a cliff or into a well, but when the appointed time comes for his death the angels just leave him alone to his own self.'"

H 1564, Ch. 26, h 9

Al-Husayn ibn Muhammad has narrated from Mu'alla ibn Muhammad from Ali ibn Asbat who has said the following:

"I heard abu al-Hassan al-Rida, *'Alayhi al-Salam*, saying, 'In the treasure mentioned in the words of Allah, the Most Majestic, the Most Holy: "Underneath the wall there was a treasure that belonged to them. . . .," (18:82) there were the following statements: 'In the name of Allah, the Beneficent, the Merciful, strange to me is the case of a person who is certain of the coming of death but he feels happy. Strange to me is the case of a person who is certain of the strict measurement of Allah but he feels depressed. Strange to me is the case of a person who is aware of all the up and down in the world with its inhabitants but he still relies on it. It is expected from a man who has understanding of Allah not to accuse Allah in His decision and not to consider Him slow in His Providence.' I then said, 'May Allah keep my soul in service for your cause, I want to write it down. The Imam gave me, I swear by Allah, the inkpot so I can write. I reached out to his hands and kissed them and then took the inkpot and wrote down the Hadith.'"

H 1565, Ch. 26, h 10

Muhammad ibn Yahya has narrated from Ahmad ibn Muhammad from Ali ibn al-Hakam from 'Abd al-Rahman al-'Arzami from his father, from abu 'Abd Allah, *'Alayhi al-Salam*, who has said the following:

"Qanber, a worker for Ali, *'Alayhi al-Salam*, loved Ali intensely. Whenever Imam went out he followed him with a sword for protection. Once at night Imam Ali saw Qanber and asked him, 'What is the matter with you?' He said, 'O Amir al-Mu'minin, I follow you for your protection.' The Imam said, 'Qamber, what is the matter with you, are you protecting me from the people of the heavens or from the people of the earth?' He said, 'I do not protect you from the people of the heavens but I protect you from the people of the earth.' The Imam said, 'The people of the earth can do nothing to me without permission from Allah from the heavens. Qamber, go back home and he obeyed.'"

H 1566, Ch. 26, h 11

Ali ibn Ibrahim has narrated from Muhammad ibn 'Isa from Yunus from the one whom he has mentioned, he has said the following:

"It was said to al-Rida, *'Alayhi al-Salam*, 'You speak of it (Your Divine Authority) and blood drips from the sword (of your enemies).' The Imam said, 'Allah has a valley that is gold. He has guarded it with ants, the weakest creature. Even if the camels of Khurasan (North East parts of Iran) try to go there they cannot reach it.'"

Chapter 27 - To Agree with the Decision (of Allah)

H 1567, Ch. 27, h 1

Ali ibn Ibrahim has narrated from his father from ibn abu 'Umayr from Jamil ibn Salih from certain shaykhs of Banu al-Najashi from abu 'Abd Allah, *'Alayhi al-Salam*, who has said the following:

"The head of obedience to Allah is patience and agreeing with the decisions of Allah in all matters whether a servant may love or dislike doing so. Of the servant of Allah anyone who agrees with the decisions of Allah in all matters which he loves or dislikes, should know that agreeing, in fact, is in his best interest."

H 1568, Ch. 27, h 2

A number of our people have narrated from Ahmad ibn 'Abd Allah from his father from Hammad ibn 'Isa from 'Abd Allah ibn Muskan from Layth al-Muradi from abu 'Abd Allah, *'Alayhi al-Salam*, who has said the following:

"Abu 'Abd Allah, *'Alayhi al-Salam*, has said, 'The most knowledgeable among people is the one who agrees with the decisions of Allah, the Most Majestic, the Most Holy.'"

H 1569, Ch. 27, h 3

It is narrated from him from Yahya ibn Ibrahim ibn abu al-Balad from 'Asim ibn Humayd from abu Hamza al-Thumali from Ali ibn al-Husayn, *'Alayhi al-Salam*, who has said the following:

"Patience and agreeing with the decisions of Allah is the head of obedience to Allah. If one exercises patience and agrees with the decisions of Allah in all the matters which he loves or dislikes, Allah, the Most Majestic, the Most Holy, will not make any decision in any of his affairs which he loves or dislikes but that the decisions are in his best interest."

H 1570, Ch. 27, h 4

Muhammad ibn Yahya has narrated from Ahmad ibn Muhammad ibn 'Isa from ibn Mahbub from Dawud al-Riqqiy from 'Ubayda al-Hadhdha' from abu Ja'far, *'Alayhi al-Salam*, who has said the following:

"The Messenger of Allah has said that Allah, the Most Majestic, the Most Holy, has said, 'Among My believing servants there are those whose religious lives can only be at their best with wealth, comfort and good health. I try them by means of wealth, comfort and good health and this makes their religious affairs to be in the best condition. Also among My believing servants there are those whose religious lives are only at their best with poverty, destitution and ailing health. I try them by means of poverty, destitution and ailing health and this helps their religious lives to be in the best condition. I know what is good for the religious matters of my believing servants. Among My believing servants there are those who strive to worship Me. They wake up from sleep leaving their comfortable pillow for Tahajjud (special prayer at night). They experiences fatigue and I allow slumber overcome them on one or two nights, a trial from Me to see if he continues, he goes to sleep and wakes up upset and angry over his own self. If I allow him to do the way he wants to worship, he may develop a sense of conceit (unwanted pride) that can lead him to mischief in his deeds. This may bring about his destruction. It can so happen due to his happiness with whatever his soul desires. He may begin to feel as if he has excelled all worshippers and has surpassed the limits of defective worship. In so doing he moves away from Me even though he thinks that he is getting closer to Me. Therefore, they must not rely on their good deeds that they do to receive rewards from Me. Even if they strive hard, tire themselves and finish their lives worshipping Me they fall short, in worshipping Me truly, in their quest for My generous rewards, My bounties in paradise and high positions near Me. They must only trust in My mercy, be happy with My generosity and always be hopeful about Me. In such cases My mercy will reach them as well as my approval and forgiveness and my pardon will provide them cover; I am Allah, the Most Beneficent, the Most Merciful, and thus I have taken such names.'"

H 1571, Ch. 27, h 5

A number of our people have narrated from Sahl ibn Ziyad from Ahmad ibn Muhammad ibn abu Nasr from Safwan al-Jammal from abu al-Hassan, the 1st, *'Alayhi al Salam*, who has said the following:

"One who has proper understanding about Allah must not feel that Allah procrastinates in sending his sustenance or accuse Him in His decisions."

H 1572, Ch. 27, h 6

Abu Ali al-Ash'ari has narrated from Muhammad ibn 'Abd al-Jabbar from Muhammad ibn Isma'il from Ali ibn al-Nu'man from 'Amr ibn al-Nuhayk Bayya' al-Harawi who has said the following:

"Abu 'Abd Allah, *'Alayhi al-Salam*, has said, 'Allah, the Most Majestic, the Most Holy, has said, "Whatever conditions I may turn My believing servant to are for his good. He then must agree with My decisions, be patient in My trial and appreciate My favors. I will then, O Muhammad, count him among the truthful ones."'"

H 1573, Ch. 27, h 7

Muhammad ibn Yahya has narrated from Ahmad ibn Muhammad ibn 'Isa from al-Hassan ibn Mahbub from Malik ibn 'Atiyah from Dawud ibn Farqad from abu 'Abd Allah, *'Alayhi al-Salam*, who has said the following:

"Of the revelations that Allah, the Most Majestic, the Most Holy, sent to Moses ibn 'Imran was as follows: 'O, Moses, son of 'Imran, I have not created anything more beloved to Me than My believing servant. I try him only because it is for his good. I give him good health just for his good. I hold back what is evil for him in favor of what is for his good. I know best in what conditions My servant works for his own best interest. He then must bear patience in My trials, appreciate My favors and agree with My decision. I count him among the truthful ones before Me if he acts according to My pleasure and obeys My command.'"

H 1574, Ch. 27, h 8

Abu Ali al-Ash'ari has narrated from Muhammad ibn 'Abd al-Jabbar from Safwan ibn Yahya from Fudayl ibn 'Uthman from ibn abu Ya'fur from abu 'Abd Allah, *'Alayhi al-Salam*, who has said the following:

"The case of a Muslim (believer) man is amazing. There is no decision that Allah, the Most Majestic, the Most Holy, makes about him but that it is in his best interest. Even if he is cut in pieces with scissors, still it is for his good. If he may possess the kingdom of the East and West of the earth, still it is for his good."

H 1575, Ch. 27, h 9

Muhammad ibn Yahya has narrated from Ahmad ibn Muhammad ibn 'Isa from ibn Sinan from Salih ibn 'Aqaba from 'Abd Allah ibn Muhammad al-Ja'fi from abu Ja'far, *'Alayhi al-Salam*, who has said the following:

"Abu Ja'far, *'Alayhi al-Salam*, has said, 'The most proper people to agree with the decisions of Allah, the Most Majestic, the Most Holy, are those who have recognized Allah, the Most Majestic, the Most Holy. Whoever agrees with the decision of Allah that is to take place anyway, Allah increases his reward. Whoever disagrees with the decision of Allah, the decision is, inevitably, applied to him but his reward becomes void.'"

H 1576, Ch. 27, h 10

Ali ibn Ibrahim has narrated from his father from al-Qasim ibn Muhammad from al-Minqari form Ali ibn Hashim ibn al-Burayd from his father who has said the following:

"Ali ibn al-Husayn, *'Alayhi al-Salam*, has said, 'Abstinence from worldly pleasures has ten levels. Its highest level is the lowest level of piety and reserve. The highest level of piety and reserve is the lowest level of certainty. The highest level of certainty is the lowest level of consent to the decision of Allah.'"

H 1577, Ch. 27, h 11

A number of our people have narrated from Ahmad ibn Muhammad ibn Khalid from Muhammad ibn Ali from Ali ibn Asbat from those whom he has mentioned from abu 'Abd Allah, *'Alayhi al-Salam*, who has said the following:

"Al-Hassan ibn Ali, *'Alayhi al-Salam*, once met 'Abd Allah ibn Ja'far and said to him, 'O, 'Abd Allah, how can a believer be a believer when he disagrees with the decision of Allah about his share and belittles his position while the ruler over him is Allah? I guarantee that Allah accepts the prayer of one in whose heart (mind) no suggestion takes place except agreement with the decisions of Allah).'"

H 1578, Ch. 27, h 12

It is narrated from him from his father from ibn Sinan from those whom he has mentioned from abu 'Abd Allah, *'Alayhi al-Salam,* who has said the following:

"I (the narrator) asked him, (abu 'Abd Allah, *'Alayhi al-Salam*), 'By what means can a believer know that he is a believer?' The Imam said, '(He can find out) by means of his submitting himself to Allah, and agreeing with whatever happiness or sadness that he may experience.'"

H 1579, Ch. 27, h 13

It is narrated from him from his father from ibn Sinan from al-Husayn ibn al-Muhtar from 'Abd Allah ibn abu Ya'fur from abu 'Abd Allah, *'Alayhi al-Salam,* who has said the following:

"The Messenger of Allah, *'Alayhi al-Salam,* never said about something that had taken place, 'Would that something else had happened.'"

Chapter 28 - Leaving It to Allah to Be the Person in Charge of Affairs, and Having Trust in Him

H 1580, Ch. 28, h 1

Muhammad ibn Yahya has narrated from Ahmad ibn Muhammad from Muhammad ibn Sinan from Mufaddal from abu 'Abd Allah who has said the following:

"Allah, the Most Majestic, the Most Holy, sent revelation to David, 'Any one among my servants who seeks protection with Me and not with any other creature, and I find this in his intention, thereafter even if all the heavens and earth and those in them conspire against him, I will most certainly find for him a way to escape. On the other hand, whoever among My servants tries to seek protection with My creatures, and I find this in his intention, I most certainly cut off from him all the means of the heavens and earth and make it (earth) extremely angry beneath him and I am not concerned in the least where he will perish.'"

H 1581, Ch. 28, h 2

Abu Ali al-Ash'ari has narrated from ibn 'Abd al-Jabbar from ibn Mahbub from abu Hafs al-'Asha' from Amr ibn Khalid from abu Hamza al-Thumali from Ali ibn al-Husayn, *'Alayhi al-Salam,* who has said the following:

"Once I walked out till I reached this wall and I leaned against it. At that time a man wearing only two pieces of white cloth was looking toward my face. He then said, 'O, Ali son of al-Husayn, *'Alayhi al-Salam,* you look very sad, as if you have suffered a great deal. Is it because of worldly things wherein the sustenance from Allah is available for all the good and bad people?' I said, 'I am not sad because of the worldly things; they are just as you said.' He asked, 'Is it then for the matters of the life hereafter, for which the promises will all come true? The Judge therein will be the forceful ruler,' or he said, 'Powerful ruler?' I said, 'This also is not the reason; it is just as you said it is.' He then asked, 'Why are you then so sad?' I said, 'It is because of the mischief of ibn Zubayr and the conditions of the people.' The Imam said, 'He then laughed and said, 'O Ali son of al-Husayn, *'Alayhi al-Salam,* have you ever come to know of anyone who prayed and Allah did not listen to his prayer?' I said, 'No, I have not known anyone as such.' He then said, 'Have you come to know of anyone who trusted Allah and He did not protect him?' I said, 'No (I have not found any such person).' He then asked, 'Have you come to know of anyone who asked Allah and he was not given anything?' I said, 'No (I have not found anyone as such).'

"The Imam said, 'The man then disappeared from my sight."

Ali ibn Ibrahim has narrated from his father from ibn Mahbub a similar Hadith.

H 1582, Ch. 28, h 3

A number of our people have narrated from Sahl ibn Ziyad from Ali ibn Hassan from his uncle 'Abd al-Rahman ibn Kathir from abu 'Abd Allah, *'Alayhi al-Salam*, who has said the following:

"Abu 'Abd Allah, *'Alayhi al-Salam*, has said, 'Wealth and glory circle around. If they find a place, where trust is found, they settle just therein.'"

A number of our people have narrated from Ahmad ibn abu 'Abd Allah from Muhammad ibn Ali from Ali ibn Hassan a similar Hadith.

H 1583, Ch. 28, h 4

Muhammad ibn Yahya has narrated from Ahmad ibn Muhammad ibn 'Isa from ibn Mahbub from 'Abd Allah ibn Sinan from abu 'Abd Allah, *'Alayhi al-Salam*, who has said the following:

"Any servan (of Allah) who comes forward to accept what Allah, the Most Majestic, the Most Holy, loves, Allah comes forward with what he (the servant) loves. Whoever seeks protection with Allah, He protects him. To whoever's rescue Allah comes He will protect him even if the skies were to fall on earth or an incident involving all the inhabitants of earth were to befall them, but the person under the protection of Allah would be among the members of the party of Allah, well guarded against all misfortunes. Is it not that Allah, the Most Majestic, the Most Holy, says, 'The pious people live in a peaceful place?'" (44:51)

H 1584, Ch. 28, h 5

A number of our people have narrated from Ahmad ibn Muhammad ibn Khalid from more than one narrator from Ali ibn Asbat from Ahmad ibn Úmar al-Hallal from Ali ibn Suwayd who has said the following:

"I asked abu al-Hassan 1st, *'Alayhi al-Salam*, about the words of Allah, the Most Majestic, the Most Holy: 'Whoever trusts Allah, He is enough protection against all (harms).' (65:3)

"The Imam said, 'Trust in Allah is of several degrees. One level of such trust is to trust Him in all matters. Whatever He does, you must remain happy and agree with His decision, knowing that He does not keep anything good and excellent from you and that the decision in the matter is in His hands. You then must leave all the affairs to Allah to be the person in charge (of all affairs) and have confidence in Him in this and other issues.'"

H 1585, Ch. 28, h 6

A number of our people have narrated from Sahl ibn Ziyad and Ali ibn Ibrahim from his father all from Yahya ibn al-Mubarak from 'Abd Allah ibn Jublah from Muáwiyah ibn Wahab from abu 'Abd Allah, *'Alayhi al-Salam*, who has said the following:

"Abu 'Abd Allah, *'Alayhi al-Salam*, has said, 'To whoever three things are given he is not denied three things. To whoever prayer is given he is given acceptance to his prayer. To whoever thankfulness is given he is given increased favors. To whoever trust is given he is given protection.' Then He said, 'Have you read in the book of Allah, the Most Majestic, the Most Holy, "Whoever places his trust in Allah, He provides him sufficient protection." (14:7) "If you be thankful We will increase the favor. Pray to Me, I will accept your prayer."'" (25:60)

H 1586, Ch. 28, h 7

Al-Husayn ibn Muhammad has narrated from Mu'alla ibn Muhammad from abu Ali from Muhammad ibn al-Hassan from al-Husayn ibn Rashid from al-Husayn ibn Úlwan who has said the following:

"We were in a gathering to seek knowledge and education. During one of the journeys I was left without any resources for my expenditures. A certain individual of my friends was concerned about who would look after my needs. I said, 'So and so will look after my needs.' He then said, 'I swear by Allah, you will not get what you need and you will not achieve what you hope to achieve.' I then asked, 'How do you know, may Allah grant you favors?' He said, 'Abu 'Abd Allah, *'Alayhi al-Salam*, told me that he has read in a certain book that Allah, the Most Blessed, the Most High, has said, "I swear by My Majesty, by My Glory, by My Greatness, by My Highness over My Throne, I will turn the hopes of all who hope in people other than Me into hopelessness, and I will dress him with the clothe of humiliation before the people, and move him away from nearness to Me. I will move him away from My additional favors. How dare he expects help from others in hardship? All hardships are under My control. He expects others to help him. He knocks on the door of the others and the key to all closed doors is in My hand and My door is open for those who pray to Me. Who is he that hopes to receive help from Me in his difficulties and I have left him in hardship? Is there anyone who had hopes in Me in a great hardship and I cutoff his hopes in Me? I have placed the hopes of My servants safe with Me. They did not agree with My safeguarding their interests. I have filled up My heavens with those who never tire from speaking of My Glory. I have commanded them not to close the doors between Me and My servants. They did not trust My words. Do they not know that if I afflict one with My hardships no one have the ability to remove them without My permission.

"Why is it then that I see him mindless of Me? I granted him favor without his asking, then I removed the favor and he did not ask Me to return it but he asked others. Has he not seen Me grant favors even before asking. How would I refuse My favors when I am asked for a favor? Am I stingy and do My servants consider Me as such? Do generosity and benevolence not originate from Me? Are not forgiveness and kindness in My hand? Am I not the center of hopes? Who is he that cuts off his hopes from Me? Are those who cut off their hopes from Me not afraid of placing their hopes in others? If the inhabitants of My heavens and the inhabitants of My earth would all have hopes in Me and I then grant each one equal to that which all of them wished to have, no shortages would take place in my kingdom even to the size of an atom. How can there be any shortages in the kingdom that I Myself am the keeper of? How hopeless is the case of those who cut off their hopes from Me? How hopeless is the case of those who disobey Me and do not expect anything from Me?"'"

H 1587, Ch. 28, h 8

Muhammad ibn Yahya has narrated from Muhammad ibn al-Hassan from certain individuals of our people from 'Abbad ibn Ya'qub al-Rawijni from Sa'id ibn 'Abd al-Rahman who has said the following:

"I was at Yanbu' with Musa ibn 'Abd Allah. My supplies for my expenses were exhausted during certain journeys. A certain person of the children of al-Husayn asked me, 'Whose assistence do you hope will help out overcome your difficult conditions?' I said, 'Musa ibn 'Abd Allah will provide for my expenses.' He then said, 'He, therefore, will not provide you any help, and you will not succeed in your quest.' I then asked, 'Why it will be as such?' He said, 'It is because I have found in certain books of my ancestors that Allah, the Most Majestic, the Most Holy, has said, ". . . He mentioned a Hadith similar to the previous Hadith."' I then said, 'O descendent of the Messenger of Allah, dictate it to me.' He dictated it to me and I said, 'I swear by Allah that I will not ask him (Musa ibn 'Abd Allah) to help me.'"

Chapter 29 - Fear and Hope

H 1588, Ch. 29, h 1

A number of our people have narrated from Ahmad ibn Muhammad from Ali ibn Hadid from Mansur ibn Yunus from al-Harith ibn al-Mughira or his father who has said the following:

"Once I asked abu 'Abd Allah, *'Alayhi al-Salam*, 'What did the will of Luqman (the person mentioned in Chapter 31 of the Holy Quran) contain?' The Imam said, 'It contained amazing things and the most amazing one was what he said to his son, "My son, be pious before Allah, the Majestic, the Glorious, such that even if you come into His presence with the good deeds of all man and Jinn, Thaqilayn, you will still fear His punishment. On the other hand your hope in Him must be so great that even if you come into His presence with all the sins of all man and Jinn, Thaqilayn, you will still be hopeful for His kindness and mercy."'"

"Abu 'Abd Allah, *'Alayhi al-Salam*, then said, 'My father has said, "There is no believing servant of Allah without the presence of two lights in his heart. There is the light of hope and the light of fear. They are such that on weighing, no one exceeds the other in any way (in lightness or heaviness)."'"

H 1589, Ch. 29, h 2

Muhammad ibn al-Hassan has narrated from Sahl ibn Ziyad from Yahya ibn al-Mubarak from 'Abd Allah ibn Jabala from Ishaq ibn 'Ammar who has said the following:

"Once abu 'Abd Allah, *'Alayhi al-Salam*, said, 'O Ishaq, have fear of Allah as if you see Him. Even if you do not see Him He sees you. If you think that He does not see you, you have certainly rejected belief. If you believe that He sees you and you disobey Him you have considered Him as the most insignificant observer.'"

H 1590, Ch. 29, h 3

Muhammad ibn Yahya has narrated from Ahmad ibn Muhammad ibn 'Isa from al-Hassan ibn Mahbub from al-Hatham ibn Waqid who has said the following:

"I heard abu 'Abd Allah, *'Alayhi al-Salam*, saying, 'Whoever fears Allah, Allah causes everything to be afraid of him. Whoever does not fear Allah, Allah frightens him from everything.'"

H 1591, Ch. 29, h 4

A number of our people have narrated from Ahmad ibn abu 'Abd Allah from his father from Hamza ibn 'Abd Allah al-Ja' fary from Jamil ibn Darraj from abu Hamza who has said the following:

"Abu 'Abd Allah, *'Alayhi al-Salam*, has said, 'Whoever has come to know Allah, he fears Allah. Whoever fears Allah, ignores his own soul in this world.'"

H 1592, Ch. 29, h 5

It is narrated from him (narrator of the Hadith above) from ibn abu al-Najran from those whom he has mentioned and who has said the following:

"Once I said to abu 'Abd Allah, *'Alayhi al-Salam*, 'Certain people commit sins and say that they hope. They continue until their death arrives.' The Imam said, 'Such people have strayed away in hopes. They lie and they do not have any hope. Whoever hopes to have something, he tries to find it. People fearing something, run away from it.'"

H 1593, Ch. 29, h 6

Ali ibn Muhammad has also narrated the above Hadith in a mafu' manner from who has said the following:

"I said to abu 'Abd Allah, *'Alayhi al-Salam*, 'Certain people of your supporters commit smaller sins and say that they have hope (in Allah's forgiveness).' The Imam said, 'They lie. They are not our supporters. They are a people whose hope has caused them to deviate. Whoever has hope in something, he works to achieve it. Whoever is afraid of something, he keeps away from it.'"

H 1594, Ch. 29, h 7

A number of our people have narrated from Ahmad ibn Muhammad ibn Khalid from certain individuals of his people from Salih ibn Hamza in a mafu' manner from abu 'Abd Allah, *'Alayhi al-Salam*, who has said the following:

"To have intense fear of Allah, the Most Majestic, the Most Holy, is part of worship. Allah has said, 'Of the servants of Allah who fear Him are the scholars.' (35:28) Allah, Whose praise is great, has said, 'Do not fear people but fear Me.' (5:44) Allah, the Most Blessed, the Most High, has said, 'For those who fear Allah, He finds a way out (in their difficulties).' (65:2) "The narrator has said that abu 'Abd Allah, *'Alayhi al-Salam*, then said, 'Love for fame and popularity (domination) will not exist in the heart of one who has fear and is concerned (about his relation toward Allah).'"

H 1595, Ch. 29, h 8

Ali ibn Ibrahim has narrated from Ahmad ibn Muhammad ibn Khalid from al-Hassan ibn al-Husayn from Muhammad ibn Sinan from abu Sa'id al-Makari from abu Hamza al-Thumali from Ali ibn al-Husayn, *'Alayhi al-Salam*, who has said the following:

"A man once set sail with his people and suffered a shipwreck. Everyone on board died except his wife who clung to a board and landed on an island where there lived a robber who had left no instance of disobedience to Allah but had committed them all. Without knowing anything about the shipwreck he found the woman standing over his head. He raised his head and asked her, 'Are you a human being or a Jinni?' She replied, 'I am a human being.' He then did not say any other word but began to behave like a husband. When he advanced for a carnal relation she panicked. He asked, 'Why have you panicked?' She said, 'I am afraid of this, pointing to the heavens.' He then asked, 'Have you done any such thing wrong against Him?' She said, 'No, I swear by His Glory that I have not done any such thing against Him.' He then said, 'You fear Him this much when you have done nothing against Him and it is only I that force you into this. In fact, I swear by Allah, I am the one who must be afraid of Him more so than you are.' The robber then moved away without speaking a word and went back to his family. He then had no other aim but to repent and return to Allah. Once as he was walking on the road, a monk joined him walking in the same direction. The day was hot and the monk suggested that they should pray to Allah to send them a piece of cloud to provide shade against the hot sun. The young man (once a robber) said, 'I do not think I have any good deed with my Lord so I dare not pray to Him.' The monk said, 'I pray and you say, Amen.' He agreed and the monk began to pray and the young man said the Amen part. Quickly a piece of cloud appeared and provided them a shadow. They walked comfortably under the shadow against the sun. The road then divided and the young man walked in one road and the monk in the other one. The shadow went along over the young man. The monk said, 'You are better than me. The prayer was accepted because of you, not because of me. Now tell me what is your story?' The young man told him the story of the woman. The monk said, 'Your sins of the past are forgiven because of fear that entered in your heart. Pay proper attention to your future behaviors.'"

H 1596, Ch. 29, h 9

Muhammad ibn Yahya has narrated from Ahmad ibn Muhammad from Ali ibn al-Nu'man from Hamza ibn Humran who has said the following:

"I heard abu 'Abd Allah, *'Alayhi al-Salam*, saying, 'Of the preserved speeches of the Holy Prophet one is his words as follows: "O people, for you there are the sources of knowledge. You must reach out to them. For you there are the end goals and you must reach them. You must know that a believer works between two frightening facts. On one side is the time that has passed and he does not know what Allah has done about it, and on the other is the time to come that he does not know how Allah will decide about. The believing servant (of Allah) must take from hisown soul for hisown soul and from his worldly life for his hereafter, during his youth before his getting old and in his lifetime before his death. I swear by the One in whose hand is the soul of Muhammad that after the worldly life there will be no chance to please anyone and there will be no other home except paradise or hell.'"

H 1597, Ch. 29, h 10

It is narrated from him (narrator of the Hadith above) from Ahmad from ibn Mahbub from Dawud al-Ruqiyy from abu 'Abd Allah, *'Alayhi al-Salam*, who has said the following:

"About the words of Allah, the Most Majestic, the Most Holy, 'For one who fears of the position of his Lord there are two gardens.'(55:46) The Imam said, 'One who knows that Allah sees him, hears what he says and knows what he does, good or evil, and it keeps him off wicked deeds, such person is the one who fears the position of his Lord and stops his soul from following his (negative) desires.'"

H 1598, Ch. 29, h 11

It is narrated from him (narrator of the Hadith above) from Ahmad ibn Muhammad from ibn Sinan from ibn Muskan from al-Hassan ibn abu Sarah who has said the following:

"I heard abu 'Abd Allah, *'Alayhi al-Salam*, saying, 'A believer is not a believer until he is fearing and hopeful. He cannot become fearing and hopeful until he comes to know what to fear and in whom to have hope.'"

H 1599, Ch. 29, h 12

Ali ibn Ibrahim has narrated from Muhammad ibn 'Isa from Yunus from Fudayl ibn 'Uthman from abu 'Ubaydah al-Hadhdha' from abu 'Abd Allah, *'Alayhi al-Salam*, who has said the following:

"A believer lives in two frightening conditions. In his life he is concerned about his sins of the past about which he does not know how Allah has decided. He is also worried about his future, for not knowing what kind of destructive sins he may get involved in. Therefore, he is always fearful and nothing serves his best interest except fear."

H 1600, Ch. 29, h 13

Ali ibn Ibrahim has narrated from his father from ibn abu 'Umayr from certain individuals of his people from abu 'Abd Allah, *'Alayhi al-Salam*, who has said the following:

"My father would say, 'In the heart of every believing servant (of Allah) there are two lights. There is the light of fear and the light of hope. On being weighed no one of these lights weighs differently from the other.'"

Chapter 30 - Hopefulness Toward Allah, the Most Majestic, the Most Holy

H 1601, Ch. 30, h 1

A number of our people have narrated from Ahmad ibn Muhammad from ibn Mahbub from Dawud ibn Kathir from abu 'Ubaydah al-Hadhdha' from abu Ja'far, *'Alayhi al-Salam*, who has said the following:

"The Messenger of Allah has said, 'Allah, the Most Blessed, the Most High, has said, "The doers of good deeds must not rely on their deeds alone to receive rewards from Me. If they strive and tire themselves (for a lifetime) to worship Me they still have shortcomings in their worship. They cannot reach the essence of worshipping Me to find what they look for. They cannot receive My grace and bounties in My paradise and high ranks near Me without My kindness. They must rely on My kindness, hope for My additional rewards, be comfortable in their hopefulness about Me. My kindness and mercy, in such cases, will reach them, from Me My gratification and forgiveness will close up to them, and My pardon will provide them cover. I am Allah, the Beneficent, the Merciful, and thus I have named Myself."'"

H 1602, Ch. 30, h 2

Ibn Mahbub has narrated from Jamil ibn Salih from Burayd ibn Mu'awiyah from abu Ja'far, *'Alayhi al-Salam*, who has said the following:

"We have found in the book of Ali, *'Alayhi al-Salam*, that the Messenger of Allah said from the pulpit, 'I swear by the One besides Whom no one else deserves to be worshipped, a believer never receives any good in this life and in the hereafter, except because of his hopefulness toward Allah, his confidence in Allah, his good moral behavior and his abstaining from backbiting the believers. I swear by the One besides Whom no one else deserves to be worshipped, Allah does not punish a believer after his repenting and asking forgiveness except because of his despair toward Allah, his shortcoming in his hope from Allah, his bad moral behaviors and his backbiting of the believers. I swear by the One besides Whom no one else deserves to be worshipped that, hope of a believer does not exist without Allah running his affairs according to the hopeful intentions of the believer. It is because nobility is of the attributes of Allah; in His hand is all good, and He considers Himself indebted toward His believing servants, who are hopeful about Him, not to allow their hope remain fruitless. Therefore, be hopeful about Allah and be interested with Him.'"

H 1603, Ch. 30, h 3

Muhammad ibn Yahya has narrated from Ahmad ibn Muhammad ibn 'Isa from Muhammad ibn Isma'il ibn Bazi' from abu al-Hassan al-Rida, *'Alayhi al-Salam*, who has said the following:

"Be hopeful about Allah, because Allah, the Most Majestic, the Most Holy, has said, 'I deal according to the thinking of My believing servant toward Me. I am good to him if he thinks good about Me and I am not good to him if he does not think good about Me.'"

H 1604, Ch. 30, h 4

Ali ibn Ibrahim has narrated from his father from al-Qasim ibn Muhammad al-Minqari from Sufyan ibn 'Uyayna who has said the following:

"I heard abu 'Abd Allah, *'Alayhi al-Salam*, saying, 'To be hopeful toward Allah means not to have hope in anyone except Allah and not to be afraid of anything but one's sins.'"

Chapter 31 -To Profess One's Shortcomings

H 1605, Ch. 31, h 1

Muhammad ibn Yahya has narrated from Ahmad ibn Muhammad ibn 'Isa from al-Hassan ibn Mahbub from Sa'D ibn abu Khalaf from abu al-Hassan Musa, *'Alayhi al-Salam*, who to one of his sons has said the following:

"My son, you must work hard and do not allow your soul to lead you out of a feeling of always falling short in worshipping Allah, the Most Majestic, the Most Holy, and in obedience to Him; Allah is not worshipped as truly as He should be worshipped."

H 1606, Ch. 31, h 2

A number of our people have narrated from Ahmad ibn abu 'Abd Allah from certain people (scholars of Kufa) of Iraq from Muhammad al-Muthanna al-Hadrami from his father from 'Uthman ibn Zayd from Jabir who has said the following:

"Once abu Ja'far, *'Alayhi al-Salam*, said to me, 'O Jabir, (I wish) Allah grants you a chance to think of yourself as falling short in your worship and having deficiencies.'"

H 1607, Ch. 31, h 3

It is narrated from him (narrator of the Hadith above) from Faddal from al-Hassan al-Jahm who has said the following:

"I heard abu al-Hassan, *'Alayhi al-Salam*, saying, 'A man of banu Israel worshipped Allah for forty years. He then offered an offering that was not accepted. He said to his soul, "Whatever I face is only because of you and there is no sin but that you are responsible therefor."' The Imam said, 'Allah, the Most Blessed, the Most High, then revealed to him, "Your blaming your soul is better than your forty years of worship."'"

H 1608, Ch. 31, h 4
Abu Ali al-Ash'ari has narrated from 'Isa ibn Ayyub from Ali ibn Mahziyar from al-Fadl ibn Yunus from abu al-Hassan, *'Alayhi al-Salam*, who has said the following:
"You should say very often, 'O Lord, do not include me among those whose beliefs are temporary and do not make me feel free of shortcomings.' I (the narrator) then asked, 'I know the meaning of people whose beliefs are temporary. They come into a religion and then abandon it. What is the meaning of, "Do not make me feel free of shortcomings?"' The Imam said, 'It is when after all the worship of Allah, the Most Majestic, the Most Holy, that you may do, you still think that you are falling far short of doing true worship. All people fall far short in their worshipping Allah truly except those to whom Allah, the Most Majestic, the Most Holy, has granted protection.'"

Chapter 32 - Obedience and Piety

H 1609, Ch. 32, h 1
Ali ibn Ibrahim has narrated from his father from Ahmad ibn Muhammad ibn abu Nasr from Muhammad brother of 'Amr from Muhammad ibn Muslim from abu Ja'far, *'Alayhi al-Salam*, who has said the following:
"Do not allow (false) religions to confuse you. Of our Shi'a and true followers are only those who obey Allah, the Most Majestic, the Most Holy."

H 1610, Ch. 32, h 2
A number of our people have narrated from Ahmad ibn Muhammad from ibn Fadal from 'Asim ibn Humayd from abu Hamza al-Thumali from abu Ja'far, *'Alayhi al-Salam*, who has said the following:
"The Messenger of Allah addressed the people during his farewell (last) visit to Makka, 'O people, I swear by Allah, everything that can take you closer to paradise and farther away from hell I have commanded you all to follow. Everything that may take you closer to hell and farther away from paradise I have prohibited you to do. You must know that the trusted spirit has inspired me that no soul dies before his supply of sustenance is completely exhausted. Be pious before Allah and do your best in search of means of sustenance. Do not allow laziness to overcome you in your search to make a living, or lead you to make a living through improper means; nothing is achievable from what is with Allah except through obedience to Him.'"

H 1611, Ch. 32, h 3
Abu Ali al-Ash'ari has narrated from Muhammad ibn Salim and Ahmad ibn abu 'Abd Allah from his father all from Ahmad ibn al-Nadr from 'Amr ibn Shamir from Jabir from abu Ja'far, *'Alayhi al-Salam*, who has said the following:
"O Jabir, do people think just claiming to be our Shi'a and saying they love us (Ahl al-Bayt) is enough for their salvation? I swear by Allah, of our Shi'a are only

those who are pious before Allah and obey Him. No one, O Jabir, would know them except by their humbleness, submissiveness, trustworthiness, their speaking frequently of Allah, fasting, prayer, virtuous deeds toward parents, good relations with neighbors, the needy, the destitute, the heavily indebted, the orphans, by their truthfulness, recitation of the Holy Quran, and restraining of their tongues except for the good of the people and their being trusted among the people of their tribe in all things. I (Jabir) then said, 'O descendent of the Messenger of Allah, today we do not find anyone with such qualities.' The Imam said, 'O Jabir, do not allow (false) religions confuse you. One should not think, since he loves Ali, *'Alayhi al-Salam*, and supports him, thereafter he does not have to be active in anything. If one says he loves the Messenger of Allah who is better than Ali, *'Alayhi al-Salam*, but does not follow his way of life or practice his tradition, his love as such is of no benefit for him. You must be pious before Allah and work to achieve things that exist with Allah. There is no family relation between one and Allah. The most beloved one to Allah, the Most Majestic, the Most Holy, is the most noble before Him, the most pious ones before Him and the most obedient ones to Him. O Jabir, I swear by Allah, nothing helps one to become nearer to Allah, the Most Blessed, the Most High, except obedience to Him. There is no immunity from hell and no one possesses any authority over Allah. Only those who obey Allah, they are our supporters. Whoever is disobedient to Allah, is our enemy. Our guardianship applies only to those who do good deeds and maintain restraint over their desires for worldly things.'"

H 1612, Ch. 32, h 4

Ali ibn Ibrahim has narrated from his father and Muhammad ibn Isma'il from Fadl ibn Shadhan all from ibn abu 'Umayr from Hisham ibn al-Hakam from abu 'Abd Allah, *'Alayhi al-Salam*, who has said the following:

"On the Day of Judgment certain people raise their necks, approach the door of paradise and knock on it. They then will be asked, 'Who are you?' They will say, 'We are the people of patience.' They will then be asked, 'In what matters did you exercise patience?' They will answer, 'We exercised patience in obeying Allah and against disobedience to Allah.' Allah, the Most Majestic, the Most Holy, will say, 'They have spoken the truth, allow them to enter into paradise.' This is in the words of Allah, the Most Majestic, the Most Holy, 'It is those who exercise patience that receive their reward without being asked to clear any accounts.'" (39:10)

H 1613, Ch. 32, h 5

Muhammad ibn Yahya from Ahmad ibn Muhammad from Muhammad ibn Sinan from Fudayl ibn 'Uthman from 'Ubaydah from abu Ja'far, *'Alayhi al-Salam*, who has said the following:

"Amir al-Mu'minin (Ali ibn abu Talib), *'Alayhi al-Salam*, would say, 'A deed with piety is never considered a little deed. How could it be considered little when it is the very thing with which deeds are accepted?'"

H 1614, Ch. 32, h 6

Hamid ibn Ziyad has narrated from al-Hassan ibn Muhammad ibn Sama'a from certain individuals of his people from Aban from 'Amr ibn Khalid from abu Ja'far, *'Alayhi al-Salam*, who has said the following:

"Abu Ja'far, *'Alayhi al-Salam*, has said, 'O the community of Shi'a, Shi'a of Muhammad, *'Alayhi al-Salam*, be the central support so that both al-Ghali and al-Tali refer to you.' A man from Ansar (people of Madina) called Sa'd, said, 'May Allah keep my soul in service for your cause, what is the meaning of al-Ghali?' The Imam said, 'They are the people who say about us what we do not say about ourselves. Thus, they are not of our people and we are not of their people.' The man then asked, 'Who are al-Tali?' The Imam said, 'They are those who search for good. They receive good instructions (from our Shi'a) and are rewarded for it.' The Imam then turned to us and said, 'I swear by Allah that we do not possess any amnesty from Allah and there is no family relation between Allah and us nor do we possess any authority over Allah. We do not seek nearness to Allah through any other means but obedience to Him. Whoever of you is obedient to Allah it (our guardianship, Wilayah) will benefit him, and whoever of you is disobedient to Allah our guardianship, Wilayah, will not benefit him. What is the matter with you? Do not be misled! What is the matter with you? Do not be misled!'"

H 1615, Ch. 32, h 7
A number of our people have narrated from Ahmad ibn Muhammad ibn Khalid from 'Uthman ibn 'Isa from Mufaddal ibn 'Umar who has said the following:
"Once I was in the presence of abu 'Abd Allah, *'Alayhi al-Salam*. We spoke about deeds and I said, 'My deeds are the weakest.' The Imam said, 'Calm down. Ask forgiveness from Allah.' Then the Imam said to me, 'A little deed with piety is better than a great deal of deeds without piety.' I then asked, 'Can there be a great deal of deeds without piety?' The Imam said, 'Yes, it is true. It is like a man who feeds people, who is kind to his neighbors and entertains people at his home, but when a door to unlawful matters opens he enters such a door. Such are deeds without piety. There can be another person who does not have such deeds but when a door to unlawful matters opens he does not enter into such doors.'"

H 1616, Ch. 32, h 8
Al-Husayn ibn Muhammad has narrated from Mu'alla ibn Muhammad from abu Dawud al-Mustariqq from Muhsin al-Maythami from Ya'qub ibn Shu'ayb who has said the following:
"I heard abu 'Abd Allah, *'Alayhi al-Salam*, saying, 'Allah, the Most Majestic, the Most Holy, does not transfer a believer from the humiliation of sins to the honor of piety before granting him freedom from wants without property, strength without tribesmen and comforting companionship without people.'"

Chapter 33 - Restraint from Worldly Matters (Sins)

H 1617, Ch. 33, h 1
Ali ibn Ibrahim has narrated from his father from ibn abu 'Umayr from abu al-Maghra' from Zayd al-Shahham from 'Amr ibn Sa'id ibn Hilal al-Thaqafi who has said the following:
"Once I said to abu 'Abd Allah, *'Alayhi al-Salam*, 'I can visit you only once every several years. Teach me, please, something to which I can hold.' The Imam said, 'I advise you to be pious before Allah, restrain from worldly matters (sins) and work hard. Note it properly that hard work without restraint from worldly matters is of no benefit.'"

H 1618, Ch. 33, h 2

Muhammad ibn Yahya has narrated from Ahmad ibn Muhammad from al-Hassan ibn Mahbub from Hadid ibn Hakim who has said the following:

"I heard abu 'Abd Allah, *'Alayhi al-Salam*, saying, 'Be pious before Allah and protect your religion by means of restraint from worldly matters (sins).'"

H 1619, Ch. 33, h 3

Abu Ali al-Ash'ari has narrated from Muhammad ibn 'Abd al-Jabbar from Safwan ibn Yahya from Yazid ibn Khalifa who has said the following:

"Once abu 'Abd Allah, *'Alayhi al-Salam*, spoke to us to advise us. He gave orders and told us to abstain from indulging (ourselves) in worldly matters. He then said, 'You must maintain restraint; one does not receive of the things with Allah except by means of restraint from worldly matters (sins).'"

H 1620, Ch. 33, h 4

A number of our people have narrated from Ahmad ibn Muhammad ibn Khalid from ibn Faddal from abu Jamilah from ibn abu Ya'fur from abu 'Abd Allah, *'Alayhi al-Salam*, who has said the following:

"Abu 'Abd Allah, *'Alayhi al-Salam*, has said, 'Hard work without restraint from worldly things (sins) is of no benefit.'"

H 1621, Ch. 33, h 5

It is narrated from him (narrator of the Hadith above) from his father from Fadalah ibn Ayyub from al-Hassan ibn Ziyad al-Sayqal from Fudayl ibn Yasar from abu Ja'far who has said the following:

"Abu Ja'far, *'Alayhi al-Salam*, has said, 'Restraining from worldly matters (sins) is the most intense form of worship.'"

H 1622, Ch. 33, h 6

Muhammad ibn Yahya has narrated from Ahmad ibn Muhammad ibn 'Isa from Muhammad ibn Isma'íl ibn Bazi' from Hanan ibn Sadir who has said that abu Sabah al-Kanani said to abu 'Abd Allah, *'Alayhi al-Salam*:

"Abu Sabah al-Kanani has said, 'We are not received well among people because of you.' The Imam said, 'How are you received among people because of me?' He said, 'As soon as we speak to a man he then says, "He is a Ja'fari (follower of Imam Ja'far al-Sadiq, *'Alayhi al-Salam*) a filthy one."' The Imam said, 'Do they reprimand you because of me?' He said, 'Yes, they do so.' The Imam said, 'I swear by Allah, how few are among you who follow Ja'far ibn Muhammad, *'Alayhi al-Salam*? My people and followers are only those who maintain forceful restraint from worldly things (sins), work for their creator, and hope to receive reward from their Lord. Only such people are of my followers.'"

H 1623, Ch. 33, h 7

Hanan ibn Sadir has narrated from abu Sara al-Ghazzal from abu Ja'far, *'Alayhi al-Salam*, who has said the following:

"Allah, the Most Majestic, the Most Holy, has said, 'O son of Adam, stay away from what I have made unlawful to you, you then will be of the people who restrain themselves from worldly matters the most.'"

H 1624, Ch. 33, h 8

Ali ibn Ibrahim has narrated from his father and Ali ibn Muhammad from al-Qasim ibn Muhammad from Sulayman al-Minqari from Hafs ibn Ghiyath who has said the following:

"I asked abu 'Abd Allah, *'Alayhi al-Salam*, what kind of people are those who restrain from worldly matters? The Imam said, 'They are those who stay away from what Allah, the Most Majestic, the Most Holy, has made unlawful.'"

H 1625, Ch. 33, h 9
Muhammad ibn Yahya has narrated from Ahmad ibn Muhammad ibn 'Isa from Ali ibn al-Nu'man from abu 'Usama who has said the following:

"I heard abu 'Abd Allah, *'Alayhi al-Salam*, saying, 'You must be pious before Allah, restrain yourself against worldly matters, work hard, speak the truth, keep the trust, have good moral behaviors, be good to your neighbors and be so good that you can attract people without preaching to them by your tongues. Be an honor for us and not a disgrace. You must take a long time during your Ruku' and Sajda (bowing down in prayer and prostration). When one of you takes a long time during his Ruku' and Sajda, Satan cries behind him, "Woe upon me, he is obedient and I disobeyed. He prostrates (before the Lord) and I refused."'"

H 1626, Ch. 33, h 10
Muhammad ibn Yahya has narrated from Ahmad ibn Muhammad ibn 'Isa from Ali ibn abu Zayd from his father who has said the following:

"Once I was in the presence of abu 'Abd Allah, *'Alayhi al-Salam*, when 'Isa ibn 'Abd Allah al-Qumi came to see him. The Imam greeted him and gave him a seat near his own seat. The Imam then said, 'O 'Isa ibn 'Abd Allah, one is not from our people, and it is not an honor that one lives in a city of a hundred thousand people and someone else (one who is not a Shi'a) therein excercises more restraint from worldly matters (sins) than he (a Shi'a) does.'"

H 1627, Ch. 33, h 11
It is narrated from him (narrator of the Hadith above) from Ahmad ibn Muhammad ibn 'Isa from ibn Faddal from Ali ibn 'Aqaba from abu Kahmas from 'Amr ibn Sa'id ibn Hilal who has said the following:

"Once I asked abu 'Abd Allah, *'Alayhi al-Salam*, to instruct me with good advice. The Imam said, 'I recommend you to be pious before Allah, restrain from worldly matters (sins) and work hard. Note that there is no benefit in hard work without restraint from worldly matters.'"

H 1628, Ch. 33, h 12
It is narrated from him (narrator of the Hadith above) from Ahmad ibn Muhammad from Ali ibn al-Hakam from Sayf ibn 'Amirah from abu al-Sabah al-Kanani from abu Ja'far, *'Alayhi al-Salam*, who has said the following:

"Abu Ja'far, *'Alayhi al-Salam*, has said, 'Support us by means of restraint from worldly matters; whoever of you will meet Allah, the Most Majestic, the Most Holy, with the quality of restraint from worldly matters will have enough good news from Allah. Allah, the Most Majestic, the Most Holy, has said, "One who obeys Allah and the Messenger is a friend of the prophets, saints, martyrs and the righteous ones to whom Allah has granted His favors. They are the best friends that one can have." (4:69)

'Of our people are the prophets, the truthful ones, the martyrs and the virtuous people.'"

H 1629, Ch. 33, h 13

Ali ibn Ibrahim has narrated from his father from ibn Mahbub from ibn Ri'ab from abu 'Abd Allah, *'Alayhi al-Salam*, who has said the following:

"We do not consider a person a believer until that person follows us in all of our orders and has firmly decided to do so. The decision to exercise restraint against worldly matters consists of following our orders and commands. You must have this beautiful quality. May Allah grant you blessings. With this Quality you defeat our enemies, and Allah will grant you delight and happiness."

H 1630, Ch. 33, h 14

Muhammad ibn Yahya has narrated from Ahmad ibn Muhammad from al-Hajjal from al-'Ala' from ibn abu Ya'fur from abu 'Abd Allah, *'Alayhi al-Salam*, who has said the following:

"Abu 'Abd Allah, *'Alayhi al-Salam*, has said, 'Preach to people without your tongue. You must show them restraint from worldly matters (sins). You should perform hard work, prayer and good deeds. Such behavior includes preaching."

H 1631, Ch. 33, h 15

Al-Husayn ibn Muhammad has narrated from Ali ibn Muhammad ibn Sa'id from Muhammad ibn Muslim from Muhammad ibn Hamza al-'Alawi who has said the following:

"'Ubayd Allah ibn Ali reported to me from abu al-Hassan the 1st, *'Alayhi al-Salam*, who has said, 'I would hear my father saying, "One of whose restraint from worldly matters (sins) ladies in their private quarters would not speak, is not of our Shi'a, and neither is one who lives in a town of ten thousand people among whom Allah has created someone restraining more from worldly matters than he is."'"

Chapter 34 - Chastity

H 1632, Ch. 34, h 1

Ali ibn Ibrahim has narrated from his father from Hammad ibn 'Isa from Hariz from Zurara from abu Ja'far, *'Alayhi al-Salam*, who has said the following:

"Abu Ja'far, *'Alayhi al-Salam*, has said, 'No obedience and worship in the sight of Allah is better than to be a chaste person in matters of (one's) stomach and genital organs."

H 1633, Ch. 34, h 2

Muhammad ibn Yahya has narrated from Ahmad ibn Muhammad from Muhammad ibn Isma'il from Hanan ibn Sadir from his father who has said the following:

"Abu Ja'far, *'Alayhi al-Salam*, has said, 'The best worship is to be chaste in the matters of stomach and genital organs.'"

H 1634, Ch. 34, h 3

A number of our people have narrated from Sahl ibn Ziyad from Ja'far ibn Muhammad al-Ash'ari from 'Abd Allah ibn Maymun al-Qaddah from abu 'Abd Allah, *'Alayhi al-Salam*, who has said the following:

"Amir al-Mu'minin (Ali ibn abu Talib), *'Alayhi al-Salam*, would say, 'Chastity is the best worship.'"

H 1635, Ch. 34, h 4

A number of our people have narrated from Ahmad ibn abu 'Abd Allah from his father from al-Nadr ibn Suwayd from Yahya ibn 'Imran al-Halabi from Mu'alla abu 'Uthman from abu Basir who has said the following:

"Once a man said to abu Ja'far, *'Alayhi al-Salam*, 'My deeds are weak and my fasting is very little but I hope to eat only what is lawful.' The narrator has said that the Imam then said, 'What kind of hard work could be considered better than chastity of stomach and chastity of genital organs?'"

H 1636, Ch. 34, h 5

Ali ibn Ibrahim has narrated from his father from al-Nawfali from al-Sakuni from abu 'Abd Allah, *'Alayhi al-Salam*, who has said the following:

"The Messenger of Allah has said, 'Of my followers who go to hell, in the case of most of them it will so happen because of two hollow things: the stomach and the genital organs (for consuming unlawful things or committing sins) .'"

H 1637, Ch. 34, h 6

Ali ibn Ibrahim has narrated from his sources of narrators who have said the following:

"The Messenger of Allah has said, 'There are three things about which I am afraid for my followers after me: misguidance after recognition of the truth, confusion because of mischief and the desires of stomach and genital organs.'"

H 1638, Ch. 34, h 7

Abu Ali al-Ash'ari has narrated from Muhammad ibn 'Abd al-Jabbar from certain individuals of his people from Maymun al-Qaddah who has said the following:

"I heard abu Ja'far, *'Alayhi al-Salam*, saying, 'There is no worship better than the chastity in matters of stomach and genital organs.'"

H 1639, Ch. 34, h 8

Muhammad ibn Yahya has narrated from Ahmad ibn Muhammad from Ali ibn al-Hakam from Sayf ibn 'Amirah from Mansur ibn Hazim from abu Ja'far, *'Alayhi al-Salam*, who has said the following:

"Abu Ja'far, *'Alayhi al-Salam*, has said, 'In the sight of Allah there is no worship more virtuous than chastity in matters of stomach and genital organs.'"

Chapter 35 - Abstaining From Unlawful Matters

H 1640, Ch. 35, h 1

Muhammad ibn Yahya has narrated from Ahmad ibn Muhammad ibn 'Isa from al-Hassan ibn Mahbub from Dawud ibn Kathir al-Riqqi from abu 'Abd Allah, *'Alayhi al-Salam*, who has said the following:

"About the words of Allah, the Most Majestic, the Most Holy, '. . . for one who has fear of the position of his Lord there are two gardens,' (55:46) the Imam said, 'Whoever knows that Allah, the Most Majestic, the Most Holy, sees him and hears whatever he says or acts for good or evil, and it keeps him back from the evil acts, such person is the "One who has fear of the position of his Lord," and thus he prohibits the soul from acting according to desires.'"

H 1641, Ch. 35, h 2

Ali ibn Ibrahim has narrated from his father from Hammad ibn 'Isa from Ibrahim ibn 'Umar al-Yamani from abu Ja'far, *'Alayhi al-Salam*, who has said the following:

"Abu Ja'far, *'Alayhi al-Salam*, has said, 'On the Day of Judgment all eyes will be weeping except three kinds of eyes: the eye that spends the night awake in the way of Allah, the eye that weeps in submission before Allah and the eye that turns away from what Allah has made unlawful to look at.'"

H 1642, Ch. 35, h 3

Ali has narrated from Muhammad ibn 'Isa from Yunus from those whom he has mentioned (in his book) from abu 'Abd Allah, *'Alayhi al-Salam*, who has said the following:

"Abu 'Abd Allah, *'Alayhi al-Salam*, has said, 'Of the things that Allah, the Majestic, the Glorious, spoke to Moses one was as follows: 'O Moses, of those who seek nearness to Me no one is like the ones who restrain from what I have made unlawful. I, therefore, open for them the garden of Eden and will not allow anyone else to share it with them.'"

H 1643, Ch. 35, h 4

Ali ibn Ibrahim has narrated from his father from ibn abu 'Umayr from Hisham ibn Salim from abu 'Ubayda from abu 'Abd Allah, *'Alayhi al-Salam*, who has said the following:

"Abu 'Abd Allah, *'Alayhi al-Salam*, has said, 'The most intensive obligation Allah has placed upon His creature is to speak of Allah (remember Him) a great deal.' The Imam then said, 'I did not mean thereby saying, "Glory belongs to Allah, all thanks belong to Allah, no one deserves to be worshipped except Allah and Allah is greater (than to be described)," even though they are a form of speaking of Allah. It is to remember Him (or speak of Him) when one encounters a lawful or an unlawful matter, thus, does not disobey Him if it is an act of worship and stays away from it if it is something unlawful to do.'"

H 1644, Ch. 35, h 5

Ibn abu 'Umayr has narrated from Hisham ibn Salim from Sulayman ibn Khalid who has said the following:

"I asked abu 'Abd Allah, *'Alayhi al-Salam*, about the words of Allah, the Most Majestic, the Most Holy, 'We shall call their deeds into Our presence and scatter them into the air as dust (turn them devoid of all virtue).' (25:23) The Imam said, 'I swear by Allah, even though their deeds may have been whiter than the Coptic gown, the nullification of such deed is because on their encountering an unlawful matter they did not stay away from it.'"

H 1645, Ch. 35, h 6

Ali has narrated from his father from al-Nawfali from al-Sakuni from abu 'Abd Allah, *'Alayhi al-Salam*, who has said the following:

"The Messenger of Allah has said, 'Whoever stays away from disobeying Allah because of fear of Allah, the Most Blessed, the Most High, Allah will make him happy on the Day of Judgment.'"

Chapter 36 - Fulfilling Obligations

H 1646, Ch. 36, h 1

A number of our people have narrated from Sahl ibn Ziyad and Ali ibn Ibrahim has narrated from his father all from ibn Mahbub from abu Hamza al-Thumali who has said the following:

"Ali ibn al-Husayn, *'Alayhi al-Salam*, has said, 'One who fulfils what Allah has made obligatory upon him is the best of people.'"

H 1647, Ch. 36, h 2

Ali ibn Ibrahim has narrated from his father from Hammad ibn 'Isa from al-Husayn al-Mukhtar from 'Abd Allah ibn abu Ya'fur from abu 'Abd Allah who has said the following:

"About the words of Allah, the Most Majestic, the Most Holy, 'Believers, have patience, help each other with patience, establish good relations with one another. . . .' (3:200), the Imam said, 'Exercise patience in fulfilling your obligations.'"

H 1648, Ch. 36, h 3

A number of our people have narrated from Sahl ibn Ziyad from 'Abd al-Rahman ibn abu Najran from Hammad ibn 'Isa from abu al-Safatij from abu 'Abd Allah, *'Alayhi al-Salam*, who has said the following:

"About the words of Allah, the Most Majestic, the Most Holy, 'Believers, have patience, help each other with patience, establish good relations with one another. . . .,' (3:200) the Imam said, 'Exercise patience in fulfilling your obligations, help each other with patience in tragedies and establish good relations with 'A'immah (plural of Imam), *'Alayhim al-Salam*.'"

In the narration of ibn Mahbub from abu al-Safatij the following is added, "Have fear of Allah, your Lord, in what He has made obligatory upon you."

H 1649, Ch. 36, h 4

Ali ibn Ibrahim has narrated from his father from al-Nawfali from al-Sakuni from abu 'Abd Allah, *'Alayhi al-Salam*, who has said the following:

"The Messenger of Allah has said, 'Fulfill what Allah has made obligatory upon you. You will then be considered the most pious of the people.'"

II 1650, Ch. 36, h 5

A number of our people have narrated from Ahmad ibn Muhammad from ibn Faddal from abu Jamilah from Muhammad al-Halabi from abu 'Abd Allah, *'Alayhi al-Salam*, who has said the following:

"Allah, the Most Blessed, the Most High, has said, 'The most beloved matter to Me through which My servant seeks to be loved is to fulfill what I have made obligatory upon him.'"

Chapter 37 - Balanced and Continuous Good Deeds

H 1651, Ch. 37, h 1

Ali ibn Ibrahim has narrated from his father from ibn abu 'Umayr from Hammad from al-Halabi who has said the following:

"Abu 'Abd Allah, *'Alayhi al-Salam*, has said, 'If a man does a good deed, he should continue for a year before ending, if he may so wish, to perform another good deed. This is because the night of destiny comes in his year in which things that Allah wills come into being.'"

H 1652, Ch. 37, h 2

Ali ibn Ibrahim has narrated from his father from Hammad ibn 'Isa from Hariz from Zurara from abu Ja'far, *'Alayhi al-Salam*, who has said the following:

"Abu Ja'far, *'Alayhi al-Salam*, has said, 'The most beloved deed in the sight of Allah, the Most Majestic, the Most Holy, is that which is continued even though it is very little.'"

H 1653, Ch. 37, h 3
Abu Ali al-Ash'ari has narrated from 'Isa ibn Ayyub from Ali ibn Mahziyar from Fadalah ibn Ayyub from Mu'awiyah ibn 'Ammar from Najbah from abu Ja'far, *'Alayhi al-Salam*, who has said the following:

"Abu Ja'far, *'Alayhi al-Salam*, has said, 'There is nothing more beloved to Allah, the Most Majestic, the Most Holy, than a deed that is continued by a servant (of Allah) even though it is very little.'"

H 1654, Ch. 37, h 4
It is narrated from him (narrator of the Hadith above) from Fadalah ibn Ayyub from Mu'awiyah ibn 'Ammar from abu 'Abd Allah, *'Alayhi al-Salam*, who has said the following:

"Ali ibn al-Husayn, *'Alayhi al-Salam*, would say, 'I love to continue a good deed even if it is very little.'"

H 1655, Ch. 37, h 5
It is narrated from him (narrator of the Hadith above) from Fadalah ibn Ayyub from al-'Ala' from Muhammad ibn Muslim from abu Ja'far, *'Alayhi al-Salam*, who has said the following:

"Ali ibn al-Husayn, *'Alayhi al-Salam*, would say, 'I love to go before my Lord with my deeds orderly and balanced.'"

H 1656, Ch. 37, h 6
A number of our people have narrated from Ahmad ibn Muhammad from Muhammad ibn Isma'il from Ja'far ibn Bashir from 'Abd al-Karim ibn 'Amr from Sulayman ibn Khalid who has said the following:

"Abu 'Abd Allah, *'Alayhi al-Salam*, has said, 'Be careful and do not give up on a good deed that you may have decided to do, before twelve lunar months end.'"

Note: The good deeds and acts of worship in the above Ahadith refer to the optional acts of worship; the obligatory ones do not decrease or increase.

Chapter 38 - The Worship

H 1657, Ch. 38, h 1
A number of our people have narrated from Ahmad ibn Muhammad from ibn Mahbub from 'Umar ibn Yazid from abu 'Abd Allah, *'Alayhi al-Salam*, who has said the following:

"Abu 'Abd Allah, *'Alayhi al-Salam*, has said, 'It is written in the Torah, "O son of Adam, devote yourself to my worship and I will fill your heart with riches and will not leave you to your own quest. It is upon Me to meet your needs and fill your heart with fear from Me. If you do not devote yourself to My worship I will fill your heart with preoccupation in worldly matters, and then I will not meet your needs and will leave you up to your own pursuit."'"

H 1658, Ch. 38, h 2
Ali ibn Ibrahim has narrated from Muhammad ibn 'Isa from abu Jamilah from abu 'Abd Allah, *'Alayhi al-Salam*, who has said the following:

"Abu 'Abd Allah, *'Alayhi al-Salam*, has said, 'Allah, the Most Blessed, the Most High, has said, "O My truthful servants, enjoy the blessings of worshipping Me in this world; you will enjoy its benefits in the next life.""

H 1659, Ch. 38, h 3

Ali ibn Ibrahim has narrated from Muhammad ibn 'Isa from Yunus from 'Amr ibn Jami' from abu 'Abd Allah, *'Alayhi al-Salam*, who has said the following:

"The Messenger of Allah has said, 'The best of the people are those who love worship (of Allah) intensely. They hold to it, love it in their hearts, accompany it with their body and are devoted in it. Such people are concerned no more about the world, whether it gives them comfort or difficulties.'"

H 1660, Ch. 38, h 4

Muhammad ibn Yahya has narrated from Ahmad ibn Muhammad ibn 'Isa from Shadhan ibn al-Khalil. The narrator has said that he wrote down from his book through the chain of his narrators who narrated in a marfu' manner from 'Isa ibn 'Abd Allah saying:

"'Isa ibn 'Abd Allah once said to abu 'Abd Allah, *'Alayhi al-Salam*, 'May Allah keep my soul in service for your cause, what is worship?' The Imam said, 'It is good intention in obedience to Allah concerning the aspects through which He is obeyed. As for you, O 'Isa, you will not be a believer until you can distinguish the abrogating from the abrogated.' I then said, 'May Allah keep my soul in service for your cause, what is distinguishing the abrogating from the abrogated?' The Imam said, 'Is it not true that you obey an Imam with good intention and in good faith, and when that Imam passes away and another Imam comes, you settle your soul on obedience to him with good intention and in good faith?' I said, 'Yes, I do so.' The Imam said, 'This is distinguishing the abrogating from the abrogated.'"

H 1661, Ch. 38, h 5

Ali ibn Ibrahim has narrated from his father from ibn Mahbub from Jamil from Harun ibn Kharijah from abu 'Abd Allah, *'Alayhi al-Salam*, who has said the following:

"Abu 'Abd Allah, *'Alayhi al-Salam*, has said, 'There are three kinds of worship: there are people who worship Allah, the Most Majestic, the Most Holy, because of fear. This kind of worship is the worship of slaves. There are people who worship Allah, the Most Blessed, the Most High, for His rewards. This is the worship of people for hire. There are people who worship Allah, the Most Majestic, the Most Holy, for His love. This is the worship of free people and this is the best kind of worship.'"

H 1662, Ch. 38, h 6

Ali has narrated from his father from al-Nawfali from al-Sakuni from abu 'Abd Allah, *'Alayhi al-Salam*, who has said the following:

"The Messenger of Allah has said, 'How ugly is poverty after riches, sin in destitution and worst of all worshipping Allah and then giving up His worship.'"

H 1663, Ch. 38, h 7

Al-Husayn ibn Muhammad has narrated from Mu'alla ibn Muhammad from al-Washsha' from 'Asim ibn Humayd from abu Hamza from Ali ibn al-Husayn, *'Alayhi al-Salam*, who has said the following:

"Ali ibn al-Husayn, *'Alayhi al-Salam*, has said, 'One who fulfills what Allah has made obligatory upon him, he, among the people, is the one who worships the most.'"

Chapter 39 - The Intention

H 1664, Ch. 39, h 1

Ali ibn Ibrahim has narrated from his father from ibn Mahbub from Malik ibn 'Atiyah from abu Hamza from Ali ibn al-Husayn, *'Alayhi al-Salam*, who has said the following:

"Ali ibn al-Husayn, *'Alayhi al-Salam*, has said, 'There can be no deed without intention.'"

H 1665, Ch. 39, h 2

Ali has narrated from his father from al-Nawfali from al-Sakuni from abu 'Abd Allah, *'Alayhi al-Salam*, who has said the following:

"The Messenger of Allah has said, 'The intention of the believer is better than his deeds, and the intention of the unbeliever is more wicked than his deeds. Everyone acts according to his intention.'"

H 1666, Ch. 39, h 3

A number of our people have narrated from Ahmad ibn Muhammad from ibn Mahbub from Hisham ibn Salim from abu Basir from abu 'Abd Allah, *'Alayhi al-Salam*, who has said the following:

"The poor believing servant (of Allah) says, 'O Lord bestow upon me such and such so that I can do so and so good deeds. If Allah, the Most Majestic, the Most Holy, finds that his intention is true He will write down for him a reward (just for his intention) equal to the degree of good deeds had his intention materialized; Allah is vastly generous.'"

H 1667, Ch. 39, h 4

A number of our people have narrated from Ahmad ibn Muhammad ibn Khalid from Ali ibn Asbat from Muhammad ibn Ishaq ibn al-Husayn from Amr from Hassan ibn Aban from abu Basir who has said the following:

"I asked abu 'Abd Allah, *'Alayhi al-Salam*, about worship, 'What kind of worshipping sets the worshipper free from obligations.' The Imam said, 'It is obedience with good intention and in good faith.'"

H 1668, Ch. 39, h 5

Ali ibn Ibrahim has narrated from his father from al-Qasim ibn Muhammad from al-Minqari from Ahmad ibn Yunus from abu Hashim who has said the following:

"Abu 'Abd Allah, *'Alayhi al-Salam*, has said, 'People of hell will remain in hell for ever because of their intention in this world to disobey Allah even if they lived here forever. People of paradise will live therein forever because of their intention in this world to worship Allah even if they lived here forever. Because of intentions these and those will remain therein forever. The Imam then recited the words of Allah, "Say, everyone does as he intends (shakilah). . . .," (17:84) the Imam said, 'It (Shakilah) means intention.'"

Chapter 40 - Part of Previous Chapter

H 1669, Ch. 40, h 1

Muhammad ibn Yahya has narrated from Ahmad ibn Muhammad ibn 'Isa from ibn Mahbub from al-Ahwal from Salam ibn al-Mustanir from abu Ja'far, 'Alayhi al-Salam, who has said the following:

"The Messenger of Allah has said, 'For every form of worship there is a strong desire and willingness, then it reduces. Whoever's worship falls within my tradition and practice, he has found the right guidance, and whoever is against my tradition is lost and his deeds are a total loss. I, however, pray, sleep, fast, eat, laugh and weep. Whoever dislikes my tradition and practice is not of my people.' He has said, 'Death is a sufficient preacher, certainty is enough wealth and worship is a complete occupation.'"

H 1670, Ch. 40, h 2

A number of our people have narrated from Sahl ibn Ziyad from al-Hajjal from Tha'labah who has said the following:

"Abu 'Abd Allah, 'Alayhi al-Salam, has said, 'Everyone has an enthusiasm and every enthusiasm has a decline. Tuba (a tree in paradise) is for those whose decline is toward a constructive side.'"

Chapter 41 - Moderation in Worship

H 1671, Ch. 41, h 1

Muhammad ibn Yahya has narrated from Ahmad ibn Muhammad ibn 'Isa from Muhammad ibn Sinan from abu al-Jarud from abu Ja'far, 'Alayhi al-Salam, who has said the following:

"The Messenger of Allah has said, 'This religion is strong (and vast). Follow it with care and do not make the servants of Allah dislike the worship of Allah, lest you become like the rider who destroys his carry-animal during a journey, thus has neither reached his destination nor has any animal to ride on.'"

Muhammad ibn Sinan has narrated from Muqrin from Muhammad ibn Sawqah from abu Ja'far, 'Alayhi al-Salam, a similar Hadith.

H 1672, Ch. 41, h 2

Ali ibn Ibrahim has narrated from his father and Muhammad ibn Isma'il from Fadl ibn Shadhan all from ibn abu 'Umayr from Hafs ibn al-Bakhtari from abu 'Abd Allah, 'Alayhi al-Salam, who has said the following:

"Abu 'Abd Allah, 'Alayhi al-Salam, has said, 'Do not cause your souls to dislike worship.'"

H 1673, Ch. 41, h 3

Muhammad ibn Yahya has narrated from Ahmad ibn Muhammad ibn 'Isa from Muhammad ibn Isma'il from Hanan ibn Sadir who has said the following:

"I heard abu 'Abd Allah, 'Alayhi al-Salam, saying, 'When Allah, the Most Majestic, the Most Holy, loves any (of His) servants who have done a little good deed, He grants him a great reward for his little deeds. He does not consider granting a great reward, for a little deed, a difficult thing at all.'"

H 1674, Ch. 41, h 4

A number of our people have narrated from Ahmad ibn Muhammad from ibn Faddal from al-Hassan ibn al-Jahm from Mansur from abu Basir from abu 'Abd Allah, *'Alayhi al-Salam*, who has said the following:

"Abu 'Abd Allah, *'Alayhi al-Salam*, has said, 'Once my father passed by during my Tawaf (walking seven times around the Ka'ba). I was young and very seriously striving to worship. He saw me sweating and said to me, "O Ja'far, my son, if Allah loves any (of His) servants, He admits him in paradise and becomes happy with him even with a very little good deed.'"

H 1675, Ch. 41, h 5

Ali ibn Ibrahim has narrated from his father from ibn abu 'Umayr from Hafs ibn al-Bakhtari and others from abu 'Abd Allah, *'Alayhi al-Salam*, who has said the following:

"Abu 'Abd Allah, *'Alayhi al-Salam*, has said, 'I strived hard in worshipping and I was young. My father said to me, "My son, I want to see you also do things other than what you are doing. Were Allah, the Most Majestic, the Most Holy, to love a servant He would become happy with him even with a very little deed."'"

H 1676, Ch. 41, h 6

Hamid ibn Ziyad has narrated from al-Khashshab from ibn Baqqah from Mu'adh ibn Thabit from 'Amr ibn Jami' from abu 'Abd Allah, *'Alayhi al-Salam*, who has said the following:

"The Messenger of Allah once said, 'O Ali, this religion is strong (and vast). Follow it with care. Do not cause your soul to hate the worship of your Lord. The extremist is like a person who during a journey destroys his riding animal and is left without any animal to ride before reaching his destination. Do good deeds like one who knows he will die very old and be cautious as one who is afraid of dying the next day.'"

Chapter 42 - One Who Has Learned to Receive Rewards from His Lord for a Certain Deed

H 1677, Ch. 42, h 1

Ali ibn Ibrahim has narrated from his father from ibn abu 'Umayr from Hisham ibn Salim from abu 'Abd Allah, *'Alayhi al-Salam*, who has said the following:

"If one learns (from a Hadith) that for a certain act there is a certain reward and he performs that act, he will receive such reward even if, in fact, it (the Hadith) may not be as such."

H 1678, Ch. 42, h 2

Muhammad ibn Yahya has narrated from Muhammad ibn al-Husayn from Muhammad ibn Sinan from 'Imran al-Za'farani from Muhammad ibn Marwan who has said the following:

"I heard abu Ja'far, *'Alayhi al-Salam*, saying, 'If one learns that there is a certain reward from Allah for a certain act and he performs such act to receive such reward, he will be given the reward even if, in fact, the Hadith may not be as such that has come to him.'"

Chapter 43 - Patience

H 1679, Ch. 43, h 1

A number of our people have narrated from Sahl ibn Ziyad from al-Hassan ibn Mahbub from Ali ibn Ri'ab from ibn abu Ya'fur from abu 'Abd Allah, *'Alayhi al-Salam*, who has said the following:

"Abu 'Abd Allah, *'Alayhi al-Salam*, has said, 'Patience is the head of belief."

H 1680, Ch. 43, h 2

Abu Ali al-Ash'ari has narrated from Ahmad ibn Muhammad ibn 'Isa from Muhammad ibn Sinan from al-'Ala' ibn Fudayl from abu 'Abd Allah, *'Alayhi al-Salam*, who has said the following:

"Abu 'Abd Allah, *'Alayhi al-Salam*, has said, 'Patience is to belief as the head is to the body. If the head is gone the body is also destroyed. So also, if patience vanishes, belief also goes away and is no more.'"

H 1681, Ch. 43, h 3

Ali ibn Ibrahim has narrated from his father from Ali ibn Muhammad al-Qasani all from al-Qasim ibn Muhammad al-Asbahani from Sulayman ibn Dawud al-Minqari from Hafs ibn Ghiyath who has said the following:

"Once abu 'Abd Allah, *'Alayhi al-Salam*, said, 'O Hafs, whoever exercises patience does so only for a short time, and whoever expresses impatience, he does so only for a short time.'

"The Imam then said, 'You must exercise patience in all of your affairs. Allah, the Most Majestic, the Most Holy, sent Muhammad, *'Alayhi al-Salam*, and commanded him to exercise patience and kindness and said, "Bear patiently whatever they say, do not yield to them and distance them gracefully (73:10). Leave the prosperous disbelievers to Me. . . ." (73:11)

'Allah, the Most Holy, the Most High, has also said, "Virtue and evil are not equal. If you respond (to evil acts) by virtuous ones, you will certainly find that your enemies will become your intimate friends (41:34). Only those who exercise patience and who have been granted a great share of Allah's favor can find such an opportunity." (41:35) The Messenger of Allah exercised patience in suffering and hardships even when they (pagans) attacked him with bones (of large animals). He became very depressed, and Allah, the Most Majestic, the Most Holy, revealed to him, "We certainly know that you feel sad about what they say against you (15:97). Glorify and praise your Lord and be with those who prostrate themselves before Allah." (15:98) They (pagans) rejected his message and caused him physical suffering so he became depressed. Allah, the Most Majestic, the Most Holy, sent him these words, "We certainly know that you (Muhammad) are sad about what they (the unbelievers) say. It is not you (alone) who has been accused of lying. The unjust have always rejected Allah's revelations. (6:33) The Messengers who lived before you were also accused of lying, but they exercised patience. They were cruelly persecuted before We gave them victory. . . ." (6:34) The Holy Prophet held to patience firmly and they (pagans) spoke of Allah, the Most Blessed, the Most High, and called His words as lies. The Messenger of Allah said, "I remained patient about myself, my family and my honor, but I cannot remain quiet when they speak ill of my Lord." Allah, the Most Majestic, the Most Holy, revealed to him these words, "We created the heavens, the earth and all that is between them in six days without experiencing any fatigue (50:38). (Muhammad), exercise patience against what they say. . . ." (50:39) The Holy Prophet thereafter exercised patience in all matters and then he was given the good news of Imamat (Divine Authority) given to his descendents who were described as (people) exercising patience. Allah, the Most Majestic, the Most Holy, has said, "We appointed from them as 'A'immah (leaders) for their exercising patience to guide the others to Our commands. They had firm belief in Our revelations." (32:24)

'Thereupon the Messenger of Allah said, "Patience is to belief as is the head to the body." Allah, the Majestic, the Glorious, appreciated this and He, the Most Majestic, the Most Holy, revealed these words: "Thus, the promises of your Lord to the children of Israel all came true because of the patience which they exercised. He destroyed all the establishments of the Pharaoh and his people." (7:137) The Messenger of Allah said, "This is good news and compensation." Allah, the Most Majestic, the Most Holy, then made it lawful for him to fight the pagans. Allah then revealed these words, "Slay the pagans wherever you find them. Capture, besiege and watch out for them. If they repent, perform prayers and pay the religious tax, set them free. Allah is Allforgiving and All-Merciful." (9:5). "Then slay them for it is the recompense that the disbelievers deserve." (2:191)

'Allah caused them to be killed by the (forces) of the Messenger of Allah and his friends, and made it a reward for his exercising patience in addition to the rewards reserved for him in the next life. Whoever exercises patience nobly will not leave this world before Allah grants him delight to his heart in the matters of his enemies, in addition to the reward that is reserved for him in the next life.'"

H 1682, Ch. 43, h 4

Muhammad ibn Yahya has narrated from Ahmad ibn Muhammad ibn 'Isa from Ali ibn al-Hakam from abu Muhammad 'Abd Allah al-Sarraj who has narrated in a marfu' manner from Ali ibn al-Husayn, *'Alayhi al-Salam*, who has said the following:

"Ali ibn al-Husayn, *'Alayhi al-Salam*, has said, 'Patience is to belief as the head is to the body. One who does not have patience has no belief.'"

H 1683, Ch. 43, h 5

Ali ibn Ibrahim has narrated from his father from Hammad ibn 'Isa from Rib'I ibn 'Abd Allah from Fudayl ibn Yasar from abu 'Abd Allah, *'Alayhi al-Salam*, who has said the following:

"Abu 'Abd Allah, *'Alayhi al-Salam*, has said, 'Patience is to belief as the head is to the body. When the head is no more so also is the body. Similarly, when patience is no more so also is belief.'"

H 1684, Ch. 43, h 6

A number of our people have narrated from Ahmad ibn Muhammad ibn Khalid from his father from Ali ibn al-Nu'man from 'Abd Allah ibn Muskan from abu Basir who has said the following:

"I heard abu 'Abd Allah, *'Alayhi al-Salam*, saying, 'A free person is free in all conditions. Even if hardships strike him he exercises patience, if afflictions batter him he does not break down even if he is taken as a captive and is overpowered and his comfort and prosperity are changed into poverty and hardships, just as in the case of Yusuf (Joseph) the truthful and trustworthy one (may Allah grant him blessings), whose freedom remained unaffected even though he was enslaved, taken as a captive and overpowered. The darkness and loneliness of the well did not harm him, nor did all that he went through until Allah granted him favors. He made the insolent tyrant into a slave for him after his being his king. He set him free and made a whole nation to be kind to him. This is how patience yields goodness. You must exercise patience and settle your soul upon patience and you will, certainly, be rewarded.'"

H 1685, Ch. 43, h 7

Muhammad ibn Yahya has narrated from Ahmad ibn Muhammad ibn 'Isa from Ali ibn al-Hakam from 'Abd Allah ibn Bukayr from Hamza ibn Humran from abu Ja'far, *'Alayhi al-Salam*, who has said the following:

"Abu Ja'far, *'Alayhi al-Salam*, has said, 'Paradise is kept behind layers of hardship and patience. Whoever exercises patience in hardship in the worldly life will go to paradise. Hell is placed behind enjoyments and desires. Whoever allows his soul to indulge in enjoyment and desires will go to hell.'"

H 1686, Ch. 43, h 8

Ali ibn Ibrahim has narrated from his father from ibn Mahbub from 'Abd Allah ibn Marhum from abu Sayyar from abu 'Abd Allah, *'Alayhi al-Salam*, who has said the following:

"When a believer is placed in his grave, prayer will be on his right al-Zakat (charity) on his left, and virtuous deeds will provide cover from above and patience will stay aside. When the two angels come to interrogate him, patience will say to the prayer, al-Zakat (charity) and virtuous deeds, 'Help your friend. Were you to become helpless then I will take over.'"

H 1687, Ch. 43, h 9

Ali has narrated from his father from Ja'far ibn Muhammad al-Ash'ari from 'Abd Allah ibn Maymun from abu 'Abd Allah, *'Alayhi al-Salam*, who has said the following:

"Once Amir al-Mu'minin (Ali ibn abu Talib), *'Alayhi al-Salam*, entered the Mosque and at the door of the Mosque he met a man who was depressed and sad. Amir al-Mu'minin (Ali ibn abu Talib), *'Alayhi al-Salam*, asked him 'What has happened to you?' He said, 'It is due to the death of my father, mother and brother. O Amir al-Mu'minin, I am afraid my gall bladder may have ruptured.' Amir al-Mu'minin (Ali ibn abu Talib), *'Alayhi al-Salam*, said, 'You must be pious before Allah and exercise patience. Tomorrow (on the Day of Judgment) you will proceed to Him. Patience in the issues (in life) is like a head to a body. If the head departs the body is destroyed, likewise, in the issues (of life), if patience departs the issues, all affairs (of life) are destroyed.'"

H 1688, Ch. 43, h 10

Muhammad ibn Yahya has narrated from Ahmad ibn Muhammad ibn 'Isa from Ali ibn al-Hakam from Sama'a ibn Mehran who has said the following:

"Once abu al-Hassan, *'Alayhi al-Salam*, said to me, 'What is holding you back from performing Hajj?' I said, 'May Allah keep my soul in service for your cause, I am indebted a great deal and my properties are gone. It is my debt that is holding me down and is worse than the loss of my properties. If someone from our people does not help me out I will not be able to do it myself.' The Imam said, 'If you exercise patience you will be envied, otherwise Allah will execute his measures whether you agree or not.'"

H 1689, Ch. 43, h 11
Muhammad ibn Yahya has narrated from Ahmad ibn Muhammad from ibn Sinan form abu al-Jarud from al-Asbagh who has said the following:

"Amir al-Mu'minin (Ali ibn abu Talib), *'Alayhi al-Salam*, has said, 'There are two kinds of patience: to exercise patience in hardship which is good and graceful, yet better than this is to exercise patience against the temptation of committing what Allah, the Most Majestic, the Most Holy, has prohibited one from doing. There are two ways of speaking of Allah: to speak of Allah the Most Majestic, the Most Holy, in suffering hardship, yet better than this is speaking of Allah (remembering Him) when facing temptation to commit what Allah has prohibited one from doing and one's patience serves as a barrier.'"

H 1690, Ch. 43, h 12
Abu Ali al-Ash'ari has narrated from al-Hassan ibn Ali al-kufi from al-'Abbas ibn 'Amir from al-'Arzami from abu 'Abd Allah, *'Alayhi al-Salam*, who has said the following:

"The Messenger of Allah has said, 'A time will come upon people when kingdom can be achieved only by committing murders and tyranny. Wealth can only be achieved through usurpation and stinginess. Love and harmony can be established only by exclusion of religion and by following desires. Those living at such a time must exercise patience in poverty despite the accessability of wealth to them, be patient against the hatred of people toward them even though they can establish love and harmony. They must exercise patience in humiliation even though they can rise with respectable (position). To each one of such persons Allah will grant a reward equal to the reward for fifty truthful people of those who have acknowledged my message.'"

H 1691, Ch. 43, h 13
A number of our people have narrated from Ahmad ibn abu 'Abd Allah from Isma'il ibn Mehran from Durust ibn abu Mansur from 'Isa ibn Bashir from abu Hamza who has said the following:

"Abu Ja'far, *'Alayhi al-Salam*, has said, 'When my father Ali ibn al-Husayn, *'Alayhi al-Salam*, was about to leave this world he held me against his chest and said, "My son, I recommend you with the same recommendation with which he (my father) advised me at the time that he was about to leave this world and with the recommendation that his father had made to him, O my son, hold to the truth with patience even if it is very bitter."'"

H 1692, Ch. 43, h 14
It is narrated from him (narrator of the Hadith above) from his father from Yunus ibn 'Abd al-Rahman who has narrated it in a marfu' manner from abu Ja'far, *'Alayhi al-Salam*, who has said the following:

"Abu Ja'far, *'Alayhi al-Salam*, has said, 'Patience is of two kinds: to exercise patience in hardship, which is good and graceful, yet, the best of patience is that which is exercised to stop one from committing what Allah has prohibited.'"

H 1693, Ch. 43, h 15
Muhammad ibn Yahya has narrated from Ahmad ibn Muhammad ibn 'Isa who has said that reported to me Yahya ibn Salim al-Ta'ifi who has said that informed me 'Amr ibn Shamir al-Yamani in a

marfu' manner from Amir al-Mu'minin (Ali ibn abu Talib), *'Alayhi al-Salam*, who has said the following:

"The Messenger of Allah has said, 'Patience is of three kinds: patience at the time of suffering hardship, patience in performing acts of obedience (worship) and patience to stop one from committing what Allah has prohibited. For one who exercises patience at the time of suffering hardship until one passes it by with grace and goodness Allah writes down three hundred degrees. Each is distant from the other as the sky and the earth. Whoever exercises patience in performing the acts of obeying (worshipping) Allah writes for him six hundred degrees. Each is apart from the other as the core of the earth to the Throne. Whoever exercises such patience that stops one from committing what Allah has prohibited, Allah writes for him nine hundred degrees. Each is apart from the other as is the core of the earth to the end of the Throne.'"

H 1694, Ch. 43, h 16

It is narrated from him (narrator of the Hadith above) from Ali ibn al-Hakam from Yunus ibn Ya'qub who has said the following:

"Abu 'Abd Allah, *'Alayhi al-Salam*, ordered me to meet al-Muffadal and offer him condolences for Isma'il (son of the Imam), 'Convey my greetings of peace to him and tell him that we have suffered the death of Isma'il but have exercised patience. You must also exercise patience as we have done. We wanted one thing but Allah, the Most Majestic, the Most Holy, decided that another thing happen, and we are submissive to the command of Allah, the Most Majestic, the Most Holy.'"

H 1695, Ch. 43, h 17

Ali ibn Ibrahim has narrated from his father from ibn abu 'Umayr from Sayf ibn 'Amirah from abu Hamza al-Thumali who has said the following:

"Abu 'Abd Allah, *'Alayhi al-Salam*, has said, 'Whoever among the believers exercises patience at the time of suffering hardship he will have a reward equal to the reward of a thousand martyrs.'"

H 1696, Ch. 43, h 18

Muhammad ibn Yahya has narrated from Ahmad ibn Muhammad ibn 'Isa from Muhammad ibn Sinan from 'Ammar ibn Marwan ibn Sama'a from abu 'Abd Allah who has said the following:

"Abu 'Abd Allah, *'Alayhi al-Salam*, has said, 'Allah, the Most Majestic, the Most Holy, granted a favor to a people but they did not appreciate it and that favor turned against them in the form of a burden. He tried another nation with hardships and sufferings but these people exercised patience and the trouble turned into bounties for them.'"

H 1697, Ch. 43, h 19

Ali ibn Ibrahim has narrated from his father and Muhammad ibn Isma'il from Fadl ibn Shadhan all from ibn abu 'Umayr from Ibrahim ibn 'Abd al-Hamid from Aban ibn abu Musafir from abu 'Abd Allah, *'Alayhi al-Salam*, who has said the following:

"About the words of Allah, the Most Majestic, the Most Holy, 'Believers, have patience, help each other with patience. . . .,' (3:200) the Imam has said, 'It means to exercise patience in suffering hardship.'"

In the narration of ibn abu Ya'fur from abu 'Abd Allah, *'Alayhi al-Salam*, it says, "Exercise patience in suffering afflictions."

H 1698, Ch. 43, h 20

A number of our people have narrated from Ahmad ibn Muhammad ibn Khalid from Muhammad ibn 'Isa from Ali ibn Muhammad ibn abu Jamilah from his grad father abu Jamilah from certain individuals of his people from who have said:

"The Imam said, 'Had patience not been created before misfortune, it would have torn the believer into pieces like an egg hit against a rock.'"

H 1699, Ch. 43, h 21

Abu Ali al-Ash'ari has narrated from Muhammad ibn 'Abd al-Jabbar from Safwan from Ishaq ibn 'Ammar and 'Abd ibn Sinan from abu 'Abd Allah, *'Alayhi al-Salam*, who has said the following:

"The Messenger of Allah has said that Allah, the Most Majestic, the Most Holy, has said, 'I have made the world a borrowing (place) for My servants. Whoever gives Me a loan I will return it ten times over up to seven hundred times over, and more if I so wish. Those who do not lend Me a loan I will take something forcibly from them. If they then exercise patience I will give three such rewards of which if I gave only one to My angels they would all become happy with Me.' The narrator has said that abu 'Abd Allah, *'Alayhi al-Salam*, recited the words of Allah, the Most Majestic, the Most Holy: '. . . those who when suffering hardship say, "We are the servants of Allah and to Him we shall all return," (2:156) it is they who will receive blessing, [one of the three rewards], and mercy from Allah, [the second of the three rewards], and who have recieved the right guidance (2:157) [the third of the three rewards]. Abu 'Abd Allah, *'Alayhi al-Salam*, then said, 'This is when Allah takes something from one forcibly.'"

H 1700, Ch. 43, h 22

Ali ibn Ibrahim has narrated from his father and Ali ibn Muhammad al-Qasani fro al-Qasim ibn Muhammad from Sulayman ibn Dawud form Yahya ibn Adam from Sharik from Jabir ibn Yazid from abu Ja'far, *'Alayhi al-Salam*, who has said the following:

"Abu Ja'far, *'Alayhi al-Salam*, has said, 'The courage to exercise patience in times of need and poverty with chastity and self-sufficiency is more than the courage needed to give charity.'"

H 1701, Ch. 43, h 23

Abu Ali al-Ash'ari has narrated from Muhammad ibn 'Abd al-Jabbar from Ahmad ibn al-Nadr from 'Amr ibn Shamir from Jabir who has said the following:

"Once I said to abu Ja'far, *'Alayhi al-Salam*, 'May Allah grant you favors, what is graceful patience?' The Imam said, 'That is the patience in which there is no complaint before the people.'"

H 1702, Ch. 43, h 24

Hamid ibn Ziyad has narrated from al-Hassan ibn Muhammad ibn Sama'a from certain individuals of his people from Aban from 'Abd al-Rahman ibn Seyabah from abu al-Nu'man from abu 'Abd Allah or abu Ja'far, *'Alayhi al-Salam*, who has said the following:

"Abu Ja'far, *'Alayhi al-Salam*, has said, 'One who does not prepare himself in patience to face the hardships of life, will remain helpless.'"

H 1703, Ch. 43, h 25

Abu Ali al-Ash'ari has narrated from Mu'alla ibn Muhammad from al-Washsha' from certain individuals of his people from abu 'Abd Allah, *'Alayhi al-Salam*, who has said the following:

"Abu 'Abd Allah, *'Alayhi al-Salam*, has said, 'We are strong to exercise patience, and our (Shi'a) followers are stronger than we are.' I then said, 'May Allah keep my soul in service for your cause, how have your followers become stronger than you are?' The Imam said, 'It is because we exercise patience in the matters that we already know, but our (Shi'a) followers exercise patience in matters of the reality of which they have no knowledge.'"

Chapter 44 - Gratitude and Thankfulness

H 1704, Ch. 44, h 1

Ali ibn Ibrahim has narrated from his father from al-Nawfali from al-Sakuni from abu 'Abd Allah, *'Alayhi al-Salam*, who has said the following:

"The Messenger of Allah has said, 'A person feeding (himself) with gratitude (before Allah) has a reward equal to the reward of a fasting person who brings himself to strict account. A person in good health who is grateful receives a reward equal to the reward of a person who suffers from an illness but exercises patience. A person who gives charity with gratitude receives a reward equal to the reward of a deprived person who is content.'"

H 1705, Ch. 44, h 2

It is narrated through the same chain of narrators:

"The Messenger of Allah has said, 'Whenever Allah opens the door of gratitude to someone He does not keep the door of increasing (bounties) hidden from him.'"

H 1706, Ch. 44, h 3

Muhammad ibn Yahya has narrated from Ahmad ibn Muhammad ibn 'Isa from Ja'far ibn Muhammad al-Baghdadi from 'Abd Allah ibn Ishaq al-Ja'fari from abu 'Abd Allah, *'Alayhi al-Salam*, who has said the following:

"Abu 'Abd Allah, *'Alayhi al-Salam*, has said, 'This is written in the Torah: "Thank (and be grateful to) those who have done favors to you, and do favors to those who thank you; bounties will not go away if you appreciate them and they will not stay all the time if you reject them. Thankfulness increases the bounties and provides security against changes (from good to worse).""""

H 1707, Ch. 44, h 4

A number of our people have narrated from Ahmad ibn abu 'Abd Allah from Muhammad ibn Ali from Ali ibn Asbat from Ya'qub ibn Salim from a man from abu Ja'far or abu 'Abd Allah, *'Alayhi al-Salam*, who has said the following:

"Abu 'Abd Allah, *'Alayhi al-Salam*, has said, 'A person in good health who is thankful for it receives the same amount of reward as a person who in an ailing health exercises patience. One who gives (charity) and is thankful (for his ability) receives the same amount of reward as the deprived person who is content.'"

H 1708, Ch. 44, h 5

It is narrated from him (narrator of the Hadith above) from Ahmad ibn Muhammad ibn abu Nasr from Dawud al-Hasin from Fadl al-Baqbaq who has said the following:

"I asked abu 'Abd Allah, *'Alayhi al-Salam*, about the words of Allah, the Most Majestic, the Most Holy, '. . . and proclaim the bounties of your Lord.' (93:11) The Imam said that in the above passage the Holy Prophet is commanded, to proclaim the special treatment that He has granted you, the distinctions that He has given you, the favors that He has presented to you and His being benevolent to you. The Imam then said, 'He (the Holy Prophet) then spoke of His religion, and of what Allah had given him and the bounties that He made available to him.'"

H 1709, Ch. 44, h 6
Hamid ibn Ziyad has narrated from al-Hassan ibn Muhammad ibn Sama'a from Wuhayb ibn Hafs from abu Basir from abu Ja'far, *'Alayhi al-Salam*, who has said the following:

"Abu Ja'far, *'Alayhi al-Salam*, has said, 'One night when the Messenger of Allah stayed in 'A'isha's chamber she said, "O Messenger of Allah, why do you tire yourself when Allah has already forgiven all of your past and future sins (that the pagans thought you had committed against them)?" He replied, 'O 'A'isha, should not I be a grateful servant?'

"The Imam said, 'The Messenger of Allah would standup on his toes worshipping, then Allah revealed this to him, 'Ta. Ha (20:1). We have not sent the Quran to make you, (Muhammad), miserable (20:2) (It is) only a reminder for those who are afraid (of disobeying Allah).'" (20:3)

H 1710, Ch. 44, h 7
A number of our people have narrated from Ahmad ibn Muhammad from ibn Faddal from Hassan ibn Jahm from abu al-Yaqdan from 'Ubayd Allah ibn al-Walid who has said the following:

"I heard abu 'Abd Allah, *'Alayhi al-Salam*, saying, 'With the existence of three factors nothing can harm one. These factors include: prayer in difficulties, asking forgiveness in sins and thankfulness for bounties.'"

H 1711, Ch. 44, h 8
A number of our people have narrated from Sahl ibn Ziyad from Yahya ibn al-Mubarak from 'Abd Allah ibn Jabalah from Mu'awiyah ibn Wahab from abu 'Abd Allah, *'Alayhi al-Salam*, who has said the following:

"Abu 'Abd Allah, *'Alayhi al-Salam*, has said, 'Whoever is granted the ability to be thankful is also granted increase in bounties. Allah, the Most Majestic, the Most Holy, has said, ". . . if you give thanks, I shall give you greater (favors). . . ."'" (14:7)

H 1712, Ch. 44, h 9
Abu Ali al-Ash'ari has narrated from Muhammad ibn 'Abd al-Jabbar from Safwan from Ishaq ibn 'Ammar from two men of our people who have said the following:

"We heard abu 'Abd Allah, *'Alayhi al-Salam*, saying, 'If upon Allah's granting a favor to a servant he acknowledges it in his heart, and expresses thanks to Him in public, as soon as his words are completed, an order is issued to give the servant more.'"

H 1713, Ch. 44, h 10
A number of our people have narrated from Ahmad ibn Muhammad ibn Khalid from certain individuals of our people from Muhammad ibn Hisham from Muyassir from abu 'Abd Allah, *'Alayhi al-Salam*, who has said the following:

"Abu 'Abd Allah, 'Alayhi al-Salam, has said, 'Not to commit unlawful acts is a form of expressing thanks for a bounty. A complete expression of thankfulness is that one says, "All praise belongs to Allah, Lord of the worlds."'"

H 1714, Ch. 44, h 11
Ali ibn Ibrahim has narrated from his father from ibn abu 'Umayr from Ali ibn 'Uyayna from 'Umar ibn Yazid who has said the following:
"I heard abu 'Abd Allah, 'Alayhi al-Salam, saying, 'Expressing one's thankfulness for any favor, no matter how great it may be, is to thank Allah, the Most Majestic, the Most Holy, for it.'"

H 1715, Ch. 44, h 12
A number of our people have narrated from Ahmad ibn Muhammad ibn Khalid from Isma'il ibn Mehran from Sayf ibn 'Amirah from abu Basir who has said the following:
"I asked abu 'Abd Allah, 'Alayhi al-Salam, 'Is there a limit for the expression of thankfulness, upon which a servant is considered a thankful one?'

"The Imam said, 'Yes, there is a limit.' I then asked, 'What is that limit?' The Imam said, 'One must thank Allah for every favor that He has done, such as family and properties. If on the property one has received there is a certain right it must be paid off as is mentioned in the words of Allah, the Most Majestic, the Most Holy, quoting certain people, "Glory belongs to Him who has made it subservient to us when we were not able to do so ourselves." (43:13) He, the Most High, has also said quoting certain people, "Lord, grant us a blessed landing from the Ark; You are the One who provides the safest landing" (23:29). Allah has also said, "(Muhammad), say, 'Lord, make me enter through a path that will lead to the Truth and come out of an exit that will take me to the Truth. Grant me supportive authority.'"'" (17:80)

H 1716, Ch. 44, h 13
Muhammad ibn Yahya has narrated from Ahmad ibn Muhammad ibn 'Isa from Mu'ammar ibn Khallad who has said the following:
"I heard Abu al-Hassan, 'Alayhi al-Salam, saying, 'One's praising Allah for His granting him bounties is considered his expressing thanks to Allah and expressing the praise of Allah, is better than the bounties one has received.'"

H 1717, Ch. 44, h 14
Muhammad ibn Yahya has narrated from Ahmad from Ali ibn al-Hakam from Safwan al-Jammal from abu 'Abd Allah, 'Alayhi al-Salam, who has said the following:
"Abu 'Abd Allah, 'Alayhi al-Salam, has said, 'For any favor that Allah may grant to any one of His servants, a small or a greater favor, if that servant says "All praise belongs to Allah," has thanked Him properly.'"

H 1718, Ch. 44, h 15
Abu Ali al-Ash'ari has narrated from 'Isa ibn Ayyub from Ali ibn Mahziyar from al-Qasim ibn Muhammad from Isma'il ibn abu al-Hassan from a man from abu 'Abd Allah, 'Alayhi al-Salam, who has said the following:

"Abu 'Abd Allah, *'Alayhi al-Salam*, has said, 'Whoever receives a favor from Allah and acknowledges it in his heart, in so doing he has expressed his thankfuness for it also.'"

H 1719, Ch. 44, h 16

Ali ibn Ibrahim has narrated from his father from ibn abu 'Umayr from Mansur ibn Yunus from abu Basir who has said the following:

"Once abu 'Abd Allah, *'Alayhi al-Salam*, said, 'One of you drinks water and for this Allah admits him into paradise.' The Imam then said, 'He picks up the bowl of water and places it in his mouth, then mentions the name of Allah and then he drinks. He then removes it from his mouth and expresses praise for Allah, even though he still has a desire to drink. He then drinks and removes the bowl of water from his mouth and expresses praise for Allah. He then drinks and then removes and expresses praise for Allah. Thus, Allah, the Majestic, the Glorious, deems his admission to paradise necessary.'"

H 1720, Ch. 44, h 17

Ibn abu 'Umayr has narrated from al-Hassan ibn 'Atiyyah from 'Umar ibn Yazid who has said the following:

"Once I said to abu 'Abd Allah, *'Alayhi al-Salam*, 'I prayed to Allah, the Most Majestic, the Most Holy, for property and He granted me. I prayed to Allah for a child and He granted me. I prayed to Him for a house and He granted me. I am afraid that it (coming true of my wishes) is a kind of leading me to my own destruction (gradually)' The Imam said, 'I swear by Allah, it is not so if it takes place along with expressing His praise.'"

H 1721, Ch. 44, h 18

Al-Husayn ibn Muhammad has narrated from Mu'alla ibn Muhammad from al-Washsha' from Hammad ibn 'Uthman who has said the following:

"Once abu 'Abd Allah, *'Alayhi al-Salam*, came out of the Mosque and his animal that he had ridden was missing. The Imam said, 'If Allah will return my animal I will thank Him the way He must be thanked.' Not long thereafter his animal was brought back. The Imam said, 'All praise belongs to Allah.' Someone then said, 'May Allah keep my soul in service for your cause, did you not say, "I will thank Allah the way He must be thanked?"' The Imam said, 'Did you not hear me saying, "All praise belongs to Allah?"'"

H 1722, Ch. 44, h 19

Muhammad ibn Yahya has narrated from Ahmad ibn Muhammad ibn 'Isa from al-Qasim ibn Yahya from his grandfather al-Hassan ibn Rashid from al-Muthanna al-Hannat from abu 'Abd Allah, *'Alayhi al-Salam*, who has said the following:

"Abu 'Abd Allah, *'Alayhi al-Salam*, has said, 'If the Messenger of Allah were to receive happy news he would say, "All praise belongs to Allah, for His granting this favor." Whenever he was to receive a sad news he would say, "All praise belongs to Allah in all conditions."'"

H 1723, Ch. 44, h 20

Ali ibn Ibrahim has narrated from his father from ibn abu 'Umayr from abu Ayyub al-Khazzaz from abu Basir from abu Ja'far, *'Alayhi al-Salam*, who has said the following:

"Abu Ja'far, *'Alayhi al-Salam*, has said, 'Say three times when you see an ailing person without making him hear it, "All praise belongs to Allah for his keeping me safe from that with which you are afflicted. Had You (the Lord) wanted You could have made me suffer from this also."' The Imam said, 'Whoever says this he will never be afflicted with such ailment.'"

H 1724, Ch. 44, h 21

Hamid ibn Ziyad has narrated from al-Hassan ibn Muhammad ibn Sama'a from more than one person from Aban ibn 'Uthman from Hafs al-Kunansi from abu 'Abd Allah, *'Alayhi al-Salam*, who has said the following:

"Abu 'Abd Allah, *'Alayhi al-Salam*, has said, 'Anyone who upon seeing an ailing person says, "All praise belongs to Allah Who has avoided afflicting me with what He has afflict you and has given preference to me over you in granting a good health. O Allah, grant me good health against the ailment with which he is afflicted." He, because of this prayer, will not suffer from such an ailment.'"

H 1725, Ch. 44, h 22

A number of our people have narrated from Ahmad ibn 'Abd Allah from 'Uthman ibn 'Isa from Khalid ibn Najih from abu 'Abd Allah, *'Alayhi al-Salam*, who has said the following:

"Abu 'Abd Allah, *'Alayhi al-Salam*, has said, 'When you see a man who is in affliction and Allah has granted you a favor, say, "O Allah, I do not ridicule him or boast, but I express Your praise for the great favors that You have done for me."'"

H 1726, Ch. 44, h 23

It is narrated from him (narrator of the Hadith above) from his father from Harun ibn al-Jahm from Hafs ibn 'Umar from abu 'Abd Allah, *'Alayhi al-Salam*, who has said the following:

"The Messenger of Allah has said, 'When you see people who are in affliction, express the praise of Allah but do not make them hear it; it may cause them to feel sad.'"

H 1727, Ch. 44, h 24

It is narrated from him (narrator of the Hadith above) from 'Uthman ibn 'Isa from 'Abd Allah ibn Muskan from abu 'Abd Allah, *'Alayhi al-Salam*, who has said the following:

"The Messenger of Allah once was on a small journey on his camel. He dismounted and prostrated five times. When he mounted the camel they said, 'O Messenger of Allah, we saw you do what we had not seen you do before.' He said, 'Yes, it is true, but Jibril came to me with much good news from Allah, the Most Majestic, the Most Holy, and I then made one prostration in gratitude for each word of good news.'"

H 1728, Ch. 44, h 25

It is narrated from him (narrator of the Hadith above) from 'Uthman ibn 'Isa from Yunus ibn 'Ammar from abu 'Abd Allah, *'Alayhi al-Salam*, who has said the following:

"When any of you may remember or speak of the bounties of Allah, the Most Majestic, the Most Holy, he should place his cheek on the soil as an expression of gratitude to Allah. If one is riding one should dismount and place one's cheek on the soil. If he is not able to do so because of his avoiding publicity, should place his cheek on the saddle. If this also cannot be done he should place his cheek on his palm, then thank Allah for the favor that He has done for him."

H 1729, Ch. 44, h 26

Ali ibn Ibrahim has narrated from his father from ibn abu 'Umayr from Ali ibn 'Atiyah from Hisham ibn Ahmar who has said the following:

"Once I was walking with abu al-Hassan, 'Alayhi al-Salam, on a certain side of the city of Madina. He joined his legs on one side of the animal he was riding, dismounted and went to prostrate on the ground. He prolonged and prolonged the prostration. He then raised his head and mounted the animal. I then said, 'May Allah keep my soul in service for your cause, you had a very long prostration.' The Imam said, 'I just remembered a favor that Allah had granted me and I loved for it to thank my Lord.'"

H 1730, Ch. 44, h 27

Ali has narrated from father from ibn abu 'Umayr from abu 'Abd Allah Sahib al-Sabiri as I know or other people from abu 'Abd Allah, 'Alayhi al-Salam, who has said the following:

"Abu 'Abd Allah, 'Alayhi al-Salam, has said, 'Of the things that Allah, the Most Majestic, the Most Holy, revealed to Moses was this: "O Moses, thank Me the way I must be thanked." Moses said, "O Lord, how can I thank You the way You must be thanked while there is no thanking that I may perform but that in it You grant me a (new) favor." Allah said, "Now you have thanked Me, for realizing that it (the ability to thank) is also from Me."'"

H 1731, Ch. 44, h 28

Ibn abu 'Umayr has narrated from ibn Ri'ab from Isma'il ibn al-Fadl who has said the following:

"Abu 'Abd Allah, 'Alayhi al-Salam, has said, 'In the morning and evening say ten times: "O Lord, every morning I find myself with a favor and the well-being of the world or the hereafter. All such favors are from You, from You alone, and no one is Your partner. All praise belongs to You and thanks to You for Your favors to me, O Lord, until You are happy with me. Thanks to You even after Your being happy with me."' If you say this you have thanked Allah for what He has granted you on that day and on that night."

H 1732, Ch. 44, h 29

Ibn abu 'Umayr has narrated from Hafs ibn al-Bakhtari from abu 'Abd Allah, 'Alayhi al-Salam, who has said the following:

"Abu Abd Allah, 'Alayhi al-Salam, has said, 'Noah would say the prayer in the previous Hadith every morning and for that reason he is called a thankful person.' The Imam said, 'The Messenger of Allah has said, "Whoever accepts the truth from Allah, gains his salvation."'"

H 1733, Ch. 44, h 30

Ali ibn Ibrahim has narrated from his father from al-Qasim ibn Muhammad from al-Minqari from Sufyan ibn 'Uyayna from 'Ammar al-Dihni who has said the following:

"Allah loves every sad heart and He loves every thankful servant. Allah, the Most Blessed, the Most High, on the Day of Judgment will say to a servant among His servants, 'Did you thank so and so?' He (that servant) will say, 'No, but I thanked You, O Lord.' Allah will say, 'You have not thanked Me because you did not thank him.' The Imam said, 'The most thankful among you to Allah is the most thankful among you to people.'"

Chapter 45 - Excellence in Moral Behaviors

H 1734, Ch. 45, h 1

Muhammad ibn Yahya has narrated from Ahmad ibn Muhammad ibn 'Isa from al-Hassan ibn Mahbub from Jamil ibn Salih from Muhammad ibn Muslim from abu Ja'far, *'Alayhi al-Salam*, who has said the following:

"Abu Ja'far, *'Alayhi al-Salam*, has said, 'Among the believers of perfect belief is one whose moral behavior is excellent.'"

H 1735, Ch. 45, h 2

Al-Husayn ibn Muhammad has narrated from Mu'alla ibn Muhammad from al-Washsha' from 'Abd Allah ibn Sinan from a man from the people of Madina from Ali ibn al-Husayn, *'Alayhi al-Salam*, who has said the following:

"Ali ibn al-Husayn, *'Alayhi al-Salam*, has said, 'The Messenger of Allah has said, "On the Day of Judgment, in the balance of a man, no other things will be as meritorious as excellence in moral behavior."'"

H 1736, Ch. 45, h 3

Muhammad ibn Yahya has narrated from Ahmad ibn Muhammad from ibn Mahbub from abu Wallad al-Hannat from abu 'Abd Allah, *'Alayhi al-Salam*, who has said the following:

"Whoever has four things, his belief is complete even if he is covered with sins from his top to his toes, and it will not harm him. They are truthfulness, safe return of the trust, bashfulness and excellent moral behavior."

H 1737, Ch. 45, h 4

A number of our people have narrated from Ahmad ibn Muhammad ibn Khalid from ibn Mahbub from 'Anbasa al-'Abid who has said the following:

"Abu 'Abd Allah, *'Alayhi al-Salam*, once said to me, 'No one comes before Allah, the Most Majestic, the Most Holy, with good deeds, besides the obligatory ones, more beloved to Allah, the Most Blessed, the Most High, than one with excellent moral behavior that has room for all people in it.'"

H 1738, Ch. 45, h 5

Abu Ali al-Ash'ari has narrated from Muhammad ibn 'Abd al-Jabbar from Safwan from Dharih from abu 'Abd Allah, *'Alayhi al-Salam*, who has said the following:

"The Messenger of Allah has said, 'The reward for one who possesses excellent moral behavior is equal to the reward for one who worships all nights and fasts all days.'"

H 1739, Ch. 45, h 6

Ali ibn Ibrahim has narrated from his father from al-Nawfali from al-Sakuni from abu 'Abd Allah, *'Alayhi al-Salam*, who has said the following:

"The Messenger of Allah has said, 'The fact for which most people from my followers will go to paradise are piety before Allah and excellence in moral behavior.'"

H 1740, Ch. 45, h 7

Ali ibn Ibrahim has narrated from his father from ibn abu 'Umayr from Husayn al-Ahmasi and 'Abd Allah ibn Sinan from abu 'Abd Allah, *'Alayhi al-Salam*, who has said the following:

"Abu 'Abd Allah, *'Alayhi al-Salam*, has said, 'Excellent moral behavior melts down sins just as the sun melts down hoarfrost.'"

H 1741, Ch. 45, h 8

It is narrated from him (narrator of the Hadith above) from his father from ibn abu 'Umayr from 'Abd Allah ibn Sinan from abu 'Abd Allah, *'Alayhi al-Salam*, who has said the following:

"Abu 'Abd Allah, *'Alayhi al-Salam*, has said, 'Virtuous deeds and excellent moral behavior develop the cities and add to longevity of life.'"

H 1742, Ch. 45, h 9

A number of our people have narrated from Sahl ibn Ziyad from Muhammad ibn 'Abd al-Hamid who has said that Yahya ibn 'Amr from 'Abd Allah ibn Sinan narrated to me from abu 'Abd Allah, *'Alayhi al-Salam*, who has said the following:

"Abu 'Abd Allah, *'Alayhi al-Salam*, has said, 'Allah, the Most Blessed, the Most High, revealed to one of His prophets this: "Excellent moral behavior melts down sins just as the sun melts down hoarfrost."'"

H 1743, Ch. 45, h 10

Muhammad ibn Yahya has narrated from Ahmad ibn Muhammad ibn 'Isa from al-Hassan ibn Ali al-Washsha' from 'Abd Allah ibn Sinan from abu 'Abd Allah, *'Alayhi al-Salam*, who has said the following:

"During the time of the Holy Prophet a man died. The gravediggers could not dig a grave for him. They complained to the Messenger of Allah saying, 'O Messenger of Allah, our picks do not work. It is as if we hit a rock.' The Messenger of Allah said, 'Why it would be as such had your man been excellent in moral behavior. Bring to me a bowl of water.' When water was brought he (the Messenger of Allah), *'Alayhi al-Salam*, immersed his hand into it and then sprinkled it on the ground. He then told them to dig. They began to dig and it was like sand falling fast upon them."

H 1744, Ch. 45, h 11

It is narrated from him (narrator of the Hadith above) from Muhammad ibn Sinan from Ishaq ibn 'Ammar from abu 'Abd Allah, *'Alayhi al-Salam*, who has said the following:

"The Imam said, 'Moral behavior is a gift that, Allah, the Most Majestic, the Most Holy, bestows upon His creature. From moral behavior comes habit and intentions.' I then asked, 'Which one is better?' The Imam said, 'A person with an established habit is not able to do anything else. The person who possesses the intention may exercise patience for worship and thus, is the better one of the two.'"

H 1745, Ch. 45, h 12

It is narrated from him (narrator of the Hadith above) from Bakr ibn Salih from al-Hassan ibn Ali from 'Abd Allah ibn Ibrahim from Ali ibn abu Ali al-Lahabi from abu 'Abd Allah, *'Alayhi al-Salam*, who has said the following:

"Abu 'Abd Allah, *'Alayhi al-Salam*, has said, 'Allah, the Most Blessed, the Most High, grants good rewards to a person of excellent moral behavior as He grants rewards to one who strives hard (does Jihad) in the way of Allah, mornings and evenings.'"

H 1746, Ch. 45, h 13

It is narrated from him (narrator of the Hadith above) from 'Abd Allah al-Hajjall from abu 'Uthman al-Qabusi from the people whom he has mentioned (in his book) from abu 'Abd Allah, 'Alayhi al-Salam, who has said the following:

"Abu 'Abd Allah, 'Alayhi al-Salam, has said, 'Allah, the Most Blessed, the Most High, has, of the moral behavior of His friends, lent to His enemies so that His friends can live with His enemies in their governments.'"

In another Hadith it is stated that had it not been as such they would not have left any of Allah's friends alive.

H 1747, Ch. 45, h 14

Ali ibn Ibrahim has narrated from his father from Hammad ibn 'Isa from al-Husayn ibn al-Mukhtar from 'Ala' ibn Kamil from abu 'Abd Allah, 'Alayhi al-Salam, who has said the following:

"In your association with people you should have the upper hand (to benefit them), if you are able to do so. A servant (of Allah) who has shortcomings in his worship may have commendable moral behavior with which Allah grants him a reward of the degree of one who worships all nights and fasts all days."

H 1748, Ch. 45, h 15

A number of our people have narrated from Ahmad ibn abu 'Abd Allah from his father from Hammad ibn 'Isa from Hariz ibn 'Abd Allah from Bahr al-Saqqa who has said the following:

"Abu 'Abd Allah, 'Alayhi al-Salam, said to me, 'O Bahr, excellent moral behavior is prosperity. Would you like me to teach you a Hadith which is not found in the hands of any of the people of Madina?' I said, 'Yes, please do so.' The Imam said, 'Once the Messenger of Allah was in the Mosque when a girl from the people of Ansar came in and he was standing there. She held to one end of his (the Messenger of Allah's) cloth, the Holy Prophet stood up. She did not say anything and he (the Holy Prophet) also did not say anything to her (he then sat down). She repeated it three times and at the fourth time the Holy Prophet stood up for her and she was behind him. She then took a piece from his cloth and returned back. People rebuked her saying, "May Allah do to you what He may decide to do. You held the Messenger of Allah as your captive. You did it three times. You said nothing to him nor did he say anything to you. What did you want from him?" She then said, "We had a patient and our people sent me to get a piece from his (the Messenger of Allah's) cloth to be used to cure the patient. When I wanted to get the piece he saw me and stood up. I then felt shy to take what I wanted when he would see me. I did not like to demand anything from him. At last I took what I wanted to get."'"

H 1749, Ch. 45, h 16

Ali ibn Ibrahim has narrated from his father from ibn abu 'Umayr from Habib al-Khath'ami from abu 'Abd Allah, 'Alayhi al-Salam, who has said the following:

"The Messenger of Allah has said, 'The meritorious ones among you are those who possess excellent moral behavior, who are easy to associate with, associate others with ease and comfort others.'"

H 1750, Ch. 45, h 17

A number of our people have narrated from Sahl ibn Ziyad from Ja'far ibn Muhammad al-Ash'ari from 'Abd Allah ibn Maymun al-Qaddah from abu 'Abd Allah, *'Alayhi al-Salam*, who has said the following:

"Amir al-Mu'minin (Ali ibn abu Talib), *'Alayhi al-Salam*, has said, 'A believer is easy to associate with and there is nothing good in one who does not associate with others or is associated with.'"

H 1751, Ch. 45, h 18

Ali ibn Ibrahim has narrated from his father from ibn abu 'Umayr from 'Abd Allah ibn Sinan from abu 'Abd Allah, *'Alayhi al-Salam*, who has said the following:

"Abu 'Abd Allah, *'Alayhi al-Salam*, has said, 'Excellence in moral behavior takes one to the level of those who worship all nights and fast all days.'"

Chapter 46 - Delightful Appearance

H 1752, Ch. 46, h 1

A number of our people have narrated from Ahmad ibn Muhammad from Ali ibn al-Hakam from al-Hassan ibn al-Husayn who has said the following:

"I heard abu 'Abd Allah, *'Alayhi al-Salam*, saying, 'The Messenger of Allah said, "O children of 'Abd al-Muttalib, you cannot reach the level of people with your wealth, but you should meet them with openness and a delightful face."'"

He has narrated also from al-Qasim ibn Yahya from his grandfather al-Hassan ibn Rashid from abu 'Abd Allah, *'Alayhi al-Salam*, a similar Hadith except that it says, "O children of Hashim."

H 1753, Ch. 46, h 2

It is narrated from him (narrator of the Hadith above) from 'Uthman ibn 'Isa from Sama'a ibn Mehran from abu 'Abd Allah, *'Alayhi al-Salam*, who has said the following:

"Abu 'Abd Allah, *'Alayhi al-Salam*, has said, 'If Allah grants to a person one of three things, He will make paradise necessary for him. They are: To give charity in poverty, to have delightful appearance in all people and to exercise justice even against one's own self.'"

H 1754, Ch. 46, h 3

Ali ibn Ibrahim has narrated from his father from ibn Mahbub from Hisham ibn Salim from abu Basir from abu Ja'far, *'Alayhi al-Salam*, who has said the following:

"Once a man came to the Messenger of Allah, saying, 'O Messenger of Allah, confer upon me good advice.' Of the advice given to him was this: 'Meet your brethren (fellow human beings) with open and delightful face.'"

H 1755, Ch. 46, h 4

It is narrated from him (narrator of the Hadith above) from ibn Mahbub from certain individuals of his people who has said the following:

"Once I asked abu 'Abd Allah, *'Alayhi al-Salam*, 'What is the limit of excellent moral behavior?' The Imam said, 'It is to be relaxed (kindhearted), to have sweet expressions and to meet one's fellow human beings with a delightful face.'"

H 1756, Ch. 46, h 5

It is narrated from him (narrator of the Hadith above) from his father from Hammad from Rib'I from Fudayl who has said the following:

"Abu Ja'far or abu 'Abd Allah, *'Alayhi al-Salam,* has said, 'Doing lawful favors to others and having a delightful appearance earns love and lead one to paradise. Stinginess and a frowning face lead one away from Allah and into fire (of hell).'"

H 1757, Ch. 46, h 6

A number of our people have narrated from Ahmad ibn Muhammad from 'Uthman ibn 'Isa from Sama'a from abu al-Hassan Musa, *'Alayhi al-Salam,* who has said the following:

"The Messenger of Allah has said, 'Delightful appearance removes ill will.'"

Chapter 47 - Truthfulness and Trust

H 1758, Ch. 47, h 1

Muhammad ibn Yahya has narrated from Ahmad ibn Muhammad ibn 'Isa from Ali ibn al-Hakam from al-Husayn ibn abu al-'Ala' from abu 'Abd Allah *'Alayhi al-Salam* who has said the following:

"Allah, the Most Majestic, the Most Holy, has not sent any prophet who would not be truthful in their words and trustworthy in returning the trust without discriminating between virtuous or otherwise people."

H 1759, Ch. 47, h 2

It is narrated from him (narrator of the Hadith above) from 'Uthman ibn 'Isa from Ishaq ibn 'Ammar and others from abu 'Abd Allah, *'Alayhi al-Salam,* who has said the following:

"Abu 'Abd Allah, *'Alayhi al-Salam,* has said, 'Do not allow their prayers or fasts mislead you. A man may develop an attachment to praying or fasting so much so that without it he may feel frightened. Try them how truthful they are in their words or how reliable they are in returning the trust.'"

H 1760, Ch. 47, h 3

A number of our people have narrated from Sahl ibn Ziyad from ibn abu Najaran from Muthanna al-Hannat from Muhammad ibn Muslim from abu 'Abd Allah, *'Alayhi al-Salam,* who has said the following:

"Abu 'Abd Allah, *'Alayhi al-Salam,* has said, 'Whoever's tongue is truthful; his deeds are clean and pure.'"

H 1761, Ch. 47, h 4

Muhammad ibn Yahya has narrated from Muhammad ibn al-Husayn from Musa ibn Sa'dan from 'Abd Allah ibn al-Qasim from 'Amr ibn abu al-Miqdam who has said the following:

"The first time I met abu Ja'far, *'Alayhi al-Salam,* he said to me, 'Learn to speak the truth before narrating al-Hadith (statements of the Holy prophet and 'A'immah).'"

H 1762, Ch. 47, h 5

Muhammad ibn Yahya has narrated from Ahmad ibn Muhammad ibn 'Isa from al-Hassan ibn Mahbub from abu Kahmas who has said the following:

"Once I said to abu 'Abd Allah, *'Alayhi al-Salam,* ''Abd Allah ibn abu Ya'fur has sent you (salam) greetings.' The Imam said, 'May salam (peace) be with you and with him. If you meet 'Abd Allah convey salam to him and say, 'Ja'far, son of Muhammad, says to you, "Consider to what level Ali (Amir al-Mu'minin ibn abu

Talib) had reached before the Messenger of Allah. You must follow his manners. Ali, *'Alayhi al-Salam*, reached the level that he reached before the Messenger of Allah because of the truthfulness in his words and his trustworthiness in returning the trust.""

H 1763, Ch. 47, h 6
Ali ibn Ibrahim has narrated from his father from ibn abu 'Umayr from abu Isma'il al-Basri from Fudayl ibn Yasar who has said the following:

"Once abu 'Abd Allah, *'Alayhi al-Salam*, said to me, 'O Fudayl, the truthfulness of a truthful person is first verified by Allah, the Most Majestic, the Most Holy. He knows that he is truthful. Then his own soul confirms; it knows his truthfulness.'"

H 1764, Ch. 47, h 7
Ibn abu 'Umayr has narrated from Mansur ibn Hazim from abu 'Abd Allah, *'Alayhi al-Salam*, who has said the following:

"Isma'il is called the truthful in his promises; he promised a man to meet him at a certain place and Isma'íl waited for him at that place for one year. Thus, Allah, the Most Majestic, the Most Holy, named him the truthful in his promise. The Imam then said, 'The man then came at that place and Isma'íl said to him, "I am still waiting for you."'"

H 1765, Ch. 47, h 8
Abu Ali al-Ash'ari has narrated from Muhammad ibn Salim from Ahmad ibn al-Nadr al-Khazzaz from his grandfather al-Rabi' ibn Sa'd who has said the following:

"Once abu Ja'far, *'Alayhi al-Salam*, said to me, 'O Rab'i, a man must keep speaking the truth until Allah writes him down as a truthful one.'"

H 1766, Ch. 47, h 9
A number of our people have narrated from Ahmad ibn Muhammad from al-Washsha' from Ali ibn abu Hamza from abu Basir who has said the following:

"I heard abu 'Abd Allah, *'Alayhi al-Salam*, saying, 'A servant (of Allah) may keep speaking the truth until he is written among the truthful ones before Allah or keep speaking lies until he is written in the (list of) liars before Allah. If a man speaks the truth, Allah, the Most Majestic, the Most Holy, will say, "He has spoken the truth and has acted virtuously." If one speaks lies, Allah, the Most Majestic, the Most Holy, will say, "He has lied and has committed evil."'"

H 1767, Ch. 47, h 10
It is narrated from him (narrator of the Hadith above) from ibn Mahbub from al-'Ala' ibn Razin from 'Abd Allah ibn abu Ya'fur from abu 'Abd Allah, *'Alayhi al-Salam*, who has said the following:

"Abu 'Abd Allah, *'Alayhi al-Salam*, has said, 'Preach and call people to the good, but not with your tongues. They must see from your hard work, truthfulness and restraint from worldly matters (sins).'"

H 1768, Ch. 47, h 11
Muhammad ibn Yahya has narrated from Ahmad ibn Muhammad ibn 'Isa from Ali ibn al-Hakam who has said that abu al-Walid, Hassan ibn Ziyad al-Sayqal has said the following:

"Abu 'Abd Allah, *'Alayhi al-Salam*, has said, 'Making one's tongue speak the truth purifies one's deeds. Having good intentions increases one's livelihood. One who betters his kind deeds toward his family is granted longevity in his life.'"

H 1769, Ch. 47, h 12

It is narrated from him (narrator of the Hadith above) from abu Talib in a marfu' manner from abu 'Abd Allah, *'Alayhi al-Salam*, who has said the following:

"Abu 'Abd Allah, *'Alayhi al-Salam*, has said, 'Do not look to the long Ruku' (bowing down on one's knees for prayer) and Sajda (prostrating in prayer) of a man. It may have become his routine; without it he may feel frightened, but look to the truthfulness in his words and his credibility in keeping the trust.'"

Chapter 48 - Bashfulness

H 1770, Ch. 48, h 1

A number of our people have narrated from Sahl ibn Ziyad from ibn Mahbub from Ali ibn Ri'ab from abu 'Ubayda al-Hadhdha' from abu 'Abd Allah, *'Alayhi al-Salam*, who has said the following:

"Abu 'Abd Allah, *'Alayhi al-Salam*, has said, 'Bashfulness is from belief and belief is in paradise.'"

H 1771, Ch. 48, h 2

Muhammad ibn Yahya has narrated from Ahmad ibn Muhammad from Muhammad ibn Sinan from ibn Muskan from al-Hassan al-Sayqal from abu 'Abd Allah, *'Alayhi al-Salam*, who has said the following:

"Abu 'Abd Allah, *'Alayhi al-Salam*, has said, 'Bashfulness, chastity, tiredness of tongue (to shun speaking useless things), not tiredness of the heart, are from belief.'"

H 1772, Ch. 48, h 3

Al-Husayn ibn Muhammad has narrated from Muhammad ibn Ahmad al-Nahdi from Mus'ab ibn Yazid from al -'Awwam ibn al-Zubayr from abu 'Abd Allah, *'Alayhi al-Salam*, who has said the following:

"Abu 'Abd Allah, *'Alayhi al-Salam*, has said, 'One whose face is thin (bashful and shy) has thin knowledge.'"

H 1773, Ch. 48, h 4

Ali ibn Ibrahim has narrated from his father from 'Abd Allah ibn al-Mughirah from Yahya brother of Daram from Mu'adh ibn Kathir from one of the two Imam (abu Ja'far or abu 'Abd Allah, *'Alayhi al-Salam*) who has said the following:

"Bashfulness and belief are tied with the same rope. If one of them goes away, the other also follows its companion."

H 1774, Ch. 48, h 5

A number of our people have narrated from Sahl ibn Ziyad from Muhammad ibn 'Isa from al-Hassan ibn Ali ibn Yaqtin from al-Fadl ibn Kathir from those whom he has mentioned (in his book) from abu 'Abd Allah, *'Alayhi al-Salam*, who has said the following:

"Abu 'Abd Allah, *'Alayhi al-Salam*, has said, 'One has no belief if he does not have bashfulness.'"

H 1775, Ch. 48, h 6

A number of our people have narrated from Ahmad ibn abu 'Abd Allah from certain individuals of our people in a marfu' manner from the Messenger of Allah who has said the following:

"There are two kinds of bashfulness: A bashfulness that comes from one's reason and the bashfulness that comes from one's foolishness. The bashfulness that comes from one's reason is knowledge and the bashfulness that comes from one's foolishness is ignorance."

H 1776, Ch. 48, h 7

Muhammad ibn Yahya has narrated from Ahmad ibn Muhammad from Bukayr ibn Salih from al-Hassan ibn Ali from 'Abd Allah ibn Ibrahim from Ali ibn abu Ali al-Lahabi from abu 'Abd Allah, *'Alayhi al-Salam*, who has said the following:

"The Messenger of Allah has said, 'If four things are found in a person, even though he may be full of sins from his top to his toes, Allah will change his sins into good deeds. The four things are: truthfulness, bashfulness, excellence in moral behavior and gratefulness.'"

Chapter 49 - Forgiveness

H 1777, Ch. 49, h 1

Ali ibn Ibrahim has narrated from his father from ibn abu 'Umayr from 'Abd Allah ibn Sinan from abu 'Abd Allah, *'Alayhi al-Salam*, who has said the following:

"The Messenger of Allah said in a sermon, 'Should I tell you what is the best faculty of creatures of this world and of the next world? It is forgiveness for those who do injustice to you, to establish good relations with those who ignore you, to do favors to those who harm you and to give to those who deprive you.'"

H 1778, Ch. 49, h 2

A number of our people have narrated from Sahl ibn Ziyad from Muhammad ibn 'Abd al-Hamid from Yunus ibn Ya'qub from Ghirrah ibn Dinar al-Riqqi from ibn Ishaq al-Subay'i in a marfu' manner from the Messenger of Allah, *'Alayhi al-Salam*, who has said the following:

"I must teach you what is the best moral behavior in this world and in the next world. You must establish relations with those who disassociate with you, give to those who deprive you and forgive those who do injustice to you."

H 1779, Ch. 49, h 3

Ali ibn Ibrahim has narrated from his father from Muhammad ibn 'Isa ibn 'Ubayd from Yunus ibn 'Abd al-Rahman from abu 'Abd Allah Nashib al-Lafa'ifi from Humran ibn 'A'Yun who has said the following:

"Abu 'Abd Allah, *'Alayhi al-Salam*, has said, 'Three things are of the noble qualities of this world and of the next world: to forgive those who do injustice to you, to establish relations with those who abandon you and to exercise forbearance when you are ignored.'"

H 1780, Ch. 49, h 4

Ali has narrated from his father and Muhammad ibn Isma'il from Fadl ibn Shadhan all from ibn abu 'Umayr from Ibrahim ibn 'Abd al-Hamid from abu Hamza al-Thumali from Ali ibn al-Husayn, *'Alayhi al-Salam*, who has said the following:

"Abu Hamza al-Thumali has said, 'I heard the Imam saying, "When it will be the Day of Judgment Allah, the Most Blessed, the Most High, will bring together all the people of the past and the later generations on one platform. Then it will be called, 'Where are the meritorious people?'" The Imam said, 'Certain necks from among the people will be raised and then the angels will meet them and ask, "What were your merits?" They will say, 'We would establish relations with those who neglected us, gave those who deprived us and forgave those who did injustice to us.' The Imam said, 'They will then be told, "You have indeed spoken the truth, enter in paradise."'"

H 1781, Ch. 49, h 5

A number of our people have narrated from Ahmad ibn Muhammad ibn Khalid from Jahm ibn al-Hakam al-Mada'ini from Isma'il ibn abu Ziyad al-Sakuni from abu 'Abd Allah, *'Alayhi al-Salam*, who has said the following:

"The Messenger of Allah has said, 'You must forgive. Forgiving increases one's respect, therefore, forgive so Allah may respect you.'"

H 1782, Ch. 49, h 6

Muhammad ibn Yahya has narrated from Ahmad ibn Muhammad ibn 'Isa from Muhammad ibn Sinan from abu Khalid al-Qammat from Humran from abu Ja'far, *'Alayhi al-Salam*, who has said the following:

"Abu Ja'far, *'Alayhi al-Salam*, has said, 'Regret for forgiving is better and easier than regret for being subjected to punishment.'"

H 1783, Ch. 49, h 7

A number of our people have narrated from Ahmad ibn abu 'Abd Allah from Sa'dan from Mu'attib who has said the following:

"Abu al-Hassan Musa, *'Alayhi al-Salam*, once was in his compound that had palm-trees. I looked at one of his slaves who had picked up a certain amount of dates. He threw it on the other side of the wall. I went and picked up what he had thrown and I brought it to the Imam. I said, 'May Allah keep my soul in service for your cause, I found him and this amount of dates.' The Imam called the slave, 'O so and so.' 'Yes, sir,' the slave replied. 'Are you hungry?' asked the Imam. 'No, sir,' replied the slave. 'Do you need clothes?' asked the Imam. 'No, sir,' replied the slave. 'What for did then you take this many dates?' inquired the Imam. 'I just wanted,' said the slave. 'Take them. They are for you. Let him go,' the Imam said to others.'"

H 1784, Ch. 49, h 8

It is narrated from him (narrator of the Hadith above) from ibn Faddal who has said the following:

"I heard abu al-Hassan, *'Alayhi al-Salam*, saying, 'Whenever two hostile parties face each other, the one who forgives to a greater degree comes out victorious.'"

H 1785, Ch. 49, h 9

Muhammad ibn Yahya from Ahmad ibn Muhammad ibn 'Isa from ibn Faddal from ibn Bukayr from Zurara from abu Ja'far, *'Alayhi al-Salam*, who has said the following:

"The Jewish woman who had poisoned the sheep to also poison the Holy Prophet was brought before him. He asked her, 'What made you do this?' She said, 'I thought that if he is a prophet it will not harm him and if he is a king people will be relieved of his troubles.' The Messenger of Allah forgave her.'"

H 1786, Ch. 49, h 10

Ali ibn Ibrahim has narrated from Muhammad ibn 'Isa from Yunus from 'Amr ibn Shamir from Jabir from abu Ja'far, *'Alayhi al-Salam*, who has said the following:

"Abu Ja'far, *'Alayhi al-Salam*, has said, 'There are three qualities with which Allah increases the respect of a Muslim: To be lenient to those who do injustice to him, to give to those who deprive him and to establish relations with those who neglect him.'"

Chapter 50 - Suppressing One's Anger

H 1787, Ch. 50, h 1

Ali ibn Ibrahim has narrated from his father from ibn abu 'Umayr from Hisham ibn al-Hakam from abu 'Abd Allah, *'Alayhi al-Salam*, who has said the following:

"I do not love to humiliate my soul even to achieve the best of the bounties. I have not swallowed a drop more beloved to me than the drop (in the form) of my anger for which I did not seek compensation from the source that had caused it to stir up."

H 1788, Ch. 50, h 2

Muhammad ibn Yahya has narrated from Ahmad ibn Muhammad ibn 'Isa from Muhammad ibn Sinan and Ali ibn al-Nu'man from 'Ammar ibn Marwan from Zayd al-Shahham from abu 'Abd Allah, *'Alayhi al-Salam*, who has said the following:

"How wonderful indeed is the drop of anger for one who curbs it with exercising patience! Great rewards are for those who go through great trials and tribulations. Allah has not loved any people without exposing them to trials and tribulations."

H 1789, Ch. 50, h 3

It is narrated from him (narrator of the Hadith above) from Ali ibn al-Nu'man and Muhammad ibn Sinan from 'Ammar ibn Marwan from abu al-Hassan the 1st, *'Alayhi al-Salam*, who has said the following:

"Be patient against the enemies (jealous) of bounties. You cannot seek a compensation from one who disobeys Allah in your case, more meritorious and better than obeying Allah in his case (exercise patience against his jealousy)."

H 1790, Ch. 50, h 4

It is narrated from him (narrator of the Hadith above) from Muhammad ibn Sinan from Thabit Mawla Ale Hariz from abu 'Abd Allah, *'Alayhi al-Salam*, who has said the following:

"To suppress one's anger in the face of the enemy, the ruling party's government, for protection (Taqiyah), is a cutting edge for those who adopt it. It is to avoid being exposed to suffering in this world and to the animosity of the ruling party in their government. Opposition to such ruling parties without maintaining protective (Taqiyah) measures is ignoring the commands of Allah. Maintain a graceful position toward people; it will grow with them in your favor. Do not deal with them as your enemies; otherwise, you make them impose burdens on you and humiliate you."

H 1791, Ch. 50, h 5

Ali ibn Ibrahim has narrated from certain individuals of his people from Malik ibn Hasin al-Sakuni who has said the following:

"Abu 'Abd Allah, *'Alayhi al-Salam*, has said, 'If a servant (of Allah) suppresses his anger, Allah, the Most Majestic, the Most Holy, increases his respect in this world and in the next world. Allah, the Most Majestic, the Most Holy, has said, ". . . who also harness their anger and forgive the people. Allah loves the righteous ones." (3:134) Allah will give them such rewards; they had suppressed their anger.'"

H 1792, Ch. 50, h 6

A number of our people have narrated from Ahmad ibn Muhammad ibn Khalid from Isma'il ibn Mehran ibn Sayf ibn 'Amirah who has said that spoke to him one who had heard from abu 'Abd Allah, *'Alayhi al-Salam*, the following:

"Abu 'Abd Allah, *'Alayhi al-Salam*, has said, 'Whoever suppressess his anger that he could let out if he wanted, Allah, on the Day of Judgment, will fill his heart with His happiness.'"

H 1793, Ch. 50, h 7

Abu Ali al-Ash'ari has narrated from Muhammad ibn 'Abd al-Jabbar from ibn Faddal from Ghalib ibn 'Uthman from 'Abd Allah ibn Mundhir from al-Wassafi from abu Ja'far, *'Alayhi al-Salam*, who has said the following:

"Abu Ja'far, *'Alayhi al-Salam*, has said, 'Whoever controls his anger which he could allow to take its course, Allah on the Day of Judgment will fill his heart with security and belief.'"

H 1794, Ch. 50, h 8

Al-Husayn ibn Muhammad has narrated from Mu'alla ibn Muhammad from al-Hassan ibn Ali al-Washsha' from 'Abd al-Karim ibn 'Amr from abu 'Usama Zayd al-Shahham from abu 'Abd Allah, *'Alayhi al-Salam*, who has said the following:

"Once the Imam said to me, 'O Zayd be patient against the enemies of the bounties (jealous people). You cannot compensate (retaliate to offset your suffering) from one who disobeys Allah through causing you to suffer, in other ways more properly, than obeying Allah in his case (in not causing any suffering to him). O Zayd Allah has chosen Islam and has selected it. Be good companions of Islam through generosity and excellence in moral behavior.'"

H 1795, Ch. 50, h 9

Ali ibn Ibrahim has narrated from Muhammad ibn 'Isa from Yunus from Hafs Bayya' al-Sabiri from abu Hamza from Ali ibn al-Husayn, *'Alayhi al-Salam*, who has said the following:

"The Messenger of Allah has said, 'Of the most beloved path to Allah, the Most Majestic, the Most Holy, there are two drops: The drop of anger that one brushes aside and repels with tolerance and the drop of suffering that one wipes off with patience.'"

H 1796, Ch. 50, h 10

Ali ibn Ibrahim has narrated from his father from Hammad from Rib'i from his chain of narrators from abu Ja'far, *'Alayhi al-Salam*, who has said the following:

"The Imam said, 'My father once said to me, "My son, there is nothing more delightful to the eyes of your father than the drop (feeling) of anger that precedes patience. My receiving the most noble of the bounties does not bring me any happiness if it may cuase humiliation to my soul."'"

H 1797, Ch. 50, h 11

Ali ibn Ibrahim has narrated from his father from ibn abu 'Umayr from Mu'awiyah ibn Wahab from Mu'adh ibn Muslim from abu 'Abd Allah, *'Alayhi al-Salam*, who has said the following:

"Bear patience against the enemies of the bounties (jealous people). You cannot compensate (your loss) from one who has disobeyed Allah in your case, in a more proper way than obeying Allah in his case."

H 1798, Ch. 50, h 12

It is narrated from him (narrator of the Hadith above) from his father from ibn abu 'Umayr from Khallad from al-Thumali from Ali ibn al-Husayn, *'Alayhi al-Salam*, who has said the following:

"I do not love to have the most noble of the bounties at the cost of humiliation to my soul. I have not swallowed any drop more beloved to me than the drop of anger for which I did not compensate from the one who caused it (my anger)."

H 1799, Ch. 50, h 13

A number of our people have narrated from Ahmad ibn Muhammad from al-Washsha' from Muthanna al-Hannat from abu Hamza who has said the following:

"Abu 'Abd Allah, *'Alayhi al-Salam*, once said to me, 'The swallowing of a servant (of Allah) of no other drop is more beloved to Allah, the Most Majestic, the Most Holy, than the drop (feeling) of anger when it runs around in his heart, and he swallows it by means of patience and forbearance.'"

Chapter 51 - Forbearance

H 1800, Ch. 51, h 1

Muhammad ibn Yahya has narrated from Ahmad ibn Muhammad ibn 'Isa from Ahmad ibn Muhammad ibn abu Nasr from Muhammad ibn 'Ubayd Allah who has said the following:

"I heard al-Rida, *'Alayhi al-Salam*, saying, 'A man cannot become a worshipper until he becomes a forbearing one. A man in the tribe of Israel wanting to become a worshipper had to keep silent for ten years before he could be considered a worshipper.'"

H 1801, Ch. 51, h 2

Muhammad ibnYahya has narrated from Ahmad ibn Muhammad from Ali ibn al-Nu'man from ibn Muskan from abu Hamza who has said the following:

"The believer's deeds are mixed with forbearance. He sits to learn and speaks to understand. He does not tell his friends about his trust and he does not hide his testimony for the enemies. He does not do any true thing to show off and does not ignore it due to shyness. If he purifies himself he fears what they may say and he asks forgiveness from Allah for what they do not know. The words of those who do not know him do not make him boastful. He fears from the record of his deeds."

H 1802, Ch. 51, h 3

Muhammad ibn Yahya has narrated from Ahmad ibn Muhammad ibn 'Isa from ibn Faddal from ibn Bukayr from Zurara from abu Ja'far, *'Alayhi al-Salam*, who has said the following:

"Ali ibn al-Husayn, *'Alayhi al-Salam*, would say, 'It is fascinating to me when a man's forbearance saves him from his anger.'"

H 1803, Ch. 51, h 4

A number of our people have narrated from Ahmad ibn Muhammad ibn Khalid from Ali ibn al-Hakam from abu Jamilah from Jabir from abu Ja'far, *'Alayhi al-Salam*, who has said the following:

"Allah, the Most Majestic, the Most Holy, loves the living person who is forbearing."

H 1804, Ch. 51, h 5

It is narrated from him (narrator of the Hadith above) from Ali ibn Hafs al-'Awsi al-Kufi in a marfu' manner from abu 'Abd Allah, *'Alayhi al-Salam*, who has said the following:

"The Messenger of Allah has said, 'Allah has never given respect to anyone because of ignorance and He has never humiliated anyone who possessed forbearance.'"

H 1805, Ch. 51, h 6

It is narrated from him (narrator of the Hadith above) from certain individuals of his people in a marfu' manner from abu 'Abd Allah, *'Alayhi al-Salam*, who has said the following:

"Abu 'Abd Allah, *'Alayhi al-Salam*, has said, 'Forbearance is enough as a helper' and he said, 'If you are not a forbearing person at least pretend to be like a forebearing person.'"

H 1806, Ch. 51, h 7

Muhammad ibn Yahya has narrated from Ahmad ibn Muhammad ibn 'Isa from 'Abd Allah al-Hajjal from Hafs ibn abu 'A'isha who has said the following:

"Abu 'Abd Allah, *'Alayhi al-Salam*, once sent one of his slaves for a certain work and he delayed. The Imam then went out to find why he has delayed so much. He found him sleeping. He sat near his head fanning to comfort him until he woke up. When he fully woke up, abu 'Abd Allah, *'Alayhi al-Salam*, said to him, 'O so and so, Allah knows, you are not supposed to do this. You sleep night and day. The night is for you to sleep and your day is for us.'"

H 1807, Ch. 51, h 8

Muhammad ibn Yahya has narrated from Ahmad ibn Muhammad from Ali ibn al-Nu'man from 'Amr ibn Shamir from Jabir from abu Ja'far, *'Alayhi al-Salam*, who has said the following:

"The Messenger of Allah has said, 'Allah certainly loves the living person who is forbearing, maintains chastity and restrains from worldly matters (sins).'"

H 1808, Ch. 51, h 9

Abu Ali al-Ash'ari has narrated from Muhammad ibn Ali ibn Mahbub from Ayyub ibn Nuh from 'Abbas ibn 'Amir from Rabi' ibn Muhammad al-Musalli from abu Muhammad from 'Imran from Sa'id ibn Yasar from abu 'Abd Allah, *'Alayhi al-Salam*, who has said the following:

"When two men dispute each other, two angels come down and say to the foolish one of the two, 'You said what you said and you were the kind to say what you said and you will be brought to account for what you have said.' Then they will say to the forbearing one of the two men, 'You exercised patience and forbearance. Allah will forgive you if you will complete it.' The Imam said, 'If the forbearing man answers back to the other man the two angels will ascend.'"

Chapter 52 - Silence and Controlling the Tongue

H 1809, Ch. 52, h 1
Muhammad ibn Yahya has narrated from Ahmad ibn Muhammad ibn 'Isa from Ahmad ibn Muhammad ibn abu Nasr who has said the following:

"Abu al-Hassan al-Rida, 'Alayhi al-Salam, has said, 'Of the signs of one's intelligence is forbearance, knowledge and silence. Silence is one of the doors of wisdom. Silence earns love and it, certainly, is the guide to all good.'"

H 1810, Ch. 52, h 2
It is narrated from him (narrator of the Hadith above) from al-Hassan ibn Mahbub from 'Abd Allah ibn Sinan from abu Hamza who has said the following:

"I heard abu Ja'far, 'Alayhi al-Salam, saying, 'Our Shi'a (followers) are just (like) mute people (do not speak uselessly).'"

H 1811, Ch. 52, h 3
It is narrated from him (narrator of the Hadith above) from al-Hassan ibn Mahbub from abu Ali al-Jawwani who has said the following:

"I saw abu 'Abd Allah, 'Alayhi al-Salam, speaking to one of his slaves called Salim, placing his hands over his (slaves) mouth, 'O Salim, control your tongue and you will have peace and do not load people over our necks.'"

H 1812, Ch. 52, h 4
It is narrated from him (narrator of the Hadith above) from 'Uthman ibn 'Isa who has said the following:

"Once I was in the presence of abu al-Hassan, 'Alayhi al-Salam, and a man said, 'Please teach me good advice.' The Imam said, 'Control your tongue and you will be respected and do not allow people to lead you to humiliation.'"

H 1813, Ch. 52, h 5
It is narrated from him (narrator of the Hadith above) from al-Haytham ibn abu Masruq from Hisham ibn Salim from abu 'Abd Allah, 'Alayhi al-Salam, who has said the following:

"The Messenger of Allah said to a man who had come to see him, 'Should I guide you to a matter with which Allah will enter you in paradise?' The man said, 'Yes, O Messenger of Allah.' The Messenger of Allah said, 'Give of what Allah has given you.' The man asked, 'What if I were more needy than the recipient?' The Messenger of Allah said, 'Then help the oppressed.' The man asked, 'What if I were weaker than the oppressed?' The Messenger of Allah then said, 'Do what an ignorant person may do, that is, guide him to good.' The man asked, 'What if I were more ignorant than him?' The Messenger of Allah said, 'Control your tongue except from good. Do you not like to have one of the above mentioned qualities in you that may lead you to paradise?'"

H 1814, Ch. 52, h 6
A number of our people have narrated from Sahl ibn Ziyad from Ja'far ibn Muhammad al- Ash'ari from ibn al-Qaddah from abu 'Abd Allah, 'Alayhi al-Salam, who has said the following:

"Luqman (who is mentioned in Chapter 31 of the Holy Quran) said to his son, 'My son, if you think speaking is silver, note it down that silence is gold.'"

H 1815, Ch. 52, h 7

Ali ibn Ibrahim has narrated from Muhammad ibn 'Isa from Yunus from al-Halabi in a marfu' manner from the Messenger of Allah who has said the following:

"Control your tongue; it is a charity that you give to yourself. He then said, 'A servant (of Allah) will not know the reality of his belief until he reserves (controls) his tongue.'"

H 1816, Ch. 52, h 8

Ali ibn Ibrahim has narrated from his father and Muhammad Isma'il from Fadl ibn Shadhan all from ibn abu 'Umayr from Ibrahim ibn 'Abd al-Hamid from 'Ubayd Allah ibn Ali al-Halabi from abu 'Abd Allah, *'Alayhi al-Salam*, who has said the following:

"About the words of Allah, the Most Majestic, the Most Holy: 'Have you not seen those who were told to control their hands. . . .' (4:77), the Imam said, 'It (their hands) stands for their tongue.'"

H 1817, Ch. 52, h 9

Ali ibn Ibrahim has narrated from Muhammad ibn 'Isa from Yunus from al-Halabi in a marfu' manner from the Messenger of Allah who has said the following:

"The salvation of a believer is in his controlling his tongue."

H 1818, Ch. 52, h 10

Yunus has narrated from Muthanna from abu Basir who has said the following:

"I heard abu Ja'far, *'Alayhi al-Salam*, saying, abu Dhar may Allah grant him blessings, would say, 'O you who seek knowledge, this tongues is the key to both good and evil. Seal your tongue as you would seal your gold and silver.'"

H 1819, Ch. 52, h 11

Hamid ibn Ziyad has narrated from al-Khashshab from ibn Baqqah from Mu'adh ibn Thabit from 'Amr ibn Jami' from abu 'Abd Allah, *'Alayhi al-Salam*, who has said the following:

"Abu 'Abd Allah, *'Alayhi al-Salam*, has said, 'Jesus would say, "Do not speak a great deal in things other than speaking of Allah. Those who speak a great deal in things other than speaking of Allah are hardhearted, but they do not know it."'"

H 1820, Ch. 52, h 12

A number of our people have narrated from Sahl ibn Ziyad from ibn abu Najran from abu Jamilah from those he has mentioned (in his book) from abu 'Abd Allah, *'Alayhi al-Salam*, who has said the following:

"There is no day wherein every part of the body does not bow down before the tongue pleading, 'We request you, for the sake of Allah, do not subject us to punishment.'"

H 1821, Ch. 52, h 13

Muhammad ibn Yahya has narrated from Ahmad ibn Muhammad ibn 'Isa from Ali ibn al-Hakam from Ibrahim ibn Mahziyar al-Asadi from abu Hamza from Ali ibn al-Husayn, *'Alayhi al-Salam*, who has said the following:

"The tongue of Adam's children addresses all parts of his body and asks, 'How is your morning?' They reply, 'We are fine, if only you leave us alone.' They further say, 'For the sake of Allah, for the sake of Allah, we plead before you to note because of only you we may find reward or face punishment.'"

H 1822, Ch. 52, h 14

Ali ibn Ibrahim has narrated from his father and Muhammad ibn Isma'il from Fadl ibn Shadhan all from ibn abu 'Umayr from Ibrahim ibn 'Abd al-Hamid from Qays abu Isma'il (he has said that he is fine and is of our people) in a marfu' manner from the Messenger of Allah, *'Alayhi al-Salam*:

"Once a man came to the Holy Prophet and said, 'O Messenger of Allah, advise me.' The Messenger of Allah, *'Alayhi al-Salam*, said, 'Control your tongue.' He then said, 'O Messenger of Allah, advise me.' The Messenger of Allah said, 'Control your tongue.' He again said, 'O Messenger of Allah, advise me.' The Messenger of Allah said, 'Control your tongue. Fie upon you, do people get thrown into fire headlong for any reason other than being a victim due to their own tongue?'"

H 1823, Ch. 52, h 15

Abu Ali al-Ash'ari has narrated from Muhammad ibn 'Abd al-Jabbar from ibn Faddal from those he narrated from abu 'Abd Allah, *'Alayhi al-Salam*, who has said the following:

"The Messenger of Allah has said, 'One who does not count his words as his deeds, his sins increase and his punishment approaches.'"

H 1824, Ch. 52, h 16

Ali ibn Ibrahim has narrated from his father from al-Nawfali from al-Sakuni from abu 'Abd Allah, *'Alayhi al-Salam*, who has said the following:

"The Messenger of Allah has said, 'Allah will punish the tongue with a punishment that no other part will suffer thereby. And the tongue will say, "O Lord, You have punished me with a punishment that no one has suffered thereby." It then will be said to the tongue, "From you came out a word that reached the East and West of the earth. It caused unlawful bloodshed, destroyed properties illegally, and caused unlawful sexual relations to take place. I swear by My Majesty and Glory to punish you with a punishment whereby no other parts of you has suffered."'"

H 1825, Ch. 52, h 17

Through the same chain of narrators it is narrated from the Messenger of Allah, *'Alayhi al-Salam*, has said, the following:

"The Messenger of Allah, *'Alayhi al-Salam*, has said, 'If there is any wickedness, it is in the tongue.'"

H 1826, Ch. 52, h 18

A number of our people have narrated from Sahl ibn Ziyad and al-Husayn ibn Muhammad from Mu'alla ibn Muhammad all from al-Washsha' who has said the following:

"I heard al-Rida, *'Alayhi al-Salam*, say, 'In the tribe of Israel if a man wanted to become a worshipper he was to keep silent for ten years before starting the deed.'"

H 1827, Ch. 52, h 19

Muhammad ibn Yahya has narrated from Ahmad ibn Muhammad from Bakr ibn Salih form al-Ghaffari from Ja'far ibn Ibrahim who has said the following:

"I heard abu 'Abd Allah, *'Alayhi al-Salam*, say, 'The Messenger of Allah has said, "If one can realize the effect of his words on his deeds, his words will decrease except for what he needs.'"

H 1828, Ch. 52, h 20

Abu Ali al-Ash'ari has narrated from al-Hassan ibn Ali al-Kufi from 'Uthman ibn 'Isa from Sa'id ibn Yasar from Mansur ibn Yunus from abu 'Abd Allah, *'Alayhi al-Salam*, who has said the following:

"It is in the wisdom of Ale (people of) Dawud: 'A person of reason must learn about the nature of his time, pay attention to his affairs and safeguard his tongue.'"

H 1829, Ch. 52, h 21

Muhammad ibn Yahya has narrated from Muhammad ibn al-Husayn from Ali ibn al-Hassan ibn Ribat from certain individuals of his people from abu 'Abd Allah, *'Alayhi al-Salam*, who has said the following:

"A believing servant (of Allah) is considered a person of good deeds as long as he does not speak. When he speaks he is considered a person of good deeds or of evil deeds."

Chapter 53 - Gentleness in Dealings

H 1830, Ch. 53, h 1

Ali ibn Ibrahim has narrated from his father from al-Nawfali from al-Sakuni from abu 'Abd Allah, *'Alayhi al-Salam*, who has said the following:

"The Messenger of Allah has said, 'There are three things for the absence of which none of one's deeds is complete: restraint from the worldly things to keep him from disobeying Allah, moral behavior with which one can gently deal with people and forbearance with which one can repel the ignorance of ignorant people.'"

H 1831, Ch. 53, h 2

Muhammad ibn Yahya has narrated from Ahmad ibn Muhammad ibn 'Isa from Ali ibn al-Hakam from al-Husayn ibn al-Hassan who has said the following:

"I heard abu Ja'far, *'Alayhi al-Salam*, say, 'Jibril (the Archangel) once came to the Holy Prophet and said, "O Muhammad, your Lord sends you greetings of peace and says to you, 'Be gentle and kind to My creatures.'"'"

H 1832, Ch. 53, h 3

It is narrated from him (narrator of the Hadith above) from Ahmad ibn Muhammad ibn 'Isa from ibn Mahbub from Hisham ibn Salim from Habib al-Sajistani from abu Ja'far, *'Alayhi al-Salam*, who has said the following:

"In the Torah it is of the words of Allah, the Most Majestic, the Most Holy, to Moses ibn 'Imran, 'O Moses, keep My secret as secret in your secrecy. Demonstrate gentleness from Me in your public life toward your enemy and My enemy among My creatures. Do not express My secret (condemnation of the enemy) for Me before them and in public that, consequently, your enemy and My enemy join to abuse Me.'"

H 1833, Ch. 53, h 4

Abu Ali al-Ash'ari has narrated from Muhammad ibn 'Abd al-Jabbar from Muhammad ibn Isma'il from ibn Bazi' from Hamza ibn Bazi' from 'Abd Allah ibn Sinan from abu 'Abd Allah, *'Alayhi al-Salam*, who has said the following:

"The Messenger of Allah has said, 'My Lord (Allah) has commanded me to be gentle to people just as He has commanded me to fulfill my obligations.'"

H 1834, Ch. 53, h 5

Ali ibn Ibrahim has narrated from Harun ibn Muslim from Mas'adah ibn Sadaqa from abu 'Abd Allah, *'Alayhi al-Salam*, who has said the following:

"The Messenger of Allah has said, 'Dealing kindly with people is half of belief and leniency to them is half of livelihood.' The Imam then said, 'Meet the virtuous people privately. Meet the criminals in public and do not be attracted to them; they will do injustice to you. There will come a time when, from the religious people, only those will be safe who are thought of as fools. They exercise patience so much so that they will be called silly.'"

H 1835, Ch. 53, h 6

Ali ibn Ibrahim has narrated from certain individuals of his people whom he has mentioned (in his book) from Muhammad ibn Sinan from Hudhayfa ibn Mansur who has said the following:

"I heard abu 'Abd Allah, *'Alayhi al-Salam*, say, 'Certain people lacked gentle dealings with others, they were expelled from the tribe of Quraysh. I swear by Allah, there was nothing wrong with their birth. On the other hand, certain people who were not from the tribe of Quraysh dealt with people gently and they were joined in the family of superior status.' The Imam then said, 'One who holds his hand back from people he only holds back one hand but they (people) hold back from him many hands.'"

Chapter 54 - Friendliness

H 1836, Ch. 54, h 1

A number of our people have narrated from Ahmad ibn Muhammad ibn Khalid from his father from who he has mentioned (in his book) from Muhammad ibn 'Abd al-Rahman ibn abu Layla from his father from abu Ja'far, *'Alayhi al-Salam*, who has said the following:

"For everything there is a lock and the lock for belief is friendliness."

H 1837, Ch. 54, h 2

Through the same chain of narrators it is narrated from abu Ja'far, *'Alayhi al-Salam*, who has said the following:

"Whoever has received a share of friendliness has received a share of belief."

H 1838, Ch. 54, h 3

Ali ibn Ibrahim has narrated from his father from Safwan ibn Yahya from Yahya al-Azraq from Hammad ibn Bashir from abu 'Abd Allah, *'Alayhi al-Salam*, who has said the following:

"Allah, the Most Blessed, the Most High, is compassionate and He loves friendliness. Of the examples of His compassion to His worshippers is His reducing and easing off of their feeling grudge, resentment and hatred that confronts their wish and their heart. It is of the examples of His compassion toward them that He calls upon them to obey one of His commands to remove a certain evil (practice) from them for compassionate reasons so that the ring and the weight of belief do not fall upon them at once to make them weak. When He wants to make such a decision (of easing up on them) He cancels one command by another command and it becomes abrogated."

H 1839, Ch. 54, h 4

Muhammad ibn Yahya has narrated from Ahmad ibn Muhammad ibn 'Isa from ibn Mahbub from Mu'awiyah ibn Wahab from Mu'adh ibn Muslim from abu 'Abd Allah, *'Alayhi al-Salam*, who has said the following:

"The Messenger of Allah has said, 'Friendliness is a blessing and detachment is evil.'"

H 1840, Ch. 54, h 5

It is narrated from him (narrator of the Hadith above) from ibn Mahbub from 'Amr ibn Shamir from Jabir from abu Ja'far, *'Alayhi al-Salam*, who has said the following:

"Allah, the Most Majestic, the Most Holy, is compassionate. He loves kindheartedness and awards for it with such things that He does not give due to rudeness."

H 1841, Ch. 54, h 6

Ali ibn Ibrahim has narrated from his father from ibn abu 'Umayr from 'Umar ibn 'Udhayna from Zurara from abu Ja'far, *'Alayhi al-Salam*, who has said the following:

"The Messenger of Allah has said, 'There is nothing in which friendliness is placed but that such thing is beautified. There is nothing from which friendliness is removed but that such thing is shunned.'"

H 1842, Ch. 54, h 7

Ali has narrated from his father from 'Abd Allah ibn al-Mughirah from 'Amr ibn abu al-Miqdam in a marfu' manner from the Holy prophet who has said the following:

"In friendliness, certainly, there are increased blessings. One dispossessed of (faculty) friendliness is deprived of goodness."

H 1843, Ch. 54, h 8

It is narrated from him (narrator of the Hadith above) from 'Abd Allah ibn al-Mughirah from those whom he has mentioned (in his book) from abu 'Abd Allah, *'Alayhi al-Salam*, who has said the following:

"If kindheartedness goes away from a family, goodness departs them also."

H 1844, Ch. 54, h 9

A number of our people have narrated from Ahmad ibn 'Abd Allah from Ibrahim ibn Muhammad al-Thaqafi from Ali ibn Mu'alla from Isma'il ibn Yasar from Ahmad ibn Ziyad ibn Arqam al-Kufi from a man from abu 'Abd Allah, *'Alayhi al-Salam*, who has said the following:

"Any family who has received their share of kindheartedness, Allah has certainly increased their livelihood. Friendliness in matters of earning a living is better than great wealth. Friendliness does not cause any weakness but a spendthrift habit leaves nothing in place. Allah, the Most Majestic, the Most Holy, is compassionate and He loves friendliness."

H 1845, Ch. 54, h 10

Ali ibn Ibrahim has narrated in a marfu' manner from Salih ibn 'Aqaba from Hisham ibn Ahmar from abu al-Hassan, *'Alayhi al-Salam*, who has said the following:

"The narrator has said, 'A conversation took place between a man of the group and me and the Imam said to me, 'Be friendly with them or else one of them may reject in anger and there is nothing good in rejection that may come from anger.'"

H 1846, Ch. 54, h 11

A number of our people have narrated from Sahl ibn Ziyad from Ali ibn Hassan from Musa ibn Bakr from abu al-Hassan Musa, *'Alayhi al-Salam*, who has said the following:

"Friendliness is half of livelihood."

H 1847, Ch. 54, h 12

Ali ibn Ibrahim has narrated from his father from al-Nawfali from al-Sakuni from abu 'Abd Allah, *'Alayhi al-Salam*, who has said the following:

"The Messenger of Allah has said, 'Allah, certainly, loves kindheartedness and He supports one to achieve it. If you ride a weak animal allow it to rest whenever needed. If it is a barren land pass it quickly, and if it is a fertile land, allow them to rest as they need.'"

H 1848, Ch. 54, h 13

A number of our people have narrated from Ahmad ibn abu 'Abd Allah from 'Uthman ibn 'Isa from 'Amr ibn Shamir from Jabir from abu Ja'far, *'Alayhi al-Salam*, who has said the following:

"The Messenger of Allah has said, 'If kindheartedness were to be seen like a creature, nothing of the creatures of Allah could have been as good as kindheartedness.'"

H 1849, Ch. 54, h 14

Abu Ali al-Ash'ari has narrated from Muhammad ibn 'Abd al-Jabbar from ibn Faddal from Tha'labi from ibn Maymun from those who narrated to him from one of them (one of the two Imams), *'Alayhi al-Salam*, who has said the following:

"Allah is compassionate and He loves kindheartedness. Of the examples of His compassion is His reducing and easing off of your feeling of grudge and hatred that confronts your wish and your heart. When He decides to change a worshipper's habits He issues a command and then changes it with an abrogating command so that the truth does not fall very heavy on him."

H 1850, Ch. 54, h 15

Ali ibn Ibrahim has narrated from his father from al-Nawfali from al-Sakuni from abu 'Abd Allah, *'Alayhi al-Salam*, who has said the following:

"The Messenger of Allah has said, 'Whenever two things accompany each other the recipient of greater reward and the most beloved of the two before Allah, the Most Majestic, the Most Holy, is the kindhearted one to its companion.'"

H 1851, Ch. 54, h 16

Abu Ali al-Ash'ari has narrated from Muhammad ibn Hassan from al-Hassan ibn al-Husayn from Fudayl ibn 'Uthman who has said the following:

"I heard abu 'Abd Allah, *'Alayhi al-Salam*, say, 'Whoever is friendly in his affairs achieves what he wants from people.'"

Chapter 55 - Humbleness

H 1852, Ch. 55, h 1

Ali ibn Ibrahim has narrated from his father from Harun ibn Muslim from Mas'adah ibn Sadaqa from abu 'Abd Allah, *'Alayhi al-Salam*, who has said the following:

"Abu 'Abd Allah, *'Alayhi al-Salam*, has said, 'Once al-Najashi (a king of Abyssinia) called to his presence Ja'far ibn abu Talib and his companions. When they came in, they found the king sitting on the ground wearing two old pieces of cloth.' The Imam said that Ja'far has said, 'We felt compassion for him in our hearts when we saw him in that condition. When he noticed our feelings from our faces he said, "All praise is due to Allah for his giving victory to Muhammad and delight to his heart. Should I give you good news?" I said, "Yes, O King." He then said, "This hour my informant people have come from your land and have informed me that Allah, the Most Majestic, the Most Holy, has granted victory to His prophet, Muhammad, *'Alayhi al-Salam*, and has destroyed his enemies. So and so are taken captive when they met each other in a land called Badr, which has a great many bushes of Arak as if I can see it, because I was a shepherd grazing the herd for my master who was from the tribe of Damrah." Ja'far then said to him, "O king, why do you sit on the ground wearing two pieces of old cloth?" He then said, "O Ja'far, we find in what Allah had revealed to Jesus that of the rights of Allah on his servants is to show humbleness when He does a favor for them. Since Allah, the Most Majestic, the Most Holy, has done a favor for me by means of granting victory to Muhammad, *'Alayhi al-Salam*, I show humility."' When this was mentioned to the Holy Prophet he said to his companions, 'Charity increases the wealth of the donor, therefore, give charity. Humbleness elevates the position of a person, therefore, be humble, Allah will raise your degree in meritorious status. Forgiveness increases the respect of a person, therefore, forgive, Allah will grant you respect.'"

H 1853, Ch. 55, h 2

Ali ibn Ibrahim has narrated from his father from ibn abu 'Umayr from Mu'awiyah ibn 'Ammar from abu 'Abd Allah, *'Alayhi al-Salam*, who has said the following:

"I heard the Imam saying, 'In heaven there are two angels who guard the servants (of Allah). Whoever is humble before Allah, they raise him up, and whoever is arrogant, they bring him low.'"

H 1854, Ch. 55, h 3

Ibn abu 'Umayr has narrated from 'Abd al-Rahman ibn al-Hajjaj from abu 'Abd Allah, *'Alayhi al-Salam*, who has said the following:

"In a Thursday evening the Messenger of Allah had completed his day's fasting and dinner was served in the Mosque of Quba. He asked, 'Is there any drink?' Aws ibn Khuli brought him a bowl of milk mixed with honey. When he touched it with his lips he moved it away saying, 'There are two drinks each of which is enough drink. I will not drink it and I am not making unlawful to drink it, but I want to be humble before Allah. Whoever is humble before Allah, He raises him up, and whoever is arrogant, Allah brings him low. Whoever economizes in his living Allah grants him sustenance. Whoever is a spendthrift, Allah deprives him. Whoever speaks of death very often, Allah loves him.'"

H 1855, Ch. 55, h 4

Al-Husayn ibn Muhammad has narrated from Mu'alla ibn Muhammad from al-Hassan ibn Ali al-Washsha' from Dawud al-Hammar from abu 'Abd Allah, *'Alayhi al-Salam*, a similar Hadith in which he has said the following:

"Whoever speaks of Allah very often, Allah will provide him shadow in His paradise."

H 1856, Ch. 55, h 5

A number of our people have narrated from Ahmad ibn Muhammad ibn Khalid from ibn Faddal from al-'Ala' ibn Razin from Muhammad ibn Muslim who has said the following:

"I heard abu Ja'far, *'Alayhi al-Salam*, saying, 'Once an angel came to the Messenger of Allah and said, "Allah, the Most Majestic, the Most Holy, gives you the choice to be a servant and a humble messenger, or to be an angel and a messenger." He looked to Jibril who made a gesture with his hand to be humble. He (the Messenger of Allah) said, "I want to be a humble servant and a messenger." The messenger (the angel) said, "Despite this, there is no reduction in what is with your Lord." The Imam said, "With him were the keys to the treasures of earth."'"

H 1857, Ch. 55, h 6

Ali ibn Ibrahim has narrated from his father from al-Nawfali from al-Sakuni from abu 'Abd Allah, *'Alayhi al-Salam*, who has said the following:

"It is of humbleness to be happy with one seat instead of another seat, to initiate the greeting of peace to one who meets him and to avoid extreme argumentation even though one is right, and should not love to be praised for piety."

H 1858, Ch. 55, h 7

Ali ibn Ibrahim has narrated from his father from ibn abu 'Umayr from Ali ibn Yaqtin from his narrators from abu 'Abd Allah, *'Alayhi al-Salam*, who has said the following:

"Allah, the Most Majestic, the Most Holy, sent revelation to Moses asking, 'Moses, do you know why I chose you to speak to instead of My other creatures?' He asked, 'My Lord, why did You do so?' The Imam said, 'Allah, the Most Blessed, the Most High, revealed to Moses, "Moses, I turned My creatures upside down and I did not find anyone of a more humble soul than you. O Moses, whenever you prayed you had been placing your cheek on the soil," or he said, 'On earth.'"

H 1859, Ch. 55, h 8

Ali ibn Ibrahim has narrated from his father from ibn abu 'Umayr from Hisham ibn Salim from abu 'Abd Allah, *'Alayhi al-Salam*, who has said the following:

"Once, Ali ibn al-Husayn, *'Alayhi al-Salam*, was passing by the lepers while riding his donkey. They were having their lunch so they invited him to join them for food. The Imam said, 'Had I not been fasting I would have joined you.' When he returned home he asked that good food be prepared. He then invited the lepers for food and he (Ali ibn al-Husayn), *'Alayhi al-Salam*, joined them at the table.'" (Leprosy is a contagious disease.)

H 1860, Ch. 55, h 9

A number of our people have narrated from Ahmad ibn 'Abd Allah from 'Uthman ibn 'Isa from Harun ibn Kharijah from abu 'Abd Allah, *'Alayhi al-Salam*, who has said the following:

"Abu 'Abd Allah, *'Alayhi al-Salam*, has said, 'It is of the humbleness of a man to sit below the seat that is proper for his dignity.'"

H 1861, Ch. 55, h 10

It is narrated from him (narrator of the Hadith above) from ibn Faddal and Muhsin ibn Ahmad from Yunus ibn Ya'qub who has said the following:

"Once abu 'Abd Allah, *'Alayhi al-Salam*, looked at a man of the people of Madina carrying something that he had purchased for his family. On seeing the Imam the man felt embarrassed. Abu 'Abd Allah, *'Alayhi al-Salam*, said to him, 'I can see that you carry what you have purchased for your family. I swear by Allah, had it not been because of the people of Madina I would have loved to buy things for my family and myself carry it to them.'"

H 1862, Ch. 55, h 11

It is narrated from him (narrator of the Hadith above) from his father from 'Abd Allah ibn al-Qasim from 'Amr ibn abu al-Miqdam from abu 'Abd Allah, *'Alayhi al-Salam*, who has said the following:

"Of the things that Allah, the Most Majestic, the Most Holy, revealed to David was this: 'O Dawud (David), just as the closest people to Allah are the humble people, arrogant people are the farthest from Allah.'"

H 1863, Ch. 55, h 12

It is narrated from him (narrator of the Hadith above) from his father from Ali ibn al-Hakam in a marfu' manner from abu Basir who has said the following:

"Once I went to see abu al-Hassan Musa, *'Alayhi al-Salam*, and it was in the year that abu 'Abd Allah, *'Alayhi al-Salam*, had passed away. I asked, 'May Allah keep my soul in service for your cause, how is it that you offered a sheep as sacrifice and so and so offered a camel?' The Imam said, 'O abu Muhammad, Noah was in the ark in which there were things that Allah wanted. The ark was commanded to go seven times around the house. That is Tawaf al-Nisa' (walking seven times around the House for women). Noah left the ark free. Allah, the Most Majestic, the Most Holy, inspired the mountains of His decision to allow the ark of Noah, His servant, land on one of the mountains. They all raised and stretched themselves higher. Only Mount Judi which is a mountain near you remained humble. The ark then placed itself on Mount Judi.' The Imam said, 'Noah then said, "O Mari atqan," an Assyrian expression, meaning O Lord, make things go well.' I (the narrator) then thought abu al-Hassan, *'Alayhi al-Salam*, was applying it to his own case.'"

H 1864, Ch. 55, h 13

It is narrated from him (narrator of the Hadith above) from a number of his people from Ali ibn Asbat from al-Hassan ibn al-Jahm from abu al-Hassan al-Rida, *'Alayhi al-Salam*, who has said the following:

"Humbleness is a form of behavior that one expects others to behave that way toward him."

"In another Hadith the narrator asked, 'What is the definition of humbleness for which a servant (of Allah) could be considered humble?' The Imam said, 'There are several levels of humbleness. One is to know the value of one's soul to place it at the position that it deserves with a peaceful heart and should not love to behave toward others in a way different from what he loves others to behave toward him. If he may find an evil behavior he should change it to a virtuous one. Those who suppress their anger are safe from people and Allah loves those who do good.'"

Chapter 56 - Love for the Sake of Allah and Hate for the Sake of Allah

H 1865, Ch. 56, h 1

A number of our people have narrated from Ahmad ibn Muhammad ibn 'Isa and Ahmad ibn Muhammad ibn Khalid and Ali ibn Ibrahim has narrated from his father and Sahl ibn Ziyad all from ibn Mahbub from Ali ibn Ri'ab from abu 'Ubaydah al-Hadhdha' from abu 'Abd Allah, *'Alayhi al-Salam*, who has said the following:

"Abu 'Abd Allah, *'Alayhi al-Salam*, has said, 'Whoever loves for the sake of Allah, hates for the sake of Allah and gives for the sake of Allah, he is of those whose belief is complete.'"

H 1866, Ch. 56, h 2

Ibn Mahbub has narrated from Malik ibn 'Atiyah from Sa'id al-A'raj from abu 'Abd Allah, *'Alayhi al-Salam*, who has said the following:

"The strongest ring of belief to hold onto is to love for the sake of Allah and hate for the sake of Allah, to give for the sake of Allah and deny for the sake of Allah."

H 1867, Ch. 56, h 3

Ibn Mahbub has narrated from abu Ja'far ibn Muhammad al-Nu'man al-Ahwal Sahib al-Taq from Salam ibn al-Mustanir from abu Ja'far, *'Alayhi al-Salam*, who has said the following:

"The Messenger of Allah has said, 'Love of a believer for another believer only for the sake of Allah is of the greatest branches of belief. It is certain that whoever loves for the sake of Allah, hates for the sake of Allah, gives for the sake of Allah and denies for the sake of Allah is of the chosen people of Allah.'"

H 1868, Ch. 56, h 4

Al-Husayn ibn Muhammad has narrated from Mu'alla ibn Muhammad from al-Hassan ibn Ali al-Washsha' from Ali ibn abu Hamza from abu Basir from abu 'Abd Allah, *'Alayhi al-Salam*, who has said the following:

"Abu Basir has said, 'I heard the Imam saying, "Those who love each other for the sake of Allah, on the Day of Judgment will be seen on the pulpits of light. The light of their faces, the light of their bodies and the light of their pulpits will light up all things so much so that they will become known for it, and they will be called people loving for the sake of Allah."'"

H 1869, Ch. 56, h 5

Ali ibn Ibrahim has narrated from his father from Hammad from Hariz from Fudayl ibn Yasar who has said the following:

"I asked abu 'Abd Allah, *'Alayhi al-Salam*, 'Are love and hate part of belief?' The Imam asked, 'Is belief anything but love and hate?' He then read the words of Allah, '. . . But Allah has endeared belief to you and has made it attractive to your hearts. He has made disbelief, evil deeds and disobedience hateful to you. Such people will have the right guidance.'" (49:7)

H 1870, Ch. 56, h 6

A number of our people have narrated from Ahmad ibn abu 'Abd Allah from Muhammad ibn 'Isa from abu al-Hassan Ali ibn Yahya (as far as I know) from 'Amr ibn Mudrik al-Ta'i from abu 'Abd Allah, *'Alayhi al-Salam*, who has said the following:

"The Messenger of Allah once asked his companions, 'Which ring of belief is stronger to hold on to?' They said, 'Allah and His Messenger know best.' Certain individuals among them said, 'It is prayer,' others said, 'It is al-Zakat (charity)', a few of them said, 'It is fasting', others said, 'It is Hajj and 'Umrah' and still others said, 'It is Jihad (hard work against the enemies).'

"The Messenger of Allah then said, 'For everything you said there is a merit but is not such a ring. In fact the strongest ring of belief to hold on to is love for the sake of Allah, hate for the sake of Allah, support and love those who have received authority from Allah and to disassociate from the enemies of Allah.'"

H 1871, Ch. 56, h 7

It is narrated from him (narrator of the Hadith above) from Muhammad ibn Ali from 'Umar ibn Jabalah from al-Ahmasi from abu al-Jarud from abu Ja'far, *'Alayhi al-Salam*, who has said the following:

"The Messenger of Allah has said, 'Those who love each other for the sake of Allah, on the Day of Judgment will be found on a land of green emerald in the shadow of the Throne to His right - His both hands are right - their faces intensely white and brighter than the shining sun. Every angel close to Allah and every prophet who is a messenger also will envy their position. People will ask, "Who are they?" It will be said, "They are those who loved each other for the sake of Allah."'"

H 1872, Ch. 56, h 8

It is narrated from him (narrator of the Hadith above) from his father from al-Nadr ibn Suwayd from Hisham ibn Salim from abu Hamza al-Thumali from Ali ibn al-Husayn, *'Alayhi al-Salam*, who has said the following:

"When Allah, the Majestic, the Glorious, will gather together all the people of the past and the later generations, a caller whom everyone will hear will call, 'Where are those whose love was just for the sake of Allah?' Certain necks will rise from among the people and it will be said to them, 'Go to paradise without any questions asked.' The Imam said, 'The angels will meet them asking, "Where are you going?" They will say, "We are going to paradise without any questions asked." The Imam said, "The angels will ask, 'What kind of people are you?' They will say, 'We are the people who loved just for the sake of Allah.' The Imam said, 'The angels will ask, "What were your deeds?" They will reply, "We loved for the sake of Allah and hated just for the sake of Allah." The Imam said, 'The angels will say, "How wonderful is the reward of the doers of good deeds!"'"

H 1873, Ch. 56, h 9

It is narrated from him (narrator of the Hadith above) from Ali ibn Hassan from those he has mentioned (in his book) from Dawud ibn Farqad from abu 'Abd Allah, *'Alayhi al-Salam*, who has said the following:

"Abu 'Abd Allah, *'Alayhi al-Salam*, has said, 'Three things are of the signs of a believer: His knowledge of Allah, who to love and who to hate.'"

H 1874, Ch. 56, h 10

Ali ibn Ibrahim has narrated from his father from ibn abu 'Umayr from Hisham ibn Salim and from Hafs ibn al-Bakhtari from abu 'Abd Allah, *'Alayhi al-Salam*, who has said the following:

"The man loves you (followers of Ahl al-Bayt) without knowing your belief and Allah admits him to paradise because he loves you. A man hates you without knowing what your belief is and Allah then admits him in the fire for hating you."

H 1875, Ch. 56, h 11

A number of our people have narrated from Ahmad ibn Muhammad ibn Khalid from ibn al-'Arzami from his father from Jabir al-Juhfi from abu Ja'far, *'Alayhi al-Salam*, who has said the following:

"If you like to know whether there is anything good in you, look into your heart. If it loves people who obey Allah and hates those who disobey Him, then there is good in you and Allah loves you. If it hates the people who obey Allah and loves those who disobey Allah, then there is nothing good in you and Allah hates you. A man is with what he loves."

H 1876, Ch. 56, h 12

It is narrated from him (narrator of the Hadith above) from abu Ali al-Wasiti from al-Husayn ibn Aban from those whom he has mentioned (in his book) from abu Ja'far, *'Alayhi al-Salam*, who has said the following:

"If a man loves another man just for the sake of Allah, Allah will give him good rewards for his loving him, even if that man is of the people of the fire, in the knowledge of Allah. If a man hates another man just for the sake of Allah, Allah will give him good reward for his hating him, even if that man is of the people of paradise, in the knowledge of Allah."

H 1877, Ch. 56, h 13

Muhammad ibn Yahya has narrated from Ahmad ibn Muhammad ibn 'Isa from al-Husayn ibn Sa'id from al-Nadr ibn Suwayd from Yahya al-Halabi from Bashir al-Kannasi from abu 'Abd Allah, *'Alayhi al-Salam*, who has said the following:

"Sometimes love is for the sake of Allah and the Messenger of Allah and sometimes it is for the sake of worldly matters. For love, which is for the sake of Allah and the Messenger of Allah, the reward is with Allah. For love that is for the sake of worldly matters there is nothing."

H 1878, Ch. 56, h 14

A number of our people have narrated from Ahmad ibn Muhammad ibn Khalid from 'Uthman ibn 'Isa from Sama'a ibn Mehran from abu 'Abd Allah, *'Alayhi al-Salam*, who has said the following:

"Of the two Muslims who meet each other, the more meritorious is the one who loves his companion more intensely."

H 1879, Ch. 56, h 15

It is narrated from him (narrator of the Hadith above) from Ahmad ibn abu Nasr and ibn Faddal from Safwan al-Jammal from abu 'Abd Allah, *'Alayhi al-Salam*, who has said the following:

"Of the two believers who meet each other, the more meritorious one is the one who loves his brethren more intensely."

H 1880, Ch. 56, h 16

Al-Husayn ibn Muhammad has narrated from Muhammad ibn 'Imran al-Subay'i from 'Abd Allah ibn Jabalah from Ishaq ibn 'Ammar from abu 'Abd Allah, *'Alayhi al-Salam*, who has said the following:

"Whoever does not love because of religion and does not hate because of religion has no religion."

Chapter 57 - Condemnation of Worldly Matters and Abstaining Thereby

H 1881, Ch. 57, h 1

Muhammad ibn Yahya has narrated from Ahmad ibn Muhammad ibn 'Isa from al-Hassan ibn Mahbub from al-Hatham ibn Waqid al-Hariri from abu 'Abd Allah, *'Alayhi al-Salam*, who has said the following:

"One who abstains from worldly matters Allah establishes wisdom in his heart, makes his tongue speak it, and opens his eyes to see the defects of the world, its sicknesses and the cures for them. He takes him out of the world safely to the house of peace."

H 1882, Ch. 57, h 2

Ali ibn Ibrahim has narrated from his father and Ali ibn Muhammad al-Qasani all from al-Qasim ibn Muhammad from Sulayman ibn Dawud al-Minqari from Hafs ibn Ghiyath from abu 'Abd Allah, *'Alayhi al-Salam*, who has said the following:

"I heard abu 'Abd Allah, *'Alayhi al-Salam*, say, 'All the good is placed in a house and the key to that house is abstinence from worldly matters.' The Imam then said, 'The Messenger of Allah has said, "A man will not sense the sweetness of belief in his heart until he is free of all concerns about worldly matters."' The Imam then said, 'Before abstaining from the worldly things, to sense the sweetness of belief in you is like a prohibited thing.'"

H 1883, Ch. 57, h 3

Ali ibn Ibrahim has narrated from Muhammad ibn 'Isa from Yunus from abu Ayyub al-Khazzaz from abu Hamza from abu Ja'far, *'Alayhi al-Salam*, who has said the following:

"Amir al-Mu'minin (Ali ibn abu Talib), *'Alayhi al-Salam*, has said, 'The most supportive, of religious moral behavior, is abstinence from worldly matters.'"

H 1884, Ch. 57, h 4

Ali ibn Ibrahim has narrated from his father and Ali ibn Muhammad from al-Qasim ibn Muhammad from Sulayman ibn Dawud al-Minqari from Ali ibn Hashim ibn al-Burayd from his father has said the following:

"A man asked Ali ibn al-Husayn, *'Alayhi al-Salam*, about renunciation of worldly matters. The Imam said, 'It consists of ten issues. The highest degree of renunciation of worldly matters is the lowest stage of abstinence in worldly matters (sins). The highest stage of abstinence in worldly matters is the lowest degree of certainty. The highest stage of certainty is the lowest stage of consent. It is renunciation of worldly matters that is mentioned in the words of Allah, the Most Majestic, the Most Holy, '. . . so that you would neither grieve over what you have lost nor become much happy about what Allah has granted to you. . . .'" (57:23)

H 1885, Ch. 57, h 5

It is reported through the same chain of narrators he has narrated from al-Minqari from Sufyan ibn 'Uyayna who has said the following:

"I heard abu 'Abd Allah, *'Alayhi al-Salam*, say, 'Any heart in which there is doubt or that considers anything as a partner of Allah, such heart is a failure. The only purpose for their (servants of Allah's) renunciation of worldly things is to evacuate them from their heart for the matters of next life.'"

H 1886, Ch. 57, h 6
Ali has narrated from his father from ibn Mahbub from al-'Ala' ibn Razin from Muhammad ibn Muslim from abu 'Abd Allah, *'Alayhi al-Salam*, who has said the following:

"Amir al-Mu'minin (Ali ibn abu Talib), *'Alayhi al-Salam*, has said, 'Of the signs of one's interest in the rewards of the next life is his renunciation of immediate attraction of worldly matters. Renunciation of worldly matters does not reduce one's share of what Allah, the Most Majestic, the Most Holy, has assigned for him despite his renunciation of worldly matters. One's greed in immediate attraction of worldly matters does not increase anything for him even if he exercises greed. The real loser is one who is deprived from his share of the next life."

H 1887, Ch. 57, h 7
Muhammad ibn Yahya has narrated from Ahmad ibn Muhammad from Muhammad ibn Yahya al-Khath'ami from Talha ibn Zayd from abu 'Abd Allah, *'Alayhi al-Salam*, who has said the following:

"Abu 'Abd Allah, *'Alayhi al-Salam*, has said, 'Every one of things the Messenger of Allah liked from this world was associated with suffering, hunger or fear.'"

H 1888, Ch. 57, h 8
A number of our people have narrated from Ahmad ibn Muhammad ibn Khalid from al-Qasim ibn Yahya from his grandfather al-Hassan ibn Rashid from 'Abd Allah ibn Sinan from abu 'Abd Allah, *'Alayhi al-Salam*, who has said the following:

"Once, the Holy Prophet came out very depressed. An angel came to him with the key to the treasures of the earth and said, 'O Muhammad, these are the keys to the treasures of the earth and your Lord says, "Open these treasures and take whatever you want. It will not cause any reduction in your reward with Me." The Messenger of Allah then said, 'This world is home for the homeless. Only those who have no power of reason accumulate for this world.' The angel then said, 'I swear by the One Who has sent you with truth as a prophet that I heard what you just said from an angel saying it in the fourth heaven at the time these keys were given to me.'"

H 1889, Ch. 57, h 9
Ali ibn Ibrahim has narrated from his father from ibn abu 'Umayr from Jumayl ibn Darraj from abu 'Abd Allah, *'Alayhi al-Salam*, who has said the following:

"The Messenger of Allah, *'Alayhi al-Salam*, once passed by a kid of a goat that was dead, with ears cut and was thrown on the trash collection site of a people. He asked those people how much it was worth. They replied, 'Even when alive it was worth less than a dirham.' The Holy Prophet then said, 'I swear by the One in whose hand is my soul that this world in the sight of Allah is worth less than this (dead) goat is in the eyes of the people who own it.'"

H 1890, Ch. 57, h 10
Ali ibn Ibrahim has narrated from his father from Muhammad ibn Ali al-Qasani from those he has mentioned (in his book) from 'Abd Allah ibn al-Qasim from abu 'Abd Allah, *'Alayhi al-Salam*, who has said the following:

"Abu 'Abd Allah, *'Alayhi al-Salam*, has said, 'When Allah wants good for a servant (of Allah) He makes him reduce his interest in worldly matters, grants him good understanding in religion, and shows him his shortcomings. Whoever receives these things receives the good of both this and the next life.' The Imam then said, 'For the seekers of truth no other door is better than abstinence from worldly matters and this is exactly opposite to what the enemies of the truth search for.' I (the narrator) then asked, 'May Allah keep my soul in service for your cause, abstinence in what?' The Imam said, 'It is abstinence in desire for worldly matters, except one who exercises graceful patience. It (the worldly life) is only few days. It is unlawful for you to sense the test of belief without reducing your interest in worldly things.' I (the narrator) heard abu 'Abd Allah, *'Alayhi al-Salam*, saying, 'When the believer evacuates worldly matters from his self he gains new heights. He then senses the sweetness of the love for Allah and to the people of the world he looks like those whose power of reason is mixed and confused. In fact, they have become mixed with the love of Allah and have cut off all business with the others.' I (the narrator) heard the Imam saying, 'When a heart is cleared, the earth will look small for him until he gains real height.'"

H 1891, Ch. 57, h 11

Ali has narrated (from his father) from Ali ibn Muhammad al-Qasani from al-Qasim ibn Muhammad from Sulayman ibn Dawud al-Minqari from 'Abd al-Razzaq ibn Hammam from Mu'ammar ibn Rashid from al-Zuhri Muhammad ibn Muslim ibn Shihab who has said the following:

"Ali ibn al-Husayn, *'Alayhi al-Salam*, was asked, 'Which deed is more meritorious in the sight of Allah, the Most Majestic, the Most Holy?' The Imam said, 'No deed, after knowing Allah, the Most Majestic, the Most Holy, and the Messenger of Allah is more meritorious than to dislike (and hate) the world. It has many branches. Sins have many branches. The first disobedience to Allah was because of arrogance that Satan committed when he refused boastfully and became of those who reject (the command of Allah). Greed was the sin of Adam and Eve. Allah, the Most Majestic, the Most Holy, has said, 'We told Adam to stay with his spouse (Eve) in the garden and enjoy the foods therein. We (also) told them to stay away from going near a certain tree lest they might become one of the transgressors.' (2:35) They took what they did not need and this remains in their descendents to the Day of Judgment. For this reason most of the things that the children of Adam want they do not need. Then it is jealousy because of which the son of Adam committed disobedience and murdered his brother out of jealousy. From this branch comes love for women, love for the world, love for leadership, love for comfort, love to speak, love for higher position and wealth. They are seven characteristics and all of them are gathered together in the love for the world. The prophets and scholars after knowing this have said: 'Love for the world is the head of all sins.' There are two worlds: the world of bare necessities and the condemned world.'"

H 1892, Ch. 57, h 12

Ali ibn Ibrahim has narrated from his father from ibn abu 'Umayr from ibn Bukayr from abu 'Abd Allah, *'Alayhi al-Salam*, who has said the following:

"The Messenger of Allah has said, 'Seeking worldly benefits amounts to one's disadvantages of the next world and seeking the advantages of the next world may become losses in the benefits of this world. You must then cause losses to worldly benefits; it is better to suffer worldly losses (than to suffer losses in the next life).'"

H 1893, Ch. 57, h 13

Muhammad ibn Yahya has narrated from Ahmad ibn Muhammad ibn 'Isa from Ali ibn al-Hakam from abu Ayyub al-Khazzaz from abu 'Ubaydah al-Hadhdha' who has said the following:

"I asked abu Ja'far, *'Alayhi al-Salam*, '(I request you to) teach me a Hadith that can benefit me.' The Imam said, 'O abu 'Ubaydah, speak of death very often. No one speaks of death very often but that it reduces his interest in worldly matters.'"

H 1894, Ch. 57, h 14

It is narrated from him (narrator of the Hadith above) from Ali ibn al-Hakam from al-Hakam ibn Ayman from Dawud al-Abzari who has said the following:

"Abu Ja'far, *'Alayhi al-Salam*, has said, 'There is an angel that announces every day, "O sons of Adam, reproduce for death, accumulate for annihilation and build for destruction."'"

H 1895, Ch. 57, h 15

It is narrated from him (narrator of the Hadith above) from Ali ibn al-Hakam from 'Amr ibn Aban from abu Hamza from abu Ja'far, *'Alayhi al-Salam*, who has said the following:

"Ali ibn al-Husayn, *'Alayhi al-Salam*, has said, 'The world has begun to move backwards and the next world is moving forward. Each world has its sons. Therefore, you must be of the sons of the next world and not the sons of this world. You must be of those who have reduced their interest in worldly matters and of those seriously interested in the next life. You must know that those with reduced interest in worldly matters have taken the earth as their habitat, the soil as their bedding, water as their perfume and have cut themselves off this world in all seriousness.'

"Note that those who are interested in paradise have harnessed their worldly desires and those who are afraid of the fire have turned away from prohibited matters. Whoever reduces his interests in worldly matters, hardships become easy for him.

"Note that there are the servants of Allah who are as if they, actually, see the people of paradise in paradise live forever and the people of fire in the fire in huge suffering. Instead of evil coming from them it is absolute peace, the hearts of these servants of Allah are sad, their soul chaste, and their needs are very light. They exercise patience for a few short days followed by a very long lasting comfort. At night they stand up straight with their feet side by side and tears come down their cheeks. They plead before their Lord and struggle to set their neck free (of sins). In the day they are forbearing scholars, very virtuous and pious. They are slim like an arrow without fins; it is caused by their fear (for possible suffering in the next life) during their worship. On looking to them one may think they suffer from illness. They, in fact, have no illness, or any confusion in their reasoning power, but they have plunged into a tremendously great issue; it is the issue of the fire and all that it involves."

H 1896, Ch. 57, h 16

It is narrated from him (narrator of the Hadith above) from Ali ibn al-Hakam from abu 'Abd Allah al-Mu'min from Jabir who has said the following:

"Once I went to visit abu Ja'far, *'Alayhi al-Salam*, and he said, 'O Jabir, I swear by Allah, I am very sad and my heart is pre-occupied.' I then asked, 'May Allah keep my soul in service for your cause, what has pre-occupied your heart and what is the reason for your sadness?' The Imam said, 'O Jabir, if the religion of Allah in its pure form may enter one's heart it preoccupies the heart above everything else. O Jabir, what is the world and what can one think it can be? Is it more than food to eat, clothes to wear and a woman whom you may find?'

"O Jabir, the believers are not satisfied with remaining in it (world) and they do not feel safe from the coming of the next life. O Jabir, the next life is the permanent house and this world is finishing and passing but the people of this world are neglectful. The believers are of deep understanding, people of thinking, of learning lessons and their speaking of Allah, Most Glorious is Whose name, is not silenced by means of what their ears hear. Their eyes are not blinded in speaking of Allah due to what they see of the worldly attractions (around). They have suceeded in gaining the rewards of the next life just as they have succeeded in gaining that knowledge.

"O Jabir, you must know that people of piety are of smallest expenses and the most helpful to others. If you speak of them they will assist you and if you forget them they will speak of you. They are the most outspoken for the commands of Allah and steadfast in obeying the orders of Allah. They have discontinued their love (for others) with love for their Lord and they have cut themselves off from the world to obey their owner and king. They look to Allah, the Most Majestic, the Most Holy, and to His love with their hearts, and have learned that this is what they must look at due to its great position. Thus they have considered the world a temporary place to stay and then leave forever, or like a property that one finds in his dream and upon waking finds no trace of it. I give you this example because to people of reason and knowledge of Allah it is like fast-passing shadow. O Jabir, protect what Allah, the Most Majestic, the Most Holy, expects you to protect of His religion and wisdom. Never ask of things that are for you with Him but ask of His things that are with your soul. If the world is other than what I described for you, then consider it a house (a correctional facility) where you can seek to reform yourself. I swear by my life that many are those who are greedy for a certain matter but it makes them miserable when they achieve it and many are those who dislike a certain matter but it makes them fortunate when they find it. This is mentioned in the words of Allah, the Most Majestic, the Most Holy, 'So that Allah would test the faith of the believers, and deprive the unbelievers of (His) blessings.'" (3:141)

Note: "House (correctional facility) and reform" is a reference to verse, 24, 84, 57, 35 and 24 of Chapters, 41, 16, 30, 45 and 41, respectively.

H 1897, Ch. 57, h 17

It is narrated from him (narrator of the Hadith above) from Ali ibn al-Hakam from Musa ibn Bakr from abu Ibrahim, *'Alayhi al-Salam*, who has said the following:

"Abu Dhar, may Allah grant him favors, has said, 'May Allah renounce the world, on my behalf, except for two loaves of barley bread daily, one for my lunch and the other for my dinner and two woolen pieces of cloth which I use one as a shirt and the other as trousers.'"

H 1898, Ch. 57, h 18

It is narrated from him (narrator of the Hadith above) from Ali ibn al-Hakam from al-Muthanna from abu Basir from abu 'Abd Allah, *'Alayhi al-Salam*, who has said the following:

"Abu Dhar, may Allah grant him favors, has said in his sermons, 'O you who are found of knowledge, consider worldly things as nothing except what is beneficial in it, and its evil is harmful to people except those to whom Allah has done favors. O you who are found of knowledge do not allow your family and property to preoccupy you so you forget all about your soul. One day you will leave them like a mere guest among them does. You then will depart to be with others. This world and the next world are like two places to move from one to the other. Between death and resurrection, it is like a short nap after which you wake up. O you, who are found of knowledge, send forward supplies for yourself before Allah, the Most Majestic, the Most Holy; you will be rewarded for your knowledge. You shall reap as you sow, O you who are found of knowledge.'"

H 1899, Ch. 57, h 19

A number of our people have narrated from Ahmad ibn Muhammad ibn Khalid from al-Qasim ibn Yahya from his grand father al-Hassan ibn Rashid from abu 'Abd Allah, *'Alayhi al-Salam*, who has said the following:

"The Messenger of Allah has said, 'What do I have to do with the world. My case with the world is like a traveler who finds a tree in his day of journey and uses its shadow for a short rest and then continues for the rest of his journey, leaving the tree behind.'"

H 1900, Ch. 57, h 20

Ali ibn Ibrahim has narrated from Muhammad ibn 'Isa from Yahya ibn 'Aqaba al-Azdi from abu 'Abd Allah, *'Alayhi al-Salam*, who has said the following:

"Abu Ja'far, *'Alayhi al-Salam*, has said, 'The case of a person who is greedy in worldly matters is like the case of a silkworm. The more it wraps silk around itself the more difficult it becomes for it to get out until at last it dies therein in sorrow.' The narrator has said that abu 'Abd Allah, *'Alayhi al-Salam*, then said, 'Of the advice of Luqman to his son was this: 'My son, people before you collected for their children but their collection never remained in place, nor were those for whom the collection was made. You are only a servant for hire. You are ordered to perform a deed and receive payment for it. Do your deed and receive payment. Do not be like the sheep who, finds a green farm and keeps eating until fatness kills it. Take the world as a bridge to cross a river and leave it when you are on the other side. Never return to it until the end of time. Destroy it and never repair it; you are not ordered to build it.

"Bear in mind that tomorrow you will be questioned before Allah, the Most Majestic, the Most Holy, of four things. You will be asked about your youth, how you made it old, about your life span, how you finished it, and about your

124

properties, how you earned them and how you spent them. Wake up for these questions and prepare the answers. Do not regret for what you have missed of worldly things. The little worldly things do not last very long and more of the worldly things are not without misfortune. Be cautious, work hard in your affairs, remove the curtain before you. Get involved in the lawful matters of your Lord, renew repentance in your heart, work hard when you are free and before you are targeted (by the angel of death) for dying and judgment is issued that separates you from your goal.'"

H 1901, Ch. 57, h 21

Ali ibn Ibrahim has narrated from his father from ibn Mahbub from certain individuals of his people from ibn abu Ya'fur who has said the following:

"I heard abu 'Abd Allah, *'Alayhi al-Salam*, saying, 'Of the things that Allah, the Most Majestic, the Most Holy, spoke to Moses was this: "O Moses, do not rely upon the world like the unjust ones or like those who take it as their parents. O Moses, were I to leave you in the care of your own soul, lover of worldly things and its attraction would overcome you. O Moses, race in good, the people of goodness and compete with them in goodness; goodness is like its name. Leave alone of worldly matters what is beyond the bare necessities. Do not allow your eyes to look to every attractive matter that is left to its own self (considered as worthless). Note that every misfortune emerges from the love for the world. No one of you should feel excited for great wealth; with bigger wealth sins in the obligatory rights may increase. No one must feel happy because of people's happiness with him until he learns whether Allah is also happy with him or not. No creature must be excited about people obeying him; people's obeying him and following him on something other than the right thing is destruction for him as well as his followers.'"

H 1902, Ch. 57, h 22

Ali ibn Ibrahim has narrated from his father from 'Abd Allah ibn al-Mughirah from Ghiyath ibn Ibrahim from abu 'Abd Allah, *'Alayhi al-Salam*, who has said the following:

"It is in the book of Ali, *'Alayhi al-Salam*, 'The example of the world is like a snake which is of soft touch and has deadly poison inside. People of reason stay away from it and ignorant children wish to feel it.'"

H 1903, Ch. 57, h 23

Ali ibn Ibrahim has narrated from Muhammad ibn 'Isa from Yunus from abu Jamilah who has said the following:

"Abu 'Abd Allah, *'Alayhi al-Salam*, has said, 'Amir al-Mu'minin (Ali ibn abu Talib), *'Alayhi al-Salam*, wrote to one of his companions to advise him. "I recommend that you and I be pious before the One whose disobedience is not lawful. Besides Him, in no one else is placing any hope worthwhile. Sufficiency is not achieveable without Him. Whoever is pious before Allah, the Most Majestic, the Most Holy, is strong and satisfied with food and drink, his reason soars above the people of the world. His body is with the people of the world, but his heart and power of reason examine the next life. The light of his heart extinguishes what his eyes see of the love of the world. He considers unlawful things in it filthy and stays away from its doubtful things. He, I swear by Allah, suffers losses in even clean lawful matters except small pieces for the bare necessities that keep him standing to survive and clothes, to cover his privacy, of the roughest and thickest quality that he can find. He did not find anything in which to place his trust and hope in the needed circumstances, so he placed his trust and hope in the Creator of all things. He worked hard and struggled intensely, and suffered fatigue until his ribs appeared and his eyes sunk. Allah, then, in exchange for this, strengthened his body and intensified his power of reason. What He has stored for him in the next life is much greater. Reject the world. Love of the world makes one blind, deaf and dumb and it bends the necks in humiliation. Compensate for what is left of your life and do not leave your task for tomorrow or after tomorrow. Those who were before were destroyed because of their dependence on false hope and temptation, until the command of Allah came suddenly when they were neglectful. They were transferred on (pieces of) wood to their dark and narrow graves. Their children and family abandoned them there. He was then left to Allah with a submissive heart. Those who reject the world with firmness will face no defeat or betrayal. May Allah help us and you in obeying Him, and may Allah give us and you the opportunity to do what He likes.'"

H 1904, Ch. 57, h 24

Ali ibn Ibrahim has narrated from his father from 'Abd Allah ibn Mughirah and others from Talha ibn Zayd from abu 'Abd Allah, *'Alayhi al-Salam,* who has said the following:

"The case of the world is like the water of the ocean. The more a thirsty person drinks from it, the thirstier he becomes, consequently, it kills him."

H 1905, Ch. 57, h 25

Al-Husayn ibn Muhammad has narrated from Mu'alla ibn Muhammad from al-Washsha' who has said the following:

"I heard al-Rida, *'Alayhi al-Salam,* say, 'Jesus son of Mary (peace be upon him) said to his disciples, "O Israelites, do not regret for what you may miss of the world, just as the people of the world (who have no religion) do not regret for what they miss of religion when they find their worldly materials."'"

Chapter 58 - Additional Ahadith on the Above Subject

H 1906, Ch. 58, h 1

Al-Husayn ibn Muhammad al-Ash'ari has narrated from Mu'alla ibn Muhammad from al-Hassan ibn Ali al-Washsha' from 'Asim ibn Humayd from abu 'Ubaydah from abu Ja'far, *'Alayhi al-Salam,* who has said the following:

"Allah, the Most Majestic, the Most Holy, says, 'I swear by My Majesty, Glory, Greatness, Height and the height of My position, if anyone of My servant acts as I wish instead of acting according to his own wish, I will protect his lost and straying property and guarantee to provide him sustenance from the heavens and earth, and I will be for him (his supporter) in his business with every merchant.'"

H 1907, Ch. 58, h 2

Muhammad ibn Yahya has narrated from Ahmad ibn Muhammad from ibn Mahbub from al-'Ala' ibn Razin from ibn Sinan from abu Hamza from abu Ja'far, *'Alayhi al-Salam,* who has said the following:

"Allah, the Most Majestic, the Most Holy, has said, 'I Swear by My Majesty, My Glory, My Greatness, Beauty and Height of My Highness, if anyone of My servant acts as I wish instead of his own wish in anything of worldly matters I will make him feel rich in his soul and concentrate on his affairs of the next life. I guarantee to provide his sustenance from the heavens and earth, and I will be for him (to support) in all of his dealings with each and every merchant.'"

Chapter 59 - Contentment

H 1908, Ch. 59, h 1

Muhammad ibn Yahya has narrated from Ahmad ibn Muhammad ibn 'Isa from Muhammad ibn Sinan from 'Ammar ibn Marwan from Zayd al-Shahham from 'Amr ibn Hilal who has said the following:

"I heard abu Ja'far, *'Alayhi al-Salam*, saying, 'You must never allow your eyes aim for one who is above you (in worldly matters that may tempt you wish for his opportunity). The words of Allah, the Most Majestic, the Most Holy, to His Messenger are enough evidence to support it. "Let not their property and children tempt you. . . ." (9:55) 'Do not yearn for other people's property and wives and do not grieve. . . .' (15:88) If you sense such a feeling then consider the life of the Messenger of Allah. He lived on barley loaves and sweetness from dates. For fuel he would use palm tree twigs if he could find them.'"

H 1909, Ch. 59, h 2

Al-Husayn ibn Muhammad ibn 'Amir has narrated from Mu'alla ibn Muhammad from Salih ibn abu Hammad all from al-Washsha' from Ahmad ibn 'A'id from abu Khadijah Salim ibn Mukram from abu 'Abd Allah, *'Alayhi al-Salam*, who has said the following:

"The Messenger of Allah has said, 'Whoever asks us for help, we help, and whoever shows himself as rich, even though not so in reality, Allah will make him rich.'"

H 1910, Ch. 59, h 3

Muhammad ibn Yahya has narrated from Ahmad ibn Muhammad ibn 'Isa from al-Hassan ibn Mahbub from al- Haytham ibn Waqid from abu 'Abd Allah, *'Alayhi al-Salam*, who has said the following:

"Whoever is happy with the little sustenance (that Allah has given him), Allah becomes happy with his little good deeds."

H 1911, Ch. 59, h 4

A number of our people have narrated from Ahmad ibn abu 'Abd Allah from his father from 'Abd Allah ibn al-Qasim from 'Amr ibn abu al-Miqdam from abu 'Abd Allah, *'Alayhi al-Salam*, who has said the following:

"It is written in the Torah: 'O sons of Adam, be as you like to be. You shall reap as you sow. Whoever becomes happy with Allah for a little amount of sustenance, Allah will accept his little good deeds. Whoever becomes happy with the little but lawful, his expenses become light, his earnings pure and he will be out of the limits (environments) of sins.'"

H 1912, Ch. 59, h 5

Ali ibn Ibrahim has narrated from Muhammad 'Isa from Muhammad ibn 'Arafah from abu al-Hassan al-Rida, *'Alayhi al-Salam*, who has said the following:

"Whoever is not satisfied with anything but a large quantity of sustenance, his deeds will not be enough unless they are a great deal. Whoever is comfortable with little amount of sustenance, even little good deeds will be sufficient for him."

H 1913, Ch. 59, h 6

Ali ibn Ibrahim has narrated from his father from ibn abu 'Umayr from Hisham ibn Salim from abu 'Abd Allah, *'Alayhi al-Salam*, who has said the following:

"Amir al-Mu'minin (Ali ibn abu Talib), *'Alayhi al-Salam*, would say, 'O sons of Adam, if you want from the world that much that is sufficient for you, the little that is there will suffice you. However, if you are not satisfied with basic necessities but want more than the basic needs, then the whole thing that is there will not be sufficient for you.'"

H 1914, Ch. 59, h 7

Muhammad ibn Yahya has narrated from Muhammad ibn al-Husayn from 'Abd al-Rahman ibn Muhammad al-Asadi from Salim ibn Mukram from abu 'Abd Allah, *'Alayhi al-Salam*, who has said the following:

"At one time, among the companions of the Messenger of Allah, the financial conditions of one man became very difficult and his wife suggested that he see the Messenger of Allah about it. He went to the Holy Prophet and, when the Holy Prophet saw him, he said, 'Whoever asks us for help, we help, but whoever appears to be rich when, in fact, he is not so, Allah will make him rich.' The man thought the Holy Prophet had addressed him only. He returned to his wife and told her the story. She said, 'The Messenger of Allah is only a man. Let him know what you need.' He went back and, when the Messenger of Allah saw him, he said, 'Whoever asks us for help we help but whoever appears to be rich when, in fact, he is not so, Allah will make him rich.' This was repeated with that man three times. Thereafter, he borrowed a pick and went to the mountains, climbed it and cut down a certain amount of firewood. He climbed down and sold the firewood for half a mud (a certain measure) of flour, came home and used it for food. The next day he did the same thing and saved a little on the side until he was able to buy a pick of his own and sometime later he bought two young camels and a slave and then he became rich until he became very affluent. One day he went to see the Holy Prophet. He informed him of his whole story. The Holy Prophet said, 'I told you, whoever asks us for help we help, but whoever appears to be rich when, in fact, he is not so, Allah will make him rich.'"

H 1915, Ch. 59, h 8

A number of our people have narrated from Ahmad ibn Muhammad ibn Khalid from Ali ibn al-Hakam from al-Husayn ibn al-Farat from 'Amr ibn Shamir from Jabir from abu Ja'far, *'Alayhi al-Salam*, who has said the following:

"The Messenger of Allah has said, 'Whoever wants to be the richest among the people, what is with Allah should be more reliable to him than what is in the hands of others.'"

H 1916, Ch. 59, h 9

It is narrated from him (narrator of the Hadith above) from ibn Faddal from 'Asim ibn Humayd from abu Hamza from abu Ja'far or abu 'Abd Allah, *'Alayhi al-Salam*, who has said the following:

"Whoever is content with what Allah has given him for his sustenance is the richest person of the people."

H 1917, Ch. 59, h 10

It is narrated from him (narrator of the Hadith above) from ibn Faddal from ibn Bukayr from Hamza ibn Humran who has said the following:

"A man complained before abu 'Abd Allah, *'Alayhi al-Salam*, that he works and earns but is not content and his soul's desires compel him to find more. The man asked the Imam to teach him something to benefit him. Abu 'Abd Allah, *'Alayhi al-Salam*, said, 'If it (earnings) is enough for your necessities then it should make you rich. Thus, the minimum should suffice you. If this does not suffice then all things that are there will not suffice you.'"

H 1918, Ch. 59, h 11

It is narrated from him (narrator of the Hadith above) from a number of our people have narrated from Hannan ibn Sadir in a marfu' manner from Amir al-Mu'minin (Ali ibn abu Talib), *'Alayhi al-Salam*, who has said the following:

"Whoever is content, with worldly matters, with bare necessities, the minimum suffices him. Whoever is not content, with worldly matters, with bare necessities, then nothing will be able to suffice him."

Chapter 60 - Adequacy

H 1919, Ch. 60, h 1

Ali ibn Ibrahim has narrated from his father from more than one person from 'Asim from ibn Hamid from abu 'Ubaydah al-Hadhdha' who has said the following:

"I heard abu Ja'far, *'Alayhi al-Salam*, say, 'The Messenger of Allah has said, "Allah, the Most Majestic, the Most Holy, says, 'The most envied person among My servants is a man whose needs are light, has a good share in prayer, who performs the worship of his Lord unseen, is obscure among the people, whose expenses are within the limits of bare necessities with which he exercises patience, whose death is quick (like a dead person free from worldly desires) and whose heirs and mourners are very few.'"

H 1920, Ch. 60, h 2

Ali ibn Ibrahim has narrated from his father from al-Nawfali from al-Sakuni from abu 'Abd Allah, *'Alayhi al-Salam*, who has said the following:

"Tuba (a tree in paradise) is for those who have become Muslims and whose expenses are within the limits of bare necessities."

H 1921, Ch. 60, h 3

Al-Nawfali has narrated from al-Sakuni from abu 'Abd Allah, *'Alayhi al-Salam*, who has said the following:

"The Messenger of Allah has said, 'O Allah, grant Muhammad, the family of Muhammad and those who love Muhammad and the family of Muhammad, chastity in their personality, and sustenance enough for their exact necessities. Give those who hate Muhammad and the family of Muhammad, property and children.'"

H 1922, Ch. 60, h 4

A number of our people have narrated from Ahmad ibn Muhammad ibn Khalid from Ya'qub ibn Yazid from Ibrahim ibn Muhammad al-Nawfali in a marfu' manner from Ali ibn al-Husayn, *'Alayhi al-Salam*, who has said the following:

"The Messenger of Allah once passed by a shepherd of camels and asked him for a drink and he said, 'The milk in their udder is for the morning drink of the people of the village and the milk in the containers is for their evening drink.' The Messenger of Allah then prayed, 'O Lord, give him many children and much wealth.' The Messenger of Allah then passed by a shepherd of sheep and sent his people to ask him for a drink. He milked them and poured it from his milk container altogether in the container for the Messenger of Allah. Along with all the milk he also sent a sheep for him, saying, 'This is what we have and we can bring you more if you like.' The Imam said, 'The Messenger of Allah prayed for him, "O Lord, give him sustenance adequate only for his bare necessities." A certain man of his companion then asked, 'O Messenger of Allah, how is it that you prayed for the shepherd who refused to give you any milk in such a way that we all love. However, for the one who readily provided what you asked, you prayed for him with a prayer that we all dislike?' The Messenger of Allah said, 'The little thing that is adequate is better than a great deal that diverts one's mind (from Allah). O Lord, grant to Muhammad and the family of Muhammad only that much which is adequate for them.'"

H 1923, Ch. 60, h 5

It is narrated from him (narrator of the Hadith above) from his father from abu al-Bakhtari from abu 'Abd Allah, *'Alayhi al-Salam*, who has said the following:

"Allah, the Most Majestic, the Most Holy, has said, 'I find My believing servant depressed if I provide his sustenance in stringent measures; a condition that is closer to Me but I find My believing servant happier when I provide his sustenance plentifully; however, such condition is further away from Me.'"

H 1924, Ch. 60, h 6

Al-Husayn ibn Muhammad has narrated from Ahmad ibn Ishaq from Bakr ibn Muhammad al-Azdi from abu 'Abd Allah, *'Alayhi al-Salam*, who has said the following:

"The Messenger of Allah has said that Allah, the Most Majestic, the Most Holy, has said, 'The most enviable among My friends is a believer who has his share of salvation, performs the worship of his Lord well, worships Allah privately, is obscure among people and no finger rises to point him out. His sustenance is only adequate for his basic needs and he bears it patiently. I cause him to die faster, thus his legacy is little and his mourners are very few.'"

Chapter 61 - Promptness in Good Deeds

H 1925, Ch. 61, h 1

Muhammad ibn Yahya has narrated from Ahmad ibn Muhammad ibn 'Isa from Ali ibn al-Nu'man who has that narrated to him Hamzah ibn Humran who has said the following:

"I heard abu 'Abd Allah, *'Alayhi al-Salam*, saying, 'When one of you intends to do a good deed, he should do it without delay; a servant (of Allah) perhaps performs a prayer or fasts for a day, thereupon, it is said to him, "Do whatever you like (other good deeds) after this act, Allah has already granted you forgiveness. (One may not know which of his worships has been accepted.)'"

H 1926, Ch. 61, h 2

It is narrated from him (narrator of the Hadith above) from Ali ibn al-Hakam from abu Jamilah who has said the following:

"Abu 'Abd Allah, *'Alayhi al-Salam*, has said, 'Begin your day with a good deed, dictate to your guards (angels on both shoulders) good in the beginning and in the end of the day, all that is in between is forgiven if Allah so wills.'"

H 1927, Ch. 61, h 3

It is narrated from him (narrator of the Hadith above) from ibn abu 'Umayr from Marazim ibn Hakim from abu 'Abd Allah, *'Alayhi al-Salam*, who has said the following:

"My father, *'Alayhi al-Salam*, would say, 'When you intend to perform a good deed, do not delay; you may not know what happens next.'"

H 1928, Ch. 61, h 4

Ali ibn Ibrahim has narrated from his father from ibn abu 'Umayr from ibn 'Udhayna from Zurara from abu Ja'far, *'Alayhi al-Salam*, who has said the following:

"The Messenger of Allah has said, 'Of the good deeds that Allah loves is that which is done without delays.'"

H 1929, Ch. 61, h 5

A number of our people have narrated from Ahmad ibn Muhammad ibn Khalid from Ali ibn al-Hakam from Aban ibn 'Uthman from Bashir ibn Yasar from abu 'Abd Allah, *'Alayhi al-Salam*, who has said the following:

"When you intend to perform anything good, then do not delay. A man may fast on a hot day and hope thereby to receive what is with Allah, and Allah then sets him free from fire. Do not underestimate the good deeds with which one may seek nearness to Allah, the Most Majestic, the Most Holy, even if it is a piece of a date."

H 1930, Ch. 61, h 6

It is narrated from him (narrator of the Hadith above) from ibn Faddal from ibn Bukayr from certain individuals of our people from abu 'Abd Allah, *'Alayhi al-Salam*, who has said the following:

"Whoever intends to perform a good deed should act fast and do not delay. Perhaps a servant (of Allah) performs a deed and Allah, the Most Blessed, the Most High, says, 'I have granted you forgiveness and will never write down anything against you.' Whoever intends to perform an evil deed he must not do it. Perhaps a man does an evil deed and Allah, the Most Holy, sees it and says, "I swear by My Majesty and Glory to never forgive you hereafter."'"

H 1931, Ch. 61, h 7

Ali has narrated from his father from ibn abu 'Umayr from Hisham ibn Salim from abu 'Abd Allah, *'Alayhi al-Salam*, who has said the following:

"When you intend to perform a good deed, do not delay doing it; Allah, the Most Majestic, the Most Holy, perhaps finds a servant (of Allah) during a good deed of obedience and He, the Most Majestic, the Most Holy, may say, 'I will never subject you to punishment hereafter.' If you intend to do an evil deed, you must not do it; perhaps Allah finds a servant during an act of disobedience and may say, "I swear by My Majesty and Glory to never forgive you hereafter."'

H 1932, Ch. 61, h 8

Abu Ali al-Ash'ari has narrated from Muhammad ibn 'Abd al-Jabbar from ibn Faddal from abu Jamilah from Muhammad ibn Humran from abu 'Abd Allah, *'Alayhi al-Salam*, who has said the following:

"When one of you intends to perform a good deed or establish good relations there will be two Satans, one on each side. He, thus, should perform it immediately before they prevent him from the good deed."

H 1933, Ch. 61, h 9

Muhammad ibn Yahya has narrated from Ahmad ibn Muhammad from Muhammad ibn Sinan from abu al-Jarud who has said the following:

"I heard abu Ja'far, *'Alayhi al-Salam*, say, 'Whoever intends to perform a good deed he should do it without delay; Satan keeps an eye on anything that is delayed.'"

H 1934, Ch. 61, h 10

Muhammad ibn Yahya has narrated from Muhammad ibn al-Husayn from Ali ibn Asbat from al-'Ala' from Muhammad ibn Muslim who has said the following:

"I heard abu Ja'far, *'Alayhi al-Salam*, say, 'Allah has made good deeds heavy for the people of the world like its weight in their balance on the Day of Judgment. Allah, the Most Majestic, the Most Holy, has made evil of a light weight on the people of the world just as it will be of a light weight (no value) in their balance on the Day of Judgment.'"

Chapter 62 - Fairness and Justice

H 1935, Ch. 62, h 1

Muhammad ibn Yahya has narrated from Ahmad ibn Muhammad ibn 'Isa from Ali ibn al-Hakam from al-Hassan ibn Hamza from his grand father from abu Hamza al-Thumali from Ali ibn al-Husayn, *'Alayhi al-Salam*, who has said the following:

"The Messenger of Allah at the end of his sermon would say, 'Tuba (a tree in paradise) is for those whose moral behavior is polite, whose consciences are clean, whose privacy as well as public matters are all well, who give the excess in their properties in charity, who hold back their unnecessary words and yield to justice for people against their own souls.'"

H 1936, Ch. 62, h 2

It is narrated from him (narrator of the Hadith above) from Muhammad ibn Sinan from Mu'awiyah ibn Wahab from abu 'Abd Allah, *'Alayhi al-Salam*, who has said the following:

"Whoever likes to guarantee four things for me, I guarantee four homes in paradise. (He should guarantee me) to give charity without fear from his poverty, to speak out loud the greetings of peace in the world and quit excessive argumentation even though he is on the side of right. He must yield to justice for people against his own soul."

H 1937, Ch. 62, h 3

It is narrated from him (narrator of the Hadith above) from al-Hassan ibn Ali ibn Faddal from Ali ibn 'Aqaba from Jarud from abu al-Mundhir who has said the following:

"I heard abu 'Abd Allah, *'Alayhi al-Salam*, saying, 'The masters of good deeds are three things: To yield to justice for people against one's own soul. So what you do not like to happen to you, do not agree to happen to people also, to cooperate with your fellow believer in matters of properties and to speak of Allah in all conditions: not just saying, 'Glory belongs to Allah, all praise belongs to Allah and no one deserves to be worshipped except Allah, but that if in case Allah, the Most Majestic, the Most Holy, has commanded you to do a certain thing, you must obey the command, and if it is a case you know that Allah, the Most Majestic, the Most Holy, has prohibited you to do, you must stay away form it.'"

H 1938, Ch. 62, h 4

A number of our people have narrated from Ahmad ibn Muhammad ibn Khalid from Ibrahim ibn Muhammad al-Thaqafi from Ali ibn Mu'alla from Yahya ibn Ahmad Fadl ibn Shadhan abu Muhammad al-Maythami from Rumi ibn Zurara from his father from abu Ja'far, *'Alayhi al-Salam*, who has said the following:

"Amir al-Mu'minin (Ali ibn abu Talib), *'Alayhi al-Salam*, has said in one of his speeches, 'You must note that due to a person's yielding to justice for people against his own self, Allah increases his respect and honor.'"

H 1939, Ch. 62, h 5

It is narrated from him (narrator of the Hadith above) from 'Uthman ibn 'Isa from 'Abd Allah ibn Muskan from Muhammad ibn Muslim from abu 'Abd Allah Who has said the following:

"Three people of all creatures will be the closest to Allah, the Most Majestic, the Most Holy, on the Day of Judgment until all accounting is finished: a man whose power does not lead him in anger to do injustice to his subjects, a man who mediates between two people and does not lean toward anyone of them even to the size of a grain of barley (needle's head), and a man who speaks the truth regardless, it is for or against his own self."

H 1940, Ch. 62, h 6

It is narrated from him (narrator of the Hadith above) from his father from al-Nadr ibn Suwayd from Hisham ibn Salim from Zurara from al-Hassan al-Bazzaz from abu 'Abd Allah, *'Alayhi al-Salam*, who has said the following:

"In a Hadith he has said, 'What is the most forceful obligation from Allah upon His creatures? I must ask you.' The Imam mentioned three things of which the first was yielding to justice for people against one's own soul."

H 1941, Ch. 62, h 7

Ali ibn Ibrahim has narrated from his father from al-Nawfali from al-Sakuni from abu 'Abd Allah, *'Alayhi al-Salam*, who has said the following:

"The Messenger of Allah has said, 'The masters of deeds are yielding to justice for people against your own soul, cooperation with your fellow believers for the sake of Allah and to speak of and remember Allah, the Most Majestic, the Most Holy, in all conditions.'"

H 1942, Ch. 62, h 8

Ali has narrated from his father from ibn Mahbub from Hisham ibn Salim from Zurara from al-Hassan al-Bazzaz who has said the following:

"Once abu 'Abd Allah, *'Alayhi al-Salam*, said to me, 'Should I tell you about what Allah has emphatically made obligatory on His creatures (are three things)?' I said, 'Yes, please do so.' The Imam said, 'You must yield to justice for people against your own soul, cooperate with your fellow believers, and speak of and remember Allah in all places. I, however, do not mean thereby saying, 'Glory belongs to Allah, all praise belongs to Allah, no one deserves to be worshipped except Allah, and Allah is greater than (can be described), although, it also is speaking of Allah. It is speaking of and remembering Allah, the Most Majestic, the Most Holy, in all places whenever you are faced with a deed of obedience or prohibition.'"

H 1943, Ch. 62, h 9

Ibn Mahbub has narrated from abu 'Usamah who has said the following:

"Abu 'Abd Allah, *'Alayhi al-Salam*, has said, 'The believer is not tried with anything more difficult than three depriving things.' It was asked, 'What are they?' The Imam said, 'They are to cooperate with one who has an established relation with you with whatever financial means available, to yield to justice for people against one's own soul and to speak of and remember Allah very often. I, however, do not mean thereby saying, 'All glory belongs to Allah, all praise belongs to Allah, and no one deserves to be worshipped except Allah. Speaking of Allah, and remembering Him is to do so (remember Him) when facing something that He has made lawful or that He has prohibited.'"

H 1944, Ch. 62, h 10

A number of our people have narrated from Ahmad ibn abu 'Abd Allah from Yahya ibn Ibrahim ibn abu al-Bilad from his father from his grandfather, abu al-Bilad in a marfu' manner saying:

"Once an Arab man came to the Holy Prophet when he was about to leave for an armed campaign. The Arab held on to the harness of the horse of the Holy Prophet and said, 'O Messenger of Allah, teach me a deed with which I can go to paradise.' He said, 'Do to people what you like them to do to you, and do not do anything to people that you do not like to be done to you. Now allow the horse to go.'"

H 1945, Ch. 62, h 11

Abu Ali al-Ash'ari has narrated from al-Hassan ibn Ali al-Kufi from 'Ubays ibn Hisham from 'Abd al-Karim from al-Halabi from abu 'Abd Allah, *'Alayhi al-Salam*, who has said the following:

"Justice is sweeter than water for a thirsty man. How vast is justice if exercised on an issue, even if it is a little one!"

H 1946, Ch. 62, h 12

Ali ibn Ibrahim has narrated from his father from ibn Mahbub from certain individuals of his people from abu 'Abd Allah, *'Alayhi al-Salam*, who has said the following:

"Whoever yields to justice for people against his own soul is accepted to judge others' cases."

H 1947, Ch. 62, h 13

Muhammad ibn Yahya has narrated from Ahmad ibn Muhammad ibn 'Isa from Muhammad ibn Sinan from Yusuf ibn 'Imran ibn Maytham from Ya'qub ibn Shu'ayb from abu 'Abd Allah, *'Alayhi al-Salam*, who has said the following:

"Allah, the Most Majestic, the Most Holy, sent a revelation to Adam that said, 'I will gather together all words for you in four words.' He asked, 'O Lord, what are they?' He said, 'One is for Me, one for you, one between Me and you and one between you and other people.' He then said, 'O Lord, explain them to me so I can learn.' He said, 'The one for Me is to worship Me and do not consider anything as My partner. The one for you is that I will reward you for your deed with something that you need most. The one between Me and you is that you pray and I will accept and answer your prayers. The one between you and people is that you must like for people what you like for yourself and dislike for people what you dislike to happen to you.'"

H 1948, Ch. 62, h 14

Abu Ali al-Ash'ari has narrated from Muhammad ibn 'Abd al-Jabbar from ibn Faddal from Ghalib ibn 'Uthman from Ruh ibn 'Ukht (nephew) of Mu'alla from abu 'Abd Allah, *'Alayhi al-Salam*, who has said the following:

"Be pious before Allah and practice justice; you blame other people for not doing justice to others."

H 1949, Ch. 62, h 15

It is narrated from him (narrator of the Hadith above) from ibn Mahbub from Mu'awiyah ibn Wahab from abu 'Abd Allah, *'Alayhi al-Salam*, who has said the following:

"Justice is sweeter than honey, softer than butter and smells sweeter than musk."

H 1950, Ch. 62, h 16

A number of our people have narrated from Ahmad ibn Muhammad ibn Khalid from Isma'il ibn Mehran from 'Uthman ibn Jabalah from abu Ja'far, *'Alayhi al-Salam*, who has said the following:

"The Messenger of Allah has said, 'Whoever has three things, or even one of them, will have a place under the shadow of the Throne of Allah on the Day when nothing will have any shadows (protective shelter). A man who gives to others what he asks from them, one who does not prevent another man from a forward position or move backward except after knowing that his own moving forward is what Allah wants. A Muslim does not blame his Muslim brethren for a shortcoming until he removes such shortcoming from his own self; as soon one removes one defect from his soul another shortcoming and defect emerges. To be occupied with correcting one's own self is a full time occupation (to deal with before getting involved in people).'"

H 1951, Ch. 62, h 17

It is narrated from him (narrator of the Hadith above) from 'Abd al-Rahman ibn Hammad al-Kufi from 'Abd Allah ibn Ibrahim al-Ghifari from Ja'far ibn Ibrahim al-Ja'fari from abu 'Abd Allah, *'Alayhi al-Salam*, who has said the following:

"The Messenger of Allah has said, 'Whoever comforts the poor with his property and yields to justice for people against his own soul indeed is a believer."

H 1952, Ch. 62, h 18

Muhammad ibn Yahya has narrated from Ahmad ibn Muhammad from Muhammad ibn Sinan from Khalid ibn Nafi' Bayya' al-Sabiri from Yusuf al-Bazzaz who has said the following:

"I heard abu 'Abd Allah, *'Alayhi al-Salam*, say, 'If two people disagree in something, one of them gives half as much to his companion, but if he would not accept, it will be compensated for him (recipient of more than half for his injustice).'"

H 1953, Ch. 62, h 19

Muhammad ibn Yahya has narrated from Ahmad ibn Muhammad from ibn Mahbub from abu Ayyub from Muhammad ibn Qays from abu Ja'far, *'Alayhi al-Salam*, who has said the following:

"Allah has a paradise wherein no one is admitted except three kinds of people of whom one is he who judges himself with the truth."

H 1954, Ch. 62, h 20

Ali ibn Ibrahim has narrated from his father from ibn abu 'Umayr from Hammad from al-Halabi from abu 'Abd Allah, *'Alayhi al-Salam*, who has said the following:

"Justice is sweeter than water is for a thirsty man. How vast is justice when it is practiced in an issue even though it would be very little!"

Chapter 63 - Independence from People

H 1955, Ch. 63, h 1

Muhammad ibn Yahya has narrated from Ahmad ibn Muhammad ibn 'Isa from al-Hassan ibn Mahbub from 'Abd Allah ibn Sinan from abu 'Abd Allah, *'Alayhi al-Salam*, who has said the following:

"The nobility of the believer is in his worship at night and his honor is in his independence from people."

H 1956, Ch. 63, h 2

Ali ibn Ibrahim has narrated from his father and Ali ibn Muhammad al-Qasani all from al-Qasim ibn Muhammad from Sulayman ibn Dawud al-Minqari from Hafs ibn Ghiyath who has said the following:

"Abu 'Abd Allah, *'Alayhi al-Salam*, has said, 'If any of you would like not to be rejected when asking his Lord (Allah) for something, you must abolish all of your hope in people and place your hope in no one except Allah. When Allah, the Most Majestic, the Most Holy, finds this in one's heart, He then will not reject one's prayers and grant one's wishes.'"

H 1957, Ch. 63, h 3

Through the same chain of narrators it is narrated from al-Minqari from 'Abd al-Razzaq from Mu'ammar from al-Zuhri from Ali ibn al-Husayn, *'Alayhi al-Salam*, who has said the following:

"I saw all good gathered together in cutting off of yearning for what belongs to people and in not having any hope in people in anything and in leaving his affairs in the hands of Allah, the Most Majestic, the Most Holy, in all matters. Allah, the Most Majestic, the Most Holy, will answer him in all things."

H 1958, Ch. 63, h 4

Muhammad ibn Yahya has narrated from Ahmad ibn Muhammad from Ali ibn al-Hakam from al-Husayn ibn abu al-'Ala' from 'Abd al-'Ala' ibn 'A'yun who has said the following:

"I heard abu 'Abd Allah, *'Alayhi al-Salam*, say, 'Asking people for help is seeking to abolish one's respect, as well as one's bashfulness. Placing no hope in what is in the hands of people is dignity for a believer in his religion and greed is poverty at hand.'"

H 1959, Ch. 63, h 5

A number of our people have narrated from Ahmad ibn Muhammad ibn Khalid from Ahmad ibn Muhammad ibn abu Nasr who has said the following:

"Once I said to abu al-Hassan al-Rida, *'Alayhi al-Salam,* 'May Allah keep my soul in service for your cause, please write for me to Isma'il ibn Dawud al-Katib. I hope I will receive something from him.' The Imam said, 'I resent that you ask from him or similar persons. Allow it (financial help) to be paid from my property.'"

H 1960, Ch. 63, h 6

It is narrated from him (narrator of the Hadith above) from his father from Hammad ibn 'Isa from Mu'awiyah ibn 'Ammar from Najam ibn Hatim al-Ghanawi from abu Ja'far, *'Alayhi al-Salam,* who has said the following:

"A believer's having no hope in (what is in the hands of) people, is his respect and power in his religion. Have you not heard the words of Hatim, 'When I decided not to have any hope I found it to be independence, when I made the soul to know it. Greed is poverty?'" (The quote is due to its popularity not as evidence).

H 1961, Ch. 63, h 7

Muhammad ibn Yahya has narrated from Ahmad ibn Muhammad ibn 'Isa from Muhammad ibn Sinan from 'Ammar al-Sabati from abu 'Abd Allah, *'Alayhi al-Salam,* who has said the following:

"Amir al-Mu'minin (Ali ibn abu Talib), *'Alayhi al-Salam,* would say, 'In your heart you must have both hope in people and independence from them. Your hope and need in people must be in the form of speaking to them softly and with a delightful appearance. Your independence from them must be in the form of maintaining dignity and safety of your respect.'"

Ali ibn Ibrahim has narrated from his father from Ali ibn Mu'bid who has that narrated to him Ali ibn 'Umar from Yahya ibn 'Imran from abu 'Abd Allah, *'Alayhi al-Salam,* who has said the following:

"Amir al-Mu'minin (Ali ibn abu Talib), *'Alayhi al-Salam,* would say . . ." then he mentioned a Hadith similar to the one above.'"

Chapter 64 - Good Relation with Relatives

H 1962, Ch. 64, h 1

Ali ibn Ibrahim has narrated from his father from ibn abu 'Umayr from Jamil ibn Darraj who has said the following:

"I asked abu 'Abd Allah, *'Alayhi al-Salam,* about the words of Allah, Most Glorious is Whose name, '. . . have fear of the One by whose name you swear to settle your differences and have respect for your relatives. Allah certainly keeps watch over you.' (4:1)

"The Imam said, 'It refers to the relatives of people. Allah, the Most Majestic, the Most Holy, has commanded to maintain good relations with relatives and has mentioned it with greatness. Consider that He has placed it next to His own name together with piety.'"

H 1963, Ch. 64, h 2

Muhammad ibn Yahya has narrated from Ahmad ibn Muhammad ibn 'Isa from Ali ibn al-Nu'man from Ishaq ibn 'Ammar who has said the following:

"It is narrated to me from abu 'Abd Allah, *'Alayhi al-Salam*, who has said that once a man came to the Holy Prophet and said, 'O Messenger of Allah, my family has refused to do anything for me but to cut off and abuse me, and I also want to reject them.' He (the Messenger of Allah) said, 'If you do so, Allah will reject all of you.' He then asked, 'What should I do?' He (the Messenger of Allah) said, 'Maintain good relations with whoever cuts you off, give to those who deprive you, and forgive those who do injustice to you. If you do this, you will have support for this from Allah.'"

H 1964, Ch. 64, h 3

It is narrated from him (narrator of the Hadith above) from Ahmad ibn Muhammad ibn 'Isa from Ahmad ibn Muhammad ibn abu Nasr from Muhammad ibn 'Ubayd Allah who has said the following:

"Abu al-Hassan al-Rida, *'Alayhi al-Salam*, has said, 'A man who maintains good relations with his relatives, if he may have only three years to live, Allah, because of his good relations with relatives, will prolong his life up to thirty years; Allah does whatever He wants.'"

H 1965, Ch. 64, h 4

It is narrated from him (narrator of the Hadith above) from Ali ibn al-Hakam from Khattab al-A'War from abu Hamza who has said the following:

"Abu Ja'far, *'Alayhi al-Salam*, has said, 'Having good relations with relatives cleanses ones deeds, increases ones wealth, repulses misfortunes, makes reckoning easier and delays the coming of death.'"

H 1966, Ch. 64, h 5

It is narrated from him (narrator of the Hadith above) from al-Hassan ibn Mahbub from 'Amr ibn abu al-Miqdam from Jabir from abu Ja'far, *'Alayhi al-Salam*, who has said the following:

"The Messenger of Allah has said, 'I ask my followers who are present, those who are not present, those in the back of men and in the wombs of women to the Day of Judgment to maintain good relations with their relatives even though they are far away at a distance of one year's journey; it is part of religion.'"

H 1967, Ch. 64, h 6

It is narrated from him (narrator of the Hadith above) from Ali ibn al-Hakam from Hafs from abu Hamza from abu 'Abd Allah, *'Alayhi al-Salam*, who has said the following:

"Maintaining good relations with relatives improves moral behavior, opens the ability for generosity, helps one's soul agree easily to be generous, increases one's means of sustenance and delays the coming of death."

H 1968, Ch. 64, h 7

Al-Husayn ibn Muhammad has narrated from Mu'alla ibn Muhammad from al-Hassan ibn Ali al-Washsha' from Ali ibn abu Hamza from abu Basir from abu 'Abd Allah, *'Alayhi al-Salam*, who has said the following:

"I heard abu 'Abd Allah, *'Alayhi al-Salam*, saying, 'Kindred relations hold fast to the Throne (of the Lord) and say, "Establish those who establish me and cut off those who cut me off. This is the kindred relation of the family of Muhammad, *'Alayhi al-Salam*, that is mentioned in the words of Allah, the Most Majestic, the Most Holy, '. . . who maintain all the proper relations that Allah has commanded them to maintain. . .,' (13:21) and the kindred relation of all relatives.'"

H 1969, Ch. 64, h 8
Muhammad ibn Yahya has narrated from Ahmad ibn Muhammad from ibn Mahbub from Malik ibn 'Atiyah from Yunus ibn 'Ammar who has said the following:

"Abu 'Abd Allah, *'Alayhi al-Salam*, has said, 'The first among the parts of human body that will speak on the Day of Judgment will be (that through which) kindred relation (comes into being). It will say, "O Lord, keep good relations with those who kept me properly in the worldly life, and cut off in this life Your good relations with those who cut me off in the worldly life.'"

H 1970, Ch. 64, h 9
It is narrated from him (narrator of the Hadith above) from Ahmad ibn Muhammad ibn abu Nasr from abu al-Hassan al-Rida, *'Alayhi al-Salam*, who has said the following:

"Abu 'Abd Allah, *'Alayhi al-Salam*, has said, 'Maintain your kindred relations well even if it is a help with a drink of water. The best in such relations are not to cause any suffering to relatives. Keeping good relations with relatives delays the coming of death and brings love among them."

H 1971, Ch. 64, h 10
Ali ibn Ibrahim has narrated from his father from Hammad ibn 'Isa from Hariz ibn 'Abd Allah from Fudayl ibn Yasar who has said the following:

"Abu Ja'far, *'Alayhi al-Salam*, has said, 'Kindred relation will hold to the Throne (of the Lord) on the Day of Judgment and say, "O Lord, establish good relations with those who establish me and cut off good relations with those who cut me off.'"

H 1972, Ch. 64, h 11
Muhammad ibn Yahya has narrated from Ahmad ibn Muhammad ibn 'Isa from Muhammad ibn Isma'il ibn Bazi' from Hanan ibn Sadir from his father from abu Ja'far, *'Alayhi al-Salam*, who has said the following:

"Abu Dhar (may Allah be pleased with him) has said, 'I heard the Messenger of Allah saying, "On the Day of Judgment the bridge will stand on two pillars: the kindred relations and safe keeping of trust. Those who maintain good relations with relatives and return the trust will pass the bridge safely to paradise but when the abuser of trust and neglector of good relations with relatives will try to pass the bridge no other deeds will benefit him and he will be thrown off the bridge into the fire.'"

H 1973, Ch. 64, h 12
A number of our people have narrated from Ahmad ibn Muhammad ibn Khalid from his father from ibn abu 'Umayr from Hafs ibn Qart from abu Hamza from abu Ja'far, *'Alayhi al-Salam*, who has said the following:

"Abu Ja'far, *'Alayhi al-Salam*, has said, 'Maintaining good relations with relatives improves moral behavior, strengthens the ability to be generous with the pleasure of one's soul, increases one's means of sustenance and delays the coming of death.'"

H 1974, Ch. 64, h 13

It is narrated from him (narrator of the Hadith above) from 'Uthman ibn 'Isa from Khattab al-'A'War from abu Hamza who has said the following:

"Abu Ja'far, *'Alayhi al-Salam*, has said, 'Maintaining good relations with relatives cleanses the deeds, repulses misfortunes, increases wealth, delays the coming of death, enlarges ones share of sustenance and brings love to the family. Therefore, one must be pious before Allah and maintain good relations with one's relatives.'"

H 1975, Ch. 64, h 14

Ali ibn Ibrahim has narrated from his father and Muhammad ibn Isma'il have narrated from Fadl ibn Shadhan all from ibn abu 'Umayr from Ibrahim ibn 'Abd al-Hamid from al-Hakam al-Hannat who has said the following:

"I heard abu 'Abd Allah, *'Alayhi al-Salam*, say, 'Maintaining good relations with relatives, and keeping good neighborly relations develop towns and increase lifespans.'"

H 1976, Ch. 64, h 15

A number of our people have narrated from Sahl ibn Ziyad from Ja'far ibn Muhammad al-Ash'ari from 'Abd Allah b Maymun al-Qaddah from abu 'Ubaydah al-Hadhdha' from abu Ja'far, *'Alayhi al-Salam*, who has said the following:

"The Messenger of Allah has said, 'The good deed with the quickest reward is maintaining good relations with relatives.'"

H 1977, Ch. 64, h 16

Ali ibn Ibrahim has narrated from his father from al-Nawfali from al-Sakuni from abu 'Abd Allah, *'Alayhi al-Salam*, who has said the following:

"The messenger of Allah has said, 'One who likes to delay the coming of his death and increase his means of living should maintain good relations with relatives.'"

H 1978, Ch. 64, h 17

Ali ibn Ibrahim has narrated from his father from Safwan ibn Yahya from Ishaq ibn 'Ammar who has said the following:

"Abu 'Abd Allah, *'Alayhi al-Salam*, has said, 'We do not know of anything that may increase one's lifespan like maintaining good relations with relatives does. It is so much so that a man's life span may have only three years been left, but he maintains good relations with relatives, Allah will increase his life to last for thirty years. The total will be thirty-three years, thus the appointed time for his death will be after thirty-three years. In such case, if one is of the neglectors of good relations with relatives will live only for three years.'"

Al-Husayn ibn Muhammad has narrated from Mu'alla ibn Muhammad from al-Hassan ibn Ali al-Washsha' from abu al-Hassan al-Rida, *'Alayhi al-Salam*, a similar Hadith.

H 1979, Ch. 64, h 18

Ali ibn Ibrahim has narrated from his father from certain individuals of his people from 'Amr ibn Shamir from Jabir from abu Ja'far, *'Alayhi al-Salam*, who has said the following:

"When Amir al-Mu'minin (Ali ibn abu Talib), *'Alayhi al-Salam*, left Madina for Basra, on his way he stopped at al-Rabadhah (a place near Jaddah). A man from Muharib (a tribe) came and said, 'O Amir al-Mu'minin, I have been shouldering many responsibilities for my people and I have asked quite a few of them to help and cooperate with me, instead they have been very harsh to me. O Amir al-Mu'minin, command them to help me and encourage them to cooperate with me.' The Imam asked, 'Where are they?' He said, 'Those are a few of them as you may see.' The man has said, 'The Imam directed his horse to their direction, which began to move faster than trudge. Certain men from his companions followed, but they had difficulty catching up with him, and he would slow down for them until he reached the people and offered them greetings of peace. He asked them about their lack of cooperation with one of their own people. They complained before the Imam and he complained against them. Amir al-Mu'minin (Ali ibn abu Talib), *'Alayhi al-Salam*, said, 'A man must maintain good relations with relatives; they are more deserving of benefitting from his virtuous deeds and achievements. The relatives must maintain good relations with one of their own in times of need when things are against him. Those who maintain good relations with relatives and help financially are rewarded. Those who cut off good relations with relatives and turn away commit a sin.' The man has said, 'The Imam then turned his horse around and directed it to move.'"

H 1980, Ch. 64, h 19
Muhammad ibn Yahya has narrated from Ahmad ibn Muhammad ibn 'Isa from 'Uthman ibn 'Isa from Yahya from abu 'Abd Allah, *'Alayhi al-Salam*, who has said the following:

"Amir al-Mu'minin (Ali ibn abu Talib), *'Alayhi al-Salam*, has said, 'A man must never turn away from his relatives, even if he is wealthy and has many children. He must not fail to love them, must not ignore their honor, their defense with his hands and tongue. They are the strongest defending power behind him and the most kind to him, who care the most for his affairs if a misfortune may befall him or is suffering from a hardship. One who holds back from his kin's people only holds back one hand, and they hold back many hands from him. Whoever shows kindness to his friends finds love with them. Whoever extends his hands in charitable ways when he is able to do so Allah replaces for him in this world and will grant manifold of rewards in the next life. The truthful tongue of a man is a thing that Allah makes serve him among the people better than the property that he consumes or leaves as his legacy. No one of you must ever assume boastfulness and arrogance in his soul and distance himself from his relatives, even if he is a wealthy one. No one of you must ever reduce his good relations with his brother or distance from him when he is poor. No one of you must ever neglect relatives. Kindred relation has a characteristic that holding back from it does not benefit one and spending for it does not harm a person.'"

H 1981, Ch. 64, h 20
A number of our people have narrated from Ahmad ibn abu 'Abd Allah from 'Uthman ibn 'Isa from Sulayman ibn Hilal who has said the following:

"Once I said to abu 'Abd Allah, *'Alayhi al-Salam*, 'The family of so and so helps each other and maintains good relations.' The Imam said, 'Their wealth will increase and their persons will increase. They will remain as such as long as they will not neglect their good relations, if they neglect then they will lose.'"

H 1982, Ch. 64, h 21

It is narrated from him (narrator of the Hadith above) from more than one person from Ziyad al-Qandy from 'Abd Allah ibn Sinan from abu 'Abd Allah, *'Alayhi al-Salam*, who has said the following:

"The Messenger of Allah has said, 'A people who are evil doers and not of the virtuous ones but maintain good relations with relatives, their wealth increases, and they live longer. Can one imagine their benefits had they been virtuous and of good deeds?'"

H 1983, Ch. 64, h 22

It is narrated from him (narrator of the Hadith above) from al-Qasim ibn Yahya from his grandfather al-Hassan ibn Rashid from abu Basir from abu 'Abd Allah, *'Alayhi al-Salam*, who has said the following:

"Amir al-Mu'minin (Ali ibn abu Talib), *'Alayhi al-Salam*, has said, 'One must maintain good relations with relatives. Even offering the greeting of peace should not be held back from them. Allah, the Most Blessed, the Most High, says, "Have fear of the One by whose name you swear to settle your differences and have respect for your relatives. Allah certainly keeps watch over you."' (4:1)

H 1984, Ch. 64, h 23

Muhammad ibn Yahya has narrated from Ahmad ibn Muhammad ibn 'Isa from Ali ibn al-Hakam from Safwan al-Jammal who has said the following:

"Once a conversation took place between abu 'Abd Allah, *'Alayhi al-Salam*, and 'Abd Allah ibn al-Hassan and it had become quite noisy and people had gathered around. They departed from each other that evening. The next morning I was out for a task and I saw abu 'Abd Allah, *'Alayhi al-Salam*, at the door of 'Abd Allah ibn al-Hassan who was saying, 'O girl, tell abu Muhammad to come out.' He came out and said, 'O abu 'Abd Allah what has made you come out this early?' He replied, 'Last night I read a verse of the book of Allah, the Majestic, the Glorious, and it worried me.' He asked, 'Which verse is it?' He said, 'It is the words of Allah, Most Glorious, Most Majestic is Whose mention, ". . . who maintain all the proper relations that Allah has commanded them to maintain, who have fear of their Lord and the hardships of the Day of Judgment," (13:21) He said, 'You have spoken the truth. It seems I have never come across this verse in the book of Allah, the Most Majestic, the Most Holy.' They both wept and hugged each other.'"

H 1985, Ch. 64, h 24

It is narrated from him (narrator of the Hadith above) from Ali ibn al-Hakam from 'Abd Allah ibn Sinan who has said the following:

"Once, I said to abu 'Abd Allah, *'Alayhi al-Salam*, 'I have a cousin and with him I maintain the good relations that should be maintained with relatives, but he cuts it off. I establish it again and he cuts it off to the extent that I have begun to think of cutting it off also. Will you grant me permission do so?' The Imam said, 'When you established the relation and he cut it off Allah, the Most Majestic, the Most Holy, established it for both of you. If both of you cut it off, Allah will also cut you off.'"

H 1986, Ch. 64, h 25

It is narrated from him (narrator of the Hadith above) from Ali ibn al-Hakam from Dawud ibn Farqad who has said the following:

"Once abu 'Abd Allah, *'Alayhi al-Salam*, said to me, 'I love to show Allah humbling of my neck for my relatives and that I hasten to do good to my relatives and maintain good relations with them before they become independent of me.'"

H 1987, Ch. 64, h 26

It is narrated from him (narrator of the Hadith above) from al-Washsha' from Muhammad ibn Fudayl al-Sayrafi from al-Rida, *'Alayhi al-Salam*, who has said the following:

"The kindred relation of the family of Muhammad, the 'A'immah (people who possess Divine Authority), *'Alayhim al-Salam*, holds to the Throne (of the Lord) and says, 'O Lord establish good relations with those who establish good relations with me and cut off with those who cut off with me.' Thereafter it is applicable to the kindred relations of the believers. The Imam then read this verse: 'Have fear of the One by whose name you swear to settle your differences and have respect for your relatives. . . .'" (4:1)

H 1988, Ch. 64, h 27

A number of our people have narrated from Ahmad ibn abu 'Abd Allah from ibn Faddal from ibn Bukayr from 'Umar ibn Yazid who has said the following:

"Once I asked abu 'Abd Allah, *'Alayhi al-Salam*, about the words of Allah, the Most Majestic, the Most Holy, '. . . who maintain all the proper relations that Allah has commanded them to maintain, who have fear of their Lord and the hardships of the Day of Judgment.' (13:21) The Imam said, "It refers to your relatives.'"

H 1989, Ch. 64, h 28

Ali ibn Ibrahim has narrated from his father from ibn abu 'Umayr from Hammad ibn 'Uthman and Hisham ibn al-Hakam and Durust ibn abu Mansur from 'Umar ibn Yazid who has said the following:

"Once I asked abu 'Abd Allah, *'Alayhi al-Salam*, about the words of Allah, '. . . who maintain all the proper relations that Allah has commanded them to maintain, who have fear of their Lord and the hardships of the Day of Judgment.' (13:21) The Imam said, 'It was revealed about the family of Muhammad, *'Alayhi al-Salam*, and can also apply to your relatives.' Then the Imam said, 'Do not be of those who say about something that it is about one thing only.'"

H 1990, Ch. 64, h 29

A number of our people have narrated from Ahmad ibn abu 'Abd Allah from Muhammad ibn Ali from abu Jamilah from al-Wassafi from Ali ibn al-Husayn, *'Alayhi al-Salam*, who has said the following:

"The Messenger of Allah has said, 'Whoever loves Allah's giving him a long life and increasing his means of sustenance, he should maintain good relations with relatives; kindred relation, will have a sharp tongue on the Day of Judgment and it will say, "O Lord, establish good relations with those who maintained me properly and cut off those who cut me off. A man could be seen on the ways of good deeds but when the kindred relation that he had cut off would come he will be thrown into the depth of fire.'"

H 1991, Ch. 64, h 30

Ali ibn Muhammad has narrated from Salih ibn abu Hammad from al-Hassan ibn Ali from Safwan from al-Jahm ibn Hamid who has said the following:

"I asked abu 'Abd Allah, *'Alayhi al-Salam*, 'I have certain relatives who are not in my way (my belief). Do they have any rights on me?' The Imam said, 'Yes, it is the right of maintaining good relations with relatives that is not cut off by any means. Had they been in the same way as your way they would have had two rights: The right of relatives and the right because of Islam.'"

H 1992, Ch. 64, h 31

Muhammad ibn Yahya has narrated from Ahmad ibn Muhammad from ibn Mahbub from Ishaq ibn 'Ammar who has said the following:

"I heard abu 'Abd Allah, *'Alayhi al-Salam*, say, 'Maintaining good relations with relatives and virtuous deeds ease off the giving of accounts on the Day of Judgment and safeguard against sins. Maintain good relations with relatives and do virtuous deeds to your brothers, even if it is in the form of offering the greeting of peace or responding to the same.'"

H 1993, Ch. 64, h 32

Ali ibn Ibrahim has narrated from Muhammad ibn 'Isa from Yunus from 'Abd al-Samad ibn Bashir who has said the following:

"Abu 'Abd Allah, *'Alayhi al-Salam*, has said, 'Maintaining good relations with relatives eases off the giving of accounts on the Day of Judgment, delays the coming of death and safeguards against misfortunes. Giving charity at night extinguishes the wrath of the Lord.'"

H 1994, Ch. 64, h 33

Ali has narrated from his father from ibn abu 'Umayr from Husayn ibn 'Uthman from those whom he has mentioned (in his book) from abu 'Abd Allah, *'Alayhi al-Salam*, who has said the following:

"Maintaining good relations with relatives cleanses the deeds, increases wealth, eases off the giving of accounts on the Day of Judgment, repels misfortunes and increases one's means of sustenance."

Chapter 65 - Kindness to Parents

H 1995, Ch. 65, h 1

Muhammad ibn Yahya has narrated from Ahmad ibn Muhammad ibn 'Isa and Ali ibn Ibrahim from his father all from al-Hassan ibn Mahbub from abu Wallad al-Hannat who has said the following:

"I asked abu 'Abd Allah, *'Alayhi al-Salam*, about the meaning of 'kindness' in the words of Allah, the Most Majestic, the Most Holy, '. . . and that you must be kind to your parents. . . .' (17:23) The Imam said, 'It means to behave with them in a good manner, not to make them ask you for help, even though they are self-sufficient. Allah, the Most Majestic, the Most Holy, has said, "You can never have extended virtue and righteousness unless you spend part of what you dearly love for the cause of Allah."' (3:92)

"The narrator has said that the Imam then said, 'The words of Allah, the Most Majestic, the Most Holy, "If either or both of your parents should become advanced in age, do not express to them words which show your slightest disappointment. Never shout at them but always speak to them with kindness," (17:23) if they say harsh words to you, do not say 'Uff (expression of disappointment) to them, and do not shout at them if they beat you. Allah has said, 'Speak kind words to them.' The Imam said, 'If they beat you say to them, "May Allah forgive you," and this will be the kind and noble word from you.' Allah has said, "Be humble and merciful toward them. . . ." (17:24) The Imam said, 'Do not have an eyeful look at them except with kindness and tender heart, do not raise your voice over their voice or your hands over their hands and do not walk in front of them.'"

H 1996, Ch. 65, h 2
Ibn Mahbub has narrated from Khalid ibn Nafi' al-Bajali from Muhammad ibn Marwan who has said the following:

"I heard abu 'Abd Allah, 'Alayhi al-Salam, saying, 'Once a man came to the Holy Prophet and said, "O Messenger of Allah, give me a good advice." The Messenger of Allah said, 'Do not consider anything as partner of Allah even if you are tortured with fire except when your heart is confident with belief. You must obey your parents and be good to them whether living or dead. If they order you to leave your property and family you must do so; it is of belief.'"

H 1997, Ch. 65, h 3
Ali ibn Ibrahim has narrated from his father from ibn abu 'Umayr from Sayf from abu 'Abd Allah, 'Alayhi al-Salam, who has said the following:

"On the Day of Judgment something will suddenly come behind the believer, rush him forward and admit him in paradise. It will be said, 'This is kindness.'"

H 1998, Ch. 65, h 4
Al-Husayn ibn Muhammad has narrated from Mu'alla ibn Muhammad from al-Washsha' from Mansur ibn Hazim from abu 'Abd Allah, 'Alayhi al-Salam, who has said the following:

"I asked abu 'Abd Allah, 'Alayhi al-Salam, 'Which deed is the best?' The Imam said, 'Prayer in its proper time, kindness to parents and hard work to strive for the cause of Allah, the Most Majestic, the Most Holy.'"

H 1999, Ch. 65, h 5
Ali ibn Ibrahim has narrated from Muhammad ibn 'Isa ibn 'Ubayd from Yunus ibn 'Abd al-Rahman from Durust ibn abu Mansur from abu al-Hassan Musa, 'Alayhi al-Salam, who has said the following:

"Once, a man asked the Messenger of Allah, 'What is the right of the father on the son?' The messenger of Allah said, 'The son must not address his father by his name (first name), must not walk in front of him, must not take a seat before him, and must not cause people to abuse him.'"

H 2000, Ch. 65, h 6
A number of our people have narrated from Ahmad ibn Muhammad ibn Khalid from his father from 'Abd Allah ibn Bahr from 'Abd Allah ibn Muskan from those whom he has mentioned from abu 'Abd Allah, 'Alayhi al-Salam, who has said the following:

"Once the Imam spoke to 'Abd al-Wahid al-Ansari, while I was present, about kindness to parents mentioned in the words of Allah, the Most Majestic, the Most Holy, 'Be kind to parents.' We thought it was the verse in Chapter Seventeen that says, '. . . the Lord has ordained that you must not worship anyone other than Him and that you must "Be kind to your parents. . . .' (17:23) Later I asked the Imam and he said, 'It was verse 14-15 of Chapter 31, that says, "(Concerning his parents), We advised the man, (to be good to parents). . . . (31:14) If they try to force you to consider things equal to Me, which you cannot justify to be equal to Me, do not obey them." (31:15) The Imam then said, 'This shows greater significance of maintaining good relations with them in all cases.' I asked about: 'If they try to force you to consider things equal to Me, which you cannot justify to be equal to Me, do not obey them.' (31:15) The Imam said, 'It, in fact, is a command to establish good relations with parents even if they struggle to make him consider things equal to Allah. It only shows the greatness of the rights of parents.'"

(Note: al-Majlisi in Mir'at al-'Uqul has expressed concern about the authenticity of this Hadith. For details one may refer to this work.)

H 2001, Ch. 65, h 7
It is narrated from him (narrator of the Hadith above) from Muhammad ibn Ali from al-Hakam ibn Miskin from Muhammad ibn Marwan who has said the following:
"Abu 'Abd Allah, 'Alayhi al-Salam, has said, 'Nothing prevents any of you from doing kindness to your parents, who are living or dead, in the form of prayer for them, giving charity on their behalf, performing Hajj and fasting on their behalf. These are things that one can do for them. He will also receive similar credit, thus, Allah, the Most Majestic, the Most Holy, will grant him a great deal of good rewards for his kindness to his parents.'"

H 2002, Ch. 65, h 8
Muhammad ibn Yahya has narrated from Ahmad ibn Muhammad ibn 'Isa from Mu'ammar ibn Khallad who has said the following:
"I asked abu al-Hassan al-Rida, 'Alayhi al-Salam, 'Can I pray for my parents who do not know the truth?' The Imam said, 'Pray for them and give charity on their behalf. If they are living and do not know the truth, be kind to them; the Messenger of Allah has said, "Allah has sent me with (message of) kindness and not to punish.'"

H 2003, Ch. 65, h 9
Ali ibn Ibrahim has narrated from his father from ibn abu 'Umayr from Hisham ibn Salim from abu 'Abd Allah who has said the following:
"Once a man came to the Holy Prophet and said, 'O Messenger of Allah, to whom should I be kind?' The Messenger of Allah said, 'Be kind to your mother.' The man asked, 'Then whom?' The Messenger of Allah said, 'Your mother.' The man asked, 'Then whom?' The Messenger of Allah said, 'Your mother.' The man asked, 'Then whom?' The Messenger of Allah said, "Be kind to your father."

H 2004, Ch. 65, h 10
Abu Ali al-Ash'ari has narrated from Muhammad ibn Salim from Ahmad ibn al-Nadr from 'Amr ibn Shamir from Jabir from abu 'Abd Allah, 'Alayhi al-Salam, who has said the following:
"Once a man came to the Messenger of Allah and said, 'I am interested in Jihad (joining the army) O Messenger of Allah. I am active and light.' The Imam said, 'The Holy Prophet said, "Do Jihad (join the army) in the way of Allah, if you will

be killed you will be living with Allah and will receive sustenance. If you die you will receive your reward from Allah, and if you return you will return free from sins as in the day you were born." The man then said, 'O Messenger of Allah, my parents are old and they think my presence is a comfort for them and they do not like my going out.' The Messenger of Allah then said, 'Stay with your parents, I swear by the One in whose hand is my soul, that your parents' receiving comfort from your presence with them for one day and night is more virtuous than Jihad for one year.'"

H 2005, Ch. 65, h 11
A number of our people have narrated from Ahmad ibn Muhammad ibn Khalid from Ali ibn al-Hakam from Mu'awiyah ibn Wahab from Zakariya ibn Ibrahim who has said the following:

"I was a Christian, then I became a Muslim. I went for Hajj, where I met abu 'Abd Allah, 'Alayhi al-Salam, and I said to him, 'I was a Christian and I have become a Muslim.' The Imam asked, 'What have you seen in Islam?' I said, 'They are the words of Allah, the Most Majestic, the Most Holy, ". . . before, you did not even know what a Book or belief was, but We have made the Quran as a light by which We guide whichever of Our servants We want."' (42:52) The Imam said, 'Allah has certainly granted you guidance.' The Imam then said three times: 'O Allah, guide him. Son, ask whatever you want to ask.' I then said, 'My parents and my family are Christians and my mother is blind. I live with them. Can I eat from their utensils with them?' The Imam asked, 'Do they eat pork?' I said, 'No, they do not even touch it.' The Imam said, 'There is no offense in your eating with them. Take good care of your mother and be kind to her. When she will die do not leave her to others. You must do everything that she will need (for her funeral). Do not tell anyone of your meeting with me until you will meet me at Mina, if Allah would so will.' I (the narrator) met him at Mina and people were around him as if he were the teacher of children. He asks a question then the other asks a question and so on. I returned to Kufa and I would act more kindly toward my mother. I would feed my mother, wash her clothes, her head and would serve her in other ways.' She said, 'My son, you did not do all this for me when you followed my religion. What is all that I see from you after you left and accepted the religion of submission (Islam)?' I said, 'A man from the descendents of our prophet has commanded me to do all this.' She then asked, 'Is this man a prophet?' I said, 'No, but he is a descendent of a prophet.' She said, 'My son, he is a prophet; these are of the teachings of the prophets.' I said, 'Mother, there will be no other prophet after our prophet. He is a descendent of our prophet.' She then said, 'Your religion is the best religion. Explain it to me.' I then explained to her and she accepted Islam. I taught her more. She prayed, Zuhr, 'Asr, Maghrib and 'Isha' prayers. Thereafter something happened to her at night and she said, 'Son, explain and repeat to me what you told me about Islam and I repeated it to her. She affirmed them and then she died. In the morning the Muslims were the ones who helped with her funeral and washed her. I was the one who prayed on her body and climbed down in her grave (to place her body to rest).'"

H 2006, Ch. 65, h 12

Muhammad ibn Yahya has narrated from Ahmad ibn Muhammad ibn 'Isa from Ali ibn al-Hakam a number of our people from Ahmad ibn abu 'Abd Allah from Isma'il ibn Mehran all from Sayf ibn 'Amirah from 'Abd Allah ibn Muskan from 'Ammar ibn Hayyan who has said the following:

"Once I explained to abu 'Abd Allah, *'Alayhi al-Salam*, how kind my son Isma'il was to me. The Imam said, 'I loved him before and this has increased my love for him. Once, the sister of the Messenger of Allah (through breast-feeding) visited him. When he saw her he became very happy to see her, prepared a seat for her, began to talk to her and smiled at her. She left and her brother came. The Holy Prophet did not behave toward him as he did to her. He was asked, 'O Messenger of Allah, you behaved toward his sister differently from the way you behaved toward him, and he is a man.' The Messenger of Allah said, 'It was because she was more kind to her parents than he was.'"

H 2007, Ch. 65, h 13

Muhammad ibn Yahya has narrated from Ahmad ibn Muhammad ibn 'Isa from Ali ibn al-Hakam from Sayf ibn 'Amirah from 'Abd Allah ibn Muskan from Ibrahim ibn Shu'ayb who has said the following:

"Once I said to abu 'Abd Allah, *'Alayhi al-Salam*, 'My father has become very old and weak. We pick him up and help him for the restrooms.' The Imam said, 'If you can, you should do all of this for him and feed him with your own hand; it is paradise for you tomorrow.'"

H 2008, Ch. 65, h 14

It is narrated from him (narrator of the Hadith above) from Ali ibn al-Hakam from Sayf ibn 'Amirah from abu al-Sabbah from Jabir who has said the following:

"I heard a man saying to abu 'Abd Allah, *'Alayhi al-Salam*, 'My parents are against us (our belief).' The Imam said, 'Be kind to them just as Muslims who follow us are kind (to their parents).'"

H 2009, Ch. 65, h 15

Ali ibn Ibrahim has narrated from his father and Muhammad ibn Yahya from Ahmad ibn Muhammad all from ibn Mahbub from Malik ibn 'Atiyyah from 'Anbasah ibn Mus'ab from abu Ja'far, *'Alayhi al-Salam*, who has said the following:

"There are three things in which Allah, the Most Majestic, the Most Holy, has not given any concession: safely returning of the trust to appropriate people, regardless of their being good or evil people, keeping the promise for good or evil people, and being kind to parents whether of good or of evil manners."

H 2010, Ch. 65, h 16

Ali ibn Ibrahim has narrated from his father from al-Nawfali from al-Sakuni from abu 'Abd Allah, *'Alayhi al-Salam*, who has said the following:

"Abu 'Abd Allah, *'Alayhi al-Salam*, has said, 'It is of tradition and virtue to adopt al-Kunyah (like abu' meaning father of or 'Ibn') of the name of one's father.'"

H 2011, Ch. 65, h 17

Al-Husayn ibn Muhammad has narrated from Mu'alla ibn Muhammad and Ali ibn Muhammad from Salih ibn abu Hammad all from al-Washsha' from Ahmad ibn 'Ai'z from abu Khadijah Salim ibn Mukram from Mu'alla ibn Khanis from abu 'Abd Allah Who has said the following:

"Once a man came to the Holy Prophet and asked about kindness to parents. The Holy Prophet said, 'Be kind to your mother, be kind to your mother, be kind to your mother, be kind to your father, be kind to your father, and be kind to your father. He began with mother before the father.'"

H 2012, Ch. 65, h 18
Al-Washsha' has narrated from Ahmad ibn 'Ai'z from abu Khadijah from abu 'Abd Allah, *'Alayhi al-Salam*, who has said the following:
"Once a man came to the Holy Prophet and said, 'I had a daughter and I brought her up until she became an adult. I then dressed her up in beautiful clothes, took her to the well and threw her therein to her death and the last thing I heard from her was; O father! What is the expiation for it?' The Messenger of Allah asked, 'Do you have a living mother?' He said, 'No, I do not.' The Messenger of Allah asked, 'Do you have a living maternal aunt?' He said, 'Yes, I do.' The Messenger of Allah said, 'Be kind to her; she is like a mother, this will serve as expiation for what you have done.' Abu Khadijah has said, 'I asked abu 'Abd Allah, *'Alayhi al-Salam*, 'When was this?' The Imam said, 'It was in the time of Jahiliyah (age of darkness). They would kill the girls for fear of being taken captive and giving birth to other people.'"

H 2013, Ch. 65, h 19
Muhammad ibn Yahya has narrated from Ahmad ibn Muhammad from Muhammad ibn Isma'il ibn Bazi' from Hannan ibn Sadir from his father who has said the following:
"I asked abu Ja'far, *'Alayhi al-Salam*, 'Can a son pay back (for the favors of) a father?' The Imam said, 'There is no payment for him except two things: if the father is a slave and the son buys him and sets him free, or the father is in debt and the son pays it off.'"

H 2014, Ch. 65, h 20
Ali ibn Ibrahim has narrated from Muhammad ibn 'Isa from Yunus ibn 'Abd al-Rahman from 'Amr ibn Shamir from Jabir who has said the following:
"Once a man came to the Messenger of Allah and said, 'I am a young and active man and love Jihad (joining the army), but my mother does not like it.' The Holy Prophet said, 'Go back and stay with your mother. I swear by the One Who has sent me with the truth as a prophet that her feeling comfort because of your presence for one night is better for your Jihad in the way of Allah for one year."

H 2015, Ch. 65, h 21
Al-Husayn ibn Muhammad has narrated from Mu'alla ibn Muhammad from al-Hassan ibn Ali from 'Abd Allah ibn Sinan from Muhammad ibn Muslim from abu Ja'far, *'Alayhi al-Salam*, who has said the following:
"A servant (of Allah) may have been kind to his parents during their lifetime but when they die he does not pay their debts, and does not ask forgiveness for them. Allah writes him as unkind (person) to parents. One may have been unkind to parents during their lifetime but after their death, when he pays off their debts and asks forgiveness for them, Allah, the Most Majestic, the Most Holy, writes him down to be among the people who are kind to their parents."

Chapter 66 - Concern for the Affairs of the Muslims, Giving Them Good Advice and to Benefit Them

H 2016, Ch. 66, h 1

Ali ibn Ibrahim has narrated from his father from al-Nawfali from al-Sakuni from abu 'Abd Allah, *'Alayhi al-Salam*, who has said the following:

"The Messenger of Allah has said, 'Whoever does not feel any concern about the affairs of Muslims is not a Muslim anymore.'"

H 2017, Ch. 66, h 2

It is reported through the same chain of narrators who has said the following:

"The Messenger of Allah has said, 'The most assiduous worshipper among the people is the one whose inner center is most clean and whose heart is most peaceful toward Muslims.'"

H 2018, Ch. 66, h 3

Ali ibn Ibrahim has narrated from his father from Ali ibn Muhammad al-Qasani from al-Qasim ibn Muhammad from Sulayman ibn Dawud al-Minqari from Sufyan ibn 'Uyayna who has said the following:

"I heard abu 'Abd Allah, *'Alayhi al-Salam*, say, 'You must, for the sake of Allah, offer good advice to His creatures; you will not meet Him with any deed better than this.'"

H 2019, Ch. 66, h 4

Muhammad ibn Yahya has narrated from Ahmad ibn Muhammad ibn 'Isa from ibn Mahbub from Muhammad al-Qasim al-Hashimi from abu 'Abd Allah, *'Alayhi al-Salam*, who has said the following:

"Whoever does not feel any concern about the affairs of Muslims is not a Muslim any longer."

H 2020, Ch. 66, h 5

It is narrated from him (narrator of the Hadith above) from Salmah ibn al-Khattab from Sulayman ibn Sama'a from his uncle 'Asim al-Kuzi from abu 'Abd Allah, *'Alayhi al-Salam*, who has said the following:

"The Holy Prophet has said, 'Whoever does not feel any concern for the affairs of Muslims is no longer one of them. Whoever hears a man calling, "O Muslims, help" and one does not respond, he is not a Muslim.'"

H 2021, Ch. 66, h 6

Ali ibn Ibrahim has narrated from his father from al-Nawfali from al-Sakuni from abu 'Abd Allah, *'Alayhi al-Salam*, who has said the following:

"The Messenger of Allah has said, 'The creatures are the dependents of Allah. The most beloved creature to Allah is the one who is most beneficial to Allah's dependents (like family members) and who provides the utmost happiness to a family.'"

H 2022, Ch. 66, h 7

A number of our people have narrated from Ahmad ibn Muhammad ibn Khalid from Ali ibn al-Hakam from Sayf ibn 'Amirah who has said the following:

"The person who had heard abu 'Abd Allah, *'Alayhi al-Salam*, narrated to me the following: He had heard the Imam say, 'The Messenger of Allah was asked, "Who was the most beloved of people to Allah?" The Messenger of Allah replied, 'The most beneficial one to people is the most beloved to Allah.'"

H 2023, Ch. 66, h 8

It is narrated from him (narrator of the Hadith above) from Ali ibn al-Hakam from al-Muthanna ibn al-Walid al-Hannat from Futr ibn Khalifah from 'Amr ibn Ali ibn al-Husayn from his father, *'Alayhi al-Salam*, who has said the following:

"The Messenger of Allah has said, 'One who repulses a transgressor from Muslim's (waters) or fire, will as a matter of necessity go to paradise.'"

H 2024, Ch. 66, h 9

It is narrated from him (narrator of the Hadith above) from ibn Faddal from Tha'labah ibn Maymun from Mu'awiyah ibn 'Ammar from abu 'Abd Allah, *'Alayhi al-Salam*, who has said the following:

"About the words of Allah, the Majestic, the Glorious, '. . . speak righteous words to people. . . .' (2:83), the Imam said it means, 'Do not say anything about a people except good until you actually learn all about it.'"

H 2025, Ch. 66, h 10

It is narrated from him (narrator of the Hadith above) from ibn abu Najran from abu Jamilah al-Mufaddal ibn Salih from Jabir ibn Yazid from abu Ja'far, *'Alayhi al-Salam*, who has said the following:

"About the words of Allah, the Most Majestic, the Most Holy, '. . . speak righteous words to people, . . .' (2:83) the Imam said, 'It means say to people the best of that which you love to be said about you.'"

H 2026, Ch. 66, h 11

A number of our people have narrated from Sahl ibn Ziyad from Yahya ibn al-Mubarak from 'Abd Allah ibn Jabalah from a man from abu 'Abd Allah, *'Alayhi al-Salam*, who has said the following:

"About the words of Allah, the Most Majestic, the Most Holy: '. . . He has blessed me no matter where I dwell, . . .' (19:31) the Imam said, '"Blessed" means, the most beneficial to people.'"

Chapter 67 - High Regards for the Elderly

H 2027, Ch. 67, h 1

Ali ibn Ibrahim has narrated from his father from ibn abu 'Umayr from certain individuals of his people from abu 'Abd Allah, *'Alayhi al-Salam*, who has said the following:

"The Messenger of Allah has said, 'Of high regard toward Allah, is having high regard for a Muslim who has grown a beard.'"

H 2028, Ch. 67, h 2

A number of our people have narrated from Ahmad ibn Muhammad in a marfu' manner from abu 'Abd Allah, *'Alayhi al-Salam*, who has said the following:

"Whoever does not consider our elders as dignified and does not show kindness to our people who are yet to grow up, is not from our people."

H 2029, Ch. 67, h 3

Ali ibn Ibrahim has narrated from his father from ibn abu 'Umayr from 'Abd Allah ibn Aban from al-Wassafi who has said the following:

"Abu 'Abd Allah, *'Alayhi al-Salam*, has said, 'Consider your grown up people as great and maintain good relations with relatives. No other way is better to maintain good relations with relatives than keeping all troubles away from them.'"

Chapter 68 - The Believer's Mutual Brotherhood

H 2030, Ch. 68, h 1

A number of our people have narrated from Ahmad ibn Muhammad ibn Khalid from 'Uthman ibn 'Isa from al-Mufaddal ibn 'Umar who has said the following:

"Abu 'Abd Allah, *'Alayhi al-Salam*, has said, 'The believers are but brothers, sons of one father and mother (in the original creation). If one of them may have an distressed vein, others will remain awake all night because of his pain.'"

H 2031, Ch. 68, h 2

It is narrated from him (narrator of the Hadith above) from his father from Fadalah ibn Ayyub from 'Amr ibn Aban from Jabir al-Juhfi who has said the following:

"Once I became depressed in the presence of abu Ja'far, *'Alayhi al-Salam*, and asked him, 'May Allah keep my soul in service for your cause, why is it that sometimes I feel depressed without any apparent cause or incident? Even my family and friends notice it on my face.' The Imam said, 'Yes O Jabir, Allah, the Most Majestic, the Most Holy, has created the clay of the believers from the clay of paradise and has made the fragrance of His spirit flow through it; thus, a believer is a brother (in belief) of a believer from his father and mother. When a spirit of those spirits is distressed anywhere with a sadness the other spirits also feel sad; this is from that (clay of paradise).'"

H 2032, Ch. 68, h 3

Muhammad ibn Yahya has narrated from Ahmad ibn Muhammad ibn 'Isa from ibn Faddal from Ali ibn 'Uqbah from abu 'Abd Allah, *'Alayhi al-Salam*, who has said the following:

"The believer is a brother (in belief) of a believer, his eyes and his guide. He does not violate his trust, does not do injustice to him, or deceive him, and does not promise him only to ignore it later on.'"

H 2033, Ch. 68, h 4

Muhammad ibn Yahya has narrated from Ahmad ibn Muhammad ibn 'Isa and A number of our people have narrated from Sahl ibn Ziyad all from ibn Mahbub from Ali ibn Ri'ab from abu Basir who has said the following:

"I heard abu 'Abd Allah, *'Alayhi al-Salam*, say, 'The believer is the brother (in belief) of the believer. They are like the same body. If one part complains of pain the rest of the body also feels it. Their spirits are from one spirit. The spirit of the believer's connection with the spirit of Allah is stronger than the connection of the sun's rays to the sun.'"

H 2034, Ch. 68, h 5

A number of our people have narrated from Sahl ibn Ziyad from 'Abd al-Rahman ibn abu Najran from Muthanna al-Hannat from al-Harith ibn al-Mughirah who has said the following:

"Abu 'Abd Allah, *'Alayhi al-Salam*, has said, 'A Muslim is the brother (in belief) of a Muslim, he is his eyes, his mirror and his guide. He does not violate his trust, does not deceive him, does not do injustice to him, does not call him a liar and does not speak ill behind his back.'"

H 2035, Ch. 68, h 6

Ali ibn Ibrahim has narrated from his father from ibn abu 'Umayr from Hafs ibn al-Bakhtari who has said the following:

"Once I was in the presence of abu 'Abd Allah, *'Alayhi al-Salam*, when a man came in and the Imam asked me, 'Do you love him?' I said, 'Yes, I love him.' The Imam asked me, 'How would you not love him when he is your brother (in belief), your partner in religion, your supporter against your enemies and someone other than you provides his sustenance?'"

H 2036, Ch. 68, h 7

Abu Ali al-Ash'ari has narrated from al-Husayn ibn al-Hassan from Muhammad ibn 'Uramah from certain individuals of his people from Muhammad ibn al-Husayn from Muhammad ibn Fudayl from abu Hamza who has said the following:

"I heard abu Ja'far, *'Alayhi al-Salam*, say, 'The believer is the brother (in belief) of the believer from his father and mother; Allah, the Most Majestic, the Most Holy, has created believers from the clay of paradise and has made the fragrance of paradise flow in their forms; thus, they are brothers from father and mother.'"

H 2037, Ch. 68, h 8

Muhammad ibn Yahya has narrated from Ahmad ibn Muhammad ibn 'Isa from al-Hajjal from Ali ibn 'Uqbah from abu 'Abd Allah, *'Alayhi al-Salam*, who has said the following:

"The believer is the brother (in belief) of the believer, his eyes and his guide. He does not violate his trust, does not do injustice to him, does not deceive him and does not promise him only to ignore it later on.'"

H 2038, Ch. 68, h 9

Ahmad ibn Muhammad ibn 'Isa has narrated from Ahmad ibn abu 'Abd Allah from a man from Jamil who has said the following:

"I heard abu 'Abd Allah, *'Alayhi al-Salam*, saying, 'The believers are like servants for each other.' I asked, 'How can they be each other's servants?' The Imam said, 'They benefit each other. . . . (all of this Hadith is not mentioned)'"

H 2039, Ch. 68, h 10

Ali ibn Ibrahim has narrated from his father and Muhammad ibn Yahya from Ahmad ibn Muhammad ibn 'Isa all from ibn abu 'Umayr from Isma'il al-Basri from Fudayl ibn Yasar who has said the following:

"I heard abu Ja'far, *'Alayhi al-Salam*, say, 'Once a few Muslims set on a journey but they lost the way and faced severe thirst. They shrouded themselves holding to the roots of a tree. Suddenly an old man in white clothes appeared and told them to get up saying that they had no problems and gave them water. They drank water to their satisfaction and asked him, 'Who are you?' He said, 'I am from Jinn who pledged allegiance to the Messenger of Allah. I heard the Messenger of Allah saying, "A believer is a brother of a believer, his eyes and his guide. How could you lose your lives in my presence?"'"

H 2040, Ch. 68, h 11

Ali ibn Ibrahim has narrated from his father and Muhammad ibn Isma'il from Fadl ibn Shadhan all from Hammad ibn 'Isa from Rib'i from Fudayl ibn Yasar who has said the following:

"I heard abu 'Abd Allah, *'Alayhi al-Salam*, saying, 'A Muslim is the brother of a Muslim. He does not do injustice to him, does not betray him, does not speak ill of one behind his back, does not violate his trust and does not deprive him.' Rib'i has said, 'Certain individuals of our people asked me in Madina saying, "I have heard Fudayl saying what just you said." I then said to him, 'Yes, it is true.' He then said, 'I heard abu 'Abd Allah, *'Alayhi al-Salam*, saying, "A Muslim is the brother of a Muslim. He does not do injustice to him, does not deceive him, does not betray him, does not speak ill of one behind his back, does not violate his trust and does not deprive him."'"

Chapter 69 - The Rights of One Who Accepts the Belief and Then Severs Away

H 2041, Ch. 69, h 1

Ali ibn Ibrahim has narrated from Harun ibn Muslim from Mas'adah ibn Sadaqah who has said the following:

"I heard abu 'Abd Allah, *'Alayhi al-Salam*, saying, when he was asked about belief, and the rights of the believer, his brotherhood and how he is and by what means it is proved and is invalidated, 'The belief is of two aspects. One is that which is manifested to you from your companion. If he manifests like what you believe in, his Wilayah (right of one guardianship) is established as well as his brotherhood unless he then manifests the opposite of what he had manifested before. He then will be out of the rights that were established. That which he manifests later suspends his rights unless he then claims it to be for purposes of protection (Taqiyah). Despite this, it is to be seen, if it is of the cases where use of protective measures (Taqiyah) is applicable or not, if not then his claim is not accepted. For use of protective measures there are specific instances. Whoever misuses them will not have the benefits thereby. Of such examples one is when there are evil people whose rules and judgments are against the judgment and actions of truth. In such conditions, if the believer may use the protective measures to the limits that do not harm ones religion, such use is permissible.'"

Chapter 70 - Brotherhood in Belief is Not Due to Religion, It is only a Way of Recognition

H 2042, Ch. 70, h 1

Muhammad ibn Yahya has narrated from Ahmad ibn Muhammad ibn 'Isa from Muhammad ibn Sinan from Hamza ibn Muhammad al-Tayyar from his father from abu Ja'far, *'Alayhi al-Salam*, who has said the following:

"You have not become brothers on the basis of this belief (of Shi'a Muslims) but you have recognized each other because of it.'"

H 2043, Ch. 70, h 2

It is narrated from him (narrator of the Hadith above) from Ahmad ibn Muhammad from 'Uthman ibn 'Isa from ibn Muskan and Sama'a all from abu 'Abd Allah, *'Alayhi al-Salam*, who has said the following:

"You have not become brothers on the basis of this matter (Walayah the belief of the Shi'a Muslims); it is only that you have recognized each other by means of Walayah."

Chapter 71 - The Rights of a Believer on His Brother (in Belief) and His Duty to Observe Such Rights

H 2044, Ch. 71, h 1

Muhammad ibn Yahya has narrated from Ahmad ibn Muhammad ibn 'Isa from Ali ibn al-Hakam from Sayf ibn 'Amirah from 'Amr ibn Shamir from Jabir from abu Ja'far, *'Alayhi al-Salam*, who has said the following:

"Of the rights of the believer on his believing brother (in belief) is to satisfy his hunger, provide covering for his privacy, facilitate his hardships and pay off his debts. When he dies, look after his family and children."

H 2045, Ch. 71, h 2

It is narrated from him (narrator of the Hadith above) from Ali ibn al-Hakam from 'Abd Allah ibn Bukayr al-Hajari from Mu'alla ibn Khanis from abu 'Abd Allah, *'Alayhi al-Salam*, who has said the following:

"Once I asked the Imam, 'What are the rights of the Muslim on the Muslim?' The Imam said, 'He has seven categories of rights that are obligatory, each of which is compulsory. If he jeopardizes a single one of them he is out of the domain of guardianship (Walayah) of Allah and obedience to Him. There will be no share for Allah in him.' I then said, 'May Allah keep my soul in service for your cause, what are these rights?' The Imam said, 'O Mu'alla, I am afraid you may jeopardize them and may not protect them. You learn them but do not act up on them.' I (the narrator) then said, 'There is no power without the power of Allah.' The Imam said, 'Of those rights the easiest to fulfill is to love for him what you love for yourself and dislike for him what you dislike for yourself. The second right is to avoid (stirring) his anger, follow his wishes and obey his commands. The third right is to support him with your soul, property, tongue, hands and legs. The fourth right is to be his eyes, his guide and his mirror. The fifth right is that you must not be satisfied with food while he is hungry, with drinks while he is thirsty, and that you dress up in finery while he does not have any clothes. The sixth right is not to allow yourself to have a servant while your brother in belief does not have any servant. It then is necessary to send your servant to wash his clothes, prepare food and his bed for him. The seventh right is to keep his share handsomely, accept his invitations, visit him when he is ill, attend his funeral and if he needs something, initiate to fulfill it and do not delay until he asks you for help. You must hurry quickly and when you do so you have connected your guardianship with his guardianship and vice versa.'"

H 2046, Ch. 71, h 3

It is narrated from him (narrator of the Hadith above) from Ahmad ibn Muhammad ibn 'Isa from Ali ibn Sayf from his father, Sayf from 'Abd al-'Ala' ibn 'A'Yun who has said the following:

"Once certain individual of our people wrote to abu 'Abd Allah, *'Alayhi al-Salam*, asking him about certain issues and they ordered me to ask the Imam about the rights of the Muslim on his Muslim brother and I asked the Imam but he did not answer me. When I went to say farewell to him I said, 'I asked you that question but you did not answer me.' The Imam said, 'I am afraid you may disregard them. Of the obligations most pressing that Allah has made obligatory upon His creature are three things: a man's yielding to justice against his own soul so as not to accept for his brother (in belief) what he does not accept for his own self, to assist his brother with his property and speak of Allah in all conditions. I do not mean thereby, saying, 'Glory belongs to Allah and all praise belongs to Allah. Truly speaking of and remembering Allah is to stay away from whatever He has prohibited.'"

H 2047, Ch. 71, h 4

It is narrated from him (narrator of the Hadith above) from Ahmad ibn Muhammad from al-Hassan ibn Mahbub from Jamil from Marazim from abu 'Abd Allah, *'Alayhi al-Salam*, who has said the following:

"Allah the best way to worship is to fulfil (protect) the rights of the believer."

H 2048, Ch. 71, h 5

Ali ibn Ibrahim has narrated from his father from Hammad ibn 'Isa from Ibrahim ibn 'Umar al-Yamani from abu 'Abd Allah, *'Alayhi al-Salam*, who has said the following:

"Of the rights of the Muslim on the Muslim is that he must not satisfy himself with food while his Muslim brother is hungry. One must not satisfy himself with water while one's Muslim brother is thirsty, and one must not dress up in finery while his Muslim brother is in need of clothes. How great is the right of the Muslim on his Muslim brother! The Imam then said, 'Love for your Muslim brother what you love for yourself. Ask him when you need him and when he needs you, you must help him and do not frustrate him, but be his supporter; he is your supporter. When he is absent protect his interests in his absence and when he is present visit, honor and respect him; you are from him and he is from you. If he is disappointed with you do not keep away from him before asking him to forgive you and if he gains something, thank Allah for it. If he suffers from something then support him. If he is subjected to a plot, assist him. If a man says to his brother, fie up on you, the relation of guardianship between them remains no longer. If he says, 'You are my enemy, one of them will become an unbeliever. If he accuses him, belief in his heart melts like salt melts in water.' The narrator has said that it is reported to me that the Imam said, 'The light of the believer shines to the inhabitants of the heavens like the stars shine to the inhabitants of earth.' And he said, 'The believer is the friend of Allah Who helps him and grants him favors. He does not say about Him but the truth and he is not afraid of any one other than Him.'"

H 2049, Ch. 71, h 6

Abu Ali al-Ash'ari has narrated from Muhammad ibn 'Abd al-Jabbar from ibn Faddal from Ali ibn 'Uqbah from abu 'Abd Allah, *'Alayhi al-Salam*, who has said the following:

"Of the rights of Muslin on a Muslim is to offer him the greeting of peace upon meeting him, visit him when he is ill, protect his interest when he is absent, say,

'May Allah bless you' when he sneezes, accept his invitation and take part in the procession for his funeral."

A number of our people have narrated from Ahmad ibn Muhammad ibn Khalid from ibn Faddal from Ali ibn 'Uqbah a similar Hadith.

H 2050, Ch. 71, h 7

Ali ibn Ibrahim has narrated from his father from ibn abu 'Umayr from Mansur ibn Yunus from abu al-Mamun al-Harithi who has said the following:

"Once I asked abu 'Abd Allah, *'Alayhi al-Salam*, 'What are the rights of the believer on the believer?' The Imam said, 'Of the rights of the believer on the believer is to have compassion for him in his heart, assist him with his property, protect his interests in his absence in the matters of his family and support him against those who do injustice to him. If a benefit is distributed among the Muslims in his absence his believing brother should secure his share thereof. When he dies, he should visit his gravesite, must not do injustice to him, must not deceive him, must not violate his trust, must not betray him, must not call him a liar, must not say to him, 'Fie upon you.' If he says fie up on you then no guardianship (Walayah) relations will remain between them. If he says, 'You are my enemy,' one of them becomes an unbeliever and if he accuses him, belief in his heart will melt as salt melts in water.'"

H 2051, Ch. 71, h 8

Muhammad ibn Yahya has narrated from Ahmad ibn Muhammad ibn 'Isa from ibn abu 'Umayr from abu Ali Sahib al-Kalal from Aban ibn Taghlib who has said the following:

"Once I was performing Tawaf (walking seven times around the Ka'ba) along with abu 'Abd Allah, *'Alayhi al-Salam*, when a man from our people came up asking me to go with him for a certain need and hinted to me for that purpose, but I did not like to leave abu 'Abd Allah, *'Alayhi al-Salam*, and go with him. I was still performing Tawaf when he made a gesture for the same purpose and abu 'Abd Allah, *'Alayhi al-Salam*, saw him and said to me, 'O Aban, does he want you?.' I said, 'Yes, he does so.' The Imam asked, 'Who is he?' I said, 'He is a man from our people.' The Imam asked, 'Is he of the belief that you are?' I said, 'Yes, he is.' The Imam said, 'Then go to him.' I asked, 'Should I discontinue Tawaf?' The Imam said, 'Yes, do so.' I asked, 'Even if it is a compulsory Tawaf?' The Imam said, 'Yes, even if it is such.' I (the narrator) then went with him. Later I went to meet the Imam and I said to him, 'Please tell me about the rights of the believer on the believer.' The Imam asked, 'O Aban, ignore it and do not repeat.' I said, 'Yes, may Allah keep my soul in service for your cause, but I still like to bring up the question. The Imam said, 'O Aban, are you ready to share with him parts of your property?' He then looked at me and found out what was going on in my mind and he asked, 'O Aban do you know what Allah, the Most Majestic, the Most Holy, has said about the self-abnegating people?' I said, 'Yes, may Allah keep my soul in service for your cause, I know about it.' The Imam said, 'If you share with him you have not practiced self-abnegation, but you both are equal. You give him preference only if you give him from the other half also.'"

H 2052, Ch. 71, h 9

A number of our people have narrated from Ahmad ibn Muhammad ibn Khalid from his father from Fadalah ibn Ayyub from 'Amr ibn Aban from 'Isa ibn abu Mansur who has said the following:

"Once ibn abu Ya'fur, 'Abd Allah ibn Talha and I were in the presence of abu 'Abd Allah, *'Alayhi al-Salam*, who on his own initiation said, 'O ibn abu Ya'fur, the Messenger of Allah has said, "There are six things that if found in a person, he will be before Allah, the Most Majestic, the Most Holy, to the right of Allah (to the right of the Throne of Allah)."' Ibn abu Ya'fur then asked, 'What are those things, may Allah keep my soul in service for your cause?' The Imam said, 'A man must love for his Muslim brother what he loves for the most beloved person of his family and dislike for his Muslim brother what he dislikes for the most beloved person of his family and enlighten him in Walayah (the position of people who possess Divine Authority).' Ibn abu Ya'fur then wept and asked, 'How does he enlighten about Walayah?' The Imam said, 'O ibn abu Ya'fur, if he is of the same level (of belief), he should encourage him, show happiness in his happiness and express sadness if he is sad. If he has the means to facilitate him he should do so if not he should pray to Allah for him.'

"The narrator has said that abu 'Abd Allah, *'Alayhi al-Salam*, then said, 'Three things are for you and three things are for us. What is for us is that you must learn about our excellent merits, follow our footsteps and wait for our end results (Divine Kingdom) to take place. Whoever has these facts will be before Allah, the Most Majestic, the Most Holy, and those below them will receive light from their light. On seeing those who will be to the right of Allah, the ones below will not feel happy because of the enviable merits of the persons above.' Ibn abu Ya'fur then asked, 'How is it that they will not see when they are on the right of Allah?' The Imam said, 'O ibn abu Ya'fur, they are veiled with the light of Allah. Are you not aware of the Hadith that the Messenger of Allah said, 'Allah has a creature on the right of the Throne before Allah and on the right of Allah their faces are whiter than snow and brighter than the sun of the midday. Someone asks, 'Who are they?' It will be said, 'These are the ones who loved each other in the Glory of Allah.'"

H 2053, Ch. 71, h 10

It is narrated from him (narrator of the Hadith above) from 'Uthman ibn 'Isa from Muhammad ibn 'Ajlan who has said the following:

"Once, I was in the presence of abu 'Abd Allah, *'Alayhi al-Salam*, when a man came and offered the greeting of peace. The Imam asked, 'How are your brothers (in belief) whom you have left behind?' He praised, admired and extolled them. The Imam asked, 'Do their wealthy ones visit their poor ones?' He said, 'It is very rare.' The Imam asked, 'Do their rich ones reach out to the poor ones?' He said, 'It is very rare.'

"The Imam asked, 'Do their rich ones maintain good relations with their poor ones financially?' He said, 'You are speaking of the moral behavior that is practiced very rarely in our people.' The narrator has said that the Imam then asked, 'Why do you then think they are Shi'a (Muslims)?'"

H 2054, Ch. 71, h 11

Abu Ali al-Ash'ari has narrated from Muhammad ibn Salim from Ahmad ibn al-Nadr from abu Isma'il who has said the following:

"Once I said to abu Ja'far, *'Alayhi al-Salam*, 'May Allah keep my soul in service for your cause, there is a great number of Shi'a in our area. The Imam asked, 'Are their rich ones kind to their poor ones? Do their virtuous ones forgive their sinful ones? Do they assist each other financially?' I said, 'No, they do not do so.' The Imam said, 'They are not Shi'a. Shi'a are those who do these things.'"

H 2055, Ch. 71, h 12

Muhammad ibn Yahya has narrated from Ahmad ibn Muhammad ibn 'Isa from Muhammad ibn Sinan from al-'Ala' ibn Fudayl from abu 'Abd Allah, *'Alayhi al-Salam*, who has said the following:

"Abu Ja'far, *'Alayhi al-Salam*, would say, 'Dignify your people, honor them and do not be aggressive toward each other, do not harm each other and do not be jealous of each other. You must never be miserly and always be sincere servants of Allah.'"

H 2056, Ch. 71, h 13

Abu Ali al-Ash'ari has narrated from Muhammad ibn 'Abd al-Jabbar from ibn Faddal from 'Amr ibn Aban from Sa'id ibn al-Hassan who has said the following:

"Abu Ja'far, *'Alayhi al-Salam*, once asked me, 'Does your brother (in belief) come to you, stretch his hand in your pocket and take what he needs and you do not push him aside?' I said, 'I do not know that such things happen among us.' Abu Ja'far, *'Alayhi al-Salam*, then said, 'There is nothing then.' I said, 'It is destruction then.' The Imam said, 'The people have not yet recieved their power of reason.'"

H 2057, Ch. 71, h 14

Ali ibn Ibrahim has narrated from al-Husayn ibn al-Hassan from Muhammad ibn 'Uramah in a marfu' manner from Mu'alla ibn Khanis who has said the following:

"Once I asked abu 'Abd Allah, *'Alayhi al-Salam*, about the rights of the believer. The Imam said, 'There are seventy categories of rights but I will only tell you of seven; I am compassionate for you and I fear you may not be able to bear it.' I said, 'Yes, I will bear it, if Allah so wills.' The Imam said, 'You must not satisfy yourself with food while he is hungry, you must not dress up in finery while he may not have any clothes. You must be as his guide, as his shirt (a means of protection) that he wears, his tongue with which he speaks and love for him what you love for yourself. If you have a maiden servant, send her to prepare his bed and try to serve him during the day or night. If you do this you have connected your guardianship with our guardianship and with the guardianship of Allah, the Most Majestic, the Most Holy.'"

H 2058, Ch. 71, h 15

A number of our people have narrated from Ahmad ibn Muhammad from Ali ibn al-Hakam from abu al-Maghra' from abu 'Abd Allah, *'Alayhi al-Salam*, who has said the following:

"The Muslim is the brother of the Muslim (in belief). He does not do injustice to him, does not betray him, and does not violate his trust. It is worthwhile for the Muslims to be assiduous in maintaining good relations with each other, be kind to each other, assist the needy ones financially and be compassionate toward each other so that they can be as Allah, the Most Majestic, the Most Holy, has commanded them to be, 'Compassionate toward each other,'(48:29) kind to one another and feel sad for their absence from them. You should be just as the group of Ansar (the supporters) was in the lifetime of the Messenger of Allah, *'Alayhi al-Salam*, as mentioned in (48:29).'"

H 2059, Ch. 71, h 16

Ali ibn Ibrahim has narrated from his father from al-Nawfali from al-Sakuni from abu 'Abd Allah, *'Alayhi al-Salam*, who has said the following:

"The Messenger of Allah has said, 'It is a right upon a Muslim to inform his brothers (in belief) of his decision to go on a journey. It is a right upon his Muslim brothers to visit him when he returns from the journey.'"

Chapter 72 - Compassion and Leniency

H 2060, Ch. 72, h 1

A number of our people have narrated from Ahmad ibn Muhammad ibn Khalid from al-Hassan ibn Mahbub from Shu'ayb al-'Aqar Qufi who has said the following:

"I heard abu 'Abd Allah, *'Alayhi al-Salam*, saying to his companions, 'Be pious before Allah and be virtuous brothers who love each other for the sake of Allah, and maintain good relations leniently. Visit one another, meet and speak of our cause and preserve it.'"

H 2061, Ch. 72, h 2

Muhammad ibn Yahya has narrated from Ahmad ibn Muhammad ibn 'Isa from Muhammad ibn Sinan from Kulayb al-Saydawi from abu 'Abd Allah, *'Alayhi al-Salam*, who has said the following:

"Maintain good relations among yourselves, do good to each other, be compassionate with one another and be virtuous brothers as Allah, the Most Majestic, the Most Holy, has commanded you to be."

H 2062, Ch. 72, h 3

It is narrated from him (narrator of the Hadith above) from Muhammad ibn Sinan from 'Abd Allah ibn Yahya al-Kahili who has said the following:

"I heard abu 'Abd Allah, *'Alayhi al-Salam*, saying, 'Maintain good relations among yourselves, do good to one another, be compassionate and lenient to each other.'"

H 2063, Ch. 72, h 4

It is narrated from him (narrator of the Hadith above) from Ali ibn al-Hakam from abu al-Mighra' from abu 'Abd Allah, *'Alayhi al-Salam*, who has said the following:

"It is worthwhile for a Muslim to work assiduously to maintain good relations, to cooperate in kindness and assistance for the needy and to be compassionate to each other. Live out this so that you can be as Allah, the Most Majestic, the Most Holy, has commanded you to be, '. . . compassionate to each other, . . .' (48:29) show kindness to each other and feel sad for their absence from you. You should be just as the group of Ansar (the supporters) was in the lifetime of the Messenger of Allah, *'Alayhi al-Salam*, as mentioned in (48:29).'"

Chapter 73 - Visiting Brothers (in Belief)

H 2064, Ch. 73, h 1

Muhammad ibn Yahya has narrated from Ahmad ibn Muhammad ibn 'Isa from Ali ibn Faddal from Ali ibn 'Aqaba from abu Hamza from abu 'Abd Allah, *'Alayhi al-Salam*, who has said the following:

"Whoever visits his brother (in belief) for the sake of Allah and for no other reason, seeking thereby the promise of Allah, and to achieve what is with Allah, Allah will appoint seventy thousand angels who applaud, 'How beautiful is what you have done and how beautiful is paradise (for you).'"

H 2065, Ch. 73, h 2

It is narrated from him (narrator of the Hadith above) from Ali ibn al-Nu'man from ibn Muskan from Khaythamah who has said the following:

"Once I went to see abu Ja'far, *'Alayhi al-Salam*, to say farewell. He said, 'O Khaythamah, convey our greeting of peace to whoever of our followers you may see and advise them to be pious before Allah, the Most Great, that their rich ones look after their poor ones, the stronger ones look after their weaker ones, that the living attend the funeral of those who have just died, that they must meet each other in their homes; their meeting as such is life for our cause. May Allah bless the man who preserves our cause. O Khaythamah, inform our followers that we cannot make them independent of Allah in anything without good deeds and that they will not benefit from our Divine Authority without (al-Wari') refraining from worldly attractions (sins). Of the people who regret on the Day of Judgment, most intensely will be the ones who describe justice but do not practice it (explain the right belief but do not establish one).'"

H 2066, Ch. 73, h 3

Ali ibn Ibrahim has narrated from his father from Hammad ibn 'Isa from Ibrahim ibn 'Umar al-Yamani from Jabir from abu Ja'far, *'Alayhi al-Salam*, who has said the following:

"The Messenger of Allah has said, 'Jibril spoke to me that Allah, the Most Majestic, the Most Holy, sent an angel to earth and the angel began walking until he came to a door where a man was asking for permission from the people of the house. The angel asked him, 'What do you need from the owner of this house?' He replied, 'He is a Muslim brother (in belief). I have come to visit him for the sake of Allah, the Most Blessed, the Most High.' The angel then asked, 'Is that the only reason for your visit?' The man said, 'Nothing else has brought me here but that.' The angel then said, 'I am the Messenger of Allah to you and He sends you the greeting of peace and says, 'I have made paradise obligatory for you.' The angel then said, 'Allah, the Most Majestic, the Most Holy, says, 'Whoever of the Muslims visits an other Muslim, in fact, has not visited him but he has visited Me and his reward from Me is paradise.'"

H 2067, Ch. 73, h 4

Ali has narrated from his father from ibn abu 'Umayr from Ali al-Nahdi from al-Husayn from abu 'Abd Allah, *'Alayhi al-Salam*, who has said the following:

"Whoever visits his brother (in belief) for the sake of Allah, Allah, the Most Majestic, the Most Holy, then says, 'You in fact, have visited Me and with Me is your reward and I will not accept anything for your reward except paradise.'"

H 2068, Ch. 73, h 5

A number of our people have narrated from Ahmad ibn Muhammad from Ali ibn al-Hakam from Sayf ibn 'Amirah from Ya'qub ibn Shu'ayb who has said the following:

"I heard abu 'Abd Allah, *'Alayhi al-Salam*, saying, 'Whoever visits his brother (in belief) in a side of the city just to please Allah, has visited Him, and it becomes a responsibility for Allah to honor His visitor.'"

H 2069, Ch. 73, h 6

It is narrated from him (narrator of the Hadith above) from Ali ibn al-Hakam from Sayf ibn 'Amirah from Jabir from abu Ja'far, *'Alayhi al-Salam*, who has said the following:

"The Messenger of Allah has said, 'If one visits his brother (in belief) in his house, Allah, the Most Majestic, the Most Holy, will say, 'You are My guest and My visitor, your service is on Me and I, for your loving him, have made paradise obligatory for you.'"

H 2070, Ch. 73, h 7

It is narrated from him (narrator of the Hadith above) from Ali ibn al-Hakam from Ishaq ibn 'Ammar from abu Ghirrah who has said the following:

"I heard abu 'Abd Allah saying, 'If one visits his brother (in belief) for the sake of Allah, in his illness or in good health, not to deceive or to receive something, Allah will appoint seventy thousand angels to applaud behind him, "How beautiful is your deed! How beautiful is paradise for you! You are the visitor of Allah and the delegate to the Most Beneficent one." This happens until he comes home.' Yasyr then asked, 'May Allah keep my soul in service for your cause, is it so even if the place of visitation is far away?' The Imam said, 'Yes, O Yasyr, even if the place of visitation is at a distance of one year's journey; Allah is generous and the angles are a great many. They escort him until he reaches his home.'"

H 2071, Ch. 73, h 8

Ali ibn Ibrahim has narrated from his father from ibn abu 'Umayr from Ali ibn al-Nahdi from abu 'Abd Allah, *'Alayhi al-Salam*, who has said the following:

"If one visits his brother (in belief) due to Allah's relation and for the sake of Allah, on the Day of Judgment he will come, walking elegantly in a Coptic gown of light and will not pass by anything but that it will shine until he will come before Allah, the Most Majestic, the Most Holy, and Allah, the Most Majestic, the Most Holy, will say, 'Welcome.' When He will say welcome, He, the Most Majestic, the Most Holy, will make his reward very handsome.'"

H 2072, Ch. 73, h 9

Muhammad ibn Yahya has narrated from Ahmad ibn Muhammad ibn 'Isa from Muhammad ibn Khalid and al-Husayn ibn Sa'id from al-Nadr ibn Suwayd from Yahya ibn 'Imran al-Halabi from Bashir from abu Hamza from abu Ja'far, *'Alayhi al-Salam*, who has said the following:

"If a Muslim (believing) servant (of Allah) comes out of his house to visit his brother, due to Allah's relation, not for any other reason and just because of Allah, with interest in what is with Allah, Allah, the Majestic, the Glorious, appoints seventy thousand angels who applaud behind him until he comes home, 'How beautiful is your deed! How beautiful is paradise for you!'"

H 2073, Ch. 73, h 10

Al-Husayn ibn Muhammad has narrated from [Ahmad ibn Muhammad] from Ahmad ibn Ishaq from Bakr ibn Muhammad from abu 'Abd Allah, *'Alayhi al-Salam*, who has said the following:

"Whenever a Muslim visits his Muslim brother, due to Allah's relation, and for the sake of Allah, Allah, the Majestic, the Glorious, will say, 'O visitor, how beautiful is your deed! How beautiful is paradise as your reward!'"

H 2074, Ch. 73, h 11

Muhammad ibn Yahya has narrated from Ahmad ibn Muhammad from A number of our people have narrated from Sahl ibn Ziyad all from ibn Mahbub from abu Ayyub from Muhammad ibn Qays from abu Ja'far, *'Alayhi al-Salam*, who has said the following:

"Allah, the Most Majestic, the Most Holy, has a paradise wherein no one can go except three: (a) a man who issues judgment against himself with truth, (b) a man who visits his brother, due to Allah's relation, and (c) a man who gives preference to his believing brother (in belief), due to Allah's relation.'"

H 2075, Ch. 73, h 12

Muhammad ibn Yahya has narrated from Muhammad ibn al-Husayn from Muhammad ibn Isma'il ibn Bazi' from Salih ibn 'Aqabah from 'Abd Allah ibn Muhammad al-Juhfi from abu Ja'far, *'Alayhi al-Salam*, who has said the following:

"When the believer leaves home to visit his brother (in belief), Allah, the Most Majestic, the Most Holy, appoints an angel to place one wing on earth and one wing in the sky to provide him shadow. When he arrives at his house, the Almighty Allah, the Most Blessed, the Most High, will say, 'O servant (of Allah) who has observed My right with greatness, and followed the tradition of My prophet, it is a right with Me to grant you dignity. Ask Me and I will give you, pray to Me I will answer and if you remain silent I will initiate.' When he returns, the angel will escort him with his wings providing shadow for him until he arrives at his home. Then Allah, the Most Blessed, the Most High, will say, 'O servant (of Allah) who has observed My right with greatness, it is a right with Me to give you honor and I have made it necessary that you be admitted into My paradise. I have granted you permission to intercede for My servants.'"

H 2076, Ch. 73, h 13

Salih ibn 'Aqabah has narrated from 'Aqabah from abu 'Abd Allah, *'Alayhi al-Salam*, who has said the following:

"Visiting the believing brother (in belief) is certainly better than setting free ten believing slaves. Whoever sets free a believing slave for each part of the body of the slave, one part of his body will be protected against fire, and even the private part will be protected."

H 2077, Ch. 73, h 14

Salih ibn 'Aqabah has narrated from Safwan al-Jammal from abu 'Abd Allah, *'Alayhi al-Salam*, who has said the following:

"Whichever three believing brothers (in belief) come together to a brother (in belief) of theirs from whose evils they feel safe, who are not afraid of his rebellion, and who have good hopes in him, if they pray to Allah their prayers will be answered, if they ask, their wish will be granted, if they ask for more it will be increased and if they remain silent, He will initiate."

H 2078, Ch. 73, h 15

Ali ibn Ibrahim has narrated from his father from ibn abu 'Umayr from abu Ayyub who has said the following:

"I heard abu Hamza saying, 'I heard the good servant (of Allah) saying, "Whoever visits his believing brother (in belief) for the sake of Allah and for no other reason, seeking thereby the reward from Allah, the promise of Allah, the Most Majestic, the Most Holy, will come true and Allah, the Most Majestic, the Most Holy, will appoint seventy thousand angels, from the time he leaves his home to the time he returns home, applaud behind him, 'How beautiful is your deed! How beautiful is paradise for you! You have found a dwelling in paradise.'"

H 2079, Ch. 73, h 16

Ali ibn Ibrahim has narrated from his father from al-Nawfali from al-Sakuni from abu 'Abd Allah, *'Alayhi al-Salam*, who has said the following:

"Amir al-Mu'minin (Ali ibn abu Talib), *'Alayhi al-Salam*, has said, 'Meeting of brothers (in belief) is a great opportunity, even if they are very few.'"

Chapter 74 - Greeting with Handshake

H 2080, Ch. 74, h 1

A number of our people have narrated from Ahmad ibn Muhammad from ibn Faddal from Tha'labah ibn Mayamun from Yahya ibn Zakariya from abu 'Ubaydah who has said the following:

"'Ubaydah has said, 'Once I was a partner of abu Ja'far, *'Alayhi al-Salam*, on a journey. During the journey, first I would take my seat in the carriage set up on the back of the carry animal and then he would take his seat. He after settling down on his place properly would offer me the greeting of peace and ask a question like a person who has never met the other person. He would also shake hands.' The narrator has said, 'He after dismounting would do so before me and after finding our places on the ground he would offer the greeting of peace and ask questions like he had never met me.' I then said, 'O descendent of the Messenger of Allah, you do things that no one before us has done. Doing (such formalities) only once is more than enough.' The Imam asked, 'Do you know what is in a handshake? The believers meet and shake hands, the sins continue falling off of them just like leaves fall off the trees, and Allah looks upon them until they depart from each other.'"

H 2081, Ch. 74, h 2

It is narrated from him (narrator of the Hadith above) from ibn Faddal from Ali ibn 'Uqbah from abu Khalid al-Qammat from abu Ja'far, *'Alayhi al-Salam*, who has said the following:

"When the believing people meet and shake hands Allah inserts His hand between their hands and shakes hands with the one whose love for his brother (in belief) is more intense.'"

H 2082, Ch. 74, h 3

Ibn Faddal has narrated from Ali ibn 'Uqbah from Ayyub from al-Sumayda' from Malik ibn 'A'Yun al-Juhni from abu Ja'far, *'Alayhi al-Salam*, who has said the following:

'When two believing people meet and shake hands Allah, the Most Majestic, the Most Holy, inserts His hand between their hands and faces the one whose love for his brother (in belief) is more intense. When Allah, the Most Majestic, the Most Holy, turns His face to them their sins begin to fall like leaves from trees.'"

H 2083, Ch. 74, h 4

Ali ibn Ibrahim has narrated from his father from ibn abu 'Umayr from Hisham ibn Salim from abu 'Ubaydah al-Hadhdha' from abu Ja'far, *'Alayhi al-Salam*, who has said the following:

"When two believing people meet and shake hands Allah, the Most Majestic, the Most Holy, turns His face (direction, aspect) to them and sins began to fall from them like leaves fall from trees.'"

H 2084, Ch. 74, h 5

A number of our people have narrated from Sahl ibn Ziyad from Ahmad ibn Muhammad ibn abu Nasr from Safwan al-Jammal from abu 'Ubaydah al-Hadhdha' who has said the following:

"Once I was a partner of abu Ja'far, *'Alayhi al-Salam*, on a journey on one side of the carriage on the camel from Madina to Makka. On the way he dismounted for rest and, when he returned, he asked me for a handshake. He squeezed my hand so hard that my fingers began to hurt. He then said, 'O abu 'Ubaydah, when two Muslims meet, shake hands and crisscross their fingers, their sins begin to fall from them like leaves fall from trees on a fall day.'"

H 2085, Ch. 74, h 6

Ali ibn Ibrahim has narrated from Muhammad ibn 'Isa from Yunus from Yahya al-Halabi from Malik al-Juhni who has said the following:

"Abu Ja'far, *'Alayhi al-Salam*, once said to me, 'O Malik, you are of our followers (Shi'a). Are you aware that you go to extremes in our cause? No one is able to describe Allah. Just as no one is able to describe Allah, no one is able to describe us. Just as no one is able to describe us, no one is able to describe the believer. When a believer meets the believer and shakes hands, Allah continues looking at them and sins fall from their faces like leaves fall from trees until they depart each other. How then is one able to describe one who is as such?'"

H 2086, Ch. 74, h 7

Muhammad ibn Yahya has narrated from Ahmad ibn Muhammad ibn 'Isa from 'Umar ibn 'Abd al-'Aziz from Muhammad ibn Fudayl from abu Hamza who has said the following:

"Once I was a partner of abu Ja'far, *'Alayhi al-Salam*, on a journey. On the way we unloaded our luggage and he walked a little and came back, held my hand and squeezed it hard. I asked, 'May Allah keep my soul in service for your cause, 'Was I not with you in the carriage?' The Imam asked, 'Did you not know that when the believer comes around, and holds the hand of his brother (in belief), Allah faces them and looks at them. He continues facing them and says to the sins to fall off of them and they began to fall, O abu Hamza, like leaves that fall from trees. They then depart and there no sins will be left on them.'"

H 2087, Ch. 74, h 8

Ali ibn Ibrahim has narrated from his father from ibn abu 'Umayr from Hisham ibn Salim who has said the following:

"Once I asked abu 'Abd Allah, *'Alayhi al-Salam*, 'How often is this handshake?' The Imam said, 'It is just after going around a palm tree.'"

H 2088, Ch. 74, h 9

Muhammad ibn Yahya has narrated from Ahmad ibn Muhammad ibn 'Isa from Muhammad ibn Sinan from 'Amr ibn al-Afraq from abu 'Ubaydah from abu Ja'far, *'Alayhi al-Salam*, who has said the following:

"It is a good idea for the believers to shake each other's hands after one of them remains out of sight, even because of a tree in between."

H 2089, Ch. 74, h 10

A number of our people have narrated from Ahmad ibn Muhammad ibn Khalid from certain individuals of his people from Muhammad ibn al-Muthanna from his father from 'Uthman ibn Zayd from Jabir from abu Ja'far, *'Alayhi al-Salam*, who has said the following:

"The Messenger of Allah has said, 'Whenever any of you meets his Muslim brother (in belief) he should offer him the greeting of peace and shake his hand; Allah, the Most Majestic, the Most Holy, has honored the angels with it and you should also do what the angels do.'"

H 2090, Ch. 74, h 11

It is narrated from him (narrator of the Hadith above) from Muhammad ibn Ali from abu Baqqah from Sayf ibn 'Amirah from 'Amr ibn Shamir from Jabir from abu Ja'far, *'Alayhi al-Salam*, who has said the following:

"The Messenger of Allah has said, 'Whenever you meet, you should do so by offering the greeting of peace and shaking hands and depart each other with a plea to Allah for forgiveness.'"

H 2091, Ch. 74, h 12

It is narrated from him (narrator of the Hadith above) from Musa ibn al-Qasim from his grandfather, Mu'awiyah ibn Wahab or from others from Razin from abu 'Abd Allah, *'Alayhi al-Salam*, who has said the following:

"During an armed expedition the Muslims, along with the Messenger of Allah, each time after passing through a wooded area on reaching the open would look at each other and shake hands."

H 2092, Ch. 74, h 13

It is narrated from him (narrator of the Hadith above) from his father from those who narrated to him from Zayd ibn al-Jahm al-Hilali from Malik ibn 'Ayun from abu Ja'far, *'Alayhi al-Salam*, who has said the following:

"When two people shake hands, the one who continues holding his hand will receive greater reward than the one who releases early. However, the sins fall off of them until no sins remain."

H 2093, Ch. 74, h 14

A number of our people have narrated from Sahl ibn Ziyad from Yahya ibn al-Mubarak from 'Abd Allah ibn Jabalah from Ishaq ibn 'Ammar who has said the following:

"Once I went to see abu 'Abd Allah, *'Alayhi al-Salam*, and he looked at me frowning. I asked, 'May I know how I have disappointed you?' The Imam said, 'It is that which has changed you toward your brothers (in belief). It has come to my notice, O Ishaq, that you have appointed someone at your door to drive away the poor people of the Shi'a (our followers).' I then said, 'May Allah keep my soul in service for your cause, I was afraid of publicity.' The Imam asked, 'Why did you not fear misfortune? Did you not know that when two believing people meet and shake each other's hands Allah, the Most Majestic, the Most Holy, sends blessings upon them and ninety-nine parts of the reward go to the one who loves his believing brother (in belief) more intensely. If they love equally blessings (of Allah) encompass them both? When they sit to speak to each other the guardian angels will say to each other, 'Leave them alone, perhaps they have certain secret matters to discuss, and Allah has provided cover for them.' I then said, 'Has Allah not said, '. . . since the two scribes are sitting on each of his shoulders, he does not utter a word that is not recorded immediately by the watchful scribes.' (50:17) The Imam said, 'O Ishaq, if the scribes do not hear, the One who know all secrets hears and sees.'"

H 2094, Ch. 74, h 15

It is narrated from him (narrator of the Hadith above) from Isma'il ibn Mehran from Ayman ibn Muhriz from abu 'Abd Allah, *'Alayhi al-Salam*, who has said the following:

"When shaking hands with people, the Messenger of Allah had never been the first to discontinue the handshake."

H 2095, Ch. 74, h 16

Ali ibn Ibrahim has narrated from his father from Hammad from Rib'i from Zurara who has said the following:

"I heard abu Ja'far, *'Alayhi al-Salam*, saying, 'Allah, the Most Majestic, the Most Holy, cannot be described and how can He be described when He says in His book, "They have not revered (honored and respected) Allah properly. . . ."" (22:74) He cannot be described through measurement. He is greater than such measures of respect. The Holy Prophet cannot be described and respected. How can a servant (of Allah) be described whom Allah, the Most Majestic, the Most Holy, has veiled with seven things (no explanation for this seven is available). He has made obedience to him on earth like the obedience to His own self in heavens saying, 'Take only what the Messenger gives to you and desist from what he forbids you,' (59:7) whoever obeys him has obeyed Me and whoever disobeys him has disobeyed Me. He (Allah) made him to be the in charge person of the affairs. We also cannot be described and how can a people be described from whom Allah has removed all rijs (uncleanness), which, applies to doubt (doubt is uncleanness). The believing people also cannot be described. When the believer meets his brother (in belief) and they shake hands Allah continues looking at them and the sins fall from their faces like leaves fall off trees.'"

H 2096, Ch. 74, h 17

Muhammad ibn Yahya has narrated from Ahmad ibn Muhammad ibn 'Isa from Ali ibn al-Nu'man from Fudayl ibn 'Uthman from abu 'Ubaydah who has said the following:

"I heard abu Ja'far, *'Alayhi al-Salam*, saying, 'When two believing people meet and shake hands, Allah turns to them with His face and sins began to fall from their faces until they depart from each other.'"

H 2097, Ch. 74, h 18

Ali ibn Ibrahim has narrated from his father from al-Nawfali from al-Sakuni from abu 'Abd Allah, *'Alayhi al-Salam*, who has said the following:

"Abu 'Abd Allah, *'Alayhi al-Salam*, has said, 'Do shake hands, it removes jealousy."

H 2098, Ch. 74, h 19

A number of our people have narrated from Sahl ibn Ziyad from Ja'far ibn Muhammad al-Ash'ari from ibn al-Qaddah from abu 'Abd Allah, *'Alayhi al-Salam*, who has said the following:

"The Holy Prophet once met Hudhayfah and he extended his hand, but Hudhayfah held his hand back. The Holy Prophet asked, 'How is it, O Hudhayfah, that I extended my hand to you and you held your hand back?' Hudhayfah then said, 'O Messenger of Allah, your hand is attractive but I had not taken the shower that was required of me due to carnal relations and I did not like to touch your hand with my hand that is not formally cleansed.' The Holy Prophet then said, 'Did you not know that when the Muslims meet and shake hands, their sins fall from them like leaves from trees?'"

H 2099, Ch. 74, h 20

Al-Husayn ibn Muhammad has narrated from Ahmad ibn Ishaq from Bakr ibn Muhammad from Ishaq ibn 'Ammar who has said the following:

"Abu 'Abd Allah, *'Alayhi al-Salam*, has said, 'No one is able to describe Allah, the Most Majestic, the Most Holy, as He should be described. In the same way His Holy Prophet cannot be described. Also, the importance of the believing people cannot be described. When he meets his brother (in belief) and shakes hands, Allah looks toward them and sins began to fall from their faces like strong wind blows away leaves from trees, until they depart each other.'"

H 2100, Ch. 74, h 21

Ali ibn Ibrahim has narrated from his father from Muhammad ibn 'Isa from Yunus from Rifa'a who has said the following:

"I heard abu 'Abd Allah, *'Alayhi al-Salam*, saying, 'A handshake of believing people is better than a handshake of angels.'"

Chapter 75 - Holding in One's Arm

H 2101, Ch. 75, h 1

Muhammad ibn Yahya has narrated from Muhammad ibn al-Husayn from Muhammad ibn Isma'il ibn Bazi' from Salih ibn 'Aqabah from 'Abd Allah ibn Muhammad al-Ju'fi from abu Ja'far and abu 'Abd Allah, *'Alayhi al-Salam*, who has said the following:

"Any believer who leaves (his home) to visit his brother (in belief) because of his knowledge of the importance of such person, Allah writes for him, for every step, one good deed, deletes one evil deed, and raises him one degree in meritorious status. When he knocks at his door, the doors to heaven open to him. When they meet, shake hands and hold each other in their arm Allah turns to them with His face and expresses pride because of them to the angels and says, 'Look at My two servants who are visiting each other and love each other for My sake. It is a right upon Me not to make them suffer in fire in the hereafter. When he returns the angels, numbering equal to the number of his breaths, steps and words, will escort him. They protect him against the misfortunes of this world and the hardships of the hereafter up to a similar night next year. If he dies in between he will be exempt from presenting an account of his deeds. If the person visited would know the importance of the visitor as he knew of his importance, he also will have the same privileges."

H 2102, Ch. 75, h 2

Ali ibn Ibrahim has narrated from his father from Safwan ibn Yahya from Ishaq ibn 'Ammar from abu 'Abd Allah, *'Alayhi al-Salam*, who has said the following:

"When two believing people embrace each other, blessings engulf them. When they hold each other just for the sake of Allah and for no worldly reasons, it then will be said to them, 'You are forgiven, resume your deeds.' When they begin asking about each other the angels will say to each other, 'Keep away from them; they have secret matters and Allah has granted them cover and privacy.' I (Ishaq) then asked, 'May Allah keep my soul in service for your cause, how is it that the angels do not write their words when Allah, the Most Majestic, the Most Holy, has said, ". . . he does not utter a word which is not recorded immediately by the watchful scribes"?' (50:17) The narrator has said that abu 'Abd Allah, *'Alayhi al-Salam*, took a breath of sigh and wept so much that his tears drenched his beard, and he said, 'O Ishaq, Allah, the Most Blessed, the Most High, commands the angels to leave the believing people who meet each other alone just because of respect for them; otherwise, if the angels do not write their words or do not know them, He knows and saves them; He knows all the secrets and the hidden things.'"

Chapter 76 - Kissing

H 2103, Ch. 76, h 1

Abu Ali al-Ash'ari has narrated from al-Hassan ibn Ali al-Kufi from 'Ubays ibn Hisham from al-Husayn ibn Ahmad al-Minqari from Yunus ibn Zabyan from abu 'Abd Allah, *'Alayhi al-Salam*, who has said the following:

"In you there is a light by which you are identified in this world. It is as such that even when one of you meets his brother (in belief) he kisses him at the place of light in his forehead."

H 2104, Ch. 76, h 2

Ali ibn Ibrahim has narrated from his father from ibn abu 'Umayr from Rufa'ah ibn Musa from abu 'Abd Allah, *'Alayhi al-Salam*, who has said the following:

"No one's head or hand is kissed except those of the Messenger of Allah or one who is intended to be for the Messenger of Allah."

H 2105, Ch. 76, h 3

Ali has narrated from his father from ibn abu 'Umayr from Zayd al-Narsi from Ali ibn Mazid Sahib al-Sabiri who has said the following:

"Once I went to see abu 'Abd Allah, *'Alayhi al-Salam*, and I held and kissed his hand and the Imam said, 'This is only for the Holy Prophet or his successor.'"

H 2106, Ch. 76, h 4

Muhammad ibn Yahya has narrated from Ahmad ibn Muhammad ibn 'Isa from al-Hajjal from Yunus ibn Ya'qub who has said the following:

"Once I went to see abu 'Abd Allah, *'Alayhi al-Salam*, and I asked, 'Can I kiss your hand, please?' The Imam agreed and I kissed his hand. I then asked, 'May Allah keep my soul in service for your cause, can I kiss your head, please?' The Imam agreed and I kissed his head. Then I asked, 'Can I kiss your feet, please?' The Imam said, 'You had vowed, you had vowed, you had vowed, three and one remains, one remains, and one remains." (The Imam perhaps indicated that the narrator, in fact, had vowed to kiss the Imam's (a) hand, (b) head and (c) feet).'"

H 2107, Ch. 76, h 5
Muhammad ibn Yahya has narrated from al-'Amraki ibn Ali ibn Ja'far from abu al-Hassan, *'Alayhi al-Salam*, who has said the following:

"Whoever of the relatives kisses a relative out of compassion he has not committed any offense. A brother may kiss the cheek of his brother. Kissing an Imam is between his eyes."

H 2108, Ch. 76, h 6
It is narrated from him (narrator of the Hadith above) from Ahmad ibn Muhammad ibn Khalid from Muhammad ibn Sinan from abu al-Sabbah Mawla of Ale Sam from abu 'Abd Allah, *'Alayhi al-Salam*, who has said the following:

"Kissing on the mouth is only for the spouses and a small child."

Chapter 77 - Speak of and Remember the Brothers (in belief)

H 2109, Ch. 77, h 1
A number of our people have narrated from Ahmad ibn Muhammad ibn Khalid from his father from Fadalah ibn Ayyub from Ali ibn abu Hamza who has said the following:

"I heard abu 'Abd Allah, *'Alayhi al-Salam*, saying, 'Our Shi'a are compassionate to each other. When alone they speak of and remember Allah. To speak of us is to speak of Allah. When we are mentioned Allah is mentioned, but when our enemies are spoken of it is like speaking of Satan.'"

H 2110, Ch. 77, h 2
Muhammad ibn Yahya has narrated from Muhammad ibn al-Husayn from Muhammad ibn Isma'il ibn Bazi' from Salih ibn 'Aqabah from Yazid ibn 'Abd al-Malik from abu 'Abd Allah, *'Alayhi al-Salam*, who has said the following:

"Visit each other; in it there is a revival for your hearts and a study of our Ahadith (may take place). Our Ahadith helps you to be kind to each other. If you follow them you will find guidance and salvation in them. If you disregard them you will go astray and be destroyed. Therefore, follow them and I will assure you of your salvation."

H 2111, Ch. 77, h 3
A number of our people have narrated from Sahl ibn Ziyad from al-Washsha' from Mansur ibn Yunus from 'Abbad ibn Kathir who has said the following:

"I said to abu 'Abd Allah, *'Alayhi al-Salam*, 'Once I passed by a storyteller who said to his audience, "This is a gathering whose attendants do not suffer wickedness."' The narrator has said that abu 'Abd Allah, *'Alayhi al-Salam*, then said, 'How extremely far is it from reality!' You passed by the wrong gathering. (Astahahum al-Hufrah) How terribly wrong is their expresssion! Allah has certain angels who visit places, and they are other than the honorable scribes. When they pass by a people, who speak of Muhammad and Ale Muhammad, *'Alayhim al-Salam*, these angels say, "Stop here. You have found what you needed." They will sit down and begin to think and understand with them. When the gathering disperses they visit their people suffering due to ill health, attend their funerals and look after those of them who are absent. That is the gathering whose attendants do not suffer wickedness.'"

H 2112, Ch. 77, h 4

Muhammad ibn Yahya has narrated from Ahmad ibn Muhammad ibn 'Isa from Ali ibn al-Hakam from al-Mustawrid al-Nakha'i from those whom he has mentioned (in his book) from abu 'Abd Allah, *'Alayhi al-Salam*, who has said the following:

"Certain angels of heaven look at one, two or three people on earth speak of the excellence and praise of Muhammad and his family and they say, 'Look the small number of these people, their enemies so numerous, they still speak of the praise of Muhammad and his family, *'Alayhim al-Salam.*' The Imam then said, 'Another group of angels say to them, 'It is a favor to them from Allah that He grants to whomever He wants, Allah possesses a great deal of favors.'"

H 2113, Ch. 77, h 5

It is narrated from him (narrator of the Hadith above) from Ahmad ibn Muhammad from ibn Faddal from ibn Muskan from Muyassir who has said the following:

"Once abu Ja'far, *'Alayhi al-Salam*, asked me, 'Do you hold private gatherings wherein you say whatever you want?' I said, 'Yes, I swear by Allah, we hold private gatherings and say whatever we like to say (in praise of Muhammad and his family).' The Imam said, 'I swear by Allah, I wish I could be with you at such gatherings. I swear by Allah, I love your fragrance and your spirits. You, certainly, follow the religion of Allah, and the religion of the angels. Pay attention to restraining from the worldly attractions (sins) and assist yourselves with striving hard in work.'"

H 2114, Ch. 77, h 6

Al-Husayn ibn Muhammad and Muhammad ibn Yahya all have narrated from Ali ibn Muhammad ibn Sa'd from Muhammad ibn Muslim from Ahmad ibn Zakariya from Muhammad ibn Khalid ibn Maymun from 'Abd Allah ibn Sinan from Ghiyath ibn Ibrahim from abu 'Abd Allah, *'Alayhi al-Salam*, who has said the following:

"Abu 'Abd Allah, *'Alayhi al-Salam*, has said, 'Wherever three or more believing people gather together an equal number of angels also attend it (gathering). If they pray for a good purpose the angels say Amen! If they seek protection (from Allah) against an evil matter, the angels pray to Allah to divert it from them. If they pray so their wishes come true, the angels intercede for them before Allah and pray to Him to grant their wishes. Wherever three or more rejectors (of belief) gather together, ten times their number, Satan also attends it. If they speak Satan also speaks likewise, if they laugh, they (Satans) laugh with them. If they succeed (in abuse) against the friends of Allah, they (Satans) do the same. If any of the believing people is trapped among them and when they involve themselves in such behaviors he should move away from them so he does not become of the attendance along with Satan; the wrath of Allah, the Most Majestic, the Most Holy, is insurmountable and His condemnation is irremovable.' The Imam, *'Alayhi al-Salam*, then said, 'If he cannot do so (move away) he must condemn it in his heart and stand up even for a short while and move a little, like the time of allowing the young animal to have its share of milk while milking the mother.'"

171

H 2115, Ch. 77, h 7

Through the same chain of narrators it is narrated from Muhammad ibn Sulayman from Muhammad ibn Mahfuz from abu al-Maghra' who has said the following:

"I heard abu al-Hassan, *'Alayhi al-Salam*, saying, 'There is nothing more injurious to Satan and his soldiers than believing people's visitation of their brothers (in belief) for the sake of Allah.' The Imam said, 'When believing people meet each other, speak of Allah and speak of the praise and excellence of Ahl al-Bayt, all the flesh at the face of Satan disappear, he even cries for help due to the severity of his suffering and the angels of heaven sense it as well as the keepers of paradise and they all condemn him until all the angels close to Allah condemn him and Satan remains humiliated, frustrated and defeated.'"

Chapter 78 - To Please the Believers

H 2116, Ch. 78, h 1

A number of our people have narrated from Sahl ibn Ziyad and Muhammad ibn Yahya from Ahmad ibn Muhammad ibn 'Isa all from al-Hassan ibn Mahbub from abu Hamza al-Thumali who has said the following:

"I heard abu Ja'far, *'Alayhi al-Salam*, saying, 'The messenger of Allah has said, "Whoever pleases a believer has pleased me, and whoever pleases me has pleased Allah.""

H 2117, Ch. 78, h 2

A number of our people have narrated from Ahmad ibn Muhammad ibn Khalid from his father from a man from the people of al-Kufah called abu Muhammad from 'Amr ibn Shamir from Jabir from abu Ja'far, *'Alayhi al-Salam*, who has said the following:

"The smiling of a man for his brother (in belief) is a good deed, so also is removing a speck from him (his eyes). Allah is not worshipped with anything more beloved to Him than bringing joy to the heart of a believer."

H 2118, Ch. 78, h 3

Muhammad ibn Yahya has narrated from Ahmad ibn Muhammad ibn 'Isa from Muhammad ibn Sinan from 'Abd Allah ibn Muskan from 'Ubayd Allah ibn al-Walid al-Wassafi who has said the following:

"I heard abu Ja'far, *'Alayhi al-Salam*, saying, 'Of the private conversations that Allah, the Most Majestic, the Most Holy, made with Moses was this: 'Of my servants there are those to whom I have allotted my paradise and made them rule it.' Moses then asked, Lord, 'Who are these people to whom you have allotted your paradise and made them rule it?' The Lord said, 'They are those who bring joy to the heart of a believer.' He then said, 'A believing man once lived in the domain of a tyrant and because of fear he moved away from the tyrant into a pagan's land and he found lodging with a pagan who provided him shadow, came forward with friendly behavior and entertained him as a guest. When death approached the pagan man, Allah, the Most Majestic, the Most Holy, inspired him, 'I swear by my Majesty and Glory, had I any place for you in my paradise I would have admitted you therein, but it is forbidden for those who die as pagans. However, O fire, calm down and do not hurt him. His sustenance will be provided in both ends of the day.' I then asked the Imam, '(Does it come) from paradise?' The Imam said, 'It comes from wherever Allah wishes.'"

H 2119, Ch. 78, h 4

It is narrated from him (narrator of the Hadith above) from Bakr ibn Salih from al-Hassan ibn Ali from 'Abd Allah ibn Ibrahim from Ali ibn abu Ali from abu 'Abd Allah from his father from Ali ibn al-Husayn, *'Alayhi al-Salam*, who has said the following:

"The Messenger of Allah has said, 'Of the most beloved deed to Allah, the Most Majestic, the Most Holy, is bringing joy to the heart of the believer.'"

H 2120, Ch. 78, h 5

Ali ibn Ibrahim has narrated from his father from ibn Mahbub from 'Abd Allah ibn Sinan from abu 'Abd Allah, *'Alayhi al-Salam*, who has said the following:

"Allah, the Most Majestic, the Most Holy, sent revelations to David that said, 'One of my servants may come to Me with a good deed and I admit him in paradise.' David asked, 'Lord, what is that good deed?' The Lord said, 'It is bringing joy to the heart of my believing servant even if it is by one piece of date.' David then said, 'Lord, it is very true that one who comes to know You must not lose hope of Your kindness.'"

H 2121, Ch. 78, h 6

A number of our people have narrated from Ahmad ibn Muhammad ibn Khalid from his father from Khalaf ibn Hammad from Mufaddal ibn 'Umar from abu 'Abd Allah, *'Alayhi al-Salam*, who has said the following:

"One of you must not think that when he brings joy to the heart of a believer he has brought joy to his heart only. I swear by Allah, in fact, he has done so to our hearts and also, I swear by Allah, he has done so to (the heart of) the Messenger of Allah."

H 2122, Ch. 78, h 7

Ali ibn Ibrahim has narrated from his father and Muhammad ibn Isma'il from Fadl ibn Shadhan all from ibn abu 'Umayr from Ibrahim ibn 'Abd al-Hamid from abu al-Jarud from abu Ja'far, *'Alayhi al-Salam*, who has said the following:

"I heard abu Ja'far, *'Alayhi al-Salam*, saying, 'The most beloved of deeds to Allah, the Most Majestic, the Most Holy, is bringing joy to the heart of a believer, by means of satisfying his hunger or paying off his debt.'"

H 2123, Ch. 78, h 8

Muhammad ibn Yahya has narrated from Ahmad ibn Muhammad ibn 'Isa from al-Hassan ibn Mahbub from Sadir al-Sayrafi who has said the following:

"Abu 'Abd Allah, *'Alayhi al-Salam*, has said in a long Hadith, 'When Allah raises a believer from his grave along with him, in front, comes out a form. When and wherever the believer faces a frightening scene of the scenes of the Day of Judgment the form says to him, "Do not be afraid or sad. There is good and joyful news of the honor from Allah, the Most Majestic, the Most Holy," until he is before Allah, the Most Majestic, the Most Holy. He is held accountable very lightly and then is admitted into paradise with the form in front of him. The believer then says to the form, 'May Allah grant you blessings, you have been a very good companion ever since you came out with me from my grave and continued speaking of joy and honor from Allah until I experienced them. Who are you?' The form will say, 'I am the joy that you had brought to the heart of your believing brother (in belief) in the worldly life. Allah, the Most Majestic, the Most Holy, created me from it to carry good news to you.'"

H 2124, Ch. 78, h 9

Muhammad ibn Yahya has narrated from Muhammad ibn Ahmad from al-Sayyari from Muhammad ibn Jumhur who has said the following:

"Al-Najashiy, is a man of the landlords (community) and an agent in al-Ahwaz and Fars. Certain persons of his workers once said to abu 'Abd Allah, *'Alayhi al-Salam,* 'In the office of al-Najashiy taxes are recorded as due by me. He is a believer and believes in obedience to you. If you consider it proper, write for me a letter to him (to relieve me of the taxes).' Abu 'Abd Allah, *'Alayhi al-Salam,* wrote him, '(I begin) in the name of Allah, the Beneficent the Merciful. Send joy to the heart of your brother, Allah will send joy to your heart.'

"When the letter came he took it to him in his office. When it was private he gave him the letter and said, 'This is a letter from abu 'Abd Allah, *'Alayhi al-Salam.'* He kissed the letter and placed it on his eyes and asked, 'What do you want?' He said, 'Certain taxes are recorded in your office as due by me.' He then asked, 'How much are they?' He said, 'Ten thousand dirham.' He then called his secretary and told him to write off all the taxes due by him, and he said not to levy any taxes on him in future. Then he asked, 'Did I make you happy now?' He replied, 'Yes, may I be your servant.' He then ordered to give him an animal so he could ride, a maid servant, a male servant and a set of dress and for each item he would ask, 'Did I make you happy?' He would say, 'Yes, may I be your servant.' As long as he said, 'Yes, he increased his gifts until the last gift. He then said, 'Take the floor covering of this house wherein you gave me the letter of my master and asked me to help you in your needs.'

"I (the narrator) did so as I was told and then went to abu 'Abd Allah, *'Alayhi al-Salam,* and informed him of his story the way it had happened. The Imam enjoyed what he had done. I then said, 'O descendent of the Messenger of Allah, it seems he has made you happy by means of his favors to me.' The Imam said, 'Yes, by Allah, he certainly has made Allah and the Messenger of Allah happy.'"

H 2125, Ch. 78, h 10

Abu Ali al-Ash'ari has narrated from Muhammad ibn 'Abd al-Jabbar from al-Hassan ibn Ali ibn Faddal from Mansur from 'Ammar ibn abu al-Yaqzan from Aban ibn Taghlib who has said the following:

"Once I asked abu 'Abd Allah, *'Alayhi al-Salam,* about the rights of a believer on another believer. He has said that the Imam said, 'The right of a believer on a believer is greater than that (description). If I tell you about it you will become unbelievers. When a believer comes out of his grave a form comes out with him and says, "There is good news of honor and happiness for you from Allah." He then says to the form, 'May Allah give you good news.' He then moves with him and gives him good news as before and as they come across a frightening scene of the Day of Judgment the form says this is not against you. As they come across a good thing the form says this is for you. The form remains with him, giving him comfort and good news of what he loves until it stands with him before Allah, the Most Majestic, the Most Holy, where He orders for him to be taken to paradise. The form says to him, 'Good news for you; Allah, the Most Majestic, the Most Holy, has ordered that you be admitted in paradise.'

"The Imam said, 'He asks, "Who are you, may Allah grant you favors? You have been giving me good news from the time you came out with me from my grave. On the way you have been giving me comfort and informed me of the decision of my Lord?"' The form then says, 'I am the joy that you had sent to the heart of your believing brothers (in belief) in the worldly life. I was created from it to give you good news and comfort you in frightening conditions.'"

Muhammad ibn Yahya has narrated from Ahmad ibn Muhammad from ibn Faddal a similar Hadith.

H 2126, Ch. 78, h 11
Muhammad ibn Yahya has narrated from Ahmad ibn Muhammad from Ali ibn al-Hakam from Malik ibn 'Atiyyah from abu 'Abd Allah, *'Alayhi al-Salam*, who has said the following:

"The Messenger of Allah has said, 'The most beloved deed to Allah is the joy that you send to the heart of a believer by means of removing his hunger or relieving him of his suffering.'"

H 2127, Ch. 78, h 12
Ali ibn Ibrahim has narrated from his father from ibn abu 'Umayr from al-Hakam ibn Miskin from abu 'Abd Allah, *'Alayhi al-Salam*, who has said the following:

"Whoever sends joy to the heart of a believing man, Allah, the Most Majestic, the Most Holy, creates from that joy a creature that meets him at the time of his death and says to him, 'Good news for you, O friend of Allah, with honor from Allah and His happiness with you. The form (creature) remains with him until he is placed in his grave and speaks to him of similar good tidings. When he is raised out of the grave the form meets him and speaks to him of similar good things and remains with him. On coming across frightening things of the Day of Judgment the form gives him good news. He then asks the form, 'Who are you, may Allah grant you favors?' The form says, 'I am the joy that you sent to the heart of so and so.'"

H 2128, Ch. 78, h 13
Al-Husayn ibn Muhammad has narrated from Ahmad ibn Ishaq from Sa'dan ibn Muslim from 'Abd Allah ibn Sinan who has said the following:

"Once a man, in the presence of abu 'Abd Allah, *'Alayhi al-Salam*, recited this verse of the Holy Quran: 'Those who annoy the believing men and women without reason will bear the sin for a false accusation, a manifest offense.' (33:58) The narrator has said that abu 'Abd Allah, *'Alayhi al-Salam*, then asked, 'What then is the reward for sending joy to his heart?' I said, 'May Allah keep my soul in service for your cause, ten good deeds.' The Imam said, 'Yes, by Allah, it is one million good deeds.'"

H 2129, Ch. 78, h 14
A number of our people have narrated from Sahl ibn Ziyad from Muhammad ibn 'Uramah from Ali ibn Yahya from al-Walid ibn al-'Ala' from ibn Sinan from abu 'Abd Allah, *'Alayhi al-Salam*, who has said the following:

"Whoever sends joy to the heart of a believer he certainly has sent joy to the heart of the Messenger of Allah. If one sends joy to the heart of the Messenger of Allah such joy reaches Allah. The same is true of causing pain to the heart of a believer."

H 2130, Ch. 78, h 15

It is narrated from him (narrator of the Hadith above) from Isma'il ibn Mansur from al-Mufaddal from abu 'Abd Allah, *'Alayhi al-Salam*, who has said the following:

"Any Muslim who, on his meeting another Muslim, sends joy to his heart, Allah, the Most Majestic, the Most Holy, sends joy to his (initiator of joy) heart."

H 2131, Ch. 78, h 16

Ali ibn Ibrahim has narrated from his father from ibn abu 'Umayr from Hisham ibn al-Hakam from abu 'Abd Allah, *'Alayhi al-Salam*, who has said the following:

"Of the most beloved deeds to Allah, the Most Majestic, the Most Holy, is sending joy to the heart of a believer, by means of satisfying his hunger, relief for his suffering or paying off his debt."

Chapter 79 - Assisting a Believer in His Needs

H 2132, Ch. 79, h 1

Muhammad ibn Yahya has narrated from Ahmad ibn Muhammad ibn 'Isa from al-Hassan ibn Ali from Bakkar ibn Kardam from al-Mufaddal from abu 'Abd Allah, *'Alayhi al-Salam*, who has said the following:

"The Imam said to me, 'O Mufaddal, listen to what I say to you. Bear in mind that it is the truth. Do it and inform 'Ilyat, of your brothers (in belief).' I asked, 'May Allah keep my soul in service for your cause, what is ('Ilyah) of my brothers (in belief)?' The Imam said, 'All those interested in helping their brothers (in belief).' The narrator has said that the Imam then said, 'Whoever makes one wish of his brother (in belief) come true Allah, the Most Majestic, the Most Holy, on the Day of Judgment will make one thousand of his wishes come true of which one is his admission in paradise, as well as his relatives, those whom he knows and his brothers will be admitted into paradise, provided, they are not against belief in Walayah (Divine Authority) of 'A'immah. Whenever al-Mufaddal would ask for help from any of his brothers (in belief) he would ask, 'Do you not wish to be a 'Ilyah (brothers in belief) interested in helping believers?'"

H 2133, Ch. 79, h 2

It is narrated from him (narrator of the Hadith above) from Muhammad ibn Ziyad who has that Khalid ibn Yazid narrated to him from al-Mufaddal ibn 'Umar from abu 'Abd Allah, *'Alayhi al-Salam*, who has said the following:

"Allah, the Most Majestic, the Most Holy, has created a creature among His creatures. He has chosen to make the wishes of the poor people of the Shi'a come true so that for such good deed they can be counted among those who deserve paradise. Try to be one of them, if you succeeded, so be it.' The Imam then said, 'For us, by Allah, is the Lord. We worship Him and do not consider anything equal to him.'"

H 2134, Ch. 79, h 3

It is narrated from him (narrator of the Hadith above) from Muhammad ibn Ziyad from Hakam ibn Ayman from Sadaqah al-Ahdab from abu 'Abd Allah, *'Alayhi al-Salam*, who has said the following:

"Helping to meet the needs of a believer is better than setting free one thousand slaves and better than donating one thousand horses loaded (with good) in the way of Allah."

Ali ibn Ibrahim has narrated from his father from Muhammad ibn Ziyad a Hadith similar to the two above Ahadith.

H 2135, Ch. 79, h 4

Ali has narrated from his father from Muhammad ibn Ziyad from Sandal from abu al-Sabbah al-Kinani from abu 'Abd Allah, *'Alayhi al-Salam*, who has said the following:

"Abu 'Abd Allah, *'Alayhi al-Salam*, has said, 'To help meet the needs of a believing man is more beloved to Allah than twenty Hajj for which one spends one hundred thousand.'"

H 2136, Ch. 79, h 5

A number of our people have narrated from Ahmad ibn Muhammad ibn Khalid from his father from Harun ibn al-Jahm from Isma'il ibn 'Ammar al-Sayrafi who has said the following:

"Once I asked abu 'Abd Allah, *'Alayhi al-Salam*, 'May Allah keep my soul in service for your cause, is a believer a blessing for believers?' The Imam said, 'Yes, he is.' I then asked, 'How is he as such?' The Imam said, 'A believer who may come to his brother (in belief) for help, in fact, is a blessing from Allah whom He has lead to him and has made him a means of blessings for him. If he makes his wish come true he accepts the blessing through his help and if he refuses to help while capable to help he, in fact, has repulsed from himself blessings that Allah, the Most Majestic, the Most Holy, had lead to him and had made him (believer) a means for his receiving rewards. Allah, the Most Majestic, the Most Holy, preserves that blessing to the Day of Judgment so that the needy believer who had faced refusal may decide about it. He may avail it for himself or someone else. O Isma'il, on the Day of Judgment when he will be the judge for the blessing from Allah that is appropriated to him to who do you think he will make it available?' I said, 'I do not think he will turn it away from himself.' The Imam said, 'Do you not think? Be certain that he will not turn it away from himself. O 'Isma'il, if a believer comes to his brother (in belief) for help and he refuses to help, despite being able to help, in his grave Allah will raise a snake to keep biting his thumb to the Day of Judgment wherein he may be forgiven or made to suffer torments.'"

H 2137, Ch. 79, h 6

Ali ibn Ibrahim has narrated from his father from ibn abu 'Umayr from al-Hakam ibn Ayman from Aban ibn Taghlib who has said the following:

"I heard abu 'Abd Allah, *'Alayhi al-Salam*, saying, 'One who performs Tawaf (walking seven times around the Ka'ba for worship) Allah, the Most Majestic, the Most Holy, will write for him six thousand good deeds, delete his six thousand sins, and will raise him six thousand degrees in meritorious status.' The narrator has said that Ishaq ibn 'Ammar has added, 'His six thousand wishes will be made to come true'.

"The narrator has said that The Imam said, 'To help the wish of a believer come true is better then a Tawaf, and Tawaf. . . . (walking seven times around the Ka'ba for worship), repeating it ten times.'"

H 2138, Ch. 79, h 7

Al-Husayn ibn Muhammad has narrated from Ahmad ibn Muhammad ibn Ishaq from Bakr ibn Muhammad from abu 'Abd Allah, *'Alayhi al-Salam,* who has said the following:

"Whenever a Muslim helps make the wish of a Muslim to come true, Allah, the Most Blessed, the Most High, says, 'With Me is your reward and I will not agree to allow it to be less than paradise.'"

H 2139, Ch. 79, h 8

It is narrated from him (narrator of the Hadith above) from Sa'dan ibn Muslim from Ishaq ibn 'Ammar from abu 'Abd Allah, *'Alayhi al-Salam,* who has said the following:

"Whoever performs a single Tawaf (walking seven times around the Ka'ba for worship) of this House Allah, the Most Majestic, the Most Holy, writes down for him six thousand good deeds, deletes his six thousand sins, and raises him six thousand degrees in meritorious status until he reaches al-Multazam (a part of Ka'ba) Allah then opens seven doors of paradise for him.' I then asked, 'May Allah keep my soul in service for your cause, all these rewards just for one Tawaf (walking seven times around the Ka'ba for worship)?' The Imam said, 'Yes, and I can tell you something better than this and that is helping the wish of a Muslim to come true. It is better than a Tawaf, a Tawaf. . . . (walking seven times around the Ka'ba for worship), the Imam repeated ten times.'"

H 2140, Ch. 79, h 9

Muhammad ibn Yahya has narrated from Ahmad ibn Muhammad ibn 'Isa from ibn Mahbub from Ibrahim al-Khariqi who has said the following:

"I heard abu 'Abd Allah, *'Alayhi al-Salam,* saying, 'Whoever walks to help make the wish of his believing brother (in belief) come true, seeking thereby the reward for it with Allah until he makes it happen, Allah, the Most Majestic, the Most Holy, writes down for him a reward equal to the reward for performing Hajj and 'Umrah that are of virtuous deeds, fasting for two of the sacred months while spending this time in the Sacred Mosque performing 'I'tikaf (a certain form of worship), and if one walks with the intention to help, but does not make it come true, Allah still writes down for him the reward for one Hajj that is accepted. Therefore, be interested in good deeds.'"

H 2141, Ch. 79, h 10

A number of our people have narrated from Sahl ibn Ziyad from Muhammad ibn 'Uramah from al-Hassan ibn Ali ibn abu Hamza from his father from abu Basir who has said the following:

"Abu 'Abd Allah, *'Alayhi al-Salam,* has said, 'Compete in al-Ma'ruf, doing good to your brothers (in belief) and be of such people; in paradise there is a door called al-Ma'ruf through which no one can enter except those who have performed al-Ma'ruf (a virtuous deed) in the worldly life. If a servant (of Allah) walks to help his believing brother (in belief), Allah, the Most Majestic, the Most Holy, appoints two angels one from the right and one from the left to ask forgiveness for him from his Lord and pray for his wish to come true.' The Imam then said, 'By Allah, the Messenger of Allah becomes happier for the coming true of the wish of the needy believer than the needy believer himself.'"

H 2142, Ch. 79, h 11

A number of our people have narrated from Ahmad ibn Muhammad ibn Khalid from his father from Khalaf ibn Hammad from certain individuals of his people from abu Ja'far, *'Alayhi al-Salam*, who has said the following:

"By Allah, performing one Hajj is more beloved to me than setting free of ten slaves and up to seventy slaves. If I look after a Muslim family, satisfy their hunger and clothe them to safeguard their dignity among the people it is more beloved to me than to perform Hajj ten times and so on up to seventy Hajj."

H 2143, Ch. 79, h 12

Ali ibn Ibrahim has narrated from his father from ibn abu 'Umayr from abu Ali Sahib al-Sha'ir from Muhammad ibn Qays from abu Ja'far, *'Alayhi al-Salam*, who has said the following:

"Allah, the Most Majestic, the Most Holy, sent revelations to Moses that said, 'Of My servant there are those who perform a good deed seeking thereby nearness to Me and I help him to rule in paradise.' Moses then asked, 'Lord, what is that good deed?' Allah said, 'He walks with his brother (in belief) to help his wish come true, whether it then comes true or not.'"

H 2144, Ch. 79, h 13

Al-Husayn ibn Muhammad has narrated from Mu'alla ibn Muhammad from Ahmad ibn Muhammad ibn 'Abd Allah from Ali ibn Ja'far who has said the following:

"I heard abu al-Hassan, *'Alayhi al-Salam*, saying, 'To whomever his believing brother (in belief) comes for help, in fact, it is a blessing from Allah, the Most Blessed, the Most High, that He has lead to him. If he accepts that blessing he has connected his guardianship with our guardianship (al-Walayah) that is connected to the guardianship of Allah. If he refuses to help when he is able to help, Allah assigns a snake from fire to keep biting him in his grave until the Day of Judgment wherein he will be forgiven or made to suffer torment. If in such case (in need of help) the needy accepts his excuse it will be much worse for him.'"

H 2145, Ch. 79, h 14

Muhammad ibn Yahya has narrated from Muhammad ibn al-Husayn from Muhammad ibn Isma'il ibn Bazi' from Salih ibn 'Aqabah from 'Abd Allah ibn Muhammad al-Ju'fi from abu Ja'far, *'Alayhi al-Salam*, who has said the following:

"A believer may find his brother (in belief) needy in a certain matter that is not available to him and he intends in his heart to meet such need, Allah, the Most Blessed, the Most High, admits him in paradise just because of his intention."

Chapter 80 - Endeavor to Help a Believer

H 2146, Ch. 80, h 1

Muhammad ibn Yahya has narrated from Ahmad ibn Muhammad ibn 'Isa from Ali ibn al-Hakam from Muhammad ibn Marwan from abu 'Abd Allah, *'Alayhi al-Salam*, who has said the following:

"Abu 'Abd Allah, *'Alayhi al-Salam*, has said, 'For a believer's walking to help a believing brother (in belief) ten good deeds are written for him, ten of his sins are deleted and he is raised ten degrees in meritorious status.' The narrator has said, 'I do not know what else the Imam said, but (I do know) he (the Imam) said, 'It is equal to setting ten slaves free and performing 'I'tikaf (a certain form of worship) in the Sacred Mosque.'"

H 2147, Ch. 80, h 2

It is narrated from him (narrator of the Hadith above) from Ahmad ibn Muhammad from Mu'ammar ibn al-Khallad who has said the following:

"I heard abu al-Hassan, *'Alayhi al-Salam*, saying, 'There are servants of Allah on earth who endeavor to help people, these (helping ones) will be secure and safe on the Day of Judgment. Whoever sends joy to the heart of a believer, on the Day of Judgment, Allah will fill his heart with joy.'"

H 2148, Ch. 80, h 3

It is narrated from him (narrator of the Hadith above) from Ahmad from 'Uthman ibn 'Isa from a man from abu 'Ubaydah al-Hadhdha' who abu Ja'far, *'Alayhi al-Salam*, who has said the following:

"Abu Ja'far, *'Alayhi al-Salam*, has said, 'One who walks to help his Muslim brother (in belief) Allah will make seventy-five thousand angels to provide him shadow and for each step that he walks Allah writes for him one good deed, deletes one of his sins and raises him by one degree in meritorious satus. When he completes the help, Allah, the Most Majestic, the Most Holy, writes for him the reward for one Hajj and one 'Umrah.'"

H 2149, Ch. 80, h 4

It is narrated from him (narrator of the Hadith above) from Ahmad ibn Muhammad from Muhammad ibn Sinan from Harun ibn Kharijah from Sadaqah from a man of the people of Hulwan from abu 'Abd Allah, *'Alayhi al-Salam*, who has said the following:

"Walking to help my Muslim brother (in belief) is more beloved to me than setting free one thousand souls and donating one thousand horses, saddled and harnessed, ready for use in the way of Allah."

H 2150, Ch. 80, h 5

Ali ibn Ibrahim has narrated from his father from Hammad from Ibrahim ibn 'Umar al-Yamani from abu 'Abd Allah, *'Alayhi al-Salam*, who has said the following:

"Whoever of the believing people walks to help his believing brother, Allah, the Most Majestic, the Most Holy, writes one good deed for him for every step of his walking, deletes one sin and raises him one degree in meritorious status, adds ten good deeds thereafter and accepts his intercession in ten issues."

H 2151, Ch. 80, h 6

A number of our people have narrated from Ahmad ibn Muhammad ibn Khalid from 'Uthman ibn 'Isa from abu Ayyub al-Khazzaz from abu 'Abd Allah, *'Alayhi al-Salam*, who has said the following:

"One who endeavors to help his Muslim brother (in belief) for the sake of Allah, Allah, the Most Majestic, the Most Holy, writes for him one million good deeds, grants forgiveness to his relatives, neighbors, brothers, those whom he knows and those who has done favors for him in the worldly life. On the Day of Judgment it will be said to him, 'Find in the fire those who had done favors for you in the worldly life and take them out by the permission of Allah, the Most Majestic, the Most Holy, except people of harsh behavior against 'A'immah.'"

H 2152, Ch. 80, h 7

It is narrated from him (narrator of the Hadith above) from his father from Khalaf Hammad from Ishaq ibn 'Ammar from abu Basir from abu 'Abd Allah, *'Alayhi al-Salam*, who has said the following:

"Whoever endeavors to help his Muslim brother (in belief) and strives in it and Allah makes it (such help) possible through him, Allah, the Most Majestic, the

Most Holy, writes down for him the reward for one Hajj, one 'Umrah and 'I'tikaf (a certain form of worship) for two months in the Sacred Mosque with fasting. If he strives without success, Allah, the Most Majestic, the Most Holy, writes down for him the reward for one Hajj and one 'Umrah."

H 2153, Ch. 80, h 8
Muhammad ibn Yahya has narrated from Ahmad ibn Muhammad from al-Hassan ibn Ali from Jamil ibn Darraj from abu 'Abd Allah, *'Alayhi al-Salam*, who has said the following:

"A believer's asking help from his brother (in belief) is enough proof of the former's trust in the latter."

H 2154, Ch. 80, h 9
It is narrated from him (narrator of the Hadith above) from Ahmad ibn Muhammad from certain individuals of our people from Safwan al-Jammal who has said the following:

"Once I was in the presence of abu 'Abd Allah, *'Alayhi al-Salam*, when a man from the people of Makkah called Maymun came in and complained to him about his difficulty paying his rent. The Imam said to me, 'Stand up and help your brother (in belief).' I then left with him and Allah facilitated payment for his rent and I returned to the assembly. Abu 'Abd Allah asked, 'What did you do for your brother (in belief)?' I said, 'Allah facilitated it for him, may Allah keep the souls of my parents in service for your cause.' The Imam said, 'Your help to your Muslim brother (in belief) is more beloved to me than performing Tawaf (walking seven times around the Ka'ba for worship) around the House.' The Imam said it on his own initiation. Then the Imam said, 'Once a man came to al-Hassan ibn Ali, *'Alayhi al-Salam*, and said, "May Allah keep the souls of my parents in service for your cause, I need help with a certain matter." He put on his shoes and left with him. They passed by al-Husayn ibn Ali, *'Alayhi al-Salam*, where he was standing in prayer and he (al-Hassan) asked the man, 'Did you ask abu 'Abd Allah for help?' The man said, 'May Allah keep my soul in service for your cause, I already have done so and abu 'Abd Allah, *'Alayhi al-Salam*, said that he was in 'I'tikaf (a certain form of worship).' Al-Hassan, *'Alayhi al-Salam*, said, 'Had he helped you (were he not in 'I'tikaf), it would have been better for him than 'I'tikaf for a whole month.'"

II 2155, Ch. 80, h 10
Ali ibn Ibrahim has narrated from his father from al-Hassan ibn Ali from abu Jamilah from ibn Sinan who has said the following:

"Abu 'Abd Allah, *'Alayhi al-Salam*, has said, 'Allah, the Most Majestic, the Most Holy, has said, "Creatures are My dependents. The most beloved among them to Me is the most compassionate of them toward the others and who endeavors the most to help them."'"

H 2156, Ch. 80, h 11
A number of our people have narrated from Ahmad ibn Muhammad ibn Khalid from his father from certain individuals of his people from abu 'Ammarah who has said:

"Hammad ibn abu Hanifah during a meeting said to me, 'Repeat your Hadith to me.' I then narrate to him, 'It is narrated to us that the worshippers of Israelites on reaching the perfect stage of worshipping would become the walkers to help meet the needs of people and paid proper attention to benefit them.'"

Chapter 81 - Relief for the Suffering of a Believer

H 2157, Ch. 81, h 1
Muhammad ibn Yahya has narrated from Ahmad ibn Muhammad ibn 'Isa from ibn Mahbub from Zayd al-Shahham who has said the following:

"I heard abu 'Abd Allah, *'Alayhi al-Salam*, saying, 'One who helps his brother (in belief) who is grieved and exhausted in his suffering, relieves him of his hardships and helps him to meet his needs, Allah, the Most Majestic, the Most Holy, writes for this seventy-two blessings from Allah of which one is an immediate facilitation of his financial affairs and preserves the other seventy-one blessings for his life in the hereafter to help him in the disastrous and frightening conditions of the Day of Judgment.'"

H 2158, Ch. 81, h 2
Ali ibn Ibrahim has narrated from his father from al-Nawfali from al-Sakuni from abu 'Abd Allah, *'Alayhi al-Salam*, who has said the following:

"Abu 'Abd Allah, *'Alayhi al-Salam*, has said, 'One who provides financial help for his brother (in belief), Allah, the Most Majestic, the Most Holy, provides for him relief in seventy-three grievous conditions. One is for the worldly life and the other seventy-two in times of great grief and hardship (Day of Judgment), when people will be preoccupied with the problems of their own souls.'"

H 2159, Ch. 81, h 3
Ali ibn Ibrahim has narrated from his father from ibn abu 'Umayr from Husayn ibn Nu'aim from Musmi' abu Sayyar who has said the following:

"I heard abu 'Abd Allah, *'Alayhi al-Salam*, saying, 'For one who provides relief for his brother (in belief), Allah provides him relief in hardship in the life hereafter. He will come out of his grave with a comfortable heart. Whoever satisfies his (a believers's) hunger Allah will feed him from the fruits of paradise. One who provides drink for him Allah will quench his (the helper's) thirst with the sealed wine of paradise.'"

H 2160, Ch. 81, h 4
Al-Husayn ibn Muhammad has narrated from Mu'alla ibn Muhammad from al-Hassan ibn Ali al-Washsha' from al-Rida, *'Alayhi al-Salam*, who has said the following:

"Whoever relieves a believer from suffering, Allah will provide relief for his (helper's) heart on the Day of Judgment."

H 2161, Ch. 81, h 5
Muhammad ibn Yahya has narrated from Ahmad ibn Muhammad from al-Hassan ibn Mahbub from Jamil ibn Salih from Dharih al-Muharibi who has said the following:

"I heard abu 'Abd Allah, *'Alayhi al-Salam*, saying, 'Any believer who relieves a believer from his hardships in a constraining condition Allah will make his (helper's) needs easily met in this world and in the next.' The Imam said, 'Whoever provides cover for the private matters of a believer for which he is afraid, Allah will provide cover for his (helper's) seventy private matters of this world and in the next life.' The Imam said, 'Allah supports a believer as long as he supports his believing brother (in belief). You must benefit from the good advice and be interested in good deeds.'"

Chapter 82 - Providing Food for a Believer

H 2162, Ch. 82, h 1

Muhammad ibn Yahya has narrated from Ahmad ibn Muhammad ibn 'Isa from abu Yahya al-Wasiti from certain individuals of our people from abu 'Abd Allah, *'Alayhi al-Salam*, who has said the following:

"Paradise becomes necessary for one who satisfies the hunger of a believer. For one who satisfies the hunger of an unbeliever (for his disbelief) it becomes necessary for Allah to fill his belly with al-Zaqum, the fruit of hell, regardless of his being a believer or unbeliever."

H 2163, Ch. 82, h 2

It is narrated from him (narrator of the Hadith above) from Ahmad ibn Muhammad from 'Uthman ibn 'Isa from certain individuals of our people from abu Basir from abu 'Abd Allah, *'Alayhi al-Salam*, who has said the following:

"Abu 'Abd Allah, *'Alayhi al-Salam*, has said, 'Satisfying the hunger of a Muslim is more beloved to me than feeding a whole horizon of people.' I then asked, 'What is a horizon?' The Imam said, 'It is one hundred thousand or more people.'"

H 2164, Ch. 82, h 3

It is narrated from him (narrator of the Hadith above) from Ahmad from Safwan ibn Yahya from abu Hamza from abu Ja'far, *'Alayhi al-Salam*, who has said the following:

"The Messenger of Allah has said, 'Whoever, feeds three Muslims, Allah will feed him from three gardens in the Kingdom of the heaven, the garden of al-Firdaws, (paradise), the garden of Eden and Tuba', the tree that comes out of the garden of Eden is planted by our Lord with His own hands.'"

H 2165, Ch. 82, h 4

Ali ibn Ibrahim has narrated from his father from Hammad ibn 'Isa from Ibrahim ibn 'Umar al-Yamani from abu 'Abd Allah, *'Alayhi al-Salam*, who has said the following:

"The serving of a man's food at his home to two of the believing people to their satisfaction is more meritorious than the setting free of a human soul."

H 2166, Ch. 82, h 5

It is narrated from him (narrator of the Hadith above) from his father from Hammad from Ibrahim from abu Hamza from Ali ibn al-Husayn, *'Alayhi al-Salam*, who has said the following:

"Whoever provides food to a believer to satisfy his hunger Allah will feed him with the fruits of paradise and whoever provides water to quench the thirst of a believer Allah will quench his thirst from the wine of paradise which is in sealed containers."

H 2167, Ch. 82, h 6

A number of our people have narrated from Sahl ibn Ziyad from Ja'far ibn Muhammad al-Ash'ari from 'Abd Allah ibn Maymun al-Qaddah from abu 'Abd Allah, *'Alayhi al-Salam*, who has said the following:

"Abu 'Abd Allah, *'Alayhi al-Salam*, has said, 'If one serves food to a believer to satisfy his hunger, no one of the creatures of Allah will be able to find out how much reward he will have in the hereafter for such service, not even the angels close to Allah or a prophet Divinely commissioned to preach can find out except Allah, Lord of the worlds.' The Imam then said, 'Among the means of forgiveness of sins is feeding a hungry Muslim.' Then he read the words of Allah, the Most Majestic, the Most Holy: '. . . in a day of famine, the feeding of (9:14) an orphaned relative (9:15) and downtrodden destitute person, . . .'" (9:16)

H 2168, Ch. 82, h 7
Ali ibn Ibrahim has narrated from his father from al-Nawfali from al-Sakuni from abu 'Abd Allah, *'Alayhi al-Salam*, who has said the following:

"The Messenger of Allah has said, 'Whoever serves a drink of water to a believer who (himself) also can find water, Allah will give him seventy thousand good deeds for each drink and if he provides a drink of water when he (himself) is not able to find one it will be like setting free ten persons from the descendents of 'Isma'il.'"

H 2169, Ch. 82, h 8
A number of our people have narrated from Ahmad ibn Muhammad ibn Khalid from 'Uthman ibn 'Isa from Husayn ibn Nu'aim al-Sahhaf who has said the following:

"Once abu 'Abd Allah, *'Alayhi al-Salam*, asked, 'Do you love your brothers (in belief) O Husayn?' I said, 'Yes, I love them.' The Imam asked, 'Do you provide any benefit for their poor?' I said, 'Yes, I do so.' The Imam said, 'It is obligatory for you to love whoever loves Allah. By Allah you will not provide any benefit to any of them unless you love them. Do you invite them to your house?' I said, 'Yes, I do so. I do not eat unless there are two, three men or less or more.' Abu 'Abd Allah, *'Alayhi al-Salam*, then said, 'Their excellence over you is more than your excellence over them.' I then said, 'May Allah keep my soul in service for your cause, I feed them my food on my own table on my furnishings. How can their excellence be greater than my excellence?' The Imam said, 'Yes, it is because when they come to your house they bring with them forgiveness for you and for your family and when they leave your house they leave along with your sins and the sins of your family.'"

H 2170, Ch. 82, h 9
Ali ibn Ibrahim has narrated from his father from ibn abu 'Umayr from abu Muhammad al-Wabishi who has said the following:

"Our people were mentioned before abu 'Abd Allah, *'Alayhi al-Salam*. I said, 'I do not eat lunch or dinner without two, three or more or less of them with me.' Abu 'Abd Allah, *'Alayhi al-Salam*, said, 'Their merit over you is greater than your merit over them.' I then said, 'May Allah keep my soul in service for your cause, how can it be as such? I feed them and spent for them from my property and my family serves them.' The Imam said, 'When they come to you they come with plenty of sustenance from Allah, the Most Majestic, the Most Holy, and when they leave, they do so with forgiveness for you.'"

H 2171, Ch. 82, h 10
It is narrated from him (narrator of the Hadith above) from his father from ibn abu 'Umayr from Muhammad ibn Muqrin from 'Ubayd Allah al-Wassafi from abu Ja'far, *'Alayhi al-Salam*, who has said the following:

"Abu Ja'far, *'Alayhi al-Salam*, has said, 'Feeding a Muslim man is more beloved to me than setting free a horizon (full) of people.' I then asked, 'How many is a horizon of people?' The Imam said, 'It is ten thousand people.'"

H 2172, Ch. 82, h 11

Ali ibn Ibrahim has narrated from his father from Hammad ibn 'Isa from Rib'i who has said the following:

"Once abu 'Abd Allah, *'Alayhi al-Salam*, said, 'Whoever feeds his Muslim brother (in belief) for the sake of Allah his reward will be like the reward of a person who feeds a Fi'Am, (whole group) of people.' I then asked, 'How many is a Fi'am of people?' The Imam said, 'It is one hundred thousand people.'"

H 2173, Ch. 82, h 12

Ali ibn Ibrahim has narrated from his father from ibn abu 'Umayr from Hisham ibn al-Hakam from Sadir al-Sayrafi who has said the following:

"Abu 'Abd Allah, *'Alayhi al-Salam*, has asked, 'What prevents you from setting free a soul every day?' I said, 'My property is not enough to bear it.' The Imam said, 'Feed a Muslim every day.' I asked, 'Is it so, regardless, of his being affluent or poor?' The Imam said, 'Affluent people also desire food.'"

H 2174, Ch. 82, h 13

A number of our people have narrated from Ahmad ibn Muhammad ibn Khalid from Ahmad ibn Muhammad ibn abu Basir from Safwan al-Jammal from abu 'Abd Allah, *'Alayhi al-Salam*, who has said the following:

"A meal that (I may provide) for a Muslim brother (in belief) is more beloved to me than setting free a slave."

H 2175, Ch. 82, h 14

It is narrated from him (narrator of the Hadith above) from Isma'il ibn Mehran from Safwan al-Jammal from abu 'Abd Allah, *'Alayhi al-Salam*, who has said the following:

"Feeding one of my brothers (in belief) to his satisfaction is more beloved to me than entering your market to buy a slave and set him free."

H 2176, Ch. 82, h 15

It is narrated from him (narrator of the Hadith above) from Ali ibn al-Hakam from Aban ibn 'Uthman from 'Abd al-Rahman ibn abu 'Abd Allah from abu 'Abd Allah, *'Alayhi al-Salam*, who has said the following:

"With five Dirhams, if I enter your market to buy food to feed a few Muslim people is more beloved to me than setting free of a slave."

H 2177, Ch. 82, h 16

It is narrated from him (narrator of the Hadith above) from al-Washsha' from Ali ibn abu Hamza from abu Basir from abu 'Abd Allah, *'Alayhi al-Salam*, who has said the following:

"Muhammad ibn Ali, *'Alayhi al-Salam*, asked, 'How much is the value of setting free a slave?' The Imam said, 'It is equal to feeding a Muslim man to his satisfaction.'"

H 2178, Ch. 82, h 17

Muhammad ibn Yahya has narrated from Muhammad ibn al-Husayn ibn abu al-Khattab from Muhammad ibn Isma'il from Salih ibn 'Aqabah from abu Shabal who has said the following:

"I do not find anything equal in reward to visiting a believer except feeding him. Allah considers it His responsibility to feed, from the food of paradise, one who feeds a believer."

H 2179, Ch. 82, h 18

Muhammad has narrated from Muhammad ibn al-Husayn from Muhammad ibn Isma'il from Salih ibn 'Aqabah from Rufa'a from abu 'Abd Allah, *'Alayhi al-Salam*, who has said the following:

"Feeding a needy believer is more beloved to me than visiting him, and to visit him is more beloved to me than setting free of ten slaves."

H 2180, Ch. 82, h 19

Salih ibn 'Aqabah has narrated from 'Abd Allah ibn Muhammad and Yazid ibn 'Abd al-Malik from abu 'Abd Allah, *'Alayhi al-Salam*, who has said the following:

"Whoever feeds an affluent believer it is equal to setting free a slave from the descendents of Isma'il and rescuing him from slaughter. Whoever feeds a needy believer, it is equal in reward for him to set free one hundred slaves from the descendents of Isma'il and rescue them from being slaughtered."

H 2181, Ch. 82, h 20

Salih ibn 'Aqabah has narrated from Nasr ibn Qabus from abu 'Abd Allah, *'Alayhi al-Salam*, who has said the following:

"Abu 'Abd Allah, *'Alayhi al-Salam*, has said, 'Feeding a believer is, indeed, more beloved to me than setting free ten slaves and performing ten Hajj.' I (the narrator) then asked, 'Is it like setting free ten slaves and performing ten Hajj?' He has said that the Imam said, 'O Nasr, if you do not feed him he will die or you will humiliate him, then he will go to one who is a bitter enemy of the Imam and will ask him for help. Death is better for him than asking help from such enemy of the Imam. O Nasr, giving life to a believer is like giving life to all mankind. If you do not feed him you have caused his death, if you feed him you have given him life.'"

Chapter 83 - Providing Clothes for a Believer

H 2182, Ch. 83, h 1

Muhammad ibn Yahya has narrated from Ahmad ibn Muhammad ibn 'Isa from 'Umar ibn 'Abd al-'Aziz from Jamil ibn Darraj from abu 'Abd Allah, *'Alayhi al-Salam*, who has said the following:

"If a beleiver provides clothes for his brother (in belief) to use in winter or summer, it becomes a right with Allah to dress him with the dresses of paradise, to ease off the agony of death for him, make his grave greatly roomy. On coming out of his grave he meets the angels who give him the good news as Allah, the Most Majestic, the Most Holy, has said, 'The angels will come to them with this glad news: 'This is your day which was promised to you.'" (21:103)

H 2183, Ch. 83, h 2

It is narrated from him (narrator of the Hadith above) from Ahmad ibn Muhammad from Bakr ibn Salih from al-Hassan ibn Ali from 'Abd Allah ibn Ja'far ibn Ibrahim from abu 'Abd Allah, *'Alayhi al-Salam*, who has said the following:

"Whoever provides a poor Muslim with clothes for covering and assists him in means of his living, Allah, the Most Majestic, the Most Holy, as a reward assigns seven thousand angels to pray and ask forgiveness for him up to the time of sounding off of the trumpet (Day of Judgment) for every sin that he may have committed."

H 2184, Ch. 83, h 3

Muhammad ibn Yahya has narrated from Ahmad ibn Muhammad from Safwan from abu Hamza from abu Ja'far, *'Alayhi al-Salam*, who has said the following:

"The Messenger of Allah has said, 'Whoever provides a poor Muslim with clothes for covering and assists him in means of his living, as reward Allah, the Most Majestic, the Most Holy, assigns seventy thousand angels to pray and ask forgiveness up to the time of the sounding of the trumpet (Day of Judgment) for every sin that he may have committed.'"

H 2185, Ch. 83, h 4

Ali ibn Ibrahim has narrated from his father from Hammad ibn 'Isa from Ibrahim ibn 'Umar from abu Hamza al-Thumali from Ali ibn al-Husayn, *'Alayhi al-Salam*, who has said the following:

"Whoever provides clothes for a believer, for his reward Allah will dress him all in green.' In another Hadith he said, 'He will live under the protection of Allah as long as a fiber of that clothes is on him (believer).'"

H 2186, Ch. 83, h 5

A number of our people have narrated from Ahmad ibn Muhammad ibn Khalid from 'Uthman ibn 'Isa from 'Abd Allah ibn Sinan from abu 'Abd Allah, *'Alayhi al-Salam*, who has said the following:

"Whoever provides clothes for a believer (while in need) for covering, Allah will dress up the former with Istabraq (a kind of fine clothing) of paradise. Whoever provides clothes for a believer (while he already has enough) for covering he will live under the protection of Allah as long as anything is left of that clothing."

Chapter 84 - To Show Kindness to and Honor a Believer

H 2187, Ch. 84, h 1

Muhammad ibn Yahya has narrated from Ahmad ibn Muhammad ibn 'Isa from Ali ibn al-Hakam from al-Husayn ibn Hashim from Sa'dan ibn Muslim from abu 'Abd Allah, *'Alayhi al-Salam*, who has said the following:

"Whoever removes a speck from the face of his brother (in belief), Allah, the Most Majestic, the Most Holy, then will write down for the former ten good deeds and whoever smiles to his brother (in belief) earns one good deed."

H 2188, Ch. 84, h 2

It is narrated from him (narrator of the Hadith above) from Ahmad ibn Muhammad from 'Umar ibn 'Abd al-'Aziz from Jamil ibn Darraj from abu 'Abd Allah, *'Alayhi al-Salam*, who has said the following:

"Whoever says 'Welcome' to his brother (in belief) Allah then writes down for him 'Welcome' up to the Day of Judgment."

H 2189, Ch. 84, h 3

It is narrated from him (narrator of the Hadith above) from Ahmad ibn Muhammad ibn 'Isa from Yunus from 'Abd Allah ibn Sinan from abu 'Abd Allah, *'Alayhi al-Salam*, who has said the following:

"One who honors his Muslim brother (in belief) who has come to him, in fact, has revered Allah, the Most Majestic, the Most Holy."

H 2190, Ch. 84, h 4

It is narrated from him (narrator of the Hadith above) from Ahmad ibn Muhammad from ibn Mahbub from Nasr ibn Ishaq from al-Harith ibn al-Nu'man from al-Haytham ibn Hammad from abu Dawud from Zayd ibn Arqam who has said the following:

"The Messenger of Allah has said, 'Whoever of my followers treats his brother (in belief) with gentleness for the sake of Allah, He will provide for him servants of paradise.'"

H 2191, Ch. 84, h 5

It is narrated from him (narrator of the Hadith above) from Ahmad ibn Muhammad from Bakr ibn Salih from al-Hassan ibn Ali from 'Abd Allah ibn Ja'far ibn Ibrahim from abu 'Abd Allah, *'Alayhi al-Salam*, who has said the following:

"The Messenger of Allah has said, 'Whoever receives his Muslim brother (in belief) with honor and value and relieves his suffering continues living under the extended shadow of Allah with blessings as long as he is in there.'"

H 2192, Ch. 84, h 6

It is narrated from him (narrator of the Hadith above) from Ahmad ibn Muhammad from 'Umar ibn 'Abd al-'Aziz from Jamil from abu 'Abd Allah, *'Alayhi al-Salam*, who has said the following:

"I heard abu 'Abd Allah, *'Alayhi al-Salam*, saying, 'Of the special characteristics that Allah, the Most Majestic, the Most Holy, has given to a believer is that he is the means for the recognition and identification of the good deeds of his brothers (in belief) even if such deeds are small and little. Goodness is not in plentifulness as it is mentioned in the words of Allah, the Most Majestic, the Most Holy, in His book: 'They give preference to them over themselves, even concerning the things that they themselves urgently need. . . .' then He has said, '. . . whoever controls his greed will have everlasting happiness.' (59:9) To whoever Allah, the Most Majestic, the Most Holy, grants such recognition He loves him. Whomever Allah, the Most Blessed, the Most High, loves, He grants him reward in full measures on the Day of Judgment and without keeping any counts.' The Imam said, 'O Jamil, narrate this Hadith to your brothers (in belief); it is an exhortation to good deeds.'"

H 2193, Ch. 84, h 7

Muhammad ibn Yahya has narrated from Muhammad ibn al-Husayn from Muhammad ibn Isma'il from Salih ibn 'Aqabah from al-Mufaddal from abu 'Abd Allah, *'Alayhi al-Salam*, who has said the following:

"Believers present al-Tuhaf, (gifts) to each other.' I then asked, 'What is al-Tuhaf?' The Imam said, 'It can be a seat, a pillow, food, clothes or greetings of peace. Paradise then tries to reach out to serve them food for their good deed. Allah, the Most Majestic, the Most Holy, inspires it: 'I have made your food unlawful for the people of the world except the prophets or the successor of a prophet. When it will be the Day of Judgment Allah, the Most Majestic, the Most Holy, will inspire paradise of His decision to compensate His friends for their gifts. Thereafter, young male and female servants will come out from paradise with special trays of food covered with handkerchiefs made of pearls. When they (believers) will look into the hell and see its terrifying condition and into paradise and all that is therein their power of reason will stop in confusion and they will refuse to eat. They then will be told by someone from the foot of the Throne, 'Allah, the Most Majestic, the Most Holy, has made hell unlawful for those who have eaten the food of paradise, and then they (believers) will extend their hands and eat.'"

H 2194, Ch. 84, h 8

Muhammad ibn Yahya has narrated from Ahmad ibn Muhammad ibn 'Isa from Muhammad ibn al-Fudayl from abu Hamza from abu Ja'far, *'Alayhi al-Salam*, who has said the following:

"It is obligatory for a Muslim to cover for a Muslim seventy major sins."

H 2195, Ch. 84, h 9

Al-Husayn ibn Muhammad and Muhammad ibn Yahya have all narrated from Ali ibn Muhammad ibn Sa'd from Muhammad ibn Aslam from Muhammad ibn Ali ibn 'Uday who has said that dictated to h him Muhammad ibn Sulayman from Ishaq ibn 'Ammar who has said the following:

"Abu 'Abd Allah, *'Alayhi al-Salam*, has said, 'Be good to my friends, O Ishaq, as much as you can. No believer does something good to another believer or assists him, but that it causes a contusion to the face of Satan and injuries to his heart.'"

Chapter 85 - In the Service of Believing People

H 2196, Ch. 85, h 1

Muhammad ibn Yahya has narrated from Salmah ibn Khattab from Ibrahim ibn Muhammad al-Thaqafi from Isma'il ibn Aban from Salih ibn abu al-Aswad in a marfu' manner from abu al-Mu'tamar who has said the following:

"I heard Amir al-Mu'minin (Ali ibn abu Talib), *'Alayhi al-Salam*, saying, 'The Messenger of Allah has said, "Any Muslim who serves a group of Muslims, Allah in paradise will grant him servants equal to the number of Muslims he had served.'"

Chapter 86 - Giving Good Advice to the Believers

H 2197, Ch. 86, h 1

A number of our people have narrated from Ahmad ibn Muhammad from Ali ibn al-Hakam from 'Umar ibn Aban from 'Isa ibn abu Mansur from abu 'Abd Allah, *'Alayhi al-Salam*, who has said the following:

"It is of a believer's obligations to provide good advice to another believer."

H 2198, Ch. 86, h 2

It is narrated from him (narrator of the Hadith above) from ibn Mahbub from Mu'awiyah ibn Wahab from abu 'Abd Allah, *'Alayhi al-Salam*, who has said the following:

"It is of a believer's obligations to provide good advice to another believer face to face or in his absence."

H 2199, Ch. 86, h 3

Ibn Mahbub has narrated from ibn Ri'ab from abu 'Ubaydah al-Hadhdha' from abu Ja'far, *'Alayhi al-Salam*, who has said the following:

"It is of a believer's obligations to provide good advice to another believer."

H 2200, Ch. 86, h 4

Ibn Mahbub has narrated from 'Amr ibn Shamir from Jabir from abu Ja'far, *'Alayhi al-Salam*, who has said the following:

"The Messenger of Allah has said, 'Every man among you must provide advice to his brother (in belief) just like the advice for his own self.'"

H 2201, Ch. 86, h 5

Ali ibn Ibrahim has narrated from his father from al-Nawfali from al-Sakuni from abu 'Abd Allah, *'Alayhi al-Salam*, who has said the following:

"The Messenger of Allah has said, 'Of the people of the greatest position before Allah on the Day of Judgment will be he who is a person walking on earth the most to provide good advice to His creatures.'"

H 2202, Ch. 86, h 6

Ali ibn Ibrahim has narrated from his father from al-Qasim ibn Muhammad from al-Minqari from Sufyan ibn 'Uyaynah who has said the following:

"I heard abu 'Abd Allah, *'Alayhi al-Salam*, saying, 'You must provide good advice for the sake of Allah to His creatures; you will not meet Him with any good deed better than this.'"

Chapter 87 - Improving Good Relations Among People

H 2203, Ch. 87, h 1

Muhammad ibn Yahya has narrated from Ahmad ibn Muhammad from Muhammad ibn Sinan from Hammad ibn abu Talhah from Habib al-Ahwal who has said the following:

"I heard abu 'Abd Allah, *'Alayhi al-Salam*, saying, 'The charity that Allah loves is to improve good relations among the people when they cause devastation, and closeness when they get far away from each other.'"

It is narrated from him (narrator of the Hadith above) from Muhammad ibn Sinan from Hudhayfah ibn Mansur from abu 'Abd Allah, *'Alayhi al-Salam*, a similar Hadith.

H 2204, Ch. 87, h 2

It is narrated from him (narrator of the Hadith above) from ibn Mahbub from Hisham ibn Salim from abu 'Abd Allah, *'Alayhi al-Salam*, who has said the following:

"To improve good relations beween two people is more beloved to me than giving two Dinar in charity."

H 2205, Ch. 87, h 3

It is narrated from him (narrator of the Hadith above) from Ahmad ibn Muhammad from ibn Sinan from Mufaddal who has said the following:

"Abu 'Abd Allah, *'Alayhi al-Salam*, has said, 'When you find two of our followers disputing, settle it between them by means of paying from my property.'"

H 2206, Ch. 87, h 4

Ibn Sinan has narrated from abu Hanifah Sabiq al-Hajj who has said the following:

"Al-Mufaddal once passed us nearby, while my daughter in-law and I were disputing about a legacy. He stood by for a while and then said to us, 'Come to my house.' We went there and he settled it between us for four hundred dirhams, which he paid from his own pocket until each of us was happy with the other. He then said, 'It was not from my property. It was from the property of abu 'Abd Allah, *'Alayhi al-Salam*. He had ordered me that whenever two of our people dispute on an issue; I can settle it from his property. Payment was from the property of abu 'Abd Allah, *'Alayhi al-Salam.*'"

H 2207, Ch. 87, h 5

Ali ibn Ibrahim has narrated from his father from 'Abd Allah ibn Al-Mughirah from Mu'awiyah ibn 'Ammar from abu 'Abd Allah, *'Alayhi al-Salam,* who has said the following:

"A councilor cannot lie (is not supposed to)."

H 2208, Ch. 87, h 6

Ali has narrated from his father from ibn abu 'Umayr from Ali ibn Isma'il from Ishaq ibn 'Ammar from abu 'Abd Allah, *'Alayhi al-Salam,* who has said the following:

"About the words of Allah, the Most Majestic, the Most Holy, 'Do not swear (saying, 'By Allah') I will not do good things, or have piety, or make peace among people. . . .,' (2:224) the Imam said, "When you are called for arbitration between two people, do not say I have sworn not to do it.'"

H 2209, Ch. 87, h 7

A number of our people have narrated from Ahmad ibn Muhammad ibn Khalid from ibn Mahbub from Mu'awiyah ibn Wahab or Mu'awiyah ibn 'Ammar from abu 'Abd Allah, *'Alayhi al-Salam,* who has said the following:

"Abu 'Abd Allah, *'Alayhi al-Salam,* once said, 'Convey from me to so and so, in a few matters that he commanded me to do.' I said, 'Therefore I convey from you to them and say from myself only what you have told me to say and other things that you said.' The Imam said, 'Yes, an arbitrator cannot lie. He is the councilor, not a liar.'"

Chapter 88 - To Revive the Believer

H 2210, Ch. 88, h 1

A number of our people have narrated from Ahmad ibn Muhammad ibn Khalid from 'Uthman ibn 'Isa from Sama'a from abu 'Abd Allah, *'Alayhi al-Salam,* who has said the following:

"I asked him about the words of Allah, the Most Majestic, the Most Holy, '. . . We made it a law for the children of Israel that the killing of a person for reasons other than legal retaliation or for stopping corruption in the land is as great a sin as murdering all of mankind. However, to save a life would be as great a virtue as to save all of mankind...' (5:32)

"The Imam said, 'Whoever takes people from straying to guidance, has given them life. Whoever takes people from guidance to straying, it is as if he has murdered all of them.'"

H 2211, Ch. 88, h 2

It is narrated from him (narrator of the Hadith above) from Ali ibn al-Hakam from Aban ibn 'Uthman from Fudayl ibn Yasar who has said the following:

"I asked abu Ja'far, *'Alayhi al-Salam,* about the words of Allah, the Most Majestic, the Most Holy, in His book, ' . . . to save a life is as great a virtue as to save all of mankind. . . .' (5:32) The Imam said, 'It refers to burning or drowning someone.' I asked, 'What if someone takes him out of straying to guidance?' The Imam said, 'That is the greatest interpretation of the case in point.'"

H 2212, Ch. 88, h 3

Muhammad ibn Yahya has narrated from Ahmad and 'Abd Allah the two sons of Muhammad ibn 'Isa from Ali ibn al-Hakam from Aban a similar Hadith.

H 2213, Ch. 88, h 4

Muhammad ibn Yahya has narrated from Ahmad ibn Muhammad from Muhammad ibn Khalid from al- Nadr ibn Suwayd from Yahya ibn 'Imran al-Halabi from abu Khalid al-Qammat from Humran who has said the following:

"Once I said to abu 'Abd Allah, *'Alayhi al-Salam*, 'Can I ask you a question, may Allah keep you well?' He said, 'Yes you may do so.' I said, 'I was in a particular condition and today I am in another condition. I would go in the land to invite one or two men and women (to our belief) and Allah would save whomever He wanted. Today I do not invite anyone.' The Imam said, 'It is no offense to you to leave people to their Lord. Whomever Allah wants to guide and take out of darkness to light He does so.' The Imam then said, 'It is not an offense to you if you sense good in someone to introduce an issue.' I then said, 'Tell me about the words of Allah, the Most Majestic, the Most Holy, '. . . to save a life is as great a virtue as to save all of mankind. . . .' (5:32) The Imam said, 'It refers to burning or drowning someone. He then remained quiet and then said, 'Its greatest case in point, is that one is invited (to the truth), and he accepts it.'"

Chapter 89 - Inviting One's Own People to Belief

H 2214, Ch. 89, h 1

Muhammad ibn Yahya has narrated from Ahmad ibn Muhammad ibn 'Isa from Ali ibn al-Nu'man from 'Abd Allah ibn Muskan from Sulayman ibn Khalid who has said the following:

"Once I asked abu 'Abd Allah, *'Alayhi al-Salam*, 'I know a family who listens to me, should I invite them to this cause (belief of the Shi'a Muslims)?' The Imam said, 'Yes, Allah, the Most Majestic, the Most Holy, says in His book, 'Believers, save yourselves and your families from the fire which is fueled with people and stones . . .'" (66:6)

Chapter 90 - Not to Invite People to Belief

H 2215, Ch. 90, h 1

Ali ibn Ibrahim has narrated from his father from ibn abu 'Umayr from Kulayb ibn Mu'awiyah al-Saydawi who has said the following:

"Once abu 'Abd Allah, *'Alayhi al-Salam*, said to me, 'Beware of people.' If Allah, the Most Majestic, the Most Holy, wills good for a servant, He places a dot in his heart. He then leaves him alone and for that reason he moves around and searches it (belief).' The Imam then said, 'Were you to talk to people, say we have gone where Allah goes, we choose whoever Allah chooses. Allah chose Muhammad and we chose the family of Muhammad, *'Alayhim al-Salam*.'"

H 2216, Ch. 90, h 2

Muhammad ibn Yahya has narrated from Ahmad ibn Muhammad ibn 'Isa from Muhammad ibn Isma'il from abu Isma'il Al- Sarraj from ibn Muskan from Thabit abu Sa'id who has said the following:

"Once abu 'Abd Allah, *'Alayhi al-Salam*, said to me, 'O Thabit, what do you have to do with people? Leave the people alone and do not invite anyone to your cause (your belief). By Allah, if the inhabitants of heaven and the inhabitants of earth would come together to mislead a servant whom Allah wants to guide, they would not be able to do it. Leave the people alone and no one of you should say: "What about my brother, the son of my Uncle and my neighbor"? When Allah, the Most Majestic, the Most Holy, wills good for a servant, He cleanses his spirit and thereafter he does not listen to any principle but that he recognizes, and acknowledges it and does not hear of a wickedness but that he hates it. Then Allah places a word in his heart that serves as a focal point in his affairs.'"

H 2217, Ch. 90, h 3

Abu Ali al-Ash'ari has narrated from Muhammad ibn 'Abd al-Jabbar from Safwan ibn Yahya from Muhammad ibn Marwan from al-Fudayl who has said the following:

"Once I said to abu 'Abd Allah, *'Alayhi al-Salam,* 'Should we invite people to this cause (belief of Shi'a Muslims)?' The Imam said, 'O al-Fudayl, it is certain, when Allah wills good for a servant, He commands an angel who holds his neck until he brings him into this cause whether he likes or dislikes it.'"

H 2218, Ch. 90, h 4

Muhammad ibn Yahya has narrated from Ahmad ibn Muhammad ibn 'Isa from ibn Faddal from Ali ibn 'Uqbah from his father who has said the following:

"Once abu 'Abd Allah, *'Alayhi al-Salam,* said, 'Keep your cause (belief), for the sake of Allah and do not make it for people; what is for Allah is for Allah and what is for people cannot ascend to heaven. Do not argue with people about your religion; argumentation causes sickness to the heart. Allah, the Most Majestic, the Most Holy, has said to His Holy Prophet, '(Muhammad), you cannot guide whomever you love, but Allah guides whomever He wants. . . .' (28:56) He has also said, '. . . (Muhammad), do you force people to have faith'? (10:99). Leave the people alone; they take it from people and you take it from the Messenger of Allah and from Amir al-Mu'minin (Ali ibn abu Talib), *'Alayhim al-Salam,* and this is not equal. I heard my father saying, 'When Allah writes for a servant to enter into this cause (belief of Ahl al-Bayt) he rushes to it quicker than a bird to its nest.'"

H 2219, Ch. 90, h 5

Ali ibn Ibrahim has narrated from his father from 'Uthman from ibn 'Udhaynah from abu 'Abd Allah, *'Alayhi al-Salam,* who has said the following:

"Allah, the Most Majestic, the Most Holy, has created a people for the truth, when they pass by the door of the truth, their hearts accept it, even though they may not know it. When they pass by the door of falsehood, their hearts reject it, even though they may not know it. He has created a people for things other than this. When they pass by the door of the truth, their hearts reject it, even though they may not know it. When they pass by the door of falsehood, their hearts accept it, even though they may not know it."

H 2220, Ch. 90, h 6

Ali ibn Ibrahim has narrated from his father from ibn abu 'Umayr from 'Abd al-Hamid ibn abu al-'Ala' from abu 'Abd Allah, *'Alayhi al-Salam,* who has said the following:

"When Allah, the Most Majestic, the Most Holy, wills good for a servant, He places a dot of light in his heart, which shines his ears and heart to the extent that he becomes more eager and protective of this cause than you are. When He wills evil for a servant, He places a black dot in his heart and it darkens his ears and his heart. Then he recited this verse, 'Allah will open the hearts of whomever He wants to guide to Islam, but He will constrict the chest of one whom He has led astray, as though he were to climb high up into the sky. . . .'" (6:125)

H 2221, Ch. 90, h 7
It is narrated from him (narrator of the Hadith above) from his father from ibn abu 'Umayr from Muhammad ibn Humran from Muhammad ibn Muslim from abu 'Abd Allah, *'Alayhi al-Salam*, who has said the following:

"When Allah, the Most Majestic, the Most Holy, wills good for a servant, He places a white dot on his heart, opens up his ears and heart and assigns an angel to keep him on the right path. When He wills evil for a servant, He places a black dot in his heart and shuts down his ears and heart and assigns a Satan to mislead him."

Chapter 91 - Allah Grants Religion Only to Whomever He Loves

H 2222, Ch. 91, h 1
Muhammad ibn Yahya has narrated from Ahmad ibn Muhammad ibn 'Isa from ibn Faddal from ibn Bukayr from Hamza ibn Humran from 'Umar ibn Hanzalah who has said the following:

"Once abu 'Abd Allah, *'Alayhi al-Salam*, said to me, 'O abu al-Sakhr, Allah indeed grants the world to whoever He loves or hates. He does not grant this cause (belief) but to the chosen ones of His creatures. You, by Allah, follow my religion and the religion of my predecessors, Ibrahim and Isma'il. I do not mean thereby Ali ibn al-Husayn, Muhammad ibn Ali, *'Alayhi al-Salam*, even though they follow their (Abraham and Isma'il's) religion.'"

H 2223, Ch. 91, h 2
Al-Husayn ibn Muhammad has narrated from Mu'alla ibn Muhammad from al-Hassan ibn Ali al-Washsha' from 'Asim ibn Hamidf from Malik ibn 'Ayun al-Juhni who has said the following:

"I heard abu Ja'far, *'Alayhi al-Salam*, saying, 'O Malik, Allah grants the world to those whom He loves, and those whom He hates, but He grants His religion only to those whom He loves.'"

H 2224, Ch. 91, h 3
It is narrated from him (narrator of the Hadith above) from Mu'alla from al-Washsha' from 'Abd al-Karim ibn 'Amr al-Khath'ami from 'Umar ibn Hanzalah and Hamza ibn Humran from abu Ja'far, *'Alayhi al-Salam*, who has said the following:

"Allah gives this world to both the virtuous and evil-doing people, but He does not give belief to anyone except to His chosen creatures."

H 2225, Ch. 91, h 4
Muhammad ibn Yahya has narrated from Ahmad ibn Muhammad from Ali ibn al-Nu'man from abu Sulayman from Muyassir who has said the following:

"Abu 'Abd Allah, *'Alayhi al-Salam*, has said, 'Allah, the Most Majestic, the Most Holy, gives the world to those He loves as well as to those He hates, but He does not give belief to anyone except those He loves.'"

Chapter 92 - Sound Religion

H 2226, Ch. 92, h 1

Muhammad ibn Yahya has narrated from Ahmad ibn Muhammad from Ali ibn al-Nu'man from Ayyub ibn al-Hurr from abu 'Abd Allah, *'Alayhi al-Salam*, who has said the following:

"About the words of Allah, the Most Majestic, the Most Holy, 'Allah protected him against their evil plans. . . .,' (40:45) the Imam said, 'In fact, they perpetrated and murdered him but do you know what was protected? He (Allah) protected him against confusion in his religion.'"

H 2227, Ch. 92, h 2

Ali ibn Ibrahim has narrated from Muhammad ibn 'Isa ibn 'Ubayd from abu Jamilah who has said the following:

"abu 'Abd Allah, *'Alayhi al-Salam*, has said, 'It was in the will of Amir al-Mu'minin (Ali ibn abu Talib), *'Alayhi al-Salam*, to his companions, "You must know that this Quran is guidance day and night and it is the light in the dark night that is due to hardships and destitution. When misfortune befalls, protect yourselves with your properties. When a misfortune (to religion) befalls, protect your religion with yourselves. You must know that the destroyed, in reality, is the one whose religion is destroyed and looted, in reality, is one whose religion is looted. It is certain that there is no poverty in paradise. It is also certain that there is no prosperity in hellfire, wherein its captives are never freed and there is no cure for its blind.'"

H 2228, Ch. 92, h 3

Ali has narrated from his father from Hammad ibn 'Isa from Rib'i ibn 'Abd Allah from Fudayl ibn Yasar from abu Ja'far, *'Alayhi al-Salam*, who has said the following:

"Soundness of religion and good health is better than property. Property is a beauty of the worldly beauties and it is a good thing."

Muhammad ibn Isma'il has narrated from Fadl ibn Shadhan from Hammad from Rib'i from al-Fudayl from abu Ja'far, *'Alayhi al-Salam*, a similar Hadith.

H 2229, Ch. 92, h 4

A number of our people have narrated from Ahmad ibn Muhammad ibn Khalid from ibn Faddal from Yunus ibn Ya'qub from certain individuals of his people who has said the following:

"A man, of the companions of abu 'Abd Allah, *'Alayhi al-Salam*, would very often attend the gathering with the Imam. He remained absent for a certain time and did not attend Hajj also. Once a certain individual of his people who knew him came in and the Imam asked, 'How so and so is doing?' The narrator has said that the man then began to speak of him in very short expressions thinking that he meant thereby wealth and the world. Abu 'Abd Allah, *'Alayhi al-Salam*, then asked, 'How is his religion?' He said, 'It is just as you love.' The Imam said, 'That, by Allah, is wealth.'"

Chapter 93 - Al-Taqiyyah, Guarding and Cautiousness

H 2230, Ch. 93, h 1

Ali ibn Ibrahim has narrated from his father from ibn abu 'Umayr from Hisham ibn Salim and others from abu 'Abd Allah, *'Alayhi al-Salam*, who has said the following:

"About the words of Allah, the Most Majestic, the Most Holy, 'These will receive double reward for their forbearance, replacing evil by virtue. . . .,' (28:54) the Imam said, 'Their excercising patience with observing al-Taqiyyah (cautious protective measures) and their repelling evil by means of good deeds means: al-Taqiyyah is a good deed and publicity or disregarding al-Taqiyyah is evil.'"

H 2231, Ch. 93, h 2

Ibn abu 'Umayr has narrated from Hisham ibn Salim from abu 'Umar al-'A'jami who has said the following:

"Once abu 'Abd Allah, *'Alayhi al-Salam*, said to me, 'O abu 'Umar, nine tenths of religion is in al-Taqiyyah (cautious measures). One who does not observe al-Taqiyyah has no religion. Al-Taqiyyah must be observed in all matters except wine and wiping (a part of Wuzu) over the socks.'"

H 2232, Ch. 93, h 3

A number of our people have narrated from Ahmad ibn Muhammad ibn Khalid from 'Uthman ibn 'Isa from Sama'a from abu Basir who has said the following:

"Abu 'Abd Allah, *'Alayhi al-Salam*, has said, 'Al-Taqiyyah is of the religion of Allah.' I asked, 'Is it of the religion of Allah?' The Imam said, 'Yes, by Allah, it is of the religion of Allah. Yusuf (the prophet) had said, 'O people of the caravan of camels, you are thieves.' By Allah, they had not stolen anything and Ibrahim had said, 'I am ill', by Allah, he had no illness.'"

H 2233, Ch. 93, h 4

Muhammad ibn Yahya has narrated from Ahmad ibn Muhammad ibn 'Isa from Muhammad ibn Khalid and al-Husayn ibn Sa'id all from al-Nadr ibn Suwayd from Yahya ibn 'Imran al-Halabi from Husayn ibn abu al-'Ala' from Habib ibn Bishr who has said the following:

"Abu 'Abd Allah, *'Alayhi al-Salam*, has said, 'I heard my father saying, "By Allah, there is nothing on the face of earth more beloved to me than observing al-Taqiyyah (cautious protective measures)." O Habib, whoever observes al-Taqiyyah Allah raises him up. O Habib, whoever does not observe al-Taqiyyah Allah brings him low. O Habib, people live in peace. When that (reappearing of al-Mahdi) happens this (al-Taqiyyah) no more will happen.'"

H 2234, Ch. 93, h 5

Abu Ali al-Ash'ari has narrated from al-Hassan ibn Ali al-Kufi from al-'Abbas ibn 'Amir from Jabir al-Makfuf from 'Abd Allah ibn abu Ya'fur from abu 'Abd Allah, *'Alayhi al-Salam*, who has said the following:

"Protect your religion and veil it with al-Taqiyyah (protective measures); one who does not observe al-Taqiyyah has no belief. You in the people are like honeybees, in birds. Had birds known what is inside honeybees no honeybee would have been left and it all would have been consumed. Had people known that you love Ahl al-Bayt they might have destroyed you with their tongues, abusing you in private and in public. May Allah bless those of you who are in our Walayah (Divine Guardianship).'"

H 2235, Ch. 93, h 6

Ali ibn Ibrahim has narrated from his father from Hammad from Hariz from those who reported to him from abu 'Abd Allah, *'Alayhi al-Salam*, who has said the following:

"About the words of Allah, the Most Majestic, the Most Holy, '. . . virtue and evil are not equal. . . .', the Imam said that 'Virtue' refers to al-Taqiyyah and 'Evil' is disregarding it, and in the words of Allah, the Most Majestic, the Most Holy, 'If you respond to evil with virtuous deeds . . .', the Imam said, 'Virtue' refers to al-Taqiyyah, '. . . you will certainly find that your enemies will become your intimate friends.'" (41:34)

H 2236, Ch. 93, h 7

Muhammad ibn Yahya has narrated from Ahmad ibn Muhammad ibn 'Isa from al-Hassan ibn Mahbub from Hisham ibn Salim from abu 'Amr al-Kinani who has said the following:

"Once abu 'Abd Allah, *'Alayhi al-Salam*, said, 'O abu 'Amr, what would you do, were I to narrate a Hadith to you or give you a Fatwa (a legal opinion), and you came to me sometimes later to ask about the same issues, but I gave you a Hadith or a Fatwa that contradicts the first one, which one would you follow?' I said, 'I will follow the latest one and ignore the other one.' The Imam said, 'O abu 'Amr, you are right. Allah refuses to accept anything but to worship Him secretly. By Allah, were you to follow al-Taqiyyah it would be better for you and for me. Allah, the Most Majestic, the Most Holy, refuses to accept anything from you and I in His religion but al-Taqiyyah.'"

H 2237, Ch. 93, h 8

It is narrated from him (narrator of the Hadith above) from Ahmad ibn Muhammad from al-Hassan ibn Ali from Durust al-Wasiti who has said the following:

"Abu 'Abd Allah, *'Alayhi al-Salam*, has said, 'No one's al-Taqiyyah reached the level of strictness to that of the people of the Cave who would attend the festivities while wearing neck ties, thus, Allah gave them twice as many rewards.'"

H 2238, Ch. 93, h 9

It is narrated from him (narrator of the Hadith above) from Ahmad ibn Muhammad from al-Hassan ibn Ali ibn Faddal from Hammad ibn Waqid al-Lahham who has said the following:

"Once I came face to face to abu 'Abd Allah, *'Alayhi al-Salam*, on a road and I turned my face away and passed him by. Later I went to see him and said, 'May Allah keep my soul in service for your cause, I sometimes may turn my face away and pass you so as not to cause you any trouble.' The Imam said, 'May Allah grant you blessings, however, yesterday a man passed by me in such and such place and said, 'Upon you be peace, O abu 'Abd Allah.' What he did was not any good or beautiful.'"

H 2239, Ch. 93, h 10

Ali ibn Ibrahim has narrated from Harun ibn Muslim from Mas'adah ibn Sadaqa who has said the following:

"It was said to abu 'Abd Allah, *'Alayhi al-Salam*, 'People narrate that Ali, *'Alayhi al-Salam*, once said from the pulpit in al-Kufah, "O people, one day you will be told to abuse me. You then will do so, then you will be told to denounce me but you will not denounce me." The Imam said, 'How often has this falsehood (lie) been told about Ali, *'Alayhi al-Salam.*' The Imam then said, 'What he said was: 'One day you will be told to abuse me, you must do so then you will be told to denounce me, and I follow the religion of Muhammad, *'Alayhi al-Salam.* He did not say do not denounce me.' The person asking the question then asked, 'Do you say he must have chosen being murdered instead of denouncing?' The Imam said, 'By Allah, there was no such thing necessary for him to do. There was nothing for him but that which happened to 'Ammar ibn Yasir when people of Makkah forced him and his heart was confident with belief. Then Allah, the Most Majestic, the Most Holy, revealed His words about it, '. . . except those who are forced but their heart is confident with belief,' (16:106) to which the Holy Prophet said, 'O 'Ammar, if they would do such things again you also may do as you have already done; Allah, the Most Majestic, the Most Holy, has revealed His words about your good excuse and has commanded you to do again what you did before if they ever repeated their misdeed.'"

H 2240, Ch. 93, h 11

Muhammad ibn Yahya has narrated from Ahmad ibn Muhammad from Ali ibn al-Hakam from Hisham al-Kindy who has said the following:

"I heard abu 'Abd Allah, *'Alayhi al-Salam*, saying, 'You must never do anything that may embarrass us. A small boy causes embarrassment to his father because of his misdeeds. Be the beauty for those to whom you are devoted and do not be an embarrassment to them. Pray along with their tribes, visit their people in ill health, attend their funerals and do not allow anyone exceed you in good deeds. You have all the more reason to exceed others in good deeds. By Allah, no worship is more beloved to Allah than worshipping Him in (al-Khab').' I then asked, 'What is al-Khab'?' The Imam said, 'It is al-Taqiyyah.'"

H 2241, Ch. 93, h 12

It is narrated from him (narrator of the Hadith above) from Ahmad ibn Muhammad from Mu'ammar ibn Khallad who has said the following:

"Once I asked abu al-Hassan, *'Alayhi al-Salam*, about standing up to salute the rulers (to show respect). He said that abu Ja'far, *'Alayhi al-Salam*, has said, 'Al-Taqiyyah is my religion and the religion of my predecessors. Whoever disregards al-Taqiyyah has no belief.'"

H 2242, Ch. 93, h 13

Ali ibn Ibrahim has narrated from his father from Hammad from Rib'i from Zurara from abu Ja'far, *'Alayhi al-Salam*, who has said the following:

"Al-Taqiyyah (protective measures) is for when and wherever needed and the one involved in it knows best how to apply it."

H 2243, Ch. 93, h 14

Ali has narrated from his father from ibn Mahbub from Jamil ibn Salih from Muhammad ibn Marwan from abu 'Abd Allah, *'Alayhi al-Salam*, who has said the following:

"My father, *'Alayhi al-Salam*, has said, 'What could be more delightful to me than al-Taqiyyah; it is a shield for believing people.'"

H 2244, Ch. 93, h 15

Ali has narrated from his father from ibn abu 'Umayr from Jamil from Muhammad ibn Marwan who has said the following:

"Once abu 'Abd Allah, *'Alayhi al-Salam*, said to me, 'What was it that prevented Maytham (may Allah grant him blessings) from al-Taqiyyah?' He by Allah knew that this verse of the Holy Quran was revealed about 'Ammar and his people, '. . . unless he is forced, but his heart is confident with belief. . . .'" (16:106)

H 2245, Ch. 93, h 16

Abu Ali al-Ash'ari has narrated from Muhammad ibn 'Abd al-Jabbar from Safwan from Shu'ayb al-Haddad from Muhammad ibn Muslim from abu Ja'far, *'Alayhi al-Salam*, who has said the following:

"Al-Taqiyyah is made law to save lives. Once it (danger) is already there to take lives, then there is no al-Taqiyyah."

H 2246, Ch. 93, h 17

Muhammad ibn Yahya has narrated from Ahmad ibn Muhammad from ibn Faddal from ibn Bukayr from Muhammad ibn Muslim from abu 'Abd Allah, *'Alayhi al-Salam*, who has said the following:

"As it (time of Imam al-Mahdi) draws closer, al-Taqiyyah will be more intensely needed."

H 2247, Ch. 93, h 18

Ali ibn Ibrahim has narrated from his father from ibn abu 'Umayr from ibn 'Udhaynah from Isma'il al-Ju'fi and Mu'ammar ibn Yahya ibn Sam and Muhammad ibn Muslim and Zurara who have said the following:

"We heard abu Ja'far, *'Alayhi al-Salam*, saying, 'Al-Taqiyyah is whenever the son of Adam is compelled; Allah has made it lawful for him.'"

H 2248, Ch. 93, h 19

Ali ibn Ibrahim has narrated from Muhammad ibn 'Isa from Yunus from ibn Muskan from Hariz from abu 'Abd Allah, *'Alayhi al-Salam*, who has said the following:

"Al-Taqiyyah is a shield of Allah between Allah (His punishing) and His creatures."

H 2249, Ch. 93, h 20

Al-Husayn ibn Muhammad has narrated from Mu'alla ibn Muhammad from Muhammad ibn Jumhur from Ahmad ibn Hamza from al-Husayn ibn al-Mukhtar from abu Basir who has said the following:

"Abu Ja'far, *'Alayhi al-Salam*, has said, 'Meet them (unfriendly people) outwardly and oppose them inwardly when the rulers are childish.'"

H 2250, Ch. 93, h 21

Muhammad ibn Yahya has narrated from Ahmad ibn Muhammad ibn 'Isa from Zakariya al-Mu'min from 'Abd Allah ibn Asad from 'Abd Allah ibn 'Ata' who has said the following:

"Once I said to abu Ja'far, *'Alayhi al-Salam*, 'Two of the people of Kufah were held and it was said to them, "Denounce Amir al-Mu'minin (Ali ibn abu Talib), *'Alayhi al-Salam*. One of them did and the other did not denounce. The one who denounced was released and the other was killed.' The Imam said, 'The one who denounced was an expert of law of his religion and the one who did not denounce was in a hurry to go to paradise.'"

H 2251, Ch. 93, h 22

Ali ibn Ibrahim has narrated from his father from ibn abu 'Umayr from Jamil ibn Salih who has said the following:

"Abu 'Abd Allah, *'Alayhi al-Salam*, has said, 'Stay away from the consequences of slip and mistake (disregarding al-Taqiyyah).'"

H 2252, Ch. 93, h 23

Abu Ali al-Ash'ari has narrated from 'Abd al-Jabbar from Muhammad ibn Isma'il from Ali ibn al-Nu'man from ibn Muskan from 'Abd Allah ibn abu Ya'fur who has said the following:

"I heard abu 'Abd Allah, *'Alayhi al-Salam*, saying, 'Al-Taqiyyah for a believer is a shield and protection. One who does not observe al-Taqiyyah has no belief. A servant of Allah receives a Hadith from us and on that basis he follows the religion of Allah, the Most Majestic, the Most Holy. It then is an honor for him in this world and light for him in the next world. A servant receives a Hadith from us and he makes it public and it becomes humiliation for him in this world and Allah, the Most Majestic, the Most Holy, removes that light from him.'"

Chapter 94 - Silence and Restraint against Publicity

H 2253, Ch. 94, h 1

Muhammad ibn Yahya has narrated from Ahmad ibn Muhammad from ibn Mahbub from Malik ibn 'Atiyyah from abu Hamza from Ali ibn al-Husayn, *'Alayhi al-Salam*, who has said the following:

"I, by Allah, love to redeem two things in my followers with parts of my arms: their rush for quick response and lack of silence and restraint."

H 2254, Ch. 94, h 2

It is narrated from him (narrator of the Hadith above) from Ahmad ibn Muhammad from Muhammad ibn Sinan from 'Ammar ibn Marwan from abu 'Usamah Zayd al-Shahham who has said the following:

"Abu 'Abd Allah, *'Alayhi al-Salam*, has said, 'People were commanded to maintain two characteristics, for the loss of which they involved themselves into something else; they were patience and silent abstinence."

H 2255, Ch. 94, h 3

Ali ibn Ibrahim has narrated from his father from ibn abu 'Umayr from Yunus ibn 'Ammar from Sulayman ibn Khalid who has said the following:

"Abu 'Abd Allah, *'Alayhi al-Salam*, once said, 'O Sulayman, you follow the religion of one for whose silent abstinence Allah grants him honor, but due to his loud publicity, Allah causes his humiliation.'"

H 2256, Ch. 94, h 4

Muhammad ibn Yahya has narrated from Ahmad ibn Muhammad from Ali ibn al-Hakam from 'Abd Allah ibn Bukayr from a man who has said the following:

"Once we in a group went to see abu Ja'far, *'Alayhi al-Salam*, and said to him, 'O descendent of the Messenger of Allah, we intend to travel to Iraq, and request your recommendations.' Abu Ja'far, *'Alayhi al-Salam*, said, 'The stronger ones among you must support the weak ones, the well to do among you must reach out to the poor ones among you, do not expose our secrets and do not publicize our cause. When you receive a Hadith from us accept it only if you find sufficient, two or at least one, supporting evidence from the book of Allah, otherwise, keep it on hold and then refer it to us for verification. You must know that those waiting for this matter (coming of Imam al-Mahdi) have a reward like those who fast all the time and pray every night. Whoever will find himself with our al-Qa'im (al-Mahdi) and will come out with him to do away with our enemies he will have a reward equal to that for twenty martyrs and whoever will be killed supporting our al-Qa'im, his reward will be equal to that for fifteen martyrs.'"

H 2257, Ch. 94, h 5

It is narrated from him (narrator of the Hadith above) from Ahmad ibn Muhammad from Muhammad ibn Sinan from 'Abd al-'Ala' who has said the following:

"I heard abu 'Abd Allah, *'Alayhi al-Salam*, saying, 'Just to affirm our cause is not enough to carry it. To bear our cause is to keep it concealed and protect it from those who do not support it. Convey the greeting of peace to them and tell them, "May Allah grant blessings to those who attract people's love to himself, speak to them (common people) about what they know and conceal from them what they deny."' The Imam then said, 'By Allah, our bitter enemy, is not more of a problem bigger for us than those who speak of us things that we dislike. If you hear a servant (of Allah) publicizing (our cause) then walk to him and turn him away from it. If he did not accept your advice then leave him to one who might prove to be heavier for him and he would listen to him. There are those of you who on request meet the needs of a person with kindness. Be kind to me in my needs as you are kind to each other in your needs. If he accepts from you, that is fine, otherwise, bury his words under your feet and do not say, 'He says so and so.' This will make it difficult for you and for me. By Allah, were you to say what I say, I could confirm that you are of my companions. This is abu Hanifah and he has companions. This is al-Hassan al-Basri and he has his companions. I am a man from Quraysh of the descendents of the Messenger of Allah. I knew the book of Allah in which there is explanation for everything, the beginning of creation, the matters of heavens, the issues of earth, the matters of those in the past, the issues of the later generations, and issues of things that existed and the matters of the things that will come into existence. To me these all are as if I see them before my eyes.'"

H 2258, Ch. 94, h 6

It is narrated from him (narrator of the Hadith above) from Ahmad ibn Muhammad from Ali ibn al-Hakam from al-Rabi' ibn Muhammad al-Musalli from 'Abd Allah ibn Sulayman from abu 'Abd Allah, *'Alayhi al-Salam*, who has said the following:

"Abu 'Abd Allah, *'Alayhi al-Salam*, once said to me, 'Our cause had still been hidden until the children of Kisan began to speak of it on the roads, villages and in large places.'"

H 2259, Ch. 94, h 7

It is narrated from him (narrator of the Hadith above) from Ahmad ibn Muhammad from ibn Mahbub from Jamil ibn Salih from abu 'Ubaydah al-Hadhdha' who has said the following:

"I heard abu Ja'far, *'Alayhi al-Salam*, saying, 'By Allah, the most beloved to me of my companions are most restraining from the worldly attractions (sins), most knowledgeable in Fiqh (laws of Shari'a) and most secretive in our Hadith. Of the worst conditions among them and most disliked is the one who on hearing Hadith ascribes it to us and narrates it from us. Not only does he not accept it, also he abhors it and rejects it. He has made those who follow it turn to disbelief while he does not know. Perhaps the Hadith has come out from us and to us is ascribed and with this he will be out of our Walayah (guardianship)."'

H 2260, Ch. 94, h 8

A number of our people have narrated from Ahmad ibn Muhammad ibn Khalid from his father from 'Abd Allah ibn Yahya from Hariz from Mu'alla ibn Khanith who has said the following:

"Once abu 'Abd Allah, *'Alayhi al-Salam*, said to me, 'O Mu'alla, conceal our cause and do not make it public; to those who conceal our cause and do not publicize it, Allah grants honor in this world. He will make it a light between his eyes in the next life and lead him to paradise. O Mu'alla, whoever publicizes our cause and does not conceal it, Allah humiliates him in this world, removes the light between his eyes in the next life and will make darkness to lead him to fire. O Mu'alla, al-Taqiyyah is my religion and the religion of my predecessors. There is no religion for one who does not observe al-Taqiyyah. O Mu'alla, Allah loves to be worshipped secretly just as He loves to be worshipped publicly. O Mu'alla, one who publicizes our cause is like one who rejects it altogather.'"

H 2261, Ch. 94, h 9

Muhammad ibn Yahya has narrated from Ahmad ibn Muhammad from al-Hassan ibn Ali from Marwan ibn Muslim from 'Ammar who has said the following:

"Once abu 'Abd Allah, *'Alayhi al-Salam*, asked me, 'Did you tell anyone what I told you?' I said, 'No, I have not told anyone except Sulayman ibn Khalid.' The Imam said, 'Very good. Have you not heard the words of the poet: 'Do not allow my secret and your secret pass to a third party. Is it not the case that a secret passing two people is public?'"

H 2262, Ch. 94, h 10

Muhammad ibn Yahya has narrated from Ahmad ibn Muhammad from Ahmad ibn Muhammad ibn abu Nasr who has said the following:

"Once I asked abu al-Hassan al-Rida, *'Alayhi al-Salam*, a question. He refrained silently and said, 'If we give you everything you want, it may become evil for you and the neck of the owner of this cause will be caught tight.'

"Abu Ja'far, *'Alayhi al-Salam*, has said, 'It is the guardianship of Allah, Who told it secretly to Jibril, who secretly told it to Muhammad, *'Alayhi al-Salam*, who secretly told it to Ali, *'Alayhi al-Salam*, who secretly told it to whoever Allah wanted and then you publicize it. Who is he that has heard a word then has held it secretly?'

"Abu Ja'far, *'Alayhi al-Salam*, has said, 'It is in the wisdom of 'Ale Dawud (family of David), "It is necessary for a Muslim to have control over his soul, be attentive to his affairs and have full knowledge of the people of his time." Be pious before Allah and do not publicize our Hadith. It is a fact that Allah defends his friends and exacts recompense for His friends from His enemies. Have you considered how Allah dealt with Ale Barmak (family of Barmak) and how He recompensed for abu al-Hassan, *'Alayhi al-Salam*, when banu 'Ash'ath faced the great danger and Allah defended them for their supporting abu al-Hassan, *'Alayhi al-Salam*? In Iraq you are well aware of the deeds of those Pharaohs and the respite that Allah has given them. Therefore, you must observe piety before Allah and do not allow the worldly life to deceive you. Do not be confused about those who have been given respite. It is as if the matter (reappearance of al-Mahdi, *'Alayhi al-Salam*) is almost within your reach.'"

H 2263, Ch. 94, h 11

Al-Husayn ibn Muhammad has narrated from Mu'alla ibn Muhammad from al-Hassan ibn Ali al-Washsha' from 'Umar ibn Aban from abu Basir who has said the following:

"I heard abu 'Abd Allah, *'Alayhi al-Salam*, saying, 'The Messenger of Allah has said, "Tuba' (a tree in paradise) is for a servant who is unknown to people but Allah knows him. Such people are the torches of guidance and the fountains of knowledge. Through them every darkening calamity brightens. They do not publicize undisclosed facts and they are not quarrelsome braggarts.'"

H 2264, Ch. 94, h 12

Ali ibn Ibrahim has narrated from Muhammad ibn 'Isa from Yunus from abu al-Hassan al-Asbahani from abu 'Abd Allah, *'Alayhi al-Salam*, who has said the following:

"Amir al-Mu'minin (Ali ibn abu Talib), *'Alayhi al-Salam*, has said, 'Tuba' (a tree in paradise) is for every servant (of Allah) who is unnoticed among the people but knows people and they do not know him. Allah knows him from His side with happiness. They are the torches of guidance. Through them every darkening calamity is removed aside and for them every door to blessing opens. They do not publicize undisclosed facts and they are not quarrelsome braggarts.' He has also said, 'Speak of the good so you become known for it. Do good and be of its people and do not be hastening announcers. The best of you are those who on looking up on them one is reminded of Allah and the wicked ones among you are those who publicize undisclosed facts, cause separation among the loved ones and search for faults in the innocent people.'"

H 2265, Ch. 94, h 13

A number of our people have narrated from Ahmad ibn Muhammad from 'Uthman ibn 'Isa from those he has narrated from and who has said the following:

"Abu 'Abd Allah, *'Alayhi al-Salam*, has said, 'Control your tongues and stay home, no one will ever disturb you in particular. Zaydi people are still a protection for you and they will always be as such.'"

H 2266, Ch. 94, h 14

It is narrated from him (narrator of the Hadith above) from 'Uthman ibn 'Isa from abu al-Hassan, *'Alayhi al-Salam*, who has said the following:

"When there is something in one of your hands, if you can, do not allow the other hand to know about it.' The narrator has said that there was a man in his presence and they discussed publicity. The Imam said, 'Control your tongue and you will find honor and do not allow people to become in control of your neck to humiliate you.'"

H 2267, Ch. 94, h 15

Muhammad ibn Yahya has narrated from Ahmad ibn Muhammad ibn 'Isa from Ali ibn al-Hakam from Khalid ibn Nujayh from abu 'Abd Allah, *'Alayhi al-Salam*, who has said the following:

"Our cause is hidden and veiled by the (Divine) covenant. Whoever disregards it against us Allah will humiliate him."

H 2268, Ch. 94, h 16

Al-Husayn ibn Muhammad an Muhammad ibn Yahya all have narrated from Ali ibn Muhammad ibn Sa'd from Muhammad ibn Muslim from Muhammad ibn Sa'id ibn Ghazwan from Ali ibn al-Hakam from 'Umar ibn Aban from 'Isa ibn abu Mansur who has said the following:

"I heard abu 'Abd Allah, *'Alayhi al-Salam*, saying, 'A breath with a sigh of concern and sadness due to injustice done to us is Tasbih (speaking of the glory of Allah) and one's concern about our cause is worship, his concealing our secret is Jihad (hard work for the cause of Allah).'"

"Muhammad ibn Sa'id told me to write it down with gold. I then did not write anything better than that."

Chapter 95 - A Believer's Signs and Qualities

H 2269, Ch. 95, h 1

Muhammad ibn Ja'far has narrated from Muhammad ibn Isma'il from 'Abd Allah ibn Dahir from al-Hassan ibn Yahya from Qathm abu Qatadah al-Harrani from 'Abd Allah ibn Yunus from abu 'Abd Allah, *'Alayhi al-Salam*, who has said the following:

"Once a man called Hammam, an assiduous worshipper practicing religious rules and a hardworking man came to Amir al-Mu'minin (Ali ibn abu Talib), *'Alayhi al-Salam*, during his speech and said, 'O Amir al-Mu'minin, describe for us the qualities of the believer as if we see him before our eyes.'

"Amir al-Mu'minin (Ali ibn abu Talib), *'Alayhi al-Salam*, said, 'O Hammam, a believer is a smart, intelligent one whose delight is on his face and whose sadness is in his heart, his chest is vastly open, his soul is most humble, he criticizes one's leaning to every mortal, exhorts to go for everything good. He is not hateful, quarrelsome, scandalous, faultfinding or backbiting. He dislikes high positions (of negative nature) and is an enemy of fame and publicity. His sadness remains for a long time, his ambition is far reaching. He very often remains silent, dignified, ever remembering (the Lord), exercising patience, grateful, sad due to his thoughts, happy with his poverty, easy in his nature, kindhearted, of strong loyalty, of very little trouble, not a liar or insulting.

"When laughing, he does not burst. When angry he does not rush. His laughing is smiles, his question is to learn, his review is to understand, his knowledge is plentiful, his forbearance is great and his blessing is a great deal. He is not stingy, he does not hasten, irritate or act as an extremist, is not unjust in his judgment, or unfair due to his knowledge. His soul is more solid than a rock, his labor is more sweet than honey. He is not greedy, intolerant, violent, conceited, pretending or exaggerating. He is graceful in disputed matters, of honorable visitation, a man of justice when angry, a friend when asked. He is not adventurous, or insulting and coercive. His love is pure, he is of solid promise, of fulfilling commitment, affectionate, a keeper of good relations, forbearing, calm, of very little that is extraneous, happy with Allah, the Most Majestic, the Most Holy, and opposes his own desires. He is not rough toward his inferiors and does not indulge in what is not his business. He is a supporter of religion, a defender of believers, a stronghold for Muslims, and admiration does not affect him negatively, greed does not hurt his heart, playfulness does not change his judgment and ignorant ones cannot find the limits of his knowledge.

"His words are many and he is a determined scholar. He is not abusive or furious. He reaches out without harshness, is generous not a spendthrift, is not deceitful or treacherous, is not a faultfinder or unjust to a human being. He is a friend of the creatures, effortful on earth, assistant of the weak and a helper of the helpless. He does not violate what is hidden or uncover secrets, his trials are a great deal and his complaints very little. He remembers the good that he had seen, covers up the evil that he may observe, hides the defects, safeguards the unseen, corrects slips and forgives mistakes. He does not walk away from an advice that he can give, and he does not give up reforming an unjust instance. He is trustworthy, steadfast, pious, clean, purified and consenting. He accepts excuses, speaks of someone with grace and he is good and expects good from people.

"He accuses his soul of defects, loves for the sake of Allah with understanding and knowledge, cuts off relations for the sake of Allah with firmness and determination. Happiness does not trespass upon him and intense happiness does not make him excited. He is a reminder for the scholar and a teacher for the ignorant. He is not expected to cause a calamity. He is not feared for causing a tragedy, every effort to him is more sincere than his own and every soul is more correct than his own. He knows his defects. He is busy with his own sadness. He does not trust anyone except his Lord. He feels a stranger, lonely, dispossessed and sad. He loves for the sake of Allah, strives for the sake of Allah to follow His happiness. He does not revenge by himself for his own self. He does not make friends to make his Lord angry. He sits with the poor, is a friend of the truthful ones, a supporter of the people of truth and an assistant for those near to him. He is like a father for the orphans, like a husband for the widows, the first hope for the destitute, expected to remove every resentful matter and to relieve every difficulty.

"He is light and happy, is not frowning or sly, is strong, controlling of anger, smiling, sharp-sighted and greatly cautious. He does not ignore, and if ignored, he is forbearing. He is not stingy and if stinginess, is used against him he exercises patience. He understands, thus he is bashful, is content, independent and is self-sufficient. His bashfulness is higher than his lust, his love is higher than his jealousy and his forgiveness is higher than his hate. He does not speak without correctness and does not dress unless it is economical. He walks humbly, is submissive before his Lord in obedience and is happy with Him in all conditions. His intention is pure and sincere. His deeds are free of fraud and deceit. His observations are good lessons, his silence is thoughtful and his words are wisdom. He is advising, charitable and brotherly. He gives good advice in public and in private. He does not abandon his brother, does not backbite him and does not plot against him. He does not regret what he has missed, and does not become sad for whatever befalls him. He does not hope for what is not lawful. He does not fail in hardships and does not perpetrate in comfort. He mixes forbearance with knowledge and reason with patience. He is not lazy but is always active, of very short longing and of very few slips. (Good) is expected through him, his heart is fearful, he always speaks of his Lord, his soul is content, his ignorance is negative, his affairs are easy, he is sad for his sins, his lust is dead, his anger is controlled and his moral behaviors are lucent.

"His neighbors live safely with him, his pride is weak, he is content with whatever is determined for him, his patience is strong, his affair is well established and his remembering (the Lord) is a great deal. He meets people to learn and remains silent for safety, he asks questions to understand, and he trades to earn. He does not remain silent for good to be subjected to injustice, and does not speak to be used in doing injustice to others. His soul is tired of him and people are comfortable with him. He has tired his soul for the gains of the next life and has provided comfort to others by means of his soul. If rebellion is committed against him he exercises patience until Allah finds support for him. His distancing when distancing is needed comes in overlooking and in graceful disregard, and his closeness when closeness is needed comes as kindness and blessings. His distancing is not out of boastfulness or greatness and his closeness is not a plot or deceit. It is because he follows the footsteps of those before him, the people of goodness. Thus, he is the leader for those after him.'"

"The narrator has said that Hammam breathed very deeply and fell down unconscious. Amir al-Mu'minin (Ali ibn abu Talib), *'Alayhi al-Salam*, said, 'By Allah I was afraid of its effect for him. This is how effective advice works on people deserving such advice. Someone said, 'Why does it not apply to you, O Amir al-Mu'minin?' The Imam said, 'For everything there is an appointed time that is not surpassed and a cause that does not fail. Wait, and do not transgress. It was a blow that Satan made to flow through your tongue.'"

H 2270, Ch. 95, h 2
Ali ibn Ibrahim has narrated from his father from ibn Mahbub from Jamil ibn Salih from 'Abd Allah ibn Ghalib from abu 'Abd Allah, *'Alayhi al-Salam*, who has said the following:
"It is worthwhile of a believer to have eight qualities:

(a) Dignity in volatile conditions, (b) patience on facing a misfortune, (c) gratitude in comfortable conditions, (d) contentment with what Allah has given him for sustenance, (e) justice for enemies, (f) not to be a burden for the friends, (g) that his own body be tired of him and that (h) people be comfortable with him.'

"Knowledge is the friend of the believer, forbearance is his secretary, patience is the commander of his army, courteousness is his brother and speaking softly is his father."

H 2271, Ch. 95, h 3

Abu Ali al-Ash'ari has narrated from Muhammad ibn 'Abd al-Jabbar from ibn Faddal from Mansur ibn Yunus from abu Hamza from Ali ibn al-Husayn, *'Alayhi al-Salam*, who has said the following:

"The believer remains silent for safety and speaks to benefit. He does not speak of his trust to the friends and does not withhold his testimony for the people of distant relationships. He does not do anything good to show off and does not ignore it due to bashfulness. If he cleanses himself he fears what they (people) say, and asks forgiveness for what they do not know. The words (in his praise) of those who do not know do not make him boastful and he is afraid of the sum of his deeds."

H 2272, Ch. 95, h 4

A number of our people have narrated from Ahmad ibn Muhammad ibn Khalid from certain individuals who narrated to him in a marfu' manner from abu 'Abd Allah, *'Alayhi al-Salam*, who has said the following:

"The believer has power in religion. He is of solid determination but with soft words, his belief is in certainty, he has greed in deep understanding, is active in guidance, and virtuous in steadfastness. He has knowledge in forbearance, he is smart in friendliness, and generous in truth, modest in wealth, graceful in poverty, forgiving in power, and obedient to Allah in good advice. His desires are ending, he exsercizes restraint against desires, greed in Jihad (hard work for the cause of Allah), prayer in business, patience in hardships, dignity in volatile conditions, endurance in suffering, and gratefulness in comfortable conditions. He does not backbite or act boastfully, nor does he disregard maintaining good relations with relatives and neither is he neglectful. He is not harsh and stubborn. His eyes are not ahead of him and his stomach does not disgrace him, his private parts do not overpower him. He does not envy people; he measures but is not measured. He is not extravagant, he helps the oppressed, he has blessings for the destitute, his soul is tired of him and people receive comfort from him. He is not interested in worldly honor and does not complain because of worldly humiliation. People look forward to be closer to him but he is preoccupied with his own business. No defect is found in his judgment, no flaw is found in his opinion, and no failure takes place in his religion. He provides instruction for those who consult him and assists those who assist him. He shuns indecency and ignorance."

H 2273, Ch. 95, h 5

It is narrated from him (narrator of the Hadith above) from certain individuals of his people from in a marfu' manner from one of them (abu Ja'far or abu 'Abd Allah, *'Alayhi al-Salam,*) who has said the following:

"Amir al-Mu'minin (Ali ibn abu Talib), *'Alayhi al-Salam*, once passed by a gathering of Quraysh where he found the people in white clothes, of clear complexion, frequently laughing and who pointed out their fingers to whoever passed (near) by. Then he passed by a gathering of al-Aws and Khazraj where he found people of worn out bodies, whose necks were thinning, their colors had turned pale and were very humble in their words.

"Amir al-Mu'minin (Ali ibn abu Talib), *'Alayhi al-Salam*, wondered about his observation, he came to the Messenger of Allah and said, 'May Allah keep my soul and the souls of my parents in service for your cause, I passed by a gathering of the tribe of so and so.' He described them for the Holy Prophet. He then said, 'I also passed by a gathering of al-Aws and al-Khazraj.' He described them for the Holy Prophet. He then said, 'They all are believing people. O Messenger of Allah, describe for me the qualities of the believers.'

"The Messenger of Allah bent down his head for a while, then he raised his head and said, 'There are twenty qualities in a believer without which his belief is not complete. Of the qualities of the believing people, O Ali, is their presence in prayer, quick payment of al-Zakat (charity), feeding the destitute, placing of their hand on the heads of the orphans (to comfort them), cleansing of their clothes, and their tying up their waist with covering. They are those who do not lie when speaking, do not disregard their promise, and do not violate their trust. They tell the truth when they speak up, at night they are monks and are lions during the day. During the days they fast and stand up for worship at night. They do not harm the neighbors and the neighbors do not experience any harm from them. They are those who walk on earth in humble manners, and their steps move to the homes of the widows (to help) and in the procession for funerals. May Allah make us of the pious ones.'"

H 2274, Ch. 95, h 6
Ali ibn Ibrahim has narrated from his father from ibn abu 'Umayr from al-Qasim ibn 'Urwah from abu al-'Abbas who has said that abu 'Abd Allah, *'Alayhi al-Salam*, has said the following:
"Whoever enjoys a virtuous deed and is disgusted with a sin is a believer."

H 2275, Ch. 95, h 7
Muhammad ibn Yahya has narrated from Ahmad ibn Muhammad ibn 'Isa from Muhammad ibn al-Hassan ibn (za)'lan from abu Ishaq al-Khurasani from 'Amr ibn Jumay' al-'Abdi from abu 'Abd Allah, *'Alayhi al-Salam*, who has said the following:
"Our Shi'a (followers) look pale, with parched (lips), slim and they receive the darkening night with sadness."

H 2276, Ch. 95, h 8
Ali ibn Ibrahim has narrated from his father from Hammad ibn 'Isa from Ibrahim ibn 'Umar al-Yamani from a man from abu 'Abd Allah, *'Alayhi al-Salam*, who has said the following:
"Our Shi'a (followers) are people of guidance, of piety, of goodness, of belief and people of victory and triumph."

H 2277, Ch. 95, h 9
Muhammad ibn Yahya has narrated from Ahmad ibn Muhammad ibn 'Isa from Muhammad ibn 'Isma'il from Mansur Bazarj from Mufaddal who has said the following:
"Abu 'Abd Allah, *'Alayhi al-Salam*, has said, 'Beware of the thoughtless people. Shi'a (followers) of Ali, *'Alayhi al-Salam*, are only those whose stomach and private parts are chaste, and are intensely involved in Jihad. They work for the sake of their Creator in the hope for His rewards and for fear of His punishment. If you see such people they are the Shi'a (followers) of Ja'far ibn Muhammad, *'Alayhi al-Salam*.'"

H 2278, Ch. 95, h 10

A number of our people have narrated from Sahl ibn Ziyad from ibn Mahbub from Ali ibn Ri'ab ibn abu Ya'fur from abu 'Abd Allah, *'Alayhi al-Salam*, who has said the following:

"The Shi'a (followers) of Ali, *'Alayhi al-Salam*, were of slim and lean bellies, and withered lips. They were people of compassion, knowledge, and forbearance. They were known as of monkish practice. You should assist each other in your cause with restraint from worldly attractions (sins) and be very hard working."

H 2279, Ch. 95, h 11

Ali ibn Ibrahim has narrated from Muhammad ibn 'Isa from Yunus from Safwan al-Jammal who has said the following:

"Abu 'Abd Allah, *'Alayhi al-Salam*, has said, 'Of believers are only those who even on becoming angry do not deviate from the truth and when they become happy it does not take them into falsehood and when in power they do not take more than what is for them.'"

H 2280, Ch. 95, h 12

Muhammad ibn Yahya has narrated from Ahmad ibn Muhammad ibn 'Isa from Ali ibn al-Nu'man from ibn Muskan from Sulayman ibn Khalid who has said the following:

"Once abu Ja'far, *'Alayhi al-Salam*, said to me, 'O Sulayman, do you know who a Muslim is?' I said, 'May Allah keep my soul in service for your cause, you know better.' The Imam said, 'A Muslim is one from whose tongue and hands other Muslims are safe.' Then the Imam said, 'Do you know who a believer is?' I said, 'You know better.' The Imam said, 'A believer is one who is an accepted trustworthy person among the Muslims in their properties and lives. It is unlawful for a Muslim to be unjust toward a Muslim, betray him or push him aside in his helplessness.'"

H 2281, Ch. 95, h 13

Muhammad ibn Yahya has narrated from Ahmad ibn Muhammad from al Hassan ibn Mahbub from abu Ayyub from abu 'Ubaydah from abu Ja'far, *'Alayhi al-Salam*, who has said the following:

"A believer is one whose agreement does not lead him into sin or falsehood. When he is angry it does not take him out of speaking the words of truth, when in power it does not lead him to cross over to where he has no right."

H 2282, Ch. 95, h 14

A number of our people have narrated from Ahmad ibn Muhammad ibn Khalid from his father from abu al-Bakhtari in a marfu' manner from the Imam who has said the following:

"Believers are of serenity and soft words. They are easy to lead like the camel harnessed by the nose, who does not resist the leader who makes him sit even on a rock."

H 2283, Ch. 95, h 15

Ali ibn Ibrahim has narrated from his father from al-Nawfali from al-Sakuni from abu 'Abd Allah Who has said the following:

"Three things are of the signs of a believer: having knowledge of the existence of Allah, who to love and who dislike."

H 2284, Ch. 95, h 16

Through the same chain of narrators it is narrated from the Messenger of Allah who has said the following:

"A believer is like the tree whose leaves do not fall off in summer or in winter. They asked, 'O Messenger of Allah, what tree is it?' He said, 'It is the palm-tree.'"

H 2285, Ch. 95, h 17

A number of our people have narrated from Sahl ibn Ziyad from Muhammad ibn 'Uramah from (abu) Ibrahim al-'A'jami from certain individuals of our people from abu 'Abd Allah, *'Alayhi al-Salam*, who has said the following:

"A believer is forbearing. He is not ignorant and if he is ignored he remains forbearing. He does not do injustice and if he is oppressed he forgives. He is not stingy, if stinginess is exercised against him he exercises patience."

H 2286, Ch. 95, h 18

A number of our people have narrated from Ahmad ibn Muhammad ibn Khalid from Isma'il ibn Mehran from Mundhar ibn Jayfar from Adam abu al-Husayn al-Lu'lu'i from abu 'Abd Allah, *'Alayhi al-Salam*, who has said the following:

"A believer is one whose earning is pleasantly clean, whose moral behavior is excellent and whose conscience is not ill. He gives to charity the extra from his property and holds back the extra of his words. People do not feel threatened by his evil and he yields to justice for people against his own soul."

H 2287, Ch. 95, h 19

Abu Ali al-Ash'ari has narrated from Muhammad ibn 'Abd al-Jabbar from al-Hassan ibn Ali from abu Kahmas from Sulayman ibn Khalid from abu Ja'far, *'Alayhi al-Salam*, who has said the following:

"The Messenger of Allah has said, 'Do you want me to tell you about believers? He is one whose trustworthiness believers trust in matters of their lives and properties. Do you want me to tell you who a Muslim is? He is one from whose tongue and hands Muslims are safe. An immigrant is one who migrates from evils and desists from what Allah has prohibited. It is unlawful for believers to be unjust to a believer, betray him, backbite him or push him aside with a harmful push.'"

H 2288, Ch. 95, h 20

Muhammad ibn Yahya has narrated from Ahmad ibn Muhammad ibn 'Isa from Muhammad ibn Sinan from Mufaddal ibn 'Umar from abu Ayyub al-'Attar from Jabir who has said the following:

"Abu Ja'far, *'Alayhi al-Salam*, has said, 'The Shi'a (followers) of Ali, *'Alayhi al-Salam*, are only those who are forbearing, scholars, with parched lips and one can find signs similar to those of the monks on their faces.'"

H 2289, Ch. 95, h 21

A number of our people have narrated from Ahmad ibn Muhammad ibn Khalid from al-Hassan ibn Mahbub from 'Abd Allah ibn Sinan from Ma'ruf ibn Kharrabuz from abu Ja'far, *'Alayhi al-Salam*, who has said the following:

"Once Amir al-Mu'minin (Ali ibn abu Talib), *'Alayhi al-Salam*, prayed the morning prayer with people in Iraq. After prayer he gave a speech on having fear of Allah. He wept and made people weep. He then said, 'By Allah, I lived with a people, in the times of my beloved one, the Messenger of Allah, who were ragged, dusty and slim-bellied. Between their eyes it looked like the hooves of a goat.

They spent the night in prostration and in standing position before their Lord, only resting on their feet or forehead. They whispered to their Lord to set their necks free from the fire and, by Allah, I saw them in such condition and they still were afraid and anxious (because of the next life).'"

H 2290, Ch. 95, h 22

It is narrated from him (narrator of the Hadith above) from al-Sindy ibn Muhammad from Muhammad ibn al-Salt from abu Hamza from Ali ibn al-Husayn, *'Alayhi al-Salam*, who has said the following:

"Once Amir al-Mu'minin (Ali ibn abu Talib), *'Alayhi al-Salam*, prayed the morning prayer and remained in his place until the sun rose up to the length of a spear and then turned his face to people and said, 'By Allah I lived in the times of a people who spent the night prostrating and standing before their Lord, changing positions only to rest on their knees or forehead, as if they could hear the roaring of fire in their ears. Were Allah mentioned they swerved like branches of trees in the wind, as if the people had spent the night totally neglectful (of worship).' The narrator has said, 'The Imam, *'Alayhi al-Salam*, thereafter was never seen laughing until he passed away.'"

H 2291, Ch. 95, h 23

Ali ibn Ibrahim has narrated from Salih ibn al-Sindy from Ja'far ibn Bashir from al-Mufaddal ibn 'Umar who has said the following:

"Abu 'Abd Allah, *'Alayhi al-Salam*, has said, 'If you want to see my companions then look to those whose restraining from worldly attraction (sins) is intense, who fear their Creator in the hope for His rewards. If you find such people they are my companions.'"

H 2292, Ch. 95, h 24

A number of our people have narrated from Ahmad ibn Muhammad ibn Khalid from Muhammad ibn al-Hassan ibn Shammun from 'Abd Allah ibn 'Amr ibn al-Ash'ath from 'Abd Allah ibn Hammad al-Ansari from 'Amr ibn abu al-Miqdam from his father from abu Ja'far, *'Alayhi al-Salam*, who has said the following:

"Amir al-Mu'minin (Ali ibn abu Talib), *'Alayhi al-Salam*, has said, 'Our Shi'a (followers) spend for (the cause of) our Walayah (Divine Authority), love each other for the sake of our love, and visit each other to preserve our cause. They are those who do not commit injustice when angered, and are not excessive when they agree. They are blessings for the neighbors and peace for those who associate with them.'"

H 2293, Ch. 95, h 25

It is narrated from him (narrator of the Hadith above) from Muhammad ibn Ali from Muhammad ibn Sinan from 'Isa al-Nahriri from abu 'Abd Allah, *'Alayhi al-Salam*, who has said the following:

"The Messenger of Allah has said, 'Whoever comes to know Allah and realizes His greatness does not allow his mouth to speak or his stomach to eat. He engages his soul in fasting and standing for prayer until it is clean and exhausted.' They then said, 'May Allah keep the souls of our parents in service for your cause, O Messenger of Allah, is it not that such people are close friends of Allah?' The Messenger of Allah then said, 'The close friends of Allah kept silent and it was considered speaking of Allah, they looked and it served as a good lesson, they spoke and it was wisdom, they walked and that was blessings among the people.

Had it not been for the appointed time of their life span that was written down for them, their spirit would not have remained in their bodies for fear of torment and the desire for rewards.'"

H 2294, Ch. 95, h 26

It is narrated from him (narrator of the Hadith above) from certain individuals of his people from the people of Iraq in a marfu' manner who has said the following:

"Al-Hassan ibn Ali, *'Alayhi al-Salam*, once addressed the people saying, 'I like to tell you about one of my friends who was the greatest in my sight. The head of what was the greatest in my sight about him was the worthlessness of the world in his sight. He was free of the control of his stomach, thus, he did not have any appetite for what he could not find; he, however, would not accede when he did find it. He was out of the control of his private parts and it would not weigh his reason and opinion lightly. He was out of the control of ignorance, thus, he would not extend his hands unless he was confident of its benefits. He did not desire, become angry, or disappointed. Most of the time he remained silent, and when he spoke, he surpassed the speakers. He did not enter in arguments or take part in claims. He would not testify without the presence of a judge. He was not unaware of his brothers (in belief) and did not appropriate anything for himself without them. He was the weakest of the weak people but in serious matters he acted as an advancing lion. He did not blame anyone without a good cause. He would do what he said, and would not say what he would not do. When he became attracted to two things that he did not know which is better he would ignore that which he desired most. He would not complain for any pain before anyone unless he had known that one had a cure for it and would not consult anyone unless he had hope for good advice from him. He did not become frustrated, angered, and did not complain, desire, revenge and did not remain neglectful of his enemies. Therefore, you must acquire such noble moral behaviors if you can. You must acquire the little if you cannot bear the whole. There is no means and power without Allah.'"

H 2295, Ch. 95, h 27

Ali ibn Ibrahim has narrated from Muhammad ibn 'Isa from Yunus from Mihzam and certain individuals of our people from Muhammad ibn Ali from Muhammad ibn Ishaq al-Kahili and Abu Ali al-Ash'ari from al-Hassan ibn Ali al-Kufi from al-'Abbas ibn 'Amir from Rabi' ibn Muhammad all from Mehzam al-Asadi who has said the following:

"Abu 'Abd Allah, *'Alayhi al-Salam*, once said, 'O Mehzam, our Shi'a (followers) are those whose voices do not extend farther than their ears and their animosity do not reach beyond their bodies. They do not praise us openly, associate faultfinders with us and do not argue in our defense against our enemies. When they meet the believers they respect and honor them. When they meet the ignorant they distance themselves from him.' I (the narrator) then asked the Imam, 'May Allah keep my soul in service for your cause, how should I deal with these pretending Shi'as?' The Imam said, 'With them there are cases of distinguishing, changes and filtrations. Certain years destroy them, plagues kill them, and schisms disintegrate them. Our Shi'a (followers) do not do the barking of a dog or the craving of a crow, do not ask our enemies for help even if he may die of hunger.' The narrator has said that I then asked, 'May Allah keep my soul in service for your cause, where can I find them?' The Imam said, 'You may find them around the world. The standard of living of our Shi'a (followers) is low and their homes are transient. Although present in a place, they are not noticeable, in their absence they are not missed, of death they are not frightened, on the graves they visit each other and on being asked for help they show kindness. Their hearts do not have differences even if their homes might be different.' The Imam then said, 'The Messenger of Allah has said, "I am a city and Ali is the door. One who thinks he can enter the city but not through the door is a liar, so also is one who thinks he loves me but he hates Ali, *'Alayhi al-Salam*.'"

H 2296, Ch. 95, h 28
A number of our people have narrated from Ahmad ibn Muhammad ibn Khalid from 'Uthman ibn 'Isa from Sama'a ibn Mehran from abu 'Abd Allah, *'Alayhi al-Salam*, who has said the following:

"Whoever in his dealing with people does not do injustice to them, in his speaking does not lie to them and in his promise does not fail to keep it is among those whose backbiting is unlawful, whose kindness is complete, whose justice has become public and it is necessary to establish brotherly relations with him."

H 2297, Ch. 95, h 29
It is narrated from him (narrator of the Hadith above) from ibn Faddal from 'Asim ibn Humayd from abu Hamza al-Thumali from 'Abd Allah ibn al-Hassan from his mother, Fatimah bint al-Husayn ibn Ali, *'Alayhi al-Salam*, who has said the following:

"The Messenger of Allah has said, 'Whoever has three qualities, the quality of his belief is complete: if he is happy it does not lead him to falsehood, his anger does not lead him out of the truth and when in power does not take hold of what is not rightfully his.'"

H 2298, Ch. 95, h 30
It is narrated from him (narrator of the Hadith above) from his father from 'Abd Allah ibn al-Qasim from abu Basir from abu 'Abd Allah, *'Alayhi al-Salam*, who has said the following:

"Amir al-Mu'minin (Ali ibn abu Talib), *'Alayhi al-Salam*, has said, 'Religious people have certain signs by means of which they are recognized. Of such signs are truthfulness in their words, safekeeping of trust, steadfastness in their promise, maintaining good relations with relatives, kindness to weak ones, smaller degree of expectation from women, [or he said, yield to them in smaller degrees], excellence in moral behavior, vastness of moral discipline, following knowledge and that which leads closer to Allah, the Most Majestic, the Most Holy, with distinction. Tuba' is for them and the good ending. 'Tuba' is a tree in paradise that has its roots in the house of the Holy Prophet, Muhammad, *'Alayhi al-Salam*. 'Which quality is more graceful for a man?' The Imam said. There will be no believer with a home without a branch of that tree. No desire will emerge in their heart but that the branch will provide. A horseman may run under its shadow for a hundred years and the shadow will not end. A crow (with the longest life span in birds) may fly from its trunk upward but before reaching the top of the tree will drop death due to old age. Therefore, you must develop an interest in this. Believers are busy with themselves and people are comfortable with them. When the night grows dark they fix their faces on earth in prostration before Allah, the Most Majestic, the Most Holy, with the noblest parts of their body. They whisper to the the One Who has created them, about setting free of their necks from fire and as such you must also become.'"

H 2299, Ch. 95, h 31

It is narrated from him (narrator of the Hadith above) from Isma'il ibn Mehran from Sayf ibn 'Amirah from Sulayman ibn 'Amr al-Nakha'i who has said that narrated to him al-Husayn ibn Sayf from his brother Ali from Sulayman from those who he mentioned (in his book) from abu Ja'far, *'Alayhi al-Salam*, who has said the following:

"The Holy Prophet was asked about the best ones among the servants (of Allah). The Holy Prophet said, 'They are those who enjoy doing good deeds, and ask forgiveness when they do bad deeds, thank when they are favored, exercise patience when they suffer and forgive when they are subjected to anger.'"

H 2300, Ch. 95, h 32

Through the same chain of narrators it is narrated from abu Ja'far, *'Alayhi al-Salam*, who has said the following:

"The Holy Prophet has said, 'The best among you are those who possess al-Nuha'.' He was asked, 'O Messenger of Allah, who are possessors of al-Nuha'?' He then said, 'They are those who possess excellent moral discipline and a heavy power of reason, maintain good relations with relatives, who are kind to mothers and fathers, committed to help the poor, neighbors, orphans, who serve food (to the needy), who spread peace in the world and who pray when people sleep negligently.'"

H 2301, Ch. 95, h 33

It is narrated from him (narrator of the Hadith above) from al-Haytham al-Nahdi from 'Abd al-'Aziz ibn 'Umar from certain individuals of his people from Yahya ibn 'Imran al-Halabi who has said the following:

"Once I asked abu 'Abd Allah, *'Alayhi al-Salam*, 'Which quality is more graceful for a man?' The Imam said, 'Of such qualities are: reverence that is not a cause for any fear, magnanimity without expecting any recompense, and business, but not in worldly matters.'"

H 2302, Ch. 95, h 34

Muhammad ibn Yahya has narrated from Ahmad ibn Muhammad ibn 'Isa from al-Hassan ibn Mahbub from abu Wallad al-Hannat from abu 'Abd Allah, *'Alayhi al-Salam*, who has said the following:

"Ali ibn al-Husayn, *'Alayhi al-Salam*, has said, 'Signs of perfect religion of a Muslim are his restraining from speaking things that do not concern him, his reduced disagreement, his forbearance, patience and his excellent moral behavior.'"

H 2303, Ch. 95, h 35

Ali ibn Ibrahim has narrated from Muhammad ibn 'Isa from Yunus from Muhammad ibn 'Arafah from abu 'Abd Allah, *'Alayhi al-Salam*, who has said the following:

"The Holy Prophet once asked, 'Do you want me to tell you who is more similar to me? They replied, 'Yes, O Messenger of Allah.' The Holy Prophet then said, 'It is he whose moral behavior is most excellent, whose sheltering for protection is most gentle, who is most virtuous toward his relatives, of the most intense love for his brothers in religion, who bears the most patience for the truth, who suppresses his anger the most, whose forgiveness is most graceful and whose yielding to justice is most strict in both relaxed and irritated conditions.'"

H 2304, Ch. 95, h 36

Muhammad ibn Yahya has narrated from Ahmad ibn Muhammad from ibn Mahbub from Malik ibn 'Atiyyah from abu Hamza from Ali ibn al-Husayn, *'Alayhi al-Salam*, who has said the following:

"It is of the moral behavior of believers to spend proportionately to their standard of living, raise such standards to what is possible, fairness to people and initiation in offering the greeting of peace."

H 2305, Ch. 95, h 37

Muhammad ibn Yahya has narrated from Ahmad ibn Muhammad ibn 'Isa from ibn Faddal from ibn Bukayr from Zurara from abu Ja'far, *'Alayhi al-Salam*, who has said the following:

"A believer is stronger than a mountain. A mountain loses its parts but no loss takes place in the religion of a believer."

H 2306, Ch. 95, h 38

Ali ibn Ibrahim has narrated from Salih ibn Sindy from Ja'far ibn Bashir from Ishaq ibn 'Ammar from abu 'Abd Allah, *'Alayhi al-Salam*, who has said the following:

"A believer is of valuable assistance, of very light expenses, of excellent plans for living and does not allow to be bitten twice from the same opening."

H 2307, Ch. 95, h 39

Ali ibn Muhammad ibn Bandar has narrated from Ibrahim ibn Ishaq from Sahl ibn al-Harith from al-Dalhath servant of al-Rida, *'Alayhi al-Salam*, who has said the following:

"I heard al-Rida, *'Alayhi al-Salam*, saying, 'A believer cannot become a believer unless he has three qualities: one tradition from his Lord, one from His Holy Prophet and one from His Waliyy (one who possess Divine Authority). The tradition from his Lord is to hide his secret as Allah, the Most Majestic, the Most Holy, has said, 'He knows the unseen and He does not allow anyone to know His secrets except those of His Messengers whom He chooses.' (72:26) The tradition from the Holy Prophet is to show kindness to people. Allah, the Most Majestic, the Most Holy, commanded His Holy Prophet to be kind to people saying, 'Be forgiving, preach the truth, . . .' (7:199) The tradition from His Waliyy is to exercise patience in harsh and difficult conditions.'"

Chapter 96 - The Rarity of Believers

H 2308, Ch. 96, h 1

Muhammad ibn Yahya has narrated from Ahmad ibn Muhammad ibn 'Isa from Muhammad ibn Sinan from Qutaybah al-'A'sha' who has said the following:

"I heard abu 'Abd Allah, *'Alayhi al-Salam*, saying, 'The female believer is more valued than a male believer and a male believer is more valued than alchemy. Who among you has ever seen alchemy?'"

H 2309, Ch. 96, h 2

A number of our people have narrated from Sahl ibn Ziyad from ibn abu Najaran from Muthanna al-Hannat from Kamil al-Tammar who has said the following:

"I heard abu Ja'far, *'Alayhi al-Salam,* saying three times, 'People are animals, people are animals, people are animals, except a few of believers. Believers are rare, believers are rare, and believers are rare, (more cherished).'"

H 2310, Ch. 96, h 3

Ali ibn Ibrahim has narrated from his father from ibn Mahbub from ibn Ri'ab who has said the following:

"I heard abu 'Abd Allah, *'Alayhi al-Salam,* saying to abu Basir, 'By Allah were I to find three believers among you who keep our Hadith concealed I would not have considered it lawful to conceal any Hadith from them.'"

H 2311, Ch. 96, h 4

Muhammad ibn al-Hassan and Ali ibn Muhammad ibn Bandar have narrated from Ibrahim ibn Ishaq from 'Abd Allah ibn Hammad al-Ansari from Sadir al-Sayrafi who has said the following:

"Once I went in the presence of abu 'Abd Allah, *'Alayhi al-Salam,* and said, 'By Allah, it is your obligation not to sit (without proclaiming your leadership).' The Imam asked, 'Why O Sadir?' I said, 'Because your friends, Shi'a (followers) and supporters are so many. By Allah, were Amir al-Mu'minin (Ali ibn abu Talib), *'Alayhi al-Salam,* to have that many Shi'a (followers) as your Shi'a, friends and supporters, no one of the tribe of Tamim or 'Ady could dare to disturb him.' The Imam said, 'O Sadir, how many do you think they are?' I said, 'One hundred thousand.' The Imam said, 'One hundred thousand!' I said, 'Yes, in fact, they are up to two hundred thousand, and I said, 'Half of the world (population) is your Shi'a.'

"The narrator has said that the Imam remained calm and then said, 'Is it possible to come with us to Yanbu'?' I said, 'It is fine with me.' He then asked to bring a donkey and a mule already saddled. I hurried to ride the donkey and he said, 'O Sadir, can you consider to allow me ride the donkey?' I said, 'The mule is more beautiful and noble.' He said, 'The donkey is friendlier for me.' I then dismounted and he rode the donkey and I rode the mule. We traveled until it was time for prayer. He said, 'O Sadir, dismount and we should pray.' Then he said, 'This ground is soft, prayer is not permissible here.' We moved to a red ground and he looked to a boy who shepherded goats. He said, 'O Sadir, were I to have as many Shi'a (followers) as the number of these goats, then it would not have been permissible for me to sit (without proclaiming my leadership).' We dismounted and prayed. When we finished the prayer I turned to the goats and counted them. There were seventeen heads of goats in the flock.'"

H 2312, Ch. 96, h 5

Muhammad ibn Yahya has narrated from Ahmad ibn Muhammad ibn 'Isa from Muhammad ibn Sinan from 'Ammar ibn Marwan from Sama'a ibn Mehran who has said the following:

"A virtuous servant (of Allah), *'Alayhi al-Salam,* said to me, 'O Sama'a, they (pretending Shi'a) found their belief in their beds and they (attempt) to frighten me (ignoring al-Taqiyah). By Allah, once of the whole world and all that is therein there was only one person who worshipped Allah. Had there been anyone else, Allah, the Most Majestic, the Most Holy, would have mentioned him with him in

His words, 'Abraham was, certainly, a nation, (in terms of having a whole culture and tradition) obedient and upright person. He was not a pagan.' (16:120)

"Time passed as Allah willed. Allah then provided him comfort with Isma'il and Ishaq and they numbered three. By Allah, believers are very few and unbelievers (people of imperfect belief) are many. Do you know why that is?' I said, 'May Allah keep my soul in service for your cause, I do not know.' The Imam said, 'They (less perfect believers) have become a source of comfort for the believers who spread their secrets to the hearts (of less perfect believers) to find relief and in this they do find relief."

H 2313, Ch. 96, h 6

A number of our people have narrated from Sahl ibn Ziyad from Muhammad ibn 'Uramah from al-Nadr from Yahya ibn abu Khalid al-Qammat from Humran ibn 'Ayun who has said the following:

"Once I asked abu Ja'far, *'Alayhi al-Salam*, 'May Allah keep my soul in service for your cause, how small is our number! It is so small that all combined feasting on a goat cannot finish it.' The Imam asked, 'Do you want to hear more astonishing things? The immigrants (Muslim of Makkah) and supporters (Muslim of Madina) all went (to abu Bakr).' He (the Imam) pointed with his hands, 'except three, (Salman, abu Dhar and Miqdad) who remained as true supporters of Amir al-Mu'minin (Ali ibn abu Talib, *'Alayhi al-Salam*).' I (Humran) then asked, 'May Allah keep my soul in service for your cause, what about 'Ammar?' The Imam said, 'May Allah grant him favors, the alert man pledged allegiance (to abu Bakr) but he died as a martyr.' I (Humran) then said to myself that there is nothing better than martyrdom. The Imam looked at me and said, 'Perhaps you thought he was like one of the three. That is far remote from reality.'"

H 2314, Ch. 96, h 7

Al-Husayn ibn Muhammad has narrated from Mu'alla ibn Muhammad from Ahmad ibn Muhammad ibn 'Abd Allah from Ali ibn Ja'far who has said the following:

"I heard abu al-Hassan, *'Alayhi al-Salam*, saying, 'Not everyone who speaks of our Walayah (Divine Authority) is a believer. They, however, are made to serve as boasting morals of the believing people.'"

Chapter 97 - Accepting the Gift of Belief and to Exercise Patience in All Matters Thereafter

H 2315, Ch. 97, h 1

A number of our people have narrated from Ahmad ibn Muhammad from ibn Faddal from ibn Bukayr from Fudayl ibn Yasar from 'Abd al-Wahid ibn al-Mukhtar al-Ansari who has said the following:

"Once abu Ja'far, *'Alayhi al-Salam*, said to me, 'O 'Abd al-Wahid, nothing can harm one, if he is a person of proper understanding, who believes in our (Divine Authority), no matter what people may say about him. Although they may call him insane it will not harm him even if he lives on a mountain worshipping Allah until death approaches him.'"

H 2316, Ch. 97, h 2

Ali ibn Ibrahim has narrated from Muhammad ibn 'Isa from Yunus from ibn Muskan from Mu'alla ibn Khanis from abu 'Abd Allah, *'Alayhi al-Salam*, who has said the following:

"The Messenger of Allah has said, 'Allah, the Most Blessed, the Most High, has said, "Had there not been more than one believer on earth, he would have been sufficient for Me in place of all of My other creatures and I would have made his belief to provide him good company to help him live independent of all creatures."'"

H 2317, Ch. 97, h 3

Muhammad ibn Yahya has narrated from Ahmad ibn Muhammad ibn 'Isa from Ahmad ibn Muhammad ibn abu Nasr from al-Husayn ibn Musa from Fudayl ibn Yasar from abu Ja'far, *'Alayhi al-Salam*, who has said the following:

"One to whom Allah grants belief in this cause (our Divine Authority) will have no trouble even if he were to live on top of a mountain using plants for food until approaching of one's death."

H 2318, Ch. 97, h 4

Ali ibn Ibrahim has narrated from Muhammad ibn 'Isa from Yunus from Kulayb ibn Mu'awiyah who has said the following:

"I heard abu 'Abd Allah, *'Alayhi al-Salam*, saying, 'It does not benefit a believer to be apprehensive of his brother (in belief) of less perfect belief; believers are highly valued people in their religion.'"

H 2319, Ch. 97, h 5

It is narrated from him (narrator of the Hadith above) from Ahmad ibn Muhammad from Muhammad ibn Khalid from Faddalah ibn Ayyub from 'Umar ibn Aban and Sayf ibn abu 'Amirah from Fudayl ibn Yasar who has said the following:

"Once I went to see abu 'Abd Allah, *'Alayhi al-Salam*, in his illness that he endured and nothing was left of him except his head (due to weakness). The Imam said, I very often O Fudayl, say, 'A man to whom Allah grants belief in this cause (our Divine Authority) will have no trouble even if he were to live on a mountain until the coming of his death. O Fudayl ibn Yasar, people took to the right and left, but our Shi'a (followers) and we found guidance in the right path. O Fudayl ibn Yasar, for a believer it (belief) is better than his having all that is between the East and West. It (belief) is better for him even if he is cut in pieces. O Fudayl ibn Yasar, Allah does not do anything to believers except what is best for them. O Fudayl ibn Yasar, had the world been worth the wing of a fly, Allah, the Majestic, the Glorious, would not have allowed His enemies to drink even a drop of water from it. O Fudayl ibn Yasar, whoever finds one goal (the true belief) Allah suffices him in all other goals (affairs), however, one who has a goal in every valley Allah will be concerned the least where he may perish.'"

H 2320, Ch. 97, h 6

Muhammad ibn Yahya has narrated from Ahmad ibn Muhammad from Muhammad ibn Sinan from ibn Muskan from Mansur al-Sayqal and al-Mu'alla ibn Khanis who have said the following:

"We heard abu 'Abd Allah, *'Alayhi al-Salam*, saying, 'The Messenger of Allah has said, "Allah, the Most Majestic, the Most Holy, has said, 'I never hesitated in doing anything as I do about the death of My believing servant. I love to meet him but he dislikes death and I then hold it back from him. He prays to Me and I answer his prayers, he asks Me for help and I provide him help. Had there been even only one of my believing servants he would have been sufficient for Me of all others and I would make his belief to provide him company so that he would not feel frightened from anyone.'"

Chapter 98 - A Believer Finds Comfort With Another Believer

H 2321, Ch. 98, h 1
Ali ibn Ibrahim has narrated from Muhammad ibn 'Isa ibn 'Ubayd from Yunus from those he has mentioned (in his book) from abu 'Abd Allah, *'Alayhi al-Salam*, who has said the following:
"A believer finds comfort with another believer just as a thirsty person finds relief from cool water."

Chapter 99 - Things That Allah Removes Through a Believer

H 2322, Ch. 99, h 1
Muhammad ibn Yahya has narrated from Ali ibn al-Hassan al-Taymi from Muhammad ibn 'Abd Allah ibn Zurara from Muhammad ibn al-Fudayl from abu Hamza from abu Ja'far, *'Alayhi al-Salam*, who has said the following:
"Allah wards off destruction from a whole town just because of the existence of one believer in it."

H 2323, Ch. 99, h 2
Muhammad ibn Yahya has narrated from Ahmad ib Muhammad from ibn Mahbub from 'Abd Allah ibn Sinan from abu Hamza from abu Ja'far, *'Alayhi al-Salam*, who has said the following:
"A town in which seven believers live remains safe from torment."

H 2324, Ch. 99, h 3
Ali ibn Ibrahim has narrated from his father from ibn abu 'Umayr from more than one narrator from abu 'Abd Allah who has said the following:
"It was asked, 'In the case of punishment that descends upon a people, does it affect the believers also?' The Imam said, 'Yes, but they find salvation in the hereafter.'"

Chapter 100 - Believing People Are of Two Kinds

H 2325, Ch. 100, h 1
Muhammad ibn Yahya has narrated from Ahmad ibn Muhammad from Muhammad ibn Sinan from Nasir abu al-Hakim al-Khath'ami from abu 'Abd Allah, *'Alayhi al-Salam*, who has said the following:
"There are two kinds of believing people: one kind is true to the covenant with Allah and has kept the stipulation as Allah, the Most Majestic, the Most Holy, has said, 'Among the believers there are people who are true in their promise to Allah. . . .' (33:23) This kind of believing people do not become subject to any fear, worldly or in the hereafter. They are those who intercede for others but need no intercession. There are the kinds of believing people who are like a sprouting plant that grows straight sometimes and not so straight under certain conditions. This kind of believing people may become subject to fear in this world as well as in the next life. They need intercession but cannot intercede for anyone."

H 2326, Ch. 100, h 2

A number of our people have narrated from Sah ibn Ziyad from Muhammad ibn 'Abd Allah from Khalid al-'Ammi from Khidr ibn 'Amr from abu 'Abd Alllah, *'Alayhi al-Salam*, who has said the following:

"I heard the Imam saying, 'There are two kinds of believing people: one kind is true to the stipulations that He has made with him. He is with the prophets, the truthful ones, the martyrs and the virtuous ones. These indeed are good companions. Such ones intercede on behalf of others but they themselves do not need anyone's intercessions on their behalf. Such believers do not suffer from any frightening thing in this world or in the hereafter. There are the believers who lose balance. Such believers are like a sprouting plant that deals with the wind as it goes. Such believers face the frightening things in this world and in the hereafter. They need others intercession on their behalf but they are in good hands.'"

H 2327, Ch. 100, h 3

A number of our people have narrated from Ahmad ibn Muhammad ibn Khalid from Isma'il ibn Mehran from Yunus ibn Ya'qub from abu Maryam al-Ansari from abu Ja'far, *'Alayhi al-Salam*, who has said the following:

"Once a man in Basra stood before Amir al-Mu'minin (Ali ibn abu Talib), *'Alayhi al-Salam*, and asked, 'O Amir al-Mu'minin, speak to us of brothers (in belief).' The Imam said, 'Brothers are of two kinds: Trustworthy brothers and smiling brothers. The trustworthy brothers are one's palms, wings, the family and wealth. If they are trustworthy you may spend and work for them, be sincere to those sincere to him, and be the enemy of his enemies, conceal his secrets and faults and publicize his virtuous qualities. You (questioning person) must know that they are as rare as alchemy. On the other hand, you may enjoy the smiling brother's association that you should not cut it off from them but do not seek anything beyond it of their conscience. Do for them as much as they do for you like a happy face and sweet expressions.'"

Chapter 101 - The Matters in Which Allah Has Made a Covenant With Believing People in Exchange for Their Exercising Patience in Their Suffering

H 2328, Ch. 101, h 1

Muhammad ibn Yahya has narrated from Ahmad ibn Muhammad ibn 'Isa from Ali ibn al-Nu'man from Dawud ibn Farqad from abu 'Abd Allah, *'Alayhi al-Salam*, who has said the following:

"Allah has made a covenant with a believer (to have patience) when his words are not accepted as true and he does not avenge his enemies. A believer will not have any satisfaction without subjecting his soul to disgrace (before his own conscience); every believer is harnessed (as to his soul in the matters of worldly desires)."

H 2329, Ch. 101, h 2

A number of our people have narrated from Sahl ibn Ziyad and Muhammad ibn Yahya from Ahmad ibn Muhammad all from ibn Mahbub from abu Hamza al-Thumali from abu 'Abd Allah, *'Alayhi al-Salam*, who has said the following:

"The Messenger of Allah has said, 'Allah has made a covenant with a believer to exercise patience in the face of four kinds of misfortunes: the least serious of these is the envying of another believer against him who has the same belief, or a hypocrite that follows him (for hypocritical reason), Satan who tries to tempt him or an unbeliever against whom Jihad (working hard in the way of Allah) is necessary may cause him suffering. What then is left for a believer?"

H 2330, Ch. 101, h 3

A number of our people have narrated from Ahmad ibn Muhammad ibn Khalid from 'Uthman ibn 'Isa from ibn Muskan from abu 'Abd Allah, 'Alayhi al-Salam, who has said the following:

"A believer cannot escape one of three problems or perhaps all three at the same time: someone at home always bites him and closes his door to hurt him, a neighbor who annoys him, or someone on his way to work troubles him. Even if a believer may live on top of a mountain, Allah, the Majestic, the Glorious, sends Satan, who hurts him, but He makes his belief a source of comfort, and with it he does not feel frightened from anyone."

H 2331, Ch. 101, h 4

A number of our people have narrated from Sahl ibn Ziyad from Ahmad ibn Muhammad from ibn abu Nasr from Dawud ibn Sarhan who has said the following:

"I heard abu 'Abd Allah, 'Alayhi al-Salam, saying, 'A believer is not without four things or at least one of them at a time: he suffers from the envy of a believer and it is the most difficult one, stalking of a hypocrite, the struggle of an enemy against him or the temptation of Satan.'"

H 2332, Ch. 101, h 5

Muhammad ibn Yahya has narrated from Ahmad ibn Muhammad ibn 'Isa from ibn Sinan from 'Ammar ibn Marwan from Sama'a ibn Mehran from abu 'Abd Allah, 'Alayhi al-Salam, who has said the following:

"Allah, the Most Majestic, the Most Holy, has made His friend to become a victim of His enemy in this world."

H 2333, Ch. 101, h 6

A number of our people have narrated from Ahmad ibn Muhammad ibn Khalid from 'Uthman ibn 'Isa from Muhammad ibn 'Ajlan who has said the following:

"Once I was in the presence of abu 'Abd Allah, 'Alayhi al-Salam, when a man complained to him about something he needed. The Imam said, 'Be patient, Allah will make a way out for you.' The narrator has said that he remained quiet for a while then he turned to the man and said, 'Tell me about the jail in Kufah, how is it?' The man said, 'May Allah keep you well, it is congested, foul smelling and people are in the worst condition.' The Imam said, 'You are in a jail and expect comfort. You should bear in mind that this world is a prison for believing people'"

H 2334, Ch. 101, h 7

It is narrated from him (narrator of the Hadith above) from Muhammad ibn Ali from Ibrahim al-Hadhdha' from Muhammad ibn Saghir from his grandfather, Shu'ayb who has said the following:

"I heard abu 'Abd Allah, 'Alayhi al-Salam, saying, 'This world is a prison for believing people. Which prison is it wherein anything good may exist?"

H 2335, Ch. 101, h 8

Muhammad ibn Yahya has narrated from Ahmad ibn Muhammad ibn 'Isa from al-Hajjal from Dawud ibn abu Yazid from abu 'Abd Allah, 'Alayhi al-Salam, who has said the following:

"Abu 'Abd Allah, *'Alayhi al-Salam*, has said, 'A believer is not appreciated.'

It is narrated in another Hadith: 'This is because the virtues of a believer are taken to Allah, thus, they do not spread among the people and an unbeliever is appreciated.'"

H 2336, Ch. 101, h 9
Ali ibn Ibrahim has narrated from his father from ibn abu 'Umayr from 'Abd Allah ibn Sinan from abu 'Abd Allah, *'Alayhi al-Salam*, who has said the following:

"To every believer Allah has assigned four things: a Satan who wants to mislead him, an unbeliever who fights him, a believer who envies him - it is the most difficult one - and a hypocrite who tracks down his mistakes (for evil purposes)."

H 2337, Ch. 101, h 10
A number of our people have narrated from Sahl ibn Ziyad from ibn Mahbub from 'Amr ibn Shamir from Jabir who has said the following:

"I heard abu Ja'far, *'Alayhi al-Salam*, saying, 'When a believer dies the devils working to mislead him, now released among his neighbors, number equal to all the people of the tribe of Rabi' and Mudar.'"

H 2338, Ch. 101, h 11
Sahl ibn Ziyad has narrated from Yahya ibn al-Mubarak from 'Abd Allah ibn Jabalah from Ishaq ibn 'Ammar from abu 'Abd Allah, *'Alayhi al-Salam*, who has said the following:

"There had never been, there is no one and will never be a believer but that a neighbor causes him suffering. Even if a believer may live on an island Allah sends someone to cause him suffering."

H 2339, Ch. 101, h 12
Muhammad ibn Yahya has narrated from Ahmad ibn Muhammad ibn 'Isa from Ali ibn al-Hakam from abu Ayyub from Ishaq ibn 'Ammar from abu 'Abd Allah, *'Alayhi al-Salam*, who has said the following:

"In the past, in future and in your time there has never been a believer, whom a neighbor did not make suffer."

H 2340, Ch. 101, h 13
Ali ibn Ibrahim has narrated from his father from ibn abu 'Umayr from Mu'awiyah ibn 'Ammar who has said the following:

"I heard abu 'Abd Allah, *'Alayhi al-Salam*, saying, 'There has never been or will be a believer up to the Hour of Doom free from suffering, caused by his neighbor.'"

Chapter 102 - The Severity of the Trial of a Believer

H 2341, Ch. 102, h 1
Ali ibn Ibrahim has narrated from his father from ibn abu 'Umayr from Hisham ibn Salim from abu 'Abd Allah, *'Alayhi al-Salam*, who has said the following:

"The trial (suffering hardships in life) of the prophets is the most difficult then is that for those next to the prophets in a (spiritual) position and thereafter those similar to the previous group and so forth."

H 2342, Ch. 102, h 2

Muhammad ibn Yahya has narrated from Ahmad ibn Muhammad ibn 'Isa from al-Hassan ibn Mahbub from 'Abd al-Rahman ibn al-Hajjaj who has said the following:

"Once, trials and misfortunes and things that Allah, the Majestic, the Glorious, has specially set for the believers were mentioned in the presence of abu 'Abd Allah, *'Alayhi al-Salam,* and the qualities of the believer. The Imam said, 'The Messenger of Allah was asked, 'Who suffers the most in this world?' The Messenger of Allah said, 'The prophets suffer the most and thereafter people similar to them and then those similar in position to the second group and so forth. A believer suffers proportionate to his belief and good deeds; thus, whoever's belief is more correct as well as deeds their trails and suffering are more intense, and whoever's belief comes from a weak power of reason and whose deeds are weak their trials and suffering are less intense.'"

H 2343, Ch. 102, h 3

Muhammad ibn Yahya has narrated from Ahmad ibn Muhammad ibn 'Isa from Muhammad ibn Sinan from 'Ammar ibn Marwan from Zayd al-Shahham from abu 'Abd Allah, *'Alayhi al-Salam,* who has said the following:

"The greatest reward comes from greatest trials and suffering. There have never been a people whom Allah loved but were not put to trial."

H 2344, Ch. 102, h 4

Ali ibn Ibrahim has narrated from his father and Muhammad ibn Isma'il from Fadl ibn Shadhan all from Hammad ibn 'Isa from Rib'i ibn 'Abd Allah from Fudayl ibn Yasar from abu Ja'far, *'Alayhi al-Salam,* who has said the following:

"People who are put to the most severe trials and sufferings are the prophets, then the successors of the prophets and then those similar to the last group in position and so forth."

H 2345, Ch. 102, h 5

A number of our people have narrated from Sahl ibn Ziyad from ibn Mahbub from ibn Ri'ab from abu Basir from abu 'Abd Allah, *'Alayhi al-Salam,* who has said the following:

"Allah, the Most Majestic, the Most Holy, has His most sincere of all of His servants on earth. He does not send any gift from the heavens but that is diverted away from them (His most sincere servants) to others and no misfortune comes down but that is directed to them (His most sincere servants)."

H 2346, Ch. 102, h 6

A number of our people have narrated from Ahmad ibn Muhammad ibn Khalid from Ahmad ibn 'Ubayd from al-Husayn ibn 'Ulwan from abu 'Abd Allah, *'Alayhi al-Salam,* who has said the following:

"Sadir was present when the Imam said, 'When Allah loves a servant He deeply immerses him in misfortunes. You and we, O Sadir, live in it mornings and evenings.'"

H 2347, Ch. 102, h 7

Muhammad ibn Yahya has narrated from Ahmad ibn Muhammad ibn 'Isa from Muhammad ibn Sinan from al-Walid ibn al-'Ala' from Hammad from his father from abu Ja'far, *'Alayhi al-Salam,* who has said the following:

"When Allah, the Majestic, the Glorious, loves any of His servants He immerses him in misfortunes deeply and allows him bleed a bleeding (like sacrificial animals). When he prays to Him, He answers, 'Yes, my servant, if I like to answer your prayer quickly I have the power to do so, but if I save for you what I may save is better (for you).'"

H 2348, Ch. 102, h 8

It is narrated from him (narrator of the Hadith above) from Ahmad ibn Muhammad from ibn Mahbub from Zayd al-Zarrad from abu 'Abd Allah, *'Alayhi al-Salam*, who has said the following:

"The Messenger of Allah has said, 'The great misfortunes are matched with great rewards. When Allah loves a servant He tries him with great misfortunes. Whoever accepts it, Allah accepts him and whoever becomes angry with misfortunes, with Allah for him there is anger.'"

H 2349, Ch. 102, h 9

It is narrated from him (narrator of the Hadith above) from Ahmad ibn Muhammad from Ali ibn al-Hakam from Zakariya ibn al-Hurr from Jabir ibn Yazid from abu Ja'far, *'Alayhi al-Salam*, who has said the following:

"A believer is tried in this world proportionately to the perfection of his religion or degree of his excellence in religion (uncertainty is from the narrator)."

H 2350, Ch. 102, h 10

A number of our people have narrated from Ahmad ibn abu'Abd Allah from certain individuals of his people from Muhammad ibn al-Muthanna al-Hazrami from Muhammad ibn Bahlul ibn Muslim al-'Abdi from abu 'Abd Allah, *'Alayhi al-Salam*, who has said the following:

"The believers are like the two sides of a balance, as his belief increases in strength, his trial also increases in intensity."

H 2351, Ch. 102, h 11

Ali ibn Ibrahim has narrated from his father from ibn abu 'Umayr from abu Ayyub from Muhammad ibn Muslim from abu 'Abd Allah, *'Alayhi al-Salam*, who has said the following:

"Before forty days pass something causes sadness to a believer to remind him."

H 2352, Ch. 102, h 12

Muhammad ibn Yahya has narrated from Muhammad ibn al-Husayn from Safwan from Mu'awiyah ibn 'Ammar from Najiyah who has said the following:

"Once I said to abu Ja'far, *'Alayhi al-Salam*, 'Al-Mughirah says, 'A believer does not suffer from leprosy, bars (a form of leprosy) or so and so.'" The Imam said, 'He must be unaware of Sahib Yasin (the man mentioned in (36:20)) whose hand was paralyzed - the Imam let his fingers hanging ¬¬- and said, "It is as if I look at his paralysis. He came to the people, warning them against disbelief and the next day he was murdered." The Imam then said, 'A believer may suffer any form of misfortune and die by any form of death but does not commit suicide.'"

H 2353, Ch. 102, h 13

A number of our people have narrated from Ahmad ibn abu 'Abd Allah from his father from Ibrahim ibn Muhammad al-Ash'ari from 'Ubayd ibn Zurara who has said the following:

"I heard abu 'Abd Allah, *'Alayhi al-Salam*, saying, 'A believer has the best place in the sight of Allah, the Majestic, the Glorious, – three times. Allah tries him with misfortunes and then pulls his soul out of the parts of his body one after the other but he continues praising Allah.'"

H 2354, Ch. 102, h 14

Muhammad ibn Yahya has narrated from Ahmad ibn Muhammad ibn 'Isa from Ali ibn al-Hakam from Fudayl ibn 'Uthman from abu 'Abd Allah, *'Alayhi al-Salam*, who has said the following:

"In paradise there is a position that is accessible only to those who have gone through bodily trials of suffering in this world."

H 2355, Ch. 102, h 15

A number of our people have narrated from Ahmad ibn Muhammad ibn Khalid from his father from Ibrahim ibn Muhammad al-Ash'ari from abu Yahya al-Hannat from 'Abd Allah ibn abu Ya'fur who has said the following:

"Once I complained to abu 'Abd Allah, *'Alayhi al-Salam*, about pain. (He was often in pains). The Imam said, 'O 'Abd Allah, had a believer known about the reward for suffering from afflictions, he would have wished to be cut in pieces with scissors.'"

H 2356, Ch. 102, h 16

Muhammad ibn Yahya has narrated from Ahmad ibn Muhammad from Muhammad ibn Sinan from Yunus ibn Ribat who has said the following:

"I heard abu 'Abd Allah, *'Alayhi al-Salam*, saying, 'The people of truth had always, since their coming into being, been in suffering but that is for a short time which is followed by everlasting happiness.'"

H 2357, Ch. 102, h 17

Ali ibn Ibrahim has narrated from his father from certain individuals of his people from al-Husayn ibn al-Mukhtar from abu 'Usamah from Humran from abu Ja'far, *'Alayhi al-Salam*, who has said the following:

"Allah, the Most Majestic, the Most Holy, has an undertaking to try the believers with misfortune just as a man is committed to send gifts to his family in his absence. He holds him (believer) back from the worldly things just as the physicians hold back a patient from certain items of food."

H 2358, Ch. 102, h 18

Ali has narrated from his father from 'Abd Allah ibn al-Mughirah from Muhammad ibn Yahya al-Khath'ami from Muhammad ibn Bulul al-'Abdi who has said the following:

"I heard abu 'Abd Allah, *'Alayhi al-Salam*, saying, 'Allah has not protected the believers from the turmoil of the world but He has protected them from blindness in it and the wickedness of the next life.'"

H 2359, Ch. 102, h 19

Ali ibn Ibrahim has narrated from his father from ibn abu 'Umayr from Husayn ibn Nu'aiim al-Sahhaf from Dhurayh al-Muharibi from abu 'Abd Allah, *'Alayhi al-Salam*, who has said the following:

"Ali ibn al-Husayn, *'Alayhi al-Salam*, has said, 'I do not like a person's (total freedom from) suffering in the world from misfortunes.'"

H 2360, Ch. 102, h 20

A number of our people have narrated from Ahmad ibn abu 'Abd Allah from Nuh ibn Shu'ayb from abu Dawud al-Mustariqq in a marfu' manner from abu 'Abd Allah, *'Alayhi al-Salam*, who has said the following:

"Once, the Holy Prophet was invited for food. When he entered the house he saw a hen that had laid an egg on a wall and it fell on the top of a stake. It stayed there and did not fall off or break. The Holy Prophet expressed astonishment and the man said, 'Were you astonished because of this egg? I swear by the One who has sent you with the truth that I have never suffered any loss.' The Imam said, 'The Holy Prophet then stood up and left without having any food saying, 'One who does not suffer any losses, Allah is not interested in him.'"

H 2361, Ch. 102, h 21

It is narrated from him (narrator of the Hadith above) from Ali ibn al-Hakam from Aban ibn 'Uthman from 'Abd al-Rahman [ibn abu 'Abd Allah and abu Basir] from abu 'Abd Allah, *'Alayhi al-Salam*, who has said the following:

"The Messenger of Allah has said, 'Allah is not interested in a person in whose property or his own self there is no share (of losses).'"

H 2362, Ch. 102, h 22

Muhammad ibn Yahya has narrated from Ahmad ibn Muhammad from Muhammad ibn Sinan from 'Uthman al-Nawa' from those he has mentioned (in his book) from abu 'Abd Allah, *'Alayhi al-Salam*, who has said the following:

"Allah, the Most Majestic, the Most Holy, sets the believers into trials of all kinds and causes them to die by all kinds of deaths but He does not make them suffer the loss of their power of reason. Consider (prophet) Ayyub (Job) how Iblis (the devil) controlled his property, children, wife and all things that were his but had no control over his power of reason, which was left for him to maintain his belief in Allah only."

H 2363, Ch. 102, h 23

Muhammad ibn Yahya has narrated from Ahmad ibn Muhammad ibn 'Isa from ibn Faddal from Ali ibn 'Uqbah from Sulayman ibn Khalid from abu 'Abd Allah, *'Alayhi al-Salam*, who has said the following:

"For a servant (of Allah) there is a position with Allah that he can reach only through two qualities: Loss of his property or misfortune in his body."

H 2364, Ch. 102, h 24

It is narrated from him (narrator of the Hadith above) from ibn Faddal from Muthanna al-Hannat from abu 'Usamah from abu 'Abd Allah, *'Alayhi al-Salam*, who has said the following:

"Allah, the Most Majestic, the Most Holy, has said, 'Had my believing servant not felt sadness in his heart, I would have wrapped up the head of the unbelievers for protection with iron wrapping material so he would never experience any headaches.'"

H 2365, Ch. 102 h 25

Ali ibn Ibrahim has narrated from his father from ibn abu 'Umayr from Husayn ibn 'Uthman from 'Abd Allah ibn Muskan from abu Basir from abu 'Abd Allah, *'Alayhi al-Salam*, who has said the following:

"The Messenger of Allah has said, 'The likeness of the believers is like sprouting plants that are swirled back and forth by the winds. The believers are also turned and bent by pain and illness. The likeness of a hypocrite is that of an iron that is not affected by anything until death comes and shatters him with a (fatal) shattering.'"

H 2366, Ch. 102, h 26

Ali ibn Ibrahim has narrated from Harun ibn Muslim from Mas'adah ibn Sadaqa from abu 'Abd Allah, *'Alayhi al-Salam*, who has said the following:

"The Messenger of Allah one day said to his companions, 'Condemned is every property that is not purified by paying al-Zakat (charity), condemned is the body that is not purified once in every forty days.' He was then asked, 'O Messenger of Allah, we know how property is purified, but what is al-Zakat (purification) of the bodies?' The Messenger of Allah said, 'It is the suffering of the body from certain forms of trouble.' The narrator has said that the faces of those who heard it changed and when he noticed the change in their faces he asked them, 'Did you understand what I meant by what I just said?' They said, 'No, O Messenger of Allah.' He then said, 'What I meant was that a man suffers a scratch or a set back, a slip, or illness, or is pricked by a spike or such other things.' In his Hadith he also mentioned even sourness in the eyes."

H 2367, Ch. 102, h 27

Abu Ali al-Ash'ari has narrated from Muhammad ibn 'Abd al-Jabbar from ibn Faddal from ibn Bukayr who has said the following:

"Once I asked abu 'Abd Allah, *'Alayhi al-Salam*, 'Does a believer suffer from leprosy or similar diseases?' The Imam asked, 'Is misfortune written for anyone other than the believers?'"

H 2368, Ch. 102, h 28

Ali ibn Ibrahim has narrated from his father from ibn abu 'Umayr from his narrators, from al-Halabi from abu 'Abd Allah, *'Alayhi al-Salam*, who has said the following:

"A believer is so important to Allah that if he asks Him paradise and all that is therein, He will give it to him without any shortages caused to His kingdom. The unbeliever is so insignificant before Allah that if he asks the whole world and all that is therein, He will give it to him without any shortages caused in His kingdom. Allah is committed to sending misfortune to the believers just like one's commitment to his family in sending them souvenirs during his absence from home. He holds him back from worldly things like the physician who holds back a patient from certain food items."

H 2369, Ch. 102, h 29

Ali ibn Ibrahim has narrated from his father from ibn Mahbub from Sama'a from abu 'Abd Allah, *'Alayhi al-Salam*, who has said the following:

"It is in the book of Ali, *'Alayhi al-Salam*, that the people who suffer from the most intense form of misfortune are the prophets, then the successors of the prophets, then are people of closer position to the successors of the prophets and so on are the other groups. The trials of the believers are proportionate to their good deeds. Whoever's religion is perfect and his deeds are good, his suffering is more intense because Allah, the Most Majestic, the Most Holy, has not made this world the reward for the believers or punishment for the unbelievers. Whoever's religion is inferior and whose deeds are weak, his misfortunes are less. The misfortunes come quicker to the believers than rain to well situated land environment."

H 2370, Ch. 102, h 30

Muhammad ibn Yahya has narrated from Ahmad ibn Muhammad ibn 'Isa from Ali ibn al-Hakam from Malik ibn 'Atiyyah from Yunus ibn 'Ammar who has said the following:

"Once I said to abu 'Abd Allah, *'Alayhi al-Salam*, 'About this thing that has appeared on my face, people think Allah does not make suffer (from this) any servant in whom He is interested.' The Imam said, 'The believer among the people of Pharaoh had crippled fingers. He would extend his fingers and say, "My people follow the Messengers (of Allah)."' Then the Imam said to me, 'In the beginning of the third part of the night get up and make Wuzu and stand up for your prayer that you pray. In the last prostration of first two Rak'at say, "O the Most high, the Most great, O Beneficent, O Merciful, O the One Who listens to the prayers, O the One Who grants all good, bestow blessings upon Muhammad and his family, *'Alayhim al-Salam*, and grant me the good things of the world and of the next life and of that which You deem proper to grant me. Remove from me the evil of this world and of the hereafter and of that which You deem proper to grant and remove from me this pain - mention its name - it has angered and depressed me," Then insist pleading.' The narrator has said that before I reached al-Kufah, Allah had removed that entire thing from my face."

Chapter 103 - The Excellence of the Poor Muslims

H 2371, Ch. 103, h 1

Ali ibn Ibrahim has narrated from Muhammad ibn 'Isa from Yunus from Muhammad ibn Sinan from al-'Ala' from ibn abu Ya'fur from abu 'Abd Allah, *'Alayhi al-Salam*, who has said the following:

"The poor Muslims will stroll in the gardens of paradise forty years before the wealthy Muslims. An example of this is the case of two ships arriving at the tax collector's post. The tax collector searches one of the ships and finds it empty. He withdraws and the ship is free to go. But he finds the other ship full of goods. He then orders his people to follow the accounting procedure.'"

H 2372, Ch. 103, h 2

A number of our people have narrated from Ahmad ibn Muhammad ibn Khalid from his father from Sa'dan who has said the following:

"Abu 'Abd Allah, *'Alayhi al-Salam*, has said, 'Misfortunes are gifts from Allah and poverty is in His treasure.'"

H 2373, Ch. 103, h 3

It is narrated from him (narrator of the Hadith above) in a marfu' manner from abu 'Abd Allah, *'Alayhi al-Salam*, who has said the following:

"The Messenger of Allah has said, 'O Ali, Allah has made poverty a trust in His creatures. Whoever hides it, Allah grants him a reward equal to the reward for a fasting person who stands at night to worship Allah. One who reveals it to a person, who is able to help but does not help, it is then as if he has killed him. Although he has not killed him with a sword, or with a spear, but has done so by breaking his heart.'"

H 2374, Ch. 103, h 4

It is narrated from him (narrator of the Hadith above) from Muhammad ibn Ali from Dawud al-Hadhdha' from Muhammad ibn Saghir from his grandfather, Shu'ayb from Mufaddal who has said the following:

"Abu 'Abd Allah, *'Alayhi al-Salam*, has said, 'As the belief of a person increases in strength, his poverty intensifies.'"

H 2375, Ch. 103, h 5

Through his chain of narrators (Ali ibn Ibrahim) has said the following:

"Abu 'Abd Allah, *'Alayhi al-Salam*, has said, 'Had it not been due to the believers' pleading before Allah to increase their sustenance, He would have moved them to a poorer condition.'"

H 2376, Ch. 103, h 6

It is narrated from him (narrator of the Hadith above) from certain individuals of his people in a marfu' manner from abu 'Abd Allah, *'Alayhi al-Salam*, who has said the following:

"Whatever a servant is given of worldly things is to make him learn a lesson and whatever is withheld from him is to place him under the trial.'"

H 2377, Ch. 103, h 7

It is narrated from him (narrator of the Hadith above) from Nuh ibn Shu'ayb and abu Ishaq al-Khaffaf from a man from abu 'Abd Allah, *'Alayhi al-Salam*, who has said the following:

"For our pure Shi'a (followers) there is nothing under the rule of the unjust power more than bare necessities. Westernize or Easternize, you will never gain more than bare necessities."

H 2378, Ch. 103, h 8

Muhammad ibn Yahya has narrated from Ahmad ibn Muhammad from Muhammad ibn al-Hassan al-Ash'ari from certain individuals of his teachers from Edris ibn 'Abd Allah from abu 'Abd Allah, *'Alayhi al-Salam*, who has said the following:

"The Holy Prophet has said, 'O Ali, the need (poverty) is Allah's trust with His creatures. Whoever keeps it secret Allah grants him a reward equal to that for one who prays, but if he reveals it to one who is able to help and does not help he has killed him, not with a sword or spears, but has killed him by breaking his heart.'"

H 2379, Ch. 103, h 9

It is narrated from him (narrator of the Hadith above) from Ahmad from Ali ibn al-Hakam from Sa'dan who has said the following:

"Abu 'Abd Allah, *'Alayhi al-Salam*, has said, 'On the Day of Judgment Allah, the Majestic, the Glorious, will turn to the poor believing people, similar to an apologetic one, and will say, "I swear by My Majesty and Glory that I did not make you suffer poverty in the world, considering you insignificant. You will find out how I treat you today. Hold the hands of those who helped you in the worldly life and take them to paradise." The narrator has said that the Imam then said, 'A man from among them will say, 'O Lord, people competed in their world to marry, dress up in fine garments, to have fine food, nice houses, and riding best animals, thus, give me what you had given to them.' Allah, the Most Blessed, the Most High, will say, 'You and every one of you will have what I had given to the people of the world from its beginning to its end, seventy times as much.'"

H 2380, Ch. 103, h 10

A number of our people have narrated from Sahl ibn Ziyad from Ibrahim ibn 'Aqabah from Isma'il ibn Sahl and Isma'il ibn 'Abbad all in a marfu' manner from abu 'Abd Allah, *'Alayhi al-Salam*, who has said the following:

"There was no one of the children of Adam who was a believer but that was poor and there was no one of the children of Adam who was an unbeliever but that was rich until Ibrahim came. He said, 'O Lord, save us from the evil intentions of the unbelievers. . . .' (60:5) Thereafter Allah made these (believing people) rich as well as needy and those (unbelievers) wealthy as well as poor and needy.'"

H 2381, Ch. 103, h 11

A number of our people have narrated from Ahmad ibn Muhammad ibn Khalid from 'Uthman ibn 'Isa from those he has mentioned (in his book) from abu 'Abd Allah, *'Alayhi al-Salam*, who has said the following:

"Once a wealthy man in clean clothes came to the Messenger of Allah and sat down near the Messenger of Allah. Thereafter a poor man in not so clean clothes came and sat next to the wealthy man who then pulled his clothes away from underneath the thighs of the poor man. The Messenger of Allah then asked the wealthy man, 'Did you fear his poverty might stick to you?' The wealthy man said, 'No, that was not the reason.' The Messenger of Allah asked, 'Did you fear that something from your wealth might go to him?' He said, 'No, that was not the reason.' The Messenger of Allah said, 'Did you fear that your clothes may get dirty?' He said, 'No, that was not the reason.' The Messenger of Allah asked, 'What then was the reason?' He said, 'O Messenger of Allah, I have an associate who makes every evil thing attractive to me and vice versa in every good thing. I have decided to give half of my wealth to him (the poor man).' The Messenger of Allah asked the poor man, 'Do you accept it?' He said, 'No, I do not accept it.' The wealthy man asked the poor man, 'Why do you not accept my offer?' The poor man said, 'I am afraid, I will began to feel the way your associate makes you feel.'"

H 2382, Ch. 103, h 12

Ali ibn Ibrahim has narrated from Ali ibn Muhammad al-Qasani from al-Qasim ibn Muhammad from Sulayman ibn Dawud al-Minqari from Hafs ibn Ghiyath from abu 'Abd Allah, *'Alayhi al-Salam*, who has said the following:

"It is in the conversation of Moses, 'O Moses, when you see poverty coming say, "Welcome to the way of life of the virtuous people. When, you see wealth coming, say, 'It is a sin. I wanted to experience its punishment early (before the Day of Judgment).'"

H 2383, Ch. 103, h 13

Ali ibn Ibrahim has narrated from his father from al-Nawfali from al-Sakuni from abu 'Abd Allah, *'Alayhi al-Salam*, who has said the following:

"The Holy Prophet has said, 'Tuba (a tree in paradise) is for the destitutes who bear patience and they are the ones who observe the kingdom of heavens and earth.'"

H 2384, Ch. 103, h 14

Through the same chain of narrators he has said the following:

"The Holy Prophet has said, 'O destitute people, rejoice and be happy wholeheartedly with Allah. Allah, the Most Majestic, the Most Holy, will reward you because of your poverty, if you did not do so, you will not receive any rewards."

H 2385, Ch. 103, h 15

A number of our people have narrated from Ahmad ibn Muhammad ibn abu Nasr from 'Isa al-Farra' from Muhammad ibn Muslim from abu Ja'far, *'Alayhi al-Salam*, who has said the following:

"When it will be the Day of Judgment, Allah, the Most Blessed, the Most High, will command an announcer to announce and call before Him, 'Where are the poor people?' certain heads will rise and they will be many. Allah will say, 'My servants.' They will say, 'Yes, our Lord.' Allah will say, 'I did not make you poor considering you as insignificant. I chose you for this day. Search among the people those who helped you for My sake and compensate them on My behalf with paradise.'"

H 2386, Ch. 103, h 16

Muhammad ibn Yahya has narrated from Ahmad ibn Muhammad ibn 'Isa from Ibrahim al-Hadhdha' from Muhammad ibn Saghir from his grandfather, Shu'ayb from Mufaddal who has said the following:

"Abu 'Abd Allah, *'Alayhi al-Salam*, has said, 'Had it not been for this Shi'a's (followers) insistence on receiving more sustenance from Allah He would have moved them from their present condition to a more severe poverty."

H 2387, Ch. 103, h 17

Abu Ali al-Ash'ari has narrated from Muhammad ibn 'Abd al-Jabbar from ibn Faddal from Muhammad ibn al-Husayn ibn Kathir al-Khazzaz who has said the following:

"Once abu 'Abd Allah, *'Alayhi al-Salam*, asked me, 'Do you want to go to the market where fruits and things that you desire are sold?' I said, 'Yes, I like to go.' The Imam said, 'However, for everything that you like to buy but cannot buy there is a reward of one good deed for you.'"

H 2388, Ch. 103, h 18

Muhammad ibn Yahya has narrated from Ahmad ibn Muhammad ibn 'Isa from Muhammad ibn Sinan from Ali ibn 'Affan from Mufaddal ibn 'Umar from abu 'Abd Allah, *'Alayhi al-Salam*, who has said the following:

"Allah, the Most Exalted of praise, will apologize to His believing servants who are poor in this world just as a brother apologizes to a brother and He will say, 'I swear by my Majesty and Glory that I did not make you poor in the world considering you insignificant. Remove this curtain and look what I have given you in exchange for your poverty in the world.' The Imam said, 'He will then raise the curtain and say, '(O Lord,) your withholding the wealth of the world from me in exchange for what You have kept in reserve for me has not harmed me at all.'"

H 2389, Ch. 103, h 19

Ali ibn Ibrahim has narrated from his father from ibn abu 'Umayr from Hisham ibn al-Hakam from abu 'Abd Allah, *'Alayhi al-Salam*, who has said the following:

"When it will be the Day of Judgment certain necks of people will rise, approach the door of paradise and knock on it. They will be asked, 'Who are you?' They will say, 'We are the poor people.' They will be told, 'Show your accounts.' They will say, 'You did not give us anything. Why do you ask us for accounts?' Allah, the Most Majestic, the Most Holy, will say they have spoken the truth admit them into paradise.'"

H 2390, Ch. 103, h 20
A number of our people have narrated from Ahmad ibn Muhammad ibn Khalid from 'Uthman ibn 'Isa from Mubarak slave of Shu'ayb who has said the following:

"I heard abu al-Hassan Musa, *'Alayhi al-Salam*, saying, 'Allah, the Most Majestic, the Most Holy, says, "I have not made certain people rich because they are important to Me and I have not made certain people poor because they are insignificant to Me. It is because I wanted to try the rich through the poor. Had there been no poor, the rich ones would not have deserved paradise.'"

H 2391, Ch. 103, h 21
Ali ibn Ibrahim has narrated from Muhammad ibn 'Isa from Yunus from Ishaq ibn 'Isa from Ishaq ibn 'Ammar and al-Mufaddal ibn 'Umar who have said the following:

"Abu 'Abd Allah, *'Alayhi al-Salam*, has said, 'Our wealthy Shi'a (followers) are our trustees for our poor Shi'a. Protect us by protecting them (the poor Shi'a).'"

H 2392, Ch. 103, h 22
Ali ibn Ibrahim has narrated from his father from ibn abu 'Umayr from Hisham ibn Salim from abu 'Abd Allah, *'Alayhi al-Salam*, who has said the following:

"Amir al-Mu'minin, Ali ibn abu Talib, *'Alayhi al-Salam*, has said, 'Poverty is more beautifying for the believers than the best decorated harness with ornament is for the head of a horse.'"

H 2393, Ch. 103, h 23
A number of our people have narrated from Sahl ibn Ziyad from ibn Mahbub from 'Abd Allah ibn Ghalib from his father from Sa'id ibn al-Musayyib who has said the following:

"Once I asked Ali ibn al-Husayn, *'Alayhi al-Salam*, about the words of Allah, the Most Majestic, the Most Holy, 'Were it not that all people would become one nation, . . .' - and the Imam said, 'It (all people) stands for the followers of Muhammad, *'Alayhi al-Salam*, all of whom might turn to disbelief, - ' . . . We would have made for the unbelievers in the Beneficent, ceilings out of silver. . . .' (43:33) Had Allah done so to the followers of Muhammad, *'Alayhi al-Salam*, the believers might feel very depressed and they would not establish any marital relations with and inheritance for those turning to disbelief (thus, they might become extinct).'"

Note: To understand better, read the whole verse: 'Were it not that all people would become one nation, We would have made for the unbelievers in the Beneficent, ceilings out of silver. . . .'" (43:33

Had all unbelievers been given so much wealth, the common Muslims might have abandoned their religion considering the prosperity of the unbelievers as a sign of Allah's happiness with them. In fact, according to Allah, worldly things are of no significance at all.

Chapter 104

H 2394, Ch. 104, h 1

Muhammad ibn Yahya has narrated from Ahmad ibn Muhammad from Muhammad ibn Sinan from Aban ibn 'Abd al-Malik who has said that narrated to him Bakr ibn Arqat from abu 'Abd Allah, *'Alayhi al-Salam*, or from Shu'ayb from abu 'Abd Allah, *'Alayhi al-Salam*, who has said the following:

"Once someone came to abu 'Abd Allah, *'Alayhi al-Salam*, and said, 'May Allah keep you well, I am a man who devoutly loves you. I face a pressing need. I sought help from my family and tribe but it only has distanced me from them.' The Imam said, 'What Allah has given you is better than what He has taken from you.' The man said, 'May Allah keep my soul in service for your cause, pray for me to Allah so He will make me independent of His creatures.' The Imam said, 'Allah has assigned the sustenance of whomever He wanted to come through the hands of whomever He wanted, however, you can ask Allah to make you free of such needs that may force you to ask for help the ignoble ones of His creatures.'"

H 2395, Ch. 104, h 2

A number of our people have narrated from Sahl ibn Ziyad from Ali ibn Asbat from those he has mentioned (in his book) from abu 'Abd Allah, *'Alayhi al-Salam*, who has said the following:

"Abu 'Abd Allah, *'Alayhi al-Salam*, has said, 'Poverty is a painful death.' I (the narrator) then asked him, 'Is it poverty due to deficiency of Dirham and Dinar (units of money)?' The Imam said, 'No, in fact, it is poverty due to deficiency in religion.'"

Chapter 105 - The Heart has Two Ears in Which an Angel and Satan Blow

H 2396, Ch. 105, h 1

Ali ibn Ibrahim has narrated from his father from ibn abu 'Umayr from Hammad from abu 'Abd Allah, *'Alayhi al-Salam*, who has said the following:

"There is no heart without two ears. On one of them there is an angel who provides guidance and on the other there is a Satan (devil) who induces temptation. This one commands him and that one prohibits him. Satan commands him to disobey and the angel prohibits him from sins as it is mentioned in the words of Allah, the Most Majestic, the Most Holy, '. . . since the two scribes are sitting on each of his shoulders, he does not utter a word that is not recorded immediately by the watchful scribes.'" (50:17).

H 2397, Ch. 105, h 2

Al-Husayn ibn Muhammad has narrated from Ahmad ibn Ishaq from Sa'dan from abu Basir from abu 'Abd Allah, *'Alayhi al-Salam*, who has said the following:

"The heart has two ears. When a servant (of Allah) thinks to commit a sin the spirit of belief says to him, 'Do not do it' and Satan says, 'Do it.' When he is on her belly (for an indecent act) the spirit of belief is taken away from him.'"

H 2398, Ch. 105, h 3

Muhammad ibn Yahya has narrated from Ahmad ibn Muhammad ibn 'Isa from Ali ibn al-Hakam from Sayf ibn 'Amirah from Aban ibn Taghlib from abu 'Abd Allah, *'Alayhi al-Salam*, who has said the following:

"There is no believer but that his heart inside him has two ears. Into one of them al-Waswas and al-Khannas (two devils) blow and in the other ear an angel blows. Allah supports the believer through the angel as He has said, '. . . supported them by a Spirit from Himself . . .'" (58:22)

Chapter 106 - The Spirit Through Whom a Believer is Supported

H 2399, Ch. 106, h 1

Al-Husayn ibn Muhammad and Muhammad ibn Yahya have all narrated from Ali ibn Muhammad ibn Sa'd from Muhammad ibn Muslim from abu Salmah from Muhammad ibn Sa'id ibn Ghazwan from ibn abu Najran from Muhammad ibn Sinan from abu Khadijah who has said the following:

"Once I went to see abu al-Hassan, *'Alayhi al-Salam*, and he said to me, 'Allah, the Most Blessed, the Most High, supports a believer with a spirit from His side who attends him in all times that he performs a good deed and observes piety. The spirit remains absent in all times that he commits sins and transgresses. The spirit vibrates with joy when he does a good deed and turns into a despicable thing and lowly to earth when he commits a sin. O servants of Allah, be committed to benefit from the favors of Allah to correct and reform yourselves; it (commitment) will increase your certainty and you earn fine and valuable things. May Allah grant favors to those who think of doing good and perform it or think of committing something bad, but refrain and desist.' The Imam then said, 'We support and strengthen the spirit by means of obeying Allah and working for Him.'"

Chapter 107 - The Sins

H 2400, Ch. 107, h 1

Muhammad ibn Yahya has narrated from Ahmad ibn Muhammad ibn 'Isa from Muhammad ibn Sinan from Talhah ibn Zayd from abu 'Abd Allah, *'Alayhi al-Salam*, who has said the following:

"My father would say, 'There is nothing more destructive to the heart than sins. The heart falls on sins and remains that way until sins subdue it and then it turns upside down.'"

H 2401, Ch. 107, h 2

A number of our people have narrated from Ahmad ibn Muhammad ibn Khalid from 'Uthman ibn 'Isa from 'Abd Allah ibn Muskan from those he has mentioned (in his book) from abu 'Abd Allah, *'Alayhi al-Salam*, who has said the following:

"About the words of Allah, the Most Majestic, the Most Holy, 'What has made them remain so patient in the fire?' (2:175) The Imam said, 'What has made them so patiently do something that they know will lead them to the fire?'"

H 2402, Ch. 107, h 3

It is narrated from him (narrator of the Hadith above) from his father from al-Nadr ibn Suwayd from Hisham ibn Salim from abu 'Abd Allah, *'Alayhi al-Salam*, who has said the following:

"No vein is injured, no failure takes place, no headache or illness occurs but because of the sin. This is mentioned in the words of Allah, the Most Majestic, the Most Holy, 'Whatever hardship befalls you is the result of your own deeds. Allah pardons many of your sins.' (42:30) The Imam then said, 'Allah forgives more than what He punishes for.'"

H 2403, Ch. 107, h 4

Ali ibn Ibrahim has narrated from his father from Hammad from Hariz from Fudayl ibn Yasar from abu Ja'far, *'Alayhi al-Salam*, who has said the following:

"No failure ever takes place in the life of a servant (of Allah) except because of sin and that which Allah forgives him for is much more."

H 2404, Ch. 107, h 5

Ali has narrated from his father from al-Nawfali from al-Sakuni from abu 'Abd Allah, *'Alayhi al-Salam*, who has said the following:

"Amir al-Mu'minin, Ali ibn abu Talib, *'Alayhi al-Salam*, has said, 'You must never show your teeth (smile) when you have committed disgraceful deeds and never feel safe from misfortune to strike you due to (your) sinful deeds.'"

H 2405, Ch. 107, h 6

It is narrated from him (narrator of the Hadith above) from his father from ibn abu 'Umayr from Ibrahim ibn 'Abd al-Hamid from ibn 'Usamah who has said the following:

"I heard abu 'Abd Allah, *'Alayhi al-Salam*, saying, 'Seek refuge with Allah from His striking you at night or during the day.' I (the narrator) asked him, 'What is Allah's striking?' The Imam said, 'It is Allah's punishing for sins.'"

H 2406, Ch. 107, h 7

A number of our people have narrated from Ahmad ibn abu 'Abd Allah from his father from Sulayman al-Ja'fari from 'Abd Allah ibn Bukayr from Zurara from abu Ja'far, *'Alayhi al-Salam*, who has said the following:

"All sins are intense and severe. The most severe is that which increases flesh and blood (consumption of unlawful foods). Sins are either forgiven or one is punished for and paradise is only for the clean ones to enter."

H 2407, Ch. 107, h 8

Al-Husayn ibn Muhammad has narrated from Mu'alla ibn Muhammad from al-Washsha' from Aban from al-Fudayl ibn Yasar from abu Ja'far, *'Alayhi al-Salam*, who has said the following:

"A servant (of Allah) commits a sin it causes a serious reduction in his means of living."

H 2408, Ch. 107, h 9

Ali ibn Muhammad has narrated from Salih ibn abu Hammad from Muhammad ibn Ibrahim al-Nawfali from al-Husayn ibn Mukhtar from a man from abu 'Abd Allah, *'Alayhi al-Salam*, who has said the following:

"The Messenger of Allah has said, 'Condemned and condemned is one who worships Dirham and Dinar, condemned and condemned is one who is blind (toward the truth). Condemned and condemned is one who carries out carnal relations with animals.'"

H 2409, Ch. 107, h 10

Al-Husayn ibn Muhammad has narrated from Mu'alla ibn Muhammad from al-Washsha' from Ali ibn abu Hamza from abu Basir who has said the following:

"I heard abu Ja'far, *'Alayhi al-Salam*, saying, 'Stay away from insignificant sins because there is demand for them. One of you will say, 'I sin and ask forgiveness.' Allah, the Most Majestic, the Most Holy, has said, 'It is We who bring the dead to life and record the deeds of human beings and their consequences (of continual effects). We keep everything recorded in an illustrious Imam (leader).' (36:12) Allah, the Most Majestic, the Most Holy, in the words of Luqman, has also said, 'My son, Allah keeps the records of all the good and evil deeds, even if they are as small as a grain of mustard seed, hidden in a rock or in the heavens or the earth. Allah is subtle and All-aware.'" (31:16)

H 2410, Ch. 107, h 11
Abu Ali al-Ash'ari has narrated from Muhammad ibn 'Abd al-Jabbar from ibn Faddal from Tha'labah from Sulayman ibn Turayf from Muhammad ibn Muslim who has said the following:
"I heard abu 'Abd Allah, *'Alayhi al-Salam*, saying, 'The sin deprives the servant (of Allah) of sustenance.'"

H 2411, Ch. 107, h 12
Muhammad ibn Yahya has narrated from 'Abd Allah ibn Muhammad from Ali ibn al-Hakam from Aban ibn 'Uthman from al-Fudayl from abu Ja'far, *'Alayhi al-Salam*, who has said the following:
"A man commits a sin and it moves sustenance away from him and he (Imam) read this verse of the Holy Quran: '. . . when they swore to pluck all the fruits of the garden in the morning, (68:17) without adding, "if Allah wills" (18). A visitor (destruction) from your Lord circled (destroyed totally) around the garden during the night while they were asleep.'" (68:19)

H 2412, Ch. 107, h 13
It is narrated from him (narrator of the Hadith above) from Ahmad ibn Muhammad from ibn Faddal from ibn Bukayr from abu Basir who has said the following:
"I heard abu 'Abd Allah, *'Alayhi al-Salam*, saying, 'When a man commits a sin a black dot appears in his heart. If he then repents, the dot will disappear, if he commits more sins it will increase until it will take over his heart and he then will never have salvation.'"

H 2413, Ch. 107, h 14
It is narrated from him (narrator of the Hadith above) from Ahmad ibn Muhammad from ibn Mahbub from abu Ayyub from Muhammad ibn Muslim from abu Ja'far, *'Alayhi al-Salam*, who has said the following:
"When a servant (of Allah) prays, his prayer is supposed to be answered within a short or a longer time. The servant (of Allah) commits a sin and Allah, the Most Blessed, the Most High, says to the angel not to answer his prayer and deprive him; he is subjected to My anger and he deserves deprivation from Me."

H 2414, Ch. 107, h 15
Ibn Mahbub has narrated from Malik ibn 'Atiyyah from abu Hamza who has said the following:
"I heard abu Ja'far, *'Alayhi al-Salam*, saying, 'The amount of rain each year is the same but Allah sets it as He wills. When a people commit sins, Allah, the Most Majestic, the Most Holy, reduces their share of rain in that year and diverts it to other places such as open lands, oceans and mountains. Allah makes the beetles suffer in their hiding places by means of stopping the rain fall in that area because of the sins of those who live near by while He has created ways for it (beetles) to move away where sins are not committed.' The Imam then said, 'Learn a lesson, O people of reason.'"

H 2415, Ch. 107, h 16

Abu Ali al-Ash'ari has narrated from Muhammad ibn 'Abd al-Jabbar from ibn Faddal from ibn Bukayr from abu 'Abd Allah, *'Alayhi al-Salam*, who has said the following:

"A man commits sins and he is deprived of the prayer at night. The bad deed runs quicker (in a destructive way) into its owner than the sharp knife into the flesh."

H 2416, Ch. 107, h 17

It is narrated from him (narrator of the Hadith above) from ibn Faddal from ibn Bukayr from abu 'Abd Allah, *'Alayhi al-Salam*, who has said the following:

"One who thinks to commit a sin, must not commit it; perhaps a servant (of Allah) commits a sin and the Lord, the Most Blessed, the Most High, finds him in that condition, He will say, 'I swear by my Majesty and Glory that I will never forgive you thereafter.'"

H 2417, Ch. 107, h 18

Al-Husayn ibn Muhammad has narrated from Muhammad ibn Ahmad al-Nahdi from 'Amr ibn 'Uthman from a man from abu al-Hassan, *'Alayhi al-Salam*, who has said the following:

"It is a responsibility for Allah to expose the house wherein sin is committed, to the sun to cleanse it (subject it to ruination)."

H 2418, Ch. 107, h 19

A number of our people have narrated from Sahl ibn Ziyad from Muhammad ibn al-Hassan ibn Shammun from 'Abd Allah ibn 'Abd al-Rahman al-Asamm from Musma' ibn 'Abd al-Malik from abu 'Abd Allah, *'Alayhi al-Salam*, who has said the following:

"The Messenger of Allah has said, 'A servant (of Allah) may become imprisoned for a hundred years because of one of his sins. He will see his spouses enjoy blessings in paradise.'"

H 2419, Ch. 107, h 20

Abu Ali al-Ash'ari has narrated from 'Isa ibn Ayyub from Ali ibn Mahziyar from al-Qasim ibn 'Urwah from ibn Bukayr from Zurara from abu Ja'far who has said the following:

"In the heart of every servant (of Allah) there is a white dot. When he commits a sin a black dot appears in the white one. If he repents the black dot goes away, but if he continues committing sins the black dot enlarges until it covers the white dot and when the white dot is covered the person thereafter does not return to good things as Allah, the Most Majestic, the Most Holy, has said, 'In fact, their hearts are stained by their deeds.'" (83:14)

H 2420, Ch. 107, h 21

A number of our people have narrated from Sahl ibn Ziyad from Ali ibn Asbat from abu al-Hassan al-Rida, *'Alayhi al-Salam*, who has said the following:

"Amir al-Mu'minin, Ali ibn abu Talib, *'Alayhi al-Salam*, has said, 'Do not show your teeth (smile) if you have committed disgraceful sins. Do not feel safe from misfortunes if you have performed evil deeds.'"

H 2421, Ch. 107, h 22

Muhammad ibn Yahya and Abu Ali al-Ash'ari have narrated from al-Husayn ibn Ishaq from Ali ibn Mahziyar from Hammad ibn 'Isa from abu 'Amr al-Mada'ini who has said the following:

"I heard abu 'Abd Allah, *'Alayhi al-Salam*, saying, 'My father has said, "Allah has made a firm decision not to take away the blessing that He has granted to a servant of His until he commits a sin that subjects him to misfortune.'"

H 2422, Ch. 107, h 23

Ali ibn Ibrahim has narrated from his father from ibn Mahbub from Jamil ibn Salih from Sadir who has said the following:

"Once a man asked abu 'Abd Allah, *'Alayhi al-Salam*, about the words of Allah, the Most Majestic, the Most Holy, ' . . . They said, "Lord, make the distances of our journeys longer." They did injustice to themselves. . . .' (34:19) The Imam said, 'They were a people who lived in towns that were attached to each other, and they could see each other. There were canals with flowing water and large properties. They did not appreciate the favors of Allah, the Most Majestic, the Most Holy, and changed the manners in their souls, the comfort that Allah had granted them, thus, Allah changed the blessings they enjoyed. Allah does not change the conditions of any people until they themselves change their manners in their souls. Allah sent upon them a huge flood that drowned their towns, destroyed their homes and properties. Allah changed their gardens into two gardens that had only bitter fruits, tamarisk and a few lotus trees and then Allah said, "This was how We recompensed them for their ungratefulness and thus do We recompense the ungrateful ones.'" (34:17)

H 2423, Ch. 107, h 24

Muhammad ibn Yahya has narrated from Ahmad ibn Muhammad from Muhammad ibn Sinan from Sama'a who has said the following:

"I heard abu 'Abd Allah, *'Alayhi al-Salam*, saying, 'Allah does not take away the favor that He grants to a servant as long as he does not commit a sin that may subject him to losing Allah's favor.'"

H 2424, Ch. 107, h 25

Muhammad ibn Yahya has narrated from Ahmad ibn Muhammad fand Ali ibn Ibrahim has narrated from his father all from ibn Mahbub from al-Haytham ibn Waqid al-Jazari who has said the following:

"I heard abu 'Abd Allah, *'Alayhi al-Salam*, saying, 'Allah, the Most Majestic, the Most Holy, sent a prophet to his people and inspired him to tell his people that the Lord says, 'There has not been any inhabitants of a town or people who obeyed Me and lived happily and then changed from the condition that I loved to what I disliked, but that I also changed their condition from what they liked to what they disliked. There has not been any inhabitant of a town or a house who disobeyed Me and were suffering hardships. They then changed their condition from what I disliked to what I loved, I also then changed their condition from what they disliked to what they loved. Tell them that My favors come before My anger. Do not despair of receiving My favors; sins are not much greater to Me to forgive. Tell them not to subject themselves stubbornly to My anger and do not consider My friends insignificant; when angry, My striking is insurmountable and no one of the creatures can withstand it.'"

H 2425, Ch. 107, h 26

Ali ibn Ibrahim al-Hashimi has narrated from his grandfather, Muhammad ibn al-Hassan ibn Muhammad ibn 'Ubayd Allah from Sulayman al-Ja'fary from al-Rida, *'Alayhi al-Salam*, who has said the following:

"Allah, the Most Majestic, the Most Holy, sent revelation to one of the prophets that said, 'When I am obeyed I become happy. When I become happy I grant blessings and there is no end to My blessings. When I am disobeyed I become angry, when I become angry I condemn and My condemnation reaches seven levels (generations).'"

H 2426, Ch. 107, h 27

Muhammad ibn Yahya has narrated from Ali ibn al-Hassan from Muhammad ibn al-Walid from Yunus ibn Ya'qub from abu 'Abd Allah, *'Alayhi al-Salam*, who has said the following:

"You may feel afraid of a king because of your disobeying him. You must avoid it if you can and do not continue in such condition."

H 2427, Ch. 107, h 28

Ali ibn Ibrahim has narrated from Muhammad ibn 'Isa from Yunus in a marfu' manner from Amir al-Mu'minin, Ali ibn abu Talib, *'Alayhi al-Salam*, who has said the following:

"No pain is more painful to the heart than sins and there is no fear more intense than fear of death. Past experience is enough material for thinking and death is more than enough a preacher."

H 2428, Ch. 107, h 29

Ahmad ibn Muhammad al-Kufi has narrated from Ali ibn al-Hassan al-Maythami from al-'Abbas ibn Hilal al-Shami, Mawla of abu al-Hassan Musa, *'Alayhi al-Salam*, who has said the following:

"I heard al-Rida, *'Alayhi al-Salam*, saying, 'Whenever servants commit such sins that they had not committed before, Allah creates a new misfortune against them of which they had no knowledge.'"

H 2429, Ch. 107, h 30

Ali ibn Ibrahim has narrated from his father from ibn Mahbub from 'Abbad ibn Suhayb from abu 'Abd Allah, *'Alayhi al-Salam*, who has said the following:

"Allah, the Most Majestic, the Most Holy, has said, 'When a person who knows Me commits a sin, I subject him to the troubles from one who does not know Me.'"

H 2430, Ch. 107, h 31

A number of our people have narrated from Sahl ibn Ziyad from Ali ibn Asbat from ibn 'Arafah from abu al-Hassan, *'Alayhi al-Salam*, who has said the following:

"Allah, the Most Majestic, the Most Holy, has an announcer who announces every day and night, 'O servants of Allah, hold and stop committing sins and disobedience to Allah. Had it not been for the presence of grazing animals, breastfeeding children, bent down old people among you, torment would have definitely been poured down upon you and you would have been battered severely.'"

Chapter 108 - The Major Sins

H 2431, Ch. 108, h 1

A number of our people have narrated from Ahmad ibn Muhammad from ibn Faddal from abu Jamilah from al-Halabi from abu 'Abd Allah, *'Alayhi al-Salam*, who has said the following:

"About the words of Allah, the Most Majestic, the Most Holy, 'If you avoid violating that which has been prohibited, your (lesser) sins will be forgiven and you will be admitted into a graceful dwelling,' (4:31) the Imam said, 'Major sins are those for which Allah, the Most Majestic, the Most Holy, has made it necessary that the sinner suffer the torment of the fire.'"

H 2432, Ch. 108, h 2

It is narrated from him (narrator of the Hadith above) from ibn Mahbub who has said the following:

"Once certain individuals of our people and I wrote to abu al-Hassan, *'Alayhi al-Salam*, asking what and how many were the major sins. He wrote back to us about major sins, 'Whoever avoids the act for which Allah has decided to send one in the fire, his evil deeds are expiated, if he is of the believers. The seven acts that subject one to punishment are to commit murder, a disregard of kindness to parents, collecting unlawful interest in trade, alienating oneself from religion after accepting it, accusing married women of committing indecent acts, consuming the properties of orphans and running away from the enemy during an offensive in battle.'"

H 2433, Ch. 108, h 3

Ali ibn Ibrahim has narrated from Muhammad ibn 'Isa from Yunus from 'Abd Allah ibn Muskan from Muhammad ibn Muslim who has said the following:

"I heard abu 'Abd Allah, *'Alayhi al-Salam*, saying, 'The major sins are seven in number: Murdering a believer intentionally, Accusing a married women of committing indecent act, Running away from the enemy in the battle field during an offensive, Alienating one's self from religion after accepting it, Consuming the properties of the orphans unjustly, Consuming unlawful interest in trade after knowing it clearly and all such acts that Allah has considered to be the cause for one's being subjected to suffering in the fire.'"

H 2434, Ch. 108, h 4

Yunus has narrated from 'Abd Allah ibn Sinan who has said the following:

"I heard abu 'Abd Allah, *'Alayhi al-Salam*, saying, 'Of the major sins are disregard of good relation with parents, despair for the mercy of Allah, feeling safe from the punishment of Allah and it is narrated that the biggest of the major sins is to consider things as partners of Allah.'"

H 2435, Ch. 108, h 5

Yunus has narrated from Hammad from Nu'man al-Razi who has said the following:

"I heard abu 'Abd Allah, *'Alayhi al-Salam*, saying, 'Whoever commits fornication suffers the loss of his belief, one who drinks wine suffers the loss of belief and one who breaks intentionally the fast in the month of Ramadhan suffers the loss of his belief.'"

H 2436, Ch. 108, h 6
It is narrated from him (narrator of the Hadith above) from Muhammad ibn 'Abdahu who has said the following:

"Once I asked abu 'Abd Allah, *'Alayhi al-Salam*, 'Is it true that a fornicator does not fornicate if he is a believer?' The Imam said, 'No, it is not as such, however, when he is on her belly, belief is taken away from him and when he moves away, his belief is returned to him, if he repeats it his belief is taken away from him.' I then asked, 'Even if he wants to repeat?' The Imam said, there are many who want to repeat but do not do so.'"

H 2437, Ch. 108, h 7
Yunus has narrated from Ishaq ibn 'Ammar who has said the following:

"About the words of Allah, the Most Majestic, the Most Holy, 'Those who stay away from grave sins and indecency (should know that) for their Lamam (certain sins) your Lord's forgiveness is vast. . . .' (53:32) the Imam said, 'Indecency is fornication and theft. Lamam is when a man commits a sin, then regrets and asks forgiveness from Allah.' I then asked, 'Is there any difference between straying and disbelief?' The Imam said, 'How numerous (an indication of difference between the two) are the rings of belief!'"

H 2438, Ch. 108, h 8
Ali ibn Ibrahim has narrated from his father from ibn abu 'Umayr from 'Abd al-Rahman ibn al-Hajjaj from 'Ubayd ibn Zurara who has said the following:

"Once I asked abu 'Abd Allah, *'Alayhi al-Salam*, about the major sins. The Imam said, 'They according to the book of Ali, *'Alayhi al-Salam*, are seven: Disbelief in Allah, Murdering a soul, Disregard of good relations with parents, Consuming unlawful interest from trade with evidence, Consuming the properties of orphans unjustly, Running away from the enemy in battlefield during an offensive and Alienation from religion after accepting it.' I (the narrator) then asked, 'Are these the biggest sins?' The Imam said, 'Yes, they are.' I then asked, 'Is consuming one dirham from the property of an orphan unjustly a bigger sin or disregarding the prayer?' The Imam said, 'Disregard of the prayer is a bigger sin.'

"I then said, 'You did not mention disregard of prayer among the major sins.' The Imam said, 'What was the first item that I mentioned to you?' I said, 'It was disbelief in Allah.' The Imam said, 'One who disregards prayer is an unbeliever (that is, he is considered as such for ignoring prayer without reason?)'"

H 2439, Ch. 108, h 9
A number of our people have narrated from Ahmad ibn Muhammad ibn Khalid from Muhammad ibn Habib from 'Abd Allah ibn 'Abd al-Rahman al-Asamm from 'Abd Allah ibn Muskan from abu 'Abd Allah, *'Alayhi al-Salam*, who has said the following:

"Amir al-Mu'minin, Ali ibn abu Talib, *'Alayhi al-Salam*, has said, 'There is no believer without forty shields on him until he commits forty major sins. When he commits forty major sins, the shields are removed. Allah then sends revelations to them (angels), "Cover My servant with your wings," and the angels cover him with their wings. The Imam then said, 'He then leaves no evil deeds without committing, praising himself among people for his evil deeds. The angels will say, 'Lord, Your servant has left no evil deed uncommitted and we feel embarrassed for what he does. Allah, the Most Majestic, the Most Holy, will reveal this to them, 'Move your wings away from him.' When they do this he then is held responsible for his animosity to us (Ahl al-Bayt). At this point his privacy is disregarded in heaven and on earth and the angels will say, 'O Lord Your servant is disgraced.' Allah, the Most Majestic, the Most Holy, will reveal this to them: 'Had Allah any interest in him He would not have commanded you to remove your wings from him.'"

Ibn Faddal has narrated a similar Hadith from ibn Muskan.

H 2440, Ch. 108, h 10
Ali ibn Ibrahim has narrated from Harun ibn Muslim from Mas'adah ibn Sadaqa who has said the following:
"I heard abu 'Abd Allah, *'Alayhi al-Salam*, saying, 'Of the major sins is to Despair from the mercy of Allah and Losing hope of receiving happiness from Allah, to feel secure of the punishment of Allah, murdering a soul that Allah has made unlawful to murder, keeping good relations with parents on hold and disregarded, consuming the property of orphans unjustly, consuming unlawful interest in trade despite evidence, alienation from religion after accepting the same, accusing married women of committing indecent acts and running away from the enemy in the battlefield during an offensive.' The Imam then was asked, 'A person who commits a major sin and dies, does he lose his belief and if he will be punished will he be punished like a pagan or that his punishment will discontinue?' The Imam said, 'He will lose his Islam if he would think that such acts are lawful and for this reason he will face the most intense torment. However, if he would acknowledge that they are major sins and it is unlawful for him to commit them and that he will be punished for them and that they are unlawful, then he will be punished but not as intensely as the one mentioned before. It causes him to lose belief but not Islam.'"

H 2441, Ch. 108, h 11
Muhammad ibn Yahya has narrated from Ahmad ibn Muhammad from ibn Faddal from ibn Bukayr who has said the following:
"Once I asked abu Ja'far, *'Alayhi al-Salam*, about the words of the Messenger of Allah, 'When a person commits fornication the spirit of belief departs him,' the Imam said, 'It is mentioned in His (Allah) words, 'He has supported them with a spirit from Him,' that is the spirit that departs him.'"

H 2442, Ch. 108, h 12
Ali ibn Ibrahim has narrated from his father from Hammad from Rib'i from al-Fudayl from abu 'Abd Allah, *'Alayhi al-Salam*, who has said the following:
"The spirit of belief is moved away from him as long as he is on her belly and when he comes down the spirit returns.' The narrator has said that he then asked, 'What if one intends to commit fornication?' The Imam said, 'No, consider, if one intends to steal, will his hand be cut?'"

H 2443, Ch. 108, h 13
Ali ibn Ibrahim has narrated from his father from ibn abu 'Umayr from Mu'awiyah ibn 'Ammar from Sabah ibn Siyabah who has said the following:

"Once I was in the presence of abu 'Abd Allah, *'Alayhi al-Salam*, and Muhammad ibn 'Abdahu said, 'A fornicator fornicates. Is he still a believer?' The Imam said, 'As long as he is on her belly he is not a believer and when he stands up, belief is returned to him.' I then asked, 'What if one intends to repeat?' The Imam said, 'How many are they who intend but do not repeat!'"

H 2444, Ch. 108, h 14

Al-Husayn ibn Muhammad has narrated from Mu'alla ibn Muhammad from al-Washsha' from Aban from abu Basir who has said the following:

"I heard abu 'Abd Allah, *'Alayhi al-Salam*, saying, 'The major sins are seven: One of them is murdering a soul intentionally, considering things as a partner of Allah the Most Great, accusing a married women of committing an indecent act, consuming unlawful interest in trade with evidence, running away from the battlefield during an offensive against the enemy, alienation from religion after accepting it, disregarding to maintain good relations with parents and consuming the property of orphans unjustly.' The Imam said, 'Alienation and paganism are the same.'"

H 2445, Ch. 108, h 15

Aban has narrated from Ziyad al-Kanasi who has said the following:

"Abu 'Abd Allah, *'Alayhi al-Salam*, has said, 'A son who condemns his father when he calls him and the father who beats up his son who responds to the father's call are the same.'"

H 2446, Ch. 108, h 16

A number of our people have narrated from Ahmad ibn Muhammad ibn Khalid from his father in a marfu' manner from Muhammad ibn Dawud al-Ghanawi from Asbagh ibn Nubatah who has said the following:

"Once a man came to Amir al-Mu'minin, Ali ibn abu Talib, *'Alayhi al-Salam*, and said, 'O Amir al-Mu'minin, certain people think a servant of Allah, who is a believer, does not fornicate, commit theft, drink wine, consume unlawful interest in trade, and does not spill blood that is not lawful to spill. This has become heavy on me and my chest feels constrained when I think that this servant (of Allah) prays the way I do, pleads to Allah the way I do, marries from us and agrees we marry from them, he can inherit us and I can inherit him but is out of belief just because of a few sins.' Amir al-Mu'minin, Ali ibn abu Talib, *'Alayhi al-Salam*, said, 'You spoke the truth. I heard the Messenger of Allah saying, and evidence to it is the book of Allah, the Most Majestic, the Most Holy, 'People are of three categories and of three stages as mentioned in the book of Allah, the Most Majestic, the Most Holy: people of the right, people of the left and the foremost people. The foremost people are the Messenger prophets and non-Messenger prophets. In these people Allah has placed five spirits: The Holy Spirit, the spirit of belief, the spirit of power, the spirit of desire and the spirit of the body. With the Holy Spirit they were raised as the prophets who were Messengers and non-Messengers and with this they received the knowledge about things. With the spirit of belief they worshipped Allah and did not consider anything as His partners. With the spirit of power they performed Jihad (hard work in the way of Allah) and managed their living. With the spirit of desire they enjoyed food, lawful carnal relations with young women. With the spirit of the body they were able to move and walk around. These people are forgiven and no sin is recorded against them. Then he (the Messenger of Allah) said, 'Allah, the Most Majestic, the Most Holy, has said, 'We gave certain ones of Our Messengers preference over others. There are those to whom Allah spoke and He raised the rank of certain others. We gave authoritative proof to Jesus, son of Mary, and supported him by means of the Holy Spirit. . . .' (2:253) Then about one group He has said, 'He has supported them with a spirit from Him.' He (Allah) says that He has given them honor with it and has granted excellence over the others. These are forgiven and no sins are recorded against them.'

"He (the Messenger of Allah) then mentioned the people of the right hand and they are the believers in truth, in reality. Allah has placed four spirits in them: The spirit of belief, the spirit of power, the spirit of desire and the spirit of the body. A servant continues to perfect these four spirits and goes through conditions.' The man then asked, 'O Amir al-Mu'minin, what are these conditions?' The Imam said, 'The first condition is as Allah, the Most Majestic, the Most Holy, has said, 'Certain individuals among you will grow to an extremely old age and lose their memory. . . .' (16:70) All the spirits in him reduce and it is not a case wherein he is out of the religion of Allah. It is because the agent has returned him to the weakest point of life. He does not recognize the time for prayer, he is not able to perform Tahajjud (prayer at night) nor is he able to stand up in line with people. It is a reduction in the spirit of belief but it does not harm him. In certain ones of them the spirit of power is reduced; thus, they are not able to fight the enemy or make a living. In others the spirit of desire is reduced and a time comes when the daughters of Adam show no passion for him; he does not stand up. The spirit of the body remains with him. He moves and walks around until the angel of death comes. This condition is good because Allah, the Most Majestic, the Most Holy, is the power behind it. He faces other conditions when he is strong and young. He thinks of committing sins and the spirit of power encourages him, the spirit of desire makes it attractive to him and the spirit of the body leads him until he falls in sin. If he faces weakness in belief and it moves away from him it (belief) will not return to him before repentance. If he then repents, Allah turns to him (with forgiveness) but if he repeats the sin, Allah sends him to fire.'

"The people of the left are the Jews and the Christians as Allah, the Most Majestic, the Most Holy, has said, 'Those to whom We have given the Book (Bible) know you (Muhammad) just as good as they know their sons.' They know Muhammad and al-Walayah (the status of people who possess Divine Authority) from the Torah and the Gospel just as they know their sons in their homes. ' . . . It is clear that certain individuals among them deliberately hide the truth. (2:146) Never doubt that the essence of truth (that you are the Messenger of Allah to them) comes from your Lord.' (2:147) When they rejected what they knew Allah placed them under the trial. He removed the spirit of belief from them and allowed the three spirits to remain in them: The spirit of power, the spirit of desire and the spirit of the body. Thereafter He added them to the animals saying, 'They are like cattle or even more, straying and confused.' (25:44) The animals carry loads because of the spirit of power, feed themselves because of the spirit of desire and move around because of the spirit of the body.' The man who had asked the question then said, 'You brought life to my heart by the permission of Allah, O Amir al-Mu'minin, *'Alayhi al-Salam.*'"

H 2447, Ch. 108, h 17

Ali ibn Ibrahim has narrated from Muhammad ibn 'Isa from Yunus from Dawud who has said the following:

"Once I asked abu 'Abd Allah, *'Alayhi al-Salam,* about the words of the Messenger of Allah, 'When a man fornicates, the spirit of belief departs him.' The narrator has said that the Imam said, 'It is like the words of Allah, the Most Majestic, the Most Holy, ["... do not even think of spending for the cause of Allah worthless things that you yourselves would be reluctant to accept. ...." (2:267) The narrator has said that the Imam then said, 'Another verse is more clear than this. It is the words of Allah, the Most Majestic, the Most Holy,] " ... and supported them by means of a spirit from Him, ..." (58:22) that is the spirit that departs him.'"

H 2448, Ch. 108, h 18

Yunus has narrated from ibn Bukayr from Sulayman ibn Khalid from abu 'Abd Allah, *'Alayhi al-Salam,* who has said the following:

"The Imam said that Allah has said, 'Allah does not forgive the sin of considering others equal to Him, however, He may grant exceptions in other forms of sins that He may choose to forgive, ...' (4:48) It is a reference to the major sins and the lesser sins." I (the narrator) asked the Imam, 'Does the above exception apply to any of one's major sins?' The Imam said, 'Yes, it does apply to the major sins.'"

H 2449, Ch. 108, h 19

Yunus has narrated from Ishaq ibn 'Ammar who has said the following:

"Once I asked abu 'Abd Allah, *'Alayhi al-Salam,* 'Does the exception apply to the major sins and Allah may chose to forgive (whichever He may so choose)?' The Imam said, 'Yes, it does apply.'"

H 2450, Ch. 108, h 20

Yunus has narrated from ibn Muskan from abu Basir who has said the following:

"I heard abu 'Abd Allah, *'Alayhi al-Salam,* saying about, 'Whoever is given wisdom, certainly, has received much good. ...,' (2:269) it (such wisdom) means (having the ability to) recognize the Imam and avoid committing major sins for which Allah has made it necessary to send the perpetrators to fire.'"

H 2451, Ch. 108, h 21

Ali ibn Ibrahim has narrated from his father from ibn abu 'Umayr from Muhammad ibn Hakim who has said the following:

"I asked abu al-Hassan, *'Alayhi al-Salam,* 'Does committing a major sin remove one away from belief?' The Imam said, 'Yes, even less than major sins do. The Messenger of Allah has said, "A fornicator does not commit such a thing while he is a believer and a thief does not steal while he is a believer."'"

H 2452, Ch. 108, h 22

Ibn abu 'Umayr has narrated from Ali (ibn) al-Zayyat from 'Ubayd ibn Zurara who has said the following:

"Once ibn Qays al-Masir and 'Amr ibn Dharr - I think also abu Hanifah - came to see abu Ja'far, *'Alayhi al-Salam*. Ibn Qays al-Masir spoke and said, 'We do not expel people of our own mission and people of our own nation from belief just because of disobedience and sin.' Abu Ja'far, *'Alayhi al-Salam*, said, 'O ibn Qays, the Messenger of Allah has said, 'One does not fornicate while he is a believer, and one does not steal while he is a believer.' You and your people may go wherever you wish.'"

H 2453, Ch. 108, h 23

Ali ibn Ibrahim has narrated from Muhammad ibn 'Isa from Yunus from 'Abd Allah ibn Sinan who has said the following:

"Once I asked abu 'Abd Allah, *'Alayhi al-Salam*, about a man who commits a major sin and then dies whether it takes him away from Islam and if he will be punished, will it be like that for the pagans or will it finish on a certain time? The Imam said, 'One who commits any of the major sins considering it to be lawful it will take him away from Islam and he will face the most severe punishment. However, if he affirms that what he has done is a sin and dies, he is taken out of belief but not out of Islam and his punishment will be less severe than the one mentioned before.'"

H 2454, Ch. 108, h 24

A number of our people have narrated from Ahmad ibn Muhammad ibn Khalid from 'Abd al-'Azim ibn 'Abd Allah al-Hassani who has said the following:

"Abu Ja'far, *'Alayhi al-Salam*, narrated to me saying, 'I heard my father saying, "I heard my father, Musa ibn Ja'far, *'Alayhi al-Salam*, saying, 'Once 'Amr ibn 'Ubayd came to see abu 'Abd Allah, *'Alayhi al-Salam*, and when he offered the greeting of peace and took his seat he read the following verse of the Holy Quran, "Those who stay away from grave (major) sins and indecency . . ." (53:32) and stopped reading further. Abu 'Abd Allah, *'Alayhi al-Salam*, asked, 'What made you stop reading further?' He said, 'I like to know the major sins from the book of Allah, the Most Majestic, the Most Holy.' The Imam said, 'O 'Amr, the biggest of the major sins is to consider things as partners of Allah. Allah says, 'Whoever considers things as partners of Allah must know that Allah has forbidden their entering into paradise.' Thereafter is to despair of the mercy of Allah; Allah, the Most Majestic, the Most Holy, says, 'No one despairs from the mercy of Allah except the unbelievers.' (12:87) Another of the major sins is to feel safe from the punishment of Allah; Allah, the Most Majestic, the Most Holy, says, "No one disregards the punishment of Allah except the losing people." (7:99) Of the major sins is to disregard maintaining good relations with parents; Allah, the Most Glorious, has considered such a person oppressive and hard-hearted. (19:4) Another of the major sins is murdering, for no good reason, a person that Allah has made unlawful to murder; Allah, the Most Majestic, the Most Holy, has said, 'The punishment for one who purposely slays a believer will be to live in hell fire forever.' (4:93) Accusing a married women of committing indecent acts is a major sin; Allah, the Most Majestic, the Most Holy, has said, 'They are condemned in this world and in the next life and for them there is a great punishment.' (24:23) Consuming the property of the orphans as Allah, the Most Majestic, the Most Holy, has said, 'They eat fire in their belly and they will feel the heat of a blazing fire.' (4:10) Running away from the enemy in the battlefield; Allah, the Most Majestic, the Most Holy, says, '. . . whoever would turn back at that time, except for strategic reasons or to join another band (8:15) will incur the wrath of Allah and will dwell in hell, a terrible dwelling.' (8:16) Consuming unlawful interest in trade is among the major sins; Allah, the Most Majestic, the Most Holy, says, 'Those who take unlawful interest will stand before Allah (on the Day of Judgment) as those who suffer from a mental imbalance because of Satan's touch.' (2:275) Another major sin is performing magic: Allah, the Most Majestic, the Most Holy, says, '. . . They knew very well that one who engaged in witchcraft will have no reward in the life hereafter. . . .' (2:102) Fornication is a major sin; Allah, the Most Majestic, the Most Holy, says, '. . . those who commit fornication have committed a sin (25:68) and on the Day of Judgment their torment will be double. They will suffer forever in disgrace.' (25:69) False oath for an unlawful purpose is a major sin; Allah, the Most Majestic, the Most Holy, says, 'Those who sell their covenant with Allah and their promises for a small price will have no share in the life hereafter. . . .' (3:77) Treachery in dealing with property seized from the enemy in battle; Allah, the Most Majestic, the Most Holy, says, 'A treacherous person will be brought before Allah on the Day of Judgment with his treacherous deeds. . . .' (3:161) Not to pay al-Zakat, obligatory (charity) is a major sin; Allah, the Most Majestic, the Most Holy, says, '. . . their treasures will be heated by the fire of hell and pressed against their foreheads, sides and backs. . . .' (9:35) To present false testimony and to hide a testimony is a major sin; Allah, the Most Majestic, the Most Holy, says, 'Do not refuse to testify to what you bore witness. Whoever does so has committed a sin. . . .' (2:283) Drinking wine is a major sin; Allah, The Most Majestic, the Most High has prohibited it as He has prohibited the worship of idols and disregarding intentionally to perform prayers or anything that Allah has made obligatory; the messenger of Allah has said, 'Those who disregard, intentionally, the prayer Allah and His Messenger will have no responsibility toward such people. Disregarding one's promise and covenant and disregard of maintaining good relations with relatives are among the major sins; Allah, The Most Majestic, the Most High says, 'These . . . will have Allah's condemnation and will face the most terrible end.' (13:25)

"The narrator has said that 'Amr left sobbing and saying, 'Destroyed is one who speaks of his opinion (in religious issues) and opposes you (Imam) in the matters of excellence and knowledge.'"

Chapter 109 - Belittling Sins

H 2455, Ch. 109, h 1

Ali ibn Ibrahim has narrated from his father and Muhammad ibn Isma'il from Fadl ibn Shadhan all from ibn abu 'Umayr from Ibrahim ibn 'Abd al-Hamid from abu 'Usamah Zayd al-Shahham from abu 'Abd Allah, *'Alayhi al-Salam*, who has said the following:

"Guard against al-Muhaqqarat (sins); they will not be forgiven.' I then asked the Imam, 'What is al-Muhaqqarat?' The Imam said, 'A man commits a sin and says, "I will have Tuba (a tree in paradise) if I did not have any other sins."'

H 2456, Ch. 109, h 2

A number of our people have narrated from Ahmad ibn Muhammad from 'Uthman ibn 'Isa from Sama'a who has said the following:

"I heard abu al-Hassan, *'Alayhi al-Salam*, saying, 'Do not consider a great deal of good a great deal, and do not consider a little sin very little; little sins accumulate and become a great deal. Have fear of Allah in private so you can yield to justice against yourselves.'"

H 2457, Ch. 109, h 3

Abu Ali al-Ash'ari has narrated from Muhammad ibn 'Abd al-Jabbar from ibn Faddal and al-Hajjal all from Tha'labah from Ziyad who has said the following:

"Abu 'Abd Allah, *'Alayhi al-Salam*, has said, 'Once the Messenger of Allah stopped, during a journey on a barren land, for rest and asked his companions to collect firewood. The companions said, 'O Messenger of Allah, we are in a barren land and there is no firewood around here.' He said, 'Let everyone bring whatever he can.' They collected firewood and placed one piece over the other before him. The Messenger of Allah then said, 'This is how sins also accumulate.' Then he said, 'You must never commit al-Muhaqqarat (see Hadith 1 above) of sins; everything is in demand. You must know that the finder of sins writes them down: "It is We Who bring the dead to life and record the deeds of human beings and their consequences (of continual effects). We keep everything recorded in an illustrious Imam (leader or Book)."' (36:12)

Chapter 110 - Persistence in Sins

H 2458, Ch. 110, h 1

A number of our people have narrated from Ahmad ibn Muhammad ibn Khalid from 'Abd Allah ibn Muhammad al-Nuhayki from 'Ammar ibn Marwan al-Qandi from 'Abd Allah ibn Sinan from abu 'Abd Allah, *'Alayhi al-Salam*, who has said the following:

"Minor sins are not minor if one persists committing such sins and major sins are not major if followed by plea for forgiveness."

H 2459, Ch. 110, h 2

Abu Ali al-Ash'ari has narrated from Muhammad ibn Salim from Ahmad ibn al-Nadr from 'Amr ibn Shamir from Jabir from abu Ja'far, *'Alayhi al-Salam*, who has said the following:

"About the words of Allah, the Most Majestic, the Most Holy, '. . . and who do not knowingly persist in their mistakes,' (3:135) the Imam said, 'Persistence is when one commits and does not ask forgiveness from Allah nor say anything to himself about repentance. Such attitude is persistence in sin.'"

H 2460, Ch. 110, h 3

Ali ibn Ibrahim has narrated from his father from ibn abu 'Umayr from Mansur ibn Yunus from abu Basir who has said the following:

"I heard abu 'Abd Allah, *'Alayhi al-Salam*, saying, 'No, I swear by Allah, Allah does not accept any act of one's obedience to Him when one is persisting in disobedience to Him.'"

Chapter 111 - Roots of Disbelief

H 2461, Ch. 111, h 1
Al-Husayn ibn Muhammad has narrated from Ahmad ibn Ishaq from Bakr ibn Muhammad from abu Basir who has said the following:
"Abu 'Abd Allah, *'Alayhi al-Salam*, has said, 'The roots of disbelief are three: Greed, Self-aggrandizement and Envy. It was greed that led Adam to eat from the prohibited tree. It was Self-aggrandizement that led Satan to refuse prostration before Adam. Envy led one of the sons of Adam to murder his own brother.'"

H 2462, Ch. 111, h 2
Ali ibn Ibrahim has narrated from his father from al-Nawfali from al-Sakuni from abu 'Abd Allah, *'Alayhi al-Salam*, who has said the following:
"The Holy Prophet has said, 'The pillars of disbelief are four: Greed, Fear, Resentment and Anger.'"

H 2463, Ch. 111, h 3
A number of our people have narrated from Ahmad ibn Muhammad ibn Khalid from Nuh ibn Shu'ayb from 'Abd Allah al-Dehqan from 'Abd Allah ibn Sinan from abu 'Abd Allah, *'Alayhi al-Salam*, who has said the following:
"The Messenger of Allah has said, 'The things with which Allah was disobeyed first were six: Love of the worldly things, Love to be the leader, Love for food, Love to sleep, Love for comfort and Love of women (to such extremes that may lead one to sins).'"

H 2464, Ch. 111, h 4
Muhammad ibn Yahya has narrated from Ahmad ibn Muhammad from Muhammad ibn Sinan from Talhah ibn Zayd from abu 'Abd Allah, *'Alayhi al-Salam*, who has said the following:
"Once a man from Khath'am (a tribe) came to the Holy Prophet and asked, 'Which of the acts is more resented in the sight of Allah, the Most Majestic, the Most Holy?' The Messenger of Allah said, 'Considering things as partners of Allah.' The man asked, then what is more resented?' The Messenger of Allah said, 'Disregard of maintaining good relations with relatives.' The man asked, 'Then what is more resented?' The Messenger of Allah said, 'Commanding others to commit unlawful acts and prohibiting them to perform obligatory ones.'"

H 2465, Ch. 111, h 5
Ali ibn Ibrahim has narrated from his father from ibn abu 'Umayr from Hassan ibn 'Atiyyah from Yazid al-Sa'igh who has said the following:
"Once I said to abu 'Abd Allah, *'Alayhi al-Salam*, 'A man who is in this cause (belief of Shi'a Muslims), but the words he speaks are lies, disregards his promise, and violates his trust. What is his value?' The Imam said, 'It is very close to disbelief but he is not an unbeliever.'"

H 2466, Ch. 111, h 6

Ali ibn Ibrahim has narrated from his father from al-Nawfali from al-Sakuni from abu 'Abd Allah, *'Alayhi al-Salam*, who has said the following:

"The Messenger of Allah has said, 'Among the signs of wickedness is piercing eyes (devoid of bashfulness), hardheartedness, intense greed for worldly gains and persistence in sins.'"

H 2467, Ch. 111, h 7

Ali ibn Ibrahim has narrated from his father from Ali ibn Asbat from Dawud b al-Nu'man from abu Hamza from abu Ja'far, *'Alayhi al-Salam*, who has said the following:

"Once the Messenger of Allah addressed the people and asked, 'Should I tell you about the wicked ones among you?' They said, 'Yes, O Messenger of Allah, please do so.' The Messenger of Allah said, 'They are those of you who refuse to make any gifts (to anyone), beat up their slaves and supplies just his own self.' They thought that Allah has not created any creature most wicked than such person.

"Then the Messenger of Allah said, 'Should I tell who is most wicked than he?' They said, 'Yes, O Messenger of Allah, please do so.' The Messenger of Allah said, 'Most wicked than he is one from whom no good can be expected and from whose evil people do not feel safe.' They thought that Allah has not created anyone most wicked than he.

"The Messenger of Allah then said, 'Should I tell who is most wicked than he?' They said, 'Yes, O Messenger of Allah, please do so.' The Messenger of Allah said, 'He is a foulmouthed, profane person. When believers are mentioned before him, he abuses them and, when he is mentioned before the believers, they condemn him.'"

H 2468, Ch. 111, h 8

A number of our people have narrated from Sahl ibn Ziyad from certain individuals of his people from 'Abd Allah ibn Sinan from abu 'Abd Allah, *'Alayhi al-Salam*, who has said the following:

"The Messenger of Allah has said, 'There are three things that on being found in a person prove him to be a hypocrite, even though he may fast, pray and think that he is a Muslim: Violation of trust when he is thought of as trustworthy, lying in one's words and disregard of one's promises. Allah, the Most Majestic, the Most Holy, has said in His book, '. . . Allah does not love the treacherous ones', (8:58) also in His words, '. . . let Allah's condemnation be upon him if he lies' (24:7), and in the words of Allah, the Most Majestic, the Most Holy, 'Mention in the Book (the Quran) the story of Ishmael; he was true to his promise, a Messenger and a Prophet.'" (19:54)

H 2469, Ch. 111, h 9

Ali ibn Ibrahim has narrated from Muhammad ibn 'Isa from Yunus from certain individuals of his people from abu 'Abd Allah, *'Alayhi al-Salam*, who has said the following:

"The Messenger of Allah once asked, 'Should I tell you who is more dissimilar to me among you?' They said, 'Yes, O Messenger of Allah, please do so.' The Messenger of Allah said, 'He is an indecent, scandalous one, foulmouthed, stingy, deceitful, hateful, envious, and hardhearted who is far from being expected to do any good, and from whom all kinds of frightening evil is expected to emerge.'"

H 2470, Ch. 111, h 10

Al-Husayn ibn Muhammad has narrated from Mu'alla ibn Muhammad from Mansur ibn al-'Abbas from Ali ibn Asbat in a marfu' manner from Salman who has said the following:

"When Allah, the Most Majestic, the Most Holy, wants to destroy a person He removes bashfulness from him. When bashfulness is removed, you will not find anything in him but deceit and causing deception. When one is deceitful and deceptive, no one trusts him and when he can no longer be trusted you will not find him anything but an intensely harsh tempered one. When one is intensely harsh tempered the harness of belief is removed from him and when the harness of belief is removed from him you will find him to be nothing else but a condemned Satan."

H 2471, Ch. 111, h 11

Ali ibn Ibrahim has narrated from his father from ibn abu 'Umayr from Ibrahim ibn Ziyad al-Karkhi from abu 'Abd Allah, *'Alayhi al-Salam*, who has said the following:

"The Messenger of Allah has said, 'Three things are condemned and condemned are those who perform them: Defecating in recreational places, blocking allocated water and blocking public roads.'"

H 2472, Ch. 111, h 12

Muhammad ibn Yahya has narrated from Ahmad ibn Muhammad from ibn Mahbub from Ibrahim al-Karkhi from abu 'Abd Allah, *'Alayhi al-Salam*, who has said the following:

"The Messenger of Allah has said, 'There are three things whose performer is condemned: Defecating in recreational places, blocking allocated water and public roads.'"

H 2473, Ch. 111, h 13

A number of our people have narrated from Sahl ibn Ziyad and Ali ibn Ibrahim has narrated from his father all from ibn Mahbub from ibn Ri'ab from abu Hamza from Jabir ibn 'Abd Allah who has said the following:

"The Messenger of Allah, *'Alayhi al-Salam*, once asked, 'Should I tell you who is the most wicked among your men?' They said, 'Yes, O Messenger of Allah.' He said, 'Of the wicked ones among you is a man, accusing, boldly foulmouthed, eating all alone, refusing to give any gifts, beats up his slave and causes his family to seek refuge in others.'"

H 2474, Ch. 111, h 14

Ali ibn Ibrahim has narrated from his father from ibn abu 'Umayr from Muyassir from his father from abu Ja'far, *'Alayhi al-Salam*, who has said the following:

"The Messenger of Allah has said, 'I have condemned five things and so also has every prophet whose prayer would not miss acceptance: One who adds things to the book of Allah, ignores my Sunnah (traditions), rejects Allah's measures, legalizes things that Allah has made unlawful about my descendents and the undeserved appropriator of al-Fay' (property acquired from the enemy in battle) to himself, considering it lawful.'"

Chapter 112 - Showing Off

H 2475, Ch. 112, h 1

A number of our people have narrated from Sahl ibn Ziyad from Ja'far ibn Muhammad al-Ash'ari from ibn al-Qaddah who has said the following:

"Once abu 'Abd Allah, *'Alayhi al-Salam*, said to 'Abbad ibn Kathir al-Basri in the Mosque, 'Woe upon you, O 'Abbad, you must never show off; whoever works for someone other than Allah, He will assign him to that for which he has worked.'"

H 2476, Ch. 112, h 2

Muhammad ibn Yahya has narrated from Ahmad ibn Muhammad ibn 'Isa from ibn Faddal from Ali ibn 'Uqbah from his father who has said the following:

"I heard abu 'Abd Allah, *'Alayhi al-Salam*, saying, 'Allow your cause (Shi'a belief) to be just for the sake of Allah and do not assign it to people; whatever is for the sake of Allah is for Allah, and what is for people is unable to rise to Allah (will not be accepted).'"

H 2477, Ch. 112, h 3

Ali ibn Ibrahim has narrated from his father from ibn abu 'Umayr from abu al-Mighra' from Yazid ibn Khalifah who has said the following:

"Abu 'Abd Allah, *'Alayhi al-Salam*, has said, 'Showing off is considering things as partners of Allah. Whoever works for people, his rewards are upon the people and whoever works for Allah, his reward is before Allah.'"

H 2478, Ch. 112, h 4

Muhammad ibn Yahya has narrated from Ahmad ibn Muhammad ibn 'Isa from al-Husayn ibn Sa'id from al-Nadr ibn Suwayd from al-Qasim ibn Sulayman from Jarrah al-Mada'ini who has said the following:

"About the words of Allah, the Most Majestic, the Most Holy, '. . . whoever desires to meet his Lord should strive righteously and should worship no one besides Him,' (18:110) abu 'Abd Allah, *'Alayhi al-Salam*, has said, "A man performs a good deed and thereby he does not seek rewards from Allah but rather he wants to purify people desiring them to hear him. He has made his obedience for Allah to be shared with others." The Imam then said, 'Any servant (of Allah) who performs a good deed privately and times pass forever still, Allah will manifest its good (result) for him. Any servant (of Allah) who performs an evil deed privately and times pass forever still, Allah will uncover for him an evil (result).'"

H 2479, Ch. 112, h 5

Ali ibn Ibrahim has narrated from Muhammad ibn 'Isa ibn 'Ubayd from Muhammad ibn 'Arafah who has said the following:

"Once al-Rida, *'Alayhi al-Salam*, said to me, 'Woe upon you, O ibn 'Arafah, you must work without showing off and publicity; those who work for anyone other than Allah, He assigns him to whomever he has worked. Woe upon you, whatever one does, Allah returns it back, good (result) if it is good and evil (results) if it is bad.'"

H 2480, Ch. 112, h 6

Muhammad ibn Yahya has narrated from Ahmad ibn Muhammad from Ali ibn al-Hakam from 'Umar ibn Yazid who has said the following:

"Once I was having dinner with abu 'Abd Allah, *'Alayhi al-Salam*, and he read this verse of the Holy Quran: 'In fact, people are well-aware of their own soul (75:14) even though they make excuses.' (75:15) The Imam said, 'O abu Hafs, why should a human being seek closeness (by the form of the deed) to Allah, the Most Majestic, the Most Holy, while it is against the knowledge of Allah (in one's intention being to show off)? The Messenger of Allah has said, 'Whoever does a deed secretly, Allah returns it in a certain dress, as good rewards, were it a good deed, and in an evil form, were it an evil deed.'"

H 2481, Ch. 112, h 7

Ali ibn Ibrahim has narrated from his father from al-Nawfali from al-Sakuni from abu 'Abd Allah, *'Alayhi al-Salam*, who has said the following:

"The Holy Prophet has said, 'The angel ascends with the good deeds of a servant (of Allah) with happiness and joy and Allah, the Most Majestic, the Most Holy, will say, 'Keep them along with the records of evil people; he has not done them for Me.'"

H 2482, Ch. 112, h 8

He (Ali ibn Ibrahim) has narrated through his chain of narrators the following:

"Amir al-Mu'minin, Ali ibn abu Talib, *'Alayhi al-Salam*, has said, 'A showoff has three signs: he is very active when people are present, very lazy when he is alone and he loves to be praised in all matters.'"

H 2483, Ch. 112, h 9

A number of our people have narrated from Ahmad ibn Muhammad ibn Khalid from 'Uthman ibn 'Isa from Ali ibn Salim who has said the following:

"I heard abu 'Abd Allah, *'Alayhi al-Salam*, saying, 'Allah, the Most Majestic, the Most Holy, has said, "I am the best associate (in a deal). Whoever associates others with Me in a deed that he has done, I will not accept it; I accept only what is purely for Me.'"

H 2484, Ch. 112, h 10

Ali ibn Ibrahim has narrated from his father from ibn Mahbub from Dawud from abu 'Abd Allah, *'Alayhi al-Salam*, who has said the following:

"Whoever shows off to people an act that Allah loves and opposes Allah with what He dislikes (showoff), he will find Allah at war with him."

H 2485, Ch. 112, h 11

Abu Ali al-Ash'ari has narrated from Muhammad ibn 'Abd al-Jabbar from Safwan from Fadl abu al-'Abbas from abu 'Abd Allah who has said the following:

"Why should one of you publicize a good deed and hide an evil one? Can he not find in his own-self that it is not right? Allah, the Most Majestic, the Most Holy, has said, 'In fact, human beings are well aware of their souls.' (75:14) When the private side is correct, the public side becomes strong.'"

Al-Husayn ibn Muhammad has narrated from Mu'alla ibn Muhammad from Muhammad ibn Jumhur from Fadalah from Mu'awiyah from al-Fudayl from abu 'Abd Allah, *'Alayhi al-Salam*, a similar Hadith.

H 2486, Ch. 112, h 12

Ali ibn Ibrahim has narrated from Salih ibn Sindy from Ja'far ibn Bashir from Ali ibn abu Hamza from abu Basir who has said the following:

"Abu 'Abd Allah, *'Alayhi al-Salam*, said, 'Whenever a servant (of Allah) does a good deed secretly, not very long thereafter Allah uncovers for him good rewards. Whenever a servant (of Allah) does an evil deed secretly, very shortly thereafter Allah uncovers for him an evil return and misfortune.'"

H 2487, Ch. 112, h 13

A number of our people have narrated from Sahl ibn Ziyad from Ali ibn Asbat from Yahya ibn Bashir from his father from abu 'Abd Allah, *'Alayhi al-Salam*, who has said the following:

"Whoever wants Allah, the Majestic, the Glorious, with a small deed Allah uncovers for him a reward bigger than what he wanted. Whoever wants people with a great deal of deeds, physical effort, and with, nightly vigil, Allah, the Majestic, the Glorious, deems it necessary to belittle it (his effort) in the eyes of those for whom they (the deeds) were meant to be."

H 2488, Ch. 112, h 14

Ali ibn Ibrahim has narrated from his father from al-Nawfali from al-Sakuni from abu 'Abd Allah, *'Alayhi al-Salam*, who has said the following:

"The Messenger of Allah has said, 'There will come a time when people will be filthy from the inside but good looking from the outside due to worldly greed. They will not have any intention of seeking the rewards with Allah. Their religion will be a showoff and not for fear (from the hereafter). Allah will punish them universally, even though they may pray like a drowning person (in desperation) but it will not be accepted.'"

H 2489, Ch. 112, h 15

Muhammad ibn Yahya has narrated from Ahmad ibn Muhammad from Ali ibn al-Hakam from 'Umar ibn Yazid who has said the following:

"Once I was having dinner with abu 'Abd Allah, *'Alayhi al-Salam*, and he read this verse of the Holy Quran: 'In fact, people are well aware of their own soul (75:14) even though they make excuses.' (75:15) The Imam said, 'O abu Hafs, why should a human being make excuses before the people, opposing what Allah knows about him (his intention being to show off)? The Messenger of Allah has said, "Whoever does a deed secretly Allah will make him wear its (the deed's) garment as good rewards were it a good deed, and in an evil form were it an evil deed."'"

H 2490, Ch. 112, h 16

A number of our people have narrated from Sahl ibn Ziyad from Ali ibn Asbat from certain individuals of his people from abu Ja'far, *'Alayhi al-Salam*, who has said the following:

"Abu Ja'far, *'Alayhi al-Salam*, has said, ''Ibqa (preservation) of a deed is more difficult than performing the deed.' The narrator then asked, 'What is 'Ibqa'?' The Imam said, 'It is when a man maintains good relations with relatives or spends something just for the sake of Allah, Who has no partners. This will be recorded for him as a good deed, performed secretly. He then mentions it to people, and then it (deed performed secretly) is deleted but is recorded as a good deed performed publicly. Then he mentions it to people again and it then is deleted and is recorded as a deed to show off.'"

H 2491, Ch. 112, h 17

A number of our people have narrated from Sahl ibn Ziyad from Ja'far ibn Muhammad al-Ash'ari from ibn al-Qaddah from abu 'Abd Allah, *'Alayhi al-Salam*, who has said the following:

"Amir al-Mu'minin, Ali ibn abu Talib, *'Alayhi al-Salam*, has said, 'Be concerned and worried about (your relation with) Allah, a worry in which there are no excuses. Perform good deeds without showing off or publicity; Allah assigns one who performs a deed for something other than Him, to his own deed (and no reward from Allah).'"

H 2492, Ch. 112, h 18

Ali ibn Ibrahim has narrated from his father from ibn abu 'Umayr from Jamil ibn Darraj from Zurara who has said the following:

"Once I asked abu Ja'far, *'Alayhi al-Salam*, 'What do you say about a man who does a good deed while a human being sees him and it makes him happy?' The Imam said, 'There is no offense in it. There is no one who does not love people seeing something good come from him even though he may not have done it for such purposes (people see him doing good).'"

Chapter 113 - Seeking Leadership

H 2493, Ch. 113, h 1

Muhammad ibn Yahya has narrated from Ahmad ibn Muhammad ibn 'Isa from Mu'ammar ibn Khallad from abu al-Hassan, *'Alayhi al-Salam*, who has said the following:

"It was mentioned before the Imam that a certain man loves to have leadership. The Imam said, 'Two fierce wolves in a flock of sheep, whose shepherd is far away, are not more harmful to the flock than seeking leadership to a Muslim's religion is.'"

H 2494, Ch. 113, h 2

It is narrated from him (narrator of the Hadith above) from Ahmad ibn Sa'id ibn Janah from his brother, abu 'Amir from a man from abu 'Abd Allah, *'Alayhi al-Salam*, who has said the following:

"Abu 'Abd Allah, *'Alayhi al-Salam*, has said, 'Whoever seeks leadership is destroyed.'"

H 2495, Ch. 113, h 3

A number of our people have narrated from Ahmad ibn Muhammad ibn Khalid from his father from 'Abd Allah ibn al-Mughirah from 'Abd Allah ibn Muskan who has said the following:

"I heard abu 'Abd Allah, *'Alayhi al-Salam*, saying, 'Beware of these leaders who pretend to be leaders. I swear by Allah, shoes (people) have never marched behind a man, but that he destroys (them) and (he) is destroyed."

H 2496, Ch. 113, h 4

It is narrated from him (narrator of the Hadith above) from Muhammad ibn Isma'il ibn Bazi' and others in a marfu' manner who has said the following:

"Abu 'Abd Allah, *'Alayhi al-Salam*, has said, 'Condemned is one who seeks leadership, condemned is one who intends to become a leader and condemned is one who speaks to himself of leadership.'"

H 2497, Ch. 113, h 5

Muhammad ibn Yahya has narrated from Ahmad ibn Muhammad ibn 'Isa from al-Hassan ibn Ayyub from abu 'Aqilah al-Sayrafi who has said that Karram narrated to us from abu Hamza al-Thumali who has said the following:

"Once abu 'Abd Allah, *'Alayhi al-Salam*, said to me, 'Beware of leadership and beware of marching behind men (following them).' I (the narrator) asked, 'May Allah keep my soul in service for your cause, I understand what leadership is. However, as far as walking behind men is concerned, I must acknowledge that two thirds of what I know are but from my walking behind and following men.' The Imam said to me, 'That is not the way you think. Beware of supporting a man who does not have any (Divine) Authority but you acknowledge whatever he has said.'"

H 2498, Ch. 113, h 6

Ali ibn Ibrahim has narrated from Muhammad ibn 'Isa from Yunus from abu al-Rabi' al-Shami who has said the following:

"Once abu Ja'far, *'Alayhi al-Salam*, said to me, 'Woe upon you, O abu al-Rabi', do not seek leadership and do not be a wolf, do not eat people (consume their properties) through us so Allah makes you poor, do not say about us what we do not say about ourselves. One day you will be made to stand up (before the Judge) and will inevitably be questioned. Had you been a truthful person, we, approve you and, had you been lying, we will declare you a liar.'"

H 2499, Ch. 113, h 7

A number of our people have narrated from Sahl ibn Ziyad from Mansur ibn al-'Abbas from ibn Mayyah from his father who has said the following:

"I heard abu 'Abd Allah, *'Alayhi al-Salam*, saying, 'Whoever wants leadership is destroyed.'"

H 2500, Ch. 113, h 8

Ali ibn Ibrahim has narrated from Muhammad ibn 'Isa from Yunus from al-'Ala' from Muhammad ibn Muslim who has said the following:

"I heard abu 'Abd Allah, *'Alayhi al-Salam*, asking, 'Do you think I do not distinguish the bad from good among you? Yes, by Allah, the bad ones among you are those who love people walking behind him. Such a person is inevitably a liar or a helpless one (due to his ignorance) in his opinion.'"

Chapter 114 - Abuse of Religion for Worldly Matters

H 2501, Ch. 114, h 1

Muhammad ibn Yahya has narrated from Ahmad ibn Muhammad from Muhammad ibn Sinan from Isma'il ibn Jabir from Yunus ibn Zabyan who has said the following:

"I heard abu 'Abd Allah, *'Alayhi al-Salam*, saying, 'The Messenger of Allah has said, "Allah, the Most Majestic, the Most Holy, has said, 'Woe upon those who treacherously use religion for their worldly goals and fight those who command people to yield to justice. Woe upon those among whom the believers live frightened and hide their belief. Are they deceiving Me or that they dare to oppose Me? I swear by Myself that I will allow them to be afflicted by means of such strife whereby the most forbearing will suffer confusion.'"

Chapter 115 - Preaching Justice Without Practice

H 2502, Ch. 115, h 1

Ali ibn Ibrahim has narrated from his father from ibn abu 'Umayr from Yusuf al-Bazzaz from Mu'alla ibn Khanis from abu 'Abd Allah, *'Alayhi al-Salam*, who has said the following:

"One who, on the Day of Judgment, will regret the most is he who preaches justice but himself acts otherwise."

H 2503, Ch. 115, h 2

Muhammad ibn Yahya has narrated from Ahmad ibn Muhammad ibn 'Isa from Muhammad ibn Sinan from Qutaybah al-'A'sha' from abu 'Abd Allah, *'Alayhi al-Salam*, who has said the following:

"Of the people suffering most severely on the Day of Judgment will be one who preaches justice but acts otherwise."

H 2504, Ch. 115, h 3

Ali ibn Ibrahim has narrated from his father from ibn abu 'Umayr from Hisham ibn Salim from ibn abu Ya'fur from abu 'Abd Allah, *'Alayhi al-Salam*, who has said the following:

"Of the people who, on the Day of Judgment, will regret the most is one who preaches justice but himself does not yield to justice."

H 2505, Ch. 115, h 4

Muhammad ibn Yahya has narrated from al-Husayn ibn Ishaq from Ali ibn Mahziyar from 'Abd Allah ibn Yahya from ibn Muskan from abu Basir who has said the following:

"About the words of Allah, the Most Majestic, the Most Holy, '. . . they and rebellious ones will all be thrown headlong into hell. . . .,' (26:94) the Imam said, 'O abu Basir, they are those who preach justice by their tongues, but they themselves do not yield to justice.'"

H 2506, Ch. 115, h 5

Muhammad ibn Yahya has narrated from Ahmad ibn Muhammad ibn 'Isa from ibn abu 'Umayr from Ali ibn 'Atiyyah from Khaythamah who has said the following:

"Once abu Ja'far, *'Alayhi al-Salam*, said to me, 'Convey to our Shi'a (followers) that what is with Allah is not achievable by any other means but by good deeds. Convey to our Shi'a (followers) that of the people who, on the Day of Judgment, will regret the most is the one who preaches justice but does not yield to justice in favor of the others.'"

Chapter 116 - Disputation, Quarrels and Animosity to Men

H 2507, Ch. 116, h 1

Ali ibn Ibrahim has narrated from Harun ibn Muslim from Mas'adah ibn Sadaqa from abu 'Abd Allah, *'Alayhi al-Salam*, who has said the following:

"Amir al-Mu'minin, Ali ibn abu Talib, *'Alayhi al-Salam*, has said, 'Beware of disputations and quarrels; they create ill feelings toward the brothers (in belief) and upon these two hypocrisy grows.'"

H 2508, Ch. 116, h 2

Through the same chain of narrators he has narrated the following:

"The Holy Prophet has said, 'Whoever will find himself in the presence of Allah, the Most Majestic, the Most Holy, with three things will enter paradise through whichever gate he will like: one's proper moral discipline, one's worries and concern about and fear of Allah in secret and in public and refraining from disputations even if one is the rightful party.'"

H 2509, Ch. 116, h 3

Through the same chain of narrators he has narrated the following:

"The Holy Prophet has said, 'Whoever targets Allah in a quarrel (quarrelling with a creature is quarrelling with Him) may go through quick transitions (from truth to falsehood).'"

H 2510, Ch. 116, h 4

Ali ibn Ibrahim has narrated from Salih ibn al-Sindy from Ja'far ibn Bashir from 'Ammar ibn Marwan who has said the following:

"Abu 'Abd Allah, *'Alayhi al-Salam*, has said, 'Do not engage in a disputation against either a forbearing or a thoughtless person; a forbearing person turns into your foe and a thoughtless person will hurt you.'"

H 2511, Ch. 116, h 5

Ali has narrated from his father from ibn abu 'Umayr from al-Hassan ibn 'Atiyyah from 'Umr ibn Yazid from abu 'Abd Allah, *'Alayhi al-Salam*, who has said the following:

"The Messenger of Allah has said, 'Almost every time Jibril (Gabriel) on coming to me would say, "O Muhammad, guard (your) anger against men and animosity for them."'"

H 2512, Ch. 116, h 6

A number of our people have narrated from Ahmad ibn Muhammad from Ali ibn al-Hakam from al-Hassan ibn al-Husayn al-Kindy from abu 'Abd Allah, *'Alayhi al-Salam*, who has said the following:

"Jibril (Gabriel) said to the Holy Prophet, 'Beware of engaging in disputes against men.'"

H 2513, Ch. 116, h 7

It is narrated from him (narrator of the Hadith above) from 'Uthman ibn 'Isa from 'Abd al-Rahman ibn Siyabah from abu 'Abd Allah, *'Alayhi al-Salam*, who has said the following:

"Guard (yourself) against engaging in disputes; it causes losses and reveals defects."

H 2514, Ch. 116, h 8

Muhammad ibn Yahya has narrated from Ahmad ibn Muhammad ibn 'Isa from ibn Mahbub from 'Anbasah al-'Abid from abu 'Abd Allah, *'Alayhi al-Salam*, who has said the following:

"Beware of quarreling; it occupies the heart, causes hypocrisy and brings in hatred."

H 2515, Ch. 116, h 9

Ali ibn Ibrahim has narrated from his father from ibn abu 'Umayr from al-Hassan ibn 'Atiyyah from 'Umar ibn Yazid from abu 'Abd Allah, *'Alayhi al-Salam*, who has said the following:

"The Messenger of Allah has said, 'Almost every time Jibril (Gabriel), on coming to me, would say, "O Muhammad, guard (your) anger against men and animosity to them.'" (This Hadith is a repeat of H 5 perhaps by the scribe)

H 2516, Ch. 116, h 10
Muhammad ibn Yahya has narrated from Ahmad ibn Muhammad ibn 'Isa from Muhammad ibn Mehran from 'Abd Allah ibn Sinan from abu 'Abd Allah, *'Alayhi al-Salam*, who has said the following:

"The Messenger of Allah has said, 'Jibril (Gabriel) never came to me without advice and guidance. The last advice that he brought was: "Beware of engaging in disputations against men; it reveals the defects and eliminates one's high regard."'"

H 2517, Ch. 116, h 11
Ali ibn Ibrahim has narrated from his father and Muhammad ibn Isma'il from Fadl ibn Shadhan all from ibn abu 'Umayr from Ibrahim ibn 'Abd al-Hamid from Walid ibn Sabih who has said the following:

"I heard abu 'Abd Allah, *'Alayhi al-Salam*, saying, 'The Messenger of Allah has said, "Jibril (Gabriel) never cautioned me so emphatically about anything as he did about opposition to men."'"

H 2518, Ch. 116, h 12
A number of our people have narrated from Ahmad ibn abu 'Abd Allah from certain individuals of his people in a marfu' manner the following:

"Abu 'Abd Allah, *'Alayhi al-Salam*, has said, 'Whoever plants animosity will reap what he has sown.'"

Chapter 117 - Anger

H 2519, Ch. 117, h 1
Ali ibn Ibrahim has narrated from his father from al-Nawfali from al-Sakuni from abu 'Abd Allah, *'Alayhi al-Salam*, who has said the following:

"The Messenger of Allah has said, 'Anger spoils belief just as vinegar spoils honey.'"

H 2520, Ch. 117, h 2
Abu Ali al-Ash'ari has narrated from Muhammad ibn 'Abd al-Jabbar from ibn Faddal from Ali ibn 'Uqbah from his father from Muyassir who has said the following:

"Once anger was mentioned before abu Ja'far, *'Alayhi al-Salam*, and he said, 'Once a man is angered (unless something is done to control it) he will never become happy until he enters the fire. Therefore, whoever becomes angry with people if he is standing must sit down immediately. The filth of Satan goes away from him. Whenever one becomes angry with a relative he should reach out and touch him; when kinship is touched, it calms down.'"

H 2521, Ch. 117, h 3
Ali ibn Ibrahim has narrated from Muhammad ibn 'Isa from Yunus from Dawud ibn Farqad who has said the following:

"Abu 'Abd Allah, *'Alayhi al-Salam*, has said, 'Anger is the key to all evil.'"

H 2522, Ch. 117, h 4

A number of our people have narrated from Ahmad ibn Muhammad ibn Khalid from his father from al-Nadr ibn Suwayd from al-Qasim ibn Sulayman from abu 'Abd Allah, *'Alayhi al-Salam*, who has said the following:

"I heard my father saying, 'Once a Bedouin man came to the Messenger of Allah and said, "I live in the Sahara, please teach me comprehensive words of advice." The Messenger of Allah said, 'I command you not to become angry.' The man from the desert repeated his question three times. He then realized the fact and said, 'I will not ask for anything hereinafter. The Messenger of Allah has commanded me nothing but good.' The Imam said, 'My father has said, "What can be more severe (in harmfulness) than anger? A man becomes angry, he commits murder that is unlawful and accuses a married woman of committing indecent acts.""'"

H 2523, Ch. 117, h 5

It is narrated from him (narrator of the Hadith above) from ibn Faddal from Ibrahim ibn Muhammad al-Ash'ari from 'Abd al-'Ala who has said the following:

"Once I said to abu 'Abd Allah, *'Alayhi al-Salam*, 'Please teach me good advice that will help me learn a lesson.' The Imam said, 'Once a man came to the Messenger of Allah and said, "O Messenger of Allah, teach me an advice that will help me learn a good lesson." The Messenger of Allah said, 'Go, but do not become angry.' The man repeated his question the Messenger of Allah said three times, 'Go and do not become angry.'"

H 2524, Ch. 117, h 6

It is narrated from him (narrator of the Hadith above) from Isma'il ibn Mehran from Sayf ibn 'Amirah from the one who had heard abu 'Abd Allah, *'Alayhi al-Salam*, saying:

"Whoever controls his anger, Allah covers his defects for him.'"

H 2525, Ch. 117, h 7

It is narrated from him (narrator of the Hadith above) from ibn Mahbub from Hisham ibn Salim from Habib al-Sajistani from abu Ja'far, *'Alayhi al-Salam*, who has said the following:

"It is written in the Torah of the conversations of Musa and Allah, the Most Majestic, the Most Holy, 'O Moses, control your anger against those whom I have given you to own, I will keep my anger away from you.'"

H 2526, Ch. 117, h 8

A number of our people have narrated from Sahl ibn Ziyad from Muhammad ibn al-Hamid from Yahya ibn 'Amr from 'Abd Allah ibn Sinan who has said the following:

"Abu 'Abd Allah, *'Alayhi al-Salam*, has said, 'Allah, the Most Majestic, the Most Holy, revealed to certain persons of His prophets: "O sons of Adam, remember Me in your anger, I will remember you in My anger and will not eliminate you along with the things that I eliminate. Be happy with My support; My support is better for you than your support for your own self"'"

H 2527, Ch. 117, h 9

Abu Ali al-Ash'ari has narrated from Muhammad ibn 'Abd al-Jabbar from ibn Faddal from Ali ibn 'Uqbah from 'Abd Allah ibn Sinan from abu 'Abd Allah, *'Alayhi al-Salam*, a similar Hadith with the following addition:

"When injustice is done to you in an oppressive condition, be happy with My support; My support for you is better than your own support for yourself."

H 2528, Ch. 117, h 10

Muhammad ibn Yahya has narrated from Ahmad ibn Muhammad ibn 'Isa from ibn Mahbub from Ishaq ibn 'Ammar who has said the following:

"I heard abu 'Abd Allah, *'Alayhi al-Salam*, saying, 'It is written in the Torah: "Remember Me when you are angry so I remember you when I am angry and will not efface you along with those whom I will blot out. When injustice is done to you, accept My support; My support for you is better than your support for yourself."'"

H 2529, Ch. 117, h 11

Al-Husayn ibn Muhammad has narrated from Mu'alla ibn Muhammad and Ali ibn Muhammad from Salih ibn abu Hammad all from al-Washsha' from Ahmad ibn 'A'id from abu Khadijah from Mu'alla ibn Khanis from abu 'Abd Allah, *'Alayhi al-Salam*, who has said the following:

"Once a man said to the Holy Prophet, 'O Messenger of Allah, teach me.' The Messenger of Allah said, 'You may go and do not become angry.' The man said, 'I have taken it as a sufficient lesson.' He went to his family and found his people fighting, all of them lined up in arms. When he saw it he also armed himself and stood up in line with them and then he remembered the words of the Messenger of Allah, 'Do not become angry'. He threw away his arms and moved forward to the enemies of his people and said, 'O people, I will take responsibility for any loss of life, serious or slight injury that you may have suffered, I will pay you.' The people said, 'Whatever happened we give permission to go in your favor. It is more proper for us to make such undertakings.' The Imam then said, 'The people made peace and anger was gone.'"

H 2530, Ch. 117, h 12

A number of our people have narrated from Sahl ibn Ziyad and Ali ibn Ibrahim from his father all from ibn Mahbub from ibn Ri'ab from abu Hamza al-Thumali from abu Ja'far, *'Alayhi al-Salam*, who has said the following:

"This anger is a spark from Satan that he lights up in the hearts of the children of Adam. Whenever any of you becomes angry, his eyes turn red, his veins puff up and Satan enters into it. If any of you fears this, he must hold to the earth; in so doing the evil of Satan goes away."

H 2531, Ch. 117, h 13

A number of our people have narrated from Ahmad ibn 'Abd Allah from certain individuals of his people in a marfu' manner has said the following:

"Abu 'Abd Allah, *'Alayhi al-Salam*, has said, 'Anger darkens the heart of a wise person.' The Imam then said, 'One who loses control of his anger loses his power of reason.'"

H 2532, Ch. 117, h 14

Al-Husayn ibn Muhammad has narrated from Mu'alla ibn Muhammad from al-Hassan ibn Ali from 'Asim ibn Humayd from abu Hamza from abu Ja'far, *'Alayhi al-Salam*, who has said the following:

"The Messenger of Allah has said, 'Whoever controls his soul from hurting people, on the Day of Judgment Allah will agree to grant relief to his soul. Whoever controls his anger against people, consequently, Allah, the Most

Blessed, the Most High, will, on the Day of Judgment, hold back the fire from him."

H 2533, Ch. 117, h 15

A number of our people have narrated from Sahl ibn Ziyad from ibn Mahbub from abu Hamza from abu Ja'far, *'Alayhi al-Salam*, who has said the following:

"Whoever controls his anger against people, consequently, Allah will, on the Day of Judgment, hold back the fire from him."

Chapter 118 - Envy

H 2534, Ch. 118, h 1

Muhammad ibn Yahya has narrated from Ahmad ibn Muhammad from ibn Mahbub from al-'Ala' ibn Razin from Muhammad ibn Muslim who has said the following:

"Abu Ja'far, *'Alayhi al-Salam*, has said, 'The man may hastily commit any evil deed and then (gradually) turn in disbelief, however, envy consumes belief (immediately) just as fire consumes firewood."

H 2535, Ch. 118, h 2

It is narrated from him (narrator of the Hadith above) from Ahmad ibn Muhammad from Muhammad ibn Khalid and al-Husayn ibn Sa'id from al-Nadr ibn Suwayd from al-Qasim ibn Sulayman from Jarrah al-Mada'ini from abu 'Abd Allah, *'Alayhi al-Salam*, who has said the following:

"Envy consumes belief just as fire consumes firewood."

H 2536, Ch. 118, h 3

A number of our people have narrated from Ahmad ibn Muhammad ibn Khalid from ibn Mahbub from Dawud al-Riqqi who has said the following:

"I heard abu 'Abd Allah, *'Alayhi al-Salam*, saying, 'Be pious before Allah and do not envy each other. It was in the Shari'a of Jesus to travel in the land. During one of his journeys one of his companions, who was of short height, accompanied him very often. When they reached the sea, Jesus with correct certainty said, '(I begin) in the name of Allah,' and began to walk over the water. The short man, looking at Jesus walking over the water, also with correct certainty said, '(I begin) in the name of Allah', walked over the water and reached Jesus. At such time he felt proud of himself and said, 'This is Jesus, the Spirit of Allah who walks over the water, and I also walk over the water. Why then should he be more excellent than me?' The Imam said, 'He then sunk in the water and cried for help from Jesus, who took him out of water and asked, 'What did you say, O short man?' He replied, 'This is Jesus, the Spirit of Allah who walks over the water and I also walk over the water, and I sensed pride inside.' Jesus said to him, 'You placed yourself in a place where Allah had not placed it. Allah resented what you said. Repent and return to Allah, the Most Majestic, the Most Holy, because of what you have said.' The man repented and returned to his position that Allah had given him. Be pious before Allah and no one of you must envy the others.'"

H 2537, Ch. 118, h 4

Ali ibn Ibrahim has narrated from his father from al-Nawfali from al-Sakuni from abu 'Abd Allah, *'Alayhi al-Salam*, who has said the following:

"The Messenger of Allah has said, 'Poverty can almost be disbelief, and envy may almost overcome (disable) the power of an envying person.'"

H 2538, Ch. 118, h 5

Ali ibn Ibrahim has narrated from Muhammad ibn 'Isa from Yunus from Mu'awiyah ibn Wahab who has said the following:

"Abu 'Abd Allah, *'Alayhi al-Salam*, has said, 'Among the tragedies for religion is envy, feeling self-important and proud.'"

H 2539, Ch. 118, h 6

Yunus has narrated from Dawud al-Riqqi from abu 'Abd Allah, *'Alayhi al-Salam*, who has said the following:

"The Messenger of Allah has said, 'Allah, the Most Majestic, the Most Holy, said to Moses, "O son of 'Imran, do not envy people for what I have given them of My favors, do not focus your eyes on it (what I have given to people), and do not allow your soul to follow it; an envious person is angry with My bounties, and blocks My distribution (favors) among My servants. Whoever is as such, I am not for him, and he is not from Me.'"

H 2540, Ch. 118, h 7

Ali ibn Ibrahim has narrated from his father from al-Qasim ibn Muhammad from al-Minqari from al-Fudayl ibn 'Iyad from abu 'Abd Allah, *'Alayhi al-Salam*, who has said the following:

"A believer asks Allah for help but does not envy, and a hypocrite envies, but does not ask Allah for help."

Chapter 119 - Racism

H 2541, Ch. 119, h 1

Muhammad ibn Yahya has narrated from Ahmad ibn Muhammad ibn 'Isa from Ali ibn al-Hakam from Dawud ibn al-Nu'man from Mansur ibn Hazim from abu 'Abd Allah, *'Alayhi al-Salam*, who has said the following:

"Whoever exercises racial discrimination or it is exercised for him, he has taken off the collar of belief from his neck."

H 2542, Ch. 119, h 2

Ali ibn Ibrahim has narrated from his father from ibn abu 'Umayr from Hisham ibn Salim and Drust ibn abu Mansur from abu 'Abd Allah, *'Alayhi al-Salam*, who has said the following:

"The Messenger of Allah has said, 'Whoever practices racial discrimination or it is practiced for him has removed the collar of belief from his neck.'"

H 2543, Ch. 119, h 3

Ali ibn Ibrahim has narrated from his father from al-Nawfali from al-Sakuni from abu 'Abd Allah, *'Alayhi al-Salam*, who has said the following:

"The Messenger of Allah has said, 'Whoever has racist feelings in his heart of the size of mustard seed, on the Day of Judgment Allah will raise him with the Arabs of the time of Jahiliyah (dark age).'"

H 2544, Ch. 119, h 4

Abu Ali al-Ash'ari has narrated from Muhammad ibn 'Abd al-Jabbar from Safwan ibn Yahya from Khudr from Muhammad ibn Muslim from abu 'Abd Allah, *'Alayhi al-Salam*, who has said the following:

"On the Day of Judgment Allah will join those who practice racial discrimination with a race in fire."

H 2545, Ch. 119, h 5

A number of our people have narrated from Ahmad ibn Muhammad ibn Khalid from Ahmad ibn Muhammad ibn abu Nasr from Safwan ibn Mehran from 'Amir ibn al-Simt from Habib ibn abu Thabit from Ali ibn al-Husayn, *'Alayhi al-Salam*, who has said the following:

"Tribal and racist feelings will not enter paradise except that of Hamza ibn 'Abd al-Muttalib. When he accepted Islam he expressed such angered feelings over the story of the contents of a camel's stomach poured over the Holy Prophet."

H 2546, Ch. 119, h 6

It is narrated from him (narrator of the Hadith above) from his father from Fadalah from Dawud ibn Farqad from abu 'Abd Allah, *'Alayhi al-Salam*, who has said the following:

"The angels thought that Satan was one of them. In the knowledge of Allah he was not one of them. He (Satan) let out that which was in his soul with racist feelings and anger saying, 'You have created me from fire and You created him from clay.'"

H 2547, Ch. 119, h 7

Ali ibn Ibrahim has narrated from his father and Ali ibn Muhammad al-Qasani from al-Qasim ibn Muhammad from al-Minqari from 'Abd al-Razzaq from Mu'ammar from al-Zuhri who has said the following:

"Once, Ali ibn al-Husayn, *'Alayhi al-Salam*, was asked about racist feelings. He said, 'The racist feeling that is a sin is the one that makes a person call the evil doers of his own people better than the virtuous individuals of the other people. A man's loving his own people is not racism but it is a sin to help one's own people to commit injustice."

Chapter 120 - Arrogance

H 2548, Ch. 120, h 1

Ali ibn Ibrahim has narrated from Muhammad ibn 'Isa from Yunus from Aban from Hakim who has said the following:

"Once I asked abu 'Abd Allah, *'Alayhi al-Salam*, about a minimum degree of atheism and the Imam said, 'Arrogance is its minimum.'"

H 2549, Ch. 120, h 2

Muhammad ibn Yahya has narrated from Ahmad ibn Muhammad ibn 'Isa from Ali ibn al-Hakam from al-Husayn ibn abu al-'Ala' who has said the following:

"I heard abu 'Abd Allah, *'Alayhi al-Salam*, saying, 'Arrogance can be found in mischievous people of all sexes. Pride is the gown of Allah. Therefore, whoever disputes Allah, the Majestic, the Glorious, about His gown; it will only bring him low. Once, the Messenger of Allah was passing through one of the streets of Madina. On the way there was a black lady collecting manure (to fuel fire). She was told to move to the side to clear the way for the Messenger of Allah. She said, 'The road is wide.' Certain individuals wanted to push her aside but the Messenger of Allah said, 'Leave her alone, she is a bully.'"

H 2550, Ch. 120, h 3

A number of our people have narrated from Ahmad ibn abu 'Abd Allah from 'Uthman ibn 'Isa from al-'Ala' ibn al-Fudayl from abu 'Abd Allah, *'Alayhi al-Salam*, who has said the following:

"Abu Ja'far, *'Alayhi al-Salam*, has said, 'Majesty is the gown of Allah and pride is His loin clothe, therefore, whoever holds to any of these, Allah will throw him in hell.'"

H 2551, Ch. 120, h 4

Abu Ali al-Ash'ari has narrated from Muhammad ibn 'Abd al-Jabbar from ibn Faddal from Tha'labah from Mu'ammar ibn 'Umar ibn 'Ata' from abu Ja'far, *'Alayhi al-Salam*, who has said the following:

"Pride is the gown of Allah. An arrogant person (assuming arrogance) disputes Allah about His gown."

H 2552, Ch. 120, h 5

A number of our people have narrated from Ahmad ibn Muhammad ibn Khalid from Muhammad ibn Ali from abu Jamilah from Lath al-Muradi from abu 'Abd Allah, *'Alayhi al-Salam*, who has said the following:

"Pride is the gown of Allah and whoever disputes Allah in anything about it, Allah will throw him into the fire."

H 2553, Ch. 120, h 6

It is narrated from him (narrator of the Hadith above) from his father from al-Qasim ibn 'Urwah from 'Abd Allah ibn Bukayr from Zurara from abu Ja'far and abu 'Abd Allah, *'Alayhi al-Salam*, who have said the following:

"Whoever in his heart may have an amount of arrogance of the size of an atom he will not be able to enter paradise."

H 2554, Ch. 120, h 7

Ali ibn Ibrahim has narrated from Muhammad ibn 'Isa from Yunus from abu Ayyub from Muhammad ibn Muslim from one of them (two Imam) who has said the following:

"Whoever has an amount of arrogance in his heart of the size of a mustard seed, he will not be able to enter paradise." I then expressed astonishment saying, 'To Allah we belong and to Him we return!' The Imam asked, 'What has made you astonish?' I said, 'I have not heard such Hadith from you.' The Imam said, 'It is not the way you have thought. I meant thereby denial and rejection; it (arrogance) is rejection.'"

H 2555, Ch. 120, h 8

Abu Ali al-Ash'ari has narrated from Muhammad ibn 'Abd al-Jabbar from ibn Faddal from Ali ibn 'Uqbah from Ayyub ibn al-Hurr from 'Abd al-'Ala' from abu 'Abd Allah, *'Alayhi al-Salam*, who has said the following:

"Arrogance is when one belittles the people and calls the truth foolishness."

H 2556, Ch. 120, h 9

Muhammad ibn Yahya has narrated from Ahmad ibn Muhammad ibn 'Isa from Ali ibn al-Hakam from Sayf ibn 'Amirah from 'Abd al-'Ala' ibn 'A'Yun who has said the following:

"Abu 'Abd Allah, *'Alayhi al-Salam*, has said, 'The Messenger of Allah has said, "The biggest form of arrogance is to sink (belittle or look down upon) people and consider the truth foolishness." I (the narrator) then asked, 'What is to 'sink' the people and hoodwink the truth?' The Imam said, 'It is ignoring the truth and criticizing the people of truth. Whoever does it has disputed Allah, the Majestic, the Glorious, about His gown.""""

H 2557, Ch. 120, h 10

Ali ibn Ibrahim has narrated from his father from ibn abu 'Umayr from ibn Bukayr from abu 'Abd Allah, *'Alayhi al-Salam*, who has said the following:

"In hell there is a valley for the arrogant people and it is called 'Saqar'. It complained to Allah of excessive heat and asked Him to allow it to breathe. When it took a breath, it burnt (all of) hell."

H 2558, Ch. 120, h 11

Muhammad ibn Yahya has narrated from Ahmad ibn Muhammad ibn 'Isa from Muhammad ibn Sinan from Dawud ibn Farqad from his brother who has said the following:

"I heard abu 'Abd Allah, *'Alayhi al-Salam*, saying, 'The arrogant people will be turned into particles on whom people will walk until Allah will finalize (people's) accounts.'"

H 2559, Ch. 120, h 12

A number of our people have narrated from Ahmad ibn Muhammad ibn Khalid from more than one person from Ali ibn Asbat from his uncle, Ya'qub ibn Salim from 'Abd al-'Ala' who has said the following:

"Once I asked abu 'Abd Allah, *'Alayhi al-Salam*, 'What is arrogance?' The Imam said, 'The biggest arrogance is to hoodwink the truth and look down upon the people.' I then asked, 'What is to hoodwink the truth and belittle the people?' The Imam said, 'It is one's disregarding and ignoring the truth and his criticizing the people of the truth.'"

H 2560, Ch. 120, h 13

It is narrated from him (narrator of the Hadith above) from Ya'qub ibn Yazid from Muhammad ibn 'Umar ibn Yazid from his father who has said the following:

"Once, I said to abu 'Abd Allah, *'Alayhi al-Salam*, 'I eat good food, use good perfumes, and ride good energetic animals and a young man escorts me. Do you see anything tyrannical in it so I should avoid it? Abu 'Abd Allah, *'Alayhi al-Salam*, remained quiet for a while. He then said, 'A condemned tyrant is one who ignores people and disregards the truth.' 'Umar has said that he then said, 'I do not disregard the truth, but ignoring people is not clear for me.' The Imam said, 'Tyranny is when one considers people insignificant and acts among them repressively, such person is a tyrant.'"

H 2561, Ch. 120, h 14

Muhammad ibn Ja'far has narrated from Muhammad ibn 'Abd al-Hamid from 'Asim ibn Humayd from abu Hamza from abu Ja'far, *'Alayhi al-Salam*, who has said the following:

"The messenger of Allah has said, 'There are three kinds of people to whom, on the Day of Judgment, Allah will not speak or look to and will not purify them. They will suffer a painful punishment: an old man who fornicates, a tyrant king and an arrogant poor person."

H 2562, Ch. 120, h 15

A number of our people have narrated from Ahmad ibn Muhammad from Marwak ibn 'Ubayd from those narrated to him from abu 'Abd Allah, *'Alayhi al-Salam*, who has said the following:

"Joseph, Yusuf, peace be upon him, met his old father, Ya'qub and because of majestic feeling of a king he did not dismount. Jibril (Gabriel) descended to him and said, 'O Yusuf, (look on) your palm.' A shining light came out and went into the sky. Joseph asked, 'O Jibril (Gabriel), what was that light that came out of my palm?' He said, 'Prophet-hood was removed from your descendents as punishment for not dismounting to the old Ya'qub, thus, there will be no prophet in your descendents.'"

H 2563, Ch. 120, h 16
Ali ibn Ibrahim has narrated from his father from ibn abu 'Umayr from certain individuals of his people from abu 'Abd Allah, *'Alayhi al-Salam*, who has said the following:
"Every servant (of Allah) has in his head a certain degree of wisdom being held therein by an angel. When he expresses arrogance the angel says, 'Be humble, may Allah bring you low.' Thereafter he thinks himself to be the greatest of people but in the eyes of the people he remains the lowest of all. When he behaves humbly, Allah, the Most Majestic, the Most Holy, lifts him up. The angel then says, 'Be lofty, may Allah grant you dignity.' He thereafter remains the lowest of all people before his own soul and the most dignified in the eyes of people.'"

H 2564, Ch. 120, h 17
Muhammad ibn Yahya has narrated from Ahmad ibn Muhammad from certain individuals of his people from al-Nahdi from Yazid ibn Ishaq Sha'ar from 'Abd Allah ibn al-Mudar from 'Abd Allah ibn Bukayr who has said the following:
"Abu 'Abd Allah, *'Alayhi al-Salam*, has said, 'No one expresses arrogance but because of lowliness that he feels in his soul.' In another Hadith abu 'Abd Allah, *'Alayhi al-Salam*, has said, 'There is no man who expresses arrogance or tyranny but because of lowliness that he feels in his soul.'"

Chapter 121 - Feeling of Self-importance

H 2565, Ch. 121, h 1
Muhammad ibn Yahya has narrated from Ahmad ibn Muhammad ibn 'Isa from Ali ibn Asbat from a man of our people from Khurasan of the children of Ibrahim ibn Sayyar in a marfu' manner from abu 'Abd Allah, *'Alayhi al-Salam*, who has said the following:
"Allah knew that sin is better for believing people than feeling self-important. Were it not as such, a believer would never sin."

H 2566, Ch. 121, h 2
It is narrated from him (narrator of the Hadith above) from Sa'id ibn Janah from his brother abu 'Amir from a man from abu 'Abd Allah, *'Alayhi al-Salam*, who has said the following:
"Whoever has a feeling of self-importance is destroyed."

H 2567, Ch. 121, h 3
Ali ibn Ibrahim has narrated from his father from Ali ibn Asbat from Ahmad ibn 'Umar al-Hallal from Ali ibn Suwayd who has said the following:
"Once I asked abu al-Hassan, *'Alayhi al-Salam*, about the feeling of self-importance that destroys good deeds. The Imam said, 'The feeling of self-importance is of several degrees. Of such feeling is that one's bad deeds seem attractive to him. He considers it good and it gives him a feeling of self-

importance. He thinks that he is doing well. Of such a feeling is that a servant (of Allah) believes in his Lord and begins to like doing a favor to Allah, the Most Majestic, the Most Holy, in fact, Allah has done him the favor.'"

H 2568, Ch. 121, h 4
Ali ibn Ibrahim has narrated from his father from ibn abu 'Umayr from 'Abd al-Rahman ibn al-Hajjaj from abu 'Abd Allah, *'Alayhi al-Salam*, who has said the following:
"A man sins and then feels regretful. He then does a good deed that gives him happiness (feeling of self-importance). He then weakens. His being in a condition (regretful) is better than what he finds himself in (after a good deed with feeling of self-importance)."

H 2569, Ch. 121, h 5
Muhammad ibn Yahya has narrated from Ahmad ibn Muhammad from Muhammad ibn Sinan from Nadr ibn Qirwash from Ishaq ibn 'Ammar from abu 'Abd Allah, *'Alayhi al-Salam*, who has said the following:
"Once a scholar went to see a worshipper and asked, 'How are your prayers?' He (the worshipper) replied, 'Is a person like me questioned about his prayers? I have been worshipping Allah from such and such times.' The scholar then asked, 'How is your weeping?' He (the worshipper) said, 'I weep until my tears flow.' The scholar said, 'In fact, your laughing with fear is better than your weeping with bravado; nothing of the deeds of boastful people ascends (to heaven).'"

H 2570, Ch. 121, h 6
It is narrated from him (narrator of the Hadith above) from Ahmad ibn Muhammad from Ahmad ibn abu Dawud from certain individuals of our people from one of the two Imam, *'Alayhi al-Salam*, who has said the following:
"Two people went to a Mosque. One was a worshipper and the other a sinful one. They left the Mosque. The sinner was a true believer, but the worshipper had become a sinner. It so happened, because the worshipper went to the Mosque boastful of his worshipping, thus, his thoughts were all the time on boastfulness. The sinner was regretful for his sins and was asking forgiveness from Allah."

H 2571, Ch. 121, h 7
Ali ibn Ibrahim has narrated from Muhammad ibn 'Isa from Yunus from 'Abd al-Rahman ibn al-Hajjaj who has said the following:
"Once I asked abu 'Abd Allah, *'Alayhi al-Salam*, 'A man performs a deed and he is fearful and worried. Then he performs a good deed that gives him a feeling of self-importance.' The Imam said, 'His being in a fearful condition is better than his having a feeling of self-importance.'"

H 2572, Ch. 121, h 8
Ali ibn Ibrahim has narrated from Muhammad ibn 'Isa ibn 'Ubayd from Yunus from certain individuals of his people from abu 'Abd Allah, *'Alayhi al-Salam*, who has said the following:
"The Messenger of Allah has said, 'Once Moses was sitting when Satan came to him with a many-colored hooded cloak on him. When he approached Moses he took his cloak off, stood nearby, and offered him the greeting of peace. Moses asked, 'Who are you?' He replied, 'I am Satan.' Moses said, 'Is it you? May Allah not bring you near by.' Satan said, 'I came to offer you greetings of peace because of your closeness to Allah.' The Imam said, 'Moses then asked, 'What is this

hooded cloak for?' He said, 'With this I kidnap the hearts of the children of Adam.' Moses said, 'Tell me which sin is it that when the children of Adam commit it you feel successful?' He said, 'It is when he feels self-important, his good deeds are a great deal and his sins trivial.'

"The Imam said, 'Allah, the Most Majestic, the Most Holy, said to David, "O David, give good news to the sinners and warn the true believers." He asked, 'How should I give good news to the sinners and warn the true believers?' Allah said, 'Give good news to the sinners that I accept repentance and forgive their sins. Warn the true believers against feeling self-important due to their deeds. If I will ever make anyone settle his accounts, he is destroyed.'"

Chapter 122 - Love of and Greed for Worldly Things

H 2573, Ch. 122, h 1
Ali ibn Ibrahim has narrated from his father from ibn abu 'Umayr from Drust ibn abu Mansur from a man from abu 'Abd Allah, *'Alayhi al-Salam*, and Hisham from abu 'Abd Allah, *'Alayhi al-Salam*, who has said the following:
"Abu 'Abd Allah, *'Alayhi al-Salam*, has said, 'The head of all sins is love of this world.'"

H 2574, Ch. 122, h 2
Ali has narrated from his father from ibn Faddal from ibn Bukayr from Hammad ibn Bashir who has said the following:
"I heard abu 'Abd Allah, *'Alayhi al-Salam*, saying, 'No two fierce wolves in a flock of sheep in the absence of their shepherd, one wolf on either side is as destructive to them as the love of property and honor is to the religion of a Muslim.'"

H 2575, Ch. 122, h 3
It is narrated from him (narrator of the Hadith above) from his father from 'Uthman ibn 'Isa from abu Ayyub from Muhammad ibn Muslim from abu Ja'far, *'Alayhi al-Salam*, who has said the following:
"No two fierce wolves in a flock of sheep without a shepherd, one wolf on either side is as quick (to destroy them) as the love of property and honor (popularity) is to destroy the religion of a believer."

H 2576, Ch. 122, h 4
Muhammad ibn Yahya has narrated from Ahmad ibn Muhammad ibn 'Isa from Muhammad ibn Yahya al-Khazzaz from Ghiyath ibn Ibrahim from abu 'Abd Allah, *'Alayhi al-Salam*, who has said the following:
"Satan circles around the children of Adam in every (evil) matter (to make him sin), when he is frustrated (man did not sin) he ambushes him through his (love of) property and holds him (man) through such love by his neck."

H 2577, Ch. 122, h 5
It is narrated from him (narrator of the Hadith above) from Ahmad ibn Muhammad from Ali ibn al-Nu'man from abu 'Usamah Zayd from abu 'Abd Allah, *'Alayhi al-Salam*, who has said the following:
"The Messenger of Allah has said, 'One who is not comforted and satisfied with relief from Allah, his soul will be torn in pieces due to his sorrow for the world. One who follows his eyes to what is in the hands of the people, his depressed

condition will increase and his anguish will not cease. One who does not appreciate Allah's bounties, besides food, drinks and clothes, his deeds fall short and his suffering draws near."

H 2578, Ch. 122, h 6

A number of our people have narrated from Ahmad ibn abu 'Abd Allah from Ya'qub ibn Yazid from Ziyad al-Qandi from abu Waki' from ibn Ishaq al-Sabi'i from al-Harith al-A'War from Amir al-Mu'minin, Ali ibn abu Talib, *'Alayhi al-Salam*, who has said the following:

"The Messenger of Allah has said, 'The world and dirham (money) have destroyed those who lived before you and they will destroy you also.'"

H 2579, Ch. 122, h 7

Ali ibn Ibrahim has narrated from his father Muhammad ibn 'Isa from Yahya ibn 'Uqbah al-Azdi from abu 'Abd Allah, *'Alayhi al-Salam*, who has said the following:

"Abu Ja'far, *'Alayhi al-Salam*, has said, 'A person greedy of the worldly things is like a silkworm, the more silk it produces around itself the more difficult it becomes to come out, until it dies in sorrow.' Abu 'Abd Allah, *'Alayhi al-Salam*, then said, 'The richest person is one who is not a captive of greed.' The Imam has said, 'Do not allow your hearts to become preoccupied with what has already gone; it distracts your hearts from the task of readiness for what is to come.'"

H 2580, Ch. 122, h 8

Ali ibn Ibrahim has narrated from his father and Ali ibn Muhammad all from al-Qasim ibn Muhammad from Sulayman al-Minqari from 'Abd al-Razzaq ibn Hammam from Mu'ammar ibn Rashid from al-Zuhri Muhammad ibn Muslim ibn 'Ubayd Allah who has said the following:

"Ali ibn al-Husayn, *'Alayhi al-Salam*, was asked, 'Which deed is more excellent before Allah?' The Imam said, 'No deed, after knowing Allah, the Most Majestic, the Most Holy, and knowing the Messenger of Allah, is more excellent than hating the world. It has many branches, and the sins have branches also. The first sin committed was Arrogance, the sin of Satan, when he refused to obey (Allah), assumed arrogance and became an unbeliever. Thereafter it is Greed, the sin of Adam and Eve. When Allah, the Most Majestic, the Most Holy, told them, 'Enjoy the foods therein, but do not go near a certain tree lest you become of the transgressors.' (2:35) They took what they did not need and it remained in their descendents to the Day of Judgment. For this reason most of the things that the children of Adam want do not need them. Thereafter is Envy. It is the sin of the son of Adam who envied his brother and killed him. From this branches love for women, love for the world, love to become the leader, the love to be comfortable, the love to speak, the love to be superior and rich. They total seven characteristics and all are found in the love for the world. The prophets and the scholars after knowing this have said, 'Love for the world is the head of all sins.' The world is of two kinds: The world of bare necessities and the condemned one.'"

H 2581, Ch. 122, h 9

Through the same chain of narrators it is narrated from al-Minqari from Hafs ibn Ghiyath from abu 'Abd Allah, *'Alayhi al-Salam*, who has said the following:

"It is in the conversations of Moses: 'O Moses, the world is the home of suffering. I caused Adam to suffer in it when he made a mistake and I have condemned it. Everything in it is condemned except what is for Me. O Moses, My virtuous servants reduce their interests in the world proportionate to the degree of their knowledge, and other creatures developed interest in it proportionate to the degree of their ignorance. There is no one who for his appreciation of the world has found any delight to his eyes and no one belittled it but that he found benefits in it.'"

H 2582, Ch. 122, h 10

Muhammad ibn Yahya has narrated from Ahmad ibn Muhammad from ibn Faddal from abu Jamilah from Muhammad al-Halabi from abu 'Abd Allah, *'Alayhi al-Salam*, who has said the following:

"No two fierce wolves in a flock of sheep without a shepherd, one wolf on either side is as quick (to destroy them) as the love of property and fame is to destroy the religion of a Muslim."

H 2583, Ch. 122, h 11

A number of our people have narrated from Ahmad ibn Muhammad ibn Khalid from Mansur ibn al-'Abbas from Sa'id ibn Janah from 'Uthman ibn Sa'id from 'Abd al-Hamid ibn Ali al-Kufi from Muhajir al-Asadi from abu 'Abd Allah, *'Alayhi al-Salam*, who has said the following:

"Once Jesus, son of Mary, passed by a town, in which people, birds and animals had all died. Jesus said, 'They all have died from violence. Had they died individually they would have buried each other.' The disciples said, 'O Spirit of Allah and His word, pray to Allah to bring them to life so we may ask about their deeds and avoid them (bad ones).' Jesus prayed to his Lord and from space he was told to call them. Jesus at night stood on a high ground that dominated the town and said, 'O people of the town?' A certain individual replied, 'Yes, O the Spirit of Allah and His word.' He then said, 'Woe upon you. What kind of deeds did you have?' He said, 'We worshipped the devil, loved the world with little fear, had long hopes and neglectfully engaged in useless and playful activities.' Jesus asked, 'How was your love of the world?' He replied, 'It was like a child's love for his mother. When it came to us we rejoiced in happiness and when it went away we felt sad and cried.' He then asked, 'How was your worship of the devil?' He replied, 'It was obedience to the sinful people.' Jesus asked, 'How were the consequences of your activities?' He replied, 'We spent one night in comfort and in the morning we found ourselves in Hawiyah (a place in hell).' Jesus asked, 'What is Hawiyah?' He said, 'It is Sijjin' Jesus asked, 'What is Sijjin?' He said, 'It is a mountain of burning coal that smolders upon us to the Day of Judgment.' Jesus asked, 'What did you say and what was said to you?' He replied, 'We said, 'Return us to the worldly life so we can live piously, and it was said to us, "You are lying."' Jesus asked, 'Why do not the others of you talk to me?' He said, 'O Spirit of Allah, they are harnessed with a harness of fire which is in the hands of stern and strong angels. I was among them, but not one of them. When punishment struck it took me with them. I am hanged by a hair on the brink of hell and I do not know if I will be saved or thrown into hell.' Jesus then turned to the disciples and said, 'Friends of Allah, eating dried up bread with not so pleasant salt and sleeping on the trash collection sites is much better in good health and safety in this world and in the next life.'"

H 2584, Ch. 122, h 12

Ali ibn Ibrahim has narrated from his father from ibn abu 'Umayr from Hisham ibn Salim from abu 'Abd Allah, *'Alayhi al-Salam*, who has said the following:

"With every door to the worldly affairs that Allah opens to a servant, He also opens a door of greed to him."

H 2585, Ch. 122, h 13

Ali ibn Ibrahim has narrated from his father from al-Qasim ibn Muhammad from al-Minqari from Hafs ibn Ghiyath from abu 'Abd Allah, *'Alayhi al-Salam*, who has said the following:

"Jesus, son of Mary, peace be upon him, has said, 'You work for the worldly things while your sustenance is there without work. You do not work for the next life where you will not receive any sustenance without work. Woe upon you. You are bad scholars. You receive payments but destroy the work. Perhaps the worshippers' deeds are accepted and perhaps they will be taken out of the narrow space of this world to the darkness of the grave. How can one be of the scholars who is on his way to the next life while he is holding to the world and what is harmful to him is more beloved to him than what is beneficial to him?'"

H 2586, Ch. 122, h 14

It is narrated from him (narrator of the Hadith above) from his father from Muhammad 'Amr – as far as I know- from abu Ali al-Hadhdha' from Hariz from Zurara and Muhammad ibn Muslim from abu 'Abd Allah, *'Alayhi al-Salam*, who has said the following:

"The farthest that a servant can be from Allah, the Most Majestic, the Most Holy, is the condition wherein one has no other concern but his stomach and his genitals."

H 2587, Ch. 122, h 15

Muhammad ibn Yahya has narrated from Ahmad ibn Muhammad from ibn Mahbub from 'Abd Allah ibn Sinan and 'Abd al-'Aziz al-'Abdi from 'Abd Allah ibn abu Ya'fur from abu 'Abd Allah, *'Alayhi al-Salam*, who has said the following:

"Whoever passes the nights and days with the world as his biggest concern, Allah places poverty between his eyes, makes his affairs chaotic and he will receive of the world only what Allah has made his allocated share of the world. Whoever passes nights and the days with the next life as his biggest concern, Allah places wealth in his heart and sets his affairs in an orderly manner.'

H 2588, Ch. 122, h 16

Ali ibn Ibrahim has narrated from Muhammad ibn 'Isa from Yunus from ibn Sinan from Hafs ibn Qurt from abu 'Abd Allah, *'Alayhi al-Salam*, who has said the following:

"Whoever's entanglement with the world is greater his sorrow to leave this world becomes more intense."

H 2589, Ch. 122, h 17

Ali ibn Ibrahim has narrated from his father from ibn Mahbub from 'Abd al-'Aziz al-'Abdi from ibn abu Ya'fur who has said the following:

"I heard abu 'Abd Allah, *'Alayhi al-Salam*, saying, 'Whoever's heart is lodged with the world is ensnared with three things: a concern that never vanishes, a wish that never comes true and a hope that never materializes.'"

Chapter 123 - Greed

H 2590, Ch. 123, h 1

A number of our people have narrated from Ahmad ibn Muhammad ibn Khalid from Ali ibn Hassan from those who narrated to him from abu 'Abd Allah, *'Alayhi al-Salam*, who has said the following:

"Abu 'Abd Allah, *'Alayhi al-Salam*, has said, 'How disgraceful to a believer is a desire that humiliates him!'"

H 2591, Ch. 123, h 2

It is narrated from him (narrator of the Hadith above) from his father from those whom he has mentioned in his book from abu Ja'far, *'Alayhi al-Salam*, who has said the following:

"Abu Ja'far, *'Alayhi al-Salam*, has said, 'The worst servant is the servant who has a greed that dominates him and so also is a servant whose desires humiliate him.'"

H 2592, Ch. 123, h 3

Ali ibn Ibrahim has narrated from his father from al-Qasim ibn Muhammad from al-Minqari from 'Abd al-Razzaq from Mu'ammar from al-Zuhri who has said the following:

"Ali ibn al-Husayn, *'Alayhi al-Salam*, has said, 'I have seen all good is gathered together in eradicating of greed for what is in people's possession.'"

H 2593, Ch. 123, h 4

Muhammad ibn Yahya has narrated from Muhammad ibn Ahmad from certain individuals of our people from Ali ibn Sulayman ibn Rashid from Musa ibn Salam from Sa'dan who has said the following:

"Once I asked abu 'Abd Allah, *'Alayhi al-Salam*, 'What (deed) establishes belief firmly in a servant (of Allah)?' The Imam said, 'It is restraint from the worldly attractions (sins).' I then asked, 'What (kind of thing) removes belief from a person?' The Imam said, 'It is greed.'"

Chapter 124 - Harshness (of Manners)

H 2594, Ch. 124, h 1

A number of our people have narrated from Ahmad ibn abu 'Abd Allah from his father from those he has narrated from Muhammad ibn 'Abd al-Rahman ibn abu Layla' from abu Ja'far, *'Alayhi al-Salam*, who has said the following:

"Abu Ja'far, *'Alayhi al-Salam*, has said, 'Whoever has a share of harshness (in his behavior), belief is separated from him.'"

H 2595, Ch. 123, h 2

Muhammad ibn Yahya has narrated from Ahmad ibn Muhammad ibn 'Isa from Ali ibn al-Nu'man from 'Amr ibn Shamir from Jabir from abu Ja'far, *'Alayhi al-Salam*, who has said the following:

"The Messenger of Allah has said, 'Had harshness been among the visible creatures it would have looked the most loathsome of the creatures of Allah.'"

Chapter 125 - Evil Behavior

H 2596, Ch. 125, h 1

Ali ibn Ibrahim has narrated from his father from ibn abu 'Umayr from 'Abd Allah ibn Sinan from abu 'Abd Allah, *'Alayhi al-Salam*, who has said the following:

"Abu 'Abd Allah, *'Alayhi al-Salam*, has said, 'Wickedness and evil behavior destroys and spoils good deeds just as vinegar spoils honey.'"

H 2597, Ch. 125, h 2
Ali ibn Ibrahim has narrated from his father from al-Nawfali from al-Sakuni from abu 'Abd Allah, *'Alayhi al-Salam*, who has said the following:
"The Holy Prophet has said, 'Allah, the Most Majestic, the Most Holy, refuses to accept the repentance of a person of bad conduct.' It was asked, 'Why is it so, O Messenger of Allah?' He said, 'It is because when he repents from a sin he falls into a greater sin.'"

H 2598, Ch. 125, h 3
A number of our people have narrated from Ahmad ibn Muhammad ibn Khalid from Isma'il ibn Mehran from Sayf ibn 'Amirah from those whom he has mentioned (in his book) from abu 'Abd Allah, *'Alayhi al-Salam*, who has said the following:
"Abu 'Abd Allah, *'Alayhi al-Salam*, has said, 'Wicked and evil behavior spoils good deeds just as vinegar spoils honey.'"

H 2599, Ch. 125, h 4
It is narrated from him (narrator of the Hadith above) from Muhammad ibn Isma'il ibn Bazi' from 'Abd Allah ibn 'Uthman from al-Husayn ibn Mehran from Ishaq ibn Ghalib from abu 'Abd Allah, *'Alayhi al-Salam*, who has said the following:
"Abu 'Abd Allah, *'Alayhi al-Salam*, has said, 'Whoever's behavior is bad and evil, his soul lives in suffering.'"

H 2600, Ch. 125, h 5
A number of our people have narrated from Sahl ibn Ziyad from Muhammad ibn 'Abd al-Hamid from Yahya ibn 'Amr from 'Abd Allah ibn Sinan who has said the following:
"Abu 'Abd Allah, *'Alayhi al-Salam*, has said, 'Allah, the Most Majestic, the Most Holy, sent revelations to one of His prophets and it said, 'Bad and evil behavior spoils good deeds just as vinegar spoils honey.'"

Chapter 126 - Dimwittedness

H 2601, Ch. 126, h 1
A number of our people have narrated from Ahmad ibn Muhammad ibn Khalid from Sharif ibn Sabiq from al-Fadl ibn abu Qurrah from abu 'Abd Allah, *'Alayhi al-Salam*, who has said the following:
"Abu 'Abd Allah, *'Alayhi al-Salam*, has said, 'Dimwittedness is a bad attitude. Such an individual intimidates those below him and is humble (inferior) before those above him.'"

H 2602, Ch. 126, h 2
Muhammad ibn Yahya has narrated from Ahmad ibn Muhammad ibn 'Isa from certain individuals of his people from abu al-Maghra' from al-Halabi from abu 'Abd Allah, *'Alayhi al-Salam*, who has said the following:
"Abu 'Abd Allah, *'Alayhi al-Salam*, has said, 'Do not behave as dimwitted ones; your 'A'immah, *'Alayhim al-Salam*, have not been dimwitted people.' Abu 'Abd Allah, *'Alayhi al-Salam*, has also said, 'Whoever deals with a dimwitted person in a reciprocal manner is as if he has agreed to what he has faced and has behaved similarly (followed the footsteps of the dimwitted person).'"

H 2603, Ch. 126, h 3

Ali ibn Ibrahim has narrated from his father from ibn Mahbub from 'Abd al-Rahman ibn al-Hajjaj from abu al-Hassan Musa, *'Alayhi al-Salam*, who has said the following:

"Two people were abusing each other and the Imam said, 'The initiator is more unjust. His own sins and the sins of his companion are on him as long as the oppressed one does not transgress.'"

H 2604, Ch. 126, h 4

A number of our people have narrated from Sahl ibn Ziyad from Safwan from 'Iys ibn al-Qasim from abu 'Abd Allah, *'Alayhi al-Salam*, who has said the following:

"Abu 'Abd Allah, *'Alayhi al-Salam*, has said, 'The most hated of the creatures of Allah is one from whose tongue people are afraid.'"

Chapter 127 - Abusiveness

H 2605, Ch. 127, h 1

Muhammad ibn Yahya has narrated from Ahmad ibn Muhammad ibn 'Isa from ibn Faddal from abu al-Maghra' from abu Basir from abu 'Abd Allah, *'Alayhi al-Salam*, who has said the following:

"Abu 'Abd Allah, *'Alayhi al-Salam*, has said, 'Of the signs of the association of Satan with a person, without any doubt, is that he becomes abusive and is no more concerned about what he says or what is said about him.'"

H 2606, Ch. 127, h 2

Ali ibn Ibrahim has narrated from his father from ibn abu 'Umayr from 'Abd Allah ibn Sinan from abu 'Abd Allah, *'Alayhi al-Salam*, who has said the following:

"The messenger of Allah has said, 'If you find a man who is not concerned at all about what he says or what is said about him, he certainly is an straying person or an associate of Satan.'"

H 2607, Ch. 127, h 3

A number of our people have narrated from Ahmad ibn Muhammad ibn Khalid from 'Uthman ibn 'Isa from 'Umar ibn 'Udhaynah from Aban ibn abu 'Ayyash from Sulaym ibn Qays from Amir al-Mu'minin, Ali ibn abu Talib, *'Alayhi al-Salam*, who has said the following:

"The Messenger of Allah has said, 'Allah has made paradise unlawful for every abusive, immoral, and (persons) lacking bashfulness who is not concerned about what he says or what is said to him. If (investigated) you find him to be an straying person or a partner of Satan.' It was asked, O Messenger of Allah, 'Does Satan become a partner of people?' the Messenger of Allah said, 'Have you not read the words of Allah, the Most Majestic, the Most Holy, ' . . . share them in their properties and children. . . .' (17:64)

"The narrator has said that a man then asked a one learned in the law (the Imam), 'Is there among the people anyone who is not concerned about what he says or what is said about him?' The Imam said, 'One who disturbs people and abuses them knowing that people do not leave him without a response, such a person is the one who is not concerned about what he says or what is said about him.'"

H 2608, Ch. 127, h 4

Muhammad ibn Yahya has narrated from Ahmad ibn Muhammad ibn 'Isa from Ali ibn al-Hakam from abu Jamilah in a marfu' manner from abu Ja'far, *'Alayhi al-Salam*, who has said the following:

"Abu Ja'far, *'Alayhi al-Salam*, has said, 'Allah hates an abusive obscenity-monger.'"

H 2609, Ch. 127, h 5
Abu Ali al-Ash'ari has narrated from from Muhammad ibn Salim from Ahmad ibn al-Nadr from 'Amr ibn Nu'man al-Ju'fi who has said the following:

"Abu 'Abd Allah, *'Alayhi al-Salam*, had a friend who almost all the time accompanied him whenever he went somewhere. Once he was walking with the Imam in the shoemaker's place and his (man's) slave from Sind was walking behind them. The man looked to find where his slave was. He could not see him. He tried three times and could not find him. At the fourth time he found him and said, 'Where have you been, O son of a fornicating woman?' The narrator has said that the Imam raised his hand and hit his own forehead and said, 'All glory belongs to Allah, how you could accuse his mother? I considered you a pious person (restraining from sins). Now it shows you have no piety and restraint against evil.' The man said, 'May Allah keep my soul in service for your cause, his mother is a Sindy, (a pagan).' The Imam said, 'Did you not know that every people have a system of marriage? Stay away from me.' The narrator has said that thereafter I never saw him walk with the Imam until death separated them from each other.'

"In another Hadith it says, 'Every people have a system of marriage. It keeps them reserved and away from fornication.'"

H 2610, Ch. 127, h 6
Ali ibn Ibrahim has narrated from his father from ibn abu 'Umayr from ibn 'Udhaynah from Zurara from abu Ja'far, *'Alayhi al-Salam*, who has said the following:

"The Messenger of Allah has said, 'If obscene language had a form and shape it would have been a very ugly one.'"

H 2611, Ch. 127, h 7
Muhammad ibn Yahya has narrated from Ahmad ibn Muhammad ibn 'Isa from ibn Mahbub from 'Umar ibn Yazid from abu 'Abd Allah, *'Alayhi al-Salam*, who has said the following:

"In the tribe of Israel there was a man who prayed to Allah for a son for three years. When he found that Allah did not answer his prayer, he then asked, 'O Lord, am I far away from You and You do not hear me or You are close to me but do not answer me?' The Imam said, 'Someone came in his dream and said, 'You have prayed to Allah, the Majestic, the Glorious, for three years in an obscene language, with an oppressive heart that is impious and with untrue intentions. Stay away from obscenity, be pious before Allah and make your intention to be good.' The Imam said, 'The man followed the instruction, and prayed to Allah, only then a son was born to him.'"

H 2612, Ch. 127, h 8
A number of our people have narrated from Ahmad ibn Muhammad ibn Khalid from 'Uthman ibn 'Isa from Sama'a from abu 'Abd Allah, *'Alayhi al-Salam*, who has said the following:

"The messenger of Allah has said, 'Of the most wicked and evil servants (of Allah) are those with whom association is disliked due to their use of foul language."

H 2613, Ch. 127, h 9

A number of our people have narrated from Sahl ibn Ziyad from ibn Mahbub from ibn Ri'ab from abu 'Ubaydah from abu 'Abd Allah, *'Alayhi al-Salam*, who has said the following:

"Abu 'Abd Allah, *'Alayhi al-Salam*, has said, 'Using foul language is injustice and injustice is in the fire.'"

H 2614, Ch. 127, h 10

Muhammad ibn Yahya has narrated from Ahmad ibn Muhammad from Muhammad ibn Sinan from ibn Muskan from al-Hassan al-Sayqal who has said the following:

"Abu 'Abd Allah, *'Alayhi al-Salam*, has said, abusive, foul language and a sharp tongue is hypocrisy.'"

H 2615, Ch. 127, h 11

It is narrated from him (narrator of the Hadith above) from Ahmad ibn Muhammad from Ali ibn al-Nu'man from 'Amr ibn Shimr from Jabir from abu Ja'far, *'Alayhi al-Salam*, who has said the following:

"The Messenger of Allah has said, 'Allah hates those who use foul language and the insistant beggar."

H 2616, Ch. 127, h 12

Ali ibn Ibrahim has narrated from his father from ibn abu 'Umayr from ibn 'Udhaynah from Zurara from abu Ja'far, *'Alayhi al-Salam*, who has said the following:

"The Messenger of Allah once said to 'A'ishah, 'O 'A'ishah, had foul language had a form and shape it would have been a very ugly form and shape."

H 2617, Ch. 127, h 13

Al-Husayn ibn Muhammad has narrated from Mu'alla ibn Muhammad from Ahmad ibn Muhammad from certain individuals of his people from who has said the following:

"The Imam has said, 'Whoever uses foul language against his Muslim brother (in belief) Allah removes blessings from his livelihood, leaves him to be on his own and destroys his means of living.'"

H 2618, Ch. 127, h 14

It is narrated from him (narrator of the Hadith above) from Mu'alla from Ahmad ibn Ghassan from Sama'a who has said the following:

"Once I went to see abu 'Abd Allah, *'Alayhi al-Salam*. The Imam on his own initiation said to me, 'O Sama'a, what was that between you and your camel man? Beware of becoming abusive, loud and using foul language.' I (the narrator) then said, 'By Allah, it happened but he did injustice to me.' The Imam said, 'If he has done injustice to you, you have gained over him. This is not among my behaviors and I do not command my Shi'a (followers) to behave as such. Ask forgiveness from your Lord and do not repeat.' I then said, 'I ask forgiveness from Allah and I will not repeat.'"

Chapter 128 - Those Whose Evil is Feared

H 2619, Ch. 128, h 1

A number of our people have narrated from Ahmad ibn Muhammad ibn Khalid from 'Uthman ibn 'Isa from Sama'a from abu Basir from abu 'Abd Allah, *'Alayhi al-Salam*, who has said the following:

"One day, when the Holy Prophet was with 'A'ishah, a man asked permission to meet him. The Messenger of Allah said, 'What an evil fellow from the tribe!' 'A'ishah then went to her chamber and the Holy Prophet granted permission to the man for a meeting. When he came in, the Holy Prophet met him cheerfully, politely speaking to him until the meeting was over and the man left. 'A'ishah then asked, 'O Messenger of Allah, a while ago you said about the man what you said and then you met him in such a cheerful and polite manner!' The Messenger of Allah said, 'Of the most evil among the servants (of Allah) is one whose meeting is disliked because of his using obscene language.'"

H 2620, Ch. 128, h 2

Ali ibn Ibrahim has narrated from his father from al-Nawfali from al-Sakuni from abu 'Abd Allah, *'Alayhi al-Salam*, who has said the following:

"The Messenger of Allah has said, 'The most evil among people in the sight of Allah on the Day of Judgment will be the one whom people respect for fear from his evil manners.'"

H 2621, Ch. 128, h 3

It is narrated from him (narrator of the Hadith above) from Muhammad ibn 'Isa from 'Ubayd from Yunus from 'Abd Allah ibn Sinan who has said the following:

"Abu 'Abd Allah, *'Alayhi al-Salam*, has said, 'Whoever is feared because of his foul language will be in the fire.'"

H 2622, Ch. 128, h 4

A number of our people have narrated from Sahl ibn Ziyad from ibn Mahbub from ibn Ri'ab from abu Hamza from Jabir ibn 'Abd Allah who has said the following:

"The Messenger of Allah has said, 'The most evil among people on the Day of Judgment will be one whom people respect for fear of his evil manners'"

Chapter 129 - Tyrannical Transgression

H 2623, Ch. 129, h 1

A number of our people have narrated from Sahl ibn Ziyad from Ja'far ibn Muhammad al-Ash'ari from ibn al-Qaddah from abu 'Abd Allah, *'Alayhi al-Salam*, who has said the following:

"The Messenger of Allah has said, 'The evil most quickly facing punishment is tyrannical transgression.'"

H 2624, Ch. 129, h 2

Ali ibn Ibrahim has narrated from his father from al-Nawfali from al-Sakuni from abu 'Abd Allah, *'Alayhi al-Salam*, who has said the following:

"Satan says to his soldiers, 'Throw unto them envy and tyrannical transgression; in the sight of Allah these two are equal to considering things as partners of Allah.'"

H 2625, Ch. 129, h 3

Ali has narrated from his father from Hammad from Hariz from Misma' abu Sayyar who has said the following:

"Abu 'Abd Allah, *'Alayhi al-Salam*, once wrote a letter to me in which he had said, 'Keep in mind not to ever speak a tyrannical and transgressing word even though your own soul and tribe are more captivating to you.'"

H 2626, Ch. 129, h 4

Ali has narrated from his father from ibn Mahbub from ibn Ri'ab and Ya'qub ibn al-Sarraj all from abu 'Abd Allah, *'Alayhi al-Salam*, who has said the following:

"Amir al-Mu'minin, Ali ibn abu Talib, *'Alayhi al-Salam*, has said, 'O people, tyrannical transgression leads its associates to the fire. The first person who committed it against Allah was 'Unaq, daughter of Adam, the first one that Allah killed was 'Unaq who, when sitting occupied one acre. She had twenty fingers each of which had two fingernails like two sickles. Allah made a lion of the size of an elephant, a wolf of the size of a camel and a vulture of the size of a donkey to kill her. Allah has eliminated the transgressing tyrants in their most ideal and peaceful conditions.'"

Chapter 130 - Pride and Arrogance

H 2627, Ch. 130, h 1

Muhammad ibn Yahya has narrated from Ahmad ibn Muhammad ibn 'Isa from al-Hassan ibn Mahbub from Hisham ibn Salim from abu Hamza al-Thumali who has said the following:

"Ali ibn al-Husayn, *'Alayhi al-Salam*, has said, 'It is astonishing how one who yesterday was only a sperm and tomorrow will turn into a carcass displays arrogance and boastfulness.'"

H 2628, Ch. 130, h 2

Ali ibn Ibrahim has narrated from his father from al-Nawfali from al-Sakuni from abu 'Abd Allah, *'Alayhi al-Salam*, who has said the following:

"The Messenger of Allah has said, 'The misfortune for lineage is boastfulness and feeling self-important.'"

H 2629, Ch. 130, h 3

Abu Ali al-Ash'ari has narrated from Muhammad ibn 'Abd al-Jabbar from Muhammad ibn Isma'il from Hanan ibn 'Uqbah ibn Bashir al-Asadi who has said the following:

"Once, I said to abu Ja'far, *'Alayhi al-Salam*, 'I am 'Uqbah ibn Bashir al-Asadi and among my people my lineage is very prominent.' The narrator has said that the Imam then asked, 'What is it that makes you oblige us because of your lineage? Due to proper belief, Allah has exalted those whom people consider low. Due to disbelief, He has made low those whom people called men of dignity. No one is superior, because of any other reason, to the others except due to piety.'"

H 2630, Ch. 130, h 4

A number of our people have narrated from Ahmad ibn Muhammad ibn Khalid from 'Uthman ibn 'Isa from 'Isa ibn al-Dahhak who has said the following:

"Abu Ja'far, *'Alayhi al-Salam*, has said, 'It is astonishing how one acts boastfully and arrogantly, when it is a fact that he is created from sperm and he will soon turn into a carcass and, in between, he does not know what may happen to him.'"

H 2631, Ch. 130, h 5

Ali ibn Ibrahim has narrated from his father from al-Nawfali from al-Sakuni from abu 'Abd Allah, *'Alayhi al-Salam*, who has said the following:

"Once a man came to the Messenger of Allah and said, 'O Messenger of Allah, I am so and so son of so and so counting (boastfully) up to nine generations.' The Messenger of Allah said, 'You are the tenth of them in the fire.'"

H 2632, Ch. 130, h 6

Ali ibn Ibrahim has narrated from his father from al-Nawfali from al-Sakuni from abu 'Abd Allah, *'Alayhi al-Salam*, who has said the following:

"The Messenger of Allah has said, 'The misfortune for lineage is boastfulness.'"

Chapter 131 - Hardheartedness

H 2633, Ch. 131, h 1

A number of our people have narrated from Ahmad ibn Muhammad from 'Amr ibn 'Uthman from Ali ibn 'Isa in a marfu' manner has said the following:

"It is in the conversations of Moses with Allah, the Most Majestic, the Most Holy, 'O Moses, do not prolong your hopes in the world; it hardens your heart and the hardhearted people are far away from Me.'"

H 2634, Ch. 131, h 2

Ali ibn Ibrahim has narrated from his father from Muhammad ibn Hafs from Isma'il ibn Dabis from those whom has mentioned (in his book) from abu 'Abd Allah, *'Alayhi al-Salam*, who has said the following:

"If Allah creates a servant as an unbeliever in the beginning of his creation he will not die until He makes evil seem attractive to him so he draws nearer to evil. He then makes him turn out as arrogant and tyrannical. His heart then hardens, his behavior worsens, his face thickens (shameless), his obscenity becomes public, his bashfulness reduces and Allah opens his secrets. Thereafter unlawful dealing becomes his way of life and he does not separate from it. He then grows disobedient to Allah all the time and begins to hate obedience to Allah. He then moves on the offensive against people and is never satisfied with quarrels. Thus, you must ask Allah to grant you well-being, and you must seek to achieve it from Him.'"

H 2635, Ch. 131, h 3

Ali ibn Ibrahim has narrated from his father from al-Nawfali from al-Sakuni from abu 'Abd Allah, *'Alayhi al-Salam*, who has said the following:

"Amir al-Mu'minin, Ali ibn abu Talib, *'Alayhi al-Salam*, has said, 'There are two kinds of motivations, one from Satan and one from the angel. The motivation from the angel is tenderheartedness and sharp understanding, and the motivation from Satan is confusion and hardheartedness.'"

Chapter 132 - Injustice, Oppression

H 2636, Ch. 132, h 1

A number of our people have narrated from Ahmad ibn Muhammad ibn Khalid from his father from Harun ibn al-Jahm from al-Mufaddal ibn Salih from Sa'd ibn Tarif from abu Ja'far, *'Alayhi al-Salam*, who has said the following:

"There are three kinds of injustice: the injustice that Allah forgives, the injustice He does not forgive and the injustices that He does not leave without His judgment. The injustice that He does not forgive is to consider things to be His partners. The one that He forgives is the injustice of people against their own souls in the matters between them and Allah. The one that He does not leave without His judgment is the injustice that one person commits against the other in their dealings."

H 2637, Ch. 132, h 2

It is narrated from him (narrator of the Hadith above) from al-Hajjal from Ghalib ibn Muhammad from those whom has mentioned (in his book) from abu 'Abd Allah, 'Alayhi al-Salam, who has said the following:

"About the words of Allah, the Most Majestic, the Most Holy, '. . . your Lord keeps an eye on (al-Mirsad) (all evil-doing people),' (89:14) the Imam said, 'Al-Mirsad in this verse refers to a bridge on the way (to paradise) that is not passable for a servant who has committed injustice to others.'"

H 2638, Ch. 132, h 3

Ali ibn Ibrahim has narrated from his father from ibn abu 'Umayr from Wahab ibn 'Abd Rabbihi and 'Ubayd Allah al-Tawil from Shaykh from al-Nakha' who has said the following:

"Once I asked abu Ja'far, 'Alayhi al-Salam, 'I have been working as a governor from the time of al-Hajjaj to this time, can my repentance be accepted?' The Imam remained quiet. I repeated my question and then he said, 'No, until you pay back everything that you owe to the people.'"

H 2639, Ch. 132, h 4

Muhammad ibn Yahya has narrated from Ahmad ibn Muhammad ibn 'Isa from al-Husayn ibn Sa'id from Ibrahim ibn 'Abd al-Hamid from al-Walid ibn Sabiyh from abu 'Abd Allah, 'Alayhi al-Salam, who has said the following:

"No injustice is more severe than the one against which the oppressed cannot find any support except Allah, the Most Majestic, the Most Holy."

H 2640, Ch. 132, h 5

A number of our people have narrated from Ahmad ibn abu 'Abd Allah from Isma'il ibn Mehran from Drust ibn abu Mansur from 'Isa ibn Bashir from abu Hamza al-Thumali from abu Ja'far, 'Alayhi al-Salam, who has said the following:

"When Ali ibn al-Husayn, 'Alayhi al-Salam, was about to pass away he held me to his chest and then said, 'My son, I make my will to you as my father did to me when he was about to pass away and that which his father willed to him.' He said, 'My son, beware of the kind of injustice against which the oppressed cannot find any support except Allah.'"

H 2641, Ch. 132, h 6

It is narrated from him (narrator of the Hadith above) from his father from Harun ibn al-Jahm from Hafs ibn 'Umar from abu 'Abd Allah, 'Alayhi al-Salam, who has said the following:

"Amir al-Mu'minin, Ali ibn abu Talib, 'Alayhi al-Salam, has said, 'Whoever is afraid of retaliation should stay away from doing injustice to people.'"

H 2642, Ch. 132, h 7

Abu Ali al-Ash'ari has narrated from Muhammad ibn 'Abd al-Jabbar from Safwan from Ishaq ibn 'Ammar who has said the following:

"Abu 'Abd Allah, *'Alayhi al-Salam*, has said, 'Whoever rises in the morning without any intention of doing injustice to anyone, Allah forgives his sins that day unless it is a murder or consuming the property of the orphans unjustly.'"

H 2643, Ch. 132, h 8

Ali ibn Ibrahim has narrated from his father from al-Nawfali from al-Sakuni from abu 'Abd Allah, *'Alayhi al-Salam*, who has said the following:

"The messenger of Allah has said, 'Whoever rises in the morning without any intention of doing injustice to anyone, Allah forgives his sins.'"

H 2644, Ch. 132, h 9

Ali ibn Ibrahim has narrated from his father from ibn abu 'Umayr from Hisham ibn Salim from abu 'Abd Allah, *'Alayhi al-Salam*, who has said the following:

"Abu 'Abd Allah, *'Alayhi al-Salam*, has said, 'Whoever does injustice (financially), it (recompense) is taken from his life, property or his children.'"

H 2645, Ch. 132, h 10

Ibn abu 'Umayr has narrated from certain individuals of his people from abu 'Abd Allah, *'Alayhi al-Salam*, who has said the following:

"The Messenger of Allah has said, 'Beware of doing injustice; on the Day of Judgment there will be much darkness.'"

H 2646, Ch. 132, h 11

Muhammad ibn Yahya has narrated from Ahmad ibn Muhammad ibn 'Isa from Muhammad ibn 'Isa from Mansur from Hisham ibn Salim from abu 'Abd Allah, *'Alayhi al-Salam*, who has said the following:

"The Messenger of Allah has said, 'Be afraid of doing injustice; on the Day of Judgment there will be much darkness.'"

H 2647, Ch. 132, h 12

Ali ibn Ibrahim has narrated from his father from ibn abu 'Umayr from 'Umar ibn 'Udhaynah from Zurara from abu Ja'far, *'Alayhi al-Salam*, who has said the following:

"Abu Ja'far, *'Alayhi al-Salam*, has said, 'Whoever does injustice (financially) Allah takes it (recompense) from his life or property. However, the injustice that is between him and Allah, Allah forgives it if he repents.'"

H 2648, Ch. 132, h 13

A number of our people have narrated from Ahmad ibn Muhammad ibn Khalid from ibn abu Najaran from 'Ammar ibn Hakim from 'Abd al-'Ala' Mawla Ale Sam who has said the following:

"Once abu 'Abd Allah, *'Alayhi al-Salam*, on his own initiation said, 'Whoever does injustice, Allah makes someone to dominate him or his descendents of first or second generations.' I then asked, 'It is he who has done injustice, how will Allah make his descendents suffer?' The Imam said, 'Allah, the Most Majestic, the Most Holy, says, "Those who are concerned about the welfare of their own children after their death, should have fear of Allah (when dealing with the orphans) and guide them properly.'" (4:9)

H 2649, Ch. 132, h 14

It is narrated from him (narrator of the Hadith above) from ibn Mahbub from Ishaq ibn 'Ammar from abu 'Abd Allah, *'Alayhi al-Salam*, who has said the following:

"Allah, the Most Majestic, the Most Holy, sent revelations to one of His prophets who lived in the time of an oppressive and tyranical ruler. It said, 'Tell this tyrant, "I have not given you this opportunity to shade blood and seize properties. I have given you this opportunity only that you hold back the voices of the oppressed from coming to Me. I will not allow any oppression without justice being served, even though they (the oppressed) might be unbelievers.""

H 2650, Ch. 132, h 15
Al-Husayn ibn Muhammad has narrated from Mu'alla ibn Muhammad from al-Hassan ibn Ali al-Washsha' from Ali ibn abu Hamza from abu Basir who has said the following:
"I heard abu 'Abd Allah, *'Alayhi al-Salam*, saying, 'Whoever consumes the property of his brother (in belief) unjustly and does not return it to him, he will have to eat a chunk of fire on the Day of Judgment.'"

H 2651, Ch. 132, h 16
Muhammad ibn Yahya has narrated from Ahmad ibn Muhammad from Muhammad ibn Sinan from Talhah ibn Zayd from abu 'Abd Allah, *'Alayhi al-Salam*, who has said the following:
"Abu 'Abd Allah, *'Alayhi al-Salam*, has said, 'One acting unjustly, his supporter, and one who agrees with such act are three partners.'"

H 2652, Ch. 132, h 17
A number of our people have narrated from Ahmad ibn Muhammad from Ali ibn al-Hakam from Hisham ibn Salim who has said the following:
"I heard abu 'Abd Allah, *'Alayhi al-Salam*, saying, 'A servant (of Allah) may become oppressed and continues praying against the oppressor until he himself becomes an oppressor (for excessive praying against him).'"

H 2653, Ch. 132, h 18
A number of our people have narrated from Ahmad ibn Muhammad ibn Khalid from his father from abu Nahshal from 'Abd Allah ibn Sinan from abu 'Abd Allah, *'Alayhi al-Salam*, who has said the following:
"Whoever finds excuses for an unjust person Allah gives power to another person who will oppress him. If he prays, his prayers will not be heard and Allah will not give him any reward for his suffering injustice."

H 2654, Ch. 132, h 19
It is narrated from him (narrator of the Hadith above) from Muhammad ibn 'Isa from Ibrahim ibn 'Abd al-Hamid from Ali ibn abu Hamza from abu Basir from his father abu Ja'far, *'Alayhi al-Salam*, who has said the following:
"Allah retaliates an oppressor through another oppressor only. It is in the words of Allah, the Most Majestic, the Most Holy, 'Thus do We make the unjust friends of one another because of their evil deeds.'" (6:129)

H 2655, Ch. 132, h 20
Ali ibn Ibrahim has narrated from his father from his father al-Nawfali from his father al-Sakuni from his father abu 'Abd Allah, *'Alayhi al-Salam*, who has said the following:
"The Messenger of Allah has said, 'If one does injustice to a person and he passes away, he (the doer of injustice) must ask forgiveness from Allah for him (oppressed) and it will be the expiation for his injustice.'"

H 2656, Ch. 132, h 21

Ahmad ibn Muhammad al-Kufi has narrated from Ibrahim ibn al-Husayn from Muhammad ibn Khalaf from Musa ibn Ibrahim al-Marwazi from abu al-Hassan Musa, *'Alayhi al-Salam*, who has said the following:

"The Messenger of Allah has said, 'Whoever rises in the morning and has no intention to do injustice to anyone Allah forgives his sins."

H 2657, Ch. 132, h 22

Muhammad ibn Yahya has narrated from Ahmad ibn Muhammad ibn 'Isa from al-Hassan ibn Mahbub from Ali ibn abu Hamza from abu Basir who has said the following:

"Once two people came to see abu 'Abd Allah, *'Alayhi al-Salam*, about the differences that they had over a deal between them and when the Imam heard their case, he said, 'To achieve victory through injustice is not victory in anything good. What the oppressed takes away from the religion of the oppressor is much more than what the oppressor takes from the property of the oppressed.' The Imam then said, 'Whoever does evil to people should call it evil when it is done to him. Is it not the case that children of Adam reap what they sow? No one expects to harvest sweet from sour and vice versa. The two men then agreed to a settlement before standing up to leave.'"

H 2658, Ch. 132, h 23

A number of our people have narrated from Sahl ibn Ziyad from Ali ibn Asbat from those whom has mentioned (in his book) from abu 'Abd Allah, *'Alayhi al-Salam*, who has said the following:

"The Messenger of Allah has said, 'One who is afraid of retaliation does not do injustice to people.'"

Chapter 133 - Following Desires

H 2659, Ch. 133, h 1

Muhammad ibn Yahya has narrated from Ahmad ibn Muhammad ibn 'Isa from ibn Mahbub from abu Muhammad al-Wabishi who has said the following:

"I heard abu 'Abd Allah, *'Alayhi al-Salam*, saying, 'Be afraid of your desires just as you fear your enemies. Nothing is a more dangerous enemy to men than following their desires and what their tongues harvest.'"

H 2660, Ch. 133, h 2

A number of our people have narrated from Ahmad ibn Muhammad ibn Khalid from his father from 'Abd Allah ibn al-Qasim from abu Hamza from abu Ja'far, *'Alayhi al-Salam*, who has said the following:

"The Messenger of Allah has said, 'Allah, the Most Majestic, the Most Holy, has said, 'By My Majesty, Glory, Greatness, Supremacy, My Light, Highness, and Exalted position, whoever of the servants gives preference to his desires over My wish, I make his affairs disintegrate, confuse his world upon him, make his heart grow preoccupied with it (desire) and will not give him more than what I have determined for him. By My Majesty, Glory, Greatness, My Light, Highness, and Exalted position, any servant who gives preference to My wish over his own desire, I will assign My angels for his security, make the skies and earth to guarantee his sustenance and I will be behind each one of his business deals with the merchants and the world will come to him subdued and compelled.'"

H 2661, Ch. 133, h 3

Al-Husayn ibn Muhammad has narrated from Mu'alla ibn Muhammad from al-Washsha' from 'Asim ibn Humayd from abu Hamza from Yahya ibn 'Aqil who has said the following:

"Amir al-Mu'minin, Ali ibn abu Talib, *'Alayhi al-Salam*, has said, 'I am afraid for you from two things: following your desires and your never ending hopes of worldly matters; following of desires obstructs one from the truth and never ending hope in worldly matters makes one forget the hereafter.'"

H 2662, Ch. 133, h 4

A number of our people have narrated from Sahl ibn Ziyad from Muhammad ibn al-Hassan ibn Shammun from 'Abd Allah ibn 'Abd al-Rahman al-Asamm from 'Abd al-Rahman ibn al-Hajjaj who has said the following:

"Abu al-Hassan, *'Alayhi al-Salam*, once said to me, 'Beware of an easy climb up that has a very deep and steep climb down.'

"The narrator has said that Abu 'Abd Allah, *'Alayhi al-Salam*, would say, 'Do not leave the soul with its desires unguarded; its desires are to destroy it. Leaving the soul with its desires unguarded is hurting the soul, however, guarding the soul against its desires is medicine for its illness.'"

Chapter 134 - Evil Plans, Treachery and Deceit

H 2663, Ch. 134, h 1

Ali ibn Ibrahim has narrated from his father from ibn abu 'Umayr from Hisham ibn Salim in a marfu' manner who has said the following:

"Amir al-Mu'minin, Ali ibn abu Talib, *'Alayhi al-Salam*, has said, 'Had evil planning and deceit not been in the fire, I would have been extremely skillful in evil planning.'"

H 2664, Ch. 134, h 2

Ali has narrated from his father from al-Nawfali from al-Sakuni from abu 'Abd Allah, *'Alayhi al-Salam*, who has said the following:

"The Messenger of Allah has said, 'On the Day of Judgment all the treacherous people will come with a leader, his mouth badly deformed, and end up in the fire. All those breaking out allegiance of the Imam also will come with their hand cut off and end up in the fire.'"

H 2665, Ch. 134, h 3

It is narrated from him (narrator of the Hadith above) from his father from al-Nawfali from al-Sakuni from abu 'Abd Allah, *'Alayhi al-Salam*, who has said the following:

"The Messenger of Allah has said, 'One who makes evil plans against a Muslim is not from us.'"

H 2666, Ch. 134, h 4

Muhammad ibn Yahya has narrated from Ahmad ibn Muhammad ibn 'Isa from Muhammad ibn Yahya from Talhah ibn Zayd who has said the following:

"Once I asked abu 'Abd Allah, *'Alayhi al-Salam*, 'There are two towns of the people in the state of war against the Muslims. Each town has a king. They had a war and then made peace. Thereafter one king acted treacherously against the other king, came to the Muslims and made peace to help him against the other town.' Abu 'Abd Allah, *'Alayhi al-Salam*, said, 'It is not worthy of the Muslims to act treacherously or command people to act treacherously or fight along side the treacherous people. However, they fight the pagans wherever they find them. The covenant of the unbelievers is not effective.'"

H 2667, Ch. 134, h 5
A number of our people have narrated from Ahmad ibn Muhammad ibn Khalid from Muhammad ibn al-Hassan ibn Shammun from 'Abd Allah ibn 'Amr ibn al-Ash'ath from 'Abd Allah ibn Hammad al-Ansari from Yahya ibn 'Abd Allah ibn al-Hassan from abu 'Abd Allah, *'Alayhi al-Salam*, who has said the following:

"The Messenger of Allah has said, 'On the Day of Judgment all the treacherous people will come with an Imam whose mouth will be badly deformed and end up in the fire.'"

H 2668, Ch. 134, h 6
Ali ibn Ibrahim has narrated from his father from Ali ibn Asbat from his uncle Ya'qub ibn Salim from abu al-Hassan al-'Abdi from Sa'd ibn Tarif from al-Asbagh ibn Nubatah who has said the following:

"Amir al-Mu'minin, Ali ibn abu Talib, *'Alayhi al-Salam*, one day in his speech from the pulpit in al-Kufah said, 'O people, were it not for my intense dislike of treachery I could have been the most clever among people. You must know that in every act of treachery there is a sin of disbelief. You must also know that treachery, sins and dishonesty are all in the fire (of hell).'"

Chapter 135 - Lies and Forgery

H 2669, Ch. 135, h 1
Muhammad ibn Yahya has narrated from Ahmad ibn Muhammad ibn 'Isa from Ali ibn al-Hakam from Ishaq ibn 'Ammar from abu al-Nu'man who has said the following:

"Once abu Ja'far, *'Alayhi al-Salam*, said to me, 'O abu al-Nu'man, do not forge lies against us; it removes (your) true belief. Do not seek to be the head to become a sin and do not use people as means of your earning through us; it will make you poor. You will be held accountable and will be stopped for interrogations. If you speak the truth we will certify you and, if you lie, we will reject you.'"

H 2670, Ch. 135, h 2
A number of our people have narrated from Ahmad ibn Muhammad ibn Khalid from Isma'il ibn Mehran from Sayf ibn 'Amirah from those whom has mentioned (in his book) from abu Ja'far, *'Alayhi al-Salam*, who has said the following:

"Ali ibn al-Husayn, *'Alayhi al-Salam*, would say to his children, 'Be on your guard against lies, the small lies and the bigger lies in all the serious and trivial matters. If a man lies in a small matter, he grows bold to lie in a bigger one. Have you not noted that the Messenger of Allah has said, 'As long as a servant (of Allah) speaks the truth Allah writes him down as the truthful one and, if one continues speaking lies Allah writes him down as a liar? '"

H 2671, Ch. 135, h 3
It is narrated from him (narrator of the Hadith above) from 'Uthman ibn 'Isa from ibn Muskan from Muhammad ibn Muslim from abu Ja'far, *'Alayhi al-Salam*, who has said the following:

"Allah, the Most Majestic, the Most Holy, has created certain locks for evil. He has made wine the key to those locks. Lying is more evil than wine."

H 2672, Ch. 135, h 4

It is narrated from him (narrator of the Hadith above) from his father from those whom has mentioned (in his book) from Muhammad ibn 'Abd al-Rahman from abu Layla' from his father from abu Ja'far, *'Alayhi al-Salam*, who has said the following:

"Abu Ja'far, *'Alayhi al-Salam*, has said, 'Lying is the destruction of belief.'"

H 2673, Ch. 135, h 5

Al-Husayn ibn Muhammad has narrated from Mu'alla ibn Muhammad and Ali ibn Muhammad from Salih ibn abu Hammad all from al-Washsha' from Ahmad ibn 'A'id from abu Khadijah from abu 'Abd Allah, *'Alayhi al-Salam*, who has said the following:

"Abu 'Abd Allah, *'Alayhi al-Salam*, has said, 'Forgery against Allah and the Messenger of Allah is of the major sins.'"

H 2674, Ch. 135, h 6

Muhammad ibn Yahya has narrated from Ahmad ibn Muhammad ibn 'Isa from Ali ibn al-Hakam from Aban al-Ahmar from Fudayl ibn Yasar from abu Ja'far, *'Alayhi al-Salam*, who has said the following:

"Abu Ja'far, *'Alayhi al-Salam*, has said, 'The first one to rebuff the liar is Allah, the Most Majestic, the Most Holy, then the two angels who are with him, then he is the one who knows he is a liar.'"

H 2675, Ch. 135, h 7

Ali ibn al-Hakam has narrated (from Aban) from 'Umar ibn Yazid who has said the following:

"I heard abu 'Abd Allah, *'Alayhi al-Salam*, saying, 'A liar is destroyed by means of clear evidence (his false claims) and his followers are destroyed on ambiguous evidence (accepting a leader whose qualification is doubtful).'"

H 2676, Ch. 135, h 8

Muhammad ibn Yahya has narrated from Ahmad ibn Muhammad ibn 'Isa from ibn abu Najran from Mu'awiyah ibn Wahab who has said the following:

"I heard abu 'Abd Allah, *'Alayhi al-Salam*, saying, 'Of the signs of lies in a liar is his telling you news of heaven, earth, East and West, but when you ask him about what Allah has made unlawful and what He has made lawful, you will find nothing with him (devoid of the knowledge of Shari'a).'"

H 2677, Ch. 135, h 9

Ali ibn Ibrahim has narrated from his father from ibn abu 'Umayr from Mansur ibn Yunus from abu Basir who has said the following:

"I heard abu 'Abd Allah, *'Alayhi al-Salam*, saying, 'It is certain that a lie destroys fasting (invalidates it).' I then said, 'Who is he among us who is not such a person?' The Imam said, 'It is not as you think it is. It is forging lies against Allah, the Messenger of Allah and 'A'immah, *'Alayhim al-Salam*.'"

H 2678, Ch. 135, h 10

Muhammad ibn Yahya has narrated from Ahmad ibn Muhammad ibn 'Isa from certain individuals of his people in a marfu' manner from abu 'Abd Allah, *'Alayhi al-Salam*, who has said the following:

"It was mentioned before abu 'Abd Allah, *'Alayhi al-Salam*, that the weaver (knitting) is condemned. The Imam said, 'It is the one who weaves and fabricates lies against Allah and the Messenger of Allah.'"

H 2679, Ch. 135, h 11

A number of our people have narrated from Ahmad ibn abu 'Abd Allah from his father from al-Qasim ibn 'Urwah from 'Abd al-Hamid al-Ta'I from al-Asbagh ibn Nubatah who has said the following:

"Amir al-Mu'minin, Ali ibn abu Talib, *'Alayhi al-Salam*, has said, 'A servant (of Allah) does not sense the taste of belief until he stays away from lies, serious ones as well as trivial ones.'"

H 2680, Ch. 135, h 12

Ali ibn Ibrahim has narrated from his father from ibn abu 'Umayr from 'Abd al-Rahman ibn al-Hajjaj who has said the following:

"Once I asked abu 'Abd Allah, *'Alayhi al-Salam*, 'Is a liar one who lies about something?' The Imam said, 'No, there is no one who does not do so. It is those in whom lying becomes a thing of second nature.'"

H 2681, Ch. 135, h 13

A number of our people have narrated from Ahmad ibn abu 'Abd Allah from al-Hassan ibn Tarif from his father from those whom has mentioned (in his book) from abu 'Abd Allah, *'Alayhi al-Salam*, who has said the following:

"Abu 'Abd Allah, *'Alayhi al-Salam*, has said, 'Jesus, son of Mary has said, "One who lies, often his grace goes away."'"

H 2682, Ch. 135, h 14

It is narrated from him (narrator of the Hadith above) from 'Amr ibn 'Uthman from Muhammad ibn Salim in a marfu' manner from Amir al-Mu'minin, Ali ibn abu Talib, *'Alayhi al-Salam*, who has said the following:

"It is very proper for a Muslim man to avoid friendship and brotherhood with a liar; he lies and, even if he comes with truth, he is not believed and trusted."

H 2683, Ch. 135, h 15

It is narrated from him (narrator of the Hadith above) from ibn Faddal from Ibrahim ibn Muhammad al-Ash'ari from 'Ubayd ibn Zurara who has said the following:

"I heard abu 'Abd Allah, *'Alayhi al-Salam*, saying, 'The assistance that Allah finds (for His cause) against the liars is in (their) forgetfulness.'"

H 2684, Ch. 135, h 16

Muhammad ibn Yahya has narrated from Ahmad ibn Muhammad ibn 'Isa from abu Yahya al-Wasiti from certain individuals of our people from abu 'Abd Allah, *'Alayhi al-Salam*, who has said the following:

"Statements are of three kinds: true, false and to establish truce among people.' The narrator has said that it was asked of him, 'May Allah keep my soul in service for your cause, what is establishing truce among people?' The Imam said, 'It is when you hear something about a man that, if he himself may hear it, his soul turns filthy (with anger) but when you meet him you say, 'I heard so and so saying very good things about you, which is opposite of what you have actually heard about him.'"

H 2685, Ch. 135, h 17

Ali ibn Ibrahim has narrated from his father from Ahmad ibn Muhammad ibn abu Nasr from Hammad ibn 'Uthman from al-Hassan al-Sayqal who has said the following:

"Once I said to abu 'Abd Allah, *'Alayhi al-Salam,* 'We narrate it from abu Ja'far, *'Alayhi al-Salam,* about the words of Yusuf, "O people of the camels, you are thieves." (12:70) The Imam said, 'By Allah, they did not steal and he did not lie.'

"The narrator has said that he then said, Ibrahim said, 'In fact, it is the large one among them who has done it. Ask them if they can speak.' (22:63) The Imam said, 'By Allah, they did not do it and he did not lie.' The narrator has said that abu 'Abd Allah, *'Alayhi al-Salam,* then asked, 'What explanation do you have, O al-Sayqal?' I (the narrator) then said, 'We have no explanation, but accept it as is.' The narrator has said that the Imam then said, 'Allah loves two things and hates two things: He loves shows of arrogance between two fighting armies and loves lies to establish peace. He hates shows of arrogance on the roads and lies in the matters other than establishing reform. Ibrahim (Abraham) said, 'It is the large one who has done it,' with the intention to bring about social reform to prove that the idols cannot do such things. Yusuf (Joseph) said what he said and it was for social well-being.'"

H 2686, Ch. 135, h 18
It is narrated from him (narrator of the Hadith above) from his father from Safwan from abu Mukhallad al-Sarraj from 'Isa ibn Hassan who has said the following:
"I heard abu 'Abd Allah, *'Alayhi al-Salam,* saying, 'A person lying will be held accountable for all kinds of lies except three kinds: a man plotting in his fight will not be held accountable, a man trying to establish peace between antagonistic parties who may say something other than a party may have said with the intention to establish peace between them or a man who may promise his family something but he does not want to complete it.'"

H 2687, Ch. 135, h 19
A number of our people have narrated from Ahmad ibn Muhammad ibn Khalid from his father from 'Abd Allah ibn Mughirah from Mu'awiyah ibn 'Ammar from abu 'Abd Allah, *'Alayhi al-Salam,* who has said the following:
"Abu 'Abd Allah, *'Alayhi al-Salam,* has said, 'A reformer (a peace maker) is not a liar.'"

H 2688, Ch. 135, h 20
Muhammad ibn Yahya has narrated from Ahmad ibn Muhammad from Ali ibn al-Hakam from 'Abd Allah ibn Yahya al-Kahili from Muhammad ibn Malik from 'Abd al-'Ala' Mawla ale Sam who has said the following:
"Abu 'Abd Allah, *'Alayhi al-Salam,* stated to me a Hadith and I said, 'May Allah keep my soul in service for your cause, did you not have a (Za'm) about me a while ago of such and such nature?' The Imam said, 'No.' The narrator has said that it became very hard for me to understand and I said, 'Yes, by Allah you did have such (Za'm) about me.' The Imam said, 'No, by Allah, I did not have such (Za'm) about you.' The narrator has said that it became even more difficult for me to understand and I said, 'Yes, by Allah, you did say it.' The Imam said, 'Yes, I did say but do you not know that all (Za'm) in the Quran signify lies?'

(The word Za'm in Arabic may mean to believe, to think, to guess, to surmise and so forth. The Imam, *'Alayhi al-Salam,* explained to the narrator that in the Quran

289

this word is used to mean something not true and that he (the Imam) had not used the word "Za'm" in the sense the Holy Quran has used)

H 2689, Ch. 135, h 21

A number of our people have narrated from Sahl ibn Ziyad from Ali ibn Asbat from abu Ishaq al-Khurasani who has said the following:

"Amir al-Mu'minin, Ali ibn abu Talib, *'Alayhi al-Salam*, would say, 'Beware of lying; every hopeful strives to make his wish come true and every fearful person runs away (and I do not find this quality in you)."

H 2690, Ch. 135, h 22

Abu Ali al-Ash'ari has narrated from Muhammad ibn 'Abd al-Jabbar from Hajjal from Tha'labah from Mu'ammar ibn 'Amr from 'Ata' from abu 'Abd Allah, *'Alayhi al-Salam*, who has said the following:

"The Messenger of Allah has said, 'A peace maker is not accused of lying' and then he read the following verse of the Holy Quran: '. . . O people of camel, you are thieves.' (12:70) Then he said, 'By Allah, they did not steal and he (Joseph) did not lie.' Then he read the following verse: '. . . in fact, it is the large one among them who has done it. Ask them if they can speak.' (22: 63) Then he said, 'By Allah, they (people) did not do it (asked the idols) and he did not lie.'"

Chapter 136 - Duplicity

H 2691, Ch. 136, h 1

Muhammad ibn Yahya has narrated from Ahmad ibn Muhammad ibn 'Isa from Muhammad ibn Sinan from 'Awn al-Qalanisi from ibn abu Ya'fur from abu 'Abd Allah, *'Alayhi al-Salam*, who has said the following:

"Whoever meets the Muslims with two faces and tongues, he on the Day of Judgment will be raised with two tongues of fire."

H 2692, Ch. 136, h 2

A number of our people have narrated from Ahmad ibn Muhammad ibn Khalid from 'Uthman ibn 'Isa from abu Shaybah from al-Zuhri from abu 'Ja'far, *'Alayhi al-Salam*, who has said the following:

"The worst servant (of Allah) is a servant who has two faces and tongues. He praises his brother (in belief) on his face and backbites him in his absence. If his brother (in belief) gains something, he envies him, and if he faces difficult conditions, he betrays him."

H 2693, Ch. 136, h 3

Ali ibn Ibrahim has narrated from his father from Ali ibn Asbat from 'Abd al-Rahman ibn Hammad in a marfu' manner from the Imam who has said the following:

"Allah, the Most Blessed, the Most High, said to Jesus, son of Mary (peace be upon them), 'O Jesus, your tongue must be one tongue in private and in public so also must be your heart. I warn you against your own soul and Myself am a sufficient expert over your (activities). Two tongues are not proper for one mouth just as two swords are not proper in one sheath or two hearts in one chest, and so also are minds.'"

Chapter 137 - Abandonment and Desertion

H 2694, Ch. 137, h 1

Al-Husayn ibn Muhammad has narrated from Ja'far ibn Muhammad from al-Qasim ibn al-Rabi' and certain individuals of our people from Ahmad ibn Muhammad ibn Khalid in a marfu' manner it is in the advice to al-Mufaddal who has said the following:

"I heard abu 'Abd Allah, *'Alayhi al-Salam*, saying, 'Of the two people who depart each other to abandon and walk out on each other, one is subject to disowning and condemnation or perhaps both of them will face such conditions.' Mu'attib then said, 'May Allah keep my soul in service for your cause, one is unjust, what about the oppressed?' The Imam said, 'It is because he did not ask his brother (in belief) to maintain good brotherly relations and did not ignore his words. I heard my father saying, "Whenever two people dispute and one of them over power the other, the oppressed should turn to his companion and say to him, 'O brother (in belief), I am the unjust,'" so that forsaking and abandonment would not take place among them. Allah, the Most Blessed, the Most High, is the Judge with justice, He judges with justice for the oppressed against the oppressor.'"

H 2695, Ch. 137, h 2

Ali ibn Ibrahim has narrated from his father and Muhammad ibn Isma'il from Fadl ibn Shadhan from ibn abu 'Umayr from Hisham ibn al-Hakam from abu 'Abd Allah, *'Alayhi al-Salam*, who has said the following:

"The Messenger of Allah has said, '(Due to) walking out on another person (separation) should not continue more than three days.'"

H 2696, Ch. 137, h 3

Hamid ibn Ziyad has narrated from al-Hassan ibn Muhammad ibn Sama'a from Wuhayb ibn Hafs from abu Basir who has said the following:

"Once I asked abu 'Abd Allah, *'Alayhi al-Salam*, about a man who has forsaken his relatives who do not recognize the truth.' The Imam said, 'It is not proper for him to abandon them.'"

H 2697, Ch. 137, h 4

A number of our people have narrated from Ahmad ibn Muhammad from Ali ibn Hadid from his uncle, Murazim ibn Hakim who has said the following:

"In the presence of abu 'Abd Allah, *'Alayhi al-Salam*, there was a man from our people, also called Shalqan. The Imam had appointed him over his household expenses (included among his dependents) but he had bad manners so he was removed from the job (by Murazim). One day the Imam asked me, 'O Murazim, have you talked to 'Isa (Shalqan)?' I said, 'Yes, I have talked to him.' The Imam said, 'You have done the right thing; there is nothing good in being neglectful.'"

H 2698, Ch. 137, h 5

Muhammad ibn Yahya has narrated from Ahmad ibn Muhammad from Muhammad ibn Sinan from abu Sa'id al-Qammat from Dawud ibn Kathir who has said the following:

"I heard abu 'Abd Allah, *'Alayhi al-Salam*, saying, 'My father has said, "The Messenger of Allah has said, 'Whoever of two Muslims forsake the other and do not make peace within three days they both will be considered out of Islam and there will be no Divine Guardianship relations among them. Whoever of the two speaks first to the other, he, on the Day of Judgment, will be the first one to enter paradise."'

H 2699, Ch. 137, h 6
Ali ibn Ibrahim has narrated from his father from ibn abu 'Umayr from ibn 'Udhaynah from Zurara from abu Ja'far, *'Alayhi al-Salam*, who has said the following:
"Satan keeps throwing animosity among the believers until one of them forsakes his religion. When this happens, Satan stretches down on his back and says, 'This is my victory.' May Allah grant blessings to those who make peace between two of our friends. O believing people, unite and be compassionate to each other.'"

H 2700, Ch. 137, h 7
Al-Husayn ibn Muhammad has narrated from Ali ibn Muhammad ibn Sa'id from Muhammad ibn Muslim from Muhammad ibn Mahfuz from Ali ibn al-Nu'man from ibn Muskan from abu Basir from abu 'Abd Allah, *'Alayhi al-Salam*, who has said the following:
"As long as two Muslims continue abandoning each other, Satan enjoys it. When they meet, his (Satan's) knees began to shake and his bone joints began to come apart and he cries, 'Woe upon me; I have to face this destruction.'"

Chapter 138 - Failing to Maintain Good Relations with Relatives

H 2701, Ch. 138, h 1
Ali ibn Ibrahim has narrated from his father from ibn abu 'Umayr from 'Umar ibn 'Udhaynah from Misma' ibn 'Abd al-Malik from abu 'Abd Allah, *'Alayhi al-Salam*, who has said the following:
"The Messenger of Allah has said in a Hadith, 'It must be noted that in hatred there is shaving. I do not mean thereby shaving and tearing out of hairs, but it is shaving (destruction) of religion.'"

H 2702, Ch. 138, h 2
A number of our people have narrated from Ahmad ibn Muhammad ibn Khalid from Muhammad ibn Ali from Muhammad ibn al-Fudayl from Hudhayfah ibn Mansur who has said the following:
"Abu 'Abd Allah, *'Alayhi al-Salam*, has said, 'Be afraid of al-Haliqah; it kills men.' I then asked, 'What is al-Haliqah?' The Imam said, 'It is failing to maintain good relations with relatives.'"

H 2703, Ch. 138, h 3
Muhammad ibn Yahya has narrated from Ahmad ibn Muhammad ibn 'Isa from 'Uthman ibn 'Isa from certain individuals of our people who has said the following:
"Once I ('Isa) said to abu 'Abd Allah, *'Alayhi al-Salam*, 'My brothers and cousins have made life very difficult for me. They have forced me out of the house to another house. If I talk to them I am capable to take away what is in their hands.' The Imam said, 'Be patient. Allah will make a way out for you.' I (the narrator) changed my mind. In the year one hundred thirty-one a plague came and they all died. No one of them was left alive. I (the narrator) then went to see the Imam, *'Alayhi al-Salam*, and he asked me, 'How is the condition of your family?' I said, 'By Allah, all of them have died and not one is left alive.' The Imam said, 'It was because of their failing to maintain good relations with you, suspending you from their favors, withholding kindness from relatives and boycotting them. Do you

love and wish that they remained alive even though they caused you difficulties?' I said, 'Yes, by Allah (I do wish so).'"

H 2704, Ch. 138, h 4

It is narrated from him (narrator of the Hadith above) from Ahmad from al-Hassan ibn Mahbub from Malik ibn 'Atiyyah from abu 'Ubaydah from abu Ja'far, *'Alayhi al-Salam*, who has said the following:

"It is written in the book of Ali, *'Alayhi al-Salam*, 'There are three characteristics, that if found in anyone, he will never die before suffering their consequences: treachery, failing to maintain good relations with relatives and taking a false oath to oppose Allah thereby. Of the acts of obedience with the quickest best result is to maintain good relations with relatives. A people may happen to be unjust in their affairs but maintain good relations with relatives, their wealth increases and they grow rich. False oath and failing to maintain good relations with relatives can leave a town in ruins, empty of the inhabitants and transform the family. Transformation of family is discontinuation of the lineage and reproduction.'"

H 2705, Ch. 138, h 5

Ali ibn Ibrahim has narrated from Salih ibn al-Sindy from Ja'far ibn Bashir from 'Anbasah al-'Abid who has said the following:

"Once a man came to abu 'Abd Allah, *'Alayhi al-Salam*, and complained before him about his relatives. Abu 'Abd Allah, *'Alayhi al-Salam*, said, 'Keep your anger down and do it (maintain good relations).' The man said, 'They do and do it (act against me).' The Imam asked, 'Do you also want to act like them, if so Allah will not look to you (with kindness)?'"

H 2706, Ch. 138, h 6

Ali ibn Ibrahim has narrated from his father from al-Nawfali from al-Sakuni from abu 'Abd Allah, *'Alayhi al-Salam*, who has said the following:

"The Messenger of Allah has said, 'Do not fail to maintain good relations with relatives, even if they fail to maintain good relations with you.'"

H 2707, Ch. 138, h 7

A number of our people have narrated from Ahmad ibn abu 'Abd Allah from his father in a marfu' manner from abu Hamza al-Thumali who has said the following:

"Once Amir al-Mu'minin, Ali ibn abu Talib, *'Alayhi al-Salam*, said in one of his sermons, 'I seek refuge in Allah from sins that accelerate destruction.' The narrator has said that at this point 'Abd Allah ibn al-Kawwa' al-Yashkuri stood up and asked, 'O Amir al-Mu'minin, do sins hasten one's destruction?' The Imam said, 'Yes, it does. Woe upon you, it is failing to maintain good relations with relatives. A family lives together and cooperates with each other, even though they may happen to be a sinful people, Allah grants them sustenance. A family who fails to maintain good relations with relatives face Allah's depriving them (from benefits), even though they are pious people.'"

H 2708, Ch. 138, h 8

It is narrated from him (narrator of the Hadith above) from ibn Mahbub from Malik ibn 'Atiyyah from abu Hamza from abu Ja'far, *'Alayhi al-Salam*, who has said the following:

"Amir al-Mu'minin, Ali ibn abu Talib, *'Alayhi al-Salam*, has said, 'When they fail to maintain good relations with relatives properties are left under the control of the evil ones.'"

Chapter 139 - Causing Suffering and Disappointment to Parents (al-'Uquq)

H 2709, Ch. 139, h 1

Muhammad ibn Yahya has narrated from Ahmad ibn Muhammad ibn 'Isa from Muhammad ibn Sinan from Hadid ibn Hakim from abu 'Abd Allah, *'Alayhi al-Salam*, who has said the following:

"Minimum of al-'Uquq, (to cause disappointment) is to say 'Uff (expression of disapproval). Had Allah, the Majestic, the Glorious, known anything expressing a lesser degree of disappointment than this 'Uff, He would have prohibited it."

H 2710, Ch. 139, h 2

Ali ibn Ibrahim has narrated from his father from 'Abd Allah ibn al-Mughirah from abu al-Hassan, *'Alayhi al-Salam*, who has said the following:

"The Messenger of Allah has said, 'Be good (to parents), you will have paradise, if you cause suffering (to parents) and are hardheaded, then be prepared to suffer in the fire.'"

H 2711, Ch. 139, h 3

Abu Ali al-Ash'ari has narrated from al-Hassan ibn Ali al-Kufi from 'Ubays ibn Hisham from Salih al-Hadhdha' from Ya'qub ibn Shu'ayb from abu 'Abd Allah, *'Alayhi al-Salam*, who has said the following:

"When it will be the Day of Judgment a curtain of the curtains of paradise will rise and everything with a spirit will sense its fragrance from a distance of a five hundred years journey except one group of people.' I (the narrator) has said that then asked, 'Who is that group?' The Imam said, 'It is those who cause suffering and disappointments to their parents.'"

H 2712, Ch. 139, h 4

Ali ibn Ibrahim has narrated from his father from al-Nawfali from al-Sakuni from abu 'Abd Allah, *'Alayhi al-Salam*, who has said the following:

"The Messenger of Allah has said, 'Over and above every virtuous deed there is a virtuous deed, up to a man's accepting martyrdom and being killed for the cause of Allah. When he is killed for the cause of Allah, then there is no virtuous deed over and above it. Also, over and above every sin of causing suffering and disappointment to parents there is another sin until a man murders one of his parents, and when he does this there is nothing above this sin in the sins of causing suffering to parents.'"

H 2713, Ch. 139, h 5

A number of our people have narrated from Ahmad ibn Muhammad ibn Khalid from Isma'il ibn Mehran from Sayf ibn 'Amirah from abu 'Abd Allah, *'Alayhi al-Salam*, who has said the following:

"If one looks with anger to his parents when they are unjust to him, Allah will not accept any of his prayers."

H 2714, Ch. 139, h 6

It is narrated from him (narrator of the Hadith above) from Muhammad ibn Ali from Muhammad ibn Furat from abu Ja'far, *'Alayhi al-Salam*, who has said the following:

"The Messenger of Allah has said in one of his speeches, 'Beware of causing suffering and disappointment to parents. The fragrance of paradise can be sensed from a distance of a one thousand year journey, but those causing suffering and disappointments to parents, those failing to maintain good relations with relatives, an old fornicating man and one who drags his garments out of arrogance and boastfulness will not sense such fragrance. Greatness belongs only to Allah, Lord of the worlds.'"

H 2715, Ch. 139, h 7

It is narrated from him (narrator of the Hadith above) from Yahya ibn Ibrahim ibn abu al-Balad al-Sullami from his father from his grand father from abu 'Abd Allah, *'Alayhi al-Salam*, who has said the following:

"Had Allah known anything expressing a lesser degree of disappointment than 'Uff, He would have prohibited to use it against parents. Using the expression 'Uff is the minimum form of causing suffering and disappointment to parents. Of the cases of causing suffering and disappointment to parents is one's look and staring at them."

H 2716, Ch. 139, h 8

Ali has narrated from his father from Harun ibn al-Jahm from 'Abd Allah ibn Sulayman from abu Ja'far, *'Alayhi al-Salam*, who has said the following:

"Once, my father saw a man walking with his son who was leaning against his father's arm. My father in dislike never spoke to him until he left this world."

H 2717, Ch. 139, h 9

Abu Ali al-Ash'ari has narrated from Ahmad ibn Muhammad from Muhsin ibn Ahmad from Aban ibn 'Uthman from Hadid ibn Hakim from abu 'Abd Allah, *'Alayhi al-Salam*, who has said the following:

"Abu 'Abd Allah, *'Alayhi al-Salam*, has said, 'The minimum form of causing suffering and disappointment to parents is the expression, 'Uff. Had Allah known anything less disappointing than 'Uff, He would have prohibited it.'"

Chapter 140 - Disowning Lineage

H 2718, Ch. 140, h 1

Ali ibn Ibrahim has narrated from his father from ibn abu 'Umayr from abu Basir from abu 'Abd Allah, *'Alayhi al-Salam*, who has said the following:

"Abu 'Abd Allah, *'Alayhi al-Salam*, has said, 'It is to disbelieve Allah to disown one's lineage even though it (the lineage) is very lowly.'"

H 2719, Ch. 140, h 2

A number of our people have narrated from Ahmad ibn Muhammad from ibn Faddal from abu al-Maghra' from abu Basir from abu 'Abd Allah, *'Alayhi al-Salam*, who has said the following:

"Abu 'Abd Allah, *'Alayhi al-Salam*, has said, 'It is to disbelieve Allah to disown one's lineage even though it is very lowly.'"

H 2720, Ch. 140, h 3

Ali ibn Muhammad has narrated from Salih ibn abu Hammad from ibn abu 'Umayr from and ibn Faddal from various people from abu Ja'far and abu 'Abd Allah, *'Alayhi al-Salam*, who have said the following:

"Abu Ja'far, *'Alayhi al-Salam*, has said, 'It is to disbelieve Allah, the Most Great, to disown one's lineage even though it is very lowly.'"

Chapter 141 - One Who Causes Suffering to Muslims and Belittles Them

H 2721, Ch. 141, h 1

Muhammad ibn Yahya has narrated from Ahmad ibn Muhammad from ibn Mahbub from Hisham ibn Salim who has said the following:

"I heard abu 'Abd Allah, *'Alayhi al-Salam*, saying, 'Allah, the Most Majestic, the Most Holy, has said, "He who causes suffering to the believers has declared war against Me. He who respects and honors My believing servant should have no fear of My anger. Had there been no other creature on earth between the West and the East, except a believer with a just Imam, I would have been free of want (reason for My granting rewards) with their worship, from all that I have created on earth. The seven heavens and earths would remain up in their service and, out of their belief, I provide them company with which they did not need company from anyone besides themselves.'"

H 2722, Ch. 141, h 2

It is narrated from him (narrator of the Hadith above) from Ahmad ibn Muhammad from ibn Sinan from Mundhir ibn Yazid from al-Mufaddal ibn 'Umar who has said the following:

"I heard abu 'Abd Allah, *'Alayhi al-Salam*, saying, 'When it will be the Day of Judgment, an announcer will announce, "Where are those causing obstacles and hindrance for My friends." A people will rise who will have no flesh on their faces. It will be said, 'These are the one's who made the believers suffer; treated them with animosity, opposition, and violence in the matters of their religion. Then they will be ordered into the hell.'"

H 2723, Ch. 141, h 3

Abu Ali al-Ash'ari has narrated from Muhammad ibn 'Abd al-Jabbar from ibn Faddal from Tha'labah ibn Maymun from Hammad ibn Bashir from abu 'Abd Allah, *'Alayhi al-Salam*, who has said the following:

"The Messenger of Allah has said, 'Allah, the Most Blessed, the Most High, has said, "Whoever insults any of My friends has waged a war against Me.'"

H 2724, Ch. 141, h 4

Ali ibn Ibrahim has narrated from his father from ibn abu 'Umayr from al-Hus,ayn ibn 'Uthman from Muhammad ibn abu Hamza from those whom has mentioned (in his book) from abu 'Abd Allah, *'Alayhi al-Salam*, who has said the following:

"Abu 'Abd Allah, *'Alayhi al-Salam*, has said, 'Whoever looks down upon a believer, destitute or not, Allah, the Most Majestic, the Most Holy, continues looking down upon him and hate him until he changes his attitude as such toward a believer.'"

H 2725, Ch. 141, h 5

Muhammad ibn Yahya has narrated from Ahmad ibn Muhammad from Ali ibn al-Nu'man from ibn Muskan from Mu'alla ibn Khunayth who has said the following:

"I heard abu 'Abd Allah, *'Alayhi al-Salam*, saying, 'Allah, the Most Blessed, the Most High, says, 'Whoever insults any of My friends has waged a war against Me. I am the quickest to support My friends.'"

H 2726, Ch. 141, h 6

A number of our people have narrated from Sahl ibn Ziyad from ibn Mahbub from Hisham ibn Salim from Mu'alla ibn Khunays from abu 'Abd Allah, *'Alayhi al-Salam*, who has said the following:

"The Messenger of Allah has said, 'Allah, the Most Majestic, the Most Holy, has said, 'To cause suffering to My believing servant is certainly a declaration of animosity against Me.'"

H 2727, Ch. 141, h 7

Muhammad ibn Yahya has narrated from Ahmad ibn Muhammad ibn 'Isa from and abu Ali al-Ash'ari from Muhammad ibn 'Abd al-Jabbar all from ibn Faddal from Ali ibn 'Uqbah from Hammad ibn Bashir who has said the following:

"I heard abu 'Abd Allah, *'Alayhi al-Salam*, saying, 'The Messenger of Allah has said, "Allah, the Most Majestic, the Most Holy, has said, 'Whoever insults any of My friends has waged a war against Me. Whoever of the servant seeks closeness to Me should know that there is nothing in that matter more beloved to Me than his fulfilling his obligations and he should seek nearness to Me by performing optional acts so I may love him; when I love him I will be his ears with which he will hear, his eyes with which he will see, his tongue with which he will speak and his hands with which he will perform his activities. Whenever he prays, I answer. Whenever he will ask for help, I will help him. I have not so much hesitated in all that I do as my hesitation at the time of the death of a believer who dislikes death and I dislike disappointing him.'"

H 2728, Ch. 141, h 8

A number of our people have narrated from Ahmad ibn Muhammad ibn Khalid from Isma'il ibn Mehran from abu Sa'id al-Qammat from Aban ibn Taghlib from abu Ja'far, *'Alayhi al-Salam*, who has said the following:

"When the Holy Prophet was taken to visit the heavens, he asked, 'O Lord, how is the condition of the believers before you?' He (Allah) said, 'O Muhammad, whoever insults any of My friends has declared war against Me. I am the quickest to help My friends. I have not hesitated in any of My acts as much as I do at the time of the death of a believer who dislikes death and I dislike to disappoint him. Of My believing servants there are those who do not perform well without wealth and if I change his condition he is destroyed. Also among My believing servants are those who do not perform well unless they are poor and, if I change their condition to something else, they are destroyed. For seeking nearness to Me there is no better means for My servant than to fulfill what I have made obligatory for them and that he should seek nearness to Me through performing optional acts of worship so I will love him. When I will love him I will be his ears with which he will hear, his eyes with which he will see, his tongue with which he will speak and his hands with which he will perform his activities. Whenever he prays I will answer him and, whenever he asks a favor, I will grant him.'"

297

H 2729, Ch. 141, h 9

Ali ibn Ibrahim has narrated from his father from ibn abu 'Umayr from certain individuals of his people from abu 'Abd Allah, *'Alayhi al-Salam*, who has said the following:

"Whoever looks down upon a believer or belittles him because of his small resources or poverty, on the Day of Judgment Allah will make (his disgrace) public to all creatures."

H 2730, Ch. 141, h 10

Ali ibn Ibrahim has narrated from Muhammad ibn 'Isa from Yunus from Mu'awiyah from abu 'Abd Allah, *'Alayhi al-Salam*, who has said the following:

"The Messenger of Allah has said, 'My Lord took me for a journey and revealed to me from behind the curtain whatever He wanted to reveal, and spoke to me vocally and said to me, "O Muhammad, whoever insults any of My friends has waged a war against Me. Whoever fights Me, I fight him." I then said, 'O Lord, who is this friend of Yours? I have learned that whoever fights You, You fight him.' He said to me, 'This friend is the one with whom I have made a covenant, that he must accept your Divine Authority and Guardianship, the Divine Authority and Guardianship of the executor of your will and the Divine Authority and Guardianship of the descendents of both of you.'"

H 2731, Ch. 141, h 11

Ali ibn Ibrahim has narrated from Muhammad ibn 'Isa from Yunus from ibn Muskan from Mu'alla ibn Khunays from abu 'Abd Allah, *'Alayhi al-Salam*, who has said the following:

"The Messenger of Allah has said, 'Allah, the Most Majestic, the Most Holy, has said, "Whoever humiliates My believing servant has asked Me for a fight. I have not hesitated as much as I did at the time of the death of My believing servant. I love to meet him and he dislikes death. I then divert it from him. He prays to Me in a matter and I answer his prayer in what is better for him.'"

Chapter 142 - Those Who Seek to Find Mistakes and (Expose) Privacies of the Believers

H 2732, Ch. 142, h 1

Muhammad ibn Yahya has narrated from Ahmad ibn Muhammad ibn 'Isa from Muhammad ibn Sinan from Ibrahim and al-Fadl sons of Yazid al-Ash'ari from 'Abd Allah ibn Bukayr from Zurara from abu Ja'far and abu 'Abd Allah, *'Alayhi al-Salam*, who has said the following:

"Abu 'Abd Allah, *'Alayhi al-Salam*, has said, 'A servant (of Allah) is closest to disbelief when he assumes brotherhood (in belief) with a man and then begins to count his mistakes and slips so he can one day use them against him.'"

H 2733, Ch. 142, h 2

Muhammad ibn Yahya has narrated from Ahmad ibn Muhammad from Ali ibn al-Nu'man from Ishaq ibn 'Ammar who has said the following:

"I heard abu 'Abd Allah, *'Alayhi al-Salam*, saying, 'The Messenger of Allah has said, "O group of people who have accepted Islam with their tongue and belief has not yet purely and freely entered into their hearts, do not criticize the Muslims and do not seek to search into their privacies to find faults in them; Allah will then do the same to them and to whomever Allah will do such a thing, He may disgrace him even in the privacy of his own home.'"

It is narrated from him (narrator of the Hadith above) from Ali ibn al-Nu'man from abu al-Jarud from abu Ja'far, *'Alayhi al-Salam*, a similar Hadith.

H 2734, Ch. 142, h 3

A number of our people have narrated from Ahmad ibn Muhammad ibn Khalid from Ali ibn al-Hakam from 'Abd Allah ibn Bukayr from Zurara from abu Ja'far, *'Alayhi al-Salam*, who has said the following:

"Abu Ja'far, *'Alayhi al-Salam*, has said, 'A servant (of Allah) is closest to disbelief when he assumes brotherhood (in belief) with a man and then begins to count his mistakes and slips so he can one day use them against him.'"

H 2735, Ch. 142, h 4

It is narrated from him (narrator of the Hadith above) from al-Hajjal from 'Asim ibn Humayd from abu Basir from abu Ja'far, *'Alayhi al-Salam*, who has said the following:

"The Messenger of Allah has said, 'O group of people who have accepted Islam with their tongue and not yet with their heart, do not seek to search into the privacies of the Muslims to find faults in them; Allah will then do the same to them and to whomever Allah will do such a thing, He will bring disgrace upon him.'"

H 2736, Ch. 142, h 5

Ali ibn Ibrahim has narrated from his father from ibn abu 'Umayr from Ali ibn Isma'il from ibn Muskan from Muhammad ibn Muslim or al-Halabi from abu 'Abd Allah, *'Alayhi al-Salam*, who has said the following:

"The Messenger of Allah has said, 'Do not seek to find faults with the believers; if one seeks to find fault with his brother (in belief), Allah will find faults with him and whoever's fault Allah will seek to find, He will bring disgrace upon him and it may take place even inside his very own home.'"

H 2737, Ch. 142, h 6

A number of our people have narrated from Ahmad ibn Muhammad ibn Khalid from ibn Faddal from ibn Bukayr from Zurara from abu Ja'far, *'Alayhi al-Salam*, who has said the following:

"Abu Ja'far, *'Alayhi al-Salam*, has said, 'A servant (of Allah) is closest to disbelief when he assumes brotherhood (in belief) with a man and then begins to count his mistakes and slips so he can one day use them against him to disgrace him.'"

H 2738, Ch. 142, h 7

It is narrated from him (narrator of the Hadith above) from ibn Faddal from ibn Bukayr from abu 'Abd Allah, *'Alayhi al-Salam*, who has said the following:

"Abu 'Abd Allah, *'Alayhi al-Salam*, has said, 'A servant (of Allah) is farthest from Allah when he assumes brotherhood (in belief) with a man and keeps counting his slips and mistakes so he can one day use them against him.'"

Chapter 143 - Rebuking People

H 2739, Ch. 143, h 1

Ali ibn Ibrahim has narrated from his father from ibn abu 'Umayr from al-Husayn ibn 'Uthman from a man from abu 'Abd Allah, *'Alayhi al-Salam*, who has said the following:

"Abu 'Abd Allah, *'Alayhi al-Salam*, has said, 'Whoever rebukes a believer, Allah will debase him in this world and in the hereafter.'"

H 2740, Ch. 143, h 2

It is narrated from him (narrator of the Hadith above) from his father from ibn abu 'Umayr from Isma'il ibn 'Ammar from Ishaq ibn 'Ammar from abu 'Abd Allah, *'Alayhi al-Salam*, who has said the following:

"The Messenger of Allah has said, 'Whoever publicizes an indecent act is considered as the initiator of such deed and whoever rebukes a believer for a thing will not die before he himself commits such a thing.'"

H 2741, Ch. 143, h 3

Muhammad ibn Yahya has narrated from Ahmad ibn Muhammad ibn 'Isa from ibn Mahbub from 'Abd Allah ibn Sinan from abu 'Abd Allah, *'Alayhi al-Salam*, who has said the following:

"Abu 'Abd Allah, *'Alayhi al-Salam*, has said, 'Whoever debases a believer for a sin will not die before he himself commits such a sin.'"

H 2742, Ch. 143, h 4

A number of our people have narrated from Ahmad ibn Muhammad ibn Khalid from ibn Faddal from Husayn ibn 'Umar ibn Sulayman from Mu'awiyah ibn 'Ammar from abu 'Abd Allah, *'Alayhi al-Salam*, who has said the following:

"Abu 'Abd Allah, *'Alayhi al-Salam*, has said, 'Allah will rebuke in this world and in the next life a person who meets a believer in a reproachful manner.'"

Chapter 144 - Backbiting and Accusations

H 2743, Ch. 144, h 1

Ali ibn Ibrahim has narrated from his father from al-Nawfali from al-Sakuni from abu 'Abd Allah, *'Alayhi al-Salam*, who has said the following:

"The Messenger of Allah has said, 'Backbiting destroys the religion of a person faster than an internal cancerous disease.'

"The Imam has also said, 'The Messenger of Allah has said, "Sitting in the mosque is worship as long as it does not happen." He was asked, 'O Messenger of Allah, 'What has not happened?' He said, 'Backbiting.'"

H 2744, Ch. 144, h 2

Ali ibn Ibrahim has narrated from his father from ibn abu 'Umayr from certain individuals of his people from abu 'Abd Allah, *'Alayhi al-Salam*, who has said the following:

"Whoever says something about a believer that has not seen with his eyes and has not heard with his ears is then considered among those about whom Allah, the Most Majestic, the Most Holy, has said, 'Those who like to publicize indecency among the believers will face painful torment in this world and in the life to come. . . .'" (24:19)

H 2745, Ch. 144, h 3

Al-Husayn ibn Muhammad has narrated from Mu'alla ibn Muhammad from al-Hassan ibn Ali al-Washsha' from Dawud ibn Sarhan who has said the following:

"Once I asked abu 'Abd Allah, *'Alayhi al-Salam*, about backbiting. The Imam said, 'It is when you say about your brother in belief something about his religion that he has not done, and publicize against him something that Allah has covered up for him and he is not convicted for such crimes.'"

H 2746, Ch. 144, h 4

A number of our people have narrated from Ahmad ibn abu 'Abd Allah from his father from Harun ibn al-Jahm from Hafs ibn 'Umar from abu 'Abd Allah, *'Alayhi al-Salam*, who has said the following:

"The Holy Prophet was asked, 'What is the expiation for backbiting?' He said, 'It is to ask forgiveness from Allah for the person backbitten whenever one remembers him.'"

H 2747, Ch. 144, h 5

Muhammad ibn Yahya has narrated from Ahmad ibn Muhammad ibn 'Isa from al-Hassan ibn Mahbub from Malik ibn 'Atiyyah from ibn abu Ya'fur from abu 'Abd Allah, *'Alayhi al-Salam*, who has said the following:

"Abu 'Abd Allah, *'Alayhi al-Salam*, has said, 'Whoever accuses a believer with something that is not in him, Allah will raise him formed with the clay of Khabal, in which he will remain until he is out of what he had said.' I (the narrator) then asked, 'What is Khabal?' The Imam said, 'It is the puss that comes out from the vagina of the prostitutes.'"

H 2748, Ch. 144, h 6

Muhammad ibn Yahya has narrated from Ahmad ibn Muhammad from al-'Abbas ibn 'Amir from Aban from a man we do not know except Yahya al-Azraq who has said the following:

"Abu al-Hassan, *'Alayhi al-Salam*, once said to me, 'Anyone's mentioning a man behind his back with something that is found in him and people know is not backbiting. Whoever mentions a person behind his back with something that is found in him and people do not know it, he has backbitten him. Whoever mentions a person with something that is not found in him has accused him falsely.'"

H 2749, Ch. 144, h 7

Ali ibn Ibrahim has narrated from Muhammad ibn 'Isa from Yunus from 'Abd al-Rahman from 'Abd al-Rahman ibn Sayabah who has said the following:

"I heard abu 'Abd Allah, *'Alayhi al-Salam*, saying, 'Backbiting is when you say something about your brother (in belief) that Allah has covered up for him. However, the matters that are manifest in him like hot-temperedness and haste is not backbiting. Accusation is when you say about him what is not found in him.'"

Chapter 145 - Narration Against a Believer

H 2750, Ch. 145, h 1

Muhammad ibn Yahya has narrated from Ahmad ibn Muhammad ibn 'Isa from Muhammad ibn Sinan from Mufaddal ibn 'Umar who has said the following:

"Once abu 'Abd Allah, *'Alayhi al-Salam*, said to me, 'Whoever makes a narration against a believer intending thereby to defame him and destroy his honor to discredit him in the eyes of people, Allah moves him out of His guardianship to that of Satan, and Satan will not accept him.'"

H 2751, Ch. 145, h 2

It is narrated from him (narrator of the Hadith above) from Ahmad from al-Hassan ibn Mahbub from 'Abd Allah ibn Sinan who has said the following:

"Once I asked him (abu 'Abd Allah), *'Alayhi al-Salam*, 'Is it unlawful to publicize the secrets and privacy of a believer before another believer?' The Imam said, 'Yes, it is unlawful.' I then asked, 'Do you thereby (privacy) mean his two lower

301

organs (anus and genitals)?' The Imam said, 'It is not what you thought it is. It is to publicize his secrets and private matters.'"

H 2752, Ch. 145, h 3

Ali ibn Ibrahim has narrated from Muhammad ibn 'Isa from Yunus from al-Husayn ibn Mukhtar from Zayd from abu 'Abd Allah, *'Alayhi al-Salam*, the following:

"About the Hadith that says, 'Privacy of a believer is unlawful for another believer,' the Imam has said, 'It is not that they (genitals) are exposed and one sees certain parts of them. It is to make certain narrations against him to reproach and defame him.'"

Chapter 146 - Rejoicing at Others Troubles

H 2753, Ch. 146, h 1

A number of our people have narrated from Ahmad ibn Muhammad ibn Khalid from al-Hassan ibn Ali ibn Faddal from Ibrahim ibn Muhammad al-Ash'ari from Aban ibn 'Abd al-Malik from abu 'Abd Allah, *'Alayhi al-Salam*, who has said the following:

"Abu 'Abd Allah, *'Alayhi al-Salam*, has said, 'Do not express joy at the trouble of your brother (in belief); Allah may grant him a favor and transfer that trouble to you.' The Imam also said, 'Whoever rejoices at the suffering that has come upon his brother (in belief) he will not leave this world before going through such suffering himself.'"

Chapter 147 - Revilement

H 2754, Ch. 147, h 1

Ali ibn Ibrahim has narrated from his father from al-Nawfali from al-Sakuni from abu 'Abd Allah, *'Alayhi al-Salam*, who has said the following:

"The Messenger of Allah has said, 'Reviling a believer is like one's positioning one's self at the verge of destruction.'"

H 2755, Ch. 147, h 2

A number of our people have narrated from Ahmad ibn Muhammad ibn 'Isa from al-Husayn ibn Sa'id from Fadalah ibn Ayyub from 'Abd Allah ibn Bukayr from abu Basir from abu Ja'far, *'Alayhi al-Salam*, who has said the following:

"The Messenger of Allah has said, 'Reviling a believer is a gross sin, fighting him is disbelief, eating his flesh (backbiting) is disobedience and the illegality of consuming his property is like the illegality of spilling his blood (taking his life).'"

H 2756, Ch. 147, h 3

It is narrated from him (narrator of the Hadith above) from al-Hassan ibn Mahbub from Hisham ibn Salim from abu Basir from abu Ja'far, *'Alayhi al-Salam*, who has said the following:

"Once a man from the people of Tamim came to the Holy Prophet and said, 'Instruct me with good advice.' Of the good advice given to him was: 'Do not revile people; it only earns their animosity against you.'"

H 2757, Ch. 147, h 4

Ibn Mahbub has narrated from 'Abd al-Rahman ibn Al-Hajjaj from abu al-Hassan Musa, *'Alayhi al-Salam*, who has said the following about two people reviling:

"Abu al-Hassan Musa, *'Alayhi al-Salam*, has said, 'Of the two people reviling each other, the initiator is more unjust. He bears his own sin and the sin of his companion as long as he does not apologize to the oppressed.'"

H 2758, Ch. 147, h 5

Abu Ali al-Ash'ari has narrated from Muhammad ibn Salim from Ahmad ibn al-Nadr from 'Amr ibn Shimr from Jabir from abu Ja'far, *'Alayhi al-Salam*, who has said the following:

"Whoever testifies to the disbelief of a man will turn to one of them (one of them becomes an unbeliever). If one testifies to the disbelief of an unbeliever, he is right and if the party is a believer it turns to the testifier. You must never revile a believer."

H 2759, Ch. 147, h 6

Al-Hassan ibn Muhammad has narrated from Mu'alla ibn Muhammad from al-Hassan ibn Ali al-Washsha' from Ali ibn abu Hamza who has said the following:

"I heard one of them (the two Imam), *'Alayhi al-Salam*, saying, 'When reviling words come from the mouth of reviling people they move back and forth. They will reach the deserving party, if any; otherwise, they come back to the reviling person.'"

H 2760, Ch. 147, h 7

Muhammad ibn Yahya has narrated from Ahmad ibn Muhammad ibn 'Isa from al-Hassan ibn Ali ibn from 'Ali ibn Uqbah from 'Abd Allah ibn Sinan from abu Hamza al-Thumali who has said the following:

"I heard abu Ja'far, *'Alayhi al-Salam*, saying, 'When words of condemnation come out of the mouth of a person they move back and forth between the two to find the deserving party. If the deserving party is not found they come back to their owner (speaker of words of condemnation).'"

H 2761, Ch. 147, h 8

Abu Ali al-Ash'ari has narrated from Muhammad ibn Hassan from Muhammad ibn Ali from Muhammad ibn al-Fudayl from abu Hamza who has said the following:

"I heard abu 'Abd Allah, *'Alayhi al-Salam*, saying, 'When a man says to his believing brother (in belief), 'Uff (an expression of slight disappointment) he has moved out of his guardianship. If he says, 'You are my enemy,' one of them becomes an unbeliever. Allah does not accept the good deeds of any believer while he hides in him evil for his believing brother (in belief).'"

H 2762, Ch. 147, h 9

Muhammad ibn Yahya has narrated from Ahmad ibn Muhammad from ibn Sinan from Hammad ibn 'Uthman from Rib'i from al-Fudayl from abu Ja'far, *'Alayhi al-Salam*, who has said the following:

"Abu Ja'far, *'Alayhi al-Salam*, has said, 'Whoever reviles a believer face-to-face dies in the worst condition and deserves not to find any goodness.'"

Chapter 148 - Accusation and Evil Guessing

H 2763, Ch. 148, h 1

Ali ibn Ibrahim has narrated from his father from Hammad ibn 'Isa from Ibrahim ibn 'Umar al-Yamani from abu 'Abd Allah, *'Alayhi al-Salam*, who has said the following:

"Abu 'Abd Allah, *'Alayhi al-Salam*, has said, 'When a believer accuses his brother (in faith), belief melts away in his heart just as salt melts away in water.'"

H 2764, Ch. 148, h 2
A number of our people have narrated from Ahmad ibn Muhammad ibn Khalid from certain individuals of his people from al-Husayn ibn Hazim from Husayn ibn 'Umar ibn Yazid from his father who has said the following:
"I heard abu 'Abd Allah, *'Alayhi al-Salam*, saying, 'Whenever one accuses his brother (in belief) in his religious matters, religious relations will cease to exist between them. Whoever deals with his brother (in belief) just as he deals with other people, his religious relations (religious brotherhood) toward him all comes apart.'"

H 2765, Ch. 148, h 3
It is narrated from him (narrator of the Hadith above) from his father from those whom he has mentioned (in his book) from al-Husayn ibn al-Mukhtar from abu 'Abd Allah, *'Alayhi al-Salam*, who has said the following:
"Amir al-Mu'minin, Ali ibn abu Talib, *'Alayhi al-Salam*, has said in one of his speeches, 'Deal with the issues related to your brother (in belief) with best interpretations until you receive overwhelming evidence to support the facts. Do not act on (evil) guesswork about a word that has come from your brother (in belief) as long as you can manage to find a place for it in goodness.'"

Chapter 149 - Insincerity Toward One's Brother (in Belief)

H 2766, Ch. 149, h 1
Muhammad ibn Yahya has narrated from Ahmad ibn Muhammad from al-Hassan ibn Ali ibn al-Nu'man from abu Hafs al-'A'sha' who has said the following:
"I heard abu 'Abd Allah, *'Alayhi al-Salam*, saying, 'The Messenger of Allah has said, "Whoever works to help his brother (in belief), but is not sincere, has breached his trust with Allah and the Messenger of Allah."'"

H 2767, Ch. 149, h 2
A number of our people have narrated from Ahmad ibn Muhammad ibn Khalid from 'Uthman ibn 'Isa from Sama'a who has said the following:
"I heard abu 'Abd Allah, *'Alayhi al-Salam*, saying, 'Any believer who works to help his brother (in belief) but is not sincere enough has breached his trust with Allah and the Messenger of Allah.'"

H 2768, Ch. 149, h 3
A number of our people have narrated from Ahmad ibn Muhammad ibn Khalid and abu Ali al-Ash'ari from Muhammad ibn Hassan all from Edris ibn al-Hassan from Musabbih ibn Hilqam who has said that abu Basir narrated to him the following:
"I heard abu 'Abd Allah, *'Alayhi al-Salam*, saying, 'Whoever of our people is asked for help by any of his brothers (in belief) and does not do his best to help, has breached his trust with Allah, the Messenger of Allah and the believers.' Abu Basir has said that he then asked abu 'Abd Allah, *'Alayhi al-Salam*, 'What do you mean by "The believers"?' The Imam said, 'It applies to Amir al-Mu'minin, Ali ibn abu Talib, *'Alayhi al-Salam*, as well as 'A'immah (Leaders with Divine Authority) to the very last of them,.'"

H 2769, Ch. 149, h 4

It is narrated from both of them from Muhammad ibn Ali from abu Jamilah who has said the following:

"I heard abu 'Abd Allah, *'Alayhi al-Salam*, saying, 'Whoever walks to help his brother (in belief) but not with enough sincerity is like one who has breached his trust with Allah and the Messenger of Allah, and Allah will be his foe.'"

H 2770, Ch. 149, h 5

A number of our people have narrated from Ahmad ibn Muhammad ibn Khalid from certain individuals of his people from Husayn ibn Hazim from Husayn ibn 'Umar ibn Yazid from his father from abu 'Abd Allah, *'Alayhi al-Salam*, who has said the following:

"Abu 'Abd Allah, *'Alayhi al-Salam*, has said, 'If anyone consults his brother (in belief) and he does not help him with sincere opinions, Allah, the Majestic, the Glorious, takes away his good opinion (ability to form good opinions).'"

H 2771, Ch. 149, h 6

Ali ibn Ibrahim has narrated from Muhammad ibn 'Isa ibn 'Ubayd from Yunus from Sama'a who has said the following:

"I heard abu 'Abd Allah, *'Alayhi al-Salam*, saying, 'Any believer who walks with his brother (in belief) to help, but is not sincere enough has breached his trust with Allah and the Messenger of Allah.'"

Chapter 150 - Breach of Promise

H 2772, Ch. 150, h 1

Ali ibn Ibrahim has narrated from his father from ibn abu 'Umayr from Hisham ibn Salim who has said the following:

"I heard abu 'Abd Allah, *'Alayhi al-Salam*, saying, 'The promise of a believer to his brother (in belief) is a vow that has no expiation. Whoever violates it has initiated to violate Allah and has subjected himself to His anger as it is said in His words: "Believers, why do you preach what you do not practice? (61:2). It is most hateful in the sight of Allah if you say something and do not practice it.'" (61:3)

H 2773, Ch. 150, h 2

Ali has narrated from his father from ibn abu 'Umayr from Shu'ayb al-'Aqarqufi from abu 'Abd Allah, *'Alayhi al-Salam*, who has said the following:

"The Messenger of Allah has said, 'Whoever believes in Allah, and in the Day of Judgment, must fulfill his promise.'"

Chapter 151 - Obstructing One's Brother (in Belief)

H 2774, Ch. 151, h 1

Abu Ali al-Ash'ari has narrated from Muhammad ibn Hassan and A number of our people from Ahmad ibn Muhammad ibn Khalid all from Muhammad ibn Ali from Muhammad ibn Sinan from al-Mufaddal ibn 'Umar who has said the following:

"Abu 'Abd Allah, *'Alayhi al-Salam*, has said, 'Any believer who creates a barrier between himself and another believer, Allah, the Most Majestic, the Most Holy, will create between him and paradise seventy thousand walls, each one apart from the other by a distance of a one thousand year journey.'"

H 2775, Ch. 151, h 2

Ali ibn Muhammad has narrated from Muhammad ibn Jumhur from Ahmad ibn al-Husayn from his father from Isma'il ibn Muhammad from Muhammad ibn Sinan who has said the following:

"Once I was in the presence of al-Rida, *'Alayhi al-Salam*, and he stated to me as follows: 'O Muhammad, in the time of the children of Israel there were four believing people. One of them once went to the house where the other three had gathered together for a meeting on a certain issue among them. He knocked the door and a slave came to him. He then asked, 'Where is your master?' The slave replied, 'He is not home.' The man returned back and the slave went inside. His master asked, 'Who was at the door?' The slave replied, 'It was so and so and I told him that you were not home.' He remained quiet without regretting or blaming the slave for his false reply, nor did the other two show any concern for the return of their friend from the door and they continued talking. Next morning the man (their friend) came to the door very early and met the other three when they were leaving to go to a certain property that belonged to one of them. He offered them his greeting of peace and said, 'I also want to come with you.' They agreed but did not apologize to him for their attitude the day before. The man was needy or weak. On a certain part of the way a piece of cloud appeared over their heads with shadows and they thought it might rain. They began to move faster. When the cloud reached exactly over their heads an announcer announced from the cloud, 'O fire, strike them. I am Jibril (Gabriel), the Messenger of Allah.' Suddenly, fire from the cloud snatched the three away and the man remained frightened and astonished for what had happened to the other people. He did not know the reason. He came to the city and met Yusha' ibn Nun (peace be upon him). He explained to him what he had seen and heard. Yusha' asked, 'Did you not know that Allah had become angry with them, after that He was happy with them? It was because of the way they behaved toward you.' He asked, 'What had they done to me?' Yusha' informed him of their behavior and the man said, 'I, however, am ready to forgive them.' Yusha' said, 'Had this happened before it could have benefited them but now it does not benefit them and perhaps it may benefit them afterwards.'"

H 2776, Ch. 151, h 3

A number of our people have narrated from Sahl ibn Ziyad from Bakr ibn Salih from Muhammad ibn Sinan from Mufaddal from abu 'Abd Allah, *'Alayhi al-Salam*, who has said the following:

"If a believer creates a barrier between himself and another believer, Allah creates between him and paradise seventy thousand walls each of which will be as thick as the distance of a one thousand year journey, and of the same length will be the distance from one wall to the other wall."

H 2777, Ch. 151, h 4

Ali ibn Ibrahim has narrated from his father from Yahya ibn al-Mubarak from 'Abd Allah ibn Jabalah from 'Asim ibn Humayd from abu Hamza who has said the following:

"Once I said to abu Ja'far, *'Alayhi al-Salam*, 'May Allah keep my soul in service for your cause, what do you say about a Muslim who comes to the door of a Muslim as a visitor, or for help when he is home, and is asked permission for a meeting but does not give permission, nor does he come out to see his visitor?' The Imam said, 'O abu Hamza, if a Muslim comes to a Muslim as a visitor, or for help and he is home, and is asked permission but he does not come out to meet him, he continues living in the condemnation of Allah until the two will meet.' I (the narrator) then asked the Imam, 'May Allah keep my soul in service for your cause, will he live with the condemnation of Allah until the two will meet?' The Imam said, 'Yes, O abu Hamza.'"

Chapter 152 - Refusing to Help a Brother (in Belief)

H 2778, Ch. 152, h 1

A number of our people have narrated from Ahmad ibn Muhammad ibn Khalid and abu Ali al-Ash'ari from Muhammad ibn Hassan from Muhammad ibn Ali from Sa'dan from Husayn ibn 'Amin from abu Ja'far, 'Alayhi al-Salam, who has said the following:

"Abu Ja'far, 'Alayhi al-Salam, has said, 'Whoever exercises stinginess in assisting his Muslim brother and in helping him in his needs will run into an involvement of such an assistance that will make him sin and receive no rewards for it.'"

H 2779, Ch. 152, h 2

Ali ibn Ibrahim has narrated from Muhammad ibn 'Isa from Yunus from ibn Muskan from abu Basir from abu 'Abd Allah, 'Alayhi al-Salam, who has said the following:

"If anyone of our Shi'a (followers) comes to his brother (in belief) for help and does not help him while he is able to help, Allah will make him help other people of our enemies and on the Day of Judgment Allah will punish him for such help."

H 2780, Ch. 152, h 3

Abu Ali al-Ash'ari has narrated from Muhammad ibn Hassan from Muhammad ibn Aslam from al-Khattab ibn Mas'ab ibn Sadir from abu 'Abd Allah, 'Alayhi al-Salam, who has said the following:

"Whoever ignores assistance to his Muslim brother and the endeavor to cooperate with him will be involved in assisting someone who commits sins. It (assistance) does not bring him any rewards."

H 2781, Ch. 152, h 4

Al-Husayn ibn Muhammad has narrated from Mu'alla ibn Muhammad from Ahmad ibn Muhammad ibn 'Abd Allah from Ali ibn Ja'far from his brother abu al-Hassan, 'Alayhi al-Salam, who has said the following:

"I heard abu al-Hassan, 'Alayhi al-Salam, saying, 'Anyone whose brother (in belief) comes to him for help and support in his affairs and one does not provide any support or assistance when capable of doing so, has cut off oneself from the guardianship of Allah, the Most Majestic, the Most Holy.'"

Chapter 153 - Refusing a Believer a Thing of One's Own or Others

H 2782, Ch. 153, h 1

A number of our people have narrated from Ahmad ibn Muhammad and Abu Ali al-Ash'ari from Muhammad ibn Hassan all from Muhammad ibn Ali from Muhammad ibn Sinan from Furat ibn Ahnaf from abu 'Abd Allah, 'Alayhi al-Salam, who has said the following:

"If a believer refuses to give a needy believer something that he from his own or from another person can provide, due to such refusal on the Day of Judgment, Allah will raise him (refusing to help) with his face blackened, his eyes turned blue, his hands chained to his neck and it will be said, 'Violator of trust who breached his trust with Allah and the Messenger of Allah,' and then he is ordered into the fire.'"

H 2783, Ch. 153, h 2
Ibn Sinan has narrated from Yunus ibn Zabyan who has said the following:
"Once abu 'Abd Allah, 'Alayhi al-Salam, said to me, 'O Yunus, whoever hinders a believer's rights, because of such hindrance, Allah, the Most Majestic, the Most Holy, on the Day of Judgment will make him stand up on his feet for five hundred years until his sweat or blood flow and an announcer will announce from Allah, 'This unjust is the one who hindered the right of Allah.' The Imam said, 'He will be ridiculed for forty years and then will be ordered to the fire.'"

H 2784, Ch. 153, h 3
Muhammad ibn Sinan has narrated from Mufaddal ibn 'Umar who has said the following:
"Abu 'Abd Allah, 'Alayhi al-Salam, has said, 'If one has a home and a believer needs a place to live and is denied to use the house, Allah, the Most Majestic, the Most Holy, says, 'O My angels, My servant has denied My other servant a living place in the worldly home, by My Majesty and Glory, he will never live in My paradise.'"

H 2785, Ch. 153, h 4
Al-Husayn ibn Muhammad has narrated from Mu'alla ibn Muhammad from Ahmad ibn Muhammad ibn 'Abd Allah from Ali ibn Ja'far who has said the following:
"I heard abu al-Hassan, 'Alayhi al-Salam, saying, 'Whoever has a brother (in belief) who comes to him for help it is a favor to him from Allah, the Most Majestic, the Most Holy, Who has sent to him. If he accepted it (the favor) he has connected his guardianship with ours, which is connected with the guardianship of Allah, the Most Majestic, the Most Holy, and if he did not help while capable of helping, Allah will make a serpent from the fire to bite him in his grave up to the Day of Judgment when he may be forgiven or punished, and if the needy person accepts his (unreal) apology, it will be much worse for him.'

"I (the narrator) heard the Imam saying, 'Whoever has a brother (in belief) who comes to him for help in his needy condition, but does not provide help while capable to help, he (refusing to help) has cut off the guardianship of Allah, the Most Blessed, the Most High."

Chapter 154 - Frightening a Believer

H 2786, Ch. 154, h 1
A number of our people have narrated from Ahmad ibn Muhammad ibn Khalid from Muhammad ibn 'Isa from al-Ansari from 'Abd Allah ibn Sinan from abu 'Abd Allah, 'Alayhi al-Salam, who has said the following:
"The Messenger of Allah has said, 'Whoever looks upon a believer to frighten him, Allah, the Most Majestic, the Most Holy, will frighten him on the day when there will be no shadow (protection), accept His shadow.'"

H 2787, Ch. 154, h 2

Ali ibn Ibrahim has narrated from his father from abu Ishaq al-Khaffaf from certain people of al-Kufah from abu 'Abd Allah, *'Alayhi al-Salam*, who has said the following:

"Whoever frightens a believer with an authority and force that may harm him but is not harmed (the frightening person) will be in the fire. Whoever frightens a believer by an authority and forces to harm him and he is harmed, (the frightening person) will be raised with the Pharaoh and the people of Pharaoh in the fire."

H 2788, Ch. 154, h 3

Ali ibn Ibrahim has narrated from his father from ibn abu 'Umayr from certain individuals of his people from abu 'Abd Allah, *'Alayhi al-Salam*, who has said the following:

"Whoever helps (someone) against a believer, even with a part of a word, will meet Allah, the Most Majestic, the Most Holy, on the Day of Judgment with a writing between his eyes that will say, 'Deprived of My mercy.'"

Chapter 155 - Gossip Mongering

H 2789, Ch. 155, h 1

A number of our people have narrated from Ahmad ibn Muhammad from al-Hassan ibn Mahbub from 'Abd Allah ibn Sinan from abu 'Abd Allah, *'Alayhi al-Salam*, who has said the following:

"The Messenger of Allah has asked, 'Should I tell you who the evil ones among you are?' They said, 'Yes, O Messenger of Allah.' The Messenger of Allah said, 'They are those who spread gossip that causes separation among the loved ones and those who seek to label the innocent with faults.'"

H 2790, Ch. 155, h 2

Muhammad ibn Yahya has narrated from Muhammad ibn Ahmad from Muhammad ibn 'Isa from Yusuf ibn 'Aqil from Muhammad ibn Qays from abu Ja'far, *'Alayhi al-Salam*, who has said the following:

"Abu Ja'far, *'Alayhi al-Salam*, has said, 'Entering paradise is prohibited to spies and gossip mongers.'"

H 2791, Ch. 155, h 3

Ali ibn Ibrahim has narrated from Muhammad ibn 'Isa from Yunus from abu al-Hassan al-Asbahani from those whom has mentioned (in his book) from abu 'Abd Allah, *'Alayhi al-Salam*, who has said the following:

"Amir al-Mu'minin, Ali ibn abu Talib, *'Alayhi al-Salam*, has said, 'The evil ones among you are those who spread gossip that causes separation among the loved ones, and seek to label the innocent with defects.'"

Chapter 156 - Publicity of Confidentialities

H 2792, Ch. 156, h 1

A number of our people have narrated from Ahmad ibn Muhammad ibn Khalid from 'Uthman ibn 'Isa from Muhammad ibn 'Ajlan who has said the following:

"I heard abu 'Abd Allah, *'Alayhi al-Salam*, saying, 'Allah, the Most Majestic, the Most Holy, has criticized people for publicizing confidential matters in His words, "When they receive any news of peace or war, they announce it in public. . . ." (4:83) Therefore, be on your guard against publicity of confidential matters.'"

H 2793, Ch. 156, h 2

Ali ibn Ibrahim has narrated from Muhammad ibn 'Isa from Yunus from Muhammad al-Khazzaz from abu 'Abd Allah, *'Alayhi al-Salam*, who has said the following:

"Abu 'Abd Allah, *'Alayhi al-Salam*, has said, 'Whoever publicizes our (confidential) Hadith is like one who has denied our rights.' The Imam, *'Alayhi al-Salam*, had also said to al-Mu'alla ibn khunays, 'One who publicizes our Hadith is like one who rejects them.'"

H 2794, Ch. 156, h 3

Yunus has narrated from ibn Muskan from ibn abu Ya'fur who has said the following:

"Abu 'Abd Allah, *'Alayhi al-Salam*, has said, 'Whoever publicizes our (confidential) Hadith, Allah will take away his belief.'"

H 2795, Ch. 156, h 4

Yunus ibn Ya'qub has narrated from certain individuals of his people from abu 'Abd Allah, *'Alayhi al-Salam*, who has said the following:

"Abu 'Abd Allah, *'Alayhi al-Salam*, has said, 'Whoever publicizes our (confidential) Hadith is like one who does not kill us by mistake but he does so on purpose.'"

H 2796, Ch. 156, h 5

Yunus has narrated from al-'Ala' from Muhammad ibn Muslim who has said the following:

"I heard abu Ja'far, *'Alayhi al-Salam*, saying, 'A servant (of Allah) will be raised on the Day of Judgment, although he had not caused any bloodshed, something containing a dose or more blood will be given to him and he will be told, "This is your share of the blood of so and so." He will say, 'Lord, You know that You caused me to die and I had not committed any bloodshed.' The Lord will say, 'Yes, you did commit bloodshed. You heard such and such facts from so and so, you narrated it against his interests and transmitted it until it reached so and so tyrant, who murdered him on the basis of the narration, and this is your share of that blood.'"

H 2797, Ch. 156, h 6

Yunus has narrated from ibn Sinan from Ishaq ibn 'Ammar from abu 'Abd Allah, *'Alayhi al-Salam*, who has said the following:

"The Imam recited this verse: '. . . for they denied the evidence (of the existence of Allah) and murdered His Prophets without reason; they were disobedient transgressors.' (2:61) The Imam said, 'By Allah they did not murder them with their hands or swords but they would hear their Hadith and publicize them, causing them to be captured and murdered. It then became murder, transgression and disobedience.'"

H 2798, Ch. 156, h 7

A number of our people have narrated from Ahmad ibn abu 'Abd Allah from 'Uthman ibn 'Isa from Sama'a from abu Basir from abu 'Abd Allah, *'Alayhi al-Salam*, who has said the following:

"About the words of Allah, the Most Majestic, the Most Holy, '. . . for unjustly murdering the prophets . . .,' (3:112) the Imam said, 'By Allah, they did not murder them with their swords but they publicized their secrets, spread them against the prophets who then were murdered.'"

H 2799, Ch. 156, h 8

It is narrated from him (narrator of the Hadith above) from 'Uthman ibn 'Isa from Muhammad ibn 'Ajlan from abu 'Abd Allah, *'Alayhi al-Salam*, who has said the following:

"Allah, the Most Majestic, the Most Holy, in His words has criticized a people for publicizing confidential facts: 'When they receive any news of peace or war, they announce it in public . . .,' (4:83) therefore, be on your guard against publicizing confidential facts.'"

H 2800, Ch. 156, h 9

Ali ibn Ibrahim has narrated from his father from ibn abu 'Umayr from Husayn ibn 'Uthman from those who reported to him from abu 'Abd Allah, *'Alayhi al-Salam*, who has said the following:

"Abu 'Abd Allah, *'Alayhi al-Salam*, has said, 'Whoever publicizes our (confidential) cause is like one who murders us on purpose, and not by mistake.'"

H 2801, Ch. 156, h 10

Al-Husayn ibn Muhammad has narrated from Mu'alla ibn Muhammad from Ahmad ibn Muhammad from Nasr ibn Sa'id, Mawla abu 'Abd Allah, *'Alayhi al-Salam*, from his father who has said the following:

"I heard abu 'Abd Allah, *'Alayhi al-Salam*, saying, 'The propagator (of the confidential Hadith of 'A'immah) is in doubt (about his belief in 'A'immah) and the narrator (of confidential matter) before a stranger (unreliable audience) is an unbeliever. Whoever holds fast to the firm ring, is saved.' I (the narrator) then asked, 'What is it (the ring)?' The Imam said, 'It is submission (to the commands of 'A'immah, and acceptance of the same).'"

H 2802, Ch. 156, h 11

Ali ibn Muhammad has narrated from Salih ibn abu Hammad from a man of the people of Kufah from abu Khalid al-Kabuli from abu 'Abd Allah, *'Alayhi al-Salam*, who has said the following:

"Allah, the Most Majestic, the Most Holy, has made religion into two kingdoms; the kingdom of Adam, which is the kingdom of Allah, and the kingdom of Satan. When Allah wants to be worshipped publicly such time is the time of the kingdom of Adam. When Allah wants to be worshipped in hiding and secretly, such time is the time of the kingdom of Satan. The publisher of what Allah wants to remain secret is out of the limits and sanctuary of religion."

H 2803, Ch. 156, h 12

Abu Ali al-Ash'ari has narrated from Muhammad ibn 'Abd al-Jabbar from Safwan from 'Abd al-Rahman ibn al-Hajjaj from abu 'Abd Allah, *'Alayhi al-Salam*, who has said the following:

"Abu 'Abd Allah, *'Alayhi al-Salam*, has said, 'Whoever opens his morning activities with the publicity of our secrets Allah will make the heat of iron and the congestion of prisons dominate him.'"

Chapter 157 - Obeying the Creature in Disobedience to the Creator

H 2804, Ch. 157, h 1

Ali ibn Ibrahim has narrated from his father from al-Nawfali from al-Sakuni from abu 'Abd Allah, *'Alayhi al-Salam*, who has said the following:

"The Messenger of Allah has said, 'Whoever seeks the pleasure of people to anger Allah, Allah will make the people who praise him vilify.'"

H 2805, Ch. 157, h 2

A number of our people have narrated from Ahmad ibn Muhammad ibn Khalid from Isma'il ibn Mehran from Sayf ibn 'Amirah from 'Amr ibn Shimr from Jabir from abu Ja'far, *'Alayhi al-Salam*, who has said the following:

"The Messenger of Allah has said, 'Whoever seeks the pleasure of people with that which angers Allah, the people praising will belittle him. Whoever gives preference to Allah's obedience with that which angers people, Allah will suffice him against the animosity of every enemy, the envy of all enviers and the transgression of all transgressors. Allah, the Most Majestic, the Most Holy, will be his helper and supporter.'"

H 2806, Ch. 157, h 3

It is narrated from him (narrator of the Hadith above) from Sharif ibn Sabiq from al-Fadl ibn abu Qarrah from abu Qurrah from abu 'Abd Allah, *'Alayhi al-Salam*, who has said the following:

"Once, a man wrote al-Husayn, *'Alayhi al-Salam*, asking, 'Instruct me with good advice in two letters.' The Imam wrote back to him, 'Whoever seeks to acquire something by means of what angers Allah (his deed as such) will be most harmful to his hopes and most hastening to the coming of that which frightens him.'"

H 2807, Ch. 157, h 4

Abu Ali al-Ash'ari has narrated from Muhammad ibn 'Abd al-Jabbar from Safwan from al-'Ala' from Muhammad ibn Muslim who has said the following:

"Abu Ja'far, *'Alayhi al-Salam*, has said, 'Whoever obeys, considering it a matter of his religion, one who disobeys Allah, has no religion, and so also is one who follows what is forged against Allah as well as one who accepts as a matter of his religion, to reject any signs of Allah.'"

H 2808, Ch. 157, h 5

Ali ibn Ibrahim has narrated from his father from al-Nawfali from al-Sakuni from abu 'Abd Allah, *'Alayhi al-Salam*, from his father from Jabir ibn 'Abd Allah (al-Ansari) who has said the following:

"The Messenger of Allah has said, 'Whoever seeks the pleasure of a king by a means that anger Allah, has moved out of the religion of Allah.'"

Chapter 158 - Immediate Punishment of Sins

H 2809, Ch. 158, h 1

Ali ibn Ibrahim has narrated from his father and a number of our people have narrated from Ahmad ibn Muhammad all from Ahmad ibn Muhammad ibn abu Nasr from Aban from a man from abu Ja'far, *'Alayhi al-Salam*, who has said the following:

"The Messenger of Allah has said, 'If you find five things, then seek refuge to Allah against them: indecency has never become manifest in a people to the limit of an open performance, but that a plague and such pains that were never experienced before by their ancestors will appear among them. People who cheat in weighing and measurements face a famine, harsh conditions of living and injustice of the king. If a people deny payment of al-Zakat (charity) they will be denied rains from the skies. Were it not for the existence of animals no rain would come down upon them. If a people disregard the covenant of Allah, and the Messenger of Allah, Allah will make dominant over them their enemy and will take away certain items of their possession. If a people judge their cases by that which is not from Allah, the Most Majestic, the Most Holy, Allah, the Most Majestic, the Most Holy, will make them to suffer a civil war.'"

H 2810, Ch. 158, h 2

Ali ibn Ibrahim has narrated from his father and a number of our people have narrated from Ahmad ibn Muhammad all from ibn Mahbub from Malik ibn 'Atiyyah from abu Hamza from abu Ja'far, *'Alayhi al-Salam*, who has said the following:

"We have found in the book of the Messenger of Allah the following: after my leaving this world when fornication will turn out to be apparent among people, sudden death will take place more frequently. When weighing and measurement will become light, people will face famine and shortages of livelihood. When they deny paying al-Zakat (charity) the land will deny them its blessings of all of its farming, fruits and minerals. When people become unjust in their judgment, they will cooperate in injustice and animosity. When they disregard their covenant, Allah will make their enemies dominate them. When they fail to maintain good relations with relatives, properties will go in the hands of evildoers. When people stop commanding the fulfillment of obligations and prohibiting the unlawful matters and do not follow the virtuous people of my family, Allah will make their evil people dominate them. Their virtuous ones will pray but their prayers will not be heard."

Chapter 159 - Association with Sinful People

H 2811, Ch. 159, h 1

Ali ibn Ibrahim has narrated from his father from ibn abu 'Umayr from abu Ziyad al-Nahdi from 'Abd Allah ibn Salih from abu 'Abd Allah, *'Alayhi al-Salam*, who has said the following:

"Abu 'Abd Allah, *'Alayhi al-Salam*, has said, 'It is not proper for a believer to attend a meeting wherein Allah is disobeyed and one is not able to change it.'"

H 2812, Ch. 159, h 2

A number of our people have narrated from Ahmad ibn Muhammad from Bakr ibn Muhammad from al-Ja'fari who has said the following:

"I heard abu al-Hassan, *'Alayhi al-Salam*, saying, 'Why is it that I find you with 'Abd al-Rahman ibn Ya'qub?' I (the narrator) then said, 'It is because he is my uncle from my mother's side.' The Imam said, 'He says great heavy words about Allah. He describes Allah who is beyond description. You either sit with him and leave us or sit with us and leave him.' I then said, 'He may say anything he wants but what does that have to do with me when I say none of the things that he says?' Abu al-Hassan, *'Alayhi al-Salam*, said, 'Are you not afraid of the misfortune that may befall him and involve all of you also? Do you not know about the thing that happened to the people of Moses? The father of one of them was of the people of the Pharaoh. When the Pharaoh's horsemen approached Moses, he withdrew himself from Moses to convince his father to join Moses but his father kept moving while he argued against his father until they reached the shore and both were drowned. The news reached Moses and he said, 'He is in the mercy of Allah, but when misfortune falls there is no defense for those who are close to the sinners.'"

H 2813, Ch. 159, h 3

Abu Ali al-Ash'ari has narrated from Muhammad ibn 'Abd al-Jabbar from 'Abd al-Rahman ibn abu Najran from 'Umar ibn Yazid from abu 'Abd Allah, *'Alayhi al-Salam*, who has said the following:

"Do not associate with the heretics and do not sit with them so you may become one of them in the eyes of the people. The Messenger of Allah has said, 'A man is in the religion of his friends and associates.'"

H 2814, Ch. 159, h 4

Muhammad ibn Yahya has narrated from Muhammad ibn al-Husayn from Ahmad ibn Muhammad ibn abu Nasr from Dawud ibn Sarhan from abu 'Abd Allah, *'Alayhi al-Salam*, who has said the following:

"The Messenger of Allah has said, 'When you after me find people of heresy and skepticism express your disapproval of them and increase your condemnation, words and opposition to and evidence against them so they may not become greedy to bring destruction to Islam. You must warn people against them and against learning their heretic ideas. Allah will reward you for this and will raise your position in the next life.'"

H 2815, Ch. 159, h 5

A number of our people have narrated from Ahmad ibn Muhammad ibn Khalid from 'Uthman ibn 'Isa from Muhammad ibn Yusuf from Muyassir from abu 'Abd Allah, *'Alayhi al-Salam*, who has said the following:

"Abu 'Abd Allah, *'Alayhi al-Salam*, has said, 'It is not proper for a Muslim to establish friendship and brothehhood with a blatant sinner, a silly person or a liar.'"

H 2816, Ch. 159, h 6

It is narrated from him (narrator of the Hadith above) from 'Amr ibn 'Uthman from Muhammad ibn Salim al-Kendi from those who narrated to him from abu 'Abd Allah, *'Alayhi al-Salam*, who has said the following:

"Amir al-Mu'minin, Ali ibn abu Talib, *'Alayhi al-Salam*, from the pulpit would say, 'It is very proper for a Muslim not to establish brotherhood with three kinds of people: a vulgar, a silly or a lying person; a vulgar person polishes his acts for you and loves that you become like him. He does not help you in your religious matters and your life in the hereafter. Association with him is injustice and hardheartedness. His coming and going with you is a disgrace.

"A silly person does not show you anything good. There is no hope in his diverting any evil from you even if he may make an effort to help. Perhaps he may like to benefit you, instead he harms you. His death is better than his living, his silence is better than speaking, and his being at a distance is better than his being nearby.

"You can never have a happy life with a lying person. He narrates your words to others and the words of the others to you. Whenever he runs out of a story, he stretches one story to the other so much so that even if he may tell the truth it is not believed. He creates animosity among people and grows hatred in the hearts. Be pious before Allah and look after your souls.'"

H 2817, Ch. 159, h 7

A number of our people have narrated from Sahl ibn Ziyad from 'Amr ibn 'Uthman from Muhammad ibn 'Adhafir from certain individuals of his people from Muhammad ibn Muslim or abu Hamza from abu 'Abd Allah, *'Alayhi al-Salam*, from his father, *'Alayhi al-Salam*, who has said the following:

"Once Ali ibn al-Husayn, *'Alayhi al-Salam*, said to me, 'My son, beware of five kinds of people and do not associate with, speak to and accompany them on the road.' I then asked, 'Who are they O father?' He then said, 'You must not accompany a lying person; he is like a phantom. He tells you of what, in fact, is faraway to be very near and what, in fact, is near to be very far. You must not associate with a sinful person; he may sell you for a single loaf or even less to this or that person. You must not associate with a stingy person; he leaves you out in the cold in financial matters in your desperate conditions. You must not associate with a silly person; he may want to benefit you instead he causes you harm.

"You must not associate one who has failed to maintain good relations with relatives; I have found him as condemned in three places of the book of Allah, the Most Majestic, the Most Holy, 'If you ignore the commands of Allah, would you then also spread evil in the land and sever the ties of kinship? (47:22) Allah has condemned these people and made them deaf, dumb, and blind.' (47:23) 'Those who disregard their covenant with Allah after He has taken such a pledge from them, who sever the proper relations that Allah has commanded them to establish, and those who spread evil in the land will have Allah's condemnation instead of reward and will face the most terrible end.' (13:25) '. . . The evil doers (2:26) who break their established covenant with Him and the relations He has commanded to be kept and who spread evil in the land; these are the ones who lose a great deal.'" (2:27)

H 2818, Ch. 159, h 8

A number of our people have narrated from Ahmad ibn Muhammad from ibn Mahbub from Shu'ayb al-'Aqaqufi who has said the following:

"Once I asked abu 'Abd Allah, *'Alayhi al-Salam*, about the words of Allah, the Most Majestic, the Most Holy, 'Allah has told you (believers) in the Book that when you hear people disbelieving and mocking Allah's revelations, do not sit with them unless they change the subject. You will become like them. Allah will gather all the hypocrites and the unbelievers together in hellfire.' (4:140) The Imam said, 'It means that when you hear the man who rejects the truth, denies it and opposes 'A'immah, you then must leave him and do not sit with him no matter whoever he may be.'"

H 2819, Ch. 159, h 9

Ali ibn Ibrahim has narrated from his father from Ali ibn Asbat from Sayf ibn 'Amirah from 'Abd al-'Ala' ibn 'Ayun from abu 'Abd Allah, *'Alayhi al-Salam*, who has said the following:

"Whoever believes in Allah and in the Day of Judgment must not sit in a seat whereby an Imam is belittled or a believer is criticized."

H 2820, Ch. 159, h 10

A number of our people have narrated from Sahl ibn Ziyad from Ja'far ibn Muhammad al-Ash'ari from ibn al-Qaddah from abu 'Abd Allah, *'Alayhi al-Salam*, who has said the following:

"Amir al-Mu'minin, Ali ibn abu Talib, *'Alayhi al-Salam*, has said, 'Whoever believes in Allah and in the Day of Judgment must not stay in a place that casts doubt on one's credentials and make them murky.'"

H 2821, Ch. 159, h 11

Muhammad ibn Yahya has narrated from Ahmad ibn Muhammad from Ali ibn al-Hakam from Sayf ibn 'Amirah from 'Abd al-'Ala' who has said the following:

"I heard abu 'Abd Allah, *'Alayhi al-Salam*, saying, 'Whoever believes in Allah and in the Day of Judgment must not sit in a place where an Imam is belittled or a believer is criticized.'"

H 2822, Ch. 159, h 12

Al-Husayn ibn Muhammad has narrated from Ali ibn Muhammad ibn Sa'd from Muhammad ibn Muslim from Ishaq ibn Musa who has said that narrated to him his brother and uncle from abu 'Abd Allah, *'Alayhi al-Salam*, who has said the following:

"There are three kinds of gatherings that Allah despises and sends His anger upon the attendance therein. You must not sit there to associate with them: a gathering wherein there is one whose tongue speaks lies in his Fatwas (legal opinion), a gathering wherein our enemies are praised freshly and we are mentioned as old (of less value) ones, and a gathering wherein obstacles are created for us and you know it.' The Imam then read three verses from the book of Allah as if they were in his mouth (or as if they were on his palms): 'O believers, do not say bad words against the idols lest they (pagans) in their hostility and ignorance say such words against Allah.'(6:108) 'When you see people mocking Our revelations, turn away from them so that they may change the subject. . . .' (6:68) '(Unbelievers), do not follow whatever your lying tongues may tell you is lawful or unlawful to invent lies against Allah. . . .'" (16:116)

H 2823, Ch. 159, h 13

Through the same chain of narrators it is narrated from Muhammad ibn Muslim from Dawud ibn Farqad who has said that narrated to him Sa'id al-Jumahhi who has that narrated to him Hisham ibn Salim from abu 'Abd Allah, *'Alayhi al-Salam*, who has said the following:

"If you are caught up with the people who are bitter enemies of 'A'immah, *'Alayhim al-Salam*, and you associate with them, you must act like a person on a piece of stone heated in a furnace whereby you move away as fast as you can; Allah hates them and condemns them. If you find them, speak against any one of 'A'immah, you must move away from them; Allah's anger descend down there upon them."

H 2824, Ch. 159, h 14

Abu Ali al-Ash'ari has narrated from Muhammad ibn 'Abd al-Jabbar from Safwan from 'Abd al-Rahman ibn al-Hajjaj from abu 'Abd Allah, *'Alayhi al-Salam*, who has said the following:

"Abu 'Abd Allah, *'Alayhi al-Salam*, has said, 'Whoever sits with those who abuse the friends of Allah has certainly disobeyed Allah,the Most High.'"

H 2825, Ch. 159, h 15

A number of our people have narrated from Ahmad ibn Muhammad ibn Khalid from his father from al-Qasim ibn 'Urwah from 'Ubayd ibn Zurara from his father from abu Ja'far, *'Alayhi al-Salam*, who has said the following:

"Whoever sits in a gathering where any of 'A'immah is abused and one is able to move out of such gathering, but does not do so, Allah will dress him with humiliation in this world and punish him in the next life and take away from him the goodness that was granted to him due to his acquaintance with us.'"

H 2826, Ch. 159, h 16
Al-Husayn ibn Muhammad and Muhammad ibn Yahya have narrated from Ali ibn Muhammad ibn Sa'd from Muhammad ibn Muslim from al-Hassan ibn Ali ibn al-Nu'man who has said that his father narrated to him from Ali ibn al-Nu'man from ibn Muskan from al-Yaman ibn 'Ubayd Allah who has said the following:

"I saw Yahya ibn 'Umm Tawil standing at al-Kunasa (an open area in Kufah) calling at the peak of his voice, 'O group of friends of Allah, I disavow whatever you hear. Whoever abuses Ali, *'Alayhi al-Salam*, allow the condemnation of Allah be upon him. We renounce the people of the family of Marwan and all that they worship besides Allah.' He then would lower his voice and say, 'Do not sit with those who abuse the friends of Allah. Do not sit with those who doubt our belief and do not accept them as your judge. If any of your brothers (in belief) would need to ask you questions (help), then you have violated your trust with him (for not helping before his appeal).' He then would read, '. . . For the unjust We have prepared a fire which will engulf them with its flames. Whenever they cry for help they will be answered with water as hot as liquefied brass, which will blister their faces. How terrible is such a drink and such a resting place!'" (18:29)

Chapter 160 - Kinds of People

H 2827, Ch. 160, h 1
A number of our people have narrated from Sahl ibn Ziyad from Ali ibn Asbat from Sulaym Mawla Tirbal who has said the Hisham narrated to him from Hamza ibn al-Tayyar who has said the following:

"Once abu 'Abd Allah, *'Alayhi al-Salam*, said to me, 'People are of six categories.' I then asked, 'Can I write them down?' The Imam said, 'Yes, you can do so.' I then asked, 'What should I write?' The Imam said, 'Write down: the people promised paradise and those warned against the fire (but ignored it). Write down, ". . . others of them have already confessed their sins and have mixed virtuous deeds with sinful ones."' (9:102) I then asked, 'Who are such people?' The Imam said, 'Wahshi (assassin of Hamza) is one of them.' The Imam said, 'Write down, "There are others who have no good deeds for which they may receive any reward or sins for which they may be punished. . . ."' (9:106) The Imam said, 'Write down, "As for the really weak and oppressed men, women, and children who were not able to find any means of obtaining their freedom or of having the right guidance, (4:98) [are not able to do anything against the unbelievers or find the right guidance] perhaps Allah will forgive them; He is All-merciful and All-forgiving." (4:99) The Imam said, 'Write down the people of 'A'raf.' I asked, 'Who are they?' The Imam said, 'They are the people whose good and bad deeds measure equally. If they will be sent to the fire it will be due to their sins and if they will be sent to paradise it will be due to His kindness.'"

H 2828, Ch. 160, h 2

Ali ibn Ibrahim has narrated from Muhammad ibn 'Isa from 'Ubayd from Yunus from Hammad from Hamza ibn al-Tayyar from abu 'Abd Allah, *'Alayhi al-Salam*, who has said the following:

"People are of six categories. All of them come from three groups: people of belief, disbelief and straying. All three are the people of two promises. Allah has promised paradise and fire. There are the believers, and the unbelievers. Besides, there are the weak ones who hope in the command of Allah whereby they may be punished or forgiven and there are those who have confessed to their sins and have mixed good deeds with bad deeds. Also there are the people of 'A'raf. (Straying people are of four groups and with the other two: believing people and unbelievers total six groups)."

H 2829, Ch. 160, h 3

Ali ibn Ibrahim has narrated from his father from ibn abu 'Umayr from Hisham ibn Salim from Zurara who has said the following:

"Once Humran and I or Bukayr and I went in the presence of abu Ja'far, *'Alayhi al-Salam*, and I said, 'We use the Mitmar.' The Imam said, 'What is the Mitmar?' I said, 'It is a measuring device. Whoever of 'Alawi or none 'Alawi agrees with us we love them and whoever, 'Alawi or none 'Alawi opposes us, we disavow them.' The Imam said, 'O Zurara, the words of Allah are more true than your words. Where are those about whom Allah, the Most Majestic, the Most Holy, has said, 'As for the really weak and oppressed men, women, and children who were not able to find any means of obtaining their freedom or of having the right guidance,' (4:98) and where are those who have hope in Allah's command? Where are those who mix good deeds with bad deeds? Where are the people of 'A'raf and where are people whose hearts incline to the truth?'"

"Hammad has added in the Hadith: The voices of abu Ja'far, *'Alayhi al-Salam*, and I became loud and people at the door could hear them.

"Jamil from Zurara has added: When many words were exchanged between him and I, he said, 'O Zurara, it is a right on Allah not to send the straying people to paradise.'"

Chapter 161 - Disbelief

H 2830, Ch. 161, h1

A number of our people have narrated from Ahmad ibn Muhammad from al-Hassan ibn Mahbub from Dawud ibn Kathir al-Raqqi who has said the following:

"Once I asked abu 'Abd Allah, *'Alayhi al-Salam*, 'Are the traditions, Sunan of the Messenger of Allah like the obligations Allah, the Most Majestic, the Most Holy, has sanctioned?' The Imam said, 'Allah, the Most Majestic, the Most Holy, has sanctioned obligations that are compulsory for the servants (of Allah). Whoever ignores an obligation of the compulsory ones; does not perform it and rejects it, he becomes an unbeliever. The Messenger of Allah has commanded certain matters to be performed and they all are good deeds. One does not become an unbeliever for ignoring a few of the obligations that Allah, the Most Majestic, the

Most Holy, has commanded His servant to perform, however, he has ignored a virtue and has cut down goodness.'"

H 2831, Ch. 161, h 2

Ali ibn Ibrahim has narrated from his father from Hammad ibn 'Isa from Hariz from Zurara from abu Ja'far, 'Alayhi al-Salam, who has said the following:

"By Allah, disbelief is before paganism and it is greater in filth. The narrator has said that the Imam then mentioned the disbelief of Satan when Allah told him to bow down before Adam and refused to prostrate, that disbelief is greater than considering things partners of Allah. Whoever chooses something instead of Allah, the Most Majestic, the Most Holy, refuses to obey and commits major sins is an unbeliever. One who establishes a religion other than the religion of the believers has considered things as partners of Allah."

H 2832, Ch. 161, h 3

Ali ibn Ibrahim has narrated from Muhammad ibn 'Isa from Yunus from 'Abd Allah ibn Bukayr from Zurara from abu Ja'far, 'Alayhi al-Salam, who has said the following:

"The narrator has said that once Salim ibn abu Hafs and his companions were mentioned before abu Ja'far, 'Alayhi al-Salam, and that they denied that those who waged war against Ali, 'Alayhi al-Salam, are of the people who consider things as partners of Allah (Mushrik). Abu Ja'far, 'Alayhi al-Salam, said, 'So they think such people are unbelievers.' The Imam then said to me, 'Disbelief is before paganism.' He (the Imam) then mentioned Satan when Allah told him to prostrate, and he refused to do so. The Imam said that disbelief is before al-Shirk (paganism and considering things as partners of Allah). Whoever boldly disobeys Allah and commits major sins is an unbeliever. He has considered belief insignificant so he is an unbeliever.'"

H 2833, Ch. 161, h 4

It is narrated from him (narrator of the Hadith above) from 'Abd Allah ibn Bukayr from Zurara from Humran ibn 'A'yun who has said the following:

"Once I asked abu 'Abd Allah, 'Alayhi al-Salam, about the words of Allah, the Most Majestic, the Most Holy, 'We showed him the right path, whether he would be grateful or ungrateful.' (76:3) The Imam said, 'If he accepts it (belief), he is then grateful or rejects it; he then is an unbeliever.'"

H 2834, Ch. 161, h 5

Al-Husayn ibn Muhammad has narrated from Mu'alla ibn Muhammad from al-Hassan ibn Ali from Hammad ibn 'Uthman from 'Ubayd from Zurara who has said the following:

"Once I asked abu 'Abd Allah, 'Alayhi al-Salam, about the words of Allah, the Most Majestic, the Most Holy, 'The deeds of anyone who rejects belief, certainly, become fruitless. He, on the Day of Judgment will be of those who lose.' (5:5) The Imam said, 'It is disregarding the deeds that he has confessed to be true. Of such deeds is disregarding prayer without suffering from illness or being preoccupied.'"

H 2835, Ch. 161, h 6

A number of our people have narrated from Sahl ibn Ziyad from Ali ibn Asbat from Musa ibn Bukayr who has said the following:

"Once I asked abu al-Hassan, *'Alayhi al-Salam*, about disbelief and al-Shirk (paganism) as to which is before. The Imam said to me, 'I have not experienced your involvement in polemics among the people.' I then said, 'Hisham ibn Salim has ordered me to ask you this question.' The Imam said, 'Disbelief is before and it is denial and rejection. Allah, the Most Majestic, the Most Holy, has said, ". . . except Iblis (Satan) who abstained out of pride, and so he became one of those who deny the truth.'" (2:34)

H 2836, Ch. 161, h 7
Ali ibn Ibrahim has narrated from his father from ibn abu 'Umayr from 'Abd al-Rahman ibn al-Hajjaj from Zurara who has said the following:
"Once I asked abu Ja'far, *'Alayhi al-Salam*, 'Will a believer go in the fire?' The Imam said, 'No, by Allah.' I then asked, 'So no one will be sent in the fire except the unbelievers?' The Imam said, 'No, except whoever Allah wills.' I (the narrator) repeated my question several times and the Imam said, 'O Zurara, I say, "No," and I say, 'Except whoever Allah will wish' and you say, "No," but do not say, 'Except whoever Allah will wish.'"

Ibn abu 'Umayr has said that Hisham ibn al-Hakam and Hammad have narrated from Zurara who has said the following:

"I said to myself, 'An old man has no knowledge of polemics.' The narrator (Zurara) has said the Imam said to me, 'O Zurara, what do you say about one who says, 'I am at your command (whatever you say in matters of belief I accept). Will you kill him? What do you say about your servants and people very closely related to you? Will you kill them?'

"I (the narrator) then said to myself, 'I am the one who has no knowledge of polemics.'"

H 2837, Ch. 161, h 8
Ali ibn Ibrahim has narrated from Harun ibn Muslim from Mas'adah ibn Sadaqa who has said the following:
"I heard abu 'Abd Allah, *'Alayhi al-Salam*, saying, when he was asked about disbelief and paganism which one was first, 'Disbelief is first. Satan was the first to become an unbeliever and his disbelief was something other than al-Shirk (paganism) he did not invite to worship anyone other than Allah, he invited to such worship afterwards and thus, became a pagan.'"

H 2838, Ch. 161, h 9
Harun has narrated from Mas'adah ibn Sadaqa who has said the following:
"I heard abu 'Abd Allah, *'Alayhi al-Salam*, when he was asked, 'Why is it that a fornicator is not considered an unbeliever as one ignoring the prayer is? What is the reason and evidence?' The Imam said, 'A fornicator and so forth commits such act due to lust that influences him, while one ignoring the prayer does so due to his considering it insignificant. You do not find a fornicator contact a female for any other reason besides lust and desire that motivates him. One who ignores

the prayer does not do so for pleasure. When you negate lust and pleasure then the motive is considering it insignificant, and when this happens it is disbelief.'

"The narrator has said that abu 'Abd Allah, *'Alayhi al-Salam*, was asked, 'What is the difference between a person's looking at a female, then fornicating or to wine, then drinking it and one who ignores the prayer? Why is it that in the two aforementioned cases it is not 'considered insignificant' as is the case with ignoring prayer? What is the proof and reason that establish a difference?' The Imam said, 'Proof is that whenever you place your soul in something without any urging motive like lust and so forth, that are found in fornication and wine. In a case such as prayer in which there is no lust and desire, then it (the motive) is considering it insignificant and that is the difference between this and the other two cases.'"

H 2839, Ch. 161, h 10
Muhammad ibn Yahya has narrated from Ahmad ibn Muhammad ibn 'Isa from ibn Mahbub from 'Abd Allah ibn Sinan from abu 'Abd Allah, *'Alayhi al-Salam*, who has said the following:
"Abu 'Abd Allah, *'Alayhi al-Salam*, has said, 'Whoever doubts Allah and the Messenger of Allah is an unbeliever.'"

H 2840, Ch. 161, h 11
Ali ibn Ibrahim has narrated from his father from Safwan from Mansur ibn Hazim who has said the following:
"Once I asked abu 'Abd Allah, *'Alayhi al-Salam*, 'What if one doubts the Messenger of Allah?' The Imam said, 'He is an unbeliever.' I then asked, 'What if one doubts the disbelief of such a doubting person? Is he also an unbeliever?' The Imam did not answer me and I asked it three times. Then I noticed anger on his face?'"

H 2841, Ch. 161, h 12
Muhammad ibn Yahya has narrated from Ahmad ibn Muhammad from ibn Faddal from ibn Bukayr from 'Ubayd ibn Zurara who has said the following:
"Once I asked abu 'Abd Allah, *'Alayhi al-Salam*, about the words of Allah, the Most Majestic, the Most Holy, 'The deeds of anyone who rejects belief, certainly, become fruitless. He on the Day of Judgment will be of those who lose.' (5:5) The Imam said, 'It is he who ignores a deed that has held to be true.' I then asked, 'What kind of deed is it that has such consequences if ignored?' The Imam said, 'Of such deed is ignoring the prayer purposely not because of drunkenness or illness.'"

H 2842, Ch. 161, h 13
Ali ibn Ibrahim has narrated from his father from ibn abu 'Umayr from Muhammad ibn Hakim and Hammad from abu Masruq who has said the following:
"Once abu 'Abd Allah, *'Alayhi al-Salam*, asked me about the people of Basra and asked me, 'Who are they?' I said, 'They are Murji'a', Qadriah and Harawriah' (names of groups of certain beliefs). The Imam said, 'May Allah condemn such nations of disbelief and paganism who have no basis for worshipping Allah.'"

Note: Murji'a were those who did not believe in the true position of Amir al-Mu'minin, Ali ibn abu Talib, *'Alayhi al-Salam*, Qadriah believed in absolute free will and Harawriah was of the group who opposed Amir al-Mu'minin, Ali ibn abu Talib, *'Alayhi al-Salam*.

H 2843, Ch. 161, h 14

It is narrated from him (narrator of the Hadith above) from al-Khattab ibn Muslimah and Aban from al-Fudayl who has said the following:

"Once I went in the presence of abu Ja'far, *'Alayhi al-Salam*, and saw a man with him. As I sat down, the man stood up and left. The Imam said to me, 'O Fudayl, what is this with you?' I asked, 'What is he?' The Imam said, 'He is a Harawri.' I asked, 'Is he an unbeliever?' The Imam said, 'Yes, by Allah, he is a Mushrik (one who considers things as partners of Allah).'"

H 2844, Ch. 161, h 15

Muhammad ibn Yahya has narrated from Ahmad ibn Muhammad from ibn Mahbub from abu Ayyub from Muhammad ibn Muslim who has said the following:

"I heard abu Ja'far, *'Alayhi al-Salam*, saying, 'Anything that professing and submission carry is belief, and anything that denial and rejection carry is disbelief.'"

H 2845, Ch. 161, h 16

Al-Husayn ibn Muhammad has narrated from Mu'alla' ibn Muhammad from al-Washsha' from 'Abd Allah ibn Sinan from abu Hamza who has said the following:

"I heard abu Ja'far, *'Alayhi al-Salam*, saying, 'Amir al-Mu'minin, Ali ibn abu Talib, *'Alayhi al-Salam*, is a (means of) access that Allah has prepared. Whoever approaches through this access is a believer and whoever departs is an unbeliever.'"

H 2846, Ch. 161, h 17

A number of our people have narrated from Sahl ibn Ziyad from Yahya ibn al-Mubarak from 'Abd Allah ibn Jabalah from Ishaq ibn 'Ammar and ibn Sinan and Sama'a from abu Basir from abu 'Abd Allah, *'Alayhi al-Salam*, who has said the following:

"The Messenger of Allah has said, 'Obedience to Ali, *'Alayhi al-Salam*, is suffering (in this world) and disobedience to him is disbelief in Allah.' It was said, 'O Messenger of Allah, how can obedience to Ali, *'Alayhi al-Salam*, be suffering and disobedience to him disbelief in Allah?' The Messenger of Allah said, 'Ali, *'Alayhi al-Salam*, leads you to the truth. If you obey him you will suffer and if you disobey him you will become unbelievers in Allah, the Most Majestic, the Most Holy.'"

H 2847, Ch. 161, h 18

Al-Husayn ibn Muhammad has narrated from Mu'alla ibn Muhammad from al-Washsha' who has said that narrated to him Ibrahim ibn abu Bakr who has said the following:

"I heard abu al-Hassan Musa, *'Alayhi al-Salam*, saying, 'Ali, *'Alayhi al-Salam*, is a door of the doors of guidance. Whoever enters by the door of Ali, *'Alayhi al-Salam*, is a believer and whoever ignores this door is an unbeliever. Whoever does not enter and does not leave is among the group about whom Allah has the will and decision.'"

322

H 2848, Ch. 161, h 19

Muhammad ibn Yahya has narrated from Ahmad ibn Muhammad from Muhammad ibn Sinan from ibn Bukayr from Zurara from abu 'Abd Allah, *'Alayhi al-Salam*, who has said the following:

"Abu 'Abd Allah, *'Alayhi al-Salam*, has said, 'Had the servants (of Allah) when ignorant stood on hold and did not reject or deny they would not become unbelievers.'"

H 2849, Ch. 161, h 20

Ali ibn Ibrahim has narrated from Muhammad ibn 'Isa from Yunus from Fudayl ibn Yasar from abu Ja'far, *'Alayhi al-Salam*, who has said the following:

"Allah, the Most Majestic, the Most Holy, has appointed Ali, *'Alayhi al-Salam*, as a sign between Himself and His creatures. Those who come to know him turn into believing people and those who reject him end up as unbelievers. Those who are ignorant of him become among the straying people. Those who appoint something with him grow to be Mushrik (pagans) and those who come under his guardianship will enter paradise and those who come with his animosity will enter the fire.'"

H 2850, Ch. 161, h 21

Yunus has narrated from Musa ibn Bukayr from abu Ibrahim, *'Alayhi al-Salam*, who has said the following:

"Ali, *'Alayhi al-Salam*, is a door of the doors of paradise. Whoever approaches through him is a believer, those who depart him are unbelievers, and those who do not approach or leave are among the group about whom Allah has the will to decide."

Chapter 162 - The Aspects of Disbelief

H 2851, Ch. 162, h 1

Ali ibn Ibrahim has narrated from his father from Bakr ibn Salih from al-Qasim ibn Yazid from abu 'Amr al-Zubayri who has said the following:

"Once I said to abu 'Abd Allah, *'Alayhi al-Salam*, 'Instruct me about the kinds of disbelief (mentioned) in the book of Allah, the Most Majestic, the Most Holy.' The Imam said, 'Disbelief in the book of Allah is of five kinds:

"(1) Of disbelief is denial, which is of two kinds. (2) There is disbelief for disregarding the commands of Allah. (3) Another form of disbelief for disavowing, and (4) disbelief in the bounties is still another form of disbelief.

"Disbelief for denial is (a) denial of His Lordship and it is the belief of those who say that there is no Lord, paradise and fire. It is the belief of two kinds of atheism, called Dahriah, who say, 'It is only time that destroys us.' (45:23) It is a religion that they made for themselves on the basis of what they felt to be good with out proof and research in any of the things they say. Allah, the Most Majestic, the Most Holy, has said, 'It is only what they guess, . . .' (45:23) their religion is based on mere guessing. Allah has said, 'Those who deny your message will not believe, whether you warn them or not.' (2:6) They will not believe in the Oneness of Allah. This is one kind of disbelief.

(b) The other kind of denial is denial of knowledge. This is when the denying person denies knowing well the truth that is established before him. Allah, the Most Majestic, the Most Holy, has said, 'They rejected the evidence because of their arrogance and injustice, although their souls knew it to be true. . . .' (27:14) Allah, the Most Majestic, the Most Holy, has said, '. . . despite the fact that they had been praying for victory over the disbelievers (by the help of the truthful Prophet), they refused to accept this book, even though they knew it (to be the Truth). May Allah condemn those who hide the Truth." (2:89) This is the explanation of two kinds of disbelief.'

"The third kind of disbelief is disbelief in the bounties as Allah, the Most High, has said quoting Sulayman, '. . . This is a favor from my Lord by which He wants to test whether I am grateful or ungrateful. Whoever thanks Allah, does so for his own good. Whoever is ungrateful to Allah should know that my Lord is Self-sufficient and Benevolent.' (27:40) Allah has said, 'If you give thanks, I shall give you greater (favors), but if you deny the Truth, know that My retribution is severe.' (14:7) Allah has said, ' . . . remember Me and I shall remember you. Thank Me and do not hide the truth about Me.' (2:152)

"The fourth kind of disbelief is disbelief in the form of disregard of what Allah, the Most Majestic, the Most Holy, has commanded as in the words of Allah, the Most Majestic, the Most Holy, 'We made a covenant with you that you should not shed each other's blood or expel each other from your homeland. You accepted and bore witness to this covenant, (2:84) yet you murdered each other and forced a number of your people out of their homeland, helping each other to commit sin and to be hostile to one another. When you had expelled people from their homeland and later they had been made captives (of other people), you then paid their ransom (thinking that it was a righteous deed). Allah forbade you to expel these people in the first place. Do you believe in one part of the Book and not in the other? [They are called unbelievers due to their disregard of the commands of Allah, the Most Majestic, the Most Holy, and He has ascribed them to belief but He has not accepted it and it has been of no benefit before Him] and He has said, '. . . Those who behave in this way shall reap disgrace in this world and severe punishment on the Day of Resurrection. Allah is not unaware of things that you do.' (2:85)

"The fifth kind of disbelief is disbelief in the form of disavowing as in the words of Allah, the Most Majestic, the Most Holy, quoting Ibrahim (Abraham), 'We have rejected you. Enmity and hatred will separate us forever unless you believe in Allah only. . . .' (60:4) This is disavowing. Allah has said when mentioning (the case of) Satan and his friend of man on the Day of Judgment, 'I did not agree with your belief that I was equal to Allah. . . .' (14:22) Allah has said, '. . . you believe in idols besides Allah, only out of worldly love, but on the Day of Judgment you will reject and condemn each other . . .' (29:25) That is disavowing each other.'"

Chapter 163 (a) - Pillars and Branches of Disbelief

H 2852, Ch. 163a, h 1

Ali ibn Ibrahim has narrated from his father from Hammad ibn 'Isa from Ibrahim ibn 'Umar al-Yamani from 'Umar ibn 'Udhaynah from Aban ibn abu 'Ayyash from Sulaym ibn Qays al-Hilali from Amir al-Mu'minin, Ali ibn abu Talib, *'Alayhi al-Salam*, who has said the following:

"Disbelief is established on four pillars: Sinfulness, Extremism, Doubt and Skepticism. Sinfulness has four branches: harshness of manners, blindness of heart, neglect, and arrogance. Whoever behaves in a harsh manner belittles the truth, hates the people of profound understanding and persists in great sins. Whoever becomes blind of heart forgets to remember (the truth), follows guesses, opposes his Creator and Satan turns bold toward him. He asks forgiveness without repenting, feeling humble and without being unaware of sin. Whoever is neglectful and careless commits a crime against his own soul, turns himself upside down and thinks of his misguidance as guidance. Yearnings deceives him, remorse and pangs of guilt seize him and when the matters settle and the curtain is raised, he finds it to be what he did not expect. Whoever is arrogant to obey the commands of Allah doubts and whoever doubts, Allah overpowers him and humiliates him by His Authority and makes him little by His Glory as he has played deceit against his Honorable Lord and has gone to extremes in his affairs.

"Extremism is of four branches: Seeking profundity of opinion, disputation over an opinion, looking for deviations in it and creating a schism therein.

"Whoever seeks extreme complexity he does not return to the truth, and does not gain anything except sinking in deeper troubles. He does not finish removing one before another trouble overwhelms him. His religion sustains holes and he falls deeper in chaos. Whoever seeks disputation in an opinion and quarrels, his absurdity comes in the open due to prolonged controversy. Whoever deviates, goodness seems terrible to him and evil begins to look lovelier.

"Whoever creates a schism, his paths lead to dead end, his affairs burden him, his escape narrows if he would not follow the path of the believers.

"Doubt is of four branches: Suspicion, desire, hesitation and submission. It is mentioned in the words of Allah, the Most Majestic, the Most Holy, 'About which of the bounties of your Lord can they persistently dispute and cast doubts?' (53:55)

"In another Hadith it is said, 'It branches in suspicion, fear of truth, hesitation and submission before ignorance and ignorant people.'

"Whoever fears what is before him turns back. Whoever is suspicious of religion remains hesitant in doubts and the foremost believing people move forward before him and those behind catch up with him. He turns out to be flattened under the hooves of Satan. Whoever submits to worldly destruction and that of the next life is destroyed between the two. Whoever is saved from such condition is due to the excellence of certainty. Allah has not created any creature fewer than certainty.

"Casting doubt is of four branches: a liking of attractiveness, stimulation of soul, interpretation of crookedness and mixing of truth with falsehood.

"This is because attractiveness clashes with evidence, stimulation of soul indulges in desires and crookedness bends its companion a great bent. Hiding and mixing truth with falsehood is darkness upon darkness. That is disbelief, its pillars and branches.'"

Chapter 163 (b) - Description of Hypocrisy and Hypocrites

(This is part of the previous Hadith. The compiler has presented it in a separate Chapter).

"Amir al-Mu'minin, Ali ibn abu Talib, *'Alayhi al-Salam*, has said, 'Hypocrisy has four pillars: Desire, Neglect, Resentment and Greed.

"Desire is of four branches: disproportionate behavior, transgression, lust and insubordination. Whoever behaves disproportionately faces great risks, remains lonely and without supporters. Whoever transgresses does not remain immune to harmful consequences, his heart is not in peace and he does not control his soul against lustful matters. Whoever has not balanced his soul in lustful matters he indulges in filthy activities. Whoever acts insubordinately purposely and without evidence strays in falsehood.

"Neglect is of four branches: dishonesty, yearning, fear and procrastination. Fear and apprehension turns one away from the truth and procrastination leads to extremely reduced activities until the deadline approaches. If one does not have any yearnings he knows his true condition and measures. If he knows the true measure of his condition in which he is, he would die suddenly due to fear and apprehension. Dishonesty cuts short one's deeds.

"Resentment is of four branches: arrogance, boastfulness, egoistic, and racism. Whoever is arrogant turns his back to the truth. Whoever is boastful indulges in sins. Whoever is egoistic persists in sins. Whoever comes in the clench of racism commits injustice.

"Thus, evil is the affair that swings in deterioration, indecency, persistence and injustice on the path.

"Greed is of four branches: exhilaration, pleasure seeking, worrying and superfluity. Exhilaration is detestable before Allah. Pleasure seeking is feeblemindedness. Worrisome is a misfortune for one who is forced to carry sins. Seeking superfluity is useless, a childish manner, a vastful preoccupation and an effort to change what is of a lower quality to a better one.

"This is how hypocrisy its pillars and branches are. Allah is dominant over his servants. Speaking of Him is exalted and glory is His. He has created all things in good fashion, His hands are free, His favor is universal, His command is manifest,

His light shines, His blessing overflows, His wisdom is the source of light, His book is overriding, His evidence is overwhelming, His religion is pure, His kingdom is powerful, His word is the truth, His measures are just and His messengers have already preached. Thus, He has made evil a sin, sin a misfortune and misfortune a filth.

"He has made virtuous deeds a threshold. The threshold is repentance and repentance is purification. One who repents finds guidance. One who plots goes astray, as long as he does not repent before Allah and confess to his sins. No one dares to act, to his own destruction, against Allah, except those who are doomed.

"Allah! Allah! How vast is what He has for repentance, favors, joy and great forbearance. How severe is what is before Him of retribution, hell, and a hard grip! Whoever succeeds in obedience to Him attracts His generosity. Whoever indulges in disobedience to Him he will test the results of His disapproval and very shortly he will become regretful.'"

H 2853, Ch. 163b, h 2
Muhammad ibn Yahya has narrated from al-Husayn ibn Ishaq from Ali ibn Mahziyar from Muhammad ibn 'Abd Hamid and al-Husayn ibn Sa'id all from Muhammad ibn al-Fudayl who has said the following:
"Once I wrote to abu al-Hassan, *'Alayhi al-Salam*, asking him a question and he wrote back to me, 'The hypocrites try to deceive Allah, but He, in fact, deceives them. They stand up in prayer lazily just to show that they pray, but, in truth, they remember Allah very little. (4:142)

"They are hesitant people belonging to neither side. You can find no other way for one whom Allah has caused to go astray.' (4:143) They are not of the unbelievers, or of the believers or of the Muslims. They claim to be of belief. They change to disbelief and denial. May Allah condemn them all.'"

H 2854, Ch. 163b, h 3
Al-Husayn ibn Muhammad has narrated from Muhammad ibn Jumhur from 'Abd Allah ibn 'Abd al-Rahman al-'Assam from al-Haytham ibn Waqid from Muhammad ibn Sulayman from ibn Muskan from abu Hamza from Ali ibn al-Husayn, *'Alayhi al-Salam*, who has said the following:
"Ali ibn al-Husayn, *'Alayhi al-Salam*, has said, 'A hypocrite forbids others, but himself does not desist from prohibited matters and commands others with what he himself does not perform. When prayer is to begin he ('I'taraza) avoids it.' I (the narrator) then asked, 'O descendent of the messenger of Allah, "What is 'I'tiraz?" The Imam said, 'It is turning away. When he is in the Ruku' position (kneeling) he uses it as resting place. Toward the evening his only concern is dinner, even though he is not fasting. Toward morning his only concern is more sleep, even though he has not passed the night awake worshipping. If he speaks to you, he lies. If you trust him, he breaches it. Behind your back, he backbites you and if he promises you, he disregards his promise.'"

H 2855, Ch. 163b, h 4
It is narrated from him (narrator of the Hadith above) from ibn Jumhur from Sulayman ibn Sama'a from 'Abd al-Malik ibn Bahr in a marfu' manner a similar Hadith with the following addition:

"In, Ruku' position he rests and in Sajdah (the prostration) he acts like a crow picking up grains very fast, and sits on his heels."

H 2856, Ch. 163b, h 5
Abu Ali al-Ash'ari has narrated from al-Hassan ibn Ali al-Kufi from 'Uthman ibn 'Isa from Sa'id ibn Yasar from abu 'Abd Allah, *'Alayhi al-Salam,* who has said the following:
"The Messenger of Allah has said, 'The case of a hypocrite is like the trunk of a palm tree. His owner wants to use it in a construction but it does not fit where he wants it to fit. He then tries it in another place and it still does not fit. At last he burns it in the fire.'"

H 2857, Ch. 163b, h 6
A number of our people have narrated from Sahl ibn Ziyad from Muhammad ibn al-Hassan ibn Shammun from 'Abd Allah ibn 'Abd al-Rahman from Misma' ibn 'Abd al-Malik from abu 'Abd Allah, *'Alayhi al-Salam,* who has said the following:
"The Messenger of Allah has said, 'If humility expressed physically is more than what is in the heart, in our view it is hypocrisy.'"

Chapter 164 - Paganism Considering Things as Partners of Allah

H 2858, Ch. 164, h 1
Ali ibn Ibrahim has narrated from Muhammad ibn 'Isa from Yunus from Burayd al-'Ijli who has said the following:
"Once I asked abu Ja'far, *'Alayhi al-Salam,* of the minimum amount of belief with which one is considered a polytheist (one who considers other things as partners of Allah). The narrator has said that the Imam said, 'It is he who calls a nut a pebble and a pebble a nut and considers it his religion.'"

H 2859, Ch. 164, h 2
It is narrated from him (narrator of the Hadith above) from 'Abd Allah ibn Muskan from abu al-'Abbas who has said the following:
"Once I asked abu 'Abd Allah, *'Alayhi al-Salam,* about the minimum degree of al-Shirk (paganism). The Imam said, 'It is one's inventing an opinion and thereafter love and hate (people) on that basis.'"

H 2860, Ch. 164, h 3
A number of our people have narrated from Sahl ibn Ziyad from Yahya ibn al-Mubarak from 'Abd Allah ibn Jabalah from Sama'a from abu Basir and Ishaq ibn 'Ammar from abu 'Abd Allah, *'Alayhi al-Salam,* who has said the following:
"About the words of Allah, the Most Majestic, the Most Holy, 'Most of them do not believe in Allah; they are but pagans,' (12:106) the Imam said, 'They obey Satan without realizing it and so they grow to be pagans.'"

H 2861, Ch. 164, h 4
Ali ibn Ibrahim has narrated from Muhammad ibn 'Isa from Yunus from ibn Bukayr from Durays from abu 'Abd Allah, *'Alayhi al-Salam,* who has said the following:
"About the words of Allah, the Most Majestic, the Most Holy, 'Most of them do not believe in Allah; they are but pagans,' (12:106) the Imam said, 'Al-Shirk (paganism) is obedience and it is not worship,' and the words of Allah, the Most

Majestic, the Most Holy, ' . . . certain people worship Allah to achieve worldly gains. . . .,' (22:11) the Imam said, 'A verse comes down about a man and then it applies to his followers.' I then said, 'Do those who appoint others (as people possessing Divine Authority) instead of you (Ahl al-Bayt) worship for worldly gains?' The Imam said, 'Yes, at certain cases it is just that (al-Shirk).'"

H 2862, Ch. 164, h 5

Yunus has narrated from Dawud ibn Farqad from Hassan al-Jammal from 'Amirah who has said the following:

"I heard abu 'Abd Allah, *'Alayhi al-Salam*, saying, 'People are commanded to know us (Ahl al-Bayt), and they are referred to us and to submit to us.' The Imam then said, 'If they fast, perform prayers, testify that there is no one who deserves to be worshipped except Allah but keep it in themselves and do not refer to us for guidance, for this they will be considered Mushrik, (considering things as partners of Allah).'"

H 2863, Ch. 164, h 6

Ali ibn Ibrahim has narrated from his father from Ahmad ibn Muhammad ibn abu Nasr from 'Abd Allah ibn Yahya al-Kahili who has said the following:

"Abu 'Abd Allah, *'Alayhi al-Salam*, has said, 'If a people worship Allah alone and do not consider anything as His partner, perform the prayer, pay al-Zakat (charity), perform Hajj of the Sacred House, fast in the month of Ramadan and then say about something Allah has done or the Holy Prophet has done, "Why not is it done as such and such?" Or they find such things in their hearts, for this they will turn into Mushrik, considering things as partners of Allah.' The Imam then read this verse of the Holy Quran: 'I swear by your Lord that they will not be considered believers until they allow you to settle their disputes and then they will find nothing in their souls to prevent them from accepting your judgment, thus, submitting themselves to the will of Allah.' (4:65) Abu 'Abd Allah, *'Alayhi al-Salam*, then said, 'You must submit yourselves (to the command of Allah)'"

H 2864, Ch. 164, h 7

A number of our people have narrated from Ahmad ibn Muhammad ibn Khalid from his father from 'Abd Allah ibn Yahya from 'Abd Allah ibn Muskan from abu Basir who has said the following:

"Once I asked abu 'Abd Allah, *'Alayhi al-Salam*, about the words of Allah, the Most Majestic, the Most Holy, '. . . they (unconditionally) obeyed the rabbis and the monks. . . . as they should have obeyed Allah. . . .' (9:31) The Imam said, 'By Allah, they (rabbis and monks) did not call the people to worship them. Had they done so people would not have listened to them. They, however, made certain things lawful and unlawful as they liked and people obeyed and worshipped them without realizing the evil in such worship.'"

H 2865, Ch. 164, h 8

Ali ibn Muhammad has narrated from Salih ibn abu Hammad and Ali ibn Ibrahim has narrated from his father from ibn abu 'Umayr from a man from abu 'Abd Allah, *'Alayhi al-Salam*, who has said the following:

"Abu 'Abd Allah, *'Alayhi al-Salam*, has said, 'Whoever obeys a man in a sin has worshipped him.'"

Chapter 165 - Doubt

H 2866, Ch. 165, h 1

Ali ibn Ibrahim has narrated from Muhammad ibn 'Isa from Yunus from al-Husayn ibn Hakam who has said the following:

"Once I wrote to the virtuous servant (of Allah) saying that I had doubt and Ibrahim, peace be upon him, had said, 'Lord, show me how you will bring the dead to life?' (2: 260) and I would love that you show me something. The Imam wrote back to me, 'Ibrahim was a believer. He wanted to increase his belief. You, however, have doubt and there is nothing good in doubt.' The Imam further wrote, 'Doubt comes when there is no certainty when certainty, comes then doubting is not permissible.' He wrote further, 'Allah, the Most Majestic, the Most Holy, has said, "We did not find many among them keeping their promises. However, We did find many evil-doers among them." (7:102) The Imam said, 'It was revealed about people who doubt.'"

H 2867, Ch. 165, h 2

A number of our people have narrated from Sahl ibn Ziyad from Ali ibn Asbat from abu Ishaq al-Khurasani who has said the following:

"Amir al-Mu'minin, Ali ibn abu Talib, *'Alayhi al-Salam*, would say in his sermons, 'Do not suspect; you will doubt and do not doubt; you will become unbelievers.'"

H 2868, Ch. 165, h 3

A number of our people have narrated from Ahmad ibn Muhammad ibn Khalid from his father from Khalaf ibn Hammad from abu Ayyub al-Khazzaz from Muhammad ibn Muslim who has said the following:

"Once I was in the presence of abu 'Abd Allah, *'Alayhi al-Salam*, sitting to his left side and Zurara was sitting to his right side. Abu Basir came in and he asked, 'What do you say if one doubts in Allah?' The Imam said, 'He is an unbeliever, O abu Muhammad.' Abu Basir then asked, 'What if one has doubts in the Messenger of Allah?' The Imam said, 'He is an unbeliever.' The narrator has said that the Imam then turned to Zurara and said, 'He (such a person) is an unbeliever only if he rejects.'"

H 2869, Ch. 165, h 4

It is narrated from him (narrator of the Hadith above) from his father from al-Nadr ibn Suwayd from Yahya ibn 'Imran al-Halabi from Harun ibn Kharijah from abu Basir who has said the following:

"Once I asked abu 'Abd Allah, *'Alayhi al-Salam*, about the words of Allah, the Most Majestic, the Most Holy, 'Those who have accepted the faith and have kept it pure from injustice have achieved security and guidance.' (6:82) The Imam said, '(It means one) who has kept it (belief) pure from doubt.'"

H 2870, Ch. 165, h 5

Al-Husayn ibn Muhammad has narrated from Ahmad ibn Ishaq from Bakr ibn Muhammad from abu 'Abd Allah, *'Alayhi al-Salam*, who has said the following:

"Abu 'Abd Allah, *'Alayhi al-Salam*, has said, 'Doubts and disobedience are in the fire. It (doubt or people having doubts) is not from us nor is it directed to us.'"

H 2871, Ch. 165, h 6

A number of our people have narrated from Ahmad ibn abu 'Abd Allah from 'Uthman ibn 'Isa from a man from abu 'Abd Allah, *'Alayhi al-Salam*, who has said the following:

"Abu 'Abd Allah, *'Alayhi al-Salam*, has said, 'One who doubts in Allah after being born from Muslim parents, forever, will not end up to anything good.'"

H 2872, Ch. 165, h 7

It is narrated from him (narrator of the Hadith above) from his father in a marfu' manner from abu Ja'far, *'Alayhi al-Salam*, who has said the following:

"Abu Ja'far, *'Alayhi al-Salam*, has said, 'No deed with doubt and denial will be of any benefit.'"

H 2873, Ch. 165, h 8

It is in the advice to al-Mufaddal who has said the following:

"I heard abu 'Abd Allah, *'Alayhi al-Salam*, saying, 'One who has doubt or Zann (better than doubt and less than certainty) and lives with one of them (such conditions), Allah turns his deeds fruitless. The authority and proof for (existence of) Allah is clear authority and proof.'"

H 2874, Ch. 165, h 9

It is narrated from him (narrator of the Hadith above) from Ali ibn Asbat from al-'Ala' ibn Razin from Muhammad ibn Muslim who has said the following:

"Once I said to one of (two Imam), *'Alayhi al-Salam*, 'We find a man who worships, and strives with humility but does not believe in the truth (Shi'a belief). Will it be of any benefit for him?' The Imam said, 'O abu Muhammad, the case of Ahl al-Bayt (of Muhammad) is like that Ahl al-Bayt in the family of Israel. An individual of that family would strive for forty nights and pray, his prayers received the answer. Only one man of that family strived for forty nights and prayed but his prayer did not receive any answer. When Jesus, son of Mary came, he complained to him about his case and asked him for prayer. The Imam said that Jesus then cleansed himself, said the prayer, prayed to Allah, the Most Majestic, the Most Holy, and Allah, the Most Majestic, the Most Holy, sent revelations to Jesus that said, 'O Jesus, My servant came to Me from a door that is other than the door from which one must come to Me. He prayed and there was doubt in his heart about you. Were he to pray to Me until his neck would be cut off (disintegrate) and his fingers turn into dust, I would not answer his prayer.' The Imam said, 'Jesus then turned to the man and asked, 'Do you ask your Lord for help while you have doubt in His prophet?' The man said, 'O Spirit of Allah and His word, it has been just as you said. Pray to Allah for me to remove doubt from me.' The Imam said that Jesus than prayed for him and Allah accepted his repentance and he became like all the other ones of that family.'"

Chapter 166 - Straying

H 2875, Ch. 166, h 1

Ali ibn Ibrahim has narrated from his father from ibn abu 'Umayr from 'Abd al-Rahman ibn al-Hajjaj from Hashim Sahib al-Barid who has said the following:

"Once Muhammad ibn Muslim, abu al-Khattab and I were together and abu Khattab asked, 'What do you say about a person who does not believe in this cause (Divine Authority of Ahl al-Bayt)?' I then said, 'Anyone who does not believe in this cause is an unbeliever.' Abu al-Khattab said, 'He is not an unbeliever until all evidence is established against him, when evidence and proof is established and he did not recognize then he becomes an unbeliever.' Muhammad ibn Muslim asked him, 'Glory belongs to Allah, what has he done that for not knowing and not denying becomes an unbeliever? He is not an unbeliever if he does not deny and reject.' I (the narrator) argued and then went in the presence of abu 'Abd Allah, *'Alayhi al-Salam*, and informed him of the discussion. The Imam said, 'You have come and they both are absent. All of you may come to me tonight by the middle Jamara (pillar of stones) in Mina.'

"That night we gathered together before him. Abu al-Khattab and Muhammad ibn Muslim also were there. The Imam picked up the pillow and held it against his chest and asked us, 'What do you say about your servants, women, and people of your house? Do they not say, 'No one deserves to be worshipped except Allah?' I said, 'Yes, they do say so.' The Imam asked, 'Do they not say, Muhammad is the Messenger of Allah?' I said, 'Yes, they do say so.' The Imam asked, 'Do they not perform the prayer, fast and perform Hajj?' I said, 'Yes, they do so.' The Imam asked, 'Do they know and recognize what you believe in?' I said, 'No, they do not do so.' The Imam asked, 'What are they then in your views?' I said, 'Anyone who does not know this cause (Divine Authority of Ahl al-Bayt) is an unbeliever.' The Imam asked, 'Glory belongs to Allah, have you considered the people in the streets and the water carriers?' I said, 'Yes, I have done so.' The Imam asked, 'Do they not perform the prayer, fast, and perform Hajj? Do they not testify that no one deserves to be worshipped except Allah and that Muhammad is the Messenger of Allah?' I said, 'Yes, they do so.' The Imam said, 'Do they know and recognize what you believe in?' I said, 'No, they do not do so.' The Imam said, 'What are they then in your view?' I said, 'Anyone who does not know and recognize this cause, is an unbeliever.' The Imam said, 'Glory belongs to Allah, have you seen the Ka'bah, the Tawaf (walking seven times around the Ka'bah), the people of Yemen and their clinging to the curtain of the Ka'bah?' I said, 'Yes, I see them.' The Imam said, 'Do they not testify that no one deserves to be worshipped except Allah? That Muhammad is the Messenger of Allah? Do they not perform the prayer, fast, and perform Hajj?' I said, 'Yes they do so.' The Imam said, 'Do they know and recognize what you believe in?' I said, 'No they do not do so.' The Imam said, 'What do you say about them?' I said, 'Anyone who does not know (believe in this cause) is an unbeliever.'

"The Imam said, 'Glory belongs to Allah, this is what al-Khawarij (the group that turned against Ali, *'Alayhi al-Salam*) say.' The Imam then said, 'If you like, I may tell you.' I said, 'No, do not tell us.' The Imam said, 'It is evil against you to say what you have not heard from us.' I (the narrator) then guessed that he is turning us upon the words of Muhammad ibn Muslim (namely, one is not an unbeliever until he denies and rejects the Divine Authority of Ahl al-Bayt).'"

H 2876, Ch. 166, h 2

Ali ibn Ibrahim has narrated from Muhammad ibn 'Isa from Yunus from a man from Zurara who has said the following:

"Once I asked abu Ja'far, *'Alayhi al-Salam*, 'What do you say about marriage of the people. I have reached this age as you can see and I am not married yet.' The Imam asked, 'What prevents you from becoming married?' I said, 'What prevents me is fear that it may not be lawful to marry from them. What is your instruction?' The Imam asked, 'How can you live and you are young, can you exercise patience?' I said, 'I can buy slaves.' The Imam asked, 'Here you are, how, can slaves be lawful?' I said, 'A slave is not like a free person. If something may make me suspicious I can sell her and stay away from her.' The Imam said, 'Tell me how you make her lawful.' I (the narrator) had no answers.

"I then asked him, 'What do you say if I married?' The Imam said, 'I do not mind if you marry.' I said, 'Consider your words, 'I do not mind if you did,' it has two aspects: I do not mind if you sinned without my command. What is your command? Should I do it by your command?' The Imam said, 'The Messenger of Allah had married. There are the cases of the wives of Noah and Lot as they were in wedlock with two virtuous servants (of Allah).' I said, 'The Messenger of Allah is not of the same position as I. She was under his control and acknowledged his judgment and his religion.' The Imam asked, 'What do you think of unfaithfulness in the words of Allah, the Most Majestic, the Most Holy, 'They both were unfaithful to the two of them.' (66:9) He does not mean thereby anything other than indecent acts. The Messenger of Allah had married so and so.'

"I then said, 'May Allah keep you well, what do you command me? Should I go and marry by your command?' The Imam said to me, 'Were you to marry, you should marry al-Bulaha' of women.' I asked, 'Who are al-Bulaha' of women?' The Imam said, 'Those who observe Hijab and are chaste.' I asked, 'How is she who is in the religion of Salim ibn abu Hafsah?' The Imam said, 'No.' I said, 'How is she that is in the religion of Rabi'ah al-Ra'i?' The Imam said, 'No, but marry those who are under the guardianship of their fathers, who are not unbelievers and do not know what you believe in.' I asked, 'Is it not the case that she is either a believer or an unbeliever?' The Imam said, 'One who fasts, performs prayer, is pious before Allah and does not know what is your cause.' I said, 'Allah, the Most Majestic, the Most Holy, has said, 'It is He Who has created you. Among you there are believer and unbelievers,' (64:2) no, by Allah, there is no one in the people who is not a believer or an unbeliever.'

"The narrator has said that abu Ja'far, *'Alayhi al-Salam*, then said, 'The words of Allah are truer than your words, O Zurara. Have you not considered the words of Allah, the Most Majestic, the Most Holy, ' . . . they have mixed virtuous deeds with sinful ones. Perhaps Allah will forgive them. Allah is All-forgiving and All-merciful.' (9:102) Why has Allah said, "perhaps"?' I said, 'They are either believing people or unbelievers.'

"The narrator has said that the Imam then asked, 'What do you think of the words of Allah, the Most Majestic, the Most Holy, 'As for the really weak and oppressed men, women, and children who were not able to find any means of obtaining their freedom or of having the right guidance, . . . ' (4:98) guidance to belief?' I said, 'They are either believers or unbelievers.' The Imam said, 'By Allah they are not believing people nor unbelievers.' Then the Imam turned to me and asked, 'What do you think of the people of 'A'raf?' I said, 'They are none other than either believers or unbelievers. If they enter paradise they are believers and if they go in the fire, they are unbelievers.' The Imam said, 'By Allah, they are not believers nor are they unbelievers. Were they believers they would have entered paradise like the other believing people. Were they unbelievers they would have gone in the fire like the other unbelievers. In fact, they are people whose good and bad deeds were equal. They had shortages of deeds. They will be as Allah, the Most Majestic, the Most Holy, has said.' I asked, 'Are they of the people of paradise or of the people of the fire?' The Imam said, 'Leave them alone as Allah has done.' I asked, 'Do you leave their affairs in postponement?' The Imam said, 'Yes, I do as Allah has done. If Allah wills He will send them to paradise through his favor, and if He wills He will drive them to the fire for their sins without being unjust to them.' I said, 'Will unbelievers go to paradise?' The Imam said, 'No.' I asked, 'Will anyone other than unbelievers go in the fire?'

"The narrator has said that the Imam said, 'No, except what Allah will wish. O Zurara, I say, 'What Allah wills and you do not say what Allah wills. When you will grow up you will turn around and your knots ease up (on your opponents).'"

Note: The above Hadith is very critical of the attitude of Zurara, according to commentators. In his defense, due to his prominent position in view of the scholars, it is said that either at that time he was very young or later he matured. He believed those who did not, would not and could not believe in the Divine Authority of 'A'immah could never go to paradise. Also, it is said that perhaps the whole Hadith due to weakness in the chain of narrators is not reliable. Zurara seems unable to find any room in his heart for those who did not respect Ahl al-Bayt, *'Alayhi al-Salam*, properly.

Chapter 167 - The Feeble-Minded People

H 2877, Ch. 167, h 1
Ali ibn Ibrahim has narrated from Muhammad ibn 'Isa from Yunus from certain individuals of his people from Zurara who has said the following:
"Once I asked abu Ja'far, *'Alayhi al-Salam*, about feeble-minded (weak) people. The Imam said, 'They are those who have no means to become unbelievers and cannot find guidance to belief. They are not able to establish belief or to become unbelievers. Of such people are children and those of men and women who are of children's mentality; the pen is held back from writing to hold them responsible.'"

H 2878, Ch. 167, h 2
Ali ibn Ibrahim has narrated from his father from ibn abu 'Umayr from Jamil from Zurara from abu Ja'far, *'Alayhi al-Salam*, who has said the following:

"The feeble-minded people are those who are not able to find the means, the guidance or the way. The Imam said, 'They are not able to find the means to belief and they do not disbelieve, like children and those who are of children's mental condition, male and female.'"

H 2879, Ch. 167, h 3

A number of our people have narrated from Sahl ibn Ziyad from ibn Mahbub from ibn Ri'ab from Zurara who has said the following:

"Once I asked abu Ja'far, *'Alayhi al-Salam*, about the feeble-minded people. The Imam said, 'They are those who are not able to defend themselves against disbelief or find the means to the way in the direction of belief. They are not able to have belief and do not disbelieve.' The Imam said, 'Children and those of men and women who are of children's mental condition are among such people.'"

H 2880, Ch. 167, h 4

Muhammad ibn Yahya has narrated from Ahmad ibn Muhammad ibn 'Isa from Ali ibn al-Hakam from 'Abd Allah ibn Jundab from Sufyan ibn al-Samt al-Bajilli who has said the following:

"Once I said to abu 'Abd Allah, *'Alayhi al-Salam*, 'What do you say about the feeble-minded people?' The Imam asked me in a manner similar to one frightened, 'Have you left anyone to be considered feeble? By Allah, girls behind the curtains have heard about your cause (Divine Authority of Ahl al-Bayt) and water carriers in the street of Madina speak about it.'"

H 2881, Ch. 167, h 5

It is narrated from him (narrator of the Hadith above) from Ahmad ibn Muhammad from al-Husayn ibn Sa'id from Fudalah ibn Ayyub from 'Umar ibn Aban who has said the following:

"Once I asked abu 'Abd Allah, *'Alayhi al-Salam*, about the feeble-minded people. The Imam said, 'They are the people under guardianship.' I then asked, 'What kind of guardianship is it?' The Imam said, 'It is not a religious guardianship. It is guardianship in marriages, inheritance and social affairs. They are neither believers nor unbelievers. There are those among them for whom one may hope in the command of Allah, the Most Majestic, the Most Holy.'"

H 2882, Ch. 167, h 6

Al-Husayn ibn Muhammad has narrated from Mu'alla ibn Muhammad from al-Washsha' from Muthanna from Isma'il al-Ju'fi who has said the following:

"Once I asked abu Ja'far, *'Alayhi al-Salam*, about how much religious knowledge people must have. The Imam said, 'Religion is vast but the Khawarij (those who turned against Amir al-Mu'minin, Ali ibn abu Talib, *'Alayhi al-Salam*) group has narrowed it down upon themselves due to their ignorance.' I asked, 'May Allah keep my soul in service for your cause, can I tell you what kind of religion I believe in?' The Imam said, 'Yes, you may do so.' I said, 'I testify that no one deserves to be worshipped except Allah and I testify that Muhammad is His servant and messenger. I affirm to whatever he has brought from Allah. I love you (Ahl al-Bayt) and disavow your enemies and those who have suppressed you, kept (unjust) control over you and who have usurped your rights.' The Imam said, 'You are not ignorant of anything. This, by Allah is what we follow.' I asked, 'Is one who does not know this (cause) safe?' The Imam said, 'No, except the feeble-minded people.' I asked, 'Who are they?' The Imam said, 'Your women and children.' Then he said, 'Consider 'Umm 'Ayman. I testify that she is of the people of paradise, but she did not know what you believe.'"

H 2883, Ch. 167, h 7

Ali ibn Ibrahim has narrated from Muhammad ibn 'Isa from Yunus from ibn Muskan from abu Basir who has said the following:

"Abu 'Abd Allah, *'Alayhi al-Salam*, has said, 'Whoever knows the differences among people is not a feeble-minded person.'"

H 2884, Ch. 167, h 8

Muhammad ibn Yahya has narrated from Ahmad ibn Muhammad ibn 'Isa from ibn Mahbub from Jamil ibn Darraj who has said the following:

"Once I asked abu 'Abd Allah, *'Alayhi al-Salam*, 'I may have mentioned those feeble-minded people and I say that those people and we are in homes of paradise.' Abu 'Abd Allah, *'Alayhi al-Salam*, said, 'Allah will never do that to you.'"

H 2885, Ch. 167, h 9

It is narrated from him (narrator of the Hadith above) from Ali ibn al-Hassan al-Taymi from his two brothers, Muhammad and Ahmad sons of al-Hassan from Ali ibn Ya'qub from Marwan ibn Muslim from Ayyub ibn al-Hurr who has said the following:

"Once a man said to abu 'Abd Allah, *'Alayhi al-Salam*, while we were present, 'May Allah keep my soul in service for your cause, we are afraid that because of our sins we will be treated as feeble-minded people.' The narrator has said that the Imam said, 'No, by Allah, Allah will never do that to you.'"

Ali ibn Ibrahim has narrated from his father from ibn abu 'Umayr from a man from abu 'Abd Allah, *'Alayhi al-Salam*, a similar Hadith.

H 2886, Ch. 167, h 10

Ali ibn Ibrahim has narrated from his father from ibn abu 'Umayr from abu al-Maghra' from abu Basir from abu 'Abd Allah, *'Alayhi al-Salam*, who has said the following:

"Whoever knows the differences among people is not a feeble-minded person."

H 2887, Ch. 167, h 11

A number of our people have narrated from Sahl ibn Ziyad from Isma'il ibn Mehran from Muhammad ibn Mansur al-Khuza'i from Ali ibn Suwayd who has said the following:

"Once I asked abu al-Hassan Musa, *'Alayhi al-Salam*, about the feeble-minded people and he wrote to me, 'A feeble-minded is one to whom evidence and proof is not (or cannot be) presented and he does not know the differences among people. If he knows the differences among people he is not an enfeeble person.'"

H 2888, Ch. 167, h 12

Certain individuals of our people have narrated from Ali ibn al-Hassan from Ali ibn Habib al-Khath'ami from abu Sarah Imam of the Mosque of Banu Hilal from abu 'Abd Allah, *'Alayhi al-Salam*, who has said the following:

"Today no one is a feeble-minded person. Men have informed men and women have informed women."

Chapter 168 - People in Postponement for the Command of Allah

H 2889, Ch. 168, h 1

Muhammad ibn Yahya has narrated from Ahmad ibn Muhammad from Ali ibn al-Hakam from Musa ibn Bakr from Zurara from abu Ja'far, *'Alayhi al-Salam*, who has said the following:

"About the words of Allah, the Most Majestic, the Most Holy, '. . . there are others who have no good deeds for which they may receive any reward or sins for which they may be punished. Their fate will be in the hands of Allah. Allah is All-knowing and All-wise,' (9:106) the Imam said, 'Certain people were pagans. They murdered people like Hamza and Ja'far and similar persons from the believers. Then they accepted Islam and Allah only and gave up paganism, but did not know belief with their heart so they could be among the believers to deserve paradise. They were not in denial and a rejecting attitude as unbelievers to be subjected to fire (of hell). They are in that condition as such that it will be up to Allah to punish or accept their repentance.'"

H 2890, Ch. 168, h 2

A number of our people have narrated from Sahl ibn Ziyad from Ali ibn Hassan from Musa ibn Bakr al-Wasiti from a man who has said the following:

"Abu Ja'far, *'Alayhi al-Salam*, has said, 'Al-Murjawn were a pagan people. They murdered people like Hamza and Ja'far and similar persons from the believers. Then they accepted Islam. They accepted Allah only. They gave up paganism, but did not believe to be among believing people. They did not believe to deserve paradise. They were not in denial and a rejecting attitude to be subjected to fire (of hell). They are in that condition as such that it will be up to Allah to punish or accept their repentance.'"

Chapter 169 - People of al-'A'raf

H 2891, Ch. 169, h 1

Muhammad ibn Yahya has narrated from Ahmad ibn Muhammad from ibn Faddal from ibn Bukayr and Ali ibn Ibrahim from Muhammad ibn 'Isa from Yunus from a man all from Zurara who has said the following:

"Once, abu Ja'far, *'Alayhi al-Salam*, asked me, 'What do you say about the people of al-'A'raf?' I said, 'They are either believing people or unbelievers. If they will enter paradise they will be believing people, and if they go in fire they will be unbelievers.' The Imam then said, 'By Allah, they are not believing people nor are they unbelievers. Had they been of the believers they would have entered paradise like the believers. Were they unbelievers they would have gone in fire like the unbelievers. They, however, are a people whose good and bad deeds are equal. Their deeds fall short and they are as Allah, the Most Majestic, the Most Holy, has said they are.' I asked, 'Are they among the people of paradise or of the people of fire?' The Imam said, 'Leave them as Allah has done.' I said, 'Do you leave them in postponement?' The Imam said, 'Yes, just as Allah has done. If He will wish, He will send them in paradise through His favor, and if He will wish He will drive them to fire for their sins; He will not be doing injustice to them.' I asked, 'Will unbelievers enter paradise?' The Imam said, 'No.' I said, 'Will anyone besides unbelievers go to fire?' The Imam said, 'No, unless Allah will wish. O Zurara, I say, 'As Allah wills and you do not say, 'As Allah wills.' When you will grow up you will turn back and your knots ease up (on your opponent).'"

H 2892, Ch. 169, h 2
A number of our people have narrated from Sahl ibn Ziyad from Ali ibn Hassan from Musa ibn Bakr from a man who has said the following:

"Once abu Ja'far, *'Alayhi al-Salam*, said, 'Those who have mixed good deeds with bad deeds' are a believing people. They create in their belief such things, due to sins, that believing people censure and dislike. They are as such that perhaps Allah may accept their repentance.'"

Chapter 170 - Kinds of People Opposed to Shi'a, al-Qadriah, al-Khawarij, al-Murji'ah and People of Towns (Names of People of Certain Beliefs)

H 2893, Ch. 170, h 1
Muhammad ibn Yahya has narrated from Ahmad ibn Muhammad from Marwak ibn 'Ubayd from a man from abu 'Abd Allah, *'Alayhi al-Salam*, who has said the following:

"Abu 'Abd Allah, *'Alayhi al-Salam*, once said, 'May Allah condemn al-Qadriah, may Allah condemn al-Khawarij, may Allah condemn al-Murji'a and may Allah condemn al-Murji'a.' I asked, 'Why did you condemn these once and those twice?' The Imam said, 'These say, 'Our assassins are believers, thus our blood will stain their clothes up to the Day of Judgment. Allah has quoted a people in His book: '. . . Allah has commanded us not to believe any messenger unless he offers a burnt offering,' and (Muhammad) say, 'Messengers came to you before me with certain miracles and with that which you had asked for (burnt offering). Why, then, did you slay them if you were true in your claim?' (3:183) The Imam said, 'Between the people saying such things and the killers there was a period of five hundred years. Allah held them (the former) responsible for murder due to their condoning such an act.'"

H 2894, Ch. 170, h 2
Ali ibn Ibrahim has narrated from ibn abu 'Umayr from Muhammad ibn Hakim and Hammad ibn 'Uthman from abu Masruq who has said the following:

"Once abu 'Abd Allah, *'Alayhi al-Salam*, asked me about the people of Basra in respect to who they are. I said, 'They are Murji'a, Qadriah and Harawriah.' The Imam said, 'May Allah condemn such pagan nations who do not worship Allah on good grounds.'"

H 2895, Ch. 170, h 3
Muhammad ibn Yahya has narrated from Ahmad ibn Muhammad from Ali ibn al-Hakam from Mansur ibn Yunus from Sulayman ibn Khalid from abu 'Abd Allah, *'Alayhi al-Salam*, who has said the following:

"People of Damascus are more evil than the people of Rome, who are more evil than the people of Madina, who are more evil than the people of Makka, who disbelieve Allah openly."

Note: This Hadith, according to al-Majlisi, perhaps dates from the period of the rule of Amawides, when there were many hypocrites in those cities.

H 2896, Ch. 170, h 4

A number of our people have narrated from Ahmad ibn Muhammad ibn Khalid from 'Uthman ibn 'Isa from Sama'a from abu Basir from one of the two Imams, *'Alayhi al-Salam*, who has said the following:

"People of Makka disbelieve Allah openly and people of Madina are seventy times filthier than those of Makka."

H 2897, Ch. 170, h 5

Muhammad ibn Yahya has narrated from Ahmad ibn Muhammad ibn 'Isa from al-Husayn ibn Sa'id from Fadalah ibn Ayyub from Sayf ibn 'Amirah from abu Bakr al-Hadrami who has said the following:

"Once I asked abu 'Abd Allah, *'Alayhi al-Salam*, 'Are people of Damascus more evil than the people of Rome?' The Imam said, 'People of Rome disbelieved, but are not hostile to us. The people of Damascus have disbelieved and are hostile to us.'"

H 2898, Ch. 170, h 6

It is narrated from him (narrator of the Hadith above) from Muhammad ibn al-Husayn from al-Nadr ibn Shu'ayb from Aban ibn 'Uthman from al-Fudayl ibn Yasar from abu 'Abd Allah, *'Alayhi al-Salam*, who has said the following:

"Do not sit with them -al-Murji'a. May Allah condemn them! Allah has condemned their pagan nations which do not worship Allah on any good grounds."

Chapter 171 - People with Inclined Hearts

H 2899, Ch. 171, h 1

Muhammad ibn Yahya has narrated from Ahmad ibn Muhammad from Ali ibn al-Hakam from Musa ibn Bakr and Ali ibn Ibrahim from Muhammad ibn 'Isa from Yunus from a man all from Zurara from abu Ja'far, *'Alayhi al-Salam*, who has said the following:

"Al-Mu'allafah Qulubuhum (people with inclined hearts to Islam) were a people who had accepted Allah only and had given up the worship of things besides Allah. However, true knowledge and belief that Muhammad is the Messenger of Allah had not entered their hearts. The Messenger of Allah showed them kindness, provided them knowledge, so they might know the truth and he would teach them."

H 2900, Ch. 171, h 2

Ali ibn Ibrahim has narrated from his father from ibn abu 'Umayr from 'Umar ibn 'Udhaynah from Zurara who has said the following:

"Once I asked abu Ja'far, *'Alayhi al-Salam*, about the words of Allah, the Most Majestic, the Most Holy, 'Al-Mu'allafah Qulubuhum (the people with inclined hearts)' (9:60) the Imam said, 'They were a people who accepted Allah, the Most Majestic, the Most Holy, only, stopped worshipping things that were worshipped besides Allah, they had testified that no one deserves to be worshipped except Allah and that Muhammad is the Messenger of Allah and in that condition they had doubts about certain issue(s) that Muhammad, *'Alayhi al-Salam*, had brought. Allah, the Most Majestic, the Most Holy, commanded His Holy Prophet to attract them with financial means and gifts so that their Islam may improve and they remain steadfast in their religion which they had just accepted and professed.'

"On the day of Hunayn (a battle field) the Messenger of Allah had a meeting with leaders of Arabs from Quraysh, and others from the tribe of Mudar. Among such people were abu Sufyan ibn Harb, 'Uyaynah ibn Hasin al-Farazi and other such people. The Ansar, people of Madina, became angry and gathered around Sa'd ibn 'Ubadah. He went with them to see the Messenger of Allah at al-Ja'ranah. He asked, 'O Messenger of Allah, can I speak?' He said, 'Yes, you may speak.' He said, 'If the case of these goods that you have distributed among your tribesmen is something that has come from Allah, we agree, and if it is something else, we do not agree.' Zurara has said, 'I heard abu Ja'far saying, "The Messenger of Allah asked, 'O people of Ansar, are all of you of the opinion of your master Sa'd?'" They said, 'Our master is Allah and the Messenger of Allah.' Then they said at the third time, 'We are of the same opinion and words.' Zurara has said, 'I heard abu Ja'far, 'Alayhi al-Salam, saying, "For this reason Allah decreased the light of their belief and assigned a share for people of inclined hearts in the Holy Quran."'"

H 2901, Ch. 171, h 3
Ali has narrated from Muhammad ibn 'Isa from Yunus from a man from Zurara from abu Ja'far, 'Alayhi al-Salam, who has said the following:
"Abu Ja'far, 'Alayhi al-Salam, has said, 'Al-Mu'allafah Qulubuhum (People of inclined hearts) have never been more numerous than they are today.'"

H 2902, Ch. 171, h 4
Ali has narrated from his father from ibn abu 'Umayr from Ibrahim ibn 'Abd al-Hamid from Ishaq ibn Ghalib who has said the following:
"Abu 'Abd Allah, 'Alayhi al-Salam, once asked, 'O Ishaq, how many people can you find to whom this verse, ' . . . They are pleased when you give them something from it, but if they receive nothing, they become angry with you,' (9:58) applies? The Imam then said, 'They are more than two thirds of the people.'"

H 2903, Ch. 171, h 5
A number of our people have narrated from Sahl ibn Ziyad from Ali ibn Hassan from Musa ibn Bakr from a man who has said the following:
"Abu Ja'far, 'Alayhi al-Salam, has said, 'People of inclined hearts had never been as many as they are today. They were a people who accepted Allah only, had come out of paganism but the true knowledge about Muhammad, the Messenger of Allah had not entered their hearts as well as certain issues of what he had brought from Allah. The Messenger of Allah would meet them with kindness and after the Messenger of Allah the believers would meet them with kindness so they might receive true knowledge.'"

Chapter 172 - Hypocrites, Straying and Satan Addressed by the Call to Islam

H 2904, Ch. 172, h 1

Ali ibn Ibrahim has narrated from his father from ibn abu 'Umayr from Jamil who has said the following:

"Al-Tayyar would say to me that Satan is not among the angels. Only angels were commanded to bow down in prostration before Adam and Satan said, 'I will not bow down in prostration.' Why should Satan be called disobedient for not bowing down in prostration when he is not among the angels? The narrator has said that he and I went in the presence of abu 'Abd Allah, *'Alayhi al-Salam*. He, by Allah, presented his question very nicely saying, 'May Allah keep my soul in service for your cause, please consider Allah's, the Most Majestic, the Most Holy, calling the believers, "O believing people," are hypocrites also addressed along with the believers?' The Imam said, 'Yes, also the straying people and all who had affirmed the public call to Islam. Satan was included in the public call with them (the angles).'"

Chapter 173 (a) - About the Words of Allah, the Most High, Certain People Worship Allah with Deviance

H 2905, Ch. 173a, h 1

Ali ibn Ibrahim has narrated from his father from ibn abu 'Umayr from 'Umar ibn 'Udhaynah from al-Fudayl and Zurara who has said the following:

"Once I (Zurara) asked abu Ja'far, *'Alayhi al-Salam*, about the words of Allah, the Most Majestic, the Most Holy, 'Certain people worship Allah to achieve worldly gains. They are confident when they are prosperous, but when they face hardships they turn away from (worship). They are lost in this life and will be lost in the life to come. Such loss is indeed destructive.' (22:11)

"The Imam said, 'These were people who worshipped Allah and gave up the worship of things worshipped besides Allah. They, however, had doubt in Muhammad, *'Alayhi al-Salam*, and what he had brought from Allah. They spoke of Islam and testified that no one deserves to be worshipped except Allah, that Muhammad is the Messenger of Allah and affirmed the Holy Quran. Despite this they would doubt Muhammad, *'Alayhi al-Salam*, and what he had brought from Allah. They did not have doubt in Allah, the Most Majestic, the Most Holy. 'Certain people worship Allah with deviation,' (22:11) refers to their doubt in Muhammad, *'Alayhi al-Salam*, and what he had brought from Allah. 'When they are prosperous,' refers to well being in their health, properties and children. 'He is confident', he is happy, 'When afflictions befall him,' refers to misfortune in his body or property that he considers as an unfortunate omen and dislikes keeping up with his testimony about the truthfulness of the Holy Prophet; thus, he returns to hesitation and doubt. He becomes hostile toward Allah and the Messenger of Allah, rejects the Holy Prophet and whatever he has brought from Allah.'"

H 2906, Ch. 173a, h 2

Muhammad ibn Yahya has narrated from Ahmad ibn Muhammad from Ali ibn al-Hakam from Musa ibn Bakr from Zurara who has said the following:

"Once I asked abu Ja'far, *'Alayhi al-Salam*, about the words of Allah, the Most Majestic, the Most Holy, 'Certain people worship Allah for worldly gains.' (22:11) The Imam said, 'They were a people who accepted Allah only, gave up the worship of things worshipped besides Allah; thus they came out of paganism and did not know that Muhammad is the Messenger of Allah. Therefore they worshipped Allah with doubts in Muhammad and what he had brought from Allah. They would come to the Messenger of Allah and say (to each other), 'We will see if our properties increase, we and our children enjoy good health then we will believe that he is the Messenger of Allah; otherwise, we will think.'

"Allah, the Most Majestic, the Most Holy, has said, 'When they receive good things they enjoy confidence in it, . . .' [worldly well being], ' . . . when they suffer hardships . . .' [misfortune in his life and property], ' . . . he turns backwards,' [in doubt to paganism, thus] '. . . they suffer loses in this world and in the next life, an obvious loss. They call for help from things other than Allah that do not harm or benefit them.' (22:12) The Imam said, 'He turns to paganism and calls for help from things other than Allah and worships things besides Allah. There are those of them who learn true knowledge and belief enters their heart. They become believers. They acknowledge the truth and move from their doubtful position to belief. There are those of them who remain in doubt and still others of them return to paganism.'"

Ali ibn Ibrahim has narrated from his father from Muhammad ibn 'Isa from Yunus from a man from Zurara a similar Hadith.

Chapter 173 (b) - The Minimum of What Establishes Belief, Disbelief or Straying

H 2907, Ch. 173b, h 1

Ali ibn Ibrahim has narrated from his father from Hammad ibn 'Isa from Ibrahim ibn 'Umar al-Yamani from ibn 'Udhaynah from Aban ibn 'Uthman ibn abu 'Ayyash from Sulaym ibn Qays who has said the following:

"Once a man came to Amir al-Mu'minin, Ali ibn abu Talib, *'Alayhi al-Salam*, and asked him, 'What is the least of that with which a servant (of Allah) becomes a believer, or an unbeliever or a straying person?' I heard the Imam say, 'You asked the question, now try to understand the answer. The least of that with which one may be considered a believer is that Allah, the Most Blessed, the Most High, makes him know His Ownself, then he professes to obey Him. He (Allah) makes him know His Holy Prophet, then he professes to obey him and He makes him know His Imam, His Authority on His earth and His witness over His creatures, then he professes to obey him.'

"I then asked, 'O Amir al-Mu'minin, does this hold true even if one is ignorant of all other things besides what you just mentioned?' The Imam said, 'Yes, if he when commanded obeys and when prohibited upholds it. The least of that with which a servant (of Allah) becomes an unbeliever is that when upon a mere guess one says that this is what Allah has commanded and this is what Allah has prohibited. Then he assigns it to be his religion upon which he bases his system of guardianship (religious authority). He guesses that he obeys the one who has commanded him to do it and, in fact, he worships Satan only.'

"The least of that with which a servant (of Allah) is considered straying is when he does not know the Authority of Allah, the Most Blessed, the Most High, His witness over His servants. The Authority about whom Allah, the Most Majestic, the Most Holy, has commanded His servants to obey and has made it obligatory to love him as one's Divine Guardian.' I then said, 'O Amir al-Mu'minin, describe them (the people who possess Divine Authority) for me.' The Imam said, 'They are those whom Allah, the Most Majestic, the Most Holy, has mentioned along with His Ownself and His Holy Prophet saying, 'Believers, obey Allah, His Messenger, and your leaders (people who possess Divine Authority). . . .' (4:59) I said, 'O Amir al-Mu'minin, May Allah keep my soul in service for your cause, explain it to me.' The Imam said, 'They (people who possess Divine Authority) are those about whom the Messenger of Allah in his last sermon on the day that Allah, the Most Majestic, the Most Holy, took him (from this world) said, 'I leave among you behind me two matters. If you will hold firmly to these two you will never stray: the book of Allah and my descendents, my family. The Most Subtle and Most Expert, (Allah) has informed me that these two will never separate from each other until they will arrive before me at the pond in paradise like this - he joined his index finger and thumb - not like this - he joined his middle finger and thumb so that one may proceed before the other. You must hold firmly to these two, you will not slip, or stray and do not go before them; you will stray.'"

Chapter 174

H 2908, Ch. 174, h 1

Ali ibn Ibrahim has narrated from his father from al-Qasim ibn Muhammad from al-Minqari from Sufyan ibn 'Uyayna from abu 'Abd Allah, *'Alayhi al-Salam*, who has said the following:

"The Amawides provided people with studies of Islamic belief in generalized manner but did not allow people to study paganism, so that when they might impose it (paganism and evil deed) upon people they (people) would not consider it evil; (the Amawides preached predestination to cover up their own evil deeds)."

Chapter 175 - Establishment of Belief and its Abolishment by Allah

H 2909, Ch. 175, h 1

Muhammad ibn Yahya has narrated from Ahmad ibn Muhammad ibn 'Isa from al-Hassan ibn Mahbub from Husayn ibn Nu'aym al-Sahhaf who has said the following:

"Once I asked abu 'Abd Allah, *'Alayhi al-Salam*, 'Why is it that a man is a believer before Allah and belief is established for him, then Allah transfers him from belief to disbelief?' The narrator has said that the Imam said, 'Allah, the Most Majestic, the Most Holy, is just. He has called the servants to believe in

Him, not to disbelief and does not call anyone to disbelieve Him. Whoever believes in Allah and belief is then established for him before Allah, Allah, the Most Majestic, the Most Holy, does not transfer him thereafter from belief to disbelief.' I said, 'If a man is an unbeliever whose disbelief is established before Allah, will He transfer him from disbelief to belief?' The Imam said, 'Allah, the Most Majestic, the Most Holy, has created people - all of them - with the nature upon which He has fashioned them. They do not know belief in a way of life and a system of laws (is necessary) or that disbelief is denial (of something). Allah sent the Messengers who called people to believe in Him. Certain people are those whom Allah has guided (to the right path) and also among them are those whom He has not guided (to the right path).'"

Chapter 176 - The Transients

H 2910, Ch. 176, h 1
Muhammad ibn Yahya has narrated from Ahmad ibn Muhammad ibn 'Isa from Ali ibn al-Hakam from abu Ayyub from Muhammad ibn Muslim who has said the following:

"I heard either of the two Imams, *'Alayhi al-Salam*, saying, 'Allah, the Most Majestic, the Most Holy, has created a creature for belief and there is no transition in it. He has created a creature for disbelief and there is no transition in it. He has created a creature in between. He has deposited belief in certain individuals among them. If He wills to complete it for them He does so for them, and if He wishes to remove it from them He does so and so and so was of transient (belief) among them.'" (So and so is a reference to Muhammad ibn Miqlas al-Asadi al-Kufi)

H 2911, Ch. 176, h 2
Muhammad ibn Yahya has narrated from Ahmad ibn Muhammad from al-Husayn ibn Sa'id from Fadalah ibn Ayyub and al-Qasim ibn Muhammad al-Jawhari from Kulayb ibn Mu'awiyah al-Asadi from abu 'Abd Allah, *'Alayhi al-Salam*, who has said the following:

"Abu 'Abd Allah, *'Alayhi al-Salam*, has said, 'A servant (of Allah) may live in the morning as a believer and in the evening as an unbeliever. One may live in the morning as an unbeliever and in the evening as a believer. A people borrow belief then it is removed from them and they are called people with transient (belief).' Then the Imam said, 'So and so is among them (the last group).'"

H 2912, Ch. 176, h 3
Ali ibn Ibrahim has narrated from his father from ibn abu 'Umayr from Hafs ibn al-Bakhtari and others from 'Isa Shalqan who has said the following:

"Once I was sitting when abu al-Hassan Musa, *'Alayhi al-Salam*, passed by and with him was a goat. I (the narrator) asked him, 'O young man, do you know what your father does? He commands us to do something and then he prohibits us to do the same thing. He commanded us to be friends with abu al-Khattab and then he commanded us to condemn and disown him.' Abu al-Hassan, *'Alayhi al-Salam*, said, and he was only a young boy, 'Allah has created a creature for belief that does not vanish. He has created a creature for disbelief that does not vanish. He has created a creature in between and has deposited belief in them and they are called people with transient belief. When He wills He removes belief from them and abu al-Khattab was one in whom belief was deposited temporarily.' I (the narrator) then went in the presence of abu 'Abd Allah, *'Alayhi al-Salam*, and informed him of what I had said to abu al-Hassan and what abu al-Hassan, *'Alayhi al-Salam*, had said to me. Abu 'Abd Allah, *'Alayhi al-Salam*, then said, 'He is one of the fountains from prophet-hood.'"

H 2913, Ch. 176, h 4

Ali ibn Ibrahim has narrated from his father from Isma'il ibn Marrar from Yunus from certain individuals of our people from abu al-Hassan, *'Alayhi al-Salam*, who has said the following:

"Allah has created the prophets with prophet-hood, thus, they are nothing else but prophets. He has created the believers upon belief and they are nothing else but believers. He has deposited belief in a people. If He wills He completes it in them and if He wishes He removes it from them.' The Imam said, 'About these people it is said, ". . . the permanent and transient. . . ." (6:98) The Imam said to me, 'The belief of so and so was temporary. When he made false statements against us his belief was removed.'"

H 2914, Ch. 176, h 5

Muhammad ibn Yahya has narrated from Ahmad ibn Muhammad ibn 'Isa from al-Husayn ibn Sa'id from al-Qasim ibn Habib from Ishaq ibn 'Ammar from abu 'Abd Allah, *'Alayhi al-Salam*, who has said the following:

"Allah has formed the prophets upon their prophet-hood, thus they never, turn away therefrom. He has formed the successors of the prophets upon their successor-ship and they never turn away therefrom. He has formed certain believers upon belief and they never turn away therefrom. Belief in certain ones among them is deposited and if he prays persistently he dies upon belief."

Chapter 177 - Signs of Transience

H 2915, Ch. 177, h 1

It is narrated from him (narrator of the Hadith above) from Ahmad ibn Muhammad from Muhammad ibn Sinan from al-Mufaddal al-Ju'fi who has said the following:

"Abu 'Abd Allah, *'Alayhi al-Salam*, has said, 'Sorrow, regret and lamentation strikes one who does not benefit from what he sees and does not know upon what ground is he standing; is it beneficial for him or harmful?' I (the narrator) then asked, 'May Allah keep my soul in service for your cause, by what means are the ones who have found salvation recognized?' The Imam said, 'One whose acts agree with his words, testimony for his salvation holds true and one whose deeds do not agree with his words, his belief is transient.'"

Chapter 178 - Confusion of the Heart

H 2916, Ch. 178, h 1

Ali ibn Ibrahim has narrated from his father from ibn abu 'Umayr from Ja'far ibn 'Uthman from Sama'a from abu Basir and others who has said the following:

"Abu 'Abd Allah, *'Alayhi al-Salam*, has said, 'The heart in certain hours of the night and day has no disbelief or belief in it and it is like an old rug.' The narrator has said that the Imam then asked, 'Do you not find that in yourself? Then there

is a dot from Allah in the heart of the kind that He wills in the form of disbelief
or belief.'"

A number of our people have narrated from Sahl ibn Ziyad from Muhammad ibn
al-Husayn from Muhammad ibn abu 'Umayr a similar Hadith.

H 2917, Ch. 178, h 2
Muhammad ibn Yahya has narrated from Ahmad ibn Muhammad ibn 'Isa from al-'Abbas ibn Ma'ruf
from Hammad ibn 'Isa from al-Husayn ibn al-Mukhtar from abu Basir who has said the following:
"I heard abu Ja'far, *'Alayhi al-Salam*, saying, 'There is the heart in which there is
no belief or disbelief, like a chunk of flesh. Does any one of you feel it is as such
sometimes?'"

H 2918, Ch. 178, h 3
Muhammad ibn Yahya has narrated from al-'Amraki ibn Ali from Ali ibn Ja'far from abu al-Hassan
Musa, *'Alayhi al-Salam*, who has said the following:
"Allah has created the hearts of the believers, in which belief is wrapped up and
is unknown. When He wills to light up what is in it He sprinkles it with wisdom
and plants knowledge therein. The farmer and guardian thereof is the Lord, the
Cherisher of the worlds."

H 2919, Ch. 178, h 4
Muhammad ibn Yahya has narrated from Ahmad ibn Muhammad from Muhammad ibn Sinan from
al-Husayn ibn al-Mukhtar from abu Basir from abu 'Abd Allah, *'Alayhi al-Salam*, who has said the
following:
"The heart vibrates between the chest and the throat until it forms belief, when it
does so it rests as is in the words of Allah, the Most Majestic, the Most Holy,
'Whoever believes in Allah his heart calms down.'" (64:11)

H 2920, Ch. 178, h 5
A number of our people have narrated from Ahmad ibn Muhammad ibn Khalid from ibn Faddal from
abu Jamilah from Muhammad al-Halabi from abu 'Abd Allah, *'Alayhi al-Salam*, who has said the
following:
"The heart beats noisily inside in search of the truth. If it finds the truth it calms
down and rests.' The Imam then recited this verse: 'Allah will open the hearts of
whomever He wants to guide to Islam, but He will tighten the chest of one whom
He has led astray, as though he were climbing high up into the sky. Thus, God
places wickedness on those who do not accept the faith. (6:125)'"

H 2921, Ch. 178, h 6
Ali ibn Ibrahim has narrated from Muhammad ibn 'Isa from Yunus from abu al-Maghra' from abu
Basir who has said the following:
"I heard abu 'Abd Allah, *'Alayhi al-Salam*, saying, 'The heart in (certain) hours
of the night and day has no belief or disbelief in it. Do you not find that in
yourself? Thereafter, a dot from Allah comes in the heart of His servant in the
form that He wills. If He wills, it is with belief and if He wills, it is in disbelief.'"

H 2922, Ch. 178, h 7

A number of our people have narrated from Sahl ibn Ziyad from Muhammad ibn al-Hassan ibn Shammun from 'Abd Allah ibn 'Abd al-Rahman from 'Abd Allah ibn al-Qasim from Yunus ibn Zabyan from abu 'Abd Allah, *'Alayhi al-Salam*, who has said the following:

"Allah has created the hearts of the believers wrapped up over belief. When He wills to light it up He opens it with wisdom and plants it with knowledge. The farmer and guardian thereof is the Lord of the worlds."

Chapter 179 - About the Darkness of the Heart of the Hypocrite Even Though He Has a Tongue and the Light of the Heart of the Believer Even Though His Tongue May Fall Short

H 2923, Ch. 179, h 1

Muhammad ibn Yahya has narrated from Ahmad ibn Muhammad from Ali ibn Faddal from Ali ibn 'Uqbah from 'Amr from abu 'Abd Allah who has said the following:

"One day the Imam said to us, 'You may find a man who does not make any mistakes of the size of letter 'L' or 'W' and he is an exuberant speaker while his heart is darker than the darkest night. You may also find a man who is not able to express what is in his heart with his tongue while his heart shines like a lantern.'"

H 2924, Ch. 179, h 2

A number of our people have narrated from Ahmad ibn Muhammad ibn Khalid from his father from Harun ibn al-Jahm from al-Mufaddal from Sa'd from abu Ja'far, *'Alayhi al-Salam*, who has said the following:

"There are four kinds of hearts: the heart in which there is hypocrisy and belief, the heart that is upside down, the heart that is stamped and the heart that is Azhar and is free. I then asked, 'What is 'Azhar'? The Imam said, 'In it (the heart) there is something like a lamp. The stamped heart is the heart of hypocrite. Azhar is the heart of the believer who upon receiving favors, thanks, and in suffering exercises patience. The upside down heart is the heart of the pagans.' The Imam then read this verse: 'Can one who walks with his head hanging down be better guided than one who walks with his head upright?' (67:22) The heart with belief and hypocrisy therein was the heart of a people in Ta'if. If death seized one of them upon his hypocrisy, he perished, and if it approached him upon belief he gained salvation.'"

H 2925, Ch. 179, h 3

A number of our people have narrated from Sahl ibn Ziyad from ibn Mahbub from abu Hamza al-Thumali from abu Ja'far, *'Alayhi al-Salam*, who has said the following:

"Hearts are of three kinds: an upside down heart that holds nothing good is the heart of an unbeliever. The heart in which there is a black dot, thus, good and evil duel therein. Whichever dominates the heart defeats the other. There is the open heart. In it lamps shine and its light does not extinguish until the Day of Judgment and that is the heart of a believer.'"

Chapter 180 - The Changing Conditions of the Heart

H 2926, Ch. 180, h 1

Ali ibn Ibrahim has narrated from his father and a number of our people have narrated from Sahl ibn Ziyad and Muhammad ibn Yahya from Ahmad ibn Muhammad all from ibn Mahbub from Muhammad ibn al-Nu'man al-'Ahwal from Sallam ibn al-Mustanir who has said the following:

"Once I was in the presence of abu Ja'far, *'Alayhi al-Salam*, when Humran ibn 'A'yan came in and asked him a few things. When Humran wanted to stand up and leave he said to abu Ja'far, *'Alayhi al-Salam*, 'I like to tell you, may Allah grant you long life for us so we benefit from you more, whenever we come to you and then leave our hearts feel affectionate, we forget ourselves in the world, and what is in the hands of people of belongings seem to us insignificant. When we leave you and meet others and business people we begin to love the world.' Abu Ja'far, *'Alayhi al-Salam*, said, 'The hearts sometimes harden and at other times soften.'

"Abu Ja'far, *'Alayhi al-Salam*, then said, 'The companions of Muhammad, *'Alayhi al-Salam*, had said, 'O Messenger of Allah, we are afraid of hypocrisy.' The Imam said that the Messenger of Allah then asked, 'Why are you afraid of it?' They said, 'When we are in your presence, you remind us (of our religion), encourage us to good deeds, we feel fear, forget the world and restrain ourselves from it, as if we observe the next life, paradise and fire while we are in your presence. When we leave your presence, go to these houses, sense the smell of the children and see the family and relatives, our condition that we had in your presence changes. It is as if we are on nothing (of belief or religion). Do you fear that is hypocrisy in us?' The Messenger of Allah said, 'Beware; this is among the steps of Satan who encourages you to be interested in the world. By Allah, if you continue in such condition that you described to exist in you, the angels shake hands with you and you can walk over the water. Even if you do not commit any sin and do not need to ask Allah's forgiveness, Allah will create a creature who will sin then ask Him for forgiveness and He will forgive them. Believing people are under trial and they repent. Have you not heard the words of Allah, the Most Majestic, the Most Holy, 'Allah loves those who repent and those who cleanse themselves,' (2:222) also He has said, 'Ask your Lord for forgiveness and turn to Him in repentance.'" (11:3)

Chapter 181 - Temptation and Soul's Tale-Telling

H 2927, Ch. 181, h 1

Al-Husayn ibn Muhammad has narrated from Mu'alla ibn Muhammad from al-Washsha' from Muhammad ibn Humran who has said the following:

"Once I asked abu 'Abd Allah, *'Alayhi al-Salam*, 'What if temptation (soul's tale telling) becomes a great deal.' The Imam said, 'There is nothing in it. Say, 'No one deserves to be worshipped except Allah.'"

H 2928, Ch. 181, h 2

Ali ibn Ibrahim has narrated from his father from ibn abu 'Umayr from Jamil ibn Darraj who has said the following:

"Once I asked abu 'Abd Allah, *'Alayhi al-Salam*, 'A great thing happens in my heart.' The Imam told me to say, 'No one deserves to be worshipped except Allah.' Jamil has said, 'Whenever anything happens in my heart I say, 'No one deserves to be worshipped except Allah,' and it goes away.'"

H 2929, Ch. 181, h 3

Ibn abu 'Umayr has narrated from Muhammad ibn Muslim from abu 'Abd Allah, *'Alayhi al-Salam*, who has said the following:

"Once a man came to the Holy Prophet and said, 'O Messenger of Allah, I am destroyed,' and the Messenger of Allah said, 'Has the filthy one come to you and asked you, "Who has created you?" and you said, 'Allah has created me,' and he said, "Who has created Allah?" The man said, 'Yes, by the One Who has sent you with the truth, it was just as you said.' The Messenger of Allah said, 'That by Allah is pure belief.'

Ibn abu 'Umayr has said that I told this to 'Abd al-Rahman ibn al-Hajjaj and he said that his father narrated to him from abu 'Abd Allah, *'Alayhi al-Salam*, who has said the following:

"By saying, 'This by Allah it is pure belief' the Messenger of Allah referred to his fear of temptation and to the degree that he thought it (soul's such tale telling) is destructive.'"

H 2930, Ch. 181, h 4

A number of our people have narrated from Sahl ibn Ziyad and Muhammad ibn Yahya from Ahmad ibn Muhammad (all them) from Ali ibn Mahziyar who has said the following:

"A man wrote to abu Ja'far, *'Alayhi al-Salam*, and complained about what would pass in his mind. The Imam answered him in certain parts of his words: 'If Allah, the Most Majestic, the Most Holy, wills, He will keep you steadfast and He will not allow Satan to find way in you. Certain people complained to the Holy Prophet for what happened in their mind so much so that they liked to be blown away by the wind or being cut in pieces than to speak out of that thing in their mind. The Messenger of Allah asked, 'Do you find that?' They said, 'Yes we do.' The Messenger of Allah said, 'By the One in whose hands is my soul that it is clear belief. Whenever you sense it say, "We believe in Allah and His Messenger and there is no means and power without Allah."'"

H 2931, Ch. 181, h 5

A number of our people have narrated from Ahmad ibn Muhammad ibn Khalid from Isma'il ibn Muhammad from Muhammad ibn Bakr ibn Janah from Zakariya ibn Muhammad from ibn al-Yasa', Dawud al-Abzari has narrated from Humran from abu Ja'far, *'Alayhi al-Salam*, who has said the following:

"Once a man came to the Messenger of Allah and said, O Messenger of Allah, 'I have become a hypocrite.' The Messenger of Allah said, 'By Allah, you have not become a hypocrite, otherwise, you would not have come to me to tell me what has made you suspicious. I think the present enemy has come to you asking, "Who has created you?" You said, 'Allah has created me,' and he asked, "Who has created Allah?" The man said, 'Yes, by the One Who has sent you with the truth, it was just like that.' The Messenger of Allah said, 'Satan comes to you through the deeds and fails to overpower you. Then he comes to you from this aspect to make you slip, if this happens you must speak of Allah alone (and say, 'No one deserves to be worshipped except Allah).'"

Chapter 182 - Confessing Sins and Regret for it

H 2932, Ch. 182, h 1

Ali ibn Ibrahim has narrated from his father from ibn abu'Umayr from Ali al-Ahmasi from abu Ja'far, *'Alayhi al-Salam,* who has said the following:

"Abu Ja'far, *'Alayhi al-Salam,* has said, 'By Allah no one escapes sins except those who confess it.' The narrator has said that abu Ja'far, *'Alayhi al-Salam,* then said, 'Repenting is enough proof of one's being regretful.'"

H 2933, Ch. 182, h 2

A number of our people have narrated from Ahmad ibn Muhammad from ibn Faddal from those whom has mentioned (in his book) from abu Ja'far, *'Alayhi al-Salam,* who has said the following:

"Abu Ja'far, *'Alayhi al-Salam,* has said, 'By Allah, Allah, the Most High, wants two characteristics from people: to confess that He has granted them favors so He will increase them and to confess their sins so He will forgive them.'"

H 2934, Ch. 182, h 3

Ali ibn Ibrahim has narrated from his father from 'Umar ('Amr) ibn 'Uthman from certain individuals of his people who has said the following:

"I heard abu 'Abd Allah, *'Alayhi al-Salam,* saying, 'A man commits a sin and because of it Allah will admit him in paradise.' I asked, 'Will Allah admit him in paradise because of his sin?' The Imam said, 'Yes, he commits a sin and continues living in fear, and angry on his own self. Allah then grants him mercy and admits him in paradise.'"

H 2935, Ch. 182, h 4

Muhammad ibn Yahya has narrated from Ahmad ibn Muhammad from Muhammad ibn Sinan from Mu'awiyah ibn 'Ammar who has said the following:

"I heard abu 'Abd Allah, *'Alayhi al-Salam,* saying, 'By Allah a servant cannot get out of sin while persisting in it and a servant cannot get out of sin without confessing to it.'"

H 2936, Ch. 182, h 5

Al-Husayn ibn Muhammad has narrated from Muhammad ibn 'Imran ibn al-Hajjaj al-Subay'i (from Muhammad ibn Walid) from Yunus ibn Ya'qub who has said the following:

"I heard abu 'Abd Allah, *'Alayhi al-Salam,* saying, 'If one commits a sin and knows that Allah is aware of it, He punishes him if He so wills or forgives him if He so wills. In such case, He (Allah) forgives him even if he does not ask forgiveness.'"

H 2937, Ch. 182, h 6

A number of our people have narrated from Ahmad ibn Muhammad ibn Khalid from Muhammad ibn Ali from 'Abd al-Rahman ibn Muhammad ibn abu Hashim from 'Anbasah al-'Abid from abu 'Abd Allah, *'Alayhi al-Salam,* who has said the following:

"Abu 'Abd Allah, *'Alayhi al-Salam*, has said, 'Allah loves that a servant asks Him for help in great crimes and He hates the servant who considers trivial sins insignificant.'"

H 2938, Ch. 182, h 7
Muhammad ibn Yahya has narrated from Ahmad ibn Muhammad ibn 'Isa from Isma'il ibn Sahl from Hammad from Rib'i from abu 'Abd Allah, *'Alayhi al-Salam*, who has said the following:

"Amir al-Mu'minin, Ali ibn abu Talib, *'Alayhi al-Salam*, has said, 'Regret for an evil deed leads one to stay away from it.'"

H 2939, Ch. 182, h 8
Muhammad ibn Yahya has narrated from al-Husayn al-Daqqaq from 'Abd Allah ibn Muhammad from Ahmad ibn 'Umar from Zayd al-Qattat from Aban ibn Taghlib who has said the following:

"I heard abu 'Abd Allah, *'Alayhi al-Salam*, saying, 'If a servant commits a sin and then regrets, Allah forgives him before he asks forgiveness. If a servant receives a favor from Allah and he learns that it is from Allah, He grants him forgiveness (protection) before he offers his thanks.'"

Chapter 183 - Concealing Sins

H 2940, Ch. 183, h 1
A number of our people have narrated from Ahmad ibn Muhammad ibn Khalid from Muhammad ibn Ali from al-'Abbas Mawla al-Rida, *'Alayhi al-Salam*, who has said the following:

"I heard the Imam saying, 'To keep a good deed unnoticed is equal to seventy good deeds. Publicizing an evil deed brings humiliation and for its concealment one may receive forgiveness.'"

H 2941, Ch. 183, h 2
Muhammad ibn Yahya has narrated from Muhammad ibn Sandal from Yasir from al-Yasa' ibn Hamza from al-Rida, *'Alayhi al-Salam*, who has said the following:

"The Messenger of Allah has said, 'To keep a good deed unnoticed is equal to seventy good deeds. Publicizing an evil deed brings humiliation and for its concealment one may receive forgiveness.'"

Chapter 184 - Intending to Perform a Good or an Evil Deed

H 2942, Ch. 184, h 1
Muhammad ibn Yahya has narrated from Ahmad ibn Muhammad from Ali ibn Hadid from Jamil ibn Darraj from Zurara from one of the two Imam, *'Alayhim al-Salam*, who has said the following:

"Allah, the Most Blessed, the Most High, set for Adam in his offspring the following rules about their deeds: whoever intends to perform a good deed but does not do it, still (the reward for) one good deed will be written for him. Whoever intends to perform a good deed and actually performs it, (the reward for) ten good deeds will be written down for him. Whoever intends to commit an evil deed but does not do it, nothing will be written against him. Whoever intends to commit an evil deed and actually performs it, only one evil deed will be written against him.'"

H 2943, Ch. 184, h 2

A number of our people have narrated from Ahmad ibn abu 'Abd Allah from 'Uthman ibn 'Isa from Sama'a ibn Mehran from abu Basir from abu 'Abd Allah, *'Alayhi al-Salam*, who has said the following:

"A believer may intend to perform a good deed but does not do it, still (the reward for) one good deed will be written for him and if he actually completes it, (the reward for) ten good deeds will be written in his favor. A believer may intend to commit an evil deed but if he does not do it, nothing will be written against him."

H 2944, Ch. 184, h 3

It is narrated from him (narrator of the Hadith above) from Ali ibn Hafs al-'Awsi from Ali ibn al-Sa'ih from 'Abd Allah ibn Musa ibn Ja'far from his father, *'Alayhi al-Salam*, who has said the following:

"Once I asked him, *'Alayhi al-Salam*, if the two angels know the sin or good deed that a servant (of Allah) may intend to perform. The Imam said, 'Are the smell of a trash collection site and a sweet smelling substance the same?' I said, 'No, they are not the same.' The Imam said, 'Whenever a servant (of Allah) intends to perform a good deed his breath comes out with a good smell and the angel on the right side says to the one on the left side, 'Stand up; he intends to perform a good deed.' When he performs it his tongue serves as his pen and his saliva as ink and he writes it down for him. Whenever he intends to commit an evil deed his breath comes out with a foul smell. The angel on the left says to the one on the right, 'Stop; he intends to commit an evil deed.' For an evil act his tongue serves as the pen and his saliva as ink and he writes it down against him.'"

H 2945, Ch. 184, h 4

Muhammad ibn Yahya has narrated from Ahmad ibn Muhammad ibn 'Isa from Ali ibn al-Hakam from Fadl ibn 'Uthman al-Muradi who has said the following:

"I heard abu 'Abd Allah, *'Alayhi al-Salam*, saying, 'The Messenger of Allah has said, 'If four things are found in a person Allah will not allow his destruction to take place unless he is one of those doomed to destruction: (1) a servant (of Allah) intends to perform a good deed and actually does it, (2) even if he does not do it Allah still writes for him one good deed because of his good intention, but if he actually does perform it Allah will write ten good deeds for him. (3) One may intend to commit an evil deed and if he does not do it nothing will be written against him, however, (4) if he does commit such act he will be given seven hours. The angel for the good deeds will say to the one for the evil deeds who is on the left side, 'Do not hurry, perhaps he may perform a good deed that will cancel the evil deed as Allah, the Most Majestic, the Most Holy, says, 'The good deeds remove the bad deeds,' (11:115) if he may say, 'I ask forgiveness from Allah, besides whom no one deserves to be worshipped. He knows the unseen and the manifest, He is the most majestic, the most wise, the forgiving, the merciful, glorious and honorable and I turn in repentance to Him,' nothing will be written against him. If seven hours pass, and he performs no good deed or repentance the angel for the good deeds will say to the one for the evil deeds, 'Write it down against the wicked and deprived one that he is.'"

Chapter 185 - Repentance

H 2946, Ch. 185, h 1
Muhammad ibn Yahya has narrated from Ahmad ibn Muhammad ibn 'Isa from al-Hassan ibn Mahbub from Mu'awiyah ibn Wahab who has said the following:

"I heard abu 'Abd Allah, *'Alayhi al-Salam*, saying, 'When a servant (of Allah) repents in the form of the repentance of Nasuh (sincere advise to one's soul, or name of a person who repented in the real sense), Allah then loves him, covers and protects him in this world and in the next life.' I then asked, 'How will He cover him?' The Imam said, 'He will make the two angels forget what they have written against him. He will inspire the parts of his body to hide his sins and the places of earth to hide the sins that he had committed thereat. Allah will meet him while there will be nothing to testify anything against him.'"

H 2947, Ch. 185, h 2
Ali ibn Ibrahim has narrated from his father from ibn abu 'Umayr from abu Ayyub al-Khazzaz from Muhammad ibn Muslim from one of the two Imams, *'Alayhi al-Salam*, who has said the following:

"About the words of Allah, the Most Majestic, the Most Holy, '. . . one who has received advice from his Lord and has stopped committing sins will be rewarded for his previous good deeds . . .' (2:275) The Imam said, 'Advice means repentance.'"

H 2948, Ch. 185, h 3
A number of our people have narrated from Ahmad ibn Muhammad ibn Khalid from Muhammad ibn Ali from Muhammad ibn al-Fudayl from abu al-Sabah al-Kinani who has said the following:

"Once I asked abu 'Abd Allah, *'Alayhi al-Salam*, about the words of Allah, the Most Majestic, the Most Holy, 'Believers, turn to Allah in repentance, in a Nasuh manner, with the intention of never repeating the same sin.' (66:8) The Imam said, 'It means a servant (of Allah) repents from sins and never repeats them.'

"Muhammad ibn al-Fudayl has said, 'I asked abu al-Hassan, *'Alayhi al-Salam*, about it (repentance in a Nasuh manner) he said, 'One repents from sin and then does not repeat it. The most beloved among the servants (of Allah) to Allah, the Most High, are those who are put to trial and who repent from sins.'"

H 2949, Ch. 185, h 4
Ali ibn Ibrahim has narrated from his father from ibn abu 'Umayr from abu Ayyub from abu Basir who has said the following:

"Once I asked abu 'Abd Allah, *'Alayhi al-Salam*, about the words of Allah, the Most Majestic, the Most Holy, 'Believers, turn to Allah in repentance, "In a Nasuh manner," with the intention of never repeating the same sin.' (66:8) The Imam said, 'It is the sin that one never repeats.' I then asked, 'Who among us does not repeat?' The Imam said, 'O abu Muhammad, of His servants Allah loves those who are put to trial and the ones who repent very often.'"

H 2950, Ch. 185, h 5
Ali ibn Ibrahim has narrated from his father from ibn abu 'Umayr from certain individuals of our people in a marfu' manner from the Imam, *'Alayhi al-Salam*, who has said the following:

"Allah, the Most Majestic, the Most Holy, has given three things to the repenting people. Had any of it been given to all of those in the heavens and on earth, all have had their salvation. The following words of Allah, the Most Majestic, the Most Holy, mention those three things: 'Allah loves those who 'Repent' and those who cleanse themselves, (2:222) whomever Allah loves He will not punish him.' 'The bearers of the Throne glorify their Lord with His praise. They believe in Him and ask Him to forgive the believers. They say, "Our Lord, Your mercy and knowledge encompass all things. Forgive those who turn to You in 'Repentance' and follow Your path. Lord, save them from the torment of hell. (40:7) Lord, admit them and their fathers, spouses, and offspring who have reformed themselves to the gardens of Eden which You have promised them. You are Majestic and All-wise. (40:8)

"Lord, keep them away from evil deeds. Whomever You have saved from evil on the Day of Judgment has certainly been granted Your mercy and this is the greatest triumph.' (40:9)

"The last thing is in the words of Allah, the Most Majestic, the Most Holy, ' . . . who do not worship idols besides Allah, nor without a just cause murder a soul whom Allah has granted protection, who do not commit fornication; those who do so have committed a sin (25:68) and on the Day of Judgment their torment will be double. They will suffer forever in disgrace. (25:69) But only those who 'Repent' believe and act righteously will have their sins replaced with virtue; Allah is All-forgiving and All-merciful.'" (25:70)

H 2951, Ch. 185, h 6

Muhammad ibn Yahya has narrated from Ahmad ibn Muhammad from ibn Mahbub from al-'Ala' from Muhammad ibn Muslim from abu Ja'far, *'Alayhi al-Salam*, who has said the following:

"Once abu Ja'far, *'Alayhi al-Salam*, said, 'O Muhammad ibn Muslim, if believing people repent for their sins they will be forgiven. Believing people must resume their good deeds after repentance and forgiveness. By Allah, this is only for the believers.' I then asked, 'What if he goes back to sin after repenting and asking for forgiveness and repents again?' The Imam said, 'O Muhammad ibn Muslim, do you think a believing servant (of Allah) regrets his sins, asks forgiveness and repents but Allah does not accept his repentance?' I said, 'He, however, has done it many times. He sins, repents and asks forgiveness (from Allah).' The Imam said, 'Whenever a believing servant (of Allah) returns back for repentance and pleas for forgiveness, Allah returns to him with forgiveness; Allah is forgiving and merciful. He accepts repentance and effaces the evil deeds. You must never cause a believer to lose hope in the favor and mercy of Allah.'"

H 2952, Ch. 185, h 7

Abu Ali al-Ash'ari has narrated from Muhammad ibn 'Abd al-Jabbar from ibn Faddal from Tha'labah ibn Maymun from abu Basir who has said the following:

"Once I asked abu 'Abd Allah, *'Alayhi al-Salam*, about the words of Allah, the Most Majestic, the Most Holy, 'When a Satanic thought starts to bother the pious ones, they understand and see the light.' (7:201) The Imam said, 'It means that a servant (of Allah) intends to commit an evil deed then he realizes it and holds back and that is indicated in His words, 'They understand and see.'"

H 2953, Ch. 185, h 8

Ali ibn Ibrahim has narrated from his father from ibn abu 'Umayr from 'Umar ibn 'Udhaynah from abu 'Ubaydah al-Hadhdha' who has said the following:

"I heard abu Ja'far, *'Alayhi al-Salam*, saying, 'Allah, the Most High, is more pleased for the repentance of His servant than one who loses his animals, that carry his load and supplies, in a dark night and then finds them out. Allah is more pleased for the repentance of His servant than the person who finds his lost properties.'"

H 2954, Ch. 185, h 9

Muhammad ibn Yahya has narrated from Ahmad ibn Muhammad ibn 'Isa from Muhammad ibn Isma'il from 'Abd Allah ibn 'Uthman from abu Jamilah who has said the following:

"Abu 'Abd Allah, *'Alayhi al-Salam*, has said, 'Allah loves the servant who is put to trial (by sin) and repents, however, one without such (sinful) condition is better.'"

H 2955, Ch. 185, h 10

It is narrated from him (narrator of the Hadith above) from Ahmad ibn Muhammad from Ali ibn al-Nu'man from Muhammad ibn Sinan from Yusuf (ibn) abu Ya'qub Bayya' al-Arz from Jabir who has said the following:

"I heard abu Ja'far, *'Alayhi al-Salam*, saying, 'A person repenting from sins is like one who has not sinned. One who persists in sin and asks forgiveness is like one contemptuous of it (repentance).'"

H 2956, Ch. 185, h 11

Ali ibn Ibrahim has narrated from his father and a number of our people have narrated from Sahl ibn Ziyad all from ibn Mahbub from abu Hamza from abu Ja'far, *'Alayhi al-Salam*, who has said the following:

"Allah, the Most Majestic, the Most Holy, sent revelation to David, 'Meet My servant Daniel and say to him, 'You have disobeyed Me and I forgave you, you disobeyed Me, I forgave you, you disobeyed Me and I forgave you. If you will disobey Me the forth time I will not forgive you.' David went to meet Daniel and said, 'O Daniel, I am the Messenger of Allah and He says to you, "You disobeyed Me and I forgave you, you disobeyed Me and I forgave you, you disobeyed Me and I forgave you. If you will disobey Me the forth time I will not forgive you."' Daniel said, 'O prophet of Allah, you have conveyed your message.' In the early morning Daniel woke up and prayed to his Lord, saying, 'O Lord, Your prophet David informed me that I have disobeyed You and You forgave me, I disobeyed You and You forgave me, I disobeyed You and You forgave me and if I will disobey You the forth time You will not forgive me. I swear by Your Majesty, if You will not protect me I will certainly disobey You, I will certainly disobey You, I will certainly disobey You.'"

H 2957, Ch. 185, h 12

A number of our people have narrated from Ahmad ibn Muhammad from Musa ibn al-Qasim from his grandfather al-Hassan ibn Rashid from Mu'awiyah ibn Wahab who has said the following:

"I heard abu 'Abd Allah, *'Alayhi al-Salam,* saying, 'When a servant (of Allah) repents in the form of the repentance of Nasuh (sincerely repenting) Allah loves him and covers him up.' I then asked, 'How He covers him up?' The Imam said, 'He makes his two angels forget whatever they have written against him and Allah sends inspiration to the parts of his body and to the parts of the earth to hide his sins and he will meet Allah, the Most Majestic, the Most Holy in his meeting while there will be no one to testify anything against him for his sins.'"

H 2958, Ch. 185, h 13
A number of our people have narrated from Sahl ibn Ziyad from Ja'far ibn Muhammad al-Ash'ari from ibn al-Qaddah from abu 'Abd Allah, *'Alayhi al-Salam,* who has said the following:

"Abu 'Abd Allah, *'Alayhi al-Salam,* has said, 'The repentance of a servant (of Allah) from sins pleases Allah, the Majestic, the Glorious, more than a person's finding a dearly cherished thing that he has lost.'"

Chapter 186 - Pleading for Forgiveness

H 2959, Ch. 186, h 1
Ali ibn Ibrahim has narrated from his father from ibn abu 'Umayr from Muhammad ibn Humran from Zurara who has said the following:

"I heard abu 'Abd Allah, *'Alayhi al-Salam,* saying, 'When a servant (of Allah) commits a sin he is given respite from morning to evening. If within such time he pleaded before Allah for forgiveness no sin will be written against him.'"

H 2960, Ch. 186, h 2
It is narrated from him (narrator of the Hadith above) from his father from ibn abu 'Umayr and Abu Ali al-Ash'ari from Muhammad ibn 'Abd al-Jabbar from Safwan from abu Ayyub from abu Basir from abu 'Abd Allah, *'Alayhi al-Salam,* who has said the following:

"If one commits a sin he is given seven hours respite during the day. If he says, 'I ask forgiveness from Allah, besides Whom no one deserves to be worshipped, Who is living and controls all things, - three times - no sin will be written against him.'"

H 2961, Ch. 186, h 3
Ali ibn Ibrahim has narrated from his father and Abu Ali al-Ash'ari and Muhammad ibn Yahya all from al-Husayn ibn Ishaq from Ali ibn Mahziyar from Fadalah ibn Ayyub from 'Abd al-Samad ibn Bashir from abu 'Abd Allah, *'Alayhi al-Salam,* who has said the following:

"When a believing servant (of Allah) commits a sin Allah gives him seven hours respite. If he pleads for forgiveness from Allah within such time nothing will be written against him. If the hours pass and he did not plead for forgiveness one sin will be written against him. A believer remembers his sin even after twenty years so that he may plead to his Lord for forgiveness and He forgives him. An unbeliever forgets his sin within the same hour.'"

H 2962, Ch. 186, h 4
Humayd ibn Ziyad has narrated from al-Hassan ibn Muhammad from more than one narrator from Aban from Zayd al-Shahham from abu 'Abd Allah, *'Alayhi al-Salam,* who has said the following:

"The Messenger of Allah would plead before Allah, the Most Majestic, the Most Holy, seventy times every day.' I (the narrator) then asked, 'Would he say, 'I ask

Allah to forgive me and I turn to Him in repentance?' The Imam said, 'He, however, would say, 'I return to Allah.' I then said, 'The Messenger of Allah would yatub (repent) and would not repeat, we repent and repeat.' The Imam said, 'Allah is the source of help.'"

H 2963, Ch. 186, h 5

Muhammad ibn Yahya has narrated from Ahmad ibn Muhammad ibn 'Isa from Ali ibn al-Hakam from abu Ayyub from abu Basir from abu 'Abd Allah, *'Alayhi al-Salam*, who has said the following:

"If one commits a sin he is given seven hours time during the day. If he says, 'I plead before Allah, besides whom no one deserves to be worshipped, the living, the controlling power (over creation) and turn to Him in repentance - three times - nothing will be written against him.'"

H 2964, Ch. 186, h 6

It is narrated from him (narrator of the Hadith above) from Ahmad ibn Muhammad from ibn Faddal from Ali ibn 'Uqbah Bayya' al-Aksiyah from abu 'Abd Allah, *'Alayhi al-Salam*, who has said the following:

"A believer commits a sin and remembers it after twenty years, then he pleads before Allah for forgiveness, He still forgives him. He is made to remember so He may forgive him. An unbeliever commits a sin and forgets it within the same hour.'"

H 2965, Ch. 186, h 7

A number of our people have narrated from Ahmad ibn Muhammad ibn Khalid from ibn Mahbub from Hisham ibn Salim from those whom has mentioned (in his book) from abu 'Abd Allah, *'Alayhi al-Salam*, who has said the following:

"If a believer commits forty major sins within one day and night and then regretfully says, 'I plead before Allah, besides Whom no one deserves to be worshipped, the living, the controlling power (over creation) the inventor of the heavens and earth, possessor of glory, and honor. I ask Him to grant favors upon Muhammad and his family and to forgive me and accept my repentance. Allah, the Most Majestic, the Most Holy, will forgive all of them, however, there is no good in one who commits more than forty major sins in a day.'"

H 2966, Ch. 186, h 8

It is narrated from him (narrator of the Hadith above) from a number of our people in a marfu' manner from him, *'Alayhi al-Salam*, who has said the following:

"For everything there is a medicine and the medicine for sins is pleading (before Allah) for forgiveness."

H 2967, Ch. 186, h 9

Abu Ali al-Ash'ari and Muhammad ibn Yahya all has narrated from al-Husayn ibn Ishaq and Ali ibn Ibrahim has narrated from his father all from Ali ibn Mahziyar from al-Nadr ibn Suwayd from 'Abd Allah ibn Sinan from Hafs who has said the following:

"I heard abu 'Abd Allah, *'Alayhi al-Salam*, saying, 'If any believer commits a sin Allah, the Most Majestic, the Most Holy, gives him seven hours of a day's respite; if he repents, nothing will be written against him but if he did not repent Allah will write only one sin against him.' Thereafter 'Abbad al-Basri came to him (abu 'Abd Allah) and said, 'We have heard that you have said, 'If a servant (of Allah) commits a sin, Allah, the Most Majestic, the Most Holy, gives him seven hours of a day's respite.' The Imam said, 'I have not said as such. What I have said is 'If any believer . . .' and the rest of my words.'"

H 2968, Ch. 186, h 10
Muhammad ibn Yahya has narrated from Ahmad ibn Muhammad ibn 'Isa from Muhammad ibn Sinan from 'Ammar ibn Marwan who has said the following:

"Abu 'Abd Allah, *'Alayhi al-Salam*, has said, 'If one says, "I plead for forgiveness before Allah" one hundred times every day, Allah, the Most Majestic, the Most Holy, will forgive his seven hundred sins, but there is nothing good in a servant (of Allah) who commits seven hundred sins a day.'"

Chapter 187 - Things that Allah, the Most Majestic, the Most Holy, Gave Adam at the Time of Repentance

H 2969, Ch. 187, h 1
Ali ibn Ibrahim has narrated from his father from ibn abu 'Umayr from Jamil ibn Darraj from ibn Bukayr from abu 'Abd Allah or abu Ja'far, *'Alayhi al-Salam*, who has said the following:

"Adam said, 'O Lord, you have made Satan dominate me and made him flow in me like blood, so make something for me also.' The Lord said, 'O Adam, for your benefit I have given your offspring the advantage of not writing down against them any sin if they only intend to commit an evil deed. If they actually commit an evil deed only one evil deed is written against them. If anyone of them intends to perform a good deed one good deed is written down for him even if he did not perform it. If, however, he actually performs it ten good deeds are written for him.' Adam said, 'O Lord, increase favors upon me.' The Lord said, 'I have also assigned for your benefit that if anyone of your offspring commits a sin and then pleads before Me for forgiveness I forgive him.' Adam said, 'Lord, grant me more favors.' The Lord said, 'I, for their advantage, have made repentance available to them' or he (the Imam) said that the Lord said, 'I have extended the time for repentance in their favor up to the time the soul reaches this (throat).' Adam then said, 'Lord, this is sufficient for me.'"

H 2970, Ch. 187, h 2
A number of our people have narrated from Ahmad ibn Muhammad from ibn Faddal from those whom he has mentioned (in his book) from abu 'Abd Allah, *'Alayhi al-Salam*, who has said the following:

"The Messenger of Allah has said, 'If one repents one year before his death, Allah accepts his repentance.' Then he said, 'One year is a long time. Whoever repents one month before his death Allah accepts his repentance.' Then he said, 'One month is a long time. Whoever repents one week before his death, Allah accepts his repentance.' Then he said, 'One week is a long time. Whoever repents one day before his death, Allah accepts his repentance.' Then he said, 'One day is a long time. Whoever repents before he sees (the consequences), Allah accepts his repentance.'"

H 2971, Ch. 187, h 3
Ali ibn Ibrahim has narrated from his father from ibn abu 'Umayr from Jamil from Zurara from abu Ja'far, *'Alayhi al-Salam*, who has said the following:

"When the soul reaches this - pointing to his throat - there will be no repentance for one who has knowledge, however, there will be repentance for an ignorant person."

H 2972, Ch. 187, h 4

Muhammad ibn Yahya has narrated from Ahmad ibn Muhammad ibn 'Isa from Muhammad ibn Sinan from Mu'awiyah ibn Wahab who has said the following:

"Once we left for Makka and with us there was an old man, very religious and worshipping but did not know this cause (Shi'a Muslim belief). He would pray full (not in reduced form) on a journey and with him there was the son of his brother, also a Muslim. The old man became ill and I said to the son of his brother, 'If you introduce this cause to your uncle perhaps Allah may grant him freedom.' All of them said, 'Leave the old man alone to die in his condition; he looks just fine.' The son of his brother did not wait and said, 'Uncle, people after the Messenger of Allah proselytized (gave up their religion) except a very few people. Ali ibn abu Talib must have been obeyed just like the Messenger of Allah had been obeyed. After the Messenger of Allah it was the right of Ali to be obeyed.'

"The narrator has said that the old man sighed deeply and said, 'I am upon this (belief),' and he died. We then went in the presence of abu 'Abd Allah, *'Alayhi al-Salam*, and Ali ibn al-Sariy narrated the story before abu 'Abd Allah, *'Alayhi al-Salam*, and he said, 'He was a man of paradise.' Ali ibn al-Sariy said, 'He had no knowledge of this cause except for one Sa'ah there.' The Imam said, 'What else do you want from him. He, by Allah, has entered paradise.'"

Chapter 188 - Sins Committed from Time to Time (al-Lamam)

H 2973, Ch. 188, h 1

Ali ibn Ibrahim has narrated from his father from ibn abu 'Umayr from abu Ayyub from Muhammad ibn Muslim who has said the following:

"Once I said to abu 'Abd Allah, *'Alayhi al-Salam*, 'How do you consider the words of Allah, the Most Majestic, the Most Holy, ". . . those who avoid major sins and indecent acts except al-Lamam (sins committed from time to time). . . ." (53:33) The Imam said, 'It is the sin that one may commit then stops it, as Allah wills, and then commits it again."

H 2974, Ch. 188, h 2

Abu Ali al-Ash'ari has narrated from Muhammad ibn 'Abd al-Jabbar from Safwan from al-'Ala' from Muhammad ibn Muslim who has said the following:

"Once I read the words of Allah, the Most Majestic, the Most Holy, before one of the two Imam, *'Alayhi al-Salam*, '. . . those who avoid the major sins and indecent acts except the al-Lamam ones . . .' (53:33) The Imam said, 'It is a thing after a thing, that is, a sin after a sin that a servant (of Allah) commits.'"

H 2975, Ch. 188, h 3

Ali ibn Ibrahim has narrated from Muhammad ibn 'Isa from Yunus from Ishaq ibn 'Ammar who has said the following:

"Abu 'Abd Allah, *'Alayhi al-Salam*, has said, 'Every believer may have a sin and he shuns it for a period of time, then he commits it again and this is that which is mentioned in the words of Allah, the Most Majestic, the Most Holy, as 'Except al-Lamam' (the sins committed from time to time).' The narrator has said that I asked the Imam about the words of Allah, the Most Majestic, the Most Holy, '. . . those who avoid the major sins and the indecent acts, except the al-Lamam.' (53:33) The Imam said, 'Indecent acts are fornication and theft and al-Lamam is that which a man commits, and then pleads before Allah for forgiveness.'"

H 2976, Ch. 188, h 4

Ali ibn Ibrahim has narrated from his father from ibn abu 'Umayr from al-Harith ibn Bahram from 'Amr ibn Jumay' who has said the following:

"Abu 'Abd Allah, *'Alayhi al-Salam*, has said, 'Whoever comes to us seeking to learn Fiqh (laws of Shari'a) and the Holy Quran, allow him to come in. Whoever comes to us to make public what Allah has covered, you must move him away.' A man from the people then said, 'May Allah keep my soul in service for your cause, I have been involved in sin for a long time and I want to change to something else but I am not able to do so.' The Imam said, 'If you are true, Allah loves you. There is nothing to prevent Him from changing you to something else, it is only as such so that you can be fearing Him.'"

H 2977, Ch. 188, h 5

Ali ibn Ibrahim has narrated from his father from Hammad ibn 'Isa from (Hariz) from Ishaq ibn 'Ammar from abu 'Abd Allah, *'Alayhi al-Salam*, who has said the following:

"Any sin that may become imprinted in a believing servant (of Allah) he shuns it for a period of time then commits it again as it is mentioned in the words of Allah, the Most Majestic, the Most Holy, ' . . . those who avoid the major sins and the indecent acts except the al-Lamam . . .' (53:33) The Imam said, 'One committing al-Lamam, sins often, is he (servant) who commits such sins one after the other and it is not of his normal behavior and nature.'"

H 2978, Ch. 188, h 6

Ali ibn Ibrahim has narrated from his father and a number of our people have narrated from Sahl ibn Ziyad all from ibn Mahbub from ibn Ri'ab who has said the following:

"I heard abu 'Abd Allah, *'Alayhi al-Salam*, saying, 'A believer does not have lying, stinginess or indecent acts as part of his nature and normal behavior, perhaps he may commit certain sins in which he does not continue.' It was asked, 'Does he commit fornication?' The Imam said, 'Yes, but no child is beggotten from that seed.'"

Chapter 189 - Sins Are of Three Kinds

H 2979, Ch. 189, h 1

Ali ibn Ibrahim has narrated from his father from 'Abd al-Rahman ibn Hammad from certain individuals of his people in a marfu' manner who has said the following:

"Once Amir al-Mu'minin, Ali ibn abu Talib, *'Alayhi al-Salam*, climbed the Minbar (pulpit) in al-Kufah, praised Allah and spoke of His glory and then said, 'O people sins are of three kinds' and he remained quiet. Habbah al-'Arani, said, 'O Amir al-Mu'minin, you just said, "Sins are of three kinds, and then remained silent.' The Imam said, 'Yes, I mentioned them and wanted to explain and interpret them but a breathing problem prevented me from speaking. Yes, sins are of three kinds: A sin that is forgiven, a sin that is not forgiven and a sin for whose owner we have hopes and fears.' The man said, 'O Amir al-Mu'minin, explain them for us.'

"The Imam said, 'Yes, the sin that is forgiven is one for which Allah has punished the sinner in this world and He is by far much Forbearing and Honorable to punish His servant twice.

"The sin that is not forgiven is people's injustice to each other (in the matters of property and so forth). When Allah, the Most Blessed, the Most High, will manifest himself to His creatures, He will swear by His Ownself saying, 'By My Majesty and Glory that the injustice of the unjust cannot bypass Me, even though it is in the form of a slap for a slap, a rubbing for a slap, or blow by those having horns to those without horns.' He will retaliate for His servants from the others until no one will be left without receiving justice and thereafter they will be sent for reckoning.

"The third kind of sin is the sin that Allah has covered for His servants and has granted them repentance. He lives in fear because of his sin with hopes in his Lord. We toward him are just as he is to himself. We wish he will be granted mercy and fear for his suffering punishment.'"

H 2980, Ch. 189, h 2
Ali ibn Ibrahim has narrated from Muhammad ibn 'Isa from Yunus from ibn Bukayr from Zurara from Humran who has said the following:
"Once I asked abu Ja'far, *'Alayhi al-Salam*, about a man who is convicted and punished by stoning to death whether he will be punished in the next life for that sin again, and the Imam said, 'Allah is by far more Honorable, He will not do such a thing (punish again).'"

Chapter 190 - Quickness of Punishment for Sins

H 2981, Ch. 190, h 1
Muhammad ibn Yahya has narrated from Ahmad ibn Muhammad ibn 'Isa from al-Hassan ibn Mahbub from 'Abd Allah ibn Sinan from Hamza ibn Humran from his father from abu Ja'far, *'Alayhi al-Salam*, who has said the following:
"Of the decision of Allah, the Most Majestic, the Most Holy, in the affairs of a servant whom He honors and who has a sin, is that Allah causes him to suffer certain illnesses. If He does not do this He causes him to become needy, if He does not do this He causes death to become very difficult for him to compensate from him for the sin.'

"The Imam said, 'Also of the decision of Allah, in the case of a person who is insignificant to Him, but he has good deeds before Allah, is that He grants him good health. If He does not do this, He expands the means of living for him and if He does not do this to him also He causes death to become easy for him to match his good deed.'"

H 2982, Ch. 190, h 2

Ali ibn Ibrahim has narrated from his father from ibn abu 'Umayr from Isma'il ibn Ibrahim from Hakam ibn 'Utaybah who has said the following:

"Abu 'Abd Allah, *'Alayhi al-Salam*, has said, 'When the sins of a servant (of Allah) increase and he does not have enough good deeds to expiate them, Allah causes him to suffer sadness and depression.'"

H 2983, Ch. 190, h 3

A number of our people have narrated from Sahl ibn Ziyad from Ja'far ibn Muhammad al-Ash'ari from ibn al-Qaddah from abu 'Abd Allah, *'Alayhi al-Salam*, who has said the following:

"The Messenger of Allah has said that Allah, the Most Majestic, the Most Holy, has said, 'I swear by My Majesty and Glory, I will not take out of this world a servant whom I want to receive mercy until I will compensate from him for all the sins that he has committed. (I will do so) by causing illness in his body, constraint in the means of his living or fear for his worldly affairs. If anything is left to offset this I will cause his death to be a severe suffering.'

"I swear by My Majesty and Glory that I will not take out of this world a servant whom I want to be punished until I will fully compensate him for his good deeds in this world. This I will do either by expanding the means of his living, granting him good health in his body or by grating him peace in this world and if anything will be left without compensation I will cause his death to take place with ease.'"

H 2984, Ch. 190, h 4

A number of our people have narrated from Ahmad ibn Muhammad ibn Khalid from ibn Mahbub from Hisham ibn Salim from Aban ibn Taghlib who has said the following:

"Abu 'Abd Allah, *'Alayhi al-Salam*, has said, 'A believer may suffer a nightmare so his sins are forgiven or is bodily humiliated so his sins are forgiven.'"

H 2985, Ch. 190, h 5

Ali ibn Ibrahim has narrated from his father from ibn abu 'Umayr from al-Sariy ibn Khalid from abu 'Abd Allah, *'Alayhi al-Salam*, who has said the following:

"When Allah, the Most Majestic, the Most Holy, wants good for a servant He hastens his punishment in this world. When He wants evil for a servant He preserves his sins for him to find their consequences on the Day of Judgment."

H 2986, Ch. 190, h 6

A number of our people have narrated from Sahl ibn Ziyad from Muhammad ibn al-Hassan ibn Shammun from 'Abd Allah ibn 'Abd al-Rahman from Misma' ibn 'Abd al-Malik from abu 'Abd Allah, *'Alayhi al-Salam*, who has said the following:

"Amir al-Mu'minin, Ali ibn abu Talib, *'Alayhi al-Salam*, about the words of Allah, the Most Majestic, the Most Holy, 'Whatever hardship befalls you is the result of your own deeds. Allah pardons many of your sins,' (42:30) has said, 'The spraining of one's muscles, bumping over a stone, the slip of foot or being bruised by a piece of wood is all because of sins and what Allah forgives is much more. In the matters of whoever faces quick suffering for sins in this world, Allah, the Most Majestic, the Most Holy, is by far more Honorable and Great and will not allow a repeat of his suffering in the next life.'"

H 2987, Ch. 190, h 7

Muhammad ibn Yahya has narrated from Ahmad ibn Muhammad ibn 'Isa from al-'Abbas ibn Musa al-Warraq from Ali al-Ahmasi from a man from abu Ja'far, *'Alayhi al-Salam*, who has said the following:

"The Messenger of Allah has said, 'Anxiety and sadness continue to trouble a believer until no sin is left in him.'"

H 2988, Ch. 190, h 8

It is narrated from him (narrator of the Hadith above) from Ahmad ibn Muhammad and Ali ibn Ibrahim has narrated from his father all from ibn abu 'Umayr from al-Harith ibn Bahram from 'Amr ibn Jumay' who has said the following:

"I heard abu 'Abd Allah, *'Alayhi al-Salam*, saying, 'A believer continues facing anxiety and sadness in this world until he leaves it with no sins in him.'"

H 2989, Ch. 190, h 9

Ali ibn Ibrahim has narrated from his father from ibn abu 'Umayr from Ali al-Ahmasi from a man from abu Ja'far, *'Alayhi al-Salam*, who has said the following:

"Abu Ja'far, *'Alayhi al-Salam*, has said, 'A believer continues facing anxiety and sadness until no sin is left in him.'"

H 2990, Ch. 190, h 10

Muhammad ibn Yahya has narrated from Ahmad ibn Muhammad from Ali ibn al-Hakam from Mu'awiyah ibn Wahab from abu 'Abd Allah, *'Alayhi al-Salam*, who has said the following:

"The Messenger of Allah has said, 'Allah, the Most Majestic, the Most Holy, has said, "Any servant whom I want to admit in paradise I cause bodily suffering to expiate for his sins, if this would not be enough I then cause dying to become a severe suffering until he comes before Me without any sins, then I admit him in paradise.

"Any servant whom I want to go in fire, I grant him health in his body. If this completes compensation to him I then call him to My presence, otherwise, I grant him security from the rulers. If this completes compensation to him I then call him in My presence, otherwise, I expand the means for his living. If this completes compensation to him I then call him in My presence, otherwise, I make dying easy for him so he comes in My presence without any good deeds before Me, then I send him in fire.'"

H 2991, Ch. 190, h 11

A number of our people have narrated from Sahl ibn Ziyad from Muhammad ibn 'Uramah from Nadr ibn Suwayd from Drust ibn abu Mansur from ibn Muskan from certain individuals of our people from abu Ja'far, *'Alayhi al-Salam*, who has said the following:

"A prophet of the prophets among the descendents of Israel once passed by a man. Half of the body of the man was under the wall and the other half out of the wall. The birds had scattered it and dogs had chewed it up. Then he came to a city where the chief had passed away. His body laid in state covered with the most beautiful cloths with a huge crowed around it. He prayed to Allah saying, 'O Lord, I testify that you make just decisions, and do not do injustice. That servant of Your's never considered anything as your partner, even for a blinking of an eye, and You caused him to die that kind of death. This servant of You has not believed in You, even for a blinking of an eye, and You have caused him to die this kind of death.' Allah said, 'My servant, I am as you said I am. I make decisions with justice and do not do injustice. That servant of Mine had certain sins and I caused him to die that way so he could come in My presence without any sins. This servant of Mine had certain good deeds before Me, thus, I caused him to die this way so he would come in My presence without any good deeds before Me.'"

H 2992, Ch. 190, h 12
A number of our people have narrated from Ahmad ibn Muhammad from ibn Mahbub from abu al-Sabbah al-Kinani who has said the following:

"Once I was in the presence of abu 'Abd Allah, *'Alayhi al-Salam*, that an old man came and said, 'O abu 'Abd Allah, *'Alayhi al-Salam*, I complain to you against my sons for their failing to maintain good relations with parents and against my brothers for their injustice to me during my old age.' Abu 'Abd Allah, *'Alayhi al-Salam*, said, 'O you, for truth there is a kingdom and for falsehood there is a kingdom. Each of them is humiliated in the kingdom of the other. The least that a believer may suffer in the kingdom of falsehood is the failure of his children to maintain good relations with parents, and injustice from his brothers. Any believer who may receive comfort in the kingdom of falsehood, for this he faces suffering before his death, either in his physical health, his children or his property until Allah purifies him from what he has received in the kingdom of falsehood and will expand his share in the kingdom of truth. Exercise patience and be happy.'"

Chapter 191 - Interpretation of Sins

H 2993, Ch. 191, h 1
Al-Husayn ibn Muhammad has narrated from Mu'alla ibn Muhammad from Ahmad ibn Muhammad from al-'Abbas ibn al-'Ala' from Mujahid from his father from abu 'Abd Allah, *'Alayhi al-Salam*, who has said the following:

"The sins that change the bounties (of Allah) are transgressions, the sins that bring regret are murder, the one that brings hatred is injustice, that which brings disgrace is drinking wine, the sin which holds back the means of living is fornication, the one that hastens one's perishing is failing to maintain good relations with relatives and the sins that cause the prayers to be rejected and brings darkness (in life) is failing to maintain good relations with parents."

H 2994, Ch. 191, h 2
Ali ibn Ibrahim has narrated from his father from ibn Mahbub from Ishaq ibn 'Ammar who has said the following:

"I heard abu 'Abd Allah, *'Alayhi al-Salam*, saying, 'My father would say, "We seek refuge in Allah against the sin that hastens one's perishing, draws death closer, and vacates the towns. Such sins are failing to maintain good relations with relatives, failing to maintain good relations with parents and disregarding virtuous deeds.'"

H 2995, Ch. 191, h 3
Ali ibn Ibrahim has narrated from Ayyub ibn Nuh or certain individuals of his people from Ayyub from Safwan ibn Yahya who has said that certain individuals of our people has said the following:

"Abu 'Abd Allah, *'Alayhi al-Salam*, has said, 'When four things spread four other things appear: When fornication spreads all over, earthquakes turn out to be apparent. When injustice in governing is widespread, drops (of rain are) held back, when the rights of al-Dhimmah taxpayers are ignored, the pagans dominate the followers of Islam and when payment of al-Zakat (charity) is held back poverty spreads all over.'"

Chapter 192 - A Rare Hadith

H 2996, Ch. 192, h 1

Muhammad ibn Yahya has narrated from Ahmad ibn Muhammad ibn 'Isa from al-Hassan ibn Mahbub from 'Abd al-'Aziz al-'Abdi from ibn abu Ya'fur who has said the following:

"I heard abu 'Abd Allah, *'Alayhi al-Salam*, saying, 'Allah, the Most Majestic, the Most Holy, has said, "A servant among My believing servants commits a great sin that will make him subject to My punishment in this world and in the next life. I then see what is best for him in his next life. I then like to speed up punishment for him in this world to get even for that sin. I determine the punishment for that sin and make a decision about it. I then keep it on hold without executing and, in its execution I have a wish, and My servant does not know about it. I then hesitate many times in its execution. I then keep it on hold and do not execute; I dislike making him suffer and avoid sending affliction upon him. I then grant him forgiveness and ignore (his sin) because of love for his offsetting the sin through his many optional prayers at nights, as well as during the day, with which he tries to get closer to Me. I then divert the misfortune from him even though I had already determined, decided and had kept it on hold and for its execution I had a wish. I then write for him a great reward for the 'Would be coming misfortune' upon him. I preserve it for him, make his reward available and he does not realize it. No trouble or misfortune reaches him. I am Allah, the Honorable, the Compassionate, the Merciful.'"

Chapter 193 - Other Rare Ahadith

H 2997, Ch. 193, h 1

Muhammad ibn Yahya has narrated from Ahmad ibn Muhammad from ibn Faddal from ibn Bukayr who has said the following:

"Once I asked abu 'Abd Allah, *'Alayhi al-Salam*, about the words of Allah, the Most Majestic, the Most Holy, 'Whatever affliction befalls you is because of what your hands have obtained.'(42:30) The Imam said, '. . . He forgives a great deal,' (42:30) I (the narrator) then said, 'I did not mean in that sense. Consider what befell Ali, *'Alayhi al-Salam*, and people like him from Ahl al-Bayt (family of Holy Prophet).' The Imam said, 'The Messenger of Allah would plead, to return before Allah seventy times a day without committing any sin.'"

H 2998, Ch. 193, h 2

A number of our people have narrated from Sahl ibn Ziyad and Ali ibn Ibrahim has narrated from his father all from ibn Mahbub from Ali ibn Ri'ab who has said the following:

"Once I asked abu 'Abd Allah, *'Alayhi al-Salam*, about the words of Allah, the Most Majestic, the Most Holy, 'Whatever afflictions befall you is because of what your hands have obtained,' (42:29) do you consider whatever befell Ali and his family, *'Alayhi al-Salam*, after him was because of their deeds and acquisition of their hands despite the fact that they were members of the family of al-Taharah (cleansed by the will of Allah), the infallible people?' The Imam said, 'The Messenger of Allah would plead, to return, before Allah seventy times every day and night without any sins. Allah wants his friends, especially, to suffer so He may grant them rewards without sins.'"

H 2999, Ch. 193, h 3
Ali ibn Ibrahim has narrated in a marfu' manner has narrated from abu 'Abd Allah, *'Alayhi al-Salam*, who has said the following:
"When Ali ibn al-Husayn, *'Alayhi al-Salam*, was taken as a captive to Damascus and was made to stand before Yazid ibn Mu'awiyah, he, (Yazid) may Allah condemn him, read this verse: 'Whatever affliction befalls you is because of what your hands have obtained,' (42:30) Ali ibn al-Husayn, *'Alayhi al-Salam*, said, 'This verse is not about us. What applies to us are the words of Allah, the Most Majestic, the Most Holy, 'Whatever hardships you face on earth and in your souls, were written in the Book before the creation of souls. This is certainly easy for Allah.'" (57:22)

Chapter 194 - Allah Defends with Those Who Do Good Deeds from Those Who Do Not Do Good Deeds

H 3000, Ch. 194, h 1
Ali ibn Ibrahim has narrated from his father from Ali ibn Ma'bad from 'Abd Allah ibn al-Qasim from Yunus ibn Zabyan from abu 'Abd Allah, *'Alayhi al-Salam*, who has said the following:
"Allah defends through those of our Shi'a (followers) who perform prayer from those of our Shi'a (followers) who do not perform prayers, and if they all stop praying all of them will face destruction. Allah defends through those of our Shi'a (followers) who pay al-Zakat (charity) from those who do not pay al-Zakat and if they all stop paying al-Zakat all of them will be destroyed. Allah defends through those of our Shi'a (followers) who perform Hajj from those who do not perform Hajj and if they all stop performing Hajj all of them will be destroyed. This is indicated in the words of Allah, the Most Majestic, the Most Holy, 'Had Allah not defended one group of people through the other, the earth would have been destroyed, but Allah is generous to the worlds.' (2:251) This, by Allah, has been revealed about you and no one else is meant thereby.'"

Chapter 195 - Avoiding Sin is Easier Than Pleading for Forgiveness

H 3001, Ch. 195, h 1
Muhammad ibn Yahya has narrated from Ahmad ibn Muhammad ibn 'Isa from Ali ibn al-Hakam from certain individuals of his people from al-'Abbas al-Baqbaq who has said the following:
"Abu 'Abd Allah, *'Alayhi al-Salam*, has said, 'Amir al-Mu'minin, Ali ibn abu Talib, *'Alayhi al-Salam*, has said, "Avoiding sin is easier than pleading for forgiveness. How many are the cases of very short periods of lustful activities that cause prolonged sadness. Death disgraces the world (uncovers its worthlessness) and it has not left any happiness for the people of proper understanding.'"

Chapter 196 - Gradual Progress

H 3002, Ch. 196, h 1

A number of our people have narrated from Ahmad ibn Muhammad from Ali ibn al-Hakam from 'Abd Allah ibn Jundab from Sufyan ibn al-Samt who has said the following:

"Abu 'Abd Allah, *'Alayhi al-Salam*, has said, 'When Allah wills good for a servant upon his committing a sin He causes it to be followed by a misfortune to remind him of the need to plead for forgiveness. When Allah wills evil for a servant upon his committing a sin He causes it to be followed by his gaining bounties that make him forget the need to plead for forgiveness and continue in sin. This is indicated in the words of Allah, the Most Majestic, the Most Holy, 'We gradually lead those who have called Our revelations mere lies, to destruction. Their destruction will be such that they will not even notice how it seized them.' (7:182) This happens to them by means of His granting them bounties when they commit sins.'"

H 3003, Ch. 196, h 2

A number of our people have narrated from Sahl ibn Ziyad and Ali ibn Ibrahim has narrated from his father all from ibn Mahbub from ibn Ri'ab from certain individuals of his people who has said the following:

"Abu 'Abd Allah, *'Alayhi al-Salam*, was asked about al-'Istidraj, (gradual steps). The Imam said, 'It happens when a servant (of Allah) commits a sin he is given respite, new bounties come to him and he overlooks beseeching forgiveness for sins, thus, he is taken in gradual steps but he has not taken any notice of it.'"

H 3004, Ch. 196, h 3

Muhammad ibn Yahya has narrated from Ahmad ibn Muhammad ibn 'Isa from Muhammad ibn Sinan from 'Ammar ibn Marwan from Sama'a ibn Mehran who has said the following:

"Once I asked abu 'Abd Allah, *'Alayhi al-Salam*, about the words of Allah, the Most Majestic, the Most Holy, 'We gradually lead those who have called Our revelations mere lies to destruction. Their destruction will be such that they will not even notice how it seized them.' (7:182) The Imam said, 'It happens when a servant (of Allah) commits a sin, new bounties come to him which keeps him amused and he overlooks pleading for forgiveness for that sin.'"

H 3005, Ch. 196, h 4

Ali ibn Ibrahim has narrated from his father from al-Qasim ibn Muhammad from Sulayman (ibn Dawud) al-Minqari from Hafs ibn Ghiyath from abu 'Abd Allah, *'Alayhi al-Salam*, who has said the following:

"How many are those who suffer losses due to the bounties that Allah grant them! How many are those who gradually move to destruction due to Allah's covering their sins! How many are of the people misled due to other's praise and applause for them!'"

Chapter 197 - Evaluation of Deeds

H 3006, Ch. 197, h 1

Ali ibn Ibrahim has narrated from his father and a number of our people have narrated from Sahl ibn Ziyad all from al-Hassan ibn Mahbub from Ali ibn Ri'ab from abu Hamza from Ali ibn al-Husayn, *'Alayhi al-Salam*, who has said the following:

"Amir al-Mu'minin, Ali ibn abu Talib, *'Alayhi al-Salam*, would say, 'Time consists of three days in the middle of which you live. Yesterday that has passed in history with all that was in it and it will never return. If you had done good deeds in it you do not feel sad about it's passing into history and you feel happy about everything that you experienced in it. If you had acted extremely (bad) in it your regret is severe, for it's passing into history, due to your acting extremely (bad). While you are in the day that you live, about tomorrow you are unaware, you do not know if you will ever reach it. Perhaps your share of acting extremely (bad) in it will be just as yesterday that has passed into history.'

"One of the three days has passed and in it you had acted extremely (bad). There is the day that you are waiting for and you are not sure if you will avoid acting extremely (bad) in it. What is left is the day in which you live and it is very proper for you to use your power of reason and think about your acting extremely (bad) yesterday that passed and of the good deeds that you missed to perform when you should have performed them and the evil deeds that you should have avoided. Despite this, about tomorrow you are not certain of reaching it and whether you will perform any good deeds in it or avoid committing evil deeds that deletes the good deeds. Thus, your position toward tomorrow is like your position toward yesterday. Therefore, you must act like one who has no hope in any of the days except the day and night in which he lives. Do good deeds and save and Allah is the supporter for such task.'"

H 3007, Ch. 197, h 2

Ali ibn Ibrahim has narrated from his father from Hammad ibn 'Isa from Ibrahim ibn 'Umar al-Yamani from abu al-Hassan (Ali ibn al-Husayn), *'Alayhi al-Salam*, who has said the following:

"One who does not evaluate his deeds every day is not one of us. One must evaluate his deeds and pray to Allah to increase his good deeds, plead for forgiveness to Allah due to one's committing evil deeds and turn to Him in repentance."

H 3008, Ch. 197, h 3

Muhammad ibn Yahya has narrated from Ahmad ibn Muhammad ibn 'Isa from Ali ibn al-Nu'man from Ishaq ibn 'Ammar from abu al-Nu'man al-'Ijli from abu Ja'far, *'Alayhi al-Salam*, who has said the following:

"O abu al-Nu'man, do not allow people to deceive you about yourself; the matter will come to you and not to them. Do not spend your day in this and that; with you there is one who preserves your deeds for you. Do good deeds; I do not see anything of better result and remedy for the old sins then new good deeds.'"

A number of our people have narrated from Ahmad ibn Muhammad ibn Khalid from 'Uthman ibn 'Isa from certain individuals of our people from abu al-Nu'man a similar Hadith.

H 3009, Ch. 197, h 4

A number of our people have narrated from Ahmad ibn Muhammad ibn Khalid from 'Uthman ibn 'Isa from certain individuals of our people from abu 'Abd Allah, *'Alayhi al-Salam*, who has said the following:

"Exercise patience in worldly matters; it is only an hour. You do not find any pain or happiness in whatever has passed. The hour that has not yet arrived is unknown to you in matters of its contents. The only time is the hour in which you live. Exercise patience in it to obey Allah and exercise patience in such time in the matters of disobedience to Allah."

H 3010, Ch. 197, h 5

It is narrated from him (narrator of the Hadith above) from certain individuals of our people in a marfu' manner who has said the following:

"Abu 'Abd Allah, *'Alayhi al-Salam*, has said, 'Hold your soul responsible for yourself. If you did not do so others will not do for you.'"

H 3011, Ch. 197, h 6

It is narrated from him (narrator of the Hadith above) in a marfu' manner from abu 'Abd Allah, *'Alayhi al-Salam*, who has said the following to a man:

"You have been made the physician for your own self. Medicine is prescribed for you; signs of good health are shown to you, and the direction for medicine is given to you. It is all up to you how you treat yourself."

H 3012, Ch. 197, h 7

It is narrated from him (narrator of the Hadith above) in a marfu' manner from abu 'Abd Allah, *'Alayhi al-Salam*, who has said the following to a man:

"Make your heart a virtuous companion for yourself or like a child who does not fail to maintain good relations with parents. Consider your deeds as your father whom you follow, consider your soul as your enemy against whom you strive and consider your properties as borrowed for the safe return of which you are responsible."

H 3013, Ch. 197, h 8

It is narrated from him (narrator of the Hadith above) in a marfu' manner from abu 'Abd Allah, *'Alayhi al-Salam*, who has said the following:

"Hold back your soul from that which harms it before it departs you, strive to set it free just as you strive to make a living; your soul's well being depends upon your good deeds."

H 3014, Ch. 197, h 9

It is narrated from him (narrator of the Hadith above) from certain individuals of his people in a marfu' manner from abu 'Abd Allah, *'Alayhi al-Salam*, who has said the following:

"How many are those who seek worldly gains but can not achieve them and how many are those who had achieved worldly gains but have already departed them! Do not allow your seeking worldly gains prevent you from good deeds. You must request worldly gains from the One Who grants them and is the owner of the same. How many were those who were greedy of the worldly gains that were destroyed and whose preoccupation in them prevented them from seeking the gains of the next life until their lives finished and the appointed time approached them!

"Abu 'Abd Allah, *'Alayhi al-Salam*, has said, 'A prisoner is one whose worldly affairs imprison him so he cannot do anything for his next life.'"

H 3015, Ch. 197, h 10

It is narrated from him (narrator of the Hadith above) in a marfu' manner from abu Ja'far, *'Alayhi al-Salam*, who has said the following:

"When a man reaches the age of forty it is said to him, 'Beware, you have no excuses!' In fact, a person at the age of forty is not obliged to exercise caution against sins more than the person at the age of twenty. What is after both of them is the same (that is death) and it is not sleeping. Perform good deeds for what lies ahead of frightening conditions and stop the unnecessary words.'"

H 3016, Ch. 197, h 11

It is narrated from him (narrator of the Hadith above) from Ali ibn al-Hakam from Hassan from Zayd al-Shahham who has said the following:

"Abu 'Abd Allah, *'Alayhi al-Salam*, has said, 'Take from your soul for your soul. Take from it in good health before illness, during its strength before weakness and in its lifetime before death.'"

H 3017, Ch. 197, h 12

It is narrated from him (narrator of the Hadith above) from Ali ibn al-Hakam from Hisham ibn Salim from certain individuals of his people from abu 'Abd Allah, *'Alayhi al-Salam*, who has said the following:

"When the day comes it says, 'O son of Adam do good deeds this day so I may bear witness to it to testify (in your support) before your Lord on the Day of Judgment. I had not come to you before and will not come to you in future.' When the night comes it speaks likewise.'"

H 3018, Ch. 197, h 13

Al-Husayn ibn Muhammad has narrated from Mu'alla ibn Muhammad from Ahmad ibn Muhammad from Shu'ayb ibn 'Abd Allah from certain individuals of his people in a marfu' manner that has said the following:

"Once a man came to Amir al-Mu'minin, Ali ibn abu Talib, *'Alayhi al-Salam*, and said, 'O Amir al-Mu'minin, grant me good advice in the aspects of virtue so I may attain salvation.' Amir al-Mu'minin, Ali ibn abu Talib, *'Alayhi al-Salam*, said, 'O seeker of advice, listen carefully, understand, ascertain and practice. You must know that people are of three kinds: restraining themselves from worldly matters, exercising patience and those who are inclined toward worldly gains.

"From the hearts of restraining people sadness and happiness have moved out. He does not become happy for any of the worldly things, nor he is grieved over anything of the world that he may have missed, thus, he is comfortable.

"The person who exercises patience has hopes to have worldly gains in his heart and when he gains anything he holds his soul back from it due to such gains' bad consequences and disgrace. Were you to see his heart you would be astonished by its chastity, humility and determination.

370

"To those who are inclined to worldly gains it does not matter wherefrom worldly gains come to them, lawful or unlawful as well as whether it throws filth over their honor or destroys their souls, or takes away their kindness. They are restless in a vortex.'"

H 3019, Ch. 197, h 14

Muhammad ibn Yahya has narrated from Ahmad ibn Muhammad from Muhammad ibn Sinan from Muhammad ibn Hakim from those whom has mentioned (in his book) from abu 'Abd Allah, *'Alayhi al-Salam*, who has said the following:

"Amir al-Mu'minin, Ali ibn abu Talib, *'Alayhi al-Salam*, has said, 'What is beneficial on the Day of Judgment is not small (insignificant) and nor what is harmful for one on the Day of Judgment is small (insignificant). About whatever Allah, the Most Majestic, the Most Holy, has informed, you must be like one who has eye-witnessed them.'"

H 3020, Ch. 197, h 15

Ali ibn Ibrahim has narrated from his father and Ali ibn Muhammad al-Qasani have all narrated from al-Qasim ibn Muhammad from Sulayman al-Minqari from Hafs ibn Ghiyath who has said the following:

"Once I heard abu 'Abd Allah, *'Alayhi al-Salam*, saying, 'If you can remain unknown, then do so. There will be nothing wrong if people will not praise you. There is nothing wrong for you if people censure you if you are praiseworthy before Allah.' The Imam said, 'My father Amir al-Mu'minin, Ali ibn abu Talib, *'Alayhi al-Salam*, has said, "There is nothing good in life except for two kinds of people: a man who every day increases his good deeds and a man who every day remedies a destructive deed with repentance. How can repentance be of any benefit for him? By Allah, if he would perform a Sajdah prostration for such a length of time that his neck severs off of his body still, Allah, the Most Blessed, the Most High, will not accept his repentance without his acknowledgement of the Wilayah (Divine Authority) of our Ahl al-Bayt (family of Holy Prophet). You must know that whoever recognizes our rights can have hope for rewards because of us. He agrees, for his survival, to half of a one time meal every day, and with that which provides him covering for his privacy, his or her head, and with it, by Allah, they live in fear and apprehension and love to agree with this much as their share from the world and this is how Allah, the Majestic, the Glorious, has described them, '. . . who bring what is brought to them and whose hearts are afraid of their return to their Lord.' (23:60) What do they bring? They, by Allah, will bring along with obedience, love and (acknowledgement of) the guardianship (of Allah and Ahl al-Bayt (family of Holy Prophet) and they still will be afraid. Such fear is not due to doubts, but it is due to their fear of falling short in our love and obedience."'"

H 3021, Ch. 197, h 16

Ali ibn Ibrahim has narrated from his father from ibn Mahbub from Ibrahim ibn Mehzam from Hakam ibn Salim who has said the following:

"Once a people came to the Imam (abu Ja'far or abu 'Abd Allah, *'Alayhi al-Salam*) who granted them good advice and then said, 'If you really affirm the Holy book there is no one among you who have not observed paradise and all that it contains or the fire with all that is in it.'"

H 3022, Ch. 197, h 17

A number of our people have narrated from Ahmad ibn Muhammad ibn Khalid from 'Uthman ibn 'Isa from Sama'a who has said the following:

"I heard abu al-Hassan, *'Alayhi al-Salam*, saying, 'Do not consider a great deal of good deeds a great deal. Do not consider a little sin little; the little sins accumulate to become a great deal. Have fear of Allah in private so you can yield to justice against yourselves. Hurry up in obedience to Allah, be truthful in your words, keep the trust; it is for you. Do not be involved in what is not lawful to you; it is against you.'"

H 3023, Ch. 197, h 18

Ali ibn Ibrahim has narrated from his father from ibn Mahbub from abu Ayyub from Muhammad ibn Muslim who has said the following:

"I heard abu Ja'far, *'Alayhi al-Salam*, saying 'How excellent are good deeds after evil deeds and how disgraceful are evil deeds after good deeds!'"

H 3024, Ch. 197, h 19

A number of our people have narrated from Ahmad ibn abu 'Abd Allah from ibn Faddal from those whom has mentioned (in his book) from abu 'Abd Allah, *'Alayhi al-Salam*, who has said the following:

"You live in a period of time that is continuously reduced and in calculated days. Death comes suddenly. Whoever sows goodness will harvest what is very much sought after. Whoever sows evil will harvest regret. Every farmer finds what he has planted. The sustenance of the slow moving ones among you will not move ahead of him and the greedy will not achieve what is not assigned for him. Whoever does good, Allah grants him good and whoever safeguards against evil, Allah protects him."

H 3025, Ch. 197, h 20

Muhammad ibn Yahya has narrated from Ahmad ibn Muhammad from certain individuals of his people from al-Hassan ibn Ali ibn abu 'Uthman from Wasil from 'Abd Allah ibn Sinan from abu 'Abd Allah, *'Alayhi al-Salam*, who has said the following:

"A man came to abu Dhar and asked, 'O abu Dhar, why do we dislike death?' He said, 'It is because you have developed the world and destroyed the next life and you dislike moving from developed to that which is ruined.' The man asked, 'How do you see our moving in the presence of Allah?' He replied, 'The people of good deeds among you will be like one coming home from a journey. The evil doers among you, however, will be like a runaway slave returned to his master.' The man then asked, 'How do you see our condition before Allah?' He said, 'Present your deeds before the book of Allah. Allah has said, "The virtuous ones will live in bounties and the evil doers will live in fire." (82:14,15) The man than asked, 'Where then is the mercy of Allah?' He replied, 'The mercy of Allah is very close to the people who do good deeds.'

"Abu 'Abd Allah, *'Alayhi al-Salam*, then said, 'A man wrote to abu Dhar, may Allah be pleased with him, "O abu Dhar instruct me with a few things of knowledge." He wrote back to him, 'Knowledge is of many kinds, however, if you are able not to disappoint those whom you love, then do so. Yes, your soul is the most beloved to you. When you disobey Allah, you are doing bad and disappointing things to your own soul.'"

H 3026, Ch. 197, h 21
A number of our people have narrated from Ahmad ibn Muhammad ibn Khalid from 'Uthman ibn 'Isa from Sama'a from abu 'Abd Allah, *'Alayhi al-Salam*, who has said the following:

"I heard abu 'Abd Allah, *'Alayhi al-Salam*, saying, 'Exercise patience in the act of obedience to Allah and dictate yourselves with patience in the matters of disobeying Allah. The world is one hour. What is passed its joys and sadness do not renew. What has not yet arrived, you do not know it. Bear patience in the hour in which you live, your condition will be the one very much sought after."

H 3027, Ch. 197, h 22
Ali ibn Ibrahim has narrated from Muhammad ibn 'Isa from Yunus from a man from abu 'Abd Allah, *'Alayhi al-Salam*, who has said the following:

"Al-Khidr said to Moses, peace be upon him, 'O Moses, the best of your two days is the one before you. Consider which one it is. Then prepare the answer for it. You will be stopped for questioning. Learn your lessons from time. Time is long and also (in certain cases) short. Act as if you see the reward for your deeds so it may seem attractive due to its rewards. Anything that comes from the world is like going away from one."

H 3028, Ch. 197, h 23
A number of our people have narrated from Sahl ibn Ziyad from Ya'qub ibn Yazid from those whom has mentioned (in his book) from abu 'Abd Allah, *'Alayhi al-Salam*, who has said the following:

"It was said to Amir al-Mu'minin, Ali ibn abu Talib, *'Alayhi al-Salam*, 'Instruct us briefly with good advice.' He then said, 'For the lawful things of the world there is accountability and for the unlawful things of the world there is torment. How can you have comfort without following the traditions of your prophet? You seek what takes you to transgression and you do not agree with what is sufficient for you."

Chapter 198 - Those who Find Fault in People

H 3029, Ch. 198, h 1
Ali ibn Ibrahim has narrated from his father and A number of our people have narrated from Sahl ibn Ziyad all from ibn abu Najran from 'Asim ibn Humayd from abu Hamza al-Thumali from abu Ja'far, *'Alayhi al-Salam*, who has said the following:

"Of good deeds the quickest to bring rewards is benevolence. Of evil deeds the quickest to bring misfortune is transgression. It is enough defect for a man to find fault with others and turn a blind eye toward himself or blame people for what he himself is not able to avoid or cause suffering to one's associates for no good reason."

H 3030, Ch. 198, h 2
Muhammad ibn Yahya has narrated from Ahmad ibn Muhammad ibn 'Isa from Ali ibn al-Nu'man from ibn Muskan from abu Hamza who has said the following:

"I heard Ali ibn al-Husayn, *'Alayhi al-Salam*, saying, 'The Messenger of Allah has said, "It is enough fault in a man to find fault in people but turn a blind eye to the same that is in his own soul and to hurt his companion for no reason.'"

H 3031, Ch. 198, h 3

Muhammad ibn Yahya has narrated from al-Husayn ibn Ishaq from Ali ibn Mahziyar from Hammad ibn 'Isa from al-Husayn ibn Mukhtar from certain individuals of his people from abu Ja'far, *'Alayhi al-Salam*, who has said the following:

"It is enough fault in a man to point out people's faults but turn a blind eye to the affairs of his own soul, or consider something a fault in people while it exists in his own self from which he is not able to escape and move to something else or to cause pain to his own companion for no reason."

H 3032, Ch. 198, h 4

Ali ibn Ibrahim has narrated from Muhammad ibn 'Isa from Yunus from abu 'Abd al-Rahman al-'A'raj and 'Umar ibn Aban from abu Hamza from abu Ja'far and Ali ibn al-Husayn, *'Alayhi al-Salam*, who have said the following:

"Of the good deeds the quickest to bring reward is benevolence and of the evil deeds the quickest to bring punishment is transgression. It is enough fault in a man to look into the faults of others and turn a blind eye to his own faults or cause pain to his associates without any good reason or forbid people from that which himself is not able to avoid."

Chapter 199 - A Muslim is Not Held Responsible for His Acts of the Time of Ignorance (Pre-Islamic Paganism)

H 3033, Ch. 199, h 1

Muhammad ibn Yahya has narrated from Ahmad ibn Muhammad ibn 'Isa from ibn Mahbub from Jamil ibn Salih from abu 'Ubaydah from abu Ja'far, *'Alayhi al-Salam*, who has said the following:

"Certain people came to the Messenger of Allah after accepting Islam and said, 'O Messenger of Allah, will any of us, after accepting Islam, be held responsible for what he had done in the time of ignorance?' The Messenger of Allah said, 'Whoever is good in his Islam and corrects the certainty of his belief is not held responsible for his acts in the time of ignorance in the judgment of Allah, the Most Blessed, the Most High. Whoever's Islam is nonsense and has not corrected the certainty of his belief will be held responsible in the judgment of Allah, the Most Blessed, the Most High, for his past and later deeds.'"

H 3034, Ch. 199, h 2

Ali ibn Ibrahim has narrated from his father from al-Qasim ibn Muhammad al-Jawhari from al-Minqari from Fudayl ibn al-'Iyad who has said the following:

"Once I asked abu 'Abd Allah, *'Alayhi al-Salam*, 'Will a man who is good in Islam be held responsible for his deeds in the time of ignorance?' The Imam said, 'The Holy Prophet has said, "Whoever is good in Islam will not be held responsible for his deeds in the times of ignorance and anyone who is not good in Islam will be held responsible for his acts of the past and those thereafter.'"

Chapter 200 - Disbelief Followed by Repentance Does Not Invalidate Deeds

H 3035, Ch. 200, h 1

Ali ibn Ibrahim has narrated from his father from ibn Mahbub and others from al-'Ala' ibn Razin from Muhammad ibn Muslim from abu Ja'far, *'Alayhi al-Salam*, who has said the following:

"One who has been a believer and had performed good deeds then suffers a misfortune and turns to disbelief, then after disbelief repents, all of the good deeds that he had performed as a believer will be written down for him. Disbelief does not invalidate them if he repents after his disbelief."

Chapter 201 - People Protected from Misfortune

H 3036, Ch. 201, h 1

A number of our people have narrated from Sahl ibn Ziyad and Ali ibn Ibrahim has narrated from his father all from ibn Mahbub and others from abu Hamza from abu Ja'far, *'Alayhi al-Salam*, who has said the following:

"Allah, the Most Majestic, the Most Holy, is protective of certain people against misfortunes. He gives them life in good health, provides them sustenance in good health, causes them to die in safety, will raise them on the Day of Judgment in good health and will admit them in paradise in good health."

H 3037, Ch. 201, h 2

A number of our people have narrated from Ahmad ibn Muhammad ibn Khalid from 'Uthman ibn 'Isa from Ishaq ibn 'Ammar who has said the following:

"I heard abu 'Abd Allah, *'Alayhi al-Salam*, saying, 'Allah, the Most Majestic, the Most Holy, has created a creature that He is very acquisitively protective of. He has created them in peace and security, grants them life in peace and security, causes them to die in peace and security and will admit them in paradise in peace and security.'"

H 3038, Ch. 201, h 3

Ali ibn Ibrahim has narrated from his father and A number of our people have narrated from Sahl ibn Ziyad all from Ja'far ibn Muhammad from ibn al-Qaddah from abu 'Abd Allah, *'Alayhi al-Salam*, who has said the following:

"Allah, the Most Majestic, the Most Holy, is very protective of certain people in His creatures. He feeds them in bounties, grants them life in peace and security, will admit them in paradise with favor and mercy and He causes the misfortunes and afflictions to pass them by without harming them at all."

Chapter 202 - Nation's Exemption from Certain Issues

H 3039, Ch. 202, h 1

Al-Husayn ibn Muhammad has narrated from Mu'alla ibn Muhammad from abu Dawud al-Mustriq who has that narrated to him 'Amr ibn Marwan who has said the following:

"I heard abu 'Abd Allah, *'Alayhi al-Salam*, saying, 'The Messenger of Allah has said, "My followers are exempt from responsibility for four things: Acting mistakenly, forgetting, being coerced and compelled, and for failing to act. This has been mentioned in the words of Allah, the Most Majestic, the Most Holy,

'Lord, do not hold us responsible for our forgetfulness and mistakes. Lord, do not lay upon us the burden that You laid upon those who lived before us. Lord, do not lay upon us what we cannot afford. Ignore and forgive our sins. Have mercy upon us. You are our Lord. Help us against the unbelievers,' (2:286) also in His words, 'No one verbally denounces his faith in Allah, unless he is forced, but his heart is confident with his faith. . . .'" (16:106)

H 3040, Ch. 202, h 2
Al-Husayn ibn has narrated from Ahmad ibn Muhammad al-Hindi in a marfu' manner from abu 'Abd Allah, 'Alayhi al-Salam, who has said the following:
"The Messenger of Allah has said, 'My followers are exempt from responsibilities in nine kinds of acts and conditions:

Acting by mistake,

Out of forgetfulness,

Things they have no knowledge of,

Things they are not able to do,

Things they needed badly,

Things they are compelled to do,

Omens,

Temptations in thinking about creatures,

Feeling envy as long as it is not expressed by their tongues or hands.'"

Chapter 203 - Belief is Not Affected by Evil Deeds and Disbelief Does Not Benefit from Good Deeds

H 3041, Ch. 203, h 1
Ali ibn Ibrahim has narrated from Muhammad ibn 'Isa from Yunus from Ya'qub ibn Shu'ayb who has said the following:
"Once I asked abu 'Abd Allah, 'Alayhi al-Salam, 'Does anyone, other than the believers, has any reward with Allah for his good deeds?' The Imam said, 'No, there is no one as such.'"

H 3042, Ch. 203, h 2
It is narrated from him (narrator of the Hadith above) from Yunus from certain individuals of his people from abu 'Abd Allah, 'Alayhi al-Salam, who has said the following:
"Moses said to Khidr, 'I am honored to associate with you. Instruct me with good advice.' Khidr said, 'Hold fast to that with which nothing can harm you just as things without it will not benefit you.'"

H 3043, Ch. 203, h 3

It is narrated from him (narrator of the Hadith above) from Yunus from ibn Bukayr from abu 'Umayyah Yusuf ibn Thabit who has said the following:

"I heard abu 'Abd Allah, *'Alayhi al-Salam*, saying, 'With belief no deed can harm one and with disbelief no deed can benefit one. Consider how Allah has said it, 'What prevents their offerings from acceptance is their disbelief in Allah and His Messenger, their lack of interest in prayer and spending for the cause of Allah reluctantly, (9:54) '. . . and they die as disbelievers.'" (9:125)

H 3044, Ch. 203, h 4

Muhammad ibn Yahya has narrated from Ahmad ibn Muhammad ibn 'Isa from ibn Faddal from Tha'labah from abu 'Umayyah, Yusuf ibn Thabit ibn abu Sa'dah from abu 'Abd Allah, *'Alayhi al-Salam*, who has said the following:

"Abu 'Abd Allah, *'Alayhi al-Salam*, has said, 'With belief no deed can harm one and with disbelief no deed can benefit one.'"

H 3045, Ch. 203, h 5

Ahmad ibn Muhammad has narrated from al-Husayn ibn Sa'id from those whom has mentioned (in his book) from 'Ubaydah ibn Zurara from Muhammad ibn Marid who has said the following:

"Once I said to abu 'Abd Allah, *'Alayhi al-Salam*, 'There is a Hadith narrated to us that you have told us: 'When you recognize, do whatever you want.' The Imam said, 'Yes, I have said it.' I then asked, 'Can they even fornicate, steal and drink wine?' The Imam then said to me, 'To Allah we belong and to Him we return, by Allah they have not been fair to us. Is it fair that we will be held responsible for our deeds and they will be exempt!' What I have said is that when you recognize, do whatever you want, that is, a little good or a great deal; they will be accepted from you.'"

H 3046, Ch. 203, h 6

Ali ibn Ibrahim has narrated from his father from Muhammad ibn al-Rayyan ibn al-Salt in a marfu' manner from abu 'Abd Allah, *'Alayhi al-Salam*, who has said the following:

"Amir al-Mu'minin, Ali ibn abu Talib, *'Alayhi al-Salam*, would very often say about sin, 'O people, pay attention to your religion, pay attention to your religion. An evil deed in it (your religion) is better than a good deed in something else. An evil deed in your religion can be forgiven (by means of repenting) but a good deed in something else will not be accepted.'"

This is the end of the Book of Belief, Disbelief, Obedience and Disobedience of the Book al-Kafi and all praise belongs to Allah alone and Allah has granted blessings upon Muhammad and his family.

In the Name of Allah, the Beneficient, the Merciful

Part Two:
The Book of Prayers

Chapter 1 - The Excellence of Prayers and Strong Recommendation About It

H 3047, Ch. 1, h 1

Ali ibn Ibrahim has narrated from his father from Hammad ibn 'Isa from Hariz from Zurara from abu Ja'far, *'Alayhi al-Salam*, who has said the following:

"Allah, the Most Majestic, the Most Holy, has said, 'Those who consider themselves above the need to worship Me will soon go to hell in disgrace.' (40:60)

"The Imam said, 'This is a reference to prayer. The best form of worship is prayer (pleading before Allah for help).' I (the narrator) then asked, 'What is meant by: Ibrahim is la awwahu, prayerful and forbearing?' The Imam said, 'It means pleading for help before Allah.'"

H 3048, Ch. 1, h 2

Muhammad ibn Yahya has narrated from Ahmad ibn Muhammad from Muhammad ibn 'Isma'il and ibn Mahbub all Hanan ibn Sadir from his father who has said the following:

"Once I asked abu Ja'far, *'Alayhi al-Salam*, 'Which form of worship is better?' The Imam said, 'There is nothing more excellent before Allah, the Most Majestic, the Most Holy, than to ask and request Him to grant one from things He owns. Allah, the Most Majestic, the Most Holy, hates no one more than one who feels himself greater than to be in need of asking Allah for help, thus, he does not ask Him for help.'"

H 3049, Ch. 1, h 3

Abu Ali al-Ash'ari has narrated from Muhammad ibn 'Abd al-Jabbar from Safwan from Maysir ibn 'Abd al-'Aziz from abu 'Abd Allah, *'Alayhi al-Salam*, who has said the following:

"Abu 'Abd Allah, *'Alayhi al-Salam*, once said to me, 'O Maysir, pray and do not say that it is predetermined and it is all over. There is a position with Allah, the Majestic, the Glorious, that is not accessible without praying to Him. If a servant keeps his mouth closed and does not plead to receive help, he will not receive anything. O Maysir, there is no door that is knocked repeatedly but that sooner or later it will open up.'"

H 3050, Ch. 1, h 4

Humayd ibn Ziyad has narrated from al-Khashshab from ibn Baqqah from Mu'adh from 'Amr ibn Jumayi' from abu 'Abd Allah, *'Alayhi al-Salam*, who has said the following:

"Abu 'Abd Allah, *'Alayhi al-Salam*, has said, 'One who does not ask help from Allah, the Majestic, the Glorious, becomes needy and poor.'"

H 3051, Ch. 1, h 5

Ali ibn Ibrahim has narrated from his father from Hammad ibn 'Isa who has said the following:

"I heard abu 'Abd Allah, *'Alayhi al-Salam*, saying, 'Pray and do not say that it (belief in predetermination) is already determined and the matter is settled; prayer is worshipping. Allah, the Most Majestic, the Most Holy, has said, 'Those who consider themselves above the need to worship Me will soon go to hell in disgrace,' (40:60) 'Pray to Me, I will accept your prayers (first part of the above verse).'"

H 3052, Ch. 1, h 6
Abu Ali al-Ash'ari has narrated from Muhammad ibn 'Abd al-Jabbar from ibn abu Najran from Sayf al-Tammar who has said the following:

"I heard abu 'Abd Allah, *'Alayhi al-Salam*, saying, 'You must plead before Allah for help; you cannot seek nearness to Allah by any means better than pleading before Him for help. Do not leave your small needs without pleading before Allah for help, just because they are small; both small and large needs are in the hands of One and the same One.'"

H 3053, Ch. 1, h 7
A number of our people have narrated from Ahmad ibn Muhammad ibn 'Isa from al-Husayn ibn Sa'Id from al-Nadr ibn Suwayd from al-Qasim ibn Sulayman from 'Ubayd ibn Zurara from his father from a man who has said the following:

"Abu 'Abd Allah, *'Alayhi al-Salam*, has said, pleading before Allah for help is the form of worship about which Allah, the Most Majestic, the Most Holy, has said, 'Those who consider themselves above the need to worship Me will soon go to hell in disgrace,' (40:60) pray to Allah, the Majestic, the Glorious, and do not say that things are already determined and settled (due to predestination).'

"Zurara has said, 'The Imam thereby has meant that your belief in Allah's decision and His measures should not stop you from praying to Allah and pleading before Him for help with seriousness and enthusiasm just as he (the Imam) has said.'"

H 3054, Ch. 1, h 8
A number of our people have narrated from Sahl ibn Ziyad from Ja'far ibn Muhammad al-Ash'ari from ibn al-Qaddah from abu 'Abd Allah, *'Alayhi al-Salam*, who has said the following:

"Amir al-Mu'minin, Ali ibn abu Talib, *'Alayhi al-Salam*, has said, 'The most beloved of deeds before Allah, the Most Majestic, the Most Holy, on earth is pleading before Him for help and the best worship is chastity.' The Imam said, 'Amir al-Mu'minin, Ali ibn abu Talib, *'Alayhi al-Salam*, was a very prayerful man.'"

Chapter 2 - Pleading Before Allah for Help is a Believing Person's Weapon

H 3055, Ch. 2, h 1
A number of our people have narrated from Ahmad ibn Muhammad ibn Khalid from his father from Fadalah ibn Ayyub from al-Sakuni from abu 'Abd Allah, *'Alayhi al-Salam*, who has said the following:

"The Messenger of Allah has said, 'Pleading before Allah for help is believing people's weapons, the pillar of religion and the light of the heavens and earth.'"

H 3056, Ch. 2, h 2

Through the same chain of narrators it is narrated from Amir al-Mu'minin, Ali ibn abu Talib, *'Alayhi al-Salam*, who has said the following:

"Pleading before Allah for help is the key to success and the input for one's well being. The best prayer is what comes out of a clean chest and pious heart. In pleading before Allah for help there is the means for salvation, in sincerity there is freedom and when distress intensifies, Allah is the only One before Whom one must implore for protection."

H 3057, Ch. 2, h 3

Through his chain of narrators the narrator has said the following:

"The Holy Prophet, *'Alayhi al-Salam*, once said, 'Should I guide you to a weapon that will save you from your enemies and increase your means of living?' They said, 'Yes, (O Messenger of Allah).' The Holy Prophet said, 'Pray and plead before Allah for help night and day; prayer is the weapon of believing people.'"

H 3058, Ch. 2, h 4

A number of our people have narrated from Sahl ibn Ziyad from Ja'far ibn Muhammad al-Ash'ari from ibn al-Qaddah from abu 'Abd Allah, *'Alayhi al-Salam*, who has said the following:

"Amir al-Mu'minin, Ali ibn abu Talib, *'Alayhi al-Salam*, has said, 'Prayer is a shield for a believing person. When a door is knocked often it will sooner or later open up.'"

H 3059, Ch. 2, h 5

A number of our people have narrated from Ahmad ibn Muhammad from ibn Faddal from certain individuals of our people who has said the following:

"Al-Rida, *'Alayhi al-Salam*, would say to his disciples, 'You must keep with you the weapons of the prophets.' It was asked, 'What are the weapons of the prophets?' The Imam said, 'It is prayer, pleading before Allah for help.'"

H 3060, Ch. 2, h 6

Ali ibn Ibrahim has narrated from his father from 'Abd Allah ibn al-Mughirah from abu Sa'Id al-Bajilli who has said the following:

"Abu 'Abd Allah, *'Alayhi al-Salam*, has said, 'Prayer, pleading before Allah for help is more effective than spears.'"

H 3061, Ch. 2, h 7

It is narrated from him (narrator of the Hadith above) from his father from ibn abu 'Umayr from 'Abd Allah ibn Sinan from abu 'Abd Allah, *'Alayhi al-Salam*, who has said the following:

"Abu 'Abd Allah, *'Alayhi al-Salam*, has said, 'Prayer, pleading before Allah for help, is more effective than spears of iron.'"

Chapter 3 - Prayer Diverts Misfortune and Allah's Decision

H 3062, Ch. 3, h 1

Ali ibn Ibrahim has narrated from his father from ibn abu 'Umayr from Hammad ibn 'Uthman who has said the following:

"I heard abu 'Abd Allah, *'Alayhi al-Salam*, saying, 'Prayer and pleading before Allah for help repeals al-Qada, what is already determined, and severs it as threads are incised, even though it (threads) may have been coiled and knotted extremely strong and solid.'"

H 3063, Ch. 3, h 2
It is narrated from him (narrator of the Hadith above) from his father from ibn abu 'Umayr from Hisham ibn Salim from 'Umar ibn Yazid who has said the following:

"I heard abu al-Hassan, *'Alayhi al-Salam,* saying, 'Prayer, and pleading before Allah for help, repeals Quddira, what is already measured, and the unmeasured.' I (the narrator) then asked the Imam, 'I know the meaning of what is 'Measured', but what is the meaning of the 'Unmeasured'?' The Imam said, 'So that it (a measure, of misfortune) will not come into being.'"

H 3064, Ch. 3, h 3
Abu Ali al-Ash'ari has narrated from Muhammad ibn 'Abd al-Jabbar from Safwan from Bistam al-Zayyat from abu 'Abd Allah, *'Alayhi al-Salam,* who has said the following:

"Abu 'Abd Allah, *'Alayhi al-Salam,* has said, 'Prayer and pleading before Allah for help, repeals al-Qada', what is already determined, has already come down from heavens and is firmly established.'"

H 3065, Ch. 3, h 4
Muhammad ibn Yahya has narrated from [Ahmad ibn] Muhammad ibn 'Isa from abu Hammam Isma'Il ibn Hammam from al-Rida, *'Alayhi al-Salam,* who has said the following:

"Ali ibn al-Husayn, *'Alayhi al-Salam,* has said, 'Prayer and pleading before Allah for help, and misfortune are joined together and will remain so until the Day of Judgment. Prayer repeals misfortunes even though it (misfortune) may have already been firmly established.'"

H 3066, Ch. 3, h 5
A number of our people have narrated from Sahl ibn Ziyad from al-Hassan ibn Ali al-Washsha' from abu al-Hassan, *'Alayhi al-Salam,* who has said the following:

"Ali ibn al-Husayn, *'Alayhi al-Salam,* has said, 'Prayer and pleading before Allah for help, repels the misfortune that has already come down and that which has not yet come down.'"

H 3067, Ch. 3, h 6
Ali ibn Ibrahim has narrated from his father from Hammad ibn 'Isa from Hariz from Zurara who has said the following:

"Abu Ja'far, *'Alayhi al-Salam,* once said to me, 'Should I tell you something about a case in which even the Messenger of Allah is not an exception?' I said, 'Yes, (I like to know).' The Imam said, 'Prayer and pleading before Allah for help repeals al-Qada, what is already determined, even though it may have firmly been established. He folded his fingers together (to form a fist as a sign of firmness).'"

H 3068, Ch. 3, h 7
Al-Husayn ibn Muhammad has narrated from Mu'alla ibn Muhammad from al-Washsha' from 'Abd Allah ibn Sinan who has said the following:

"I heard abu 'Abd Allah, *'Alayhi al-Salam,* saying, 'Prayer and pleading before Allah for help, repeals what is already determined, even after it is firmly established. Thus, increase your prayers; it is the key to all favors, success and need. What is with Allah, the Most Majestic, the Most Holy, cannot be achieved by any means other than prayer and any door that is knocked very often will sooner or later open up to the one knocking.'"

H 3069, Ch. 3, h 8
Muhammad ibn Yahya has narrated from Ahmad ibn Muhammad ibn 'Isa from ibn Mahbub from abu Wallad who has said the following:

"Abu al-Hassan Musa, *'Alayhi al-Salam*, has said, 'You must pray and plead before Allah for help; pleading before Allah for help and requesting from Him repels misfortunes even though they may have already been measured and determined, Qudiya and Quddira, and are set to take place free of all obstacles except final approval, al-'Imda'. When Allah, the Most Majestic, the Most Holy, is called for help and is requested to remove a misfortune, He diverts it without fail.'"

H 3070, Ch. 3, h 9
Al-Husayn ibn Muhammad has narrated in a marfu' manner from Ishaq ibn 'Ammar who has said the following:

"Abu 'Abd Allah, *'Alayhi al-Salam*, has said, 'By means of prayer, Allah, the Most Majestic, the Most Holy, repels a thing (a misfortune) that He knows He will divert it if a plea will be made before Him. However, if the servant (of Allah) fails to pray and plead before Allah for help, the misfortune will afflict him to the extent of pulling him to pieces from the face of earth.'"

Chapter 4 - Prayer and Pleading Before Allah for Help is a Cure to all Disease

H 3071, Ch. 4, h 1
Ali ibn Ibrahim has narrated from his father from ibn abu 'Umayr from Asbat ibn Slim from al-'Ala' ibn Kamil who has said the following:

"Abu 'Abd Allah, *'Alayhi al-Salam*, once said to me, 'You must pray and plead before Allah for help; it is the cure to all diseases.'"

Chapter 5 - Whoever Prays, It is Answered

H 3072, Ch. 5, h 1
Muhammad ibn Yahya has narrated from Ahmad ibn Muhammad ibn 'Isa from al-Hassan ibn Ali from 'Abd Allah ibn Maymun al-Qaddah from abu 'Abd Allah, *'Alayhi al-Salam*, who has said the following:

"Abu 'Abd Allah, *'Alayhi al-Salam*, has said, 'Prayer and pleading before Allah for help is the means for its acceptance just as clouds are means of rain.'"

H 3073, Ch. 5, h 2
A number of our people have narrated from Sahl ibn Ziyad from Ja'far ibn Muhammad al-Ash'ari from ibn al-Qaddah from abu 'Abd Allah, *'Alayhi al-Salam*, who has said the following:

"Any servant (of Allah) who raises his hands toward Allah, the Most Majestic, the Compelling, Allah, the Most Majestic, the Most Holy, will be shy to turn him down empty-handed, and without placing in it from His favors as He wills. After praying you (every one of you) should not return his hands to normal position before wiping them over his face and head."

Chapter 6 - When One is Inspired to Pray

H 3074, Ch. 6, h 1

Ali ibn Ibrahim has narrated from his father from ibn abu 'Umayr from Hisham ibn Salim who has said the following:

"Abu 'Abd Allah, *'Alayhi al-Salam*, once asked, 'Can you tell if a misfortune is of a lengthy duration or a shorter one?' We said, 'No, we do not know.' The Imam said, 'Whenever any of you is inspired to pray then you should know that the misfortune is of a shorter duration.'"

H 3075, Ch. 6, h 2

Muhammad ibn Yahya has narrated from Ahmad ibn Muhammad ibn 'Isa from ibn Mahbub from abu Wallad who has said the following:

"Once abu al-Hassan Musa, *'Alayhi al-Salam*, said, 'Whenever a misfortune is about to arrive upon a believing servant (of Allah), if Allah, the Most Majestic, the Most Holy, inspires him to pray and plead before Allah for help, the diversion of misfortune from him will take place very shortly. Whenever a misfortune is to arrive upon a believing servant (of Allah) and he is held back from praying, that misfortune will be upon him for a lengthier period of time. Whenever a misfortune befalls you, you must pray and plead before Allah for help and appeal to Allah, the Most Majestic, the Most Holy, to move it away.'"

Chapter 7 - Prayer Before the Fall of Misfortune

H 3076, Ch. 7, h 1

Muhammad ibn Yahya has narrated from Ahmad ibn Muhammad ibn 'Isa from Ali ibn al-Hakam from Hisham ibn Salim from abu 'Abd Allah, *'Alayhi al-Salam*, who has said the following:

"Whoever prays and pleads before Allah for help before the fall of misfortune, his prayer is accepted when the misfortune arrives. The angels will say, 'It is a known voice and it is not barred from heaven.' If one does not pray and plead before Allah for help before the fall of misfortune, his prayer will not be accepted when it falls upon him. The angels will say, 'We do not know this voice.'"

H 3077, Ch. 7, h 2

Ali ibn Ibrahim has narrated from his father from Hammad ibn 'Isa from ibn Sinan from 'Anbasah from abu 'Abd Allah, *'Alayhi al-Salam*, who has said the following:

"If one fears the fall of a misfortune upon him and prays and pleads before Allah for help before its fall, Allah, the Most Majestic, the Most Holy, will never show him that misfortune."

H 3078, Ch. 7, h 3

A number of our people have narrated from Ahmad ibn Muhammad ibn Khalid from Isma'Il ibn Mehran from Mansur ibn Yunus from Harun ibn Kharijah from abu 'Abd Allah, *'Alayhi al-Salam*, who has said the following:

"Abu 'Abd Allah, *'Alayhi al-Salam*, has said, 'Prayer and pleading before Allah for help in one's enjoying well-being brings about (causes to happen) what one needs in the fall of misfortune.'"

H 3079, Ch. 7, h 4

It is narrated from him (narrator of the Hadith above) from 'Uthman ibn 'Isa from Sama'a who has said the following:

"Abu 'Abd Allah, *'Alayhi al-Salam*, has said, 'Whoever likes his prayers answered in difficult times should pray when he enjoys well-being and comfort.'"

H 3080, Ch. 7, h 5

It is narrated from him (narrator of the Hadith above) from his father from 'Ubayd Allah ibn Yahya from a man from 'Abd al-Hamid ibn Ghawwas al-Ta'I from Muhammad ibn Muslim from abu 'Abd Allah, *'Alayhi al-Salam*, who has said the following:

"My grandfather would say, 'You must pray and plead before Allah for help before the fall of misfortune; if a servant (of Allah) is prayerful and misfortune befalls him and he prays, it is then said, 'It is a familiar voice,' but if he does not pray and plead before Allah for help when misfortune befalls him, only then he prays, it then is asked, 'Where have you been before this day?'"

H 3081, Ch. 7, h 6

Al-Husayn ibn Muhammad has narrated from Mu'alla ibn Muhammad from al-Washsha' from those whom he has mentioned (in his book) from abu al-Hassan al-Awwal, *'Alayhi al-Salam*, who has said the following:

"Ali ibn al-Husayn, *'Alayhi al-Salam*, would say, 'Prayer and pleading before Allah for help after the fall of misfortune does not benefit one.'"

Chapter 8 - Certainty in (the Effectiveness of) Prayer

H 3082, Ch. 8, h 1

Ali ibn Ibrahim has narrated from his father from ibn abu 'Umayr from Sulaym al-Farra' from those whom he has mentioned (in his book) from abu 'Abd Allah, *'Alayhi al-Salam*, who has said the following:

"Abu 'Abd Allah, *'Alayhi al-Salam*, has said, 'Whenever you pray and plead before Allah for help, consider that what you have asked for has arrived at the door.'"

Chapter 9 - Praying Attentively

H 3083, Ch. 9, h 1

Ali ibn Ibrahim has narrated from his father from ibn abu 'Umayr from Sayf ibn 'Amirah from Sulayman ibn 'Amr who has said the following:

"I heard abu 'Abd Allah, *'Alayhi al-Salam*, saying, 'Allah, the Most Majestic, the Most Holy, does not accept an inattentive prayer. Whenever you may pray and plead before Allah for help, do it with an attentive heart and with certainty in its acceptance.'"

H 3084, Ch. 9, h 2

A number of our people have narrated from Sahl ibn Ziyad from Ja'far ibn Muhammad al-Ash'ari from ibn al-Qaddah from abu 'Abd Allah, *'Alayhi al-Salam*, who has said the following:

"Amir al-Mu'minin, Ali ibn abu Talib, *'Alayhi al-Salam*, has said, 'Allah, the Most Majestic, the Most Holy, does not accept the prayer from a thoughtless heart. Ali, *'Alayhi al-Salam*, would say, 'Whenever any of you may pray for a dead person, he must not do it frivolously but must strive to be serious in his prayer.'"

H 3085, Ch. 9, h 3
Muhammad ibn Yahya has narrated from Ahmad ibn Muhammad ibn 'Isa from certain individuals of his people from Sayf ibn 'Amirah from Sulaym al-Farra' from those whom he has mentioned (in his book) from abu 'Abd Allah, *'Alayhi al-Salam*, who has said the following:

"Abu 'Abd Allah, *'Alayhi al-Salam*, has said, 'Whenever you pray and plead before Allah for help, do it whole-heartedly and consider that what you have asked for has arrived at the door.'"

H 3086, Ch. 9, h 4
A number of our people have narrated from Ahmad ibn Muhammad ibn Khalid from Isma'Il ibn Mehran from Sayf ibn 'Amirah from those whom he has mentioned (in his book) from abu 'Abd Allah, *'Alayhi al-Salam*, who has said the following:

"Abu 'Abd Allah, *'Alayhi al-Salam*, has said, 'Allah, the Most Majestic, the Most Holy, does not accept a prayer coming superficially from a hardhearted attitude.'"

H 3087, Ch. 9, h 5
Ali ibn Ibrahim has narrated from his father from ibn abu 'Umayr from Hisham ibn al-Hakam from abu 'Abd Allah, *'Alayhi al-Salam*, who has said the following:

"When the Messenger of Allah prayed for rain, people were drenched so much that they thought they might be drowned and the Messenger of Allah made hand gestures to scatter the cloud, saying, 'O Lord make it to rain around us, not on us.' The Imam said, 'The clouds scattered and people asked, "O Messenger of Allah, how is it that once you prayed for rain it did not rain, then you prayed for rain and it rained?" The Messenger of Allah said, 'I prayed but I did not have much intention, then I prayed and I did.'"

Chapter 10 - Insistence in Prayer and Waiting for Answers

H 3088, Ch. 10, h 1
Ali ibn Ibrahim has narrated from his father from ibn abu 'Umayr from Husayn ibn 'Atiyyah from 'Abd al-'Aziz al-Tawil who has said the following:

"Abu 'Abd Allah, *'Alayhi al-Salam*, has said, 'Whenever a servant (of Allah) prays and pleads before Allah for help, (the will of) Allah, the Most Blessed, the Most High, is in fulfilling his needs, provided he is not in (big) haste.'"

Muhammad ibn Yahya has narrated from Ahmad ibn Muhammad ibn 'Isa from ibn abu 'Umayr from Husayn ibn 'Atiyyah from 'Abd al-'Aziz al-Tawil from abu 'Abd Allah, *'Alayhi al-Salam*, a similar Hadith.

H 3089, Ch. 10, h 2
Muhammad ibn Yahya has narrated from Ahmad ibn Muhammad ibn 'Isa and Ali ibn Ibrahim has narrated from his father all from ibn abu 'Umayr from Hisham ibn Salim and Hafs ibn al-Bakhtari and others from abu 'Abd Allah, *'Alayhi al-Salam*, who has said the following:

"If a servant (of Allah) hastens in his prayer and stands up to do what he needs, Allah, the Most Blessed, the Most High, then asks, 'Does My servant not know that I am Allah who fulfils the needs of people?'"

H 3090, Ch. 10, h 3

Muhammad ibn Yahya has narrated from Ahmad ibn Muhammad from ibn abu 'Umayr from Sayf ibn 'Amirah from Muhammad ibn Marwan from al-Walid ibn 'Uqbah al-Hajari who has said the following:

"I heard abu Ja'far, *'Alayhi al-Salam*, saying, 'By Allah, if a believing servant (of Allah) insists before Allah, the Most Majestic, the Most Holy, on praying and pleading before Allah for help, He will fulfill his needs.'"

H 3091, Ch. 10, h 4

It is narrated from him (narrator of the Hadith above) from Ahmad ibn Muhammad ibn 'Isa from al-Hajjal from Hassan from abu al-Sabbah from abu 'Abd Allah, *'Alayhi al-Salam*, who has said the following:

"Allah, the Most Majestic, the Most Holy, dislikes people insisting before one another for help but He likes it before Himself. Allah, the Most Majestic, the Most Holy, loves that one begs and requests help from Him."

H 3092, Ch. 10, h 5

Ali ibn Ibrahim has narrated from his father from ibn abu 'Umayr from Husayn al-Ahmasi from a man from abu Ja'far, *'Alayhi al-Salam*, who has said the following:

"Abu Ja'far, *'Alayhi al-Salam*, has said, 'By Allah, if a man insists before Allah, the Most Majestic, the Most Holy, on praying and pleading for help, He will accept his prayers.'"

H 3093, Ch. 10, h 6

A number of our people have narrated from Sahl ibn Ziyad from Ja'far ibn Muhammad al-Ash'ari from ibn al-Qaddah from abu 'Abd Allah, *'Alayhi al-Salam*, who has said the following:

"The Messenger of Allah has said, 'May Allah grant favors upon a servant who requests help from Allah, the Most Majestic, the Most Holy, and insists on praying and pleading before Him for help, accepted or not. He then read this verse of the Holy Quran: ". . . I worship my Lord and hope that my prayers will not be ignored."' (19:48)

Chapter 11 - Describing One's Needs

H 3094, Ch. 11, h 1

Ali ibn Ibrahim has narrated from his father from ibn abu 'Umayr from abu 'Abd Allah al-Farra' from abu 'Abd Allah, *'Alayhi al-Salam*, who has said the following:

"Allah, the Most Blessed, the Most High, knows what a servant wants when he prays and pleads before Him for help, but He loves that one's needs are brought before Him in detail. Whenever you pray, name your request.' In another Hadith it is said, 'Allah, the Most Blessed, the Most High, knows your needs and what you want, but He loves that you name (identify) in detail your needs before Him.'"

Chapter 12 - Secrecy in Prayer

H 3095, Ch. 12, h 1

Muhammad ibn Yahya has narrated from Ahmad ibn Muhammad ibn 'Isa from abu Hammam Isma'Il ibn Hammam from abu al-Hassan al-Rida, *'Alayhi al-Salam*, who has said the following:

"A servant's praying and pleading before Allah for help, privately once, is equal to seventy such prayers in public.' In another Hadith it is said: 'A prayer that you (hide from people) is better before Allah than seventy prayers made in public.'"

Chapter 13 - The Times and Conditions in Which There is Hope for Acceptance

H 3096, Ch. 13, h 1

A number of our people have narrated from Ahmad ibn Muhammad ibn Khalid from Yahya ibn Ibrahim ibn abu al-Belad from his father from Ziyad al-Shahham who has said the following:

"Abu 'Abd Allah, *'Alayhi al-Salam*, has said, 'Seek prayer in four hours: at the time of the blowing of winds, at the time of vanishing of shadows, at the time of the coming of raindrops and at the time the first drop of the blood of a believing person murdered spills. At such times the doors of the heavens open up.'"

H 3097, Ch. 13, h 2

It is narrated from him (narrator of the Hadith above) from his father from others from al-Qasim ibn 'Urwah from abu al-'Abbas Fadl al-Baqbaq who has said the following:

"Abu 'Abd Allah, *'Alayhi al-Salam*, has said, 'One's praying and pleading before Allah for help is accepted in four occasions: in al-Witr, the last Rak'at of night prayer, after dawn, after noon time and after sunset.'"

H 3098, Ch. 13, h 3

Ali ibn Ibrahim has narrated from his father from al-Nawfali from al-Sakuni from abu 'Abd Allah, *'Alayhi al-Salam*, who has said the following:

"Amir al-Mu'minin, Ali ibn abu Talib, *'Alayhi al-Salam*, has said, 'Use the opportunity for praying and pleading before Allah for help, on four occasions: at the time of reading the Holy Quran, at the time of Adhan (call for prayer) at the time it rains and at the time of the meeting of two armies (of which one sides is) for martyrdom.'"

H 3099, Ch. 13, h 4

Ali ibn Ibrahim has narrated from his father from ibn abu 'Umayr from Jamil ibn Darraj from 'Abd Allah ibn 'Ata' from abu Ja'far, *'Alayhi al-Salam*, who has said the following:

"Abu Ja'far, *'Alayhi al-Salam*, has said, 'When my father needed help from Allah he would pray for it on this hour, that is, at noon time.'"

H 3100, Ch. 13, h 5

It is narrated from him (narrator of the Hadith above) from his father from Hammad ibn 'Isa from Husayn ibn al-Mukhtar from abu Basir from abu 'Abd Allah, *'Alayhi al-Salam*, who has said the following:

"Abu 'Abd Allah, *'Alayhi al-Salam*, has said, 'Whenever any one of you feels moved, you should pray at such time; the heart does not feel moved in tenderness until it becomes sincere.'"

H 3101, Ch. 13, h 6

A number of our people have narrated from Ahmad ibn Muhammad ibn Khalid from Sharif ibn Sabiq from al-Fadl ibn abu Qurrah from abu 'Abd Allah, *'Alayhi al-Salam*, who has said the following:

"The Messenger of Allah has said, 'The best time to pray to Allah, the Most Majestic, the Most Holy, is the last part of the night' and he read this verse that quotes Ya'qub, peace be upon him, 'I shall ask my Lord to forgive you; He is All-Forgiving and All-Merciful.' (12:98) He said that he (Ya'qub) waited until the last part of the night (Sahar), then he prayed.'"

H 3102, Ch. 13, h 7

Al-Husayn ibn Muhammad has narrated from Ahmad ibn Ishaq from Su'Dan ibn Muslim from Mu'awiyah ibn 'Ammar from abu 'Abd Allah, *'Alayhi al-Salam*, who has said the following:

"Whenever my father prayed to Allah for help he would do so at noontime when the sun began to descend to the western horizon. When he intended it, first he would give something in charity, use perfume, go to the Mosque and pray to Allah for whatever he wanted."

H 3103, Ch. 13, h 8

A number of our people have narrated from Ahmad ibn Muhammad ibn Khalid from Ali ibn Hadid in a marfu' manner from abu 'Abd Allah, *'Alayhi al-Salam*, who has said the following:

"Whenever your skin feels a tingling sensation and your eyes tear up, you must pray and plead before Allah for help, it (your wish) is coming your way."

The narrator has said that Muhammad ibn Isma'il has narrated from abu Isma'il al-Sarraj from Muhammad ibn abu Hamza from Sa'id a similar Hadith.

H 3104, Ch. 13, h 9

It is narrated from him (narrator of the Hadith above) from al-Jamurani from al-Hassan ibn Ali ibn abu Hamza from Sandal from abu al-Sabbah al-Kinani from abu Ja'far, *'Alayhi al-Salam*, who has said the following:

"Allah, the Most Majestic, the Most Holy, from among His believing people loves every prayerful one. You should pray during the last part of the night until sunrise; it is the hour in which the doors of heaven open up, sustenance is distributed and people in need are granted great help."

H 3105, Ch. 13, h 10

Ali ibn Ibrahim has narrated from his father from ibn abu 'Umayr from 'Umar ibn 'Udhaynah who has said the following:

"I heard abu 'Abd Allah, *'Alayhi al-Salam*, saying, 'In a night there is an hour during which if a Muslim servant (of Allah) has the opportunity to perform a formal prayer and then plead before Allah, the Most Majestic, the Most Holy, for help, he will receive an answer every night.' I (the narrator) then asked, 'May Allah grant you well being, which hour of night is that?' The Imam said, 'It is the first one-sixth of the second half of the night.'"

Chapter 14 - Al-Raghbah (Fondness), al-Rahbah (Anxiety), al-Tadarru' (Imploration), al-Tabattul (Sincerity), al-'Ibtihal (Appealing), al-Isti'adha (Begging for Refuge), al-Mas'alah (Requesting)

H 3106, Ch. 14, h 1

A number of our people have narrated from Ahmad ibn Muhammad ibn Khalid from Isma'Il ibn Mehran from Sayf ibn 'Amirah from abu Ishaq from abu 'Abd Allah, *'Alayhi al-Salam*, who has said the following:

"Al-Raghbah means keeping the palms of your hands toward the sky. Al-Rahbah means keeping the back of your hands toward the sky. The words of Allah, the Most Majestic, the Most Holy, 'glorify the name of your Lord, with due sincerity (al-Tabattul),' (73:8) 'refers to hand gestures made in prayer with one finger. Al-Tadarru' is pointing and gesturing with two fingers, 'Ibtihal is raising both hands and stretching them up high when one's eyes tear up. It then is the time you should pray.'"

H 3107, Ch. 14, h 2

Ali ibn Ibrahim has narrated from his father from ibn abu 'Umayr from abu Ayyub from Muhammad ibn Muslim who has said the following:

"Once I asked abu Ja'far, *'Alayhi al-Salam*, about the words of Allah, the Most Majestic, the Most Holy, '. . . but they did not 'Istakanu (submit themselves to their Lord,) nor did they make themselves humble (yatadarra'un).' (23:76) The Imam said, 'Al-'Istikana, means humility and al-tadarru' means raising both hands and begging for help from (Allah) with both hands.'"

H 3108, Ch. 14, h 3

Muhammad ibn Yahya has narrated from Ahmad ibn Muhammad ibn 'Isa from Muhammad ibn Khalid and al-Husayn ibn Sa'Id all from al-Nadr ibn Suwayd from Yahya al-Halabi from abu Khalid from Marwan Bayya'al-Lu'lu from those whom he has mentioned (in his book) who has said the following:

"Once al-Raghbah (fondness) was mentioned before abu 'Abd Allah, *'Alayhi al-Salam*, and he raised his hands to the sky with his palms upward. He then turned the back of his hands upward to the sky and said, ''This way is al-Rahbah (expressing anxiety). He moved his fingers right and left and said that such is al-Tadarru'. He then raised his fingers and then lower them saying that such is al-Tabattul. He then stretched his hands in front of his face toward the Ka'bah saying that such is al-'Ibtihal only when tears flow.'"

H 3109, Ch. 14, h 4

A number of our people have narrated from Ahmad ibn Muhammad ibn Khalid from his father from Fadalah from al-'Ala' from Muhammad ibn Muslim who has said the following:

"I heard abu 'Abd Allah, *'Alayhi al-Salam*, saying, 'Once a man passed by when I was praying in my prayer with my left hand raised. The man said, 'O 'Abd Allah, (servant of Allah) pray with your right hand raised.' I then said, 'O servant of Allah, Allah, the Most Blessed, the Most High's rights apply to this hand just as they do to that hand.'

"The Imam said, al-Raghbah is raising your hands with palms upward, al-Rahbah is stretching your hands with their backs upward, al-Tadarru' is moving the index finger of your right hand right and left, al-Tabattul is moving the index finger of your left hand, raise it up and bring it down, al-'Ibtihal is stretching your hands and arms to the sky and it is only when you see reasons for weeping."

H 3110, Ch. 14, h 5

It is narrated from him (narrator of the Hadith above) from his father and others from Harun ibn Kharijah from abu Basir who has said the following:

"Once I asked abu 'Abd Allah, *'Alayhi al-Salam*, about prayer and raising hands. The Imam said, 'It is in four ways: in al-Ta'awwuz (seeking refuge) turn the palms of your hands toward the Ka'bah and in prayer for sustenance stretch your hands with their palms upward to the sky. Al-Tabattul is gesturing with index finger. Al-'Ibtihal is to raise both hands over your head with prayer and imploration. Moving your index finger before your face is in prayer when one is fearful.'"

H 3111, Ch. 14, h 6
Muhammad ibn Yahya has narratedfrom Ahmad ibn Muhammad from ibn Mahbub from abu Ayyub from Muhammad ibn Muslim who has said the following:

"Once I asked abu Ja'far, *'Alayhi al-Salam*, about the words of Allah, the Most Majestic, the Most Holy, '. . . but they did not 'Istakanu (submit themselves to their Lord,) nor did they make themselves humble (yatadarra'un)' (23:76) the Imam said, 'al-'Istikana, means humility and al-tadarru' means raising both hands and begging for help from (Allah) with both hands.'"

H 3112, Ch. 14, h 7
Ali ibn Ibrahim has narrated from his father from Hammad from Hariz from Muhammad ibn Muslim and Zurara who have said the following:

"Zurara has said, 'Once we asked abu 'Abd Allah, *'Alayhi al-Salam*, how to plead before Allah for help?' The Imam said, 'Stretch your palms.' We then asked, 'How is seeking refuge?' The Imam said, 'Turn your palm to Ka'aba, and al-Tabattul is making gestures with your finger. Al-Tadarru' is the moving of fingers and al-'Ibtihal is the stretching out of both hands.'"

Chapter 15 - Weeping

H 3113, Ch. 15, h 1
Ali ibn Ibrahim has narrated from his father from ibn abu 'Umayr from Mansur ibn Yunus from Muhammad ibn Marwan from abu 'Abd Allah, *'Alayhi al-Salam*, who has said the following:

"For everything there is weighing and measuring except tears. One drop of tears can extinguish oceans of fire. If the eyes flood with tears the face will not suffer hardships and humiliation. When tears flow out, Allah makes it forbidden for the fire and if a person weeps in a nation, such nation will receive favors."

H 3114, Ch. 15, h 2
A number of our people have narrated from Sahl ibn Ziyad from ibn Faddal from abu Jamilah and Mansur ibn Yunus from Muhammad ibn Marwan from abu 'Abd Allah, *'Alayhi al-Salam*, who has said the following:

"Every eye will be weeping on the Day of Judgment except the eye that has wept for fear of Allah. Any eye that is flooded with tears for fear of Allah, the Most Majestic, the Most Holy, Allah, the Majestic, the Glorious, will make it forbidden for the fire to burn the other parts of his body. Any eye from which tears flow over one's checks such face will not face any suffering or humiliation. Everything has weighing and measuring tools except tears with a very little of which Allah, the Most Majestic, the Most Holy, will extinguish oceans of fire. If a servant (of Allah) weeps in a nation, Allah, the Most Majestic, the Most Holy, will grant favor to that nation because of the weeping of that one servant (of Allah)."

H 3115, Ch. 15, h 3

It is narrated from him (narrator of the Hadith above) from 'Abd al-Rahman ibn abu Najran from Muthanna al-Hannat from abu Hamza from abu Ja'far, *'Alayhi al-Salam*, who has said the following:

"No drop is more beloved to Allah, the Majestic, the Glorious, than the drop of tears in the dark night for fear of Allah, and is intended to be just for Him alone."

H 3116, Ch. 15, h 4

Ali ibn Ibrahim has narrated from his father from ibn abu 'Umayr from Mansur ibn Yunus from Salih ibn Razin and Muhammad ibn Marwan and others from abu 'Abd Allah, *'Alayhi al-Salam*, who has said the following:

"Every eye on the Day of Judgment will be weeping except three eyes: the eye that was shut closed from looking at things made unlawful by (the laws of) Allah, the eye that spends the night in awake in obedience to Allah and the eye that weeps inside the night for fear of Allah."

H 3117, Ch. 15, h 5

Ibn abu 'Umayr has narrated from Jamil ibn Darraj and Drust from Muhammad ibn Marwan who has said the following:

"I heard abu 'Abd Allah, *'Alayhi al-Salam*, saying, 'everything has weighing and measuring tools except the tears. A drop of tear can extinguish oceans of fire. If the eye floods with tears, that face will not suffer anything or become humiliated. If the eye overflows with tears, Allah makes it forbidden for the fire to burn it and if a person weeps in a nation, that nation will receive favors.'"

H 3118, Ch. 15, h 6

Ibn abu 'Umayr has narrated from a man from certain individuals of his people who has said the following:

"Abu 'Abd Allah, *'Alayhi al-Salam*, has said, 'Allah, the Most Majestic, the Most Holy, sent revelations to Moses that said, "the most beloved of things to Me with which My servants can seek nearness to Me are three things." Moses then asked, 'Lord, what are they?' The Lord said, 'One's reduced interest in worldly matters, restraint from sins and weeping for fear of Me.' Moses asked, 'Lord, what is then the reward for one who would do so?' Allah, the Most Majestic, the Most Holy, sent him revelation that said, 'Moses, people with reduced interest in the world will be in paradise, those weeping for fear of Me will be in a high position with whom no one else will share and those restraining from sins for their reward will have the privilege of freedom from My searching their affairs when I search all other people.'"

H 3119, Ch. 15, h 7

A number of our people have narrated from Ahmad ibn Muhammad from 'Uthman ibn 'Isa from Ishaq ibn 'Ammar who has said the following:

"Once I said to abu 'Abd Allah, *'Alayhi al-Salam*, 'When I pray and plead before Allah for help, I like to weep but it does not come through, but if I recall members of my family who have died I may feel weeping. Is that permissible?' The Imam said, 'Yes, it is permissible. When you recall them and feel like weeping then pray to your Lord, the Most Blessed, the Most High.'"

H 3120, Ch. 15, h 8

Muhammad ibn Yahya has narrated from Ahmad ibn Muhammad ibn 'Isa from al-Hassan ibn Mahbub from 'Anbasah al-'Abid who has said the following:

"Abu 'Abd Allah, *'Alayhi al-Salam*, has said, 'If you cannot weep then make a weeping-like face.'"

H 3121, Ch. 15, h 9

It is narrated from him (narrator of the Hadith above) from ibn Faddal from Yunus ibn Ya'qub from Sa'Id ibn Yasar Bayya' al-Sabiri who has said the following:

"Once I said to abu 'Abd Allah, *'Alayhi al-Salam*, 'In my prayer I can only make a weeping-like face, but weeping does not come through.' The Imam said, 'Yes, even (tears) of the size of the head of a fly (are very good).'"

H 3122, Ch. 15, h 10

It is narrated from him (narrator of the Hadith above) from Ahmad ibn Muhammad from Ali ibn al-Hakam from Ali ibn abu Hamza who has said the following:

"Abu 'Abd Allah, *'Alayhi al-Salam*, has said to abu Basir, 'If you are afraid of something or need help, then begin with Allah and His glory and praise Him as He deserves. Then ask Allah's favors for the Holy Prophet and ask for help, try to weep even if your tears are of the size of the head of a fly. Abu 'Abd Allah, *'Alayhi al-Salam*, would say, 'a servant (of Allah) in prostration and weeping is in the nearest position to Allah, the Most Majestic, the Most Holy.'"

H 3123, Ch. 15, h 11

Ali ibn Ibrahim has narrated from his father from 'Abd Allah ibn al-Mughirah from Isma'Il al-Bajilli from abu 'Abd Allah, *'Alayhi al-Salam*, who has said the following:

"If weeping does not come through, make a weeping-like face. If of the size of the head of a fly tears come out that is your sheer good luck indeed."

Chapter 16 - Praising Allah Before Praying and Pleading for Help

H 3124, Ch. 16, h 1

Abu Ali al-Ash'ari has narrated from Muhammad ibn 'Abd al-Jabbar from Safwan ibn Yahya from al-Harith ibn al-Mughirah who has said the following:

"I heard abu 'Abd Allah, *'Alayhi al-Salam*, saying, 'You must bear in mind that whenever one of you likes to ask his Lord for help in worldly matters or of the next life, he must begin with praise of Allah, the Most Majestic, the Most Holy, thank Him and ask His favors for the Holy Prophet and then ask for help.'"

H 3125, Ch. 16, h 2

Muhammad ibn Yahya has narrated from Ahmad ibn Muhammad ibn 'Isa from ibn Faddal from ibn Bukayr from Muhammad ibn Muslim who has said the following:

"Abu 'Abd Allah, *'Alayhi al-Salam*, has said, 'It is in the book of Amir al-Mu'minin, Ali ibn abu Talib, *'Alayhi al-Salam*, "praise comes before asking for favors. Whenever you like to pray and plead before Allah, the Most Majestic, the Most Holy, for help, speak of His glory." The narrator has said that I asked the Imam, 'How should we speak of His glory?' The Imam said, 'Say, O You Who are closer to me than my jugular veins, O the One Who does without fail as He wishes, O the One Who stands between a man and his heart, O the One Who is on a high position and the One like Whom is no creature.'"

H 3126, Ch. 16, h 3

A number of our people have narrated from Ahmad ibn Muhammad ibn Khalid from his father from ibn Sinan from Mu'awiyah ibn 'Ammar from abu 'Abd Allah, *'Alayhi al-Salam*, who has said the following:

"Abu 'Abd Allah, *'Alayhi al-Salam*, has said, 'It is thanking then praising, then confession of sins then pleading before Allah for help. By Allah, no servant (of Allah) can come out of sins without confession.'"

H 3127, Ch. 16, h 4

It is narrated from him (narrator of the Hadith above) from ibn Faddal from Tha'labah from Mu'awiyah ibn 'Ammar the following:

"Mu'awiyah ibn 'Ammar has narrated from abu 'Abd Allah, *'Alayhi al-Salam*, a similar Hadith except that he said, 'Then praising and confessing sins.'"

H 3128, Ch. 16, h 5

Al-Husayn ibn Muhammad has narrated from Mu'alla ibn Muhammad from al-Hassan ibn Ali from Hammad ibn 'Uthman from al-Harith ibn al-Mughirah who has said the following:

"Abu 'Abd Allah, *'Alayhi al-Salam*, has said, 'Whenever you wish to pray and plead before Allah for help, speak of the glory of Allah, the Most Majestic, the Most Holy, thank Him, speak of His Holiness, and say that no one deserves to be worshipped except Him, praise Him and ask from Him favors for Muhammad and his family and then ask Him for help, you will receive it.'"

H 3129, Ch. 16, h 6

Abu Ali al-Ash'ari has narrated from Muhammad ibn 'Abd al-Jabbar from Safwan from 'Iys ibn al-Qasim who has said the following:

"Abu 'Abd Allah, *'Alayhi al-Salam*, has said, 'Whenever anyone of you wishes to ask for help he should praise his Lord and thank Him. When a man wants to ask a king for something, he prepares to say the best of words that he can. When you like to ask for help, speak of the Glory of Allah, the Most Majestic, the Most Compelling, thank Him and praise Him saying, "O the Most Generous in granting favors and the Best to be asked for help. O the Most Kind to those who ask for kindness, O the only One and Self-sufficient. O the One Who has no children and is not born from anyone and there is no one as His partner. O the One Who has no companion and children. O the One Who does as He wishes, commands as He wills and judges as He loves. O the One Who stands between a man and his heart, O the One Who is in a high position, O the One in Whose likeness there is no creature, O the Hearing, and the Seeing." Speak of the names of Allah, the Most Majestic, the Most Holy; they are many and ask from Him favors for Muhammad and his family and then say, 'O Lord, extend for me of Your lawful supplies with which I can save my face, return safely what is entrusted with me, maintain good relations with relatives and be helpful in my Hajj and 'Umrah.' The Imam said, 'Once a man came in the Mosque, performed two Rak'at (prayer consisting of twice kneeling) then asked Allah, the Most Majestic, the Most Holy, for help and the Messenger of Allah said, 'The servant (of Allah) hastened his Lord.' Then another man came in and prayed two Rak'at then he praised Allah, the Most

Majestic, the Most Holy, and asked from Him favors for the Holy Prophet and his family and the Messenger of Allah said, 'Ask for help you will receive it.'"

H 3130, Ch. 16, h 7

Muhammad ibn Yahya has narrated from Ahmad ibn Muhammad ibn 'Isa from Ali ibn al-Hakam from abu Kahmas who has said the following:

"I heard abu 'Abd Allah, *'Alayhi al-Salam*, saying, 'Once a man came to the Mosque and he began without praising Allah and asking from Him favors for the Holy Prophet. The Messenger of Allah said, 'The servant (of Allah) hastened his Lord.' Then another man came in and prayed, praised Allah, the Most Majestic, the Most Holy, and asked favors from Him for the Messenger of Allah. The Messenger of Allah said, 'Ask for help you will receive it.' Thereafter the Imam said, 'It is in the book of Ali, *'Alayhi al-Salam*, "Praising Allah and asking favors from Him for the Messenger of Allah should come before asking for help. When anyone comes to a man to request a favor, he loves to say to him the best words to him before asking for help.'"

H 3131, Ch. 16, h 8

Ali ibn Ibrahim has narrated from his father from 'Uthman ibn 'Isa from those whom he has mentioned (in his book) who has said the following:

"Once I said to abu 'Abd Allah, *'Alayhi al-Salam*, 'There are two verses in the book of Allah, the Most Majestic, the Most Holy, that I search for but I do not find them, (their meaning).' The Imam aked, 'What are they?' I said, 'They are the words of Allah, the Most Majestic, the Most Holy, "Call Me (for help) and I will answer you."' (40:60) We call Him and pray to Him but do not see any answer.' The Imam asked, 'Do you think He, Allah, the Most Majestic, the Most Holy, ignores His promise?' I said, 'No, He does not ignore it.' The Imam asked, 'Why is that then?' I said, 'I do not know.' The Imam said, 'I will tell you about it. Whoever obeys Allah, the Most Majestic, the Most Holy, in whatever He has commanded and then prays to Him the way prayer should be done He answers them.' I then asked, 'What is the way of prayer?' The Imam said, 'Begin the prayer by praising Allah, recall His bounties with you, thank Him, ask favors from Him for the Holy Prophet, recall your sins and confess them then seek refuge against them and such is the way of praying.' Then the Imam said, 'What is the other verse?' I said, 'It is the words of Allah, the Most Majestic, the Most Holy, '. . .He will replace whatever you spend for His cause and He is the best provider of sustanance,' (34:39) I spend but do not see any replacement.' The Imam said, 'Do you think Allah, the Most Majestic, the Most Holy, has ignored His promise?' I said, 'No.' The Imam asked, 'Why is that then?' I said, 'I do not know.' The Imam said, 'If anyone of you earns something in lawful ways and spends it in a lawful way, every dirham (unit of money) is replaced.'"

H 3132, Ch. 16, h 9

A number of our people have narrated from Sahl ibn Ziyad from Ali ibn Asbat from those whom he has mentioned (in his book) from abu 'Abd Allah, *'Alayhi al-Salam*, who has said the following:

"Abu 'Abd Allah, *'Alayhi al-Salam*, has said, 'Whoever of you wants his prayer answered must make his earning clean.'"

Chapter 17 - Praying Collectively

H 3133, Ch. 17, h 1
Ali ibn Ibrahim has narrated from his father from Ali ibn Ma'Bad from 'Ubayd Allah ibn 'Abd Allah al-Wasiti from Drust ibn abu Mansur from abu Khalid who has said the following:

"Abu 'Abd Allah, *'Alayhi al-Salam*, has said, 'If a group of forty people come together to pray and plead before Allah, the Most Majestic, the Most Holy, for help in a matter, Allah will accept their prayers. If they are not forty then four people can pray to Allah, the Most Majestic, the Most Holy, ten times still Allah will accept their prayer. If four people are not present, then one person can pray forty times. Allah the Most Majestic, the Almighty, will accept his prayer.'"

H 3134, Ch. 17, h 2
A number of our people have narrated from Ahmad ibn Muhammad ibn Khalid from Muhammad ibn Ali from Yunus ibn Ya'qub from 'Abd al-'Ala' from abu 'Abd Allah, *'Alayhi al-Salam*, who has said the following:

"Abu 'Abd Allah, *'Alayhi al-Salam*, has said, 'Whenever a group (of forty) people come together for a matter to pray and plead before Allah for help, when they disperse their prayer will be accepted.'"

H 3135, Ch. 17, h 3
It is narrated from him (narrator of the Hadith above) from al-Hajjal from Tha'labah from Ali ibn 'Uqbah from a man from abu 'Abd Allah, *'Alayhi al-Salam*, who has said the following:

"Abu 'Abd Allah, *'Alayhi al-Salam*, has said, 'Whenever something saddened my father he would call the ladies and children together. He would then pray and they would say, 'Amin.'"

H 3136, Ch. 17, h 4
Ali ibn Ibrahim has narrated from his father from al-Nawfali from al-Sakuni from abu 'Abd Allah, *'Alayhi al-Salam*, who has said the following:

"Abu 'Abd Allah, *'Alayhi al-Salam*, has said, 'A person praying and one saying 'Amin' share the reward equally.'"

Chapter 18 - Inclusiveness in Prayer

H 3137, Ch. 18, h 1
A number of our people have narrated from Sahl ibn Ziyad from Ja'far ibn Muhammad al-Ash'ari from ibn al-Qaddah from abu 'Abd Allah, *'Alayhi al-Salam*, who has said the following:

"The Messenger of Allah has said, 'Whenever anyone of you prays he should maintain inclusiveness (pray for everyone) in his prayer. This may become a reason for the acceptance of the prayer.'"

Chapter 19 - Delay in the Acceptance of Prayer

H 3138, Ch. 19, h 1
Muhammad ibn Yahya has narrated from Ahmad ibn Muhammad ibn 'Isa from Ahmad ibn Muhammad ibn abu Nasr who has said the following:

"Once I said to abu al-Hassan (al-Rida), *'Alayhi al-Salam*, 'May Allah keep my soul in service for your cause, I have been praying to Allah for help in something from the year so and so and because of delay something is happing in my heart.'

The Imam said, 'O Ahmad, beware of Satan! Do not allow him to find a way in you to despair you. Abu Ja'far, *'Alayhi al-Salam*, would say, "A believing person prays and pleads before Allah, the Most Majestic, the Most Holy, for help and help is delayed due to love for his voice and listening to his intense weeping.'" The Imam then said, 'By Allah, whatever Allah, the Most Majestic, the Most Holy, delays for believing people of the help that they may ask in this world is far better for them than helping them quickly. Such a worthless world! Abu Ja'far, *'Alayhi al-Salam*, would say, 'It is very proper for a believing person to pray for help in his comfort just like in hardships. He should not grow to be lazy after receiving help to lose interest in prayer.' You should never lose interest in prayer; it is of a very important position before Allah, the Most Majestic, the Most Holy. You should exercise patience and seek to find lawful sustenance, maintain good relations with relatives and should never make it public. We are a family who maintains good relations with those who cut off from us and do favors to those who cause us trouble. In this we find good consequences. If an affluent person in this world prays and asks for favors, his prayer receives acceptance. He may ask for more and the bounties seem insignificant to him. He does not feel satisfied with anything. When bounties are plentiful a Muslim is in a danger of violating the rights he owes and the mischief that may threaten him. Tell me about yourself. If I will say something to you, will you trust me?' I (the narrator) said, 'May Allah keep my soul in service for your cause, if I do not trust you, then whom will I trust? You possess authority from Allah over His creatures.' The Imam said, 'Your trust in Allah must be stronger; you have a covenant with Allah. Has Allah, the Most Majestic, the Most Holy, not said, "(Muhammad), if any of My servants ask you about Me, tell them that the Lord says, 'I am near; I accept the prayers of those who pray.' Allow My servants answer My call and believe in Me so that perhaps they may know the right direction.' (2:186) 'Do not despair of the mercy of Allah. Allah certainly forgives all sins. He is All-Forgiving and All-Merciful.' (39:53) 'Allah promises you forgiveness and favors. Allah is Munificent and All-Knowing.' (2:268) You must trust Allah, the Most Majestic, the Most Holy, more firmly than others. Do not allow anything to find a way in you except good; you are forgiven.'"

H 3139, Ch. 19, h 2
It is narrated from him (narrator of the Hadith above) from Ahmad from Ali ibn al-Hakam from Mansur al-Sayqal who has said the following:

"Once I asked abu 'Abd Allah, *'Alayhi al-Salam*, 'Is it possible that at one time a man prays and it is accepted and then is delayed for a period of time?' The narrator has said that the Imam then said, 'Yes, it can happen.' I then asked, 'Why is that? Is it because so he will increase his prayer and pleading?' The Imam said, 'Yes, that is right.'"

H 3140, Ch. 19, h 3
Ali ibn Ibrahim has narrated from his father from ibn abu 'Umayr from Ishaq ibn abu Hilal al-Mada'ini from Hadid from abu 'Abd Allah, *'Alayhi al-Salam*, who has said the following:

"When a servant prays, Allah, the Most Majestic, the Most Holy, says to the two angels, 'I have accepted his prayer, but keep it on hold; I love to hear his voice.'

It may also happen that a servant prays, but Allah, the Most Blessed, the Most High, says, 'Hurry up and help him quickly; I hate his voice.'"

H 3141, Ch. 19, h 4

Ibn abu 'Umayr has narrated from Sulayman Sahib al-Sabiri from Ishaq ibn 'Ammar who has said the following:

"Once I asked abu 'Abd Allah, *'Alayhi al-Salam*, 'Can a man's prayer that is accepted be kept on hold and delayed?' The Imam said, 'Yes, it can remain on hold for up to twenty years.'"

H 3142, Ch. 19, h 5

Ibn abu 'Umayr has narrated from Hisham ibn Salim from abu 'Abd Allah, *'Alayhi al-Salam*, who has said the following:

"Between the words of Allah, the Most Majestic, the Most Holy, 'Your prayer is accepted,' (10:89) and the time the Pharaoh was seized there was a forty-year timespan.'"

H 3143, Ch. 19, h 6

Ibn abu 'Umayr has narrated from Ibrahim ibn 'Abd al-Hamid from abu Basir who has said the following:

"I heard abu 'Abd Allah, *'Alayhi al-Salam*, saying, 'A believing person prays and its (the prayer's) acceptance may be delayed up to the next Friday [Day of Judgment].'"

H 3144, Ch. 19, h 7

Ali ibn Ibrahim has narrated from his father from ibn abu 'Umayr from 'Abd Allah ibn al-Mughirah from more than one individual of our people who has said the following:

"Abu 'Abd Allah, *'Alayhi al-Salam*, has said, 'A servant who is a friend of Allah may pray to Allah, the Most Majestic, the Most Holy, for a matter in his intention and Allah says to the angel guarding him, "Provide help to My servant but keep it on hold and do not hurry; I desire to hear his call and voice." On the other hand a servant who is not a friend of Allah may pray to Allah, the Most Majestic, the Most Holy, for a matter in his intention and Allah says to the angel guarding him, 'Provide him help quickly; I dislike his call and voice.'

"The Imam said, 'People will say, "This person received help due to his merit and honor and he was denied due to his worthlessness."'"

H 3145, Ch. 19, h 8

Muhammad ibn Yahya has narrated from Ahmad ibn Muhammad ibn 'Isa from ibn Mahbub from Hisham ibn Salim from abu Basir from abu 'Abd Allah, *'Alayhi al-Salam*, who has said the following:

"A believing person is fine and hopeful through the favors of Allah, the Most Majestic, the Most Holy, as long as he does not rush to despair and give up prayer.' I (the narrator) then asked the Imam, *'Alayhi al-Salam*, 'How can he rush?' The Imam said, 'He may say, "I have been praying for such and such period of time and I do not see any sign of acceptance."'"

H 3146, Ch. 19, h 9

Al-Husayn ibn Muhammad has narrated from Ahmad ibn Ishaq from Su'Dan ibn Muslim from Ishaq ibn 'Ammar from abu 'Abd Allah, *'Alayhi al-Salam*, who has said the following:

"A believing person may pray to Allah, the Most Majestic, the Most Holy, for help and Allah, the Most Majestic, the Most Holy, will say, 'Hold back the answer to his prayer for the desire in his voice and prayer.' When it will be the Day of Judgment Allah, the Most Majestic, the Most Holy, will say, 'My servant, you prayed to Me and I delayed your answer. So and so is your reward. You prayed to Me in such and such matters and I delayed your answer. Your reward is so and so.' The Imam said, 'The believing person then wishes that none of his prayers had been accepted in the worldly life. He will say so on finding such handsome rewards.'"

Chapter 20 - Asking Favors from Allah for the Holy Prophet, Muhammad and his Family, *'Alayhi al-Salam*

H 3147, Ch. 20, h 1

Ali ibn Ibrahim has narrated from his father from ibn abu 'Umayr from Hisham ibn Salim from abu 'Abd Allah, *'Alayhi al-Salam*, who has said the following:

"A prayer remains barred until one asks favors (in the form of al-Salat (the special expression called al-Salat 'Ala al-Nabiyy) from Allah for Muhammad and his family, *'Alayhi al-Salam*."

H 3148, Ch. 20, h 2

It is narrated from him (narrator of the Hadith above) from his father from al-Nawfali from al-Sakuni from abu 'Abd Allah, *'Alayhi al-Salam*, who has said the following:

"Abu 'Abd Allah, *'Alayhi al-Salam*, has said, 'Whoever prays and does not mention the Holy Prophet, his prayer remains dangled over his head. When he mentions the Holy Prophet only then his prayer is raised up (to heavens).'"

H 3149, Ch. 20, h 3

Abu Ali al-Ash'ari has narrated from Muhammad ibn 'Abd al-Jabbar from Safwan from abu 'Usama Zayd al-Shahham from Muhammad ibn Muslim from abu 'Abd Allah, *'Alayhi al-Salam*, who has said the following:

"Once a man came to the Holy Prophet and said, 'O Messenger of Allah, "I assign one third of my prayer to you. No, in fact, I assign half of my prayer to you. No, I assign all of my prayer to you." The Messenger of Allah said, 'That means that you have complete supplies for this and the next life.'"

H 3150, Ch. 20, h 4

Muhammad ibn Yahya has narrated from Ahmad ibn Muhammad from Ali ibn al-Hakam from Sayf from abu 'Usama from abu Basir who has said the following:

"Once I asked abu 'Abd Allah, *'Alayhi al-Salam*, 'What is the meaning of, "I assign all of my prayer to you?" The Imam said, 'He mentions the Holy Prophet before asking any help. He does not ask Allah, the Most Majestic, the Most Holy, anything until he begins with the Holy Prophet. He asks from Allah favors for the Holy Prophet and then asks Allah for help.'"

H 3151, Ch. 20, h 5

A number of our people have narrated from Sahl ibn Ziyad from Ja'far ibn Muhammad al-Ash'ari from ibn al-Qaddah from abu 'Abd Allah, *'Alayhi al-Salam*, who has said the following:

"The Messenger of Allah has said, 'Do not consider me as the water container of a traveler who fills up his water container and drinks from it whenever he wants. You should place me at the beginning of your prayer, at the end of it and in the middle.'"

H 3152, Ch. 20, h 6

A number of our people have narrated from Ahmad ibn Muhammad ibn Khalid from Isma'll ibn Mehran from al-Hassan ibn Ali ibn abu Hamza from his father and Husayn ibn abu al-'Ala' from abu Basir who has said the following:

"Abu 'Abd Allah, *'Alayhi al-Salam*, has said, 'Whenever the Holy Prophet is mentioned, ask from Allah favors (in the form of al-Salat) for the Holy Prophet. Ask from Allah a great deal of favors for the Holy Prophet. Whoever does so once, Allah will do the same for him one thousand times in one thousand rows of angels and nothing will be left of the creatures of Allah without doing the same for that servant because of what Allah and angels have done. Whoever is not interested in it is ignorant and deceived, Allah, the Messenger of Allah and his family disavow him.'"

H 3153, Ch. 20, h 7

A number of our people have narrated from Sahl ibn Ziyad from Ja'far ibn Muhammad al-Ash'ari from ibn al-Qaddah from abu 'Abd Allah, *'Alayhi al-Salam*, who has said the following:

"The Messenger of Allah has said, 'Whoever asks from Allah favors for me (in the form of al-Salat), Allah grants him favors and the angels pray for him. It is up to people to perform this (noble) act very little or a great deal.'"

H 3154, Ch. 20, h 8

Ali ibn Ibrahim has narrated from his father from ibn abu 'Umayr from 'Abd Allah ibn Sinan from abu 'Abd Allah, *'Alayhi al-Salam*, who has said the following:

"The Messenger of Allah has said, 'Asking from Allah favors (in the form of al-Salat) for me and my family removes hypocrisy.'"

H 3155, Ch. 20, h 9

Abu Ali al-Ash'ari has narrated from Muhammad ibn Hassan from abu 'Imran al-Azdi from 'Abd Allah ibn al-Hakam from Mu'awiyah ibn 'Ammar from abu 'Abd Allah, *'Alayhi al-Salam*, who has said the following:

"Whoever says, 'O Lord, grant favors to Muhammad and his family, one hundred times one hundred of his wishes will be granted, thirty of them in this world and the rest in the next life.'"

H 3156, Ch. 20, h 10

Muhammad ibn Yahya has narrated from Ahmad ibn Muhammad from Ali ibn al-Hakam and 'Abd al-Rahman ibn abu Najran all from Safwan al-Jammal from abu 'Abd Allah, *'Alayhi al-Salam*, who has said the following:

"Every prayer to Allah, the Most Majestic, the Most Holy, remains on hold and barred from heavens until he asks from Allah favors (in the form of al-Salat) for the Holy Prophet and his family."

H 3157, Ch. 20, h 11

It is narrated from him (narrator of the Hadith above) from Ahmad ibn Muhammad from Ali ibn al-Hakam from Sayf ibn 'Amirah from abu Bakr al-Hadrami who has said the following:

"One who had heard abu 'Abd Allah, *'Alayhi al-Salam*, narrated to me that the Imam said, 'Once a man came to the Messenger of Allah and said, "I assign half of my Salat (prayers) for you. The Messenger of Allah said, 'That is fine.' He then said, 'I assign all of my Salat, to you.' The Messenger of Allah said, 'That is fine.' When he left the Messenger of Allah said, 'He is completely sufficed in his matters of this and the next life.'"

H 3158, Ch. 20, h 12

Ali ibn Ibrahim has narrated from his father from ibn abu 'Umayr from Murazim who has said the following:

"Abu 'Abd Allah, *'Alayhi al-Salam*, has said, 'Once a man came to the Messenger of Allah and said, "O Messenger of Allah, I have assigned one third of my prayers for you." The Messenger of Allah said, 'That is good.' He then said, 'O Messenger of Allah, I have assigned half of my prayers for you.' The Messenger of Allah said, 'That is better.' He then said, 'O the Messenger of Allah, I have assigned all of my prayers for you.' The Messenger of Allah said, 'Allah, the Most Majestic, the Most Holy, will suffice you in all your needs in this world and in the next life.' A man then asked, 'May Allah grant you well being, how could he assign his prayer for him?' Abu 'Abd Allah, *'Alayhi al-Salam*, said, 'He would never pray and plead before Allah, the Majestic, the Glorious, for help before asking from Allah favors for the Holy Prophet and his family.'"

H 3159, Ch. 20, h 13

Ibn abu 'Umayr has narrated from 'Abd Allah ibn Sinan who has said the following:

"I heard abu 'Abd Allah, *'Alayhi al-Salam*, saying, 'The Messenger of Allah has said, "Raise your voices with al-Salat (asking from Allah favors for me); it removes hypocrisy.'"

H 3160, Ch. 20, h 14

Muhammad ibn Yahya has narrated from Ahmad ibn Muhammad ibn 'Isa from Ya'qub ibn 'Abd Allah from Ishaq ibn Farrukh Mawla Ale Talhah who has said the following:

"Abu 'Abd Allah, *'Alayhi al-Salam*, once said, 'O Ishaq ibn Farrukh, whoever asks from Allah al-Salat (favors) for the Holy Prophet and his family ten times, Allah and His angels will do the same for him one hundred times. Whoever asks from Allah al-Salat for the Holy Prophet and his family one hundred times, Allah and His angels will do the same for him one thousand times. Do you not hear the words of Allah, the Most Majestic, the Most Holy, "It is He who forgives you and His angels pray for you so that He will take you out of darkness into light. Allah is All-Merciful to believers.'" (33:43)

H 3161, Ch. 20, h 15

Ali ibn Ibrahim has narrated from his father from ibn abu 'Umayr from abu Ayyub from Muhammad ibn Muslim from one of the two Imams, *'Alayhi al-Salam*, who has said the following:

"On the balance there will be no other thing as heavy as asking from Allah al-Salat (favors) for the Holy Prophet and his family. A man will place his deeds on the balance and it will tilt. Then he will bring forth his deed of asking from Allah al-Salat for the Holy Prophet and his family to place on the balance and it will weigh heavy in his favor."

H 3162, Ch. 20, h 16

Ali ibn Muhammad has narrated from ibn Jumhur from his father from his narrators who has said the following:

"Abu 'Abd Allah, *'Alayhi al-Salam*, has said, 'Whoever needs help from Allah, the Majestic, the Glorious, should first ask from Allah al-Salat (favors) for the Holy Prophet and his family, then pray and plead before Allah for help, then conclude it with asking from Allah al-Salat for the Holy Prophet and his family; Honor of Allah, the Most Majestic, the Most Holy, does not allow to accept both ends of the prayer and leave out the middle; asking from Allah al-Salat for the Holy Prophet and his family is never barred from reaching His presence.'"

H 3163, Ch. 20, h 17

A number of our people have narrated from Ahmad ibn Muhammad from Muhsin ibn Ahmad from Aban al-Ahmar from 'Abd al-Salam ibn al-Nu'aym who has said the following:

"Once I said to abu 'Abd Allah, *'Alayhi al-Salam*, 'I entered the house and I did not remember any prayer except asking from Allah al-Salat (favors) for the Holy Prophet and his family.' The Imam said, 'You should know that no one has come up with something better than what you have.'"

H 3164, Ch. 20, h 18

Ali ibn Muhammad has narrated from Ahmad ibn al-Husayn from Ali ibn al-Rayyan from 'Ubayd Allah ibn 'Abd Allah al-Dehqan who has said the following:

"Once I went in the presence of abu al-Hassan al-Rida, *'Alayhi al-Salam*, and he asked me, 'What is the meaning of: ". . . remember the name of the Lord, and pray to Him." (87:15) I said, 'Whenever he remembered the name of his Lord, he stood up and prayed.' The Imam said to me, 'If so, Allah, the Most Majestic, the Most Holy, had burdened him heavily, but this is going beyond limits.' I then said, 'May Allah keep my soul in service for your cause, how is it then?' The Imam said, 'Whenever he remembered the name of his Lord, he asked from Allah al-Salat (favors) for the Holy Prophet and his family.'"

H 3165, Ch. 20, h 19

It is narrated from him (narrator of the Hadith above) from Muhammad ibn Ali from Mufaddal ibn Salih al-'Asadi from Muhammad ibn Harun from abu 'Abd Allah, *'Alayhi al-Salam*, who has said the following:

"Whenever anyone of you prays and does not mention the Holy Prophet and his family in his prayer, his prayer will be taken to a direction other than that toward paradise. The Messenger of Allah has said, 'If a person before whom my name is mentioned does not ask from Allah al-Salat (favors) for me, he will enter the fire and Allah will move him away.' He also has said, 'If a person, before whom my name is mentioned, forgets to ask from Allah al-Salat for me, he will get lost on the way of paradise.'"

H 3166, Ch. 20, h 20

Abu Ali al-Ash'ari has narrated from al-Husayn ibn Ali from 'Ubays ibn Hisham from Thabit from abu Basir from abu 'Abd Allah, *'Alayhi al-Salam*, who has said the following:

"The Messenger of Allah has said, 'If my name is mentioned before a person and he forgets to ask from Allah al-Salat (favors) for me, Allah will make him lose the way to paradise.'"

H 3167, Ch. 20, h 21

A number of our people have narrated from Sahl ibn Ziyad from Ja'far ibn Muhammad from ibn al-Qaddah from abu 'Abd Allah, *'Alayhi al-Salam*, who has said the following:

"My father once heard a man, clinging to the Ka'bah, saying, 'O Lord, grant al-Salat (favors) to Muhammad.' My father then said to him, 'O servant of Allah, do not shorten it that way. Do not do injustice to us in our rights. Say, "O Lord, grant al-Salat to Muhammad and his family."'"

Chapter 21 - The Necessary Mention of Allah, the Most Majestic, the Most Holy, in Every Gathering

H 3168, Ch. 21, h 1

A number of our people have narrated from Ahmad ibn Muhammad ibn Khalid from his father from Khalaf ibn Hammad from Rib'I ibn 'Abd Allah ibn al-Jarud al-Hudhalli from al-Fudayl ibnYasar who has said the following:

"Abu 'Abd Allah, *'Alayhi al-Salam*, has said, 'If any gathering attended by virtuous and non-virtuous people disperses without mentioning the name of Allah, the Most Majestic, the Most Holy, it (gathering) will become a regret for them on the Day of Judgment.'"

H 3169, Ch. 21, h 2

Humayd ibn Ziyad has narrated from al-Hassan ibn Muhammad ibn Sama'a from Wahab ibn Hafs from abu Basir from abu 'Abd Allah, *'Alayhi al-Salam*, who has said the following:

"If a people gather together in a place and do not make any mention of Allah, the Most Majestic, the Most Holy, or of us, that gathering will become a regret for them on the Day of Judgment.' The Imam then said, 'Abu Ja'far, *'Alayhi al-Salam*, has said, "To speak of us is to speak of Allah and speaking of our enemy is speaking of Satan."'"

H 3170, Ch. 21, h 3

Through the same chain of narrators it is narrated from abu Ja'far, *'Alayhi al-Salam*, who has said the following:

"Whoever likes to receive his reward in a correct measurement, when leaving a gathering should say, 'Glory belongs to your Lord, the Lord Who is by far more Majestic than what they (certain people) call Him to be. May peace be upon the Messengers of Allah. All praise belongs to Allah, Lord of the worlds.'"

H 3171, Ch. 21, h 4

Muhammad ibn Yahya has narrated from Ahmad ibn Muhammad ibn 'Isa from ibn Mahbub from 'Abd Allah ibn Sinan from abu Hamza al-Thumali from abu Ja'far, *'Alayhi al-Salam*, who has said the following:

"It is written in the Torah that is not changed that once Moses asked his Lord, 'O Lord, are You near me so I may whisper to You or far from me so I call You?' Allah, the Most Majestic, the Most Holy, sent him inspiration that said, 'O Moses, I am in a face-to-face meeting with anyone who speaks of Me.' Moses then said, 'Who is in Your hiding (shelter and protection) on the day when there is no hiding except Your's?' He (Allah) then said, 'Those who remember Me I then remember them. Those who love just because of Me, I love them. It is because of these beloved people that when I will to afflict the people of the earth with evil I remember them (beloved people) and spare them (people of earth) through them (beloved people).'"

H 3172, Ch. 21, h 5

Abu Ali al-Ash'ari has narrated from Muhammad ibn 'Abd al-Jabbar from Safwan ibn Yahya from Husayn ibn Zayd from abu 'Abd Allah, *'Alayhi al-Salam*, who has said the following:

"The Messenger of Allah has said, 'If a people gather together in a place and do not speak of Allah, the Most Majestic, the Most Holy, and do not ask from Allah favors al-Salat for His Holy Prophet, that gathering will become a regret and a loss for them (on the Day of Judgment).'"

H 3173, Ch. 21, h 6

A number of our people have narrated from Sahl ibn Ziyad from ibn Mahbub from ibn Ri'ab from al-Halabi from abu 'Abd Allah, *'Alayhi al-Salam*, who has said the following:

"Abu 'Abd Allah, *'Alayhi al-Salam*, has said, 'It is not an offense to speak of Allah when you are urinating; speaking of Allah, the Most Majestic, the Most Holy, is good in all conditions. Do not feel embarrassed about it.'"

H 3174, Ch. 21, h 7

Ali ibn Ibrahim has narrated from his father from al-Nawfali from al-Sakuni from abu 'Abd Allah, *'Alayhi al-Salam*, who has said the following:

"Allah, the Most Majestic, the Most Holy, sent revelations to Moses saying, 'Moses, do not be very happy about great wealth and do not avoid speaking of Me in all conditions. Great wealth causes one to forget his sins and ignoring to speak of Me hardens his heart.'"

H 3175, Ch. 21, h 8

Muhammad ibn Yahya has narrated from Ahmad ibn Muhammad ibn 'Isa from ibn Mahbub from 'Abd Allah ibn Sinan from abu Hamza from abu Ja'far, *'Alayhi al-Salam*, who has said the following:

"It is written in the Torah, which is not changed, that Moses asked his Lord saying, 'O Lord, sometimes I find myself in certain gatherings where I feel speaking of You is not worthy of Your Honor and Glory. He (Allah) said, Moses, speaking of Me is good in all conditions.'"

H 3176, Ch. 21, h 9

A number of our people have narrated from Ahmad ibn Muhammad ibn Khalid from ibn Faddal from certain individuals of his people from those whom he has mentioned (in his book) from abu 'Abd Allah, *'Alayhi al-Salam*, who has said the following:

"Allah, the Most Majestic, the Most Holy, said to Moses, 'Speak of Me a great deal during the day and night and be humble when speaking of Me, exercise patience with My misfortunes, be confident when speaking of Me, worship Me and do not consider anything as My partner. To Me is the way. O Moses, consider Me as your savings and keep your treasures with Me in the form of charitable trust.'"

H 3177, Ch. 21, h 10

Through the same chain of narrators it is narrated from abu 'Abd Allah, *'Alayhi al-Salam*, who has said the following:

"Allah, the Most Majestic, the Most Holy, has said to Moses, 'Keep your tongue behind your heart and you will remain safe. Speak of Me very often during the day and night. Do not follow a sin in its pit (sinful people) or you will regret. Sin is the promised place of the people of fire.'"

H 3178, Ch. 21, h 11

Through the same chain of narrators (it is narrated from abu 'Abd Allah, *'Alayhi al-Salam*, who has said the following):

"Abu 'Abd Allah, *'Alayhi al-Salam*, has said, 'Of the words of Allah to Moses was that He said, "O Moses do not forget Me in any condition; forgetting Me deadens a heart.'"

H 3179, Ch. 21, h 12

It is narrated from him (narrator of the Hadith above) from ibn Faddal from Ghalib ibn 'Uthman from Bashir al-Dahhan from abu 'Abd Allah, *'Alayhi al-Salam*, who has said the following:

"Allah, the Most Majestic, the Most Holy, has said, 'O sons of Adam, speak of Me in public, I will speak of you in a public that is better than your public.'"

H 3180, Ch. 21, h 13

Muhammad ibn Yahya has narrated from Ahmad ibn Muhammad ibn 'Isa from ibn Mahbub from those whom he has mentioned (in his book) from abu 'Abd Allah, *'Alayhi al-Salam*, who has said the following:

"Abu 'Abd Allah, *'Alayhi al-Salam*, has said, 'Allah, the Most Majestic, the Most Holy, has said, "Whoever speaks of Me in a group of people, I speak of him in a group of angels.'"

Chapter 22 - Speaking of Allah, the Most Majestic, the Most Holy, Very Often

H 3181, Ch. 22, h 1

A number of our people have narrated from Sahl ibn Ziyad from Ja'far ibn Muhammad al-Ash'ari from ibn al-Qaddah from abu 'Abd Allah, *'Alayhi al-Salam*, who has said the following:

"Everything has a limit where it ends except speaking of Allah which has no limit to end. Allah, the Most Majestic, the Most Holy, has sanctioned obligations. When one fulfills them, their limit is where they end. The limit for the month of Ramadan is that when one fasts that is its limit where it ends, and the limit of Hajj is that when one performs Hajj it ends. Al-Dikr (speaking of Allah) is as such that Allah, the Most Majestic, the Most Holy, does not agree with a very little of it and He has not set a limit for where it ends.' The Imam then read this verse of the Holy Quran: 'Believers, remember Allah very often (33:41) and glorify Him both in the mornings and in the evenings.' (33:42)

"The Imam said, 'Allah, the Most Majestic, the Most Holy, has not set a limit for it where it would end.' He them said, 'My father would speak of Allah very often. I would walk with him and he would speak of Allah. At the time I ate food with him he would speak of Allah. Even when speaking to people it would not stop him from speaking of Allah. I could see his tongue move saying, 'No one deserves to be worshipped except Allah.' He would gather all of us together and order us to speak of Allah until sunrise. He would command those of us who could read, to read the Holy Quran and those who could not to speak of Allah. The house in which the Holy Quran is read and Allah, the Most Majestic, the Most Holy, is spoken of therein blessings increase and angels are present, the devils run away and it shines to the people of heavens just as a diamond (shaped) star shines for the people of earth. The house in which the Holy Quran is not read, Allah is not spoken of therein, blessings in it decrease, angels move away from it and devils turn to be present therein. The Messenger of Allah once asked, 'Should I tell you about the best of your deeds, which raise your position the highest and the purest before your owner, much better for you than the world and its money and is better for you than your fighting against your enemies whom you would eliminate or else they would kill you?' They said, 'Yes.' He then said, 'Speak of Allah, the Most Majestic, the Most Holy, very often.'

"The Imam then said, 'Once a man came to the Holy Prophet and said, "Who is the best of the people in this Mosque?" He said, 'The one who speaks of Allah more than others.' The Messenger of Allah has said, 'Whoever is given a tongue that speaks of Allah very often has been granted the good for both this and the next life.'

"About the words of Allah, '. . . and do not think that by doing such deeds, you have done a great favor to Allah,' (74:6) the Imam said, 'It means do not think what you have done for the sake of Allah is a great deal.'"

H 3182, Ch. 22, h 2

Humayd ibn Ziyad has narrated from ibn Sama'a from Wahab ibn Hafs from abu Basir from abu 'Abd Allah, *'Alayhi al-Salam*, who has said the following:

"Abu 'Abd Allah, *'Alayhi al-Salam*, has said, 'Our Shi'a (followers) are those who when alone speak of Allah very often.'"

H 3183, Ch. 22, h 3

Al-Husayn ibn Muhammad has narrated from Mu'alla ibn Muhammad and A number of our people have narrated from Ahmad ibn Muhammad all from al-Hassan ibn Ali al-Washsha' from Dawud ibn Serhan from abu 'Abd Allah, *'Alayhi al-Salam*, who has said the following:

"The Messenger of Allah has said, 'Whoever speaks of Allah, the Most Majestic, the Most Holy, often Allah loves him and whoever speaks of Allah very often, two kinds of freedoms will be written for him: freedom from fire and freedom from hypocrisy.'"

H 3184, Ch. 22, h 4

Muhammad ibn Yahya has narrated from Ahmad ibn Muhammad ibn 'Isa from Ali ibn al-Hakam from Sayf ibn 'Amirah from Bakr ibn Bukayr from Zurara ibn 'A'Yun from abu 'Abd Allah, *'Alayhi al-Salam*, who has said the following:

"Tasbih of Fatimah al-Zahra, *'Alayha al-Salam*, is a form of 'Often speaking and remembering Allah' about which Allah, the Most Majestic, the Most Holy, has said, 'Believers, remember Allah very often (33:41) and glorify Him both in the mornings and in the evenings.'" (33:42)

It is narrated from him (narrator of the Hadith above) from Ali ibn al-Hakam from Sayf ibn 'Amirah from abu 'Usamah Zayd al-Shahham and Mansur ibn Hazim and Sa'id al-'A'raj from abu 'Abd Allah, *'Alayhi al-Salam*, a similar Hadith.

H 3185, Ch. 22, h 5

Al-Husayn ibn Muhammad has narrated from Mu'alla ibn Muhammad from al-Washsha' from Dawud al-Hammar from abu 'Abd Allah, *'Alayhi al-Salam*, who has said the following:

"Abu 'Abd Allah, *'Alayhi al-Salam*, has said, 'Whoever speaks of Allah, the Most Majestic, the Most Holy, very often, Allah will provide him a shadow in paradise.'"

Chapter 23 - Lightning Does Not Affect One Who Speaks of Allah

H 3186, Ch. 23, h 1

Muhammad ibn Yahya has narrated from Ahmad ibn Muhammad ibn 'Isa from Muhammad ibn Isma'Il from Muhammad ibn al-Fudayl from abu al-Sabbah al-Kinani from abu 'Abd Allah, *'Alayhi al-Salam*, who has said the following:

"A believing person may die by any form of death except lightning that will not hit him when he is speaking of Allah, the Majestic, the Glorious,."

H 3187, Ch. 23, h 2

Ali ibn Ibrahim has narrated from his father from ibn abu 'Umayr from ibn 'Udhaynah from Burayd ibn Mu'awiyah al-'Ijliy who has said the following:

"Abu 'Abd Allah, *'Alayhi al-Salam*, has said, 'lightning does not affect the speaker (of Allah).' I (the narrator) then asked, 'Who is a speaker?' The Imam said, 'One who reads one hundred verses of the Holy Quran.'"

H 3188, Ch. 23, h 3

Humayd ibn Ziyad has narrated from al-Hassan ibn Muhammad ibn Sama'a from Wahab ibn Hafs from abu Basir who has said the following:

"I asked abu 'Abd Allah, *'Alayhi al-Salam*, about the death of the believing persons. The Imam said, 'A believing person may die in any form of death, drowning, by the debris of falling buildings, or beasts may cause his death. He may die because of lightning except when speaking of Allah, the Most Majestic, the Most Holy.'"

Chapter 24 - Busy in Speaking of Allah, the Majestic, the Glorious

H 3189, Ch. 24, h 1

Ali ibn Ibrahim has narrated from his father from ibn abu 'Umayr from Hisham ibn Salim from abu 'Abd Allah, *'Alayhi al-Salam*, who has said the following:

"Allah, the Most Majestic, the Most Holy, says, 'One who is occupied in speaking of Me instead of asking Me for help, I will grant him better than what I am to grant to one who asks Me for help.'"

H 3190, Ch. 24, h 2

A number of our people have narrated from Ahmad ibn Muhammad from Muhammad ibn Isma'Il from Mansur ibn Yunus from Harun ibn Kharijah from abu 'Abd Allah, *'Alayhi al-Salam*, who has said the following:

"A servant (of Allah) may need help from Allah, the Most Majestic, the Most Holy, and he begins to praise Allah and ask from Allah al-Salat (favors) for the

Holy Prophet and his family until he forgets to ask for help but Allah, without his asking, grants him the help that he was to ask for."

Chapter 25 - Speaking of Allah, the Majestic, the Glorious, Secretly

H 3191, Ch. 25, h 1

Muhammad ibn Yahya has narrated from Ahmad ibn Muhammad ibn 'Isa from ibn Mahbub from Ibrahim ibn abu al-Belad from those whom he has mentioned (in his book) from abu 'Abd Allah, *'Alayhi al-Salam*, who has said the following:

"Abu 'Abd Allah, *'Alayhi al-Salam*, has said, 'Allah, the Most Majestic, the Most Holy, has said, "Whoever speaks of Me secretly, I speak of him in public.""

H 3192, Ch. 25, h 2

A number of our people have narrated from Ahmad ibn Muhammad ibn Khalid from Isma'Il ibn Mehran from Sayf ibn 'Amirah from Sulayman ibn 'Amr from abu al-Maghra' al-Khassaf in a marfu' manner from Amir al-Mu'minin, Ali ibn abu Talib, *'Alayhi al-Salam*, who has said the following:

"Whoever speaks of Allah, the Most Majestic, the Most Holy, secretly, has spoken of Allah very often. The hypocrites speak of Allah in public but they do not speak of Him in secret to which Allah, the Most Majestic, the Most Holy, has said, 'They stand up in prayer lazily just to show that they pray, but, in truth they speak of Allah very little.'" (4:142)

H 3193, Ch. 25, h 3

A number of our people have narrated from Ahmad ibn Muhammad ibn Khalid from ibn Faddal in a marfu' manner from The Imam, *'Alayhi al-Salam*, who has said the following:

"Allah, the Most Majestic, the Most Holy, said to Jesus, peace be upon him, 'O Jesus, speak of Me to yourself; I speak of you to Myself, speak of Me in public; I speak of you in public, which is better than man's public. O Jesus, soften your heart for Me, speak of Me very often privately and note that My happiness is in your expressing humility before Me and that you must act as a living one in such condition, and not as a dead person.'"

H 3194, Ch. 25, h 4

Ali ibn Ibrahim has narrated from his father from Hammad from Hariz from Zurara from one of the Imams, *'Alayhi al-Salam*, who has said the following:

"The angel writes down only what he hears and Allah, the Most Majestic, the Most Holy, has said, 'Speak of your Lord deep within yourselves, humbly and privately. . . .' (7:205) Thus, no one knows the reward for that act (of speaking deep within oneself) of Allah except Allah, the Most Majestic, the Most Holy, due to His greatness.'"

Chapter 26 - Speaking of Allah, the Most Majestic, the Most Holy Among Indifferent People

H 3195, Ch. 26, h 1

Ali ibn Ibrahim has narrated from his father from ibn abu 'Umayr from al-Husayn ibn al-Mukhtar from abu 'Abd Allah, *'Alayhi al-Salam*, who has said the following:

"The speaker of Allah, the Most Majestic, the Most Holy, among indifferent people is like a soldier on the offensive upon the enemies."

H 3196, Ch. 26, h 2

Ali ibn Ibrahim has narrated from his father from al-Nawfali from al-Sakuni from abu 'Abd Allah, *'Alayhi al-Salam*, who has said the following:

"The messenger of Allah has said, 'The speaker of Allah, the Most Majestic, the Most Holy, among the indifferent people is like a soldier on the offensive while others are running away. The reward for a fighter among runaway ones is paradise.'"

Chapter 27 - Praise and Glorification

H 3197, Ch. 27, h 1

Muhammad ibn Yahya has narrated from Ahmad ibn Muhammad from abu Sa'Id al-Qammat from al-Mufaddal who has said the following:

"Once I said to abu 'Abd Allah, *'Alayhi al-Salam*, 'May Allah keep my soul in service for your cause, teach me a comperehensive prayer.' The Imam said to me, 'Praise Allah; everyone who performs prayer prays for you saying, "Allah listens to (answers the prayers of) those who praise Him" (a reference to the meaning of the phrase said after Ruku' in a prayer).'"

H 3198, Ch. 27, h 2

It is narrated from him (narrator of the Hadith above) from Ali ibn al-Husayn from Sayf ibn 'Amirah from Muhammad ibn Marwan who has said the following:

"Once I asked abu 'Abd Allah, *'Alayhi al-Salam*, 'What deed is the most beloved to Allah, the Most Majestic, the Most Holy?' The Imam said, 'It is your deed of praising Him.'"

H 3199, Ch. 27, h 3

Ali ibn Ibrahim has narrated from his father from ibn abu 'Umayr from abu al-Hassan al-Anbari from abu 'Abd Allah, *'Alayhi al-Salam*, who has said the following:

"The Messenger of Allah would praise Allah everyday, three hundred sixty times, equal to the number of the veins in the body, saying 'All praise belongs to Allah, Lord of the worlds, a great deal of praise in all conditions.'"

H 3200, Ch. 27, h 4

Ali ibn Ibrahim has narrated from his father and Humayd ibn Ziyad from al-Hassan ibn Muhammad all from Ahmad ibn al-Hassan al-Mithami from Ya'qub ibn Shu'ayb who has said the following:

"I heard abu 'Abd Allah, *'Alayhi al-Salam*, saying, 'The Messenger of Allah has said that in a son of Adam there are three hundred sixty veins of which one hundred eighty are moving and one hundred eighty are quiet. If a moving vein becomes quiet one cannot sleep and if a quiet one moves one cannot sleep'. The Messenger of Allah in the morning would say, 'All praise belongs to Allah, Lord of the worlds, a great deal of praise in all conditions, three hundred sixty times and so also he would do in the evening.'"

H 3201, Ch. 27, h 5

A number of our people have narrated from Ahmad ibn Muhammad ibn Khalid from Mansur ibn al-'Abbas from Sa'Id ibn Janah who has said that narrated to him abu Mas'Ud from abu 'Abd Allah, *'Alayhi al-Salam*, who has said the following:

"Whoever says four times in the morning, 'All praise belongs to Allah, Lord of the worlds,' has completed his thanksgiving for that day and if one does the same thing in the evening he has completed his thanksgiving for the night.'"

H 3202, Ch. 27, h 6

Ali ibn Ibrahim has narrated from his father from Ali ibn Hassan from certain individuals of his people from abu 'Abd Allah, *'Alayhi al-Salam*, who has said the following:

"Abu 'Abd Allah, *'Alayhi al-Salam*, has said, 'Any prayer that does not have thanksgiving before it is incomplete. First it is thanksgiving, then praising.' I (the narrator) then asked, 'I do not know what is enough for thanksgiving?' The Imam said one should say, 'O Lord, You are the First, no one was ever before You, You are the Last and there will be no one after You, You are the Dominant and there is no one above You, You are the Inside and there is no one before You and You are the Majestic, the Wise.'"

H 3203, Ch. 27, h 7

Through the same chain of narrators it is narrated from abu 'Abd Allah, *'Alayhi al-Salam*, who has said the following:

"The least for thanksgiving is to say, 'All praise belongs to Allah who is High, so all things are subdued before Him, all praise belongs to Allah who owns all things, so He provides sustenance to all of them, all praise belongs to Allah who is inside, so He has the news of all things, all praise belongs to Allah who causes the living to die, gives life to the dead and has power over all things.'"

Chapter 28 - Plea for Forgiveness

H 3204, Ch. 28, h 1

Ali ibn Ibrahim has narrated from his father from al-Nawfali from al-Sakuni from abu 'Abd Allah, *'Alayhi al-Salam*, who has said the following:

"The Messenger of Allah has said, 'The best prayer and plea before Allah for help is the plea for forgiveness and protection against the consequences of sins.'"

H 3205, Ch. 28, h 2

A number of our people have narrated from Ahmad ibn Muhammad from Husayn ibn Sayf from abu Jamilah from 'Ubayd ibn Zurara who has said the following:

"Abu 'Abd Allah, *'Alayhi al-Salam*, has said, 'One who pleas for forgiveness often, his book of record of deeds is raised and it shines brilliantly.'"

H 3206, Ch. 28, h 3

Ali ibn Ibrahim has narrated from his father from Yasir from al-Rida, *'Alayhi al-Salam*, who has said the following:

"A plea for forgiveness is like shaking a tree from which leaves fall off. One who pleas forgiveness and commits sins is like one who derides his Lord."

H 3207, Ch. 28, h 4

A number of our people have narrated from Ahmad ibn Muhammad ibn Khalid from his father from Muhammad ibn Sinan from Talhah ibn Zayd from abu 'Abd Allah, *'Alayhi al-Salam*, who has said the following:

"The Messenger of Allah would not leave a gathering - even a small one until - he would plea for protection (forgiveness) from Allah, the Most Majestic, the Most Holy, twenty-five times."

H 3208, Ch. 28, h 5

Ali ibn Ibrahim has narrated from his father from ibn abu 'Umayr from Mu'awiyah ibn 'Ammar from al-Harith ibn al-Mughirah from abu 'Abd Allah, *'Alayhi al-Salam*, who has said the following:

"The Messenger of Allah would plea for protection seventy times everyday and turn to Allah, the Most Majestic, the Most Holy, seventy times everyday.' I (the narrator) then asked, 'Would he say, I plea for protection (forgiveness) from Allah and turn to Him?' The Imam said, 'He would say, "I plea for protection (forgiveness) from Allah, I plea for protection from Allah," seventy times. And would say, 'I return to Allah, I return to Allah,' seventy times.'"

H 3209, Ch. 28, h 6

Abu Ali al-Ash'ari has narrated from Muhammad ibn 'Abd al-Jabbar from Safwan ibn Yahya from Husayn ibn Yazid from abu 'Abd Allah, *'Alayhi al-Salam*, who has said the following:

"The Messenger of Allah has said, 'Plea for forgiveness, and the words: 'No one deserves to be worshipped except Allah' are the best forms of worship.' Allah, the Most Majestic, the Most Mighty, has said, 'Notice that Allah is the only Lord who deserves to be worshipped. Ask forgiveness for your sins. . . .'" (47:19)

Chapter 29 - Al-Tasbih, Saying, 'Glory Belongs to Allah,' Al-Tahlil, Saying, 'No One Deserves to Be Worshipped Except Allah,' Al-Takbir, Saying, 'Allah is Greater Than Can Be Described'

H 3210, Ch. 29, h 1

Ali ibn Ibrahim has narrated from his father from ibn abu 'Umayr from Hisham ibn Salim and abu Ayyub al-Khazzaz all from abu 'Abd Allah, *'Alayhi al-Salam*, who has said the following:

"Once the poor people came to the Messenger of Allah and said, 'O Messenger of Allah, the wealthy people have the means to set free slaves, we do not have it, they can go for Hajj, but we cannot, they can provide charity, but we cannot and they can join the defense army for Jihad, but we cannot do so.' The Messenger of Allah said, 'Whoever says al-Takbir of Allah, the Most Majestic, the Most Holy. "Allahu Akbar (Allah is greater than can be described)," one hundred times it will be better than setting free one hundred slaves.'

"Whoever says al-Tasbih of Allah, 'Subhana Allah (all glory belongs to Allah),' one hundred times it is better than deriving one hundred camels as a sacrificial offering.

"Whoever says, 'All praise belongs to Allah' one hundred times, it is better than offering one hundred horses, harnessed and readied with a soldier riding to move for the cause of Allah.

"Whoever says, 'No one deserves to be worshipped except Allah,' one hundred times will be the best among people in worshipping that day except for one who does more.

"The Imam then said, 'This reached the wealthy people and they followed the instruction. The poor people came to the Holy Prophet and said, "O Messenger of Allah, the wealthy people heard it and they did it." The Messenger of Allah said, 'That is an addition from Allah that He grants to whoever He wills.'"

H 3211, Ch. 29, h 2

Muhammad ibn Yahya has narrated from Ahmad ibn Muhammad ibn 'Isa from Muhammad ibn Sinan from Hammad from Rib'I from Fudayl who has said the following:

"I heard one of the two Imam, *'Alayhi al-Salam*, (abu Ja'far or abu 'Abd Allah) saying, 'Increase al-Tahlil and al-Takbir; there is nothing more beloved to Allah, the Most Majestic, the Most Holy, than al-Tahlil and al-Takbir,'"

H 3212, Ch. 29, h 3

Ali has narrated from his father from al-Nawfali from al-Sakuni from abu 'Abd Allah, *'Alayhi al-Salam*, who has said the following:

"Amir al-Mu'minin, Ali ibn abu Talib, *'Alayhi al-Salam*, has said, 'Al-Tasbih is half of the balance, al-Hamdu li Allah fills out the balance and Allahu Akbar fills from earth to heaven.'"

H 3213, Ch. 29, h 4

Muhammad ibn Yahya has narrated from Ahmad ibn Muhammad ibn 'Isa from ibn Mahbub from Malik ibn 'Atiyyah from Durays al-Kunasi from abu Ja'far, *'Alayhi al-Salam*, who has said the following:

"The Messenger of Allah once was passing by a man who was planting a plant in his yard. The Holy Prophet stopped and asked, 'Should I tell you about a plantation that has stronger roots, ripens faster and is of finer fruits?' The man said, 'Yes, O Messenger of Allah, tell me about it.' The Messenger of Allah said, 'In the morning and evenings say, "Glory belongs to Allah, all praise belongs to Allah, no one deserves to be worshipped except Allah and Allah is greater than can be described." If you say this, for each time you will have ten trees in paradise of different kinds of fruits. They are (the reward) from perpetually charitable trusts.' The Imam said that the man then said, 'I take Allah as witness that my yard is a charitable trust and the needy Muslims are its beneficiaries.' Allah, the Most Majestic, the Most Holy, then revealed the verses of the Holy Quran: 'For those who spend for the cause of Allah, observe piety, (92:5) and believe in receiving rewards from Allah, (92:6) We shall facilitate the path to bliss'" (92:7)

H 3214, Ch. 29, h 5

Ali ibn Ibrahim has narrated from his father from al-Nawfali from al-Sakuni from abu 'Abd Allah, *'Alayhi al-Salam*, who has said the following:

"The Messenger of Allah has said, 'The best form of worship is saying, 'No one deserves to be worshipped except Allah.'"

Chapter 30 - Praying for Brothers (in Belief) in Their Absence

H 3215, Ch. 30, h 1

Ali ibn Ibrahim has narrated from his father from ibn abu 'Umayr from abu al-Mighra' from al-Fudayl ibn Yasar from abu Ja'far, *'Alayhi al-Salam*, who has said the following:

"The prayer closest to acceptance and the fastest to be heard is a man's prayer for a brother (in belief) in his absence."

H 3216, Ch. 30, h 2

Muhammad ibn Yahya has narrated from Ahmad ibn Muhammad ibn 'Isa from al-Hassan ibn Mahbub from 'Abd Allah ibn Sinan from abu 'Abd Allah, *'Alayhi al-Salam*, who has said the following:

"A man's prayer for his brother (in belief) in his absence increases his sustenance and repulses misfortune."

H 3217, Ch. 30, h 3

It is narrated from him (narrator of the Hadith above) from Ahmad ibn Muhammad from Ali ibn al-Hakam from Sayf ibn 'Amirah from 'Amr ibn Shimr from Jabir from abu Ja'far, *'Alayhi al-Salam*, who has said the following:

"About the words of Allah, the Most Holy, the Most High, 'He answers the prayers of the righteously striving believers and grants them increasing favors . . .,' (42:26) the Imam said, 'This is a reference to a believing person who prays for his brother (in belief) in his absence and the angel says, "Amin." Allah, the Majestic and the Most dominant says, 'You will have twice as much you asked for you brother (in belief) and I have already granted him what you asked for due to your love for him.'"

H 3218, Ch. 30, h 4

Ali ibn Ibrahim has narrated from his father from Ali ibn Ma'Bad from 'Ubayd Allah ibn 'Abd Allah al-Wasity from Durst ibn abu Mansur from abu Khalid al-Qammat who has said the following:

"Abu Ja'far, *'Alayhi al-Salam*, has said, 'The prayer quickest to success and acceptance is one's prayer for his brother (in belief) in his absence where one starts praying for him and the angels guarding say, 'Amin' You will have twice as much you asked for him.'"

H 3219, Ch. 30, h 5

Ali ibn Muhammad has narrated from Muhammad ibn Sulayman from Isma'Il ibn Ibrahim from Ja'far ibn Muhammad al-Tamimi from Husayn ibn 'Ulwan from abu 'Abd Allah, *'Alayhi al-Salam*, who has said the following:

"The Messenger of Allah has said, 'Any believing person who prays for the believing people male and female, Allah, the Most Majestic, the Most Holy, returns to such person a reward equal to the reward for a likewise prayer with which all believing people, male and female have been praying from the beginning of time and all who will do so in future up to the Day of Judgment. A servant will be ordered and dragged to the fire and the believing people male and female will say, 'O Lord, this is the one who prayed for us, accept our intercession for him and Allah, the Most Majestic, the Most Holy, will accept their intercession about him and he will be saved.'"

H 3220, Ch. 30, h 6

Ali has narrated from his father who has said the following:

"Once I saw 'Abd Allah ibn Jundab in 'Arafat but I had not seen any stay (spending the ninth day of Dulhajj) in 'Arafat better than that. He continued stretching his hands to the sky and his tears flow on his both cheeks all the way to the ground. When people left I said to him, 'O abu Muhammad, I have never seen a wonderful performance in 'Arafat such as yours.' He said, 'By Allah I did not pray for anything but for my brothers (in belief) and that is because of abu al-Hassan Musa, *'Alayhi al-Salam*, who told me that whoever prays for his brothers (in belief) in his absence is called from the Throne, '(O servant of Allah) you will have one hundred thousand times as much reward as one may for his prayer receive,' thus, I did not like to leave one hundred thousand guaranteed for only one of mine, of which I am uncertain whether it is accepted or not.'"

H 3221, Ch. 30, h 7

A number of our people have narrated from Sahl ibn Ziyad and Ali ibn Ibrahim has narrated from his father all from ibn Mahbub from ibn Ri'ab from abu 'Ubaydah from Thuwayr who has said the following:

"I heard Ali ibn al-Husayn, *'Alayhi al-Salam*, saying, 'When the angels hear the believing person praying for his brother (in belief) in his absence or speak of him good, they say, "You are a good brother (in belief). You pray for him in his absence and speak good of him. Allah, the Most Majestic, the Most Holy, has granted you double of what you asked for him and He has praised you double of your praising him and you have excellence over him, but if they (angels) hear him speak evil of his brother (in belief), and pray against him, they will say, 'You are a bad brother for him! Stop, O you whose sins and privacy are covered, reduce your burden. Praise and thank Allah, Who has covered you, and notice that Allah, the Most Majestic, the Most Holy, knows more about His servant than you do.'"

Chapter 31 - The One Whose Prayer is Accepted

H 3222, Ch. 31, h 1

Muhammad ibn Yahya has narrated from Ahmad ibn Muhammad ibn Khalid from 'Isa ibn 'Abd Allah al-Qummi who has said the following:

"I heard abu 'Abd Allah, *'Alayhi al-Salam*, saying, 'Three people's prayers are accepted: one who has gone to performing Hajj, thus, consider how can you deal properly with his affairs in his absence, a soldier fighting for the cause of Allah, thus, consider how can you deal properly with his affairs in his absence, and a person suffering from an illness, thus, do not annoy or disturb him.'"

H 3223, Ch. 31, h 2

Al-Husayn ibn Muhammad al-Ash'ari has narrated from Mu'alla ibn Muhammad from Hassan ibn Ali al-Washsha' from 'Abd Allah ibn Sinan from abu 'Abd Allah, *'Alayhi al-Salam*, who has said the following:

"My father, *'Alayhi al-Salam*, has said, 'Five kinds of prayers are not barred from the Lord, the Most Blessed, the Most High: the prayer of an Imam who is just in his dealings, the prayer of an oppressed as Allah, the Most Majestic, the Most Holy, has said, "I will revenge for you even if it may come after a long time," the prayer of a virtuous son for his parents, the prayer of a virtuous father for his son and the prayer of a believing person for his brother (in belief) in his absence to whom it is said, 'You will have as your reward just like what you asked for him.'"

H 3224, Ch. 31, h 3
Ali ibn Ibrahim has narrated from his father from al-Nawfali from al-Sakuni from abu 'Abd Allah, *'Alayhi al-Salam*, who has said the following:

"The Messenger of Allah has said, 'Beware of the prayer of an oppressed; it climbs over the cloud and Allah, the Most Majestic, the Most Holy, looks at it and says, "Raise it up so it is accepted," and beware of the prayer of a father; it is sharper than a sword.'"

H 3225, Ch. 31, h 4
Muhammad ibn Yahya has narrated from Ahmad ibn Muhammad from al-Husayn ibn Sa'Id from his brother al-Hassan from Zar'a from Sama'a from abu 'Abd Allah, *'Alayhi al-Salam*, who has said the following:

"My father, *'Alayhi al-Salam*, would say, 'Stay away from injustice and oppression; the prayer of an oppressed climbs into the heavens.'"

H 3226, Ch. 31, h 5
Ali ibn Ibrahim has narrated from his father from ibn abu 'Umayr from Hisham ibn Salim from abu 'Abd Allah, *'Alayhi al-Salam*, who has said the following:

"Abu 'Abd Allah, *'Alayhi al-Salam*, has said, 'Whoever prays for forty believing persons and then for himself, his prayer will be accepted.'"

H 3227, Ch. 31, h 6
Muhammad ibn Yahya has narrated from Muhammad ibn al-Husayn from Ali ibn al-Nu'Man from 'Abd Allah ibn Talhah al-Nahdi from abu 'Abd Allah, *'Alayhi al-Salam*, who has said the following:

"The Messenger of Allah has said, 'The prayers of four people are not turned back before the door to heaven opens and they move to the Throne: the prayer of a father for his son, the prayer of an oppressed against his oppressor, the prayer of one who performs 'Umrah until his returning home and the prayer of a person fasting before breaking his fast.'"

H 3228, Ch. 31, h 7
Ali ibn Ibrahim has narrated from his father from al-Nawfali from al-Sakuni from abu 'Abd Allah, *'Alayhi al-Salam*, who has said the following:

"The Holy Prophet has said, 'No prayer is more quickly accepted than the prayer of one unseen for another unseen, that is, in each other's absence.'"

H 3229, Ch. 31, h 8
Ali ibn Ibrahim has narrated from his father from al-Nawfali from al-Sakuni from abu 'Abd Allah, *'Alayhi al-Salam*, who has said the following:

"The Messenger of Allah has said, 'Moses prayed and Harun said Amin and the angels said Amin. Allah, the Most Blessed, the Most High, then said, "I have accepted your prayer be steadfast", (10:89) and the prayer of one who fights for the cause of Allah will be answered just like the prayer of two of you (Moses and Harun) is accepted to the Day of Judgment.'"

Chapter 32 - One Whose Prayer is Not Accepted

H 3230, Ch. 32, h 1

Ali ibn Ibrahim has narrated from his father from Hammad ibn 'Isa from Husayn ibn Mukhtar from al-Walid ibn Sabih who has said the following:

"Once I accompanied abu 'Abd Allah, *'Alayhi al-Salam,* between Makkah and Madinah and at a certain place a beggar came and he ordered his people to help. Another beggar came he ordered his people to help, another came and he ordered to help, then the fourth one came and abu 'Abd Allah said, 'May Allah satisfy you,' and he turned to us saying, 'We still can help but I feared becoming of the three kinds of people whose prayers are not heard: a man to whom Allah has granted wealth but he spends it on a wrong cause and then asks, "O Lord, grant me wealth." His prayer is not accepted, a man who prays against his wife while Allah, the Most Majestic, the Most Holy, has made it lawful to dissolve the marriage, and a man who prays against his neighbor while Allah, the Most Majestic, the Most Holy, has made it possible for him to move away and buy another house.'"

H 3231, Ch. 32, h 2

Abu Ali al-Ash'ari has narrated from Muhammad ibn 'Abd al-Jabbar from ibn Faddal from 'Abd Allah ibn Ibrahim from Ja'far ibn Ibrahim from abu 'Abd Allah, *'Alayhi al-Salam,* who has said the following:

"The prayers of four kinds of people are not heard: a man who sits home and says, 'O Lord, grant me sustenance,' and it is said to him, "Have I not commanded you to work?" a man who is troubled by his wife so he prays for relief, but he will be asked, 'Have I not made dissolving marriage lawful?' A man who has destroyed his wealth and asks, 'O Lord, grant me wealth,' he will be asked, "Have I not commanded you to spend it moderately and have I not commanded you to make corrections?" Then the Imam read from the Holy Quran, '. . . who in their spending are neither extravagant nor stingy but maintain moderation,' (25:67) and a man who lends money to others without witnesses as evidence and it is said to him, 'Have I not commanded you to ask for witnesses as testimony?'"

Muhammad ibn Yahya has narrated from Ahmad ibn Muhammad from Ali ibn al-Hakam from 'Umar ibn abu 'Asim from abu 'Abd Allah, *'Alayhi al-Salam,* a similar Hadith.

H 3232, Ch. 32, h 3

Al-Husayn ibn Muhammad al-Ash'ari has narrated from Mu'alla ibn Muhammad from al-Washsha' from 'Abd Allah ibn Sinan from al-Walid ibn Sabih who has said the following:

"I heard abu 'Abd Allah, *'Alayhi al-Salam,* saying, 'The prayer of three kinds of people is not accepted: a man to whom Allah has granted wealth but spends it improperly and then says, "O Lord, grant me wealth," to him it is said, 'Did I not give you wealth?' A man who prays against his unjust wife, and it is said to him, 'Have I not left her affairs to you (dissolving of marriage lawful)?' A man who sits idle and prayers, 'O Lord, grant me sustenance,' and to him it is said, 'Have I not made ways how to make a living?'"

Chapter 33 - Prayer Against the Enemy

H 3233, Ch. 33, h 1

A number of our people have narrated from Sahl ibn Ziyad from Yahya ibn al-Mubarak from 'Abd Allah ibn Jabalah from Ishaq ibn 'Ammar who has said the following:

"Once I complained before abu 'Abd Allah, *'Alayhi al-Salam*, about my neighbor and what I had suffered from him. The narrator has said that the Imam said, 'Pray and plead before Allah against him.' I did so and did not have any results and I went back to the Imam to complain. He said, 'Pray against him.' I said, 'May Allah keep my soul in service for your cause, I have already done but have not seen any result.' The Imam said, 'How did you pray against him?' I said, 'When I met him I prayed against him.' The Imam said, 'Pray against him when he moves away from you.' I then did as I was told and Allah very soon granted me relief.'"

H 3234, Ch. 33, h 2

It is narrated from abu al-Hassan, *'Alayhi al-Salam*, who has said the following:

"When any of you prays against the other person he should say, 'O Lord, strike him with peerless misfortune in the night and allow his defenses to be ransacked.'"

H 3235, Ch. 33, h 3

Muhammad ibn Yahya has narrated from Ahmad ibn Muhammad ibn 'Isa from Ali ibn al-Hakam from Malik ibn 'Atiyyah from Yunus ibn 'Ammar who has said the following:

"Once I said to abu 'Abd Allah, *'Alayhi al-Salam*, 'I have a neighbor from Quraysh from the family of Muhriz who propagates against me negatively. Whenever I pass by he calls me a Rafida (rejecting successors to the Holy Prophet who are not special members of his family) and that I collect funds for Ja'far ibn Muhammad, *'Alayhi al-Salam*.' The Imam said, 'Pray to Allah against him in the last Sajdah (prostration) of the second Rak'at of Tahajjud (nightly prayer). Praise Allah, the Most Majestic, the Most Holy, and glorify Him and say, 'O Lord, so and so, son of so and so propagates against me negatively, he has caused me anger and has exposed me to danger, O Lord, strike him a quick arrow to divert him away from me, O Lord, bring the time of his death closer, eliminate his traces and make it fast, O Lord, in this hour, in this hour!' When I arrived in al-Kufa during the night and asked my family about him, how is so and so doing? They told me that he was ill. My words were not finished when I heard crying from the house of that man. They said that he had died.'"

H 3236, Ch. 33, h 4

Ahmad ibn Muhammad al-Kufi has narrated from Ali ibn al-Hassan al-Taymi from Ali ibn Asbat from Ya'qub ibn Salim who has said the following:

"Once I was in the presence of abu 'Abd Allah, *'Alayhi al-Salam*, and al-'Ala' ibn Kamil said to him, 'So and so acts against me again and again, if you consider it proper, pray to Allah, the Most Majestic, the Most Holy.' The Imam said, 'This is more than enough for you. Say, "O Lord, You are sufficient for everything and nothing is sufficient for You. Suffice me in the matters of so and so with whatever You wish, in whatever way You wish, from wherever You wish and whenever You wish.'"

H 3237, Ch. 33, h 5

Muhammad ibn Yahya has narrated from Ahmad ibn Muhammad from ibn abu Najran from Hammad ibn 'Uthman from al-Misma'I who has said that when Dawud ibn Ali killed al-Mu'alla' ibn Khunays, abu 'Abd Allah, *'Alayhi al-Salam*, said the following:

"Abu 'Abd Allah, *'Alayhi al-Salam*, said, 'I will pray to Allah against whoever has murdered my Mawla (servant) and has seized my property.' Dawud ibn Ali then said, 'You threaten me with your prayer! (But I am not afraid).' Hammad has said that al-Misma'i said that Mu'attib said to me, 'Abu 'Abd Allah, *'Alayhi al-Salam*, that night continued his Ruku' and Sajdah and, when it was morning, I hear him saying in Sajdah (prostration) "O Lord, I ask You through Your power that is strong, through Your glory that is intense, that has humbled Your creatures, grant favors to Muhammad and his family and seize him (the enemy) in this hour! Seize him in this hour!' He had not yet raised his head that we heard crying and wailing from the house of Dawud ibn Ali. Abu 'Abd Allah, *'Alayhi al-Salam*, raised his head and said, 'I prayed to Allah with a prayer and Allah, the Most Majestic, the Most Holy, sent an angel over him to hit his head with an iron bar that ruptured his bladder and caused his death.'"

Note: Dawud ibn Ali was the governor of Madinah during the rule of abu al-'Abbas al-Saffah. He ordered al-Mu'alla to identify for him every Shi'a (follower 'A'immah) of abu 'Abd Allah, *'Alayhi al-Salam*. He refused saying, 'Even if they were under my foot I would not raise it to expose them.' He was murdered and the properties of abu 'Abd Allah, *'Alayhi al-Salam*, with him was seized.

Chapter 34 - Al-Mubahalah (Pleading Before Allah for Help Against the Enemy)

H 3238, Ch. 34, h 1

Ali ibn Ibrahim has narrated from his father from ibn abu 'Umayr from Muhammad ibn Hakim from abu Masruq who has said the following:

"Once I said to abu 'Abd Allah, *'Alayhi al-Salam*, 'We speak to people and in support of our (Shi'a Muslim) belief refer them to the words of Allah, the Most Majestic, the Most Holy, 'O believers, obey Allah, His Messenger, and your leaders (who possess Divine Authority). . .' (4:59) They say, 'It applies to the commanders of the missions of armed forces.'

"We then refer them to the words of Allah, the Most Majestic, the Most Holy, 'Only Allah, His Messenger, and the true believers who are steadfast in prayer and pay alms, while they kneel during prayer, are your guardians.' (5:55) They say, 'This applies to the believing people (as a whole).'

"We refer them to the words of Allah, the Most Majestic, the Most Holy, '(Muhammad), say, "I do not ask you for any payment for my preaching to you except (your) love of (my near) relatives. . . ."' (42:23) They say, 'It applies to the relatives of the Muslims.'

"I (the narrator) then mentioned all such references that I knew of and the Imam said, 'If such is the case, call them for Al-Mubahalah (pleading before Allah for help against the enemy).' I then asked, 'How should I do that?' The Imam said, 'Correct your soul three days,' I think he said, 'Fast, take a shower and both of you go in the mountains, crisscross the fingers of your right hand with his fingers, then yield for justice against yourself (begin with yourself) and say, "O Lord, the Cherisher of the seven heavens and seven earths, the One who possesses the knowledge of the unseen and seen, the Beneficent, the Merciful, if abu Masruq has denied anyone's rights or has claimed falsehood, send upon him misfortune from the sky or a painful punishment." Then turn it to him and say, 'If so and so has rejected a truth or made a false claim, send upon him a misfortune from the sky or a painful punishment.' Then the Imam said to me, 'You will very shortly see it in him.' The narrator has said, 'I swear by Allah I could not find any creature, who could accept my call for Al-Mubahalah (pleading before Allah for help against the enemy).'"

H 3239, Ch. 34, h 2
A number of our people have narrated from Sahl ibn Ziyad from Isma'Il ibn Mehran from Mukhallad abu al-Shukr from abu Hamza al-Thumali from abu Ja'far, *'Alayhi al-Salam*, who has said the following:

"Abu Ja'far, *'Alayhi al-Salam*, has said, 'The time for al-Mubahalah is between dawn and sunrise.'"

A number of our people have narrated from Ahmad ibn Muhammad ibn Khalid from Muhammad ibn Isma'Il from Mukhallad abu al-Shukr from abu Hamza from abu Ja'far, *'Alayhi al-Salam*, a similar Hadith.

H 3240, Ch. 34, h 3
Ahmad has narrated from certain individuals of our people about al-Mubahalah this:

"Crisscross the fingers of your hand with his fingers and say, 'O Lord, if so and so has rejected a truth or has professed a falsehood, make him suffer misfortune from the sky or a painful punishment by Your command and then (the parties) renounce each other seventy times.'"

H 3241, Ch. 34, h 4
Muhammad ibn Yahya has narrated from Ahmad ibn Muhammad ibn 'Isa from ibn Mahbub from abu al-'Abbas from abu 'Abd Allah, *'Alayhi al-Salam*, who has said the following about al-Mubahalah:

"Crisscross the fingers of your hand with his fingers and say, 'O Lord, if so and so has rejected a truth or has professed a falsehood, make him suffer a misfortune from the sky or a punishment from You', and then renounce each other seventy times.'"

H 3242, Ch. 34, h 5
Muhammad ibn Yahya has narrated from Ahmad ibn Muhammad from Muhammad ibn 'Abd al-Hamid from abu Jamilah from certain individuals of his people who has said the following:

"If a man rejects the truth and if he is ready for renunciation then say, 'O Lord, the Cherisher of the seven heavens and seven earths, and Lord of the great Throne, if so and so has rejected the truth and denied it, send upon him misfortune from the sky or a painful punishment.'"

Chapter 35 - The Expressions with Which the Lord, the Most Blessed, the Most High, Has Glorified Himself

H 3243, Ch. 35, h 1

Ali ibn Ibrahim has narrated from his father from Safwan ibn Yahya from Ishaq ibn 'Ammar from certain individuals of his people from abu 'Abd Allah, *'Alayhi al-Salam*, who has said the following:

"In three hours of the day and in three hours of the night Allah, the Majestic, the Glorious, glorifies Himself. The first hours of the day begin when the distance of the sun from this side, the East, is equal to that between 'Asr (the beginning of afternoon prayer), on the West, and the start of the time of the first prayer (prayer at noon time), and the first hours of night which begin with the start of the remaining one third of the night to dawn.

"Allah says, 'I am Allah, Cherisher of the worlds, I am Allah, the Most High, the Most Great, I am Allah, the Most Majestic, the Most Wise, I am Allah, the Most Forgiving, the Most Merciful, I am Allah, the Beneficent, the Merciful, I am Allah, the Owner of the Day of Judgment, I am Allah, Who has always been and will be, I am Allah, the Creator of the good and bad, I am Allah, the Creator of paradise and fire, I am Allah, the Initiator of all things and to Me it returns, I am Allah, the only One and Self-sufficient, I am Allah, the Knower of the unseen and the seen, I am Allah, the Owner, the Holy, the Peace, the Protector, the Dominant, the Compeller, the One who is Proud, I am Allah, the Creator, the Designer, and the Shape-giver. I have all good names; I am Allah, the Great and the Most Lofty.'

"The narrator has said that abu 'Abd Allah, *'Alayhi al-Salam*, then said in his own words, 'Greatness is His dress. Whoever disputes Him in that, He (Allah) will throw him in fire.' The Imam then said, 'Whoever of the believing people prays to Him in these words turning with his heart to Allah, the Most Majestic, the Most Holy, He will grant his wish. Even if he is a person of evil fortune, I hope he will change into a person of good fortune.'"

H 3244, Ch. 35, h 2

A number of our people have narrated from Ahmad ibn Muhammad from ibn Faddal from 'Abd Allah ibn Bukayr from 'Abd Allah ibn 'A'Yun from abu 'Abd Allah, *'Alayhi al-Salam*, who has said the following:

"Allah, the Most Blessed, the Most High, glorifies Himself three times every-day and night. Whoever glorifies Allah with the words with which He has glorified Himself, and happens to be in a condition of misfortune, Allah, the Most Majestic, the Most Holy, will turn him into a condition of good fortune.

"He should say, 'You are Allah, no one deserves to be worshipped except You, the Cherisher of the worlds. You are Allah; no one deserves to be worshipped except You, the Beneficent, the Merciful. You are Allah, no one deserves to be worshipped except You, the Most Majestic, the Most (High) Great, You are Allah, no one deserves to be worshipped except You, the Owner of the Day of Judgment. You are Allah. No one deserves to be worshipped except You, the Forgiving, the Merciful. You are Allah; no one deserves to be worshipped except You, the Majestic, the Wise. You are Allah, no one deserves to be worshipped except You, from You began the creatures and to You they return. You are Allah, (besides whom) no one deserves to be worshipped. You have always been and will always be. You are Allah, (besides whom) no one deserves to be worshipped, the Creator of the good and evil. You are Allah, no one deserves to be worshipped except You, the Creator of paradise and fire. You are Allah, no one deserves to be worshipped except You, the One, Self-sufficient, who has not given birth to any one and is not born from anyone and no one is His partner. '. . . You are Allah, no one deserves to be worshipped except You, the King, the Holy, the Peace, the Protector, the Dominant, the Majestic, the Compeller, the Proud. Allah is by far more Glorious than what they call His partners. He is Allah, the Creator, the Designer, the Shape-giver; His are the most beautiful names. All that is in heavens and in the earth glorify Him and He is the Majestic, the Wise . . . – to be read to the end of Chapter 59. You are Allah, no one deserves to be worshipped except You, the Most Great for whom greatness is the dress.'"

Chapter 36 - One's Saying, No One Deserves to be Worshipped Except Allah

H 3245, Ch. 36, h 1

A number of our people have narrated from Ahmad ibn Muhammad from Muhammad ibn Ali from Muhammad ibn al-Fudayl from abu Hamza who has said the following:

"I heard abu Ja'far, *'Alayhi al-Salam*, saying, 'There is nothing greater in rewards than testifying to the truth and believing in the meaning of the testimony of belief in Allah: 'No one deserves to be worshipped except Allah', Allah, the Most Majestic, the Most Holy, Who has no equal and no one shares Him in any issue.'"

H 3246, Ch. 36, h 2

It is narrated from him (narrator of the Hadith above) from al-Fudayl ibn 'Abd al-Wahhab from Ishaq ibn 'Abd Allah from 'Ubayd Allah ibn al-Walid al-Wassafi in a marfu' manner who has said the following:

"The Messenger of Allah has said, 'Whoever (sincerely) says, 'No one deserves to be worshipped except Allah', a tree is planted for him in paradise, from red ruby that grows out of white musk, sweeter than honey, whiter than snow, of a fragrance better than musk, in which there is something like the breast of virgins, protruding from behind seventy dresses.'

"The Messenger of Allah has said, 'The best worship is the words: 'No one deserves to be worshipped except Allah.'

"He also has said, 'The best worship is pleading before Allah for forgiveness, due to the words of Allah, the Most Majestic, the Most Holy, in His book: '(you must) know that no one deserves to be worshipped except Allah. Ask forgiveness for your sins. . . .'" (47:19)

Chapter 37 - One's Saying: No One Deserves to be Worshipped Except Allah, Allah is Greater than Everyones' Description

H 3247, Ch. 37, h 1
Muhammad ibn Yahya has narrated from Ahmad ibn Muhammad ibn 'Isa in a marfu' manner from Hariz from Ya'qub al-Qummi from abu 'Abd Allah, *'Alayhi al-Salam*, who has said the following:
"The cost of paradise is (sincerely) saying: 'No one deserves to be worshipped except Allah and Allah is greater than everyones' description.'"

Chapter 38 - One's Saying: 'No One Deserves to be Worshipped Except Allah, Allah Alone, Allah Alone, Allah Alone

H 3248, Ch. 38, h 1
Muhammad ibn Yahya has narrated from Ahmad ibn Muhammad from Ali ibn al-Nu'Man from those whom he has mentioned (in his book) from abu 'Abd Allah, *'Alayhi al-Salam*, who has said the following:
"Jibril once said to the Messenger of Allah, 'Tuba (a tree in paradise) is for those among your followers who (sincerely) say: 'No one deserves to be worshipped except Allah, Allah alone, Allah alone, Allah alone.'"

Chapter 39 - One's Saying: 'No One Deserves to be Worshipped Except Allah, Alone, No One is His Partner; Ten Times

H 3249, Ch. 39, h 1
A number of our people have narrated from Ahmad ibn Muhammad from 'Amr ibn 'Uthman and Ali ibn Ibrahim has narrated from his father all from 'Abd Allah ibn al-Mughirah from ibn Muskan from abu Basir Layth al-Muradi from 'Abd al-Karim ibn 'Utbah who has said the following:
"I heard abu 'Abd Allah, *'Alayhi al-Salam*, saying, 'Whoever (sincerely) says ten times before sunrise and before sunset, 'No one deserves to be worshipped except Allah alone Who has no partner, the Kingdom is His, all praise belongs to Him, He gives life, causes death, causes death and gives life, He is living and will never die, in His hands is the good and He has power over all things,' this will be the remedy and expiation for his sins on that day.'"

H 3250, Ch. 39, h 2
Muhammad ibn Yahya has narrated from Ahmad ibn Muhammad ibn 'Isa from those whom he has mentioned (in his book) from 'Umar ibn Muhammad from abu 'Abd Allah, *'Alayhi al-Salam*, who has said the following:
"The Messenger of Allah has said, 'Whoever soon after performing the morning prayer and before raising his knees says ten times, 'No one deserves to be worshipped except Allah alone, Who has no partner, the Kingdom is His, all praise belongs to Him, He gives life, causes death, causes death and gives life, He is living and will never die, in His hands is all good and He has power over all things, and also at sunset, no servant (of Allah) will meet Allah, the Most Majestic, the Most Holy, with a deed better than this deed except one who performs the same deed.'"

Chapter 40 - One's Saying: I Testify That No One Deserves to be Worshipped Except Allah Alone Who Has No Partner and I Testify That Muhammad is His Servant and Messenger

H 3251, Ch. 40, h 1

Ali ibn Ibrahim has narrated from his father from ibn abu 'Umayr from Sa'Id from abu 'Ubaydah al-Hadhdha' from abu Ja'far, *'Alayhi al-Salam*, who has said the following:

"Whoever says, 'I testify that no one deserves to be worshipped except Allah alone, Who has no partner, and I testify that Muhammad is His servant and Messenger, Allah will write down for him one million good deeds.'"

Chapter 41 - One's Saying ten Times Everyday: I Testify That No One Deserves to be Worshipped Except Allah Alone Who Has No Partner, One Lord, the Only Self-Sufficient, Who Has Not Taken Any Companion, Nor Any Children

H 3252, Ch. 41, h 1

Muhammad ibn Yahya has narrated from Ahmad ibn Muhammad and Ali ibn Ibrahim has narrated from his father from 'Abd al-Rahman ibn abu Najran from 'Abd al-'Aziz al-'Abdi from 'Umar ibn Yazid from abu 'Abd Allah, *'Alayhi al-Salam*, who has said the following:

"Whoever says ten times everyday, 'I testify that no one deserves to be worshipped except Allah alone, Who has no partner, One Lord, the only Self-sufficient, Who has not taken any companion nor any children,' Allah will write down for him forty-five thousand good deeds, will cancel forty-five thousand of his evil deeds and will raise for him forty-five thousand degrees.'"

"In another Hadith it is stated, 'The above expression will serve him as stronghold against rulers and Satan and no major sin will engulf him.'"

Chapter 42 - One's Saying: O Allah, O Allah Ten Times

H 3253, Ch. 42, h 1

Muhammad ibn Yahya has narrated from Ahmad ibn Muhammad from his father from Ayyub ibn al-Hurr brother of 'Udaym from abu 'Abd Allah, *'Alayhi al-Salam*, who has said the following:

"Whoever says, 'O Allah, ten times, it will be said to him, 'Labbayka' (your call for help is well heard and noted). What kind of help do you need?'"

Chapter 43 - One's Saying: No One Deserves to be Worshipped Except Allah Indeed and in Truth

H 3254, Ch. 43, h 1

A number of our people have narrated from Ahmad ibn Muhammad from Muhammad ibn 'Isa al-'Armini from abu 'Imran al-Kharrat from al-Awza'I from abu 'Abd Allah, *'Alayhi al-Salam*, who has said the following:

"Whoever says ten times a day, 'No one deserves to be worshipped except Allah, indeed and in all truth, no one deserves to be worshipped except Allah, servitude and slavery is for Him, no one deserves to be worshipped except Allah, in belief and affirmation, Allah will turn to him with His face and will not turn away from him until he will enter paradise.'"

Chapter 44 - One's Saying: "O Lord, O Lord"

H 3255, Ch. 44, h 1

Muhammad ibn Yahya has narrated from Ahmad ibn Muhammad ibn 'Isa from Muhammad ibn 'Isa from Ayyub ibn al-Hurr brother of 'Udaym from abu 'Abd Allah, *'Alayhi al-Salam*, who has said the following:

"Whoever says ten times, 'O Lord.' It will be said to him, "Your call for help is well heard and noted. What kind of help do you need?'"

H 3256, Ch. 44, h 2

Ahmad ibn Muhammad and Ali ibn Ibrahim has narrated from his father all have narrated from ibn abu 'Umayr from Muhammad ibn Humran who has said the following:

"When Isma'il son of abu 'Abd Allah, *'Alayhi al-Salam*, became ill, abu 'Abd Allah, *'Alayhi al-Salam*, told him to say, 'Ten times; O Lord.' Whoever says this will be called, 'Your call is heard and well noticed, ask what kind of help do you need?'"

H 3257, Ch. 44, h 3

Muhammad ibn Yahya has narrated from Ahmad ibn Muhammad from Muhammad ibn 'Isa from Mu'awiyah from abu Basir from abu 'Abd Allah, *'Alayhi al-Salam*, who has said the following:

"Whoever says, 'O Lord, O Allah, for one full breath, it is said to him, "Your call is heard and well noticed, ask what kind of help do you need?'"

Chapter 45 - One's Sincerely Saying: "No One Deserves to Be Worshipped Except Allah"

H 3258, Ch. 45, h 1

Al-Husayn ibn Muhammad has narrated from Mu'alla ibn Muhammad and A number of our people have narrated from Ahmad ibn Muhammad all from al-Washsha' from Ahmad ibn 'Ai'z from abu al-Hassan al-Sawwaq from Aban ibn Taghlib from abu 'Abd Allah, *'Alayhi al-Salam*, who has said the following:

"O Aban, when you will arrive in al-Kufah, narrate this Hadith: 'Whoever testifies sincerely saying, "No one deserves to be worshipped except Allah," paradise becomes necessary for him. I (the narrator) then said, 'All kinds of people will come to me, shall I narrate it to them?' The Imam said, 'Yes, O Aban, when it will be the Day of Judgment and Allah will gather all the people of the past and last together, the testimony: 'No one deserves to be worshipped except Allah,' will be taken away from them except those who believe in this cause (belief of the followers of Ahl al-Baay, *'Alayhi al-Salam*).'"

Chapter 46 - One's Saying: "As Allah Wills, There are No Means and No Power Without the Help of Allah"

H 3259, Ch. 46, h 1

Muhammad ibn Yahya has narrated from Ahmad ibn Muhammad ibn 'Isa from Ali ibn al-Hakam from Hisham ibn Salim from abu 'Abd Allah, *'Alayhi al-Salam*, who has said the following:

"When a man prays and thereafter says, 'As Allah wills, there are no means and no power without the help of Allah,' Allah, the Most Majestic, the Most Holy, says, "My servant has accepted dying and has submitted himself to My command. Provide him the help that he needs.""

H 3260, Ch. 46, h 2

Muhammad ibn Yahya has narrated from Ahmad ibn Muhammad from certain individuals of his people from Jamil who has said the following:

"I heard abu 'Abd Allah, *'Alayhi al-Salam*, saying, 'Whoever says, "As Allah wills, there are no means and no power without the help of Allah," seventy times, seventy kinds of misfortunes will be diverted away from him, the least of which is al-Khanq.' I (the narrator) then asked, 'May Allah keep my soul in service for your cause, what is al-Khanq?' The Imam said, 'He will not suffer from mental illness (insanity).'"

Chapter 47 - One's Saying: I Plead Before Allah for Forgiveness, No One Deserves to be Worshipped Except Allah, the Living, the Guardian, the Possessor of Glory and Honor and to Him I Return

H 3261, Ch. 47, h 1

Muhammad ibn Yahya has narrated from Ahmad ibn Muhammad ibn 'Isa from 'Abd al-Samad from al-Husayn ibn Hammad from abu Ja'far, *'Alayhi al-Salam*, who has said the following:

"Whoever after an obligatory prayer and before moving his legs to a second position says, 'I plead before Allah for forgiveness, no one deserves to be worshipped except Allah, the Living, the Guardian, the Possessor of Glory and Honor and to Him I return,' three times Allah, the Most Majestic, the Most Holy, will forgive his sins even if they are as much as the bubbles of the ocean.'"

Chapter 48 - The Word in the Morning and Evening

H 3262, Ch. 48, h 1

Ali ibn Ibrahim has narrated from his father from Ali ibn Asbat from Ghalib ibn 'Abd Allah from abu 'Abd Allah, *'Alayhi al-Salam*, who has said the following:

"About the words of Allah, the Most Blessed, the Most High, 'All in the heavens and the earth prostrate themselves before Allah, either of their own free will or by force, just as do their shadows in the mornings and evenings,' (13:15) the Imam said, 'This is prayer before sunrise and before sunset and it is the hour in which prayers are heard.'"

H 3263, Ch. 48, h 2

A number of our people have narrated from Ahmad ibn Muhammad from ibn Faddal from abu Jamilah from Jabir from abu Ja'far, *'Alayhi al-Salam*, who has said the following:

"Satan, may Allah's condemnations be upon him, spreads the armies of the night at sunset and at sunrise. You must speak of Allah, the Most Majestic, the Most Holy, very often in these two hours and seek protection from Allah against the evils of Satan and his army, protect your little ones in those two hours; they are the hours of negligence."

H 3264, Ch. 48, h 3

Muhammad ibn Yahya has narrated from Ahmad ibn Muhammad ibn 'Isa and Ali ibn Ibrahim has narrated from his father all from ibn abu 'Umayr from al-Hassan ibn 'Atiyyah from Razin Sahib al-Anmat from one of the two Imam, *'Alayhi al-Salam*, who has said the following:

"Whoever says, 'O Lord, I ask You to be my witness, I ask Your favorite angels to be my witness and the chosen carriers of Your Throne to be my witness to my testimony: You are Allah, no one deserves to be worshipped except You, the Beneficent, the Merciful, and that Muhammad is Your servant and Your Messenger that so and so, son of so and so, (the Imam and his father should be mentioned) is my Imam and my guardian that he is a child of the Messenger of Allah, that Ali, al-Hassan and al-Husayn and so and so, *'Alayhim al-Salam*, up to him (the twelfth Imam) are my Imam and guardians. With this I live. On this I will die and will be raised (resurrected). I disavow so and so and so.' If he may die that night, he will enter paradise.'"

H 3265, Ch. 48, h 4

Muhammad ibn Yahya has narrated from Ahmad ibn Muhammad from Hajjal and Bakr ibn Muhammad from abu Ishaq al-Sha'Iri from Yazid ibn Kalthamah from abu 'Abd Allah or abu Ja'far, *'Alayhi al-Salam*, who has said the following:

"In the morning say, 'This morning I believe in Allah in the religion of Muhammad and his tradition, Sunnah, the religion of Ali and his tradition, the religion of the successors (of the Holy Prophet from his family) and their tradition. I believe in their secrets and that which is public of them, those present of them as well as those absent. I seek refuge before Allah from everything against which the Messenger of Allah, Ali and the successors (of the Holy Prophet from his family) sought refuge. I am interested in everything that was of interest to them. There are no means and no power without the help of Allah.'"

H 3266, Ch. 48, h 5

It is narrated from him (narrator of the Hadith above) from Ahmad ibn Muhammad from Ali ibn al-Hakam from abu Ayyub Ibrahim ibn 'Uthman al-Khazzaz from Muhammad ibn Muslim who has said the following:

"Abu 'Abd Allah, *'Alayhi al-Salam*, has said, 'Ali ibn al-Husayn, *'Alayhi al-Salam*, in the morning would say, "I begin in the name of Allah my day, before forgetting or hastening to other things, with the name of Allah and whatever Allah wills." If a servant (of Allah) does this, he will be rewarded for that which he may forget that day.'"

H 3267, Ch. 48, h 6

It is narrated from him (narrator of the Hadith above) from Ahmad ibn Muhammad and Ali ibn Ibrahim has narrated from his father all from ibn abu 'Umayr from 'Umar ibn Shahab and Sulaym al-Farra' from a man from abu 'Abd Allah, *'Alayhi al-Salam*, who has said the following:

"Whoever says in the evening, 'I leave myself and all that is important to me, in trust of Allah, the Most High, the Most Glorious, the Most Great, from Whose greatness all things fear, worry and waver,' three times, he will be wrapped up in a wing of the wings of Jibril, the Archangel, for protection until morning.'"

H 3268, Ch. 48, h 7

Muhammad ibn Yahya has narrated from Ahmad ibn Muhammad and Abu Ali al-Ash'ari from Muhammad ibn 'Abd al-Jabbar from al-Hajjal from Ali ibn 'Uqbah and Ghalib ibn 'Uthman from those whom he has mentioned (in his book) from abu 'Abd Allah, *'Alayhi al-Salam*, who has said the following:

"In the evening say, 'O Lord, I ask You in the approaching of Your night and retreating of Your day, in the presence of Your blessings, among the voices of prayer to You to grant al-Salat (favors) upon Muhammad and Ale (family of) Muhammad,' then pray for whatever you wish.'"

H 3269, Ch. 48, h 8

A number of our people have narrated from Sahl ibn Ziyad from Ja'far ibn Muhammad al-Ash'ari from ibn al-Qaddah from abu 'Abd Allah, *'Alayhi al-Salam*, who has said the following:

"Each coming day says to the sons of Adam, 'O son of Adam, I am a new day and a witness over you. Say good in me and do good deeds; I will testify for or against you on the Day of Judgment. You will never see me thereafter.' The Imam said that Ali, *'Alayhi al-Salam*, in the evening would say, 'Welcome to the new night, and witnessing ascribe. Both of you write down in the name of Allah.' Then he would speak of Allah, the Most Majestic, the Most Holy.'"

H 3270, Ch. 48, h 9

Ali ibn Ibrahim has narrated from his father from Salih ibn al-Sindy from Ja'far ibn Bashir from 'Abd Allah ibn Bukayr from Shahab ibn 'Abd Rabbihi who has said the following:

"I heard abu 'Abd Allah, *'Alayhi al-Salam*, saying, 'When the sun changes, speak of Allah, the Most Majestic, the Most Holy, and if there are people keeping you occupied, stand up and pray.'"

H 3271, Ch. 48, h 10

A number of our people have narrated from Ahmad ibn Muhammad ibn Khalid from Sharif ibn Sabiq from al-Fadl ibn abu Qurrah from abu 'Abd Allah, *'Alayhi al-Salam*, who has said the following:

"There are three things that the prophets inherited from Adam until they reached the Messenger of Allah. In the morning he would say, 'O Lord, I request You to grant me a belief that accompany with my heart, a certainty in the fact that nothing can affect me except what You have written, make me happy with the share that You have assigned for me.'"

Certain individuals of our people have narrated the above Hadith with this addition: "So I will not love hastening of what You have delayed, and the delay of what You have hastened, O Living, O Guardian, I plead for help through Your mercy, correct all of my affairs and do not leave me to my own soul not even for a blinking of an eye and grant al-Salat (favors) upon Muhammad and his family."

H 3272, Ch. 48, h 11

He (the above narrator) has narrated from abu 'Abd Allah, *'Alayhi al-Salam*, who has said the following:

"Abu 'Abd Allah, *'Alayhi al-Salam*, would say, 'All praise belongs to Allah Who has given us this morning and the kingdom belongs to Him. You have brought to this morning Your servant son of Your servant and son of Your female servant under Your control. O Lord, grant me sustenance through Your generosity, a sustenance from the source that I expect or did not expect, protect me against things I protect myself or cannot protect. O Lord, grant me sustenance through Your generosity and do not make me needy before any of Your creatures. O Lord, dress me up in good health and grant me the realization to thank You for it, the One, the only, O Self-sufficient O Allah Who is not born from anyone and has not given birth to anyone and no one is His partner or one of His kind. O Allah, O Beneficent, O Merciful, O the Owner of the kingdom, the Cherisher of the cherishers, the Master of the masters, O Allah, no one deserves to be worshipped except You, grant me good health through Your cure from all illnesses, and pains; I am one of Your servants and the son of Your servant and I move back and forth in Your control.'"

H 3273, Ch. 48, h 12

It is narrated from him (narrator of the Hadith above) from Muhammad ibn Ali in a marfu' manner from Amir al-Mu'minin, Ali ibn abu Talib, *'Alayhi al-Salam*, who has said the following:

"O Lord, I and this day are two creatures of Your creatures. O Lord, do not make me suffer from it and do not make it suffer from me. O Lord, do not allow it see me bold in disobeying You or committing unlawful things. O Lord, remove from me constraint and poverty, affliction and evil determination, and expression of joy from the enemy for bad things in me, and from being placed on an evil position, my property or myself.

"The Imam has said, 'Any servant (of Allah) who says in the morning or evening three times, "I accept that Allah is my Lord, Islam is my religion, Muhammad, *'Alayhi al-Salam*, is the Prophet, the Holy Quran is the text of Divine message and Ali, *'Alayhi al-Salam*, is my Imam," three times, it will be a right upon Allah, the Majestic, the Compeller to make him happy on the Day of Judgment.'

"The Imam has said that he (Ali, *'Alayhi al-Salam*) would say in the evening, 'We live in the morning thankful to Allah and we live in the evening praising Allah. All praise belongs to You as we live in the evening submitted to Your will and in peace.

"The Imam said, 'He (Amir al-Mu'minin, Ali ibn abu Talib, *'Alayhi al-Salam*) in the morning would say, "We live in the evening thankful to Allah and we live in the morning praising Allah, all praise belongs to Allah. We live in the morning submitted to Your will and in peace."'

H 3274, Ch. 48, h 13

It is narrated from him (narrator of the Hadith above) from 'Uthman ibn 'Isa from Sama'a from abu Basir from abu 'Abd Allah, *'Alayhi al-Salam*, who has said the following:

"My father, *'Alayhi al-Salam*, in the morning would say, '(I begin) in the name of Allah, with Allah, and to Allah, for the cause of Allah and on the religion of the Messenger of Allah, O Lord, to You I have submitted my soul, to You I have left my affairs, before You I have placed my trust, O Lord of the worlds. O Lord, protect me by the protection of belief, that I need against things with me, behind me, on my right, on my left from above me, from my underneath and in front of me. No one deserves to be worshipped except You. There are no means and no power without the help of Allah. We ask You to forgive us, grant us good health (and protection) against all evil, and misfortune in this world and in the hereafter. O Lord, I seek refuge with You against torment in the grave, against the pressure of the grave, and from the congestion of the grave. I seek refuge with You against the domination of the night and day. O Lord, the Cherisher of Mash'ar al-Haram (a place in Makkah), the Cherisher of the sacred town, the Lord of sacred and none sacred land; convey my greeting of peace to Muhammad and his family. O Lord, I seek refuge in Your strong coat of arms and Your community, from dying due to drowning, burning, choking, retaliation for a crime, killed with hands tied, being poisoned, being thrown in a well, being feed to beasts, by heart attack and sudden death or any form of bad death. However, cause me to die in my bed in obedience to You and Your messenger on the right path and free from being misled or in the rank that You have described in Your book: "Allah loves those who fight for His cause in battlefield formations firm as an unbreakable (metallic or) concrete wall." (61:4)

"I seek protection for myself, my children and for whatever my Lord has granted me, through: '(I begin) in the Name of Allah, the Beneficent, the Merciful (Muhammad), say, "I seek protection from the Lord of the Dawn (113:1) against the evil of whatever He has created (113:2). I seek His protection against the evil of the invading darkness, (113:3) from the evil of those who practice witchcraft (113:4) and from the evil of the envious ones."' (113:5)

"I seek protection for myself, my children and for whatever my Lord has granted me, through, '(I begin) in the name of Allah, the Beneficent, the Merciful (Muhammad), say, "I seek protection from the Cherisher of mankind, (114:1) the King of mankind, (2) the Lord of mankind (3) against the evil of the temptations of the Devils, (4) of jinn and human beings (5) who induce temptation into the hearts of mankind."' (114:6)

"He then would say, 'All praise belongs to Allah, equal to the number of what Allah has created, all praise belongs to Allah equal to what He has created. All praise belongs to Allah to the fill of what He has created. All praise belongs to Allah equal to the length of His words, all praise belongs to Allah equal to the weight of His Throne, all praise belongs to Allah as much as it can make Him happy. No one deserves to be worshipped except Allah, the Forbearing, the Honorable, and no one deserves to be worshipped except Allah, the Most High, the Most Great. Glory belongs to Allah, the Cherisher of the heavens and earths and all that is between them and He is the Lord of the great Throne. O Lord, I seek protection with You against misfortunes, and against the insults of the enemies. I seek protection with You agaisnt poverty and deafness. I seek protection with You against bad appearance in the family, belongings and children.' Then he would say, 'Al-Salat: O Lord, grant (favors) upon Muhammad and his family,' ten times.'"

H 3275, Ch. 48, h 14

A number of our people have narrated from Sahl ibn Ziyad and Ahmad ibn Muhammad and Ali ibn Ibrahim has narrated from his father all from al-Hassan ibn Mahbub from Malik ibn 'Atiyyah from abu Hamza al-Thumali from abu Ja'far, *'Alayhi al-Salam*, who has said the following:

"Whoever says in the morning before sunrise, 'Allah is greater than can be described, Allah is greater than can be described, the Most Great. I glorify Allah in the morning and in the evening, all praise belongs to Allah, Lord of the worlds, a great deal of praise. He has no partners. O Lord, grant al-Salat (favors) upon Muhammad and his family,' an angle will rush to take it (prayer) in his wing and ascend to heavens above this world and the angels will ask, "What is with you?" He will say, 'With me there are the words that a believing servant (of Allah) has said and they are such and such.' The angels will say, "May Allah grant favors upon the one who has said these words and forgive him." The Imam said, 'Through every heaven that he will pass he will say the same thing that he had said to those in the first heaven and they will say, "May Allah grant favors upon the one who has said these words and forgive him," until he arrives near the carriers of the Throne and he will say to them, 'With me there are the words that a believing servant (of Allah) has said and they are such and such,' and they will say, "May Allah grant favors to this servant and forgive him, move on to the keepers of the treasures of the sayings of the believing people. These are the words of the treasure so they will write them down in record of the treasures.'"

H 3276, Ch. 48, h 15

Humayd ibn Ziyad has narrated from al-Hassan ibn Muhammad ibn Sama'a from more than one person of his people from Aban ibn 'Uthman from 'Isa ibn 'Abd Allah from abu 'Abd Allah, *'Alayhi al-Salam*, who has said the following:

"In the morning say, 'O Lord, I seek protection from the evil of what You have created, spread and released in Your land and in Your servants. O Lord, I plead before You through Your glory, beauty, forbearance and honor for such and such favors . . . and mention your wishes.'"

H 3277, Ch. 48, h 16

Ali ibn Ibrahim has narrated from his father from Hammad ibn 'Isa from 'Abd Allah ibn Maymun from abu 'Abd Allah, *'Alayhi al-Salam*, who has said the following:

"Amir al-Mu'minin, Ali ibn abu Talib, *'Alayhi al-Salam*, would say in the morning, 'Glory belongs to Allah, the King, the Most Holy [three times]. O Lord, I seek protection against my loss of Your bounties, change in good health that You have given, Your sudden displeasure, approaching of misfortune, and the evil of what came to pass at night. O Lord, I plead before You through the majesty of Your kingdom, the intensity of Your power, the greatness of Your domain and Your power over Your creatures' . . . and mention your wishes."

H 3278, Ch. 48, h 17

Ali ibn Ibrahim has narrated from his father from Hammad from al-Husayn ibn al-Mukhtar from al-'Ala' ibn Kamil who has said the following:

"I heard abu 'Abd Allah, *'Alayhi al-Salam*, saying in the evening, 'Remember (speak of) your Lord deep within yourselves, humbly and privately, instead of shouting out loud, (in prayer) in the mornings and evenings and do not be of the heedless ones,' (7:205) and 'No one deserves to be worshipped except Allah alone, Who has no partner. To Him belongs the kingdom and all praise. He gives life, causes death, causes death and gives life and He has power over all things.' I (the narrator) said, 'In His hand is all good.' The Imam said, 'All good is in His hand, however, say as I say to you ten times and say, 'I seek protection with Allah, all Hearing and Omniscient,' at sunrise and at sunset, ten times."

H 3279, Ch. 48, h 18

Ali has narrated from his father from Hammad from Hariz from Zurara from abu Ja'far, *'Alayhi al-Salam*, who has said the following:

"One in the morning should say, 'All praise belongs to Allah, the Lord of the morning, all praise belongs to Allah, who opens the morning, [three times]. O Lord, open for me the door of the matter in which there is felicitation and good health, O Lord, prepare its way for me and show me the way out of it. O Lord, if You have decided that any of Your creatures should over power me in an evil way, seize him from all directions, front, back, right, left, above and below and suffice me by whatever means You like, whenever and however You want.'"

H 3280, Ch. 48, h 19

Abu Ali al-Ash'ari has narrated from Muhammad ibn 'Abd al-Jabbar from Muhammad ibn Isma'Il from abu Isma'Il al-Sarraj from al-Husayn ibn al-Mukhtar from a man from abu Ja'far, *'Alayhi al-Salam*, who has said the following:

"Anyone who says in the morning, 'O Lord, this morning I am under Your protection and bailsmanship, O Lord, I leave my religion, myself, my world, my hereafter, my family, and my belongings in Your trust and I seek protection with You, O Great, against the evil of all of Your creatures. I seek protection with You against the evil of the confusion of Satan and his army,' nothing will harm him that day. If in the evening he says this nothing can harm him that night by the will of Allah, the Most Blessed, the Most High.'"

H 3281, Ch. 48, h 20

A number of our people have narrated from Ahmad ibn Muhammad ibn 'Isa from al-Husayn ibn Sa'Id from 'Uthman ibn 'Isa from Ali ibn abu Hamza from abu Basir from abu 'Abd Allah, *'Alayhi al-Salam*, who has said the following:

"When you perform the Maghrib (prayer at sunset) and morning prayers say, '(I begin) in the name of Allah, the Beneficent, the Merciful, there are no means and no power without the help of Allah, the Most High, the Most Great,' seven times. Whoever says this will not suffer from leprosy, insanity as well as seventy other kinds of misfortunes. The Imam said, 'If you say in the morning and in the evening, "All praise belongs to Allah, Lord of the morning and all praise belongs to Allah, Who opens up the morning', [two times]. 'All praise belongs to Allah, who removes the night by His power and brings the morning through His favor and we enjoy good health,' then recite verses 255 of Chapter Two of the Holy Quran, the last verse of Chapter 59 and ten verses of Chapter 37: 'Your Lord, the Lord of Honor, is by far more exalted and above being considered as they describe Him. (37:180) Peace be with the Messengers (of Allah) (37:181). It is only Allah, the Lord of the worlds, Who deserves all praise.' (37:182) and, 'Glory belongs to Allah, when they (creatures) are in the morning and in the evening, (30:17) all praise belongs to Allah, in the heavens and on earth, at later evening and at noon time, (30:18) He brings out the living from the dead and the dead from the living, gives life to earth after it dies away and in a similar way you will come to life again.' (30:19) and, 'He is Glorious and Most Holy, Lord of the angels and the Spirit. (O Lord,) Your mercy comes before Your anger, no one deserves to be worshipped except You, glory belongs to You. I have committed evil deeds and wronged myself, grant me forgiveness, grant me mercy and accept my repentance; You grant acceptance to repentance; You are most Merciful.'"

H 3282, Ch. 48, h 21

Ali ibn Ibrahim has narrated from his father from ibn abu 'Umayr from Mu'awiyah ibn 'Ammar from abu 'Abd Allah, *'Alayhi al-Salam*, who has said the following:

"O Lord, all praise belongs to You. I praise You, beg assistance from You. You are my Lord, and I am Your servant. This morning I am with Your covenant and promise. I believe in Your promise and I am truthful to Your covenant as much as I can. There are no means and no power without the help of Allah, alone, Who has no partner. I testify that Muhammad is His servant and Messenger. This morning I follow the original religion of submission (Islam), and the word of sincerity, the tradition of Ibrahim and the religion of Muhammad. With this I live and will die, if Allah so wills. O Lord, grant me life, as long as You want, on this (belief) and cause me to die when You will cause me to die with this (belief), and raise me when you will with this (belief). Through this I seek Your happiness, and follow Your way. From You I beg support and to You I leave my affairs. Ale (family of) Muhammad, are my 'A'immah (plural of Imam) and no one else is my Imam. I follow them, it is they whom I love and their footsteps I follow. O Lord, allow them to be my guardians in this world and in the hereafter and make me love their friends and be the enemy of their enemies in this world and in the next life. Join me with the virtuous people and my anscestors with them.'"

H 3283, Ch. 48, h 22

Abu Ali al-Ash'ari has narrated from Muhammad ibn 'Abd al-Jabbar from Safwan from those whom he has mentioned (in his book) who has said the following:

"Once I asked abu 'Abd Allah, *'Alayhi al-Salam*, to instruct me with something that I should say in the morning and in the evening. The Imam said say, 'All praise belongs to Allah, who does as He wills, and does not do what anyone else wants. All praise belongs to Allah, as Allah loves to be praised. All praise belongs to Allah, as He deserves. O Lord, keep me in every good in which You have kept Muhammad and his family and keep me out of every evil from which You have kept out Muhammad and his family. O Lord, grant al-Salat (favors) upon Muhammad and his family.'"

H 3284, Ch. 48, h 23

A number of our people have narrated from Ahmad ibn Muhammad ibn Khalid from 'Abd al-Rahman ibn Hammad al-Kufi from 'Amr ibn Musa'B from Furat ibn al-Ahnaf from abu 'Abd Allah, *'Alayhi al-Salam*, who has said the following:

"You may give up whatever you give up but do not give up to say every morning and in the evening the following:

"O Lord, this morning I seek forgiveness from You on this day for the people of kindness and disavow the people subject to Your condemnation.

"O Lord, this morning and on this day I disavow the pagans around us, and what they worship. They were an evil people.

"O Lord, this morning and on this day make everything that You will send from the sky to earth a blessing for Your friends and a punishment for Your enemies.

"O Lord, love those who love You and be the enemy of Your enemies.

"O Lord, finish for me every sunset and sunrise with peace and belief.

"O Lord, forgive my parents and me and be kind to them just as they were kind to me for bringing me up as a small person.

"O Lord, forgive the believing male and female, Muslim male and female, their living and their dead. O Lord, You know their activities and their dwellings.

"O Lord, protect the Imam of the Muslims with the protection of belief, grant him a powerful victory, easy conquest and assign for him and for us, from before You, a supportive authority.

"O Lord, condemn so and so and the groups who deferred against Your Messenger, people possessing Authority from You after Your Messenger, the 'A'immah after him and their Shi'a (followers). I plead before You for more of Your generosity, to affirm whatever he (Your Messenger) has brought from You, submission to Your command, and to be protective of what You have commanded to follow. I do not want thereby any payment or to sell it for a little price.

"O Lord, guide me along with those whom You have granted guidance, spare me from the evil of whatever You have decided; You decide and no one can judge against You and no one who loves You is humiliated. You are blessed and high, glory belongs to You, Lord of the House, accept my prayer. And the means through which I sought nearness to You, increase them for me several times and much more. Grant us, from before You, favors and great rewards. Lord, how good is the test that You placed me in, whatever great favors You have granted me and the long time that I enjoyed good health! How much is the cover with which You have covered up my faults! All praise belongs to You, O Lord, a great deal, fine and blessed to the fill of the heavens and earth, to the fill of what my Lord wills as He loves and consents, as it should be worthwhile of my Lord, the Possessor of glory and honor.'"

H 3285, Ch. 48, h 24
It is narrated from him (narrator of the Hadith above) from Isma'il ibn Mehran from Hammad ibn 'Uthman who has said the following:

"I heard abu 'Abd Allah, *'Alayhi al-Salam*, saying, 'Whoever says, "As Allah wills it happens. There are no means and no power without the help of Allah, the Most High, the Most Great,"' one hundred times after the morning prayer, he will not suffer any hardships that day."

H 3286, Ch. 48, h 25
It is narrated from him (narrator of the Hadith above) from Isma'Il ibn Mehran from Ali ibn abu Hamza from abu Basir from abu 'Abd Allah, *'Alayhi al-Salam*, who has said the following:

"Whoever says after the Morningprayer and Maghrib (sunset) seven times, '(I begin) in the name of Allah, the Beneficent, the Merciful. There are no means and no power without the help of Allah, the Most High, the Most Great,' Allah, the Most Majestic, the Most Holy, will repel seventy kinds of misfortunes of which the least is foul smells, leprosy and insanity, and if he is listed as an unfortunate one, his name will be deleted from such list to be written down with fortunate ones.'"

H 3287, Ch. 48, h 26

In the Hadith from Su'dan from abu Basir from abu 'Abd Allah, *'Alayhi al-Salam*, a similar Hadith is narrated except this:

". . . the least of which is leprosy and insanity and if he is listed among the unfortunate ones I can hope that Allah, the Most Majestic, the Most Holy, will change him to fortunate ones."

H 3288, Ch. 48, h 27

It is narrated from him (narrator of the Hadith above) from ibn Faddal from al-Hassan ibn al-Jahm from abu al-Hassan, *'Alayhi al-Salam*, a similar Hadith except that the Imam said the following:

"Abu 'Abd Allah, *'Alayhi al-Salam*, has said, 'One should say them (expressions in Hadith 25) three times in the morning and three times in the evening and should not then fear any Satan, ruler, leprosy,' he did not say seven times. Abu al-Hassan, *'Alayhi al-Salam*, has said, 'I, however, say them one hundred times.'"

H 3289, Ch. 48, h 28

It is narrated from him (narrator of the Hadith above) from 'Uthman ibn 'Isa from Sama'a from abu 'Abd Allah, *'Alayhi al-Salam*, who has said the following:

"After performing the morning and Maghrib prayers say, '(I begin) in the name of Allah, the Beneficent, the Merciful. There are no means and no power without Allah, the Most High, the Most Great,' seven times, you will not suffer insanity, leprosy and seventy other kinds of misfortune.'"

H 3290, Ch. 48, h 29

It is narrated from him (narrator of the Hadith above) from Muhammad ibn 'Abd al-Hamid from Sa'D ibn Zayd who has said the following:

"Abu al-Hassan, *'Alayhi al-Salam*, has said, 'When you performed your Maghrib prayer before stretching your leg or speaking to anyone say one hundred times, "(I begin) in the name of Allah, the Beneficent, the Merciful. There are no means and no power without Allah, the Most High, the Most Great," and one hundred times in the morning, Allah will repel one hundred kinds of misfortune, the least of which is leprosy, Satan and rulers (unjust ones).'"

H 3291, Ch. 48, h 30

It is narrated from him (narrator of the Hadith above) from 'Abd al-Rahman ibn Hammad from 'Abd Allah ibn Ibrahim al-Ja'fari who has said the following:

"I heard abu al-Hassan, *'Alayhi al-Salam*, saying, 'In the evening when you see the sun is disappearing say, '(I begin) in the name of Allah, the Beneficent, the Merciful. All praise belongs to Allah, Who has no children, never had a partner in the kingdom, all praise belongs to Allah Who describes things and Himself is beyond description, knows and is not known. He knows the secret glance of eyes and what hearts hide. I seek protection with Allah's honorable face, with Allah's great name against the evil of what He has spread and settled, the evil under the ground, the evil of what is manifest or hidden, the evil of things in the night and during the day, the evil of abu Murrah (Satan) and what he has given birth to, the evil of false emotional attraction, the evil of what I mentioned and what I have not mentioned. All praise belongs to Allah, Cherisher of the worlds.' The Imam said, 'It is protection against beasts, Satan condemned to be stoned and his offspring.' Amir al-Mu'minin, Ali ibn abu Talib, 'Alayhi al-Salam, would say in the morning, 'Glory belongs to Allah, the King, the Most Holy, three times, O Lord, I seek protection against my loss of Your bounties, change in good health that You have given, Your sudden displeasure, the approaching of misfortune, and the evil of what came to pass in the book. O Lord, I plead before You through the majesty of Your kingdom, the intensity of Your power, the greatness of Your domain and Your power over Your creatures.'"

H 3292, Ch. 48, h 31
It is narrated from him (narrator of the Hadith above) from Muhammad ibn Ali from 'Abd al-Rahman ibn abu Hashim from abu Khadijah from abu 'Abd Allah, 'Alayhi al-Salam, who has said the following:

"Prayer before sunrise and sunset is an established Sunnah (tradition). At sunrise and sunset say, 'No one deserves to be worshipped except Allah, alone, Who has no partner. To Him belongs the Kingdom and all praise, He gives life, causes death, causes death and gives life and He does not die. In His hand is all good, He has power over all things,' ten times and then say, 'I seek protection with Allah, the Hearing, the Omniscient, against the whispers of Satan. I seek protection with You, my Lord against their approaching me. Allah is All-Hearing and Omniscient,' ten times before sunrise and sunset. If you forget, make it up as you make up the formal prayer when you forget.'"

H 3293, Ch. 48, h 32
It is narrated from him (narrator of the Hadith above) from Muhammad ibn Ali from abu Jamilah from Muhammad ibn Marwan from abu 'Abd Allah, 'Alayhi al-Salam, who has said the following:

"Say, 'I seek protection with Allah against Satan, the condemned to be stoned. I seek protection with Allah against the approach of Satan. Allah is Hearing and Omniscient.' Say, 'No one deserves to be worshipped except Allah alone, Who has no partner. He gives life and causes death. He has power over all things.' The narrator has said that a man than asked, 'Is it obligatory?' The Imam said, 'Yes, it is obligatory and limited that you say before sunrise and sunset, ten times and if you miss it then make it up during the day or night.'"

H 3294, Ch. 48, h 33
It is narrated from him (narrator of the Hadith above) from Isma'Il ibn Mehran from a man from Ishaq ibn 'Ammar from al-'Ala' ibn Kamil who has said the following:

"Abu 'Abd Allah, 'Alayhi al-Salam, has said, 'Of the prayers are such that if one forgets one should make up for it. One should say after the morning prayer, "No one deserves to be worshipped except Allah, alone Who has no partner, to Him belongs the Kingdom and all praise, He gives life, causes death, causes death, gives life, He is living and does not die, in His hand is all good and He has power over all things," ten times. One should then say, 'I seek protection with Allah, the Hearing, the Omniscient,' ten times and if one forgets any of this, he owes to make it up for them.'"

H 3295, Ch. 48, h 34

It is narrated from him (narrator of the Hadith above) from ibn Mahbub from al-'Ala' ibn Razin from Muhammad ibn Muslim who has said the following:

"Once I asked abu Ja'far, *'Alayhi al-Salam*, about Tasbih (words to glorify Allah). The Imam said, 'I do not know of anything other than Tasbih of Fatimah, *'Alayha al-Salam*, and ten times after the morning prayer, 'No one deserves to be worshipped except Allah, alone Who has no partner, to Him belongs all praise, He gives life, causes death, He has power over all things,' and then say Tasbih voluntarily as much as you wish.'"

(Tasbih of Fatimah, *'Alayha al-Salam*, consists of saying, 'Allah is greater than can be described,' thirty-four times 'all praise belongs to Allah,' thirty-three times and 'Allah is free of defects,' thirty-three times.)

H 3296, Ch. 48, h 35

Muhammad ibn Yahya has narrated from Ahmad ibn Muhammad ibn 'Isa from Muhammad ibn Sinan from Isma'll ibn Jabir from 'Ubaydah al-Hadhdha' who has said the following:

"Abu Ja'far, *'Alayhi al-Salam*, has said, 'Whoever says before dawn, "No one deserves to be worshipped except Allah alone, Who has no partner, to Him belongs the kingdom and all praise, He gives life, causes death, causes death and gives life, He is living and does not die, in His hand is all good and He has power over all things," ten times and says, 'O Lord, grant al-Salat (favors) upon Muhammad and his family,' ten times, and says, 'Allah is free of all defects,' thirty-five times, 'No one deserves to be worshipped except Allah,' thirty-five times, 'All praise belongs to Allah,' thirty-five times, he will not be written that morning among the careless ones and if he says this in the evening, he will not be written of the careless ones in that night.'"

H 3297, Ch. 48, h 36

Muhammad ibn Yahya has narrated from Ahmad ibn Muhammad ibn 'Isa from al-Husayn ibn Sa'Id from Muhammad ibn al-Fudayl who has said the following:

"Once I wrote to abu Ja'far, *'Alayhi al-Salam*, the 2nd, asking him to instruct me with a prayer. He wrote back to me, 'Say in the morning and in the evening; "Allah, Allah, Allah (is) my Lord, the Beneficent, the Merciful. I do not consider anything as His partner." If you add to it other prayers that would be fine, then ask for whatever you wish and this is for every need, by the permission of Allah, the Most High, He does as He wills.'"

H 3298, Ch. 48, h 37

Al-Husayn ibn Muhammad has narrated from Ahmad ibn Ishaq from Su'Dan from Dawud al-Raqqi from abu 'Abd Allah, *'Alayhi al-Salam*, who has said the following:

"Do not miss saying in the morning and in the evening three times this, 'O Lord, place me in Your strong coat of arms in which You place whomever You will'; my father would say that this is of the prayer that is treasured.'"

H 3299, Ch. 48, h 38

Ali ibn Muhammad has narrated from certain individuals of his people from Muhammad ibn Sinan from abu Sa'Id al-Mukari from abu Hamza who has said the following:

"Once I asked abu Ja'far, *'Alayhi al-Salam*, 'What is the meaning of: ". . . and about Abraham who fulfilled his duty (to Allah)?"' (53:37) The Imam said, 'They were certain words that he would say very often.' I then asked, 'What were they?' The Imam said, 'In the morning he would say, "I live in this morning. To my Lord belongs all praise. This morning I do not accept anything as partner of Allah. I do not worship anything besides Allah and I do not accept anything as my guardians besides Allah,"' three times. In the evening he would say them three times. The Imam said, 'Thus, Allah, the Most Majestic, the Most Holy, revealed in His book, ". . . and about Abraham who fulfilled his duty (to Allah)."' (53:37) I (the narrator) then asked, 'What is the meaning of: ". . . (Noah) was a thankful servant (of Allah)?"' (17:3) The Imam said, 'It was certain words that he would say very often.' I then asked, 'What were they?' The Imam said, 'In the morning he would say, "This morning I ask You (O Allah), to be my witness that all the bounties with me or good fortune in religion or worldly, all are from You alone. You have no partner; all praise belongs to You and for this You deserve thanks very much."' He would say in the morning three times and in the evening three times.' I (the narrator) then asked about His words concerning Yahya (John): '. . . We gave him compassion and purity. He was a pious human being.' (19:13) The Imam said, 'Allah showed compassion.' I then asked, 'What was the degree of Allah's compassion?' The Imam said, 'It was as such that whenever John would say, 'O Lord,' Allah, the Most Majestic, the Most Holy, would say, 'You are well heard and noticed, O John.'"

Chapter 49 - Prayer Before Sleeping and After Waking Up

H 3300, Ch. 49, h 1

Ali ibn Ibrahim has narrated from his father and Al-Husayn ibn Muhammad have narrated from Ahmad ibn Ishaq all from Bakr ibn Muhammad from abu 'Abd Allah, *'Alayhi al-Salam*, who has said the following:

"Whoever at the time of going to bed says three times, 'All praise belongs to Allah, Who is High, thus, He is Dominant. All praise belongs to Allah, Who is hidden, thus, He knows. All praise belongs to Allah, Who owns, thus, He has measured (all things), all praise belongs to Allah, Who gives life to the dead, and causes the living to die, and He has power over all things,' he will come out of sins just like the day he was born from his mother.'"

H 3301, Ch. 49, h 2

Muhammad ibn Yahya has narrated from Ahmad ibn Muhammad in a marfu' manner from abu 'Abd Allah, *'Alayhi al-Salam*, who has said the following:

"When any of you is about to go to your bed you should say, 'O Lord, I have placed my soul in Your custody, keep it secure in a place that You like, and forgive, and if You return it to my body, return it with belief, and with knowledge of the rights of Your friends until it will die upon such belief.'"

H 3302, Ch. 49, h 3

Humayd ibn Ziyad has narrated from al-Husayn ibn Muhammad from more than one person from Aban ibn 'Uthman from Yahya ibn al-'Ala' from abu 'Abd Allah, *'Alayhi al-Salam*, who has said the following:

"At bedtime he (abu 'Abd Allah, *'Alayhi al-Salam*) would say, 'I believe in Allah and reject the devil. O Lord, protect me in my sleep and when I am awake.'"

H 3303, Ch. 49, h 4

Ali ibn Ibrahim has narrated from his father from ibn abu 'Umayr from Jamil ibn Darraj from Muhammad ibn Marwan who has said the following:

"Once abu 'Abd Allah, *'Alayhi al-Salam*, said, 'Should I tell you about what the Messenger of Allah would say when going to his bed?' I said, 'Yes, please do so.' The Imam said, 'He would read verse 255 of Chapter two and say, "(I begin) in the name of Allah, I believe in Allah, and reject the devil. O Lord, protect me in my sleep and when I am awake.'"

H 3304, Ch. 49, h 5

A number of our people have narrated from Ahmad ibn Muhammad from his father from 'Abd Allah ibn Maymun from abu 'Abd Allah, *'Alayhi al-Salam*, who has said the following:

"Amir al-Mu'minin, Ali ibn abu Talib, *'Alayhi al-Salam*, would say, 'O Lord, I seek protection with You against wet dreams and bad dreams and from Satan playing with me during my sleep or when awake.'"

H 3305, Ch. 49, h 6

Muhammad ibn Yahya has narrated from Ahmad ibn Muhammad ibn 'Isa from Muhammad ibn Khalid and al-Husayn ibn Sa'Id all from al-Qasim ibn 'Urwah from Hisham ibn Salim from abu 'Abd Allah, *'Alayhi al-Salam*, who has said the following:

"Tasbih of Fatimah al-Zahra', *'Alayha al-Salam*, should be said when you are about to go to your bed. It is saying, 'Allah is greater than can be described, thirty-four times, all praise belongs to Allah, thirty-three times and Allah is free of defects,' thirty-three times. Recite verse 255 of Chapter two, Chapters 113, 114, ten verses from the beginning of Chapter 37 and ten verses from the end of Chapter 37.'"

H 3306, Ch. 49, h 7

It is narrated from him (narrator of the Hadith above) from Ahmad ibn Muhammad from al-Husayn ibn Sa'Id from Fadalah ibn Ayyub from Dawud ibn Farqad from his brother that Shahab ibn 'Abd Rabbihi asked him to ask help from abu 'Abd Allah, *'Alayhi al-Salam*:

"Ask the Imam, 'A woman frightens me in my dream at night.' The narrator has said that the Imam said, 'Tell him to take rosary beads (sabhah) and say, 'Allah is greater than can be described, thirty-four times, all praise belongs to Allah, thirty-three times, Allah is free of defects, thirty-three times,' then say, "No one deserves to be worshipped except Allah, alone Who has no partner, to Him belongs the Kingdom, all praise belongs to Him, He gives life, causes death, causes death and gives life, in His hand is all good, for Him is the changing of the night and the day and He has power over all things, ten times.'"

H 3307, Ch. 49, h 8

Muhammad ibn Yahya has narrated from Ahmad ibn Muhammad from Ali ibn al-Hakam from Mu'awiyah ibn Wahab who has said the following:

"One night the son of Abu 'Abd Allah, *'Alayhi al-Salam*, came to him and said, 'Father I want to go to sleep.' He said son, say, 'I testify that no one deserves to be worshipped except Allah, that Muhammad, *'Alayhi al-Salam*, is the servant and messenger of Allah. I seek protection with the greatness of Allah. I seek protection with majesty of Allah, I seek protection with the power of Allah, I seek protection with the glory of Allah, I seek protection with the authority of Allah; He has power over all things. I seek protection with the immunity of Allah, I seek protection with the forgiveness of Allah, I seek protection with the mercy of Allah, against the evil of poisonous reptiles and insects, against the evil of small and large animals during the day or night, against the evil of sinful Jinn and human beings, against the evil of the sinful Arab and non-Arab people, against the evil of lightning and cold. O Lord, grant al-Salat (favors) upon Muhammad, Your servant and messenger.' Mu'awiyah has said that each time the name of the Holy Prophet was mentioned, the boy kept saying "The noble and blessed," and asked the Imam, 'Can I say, "The noble and blessed?"' The Imam said, 'Yes, son, "The noble and blessed."'"

H 3308, Ch. 49, h 9

Ali ibn Ibrahim has narrated from his father from certain individuals of his people from Mufaddal ibn 'Umar who has said the following:

"Abu 'Abd Allah, *'Alayhi al-Salam*, said to me, 'If you can, do not go to sleep without seeking protection with eleven letters.' I then asked, 'What are they?' The Imam told me to say, 'I seek protection with the majesty of Allah, I seek protection with the power of Allah, I seek protection with the glory of Allah, I seek protection with the authority of Allah, I seek protection with the beauty of Allah, I seek protection with the defense of Allah, I seek protection with the prevention of Allah, I seek protection with the community of Allah, I seek protection with the possession of Allah, I seek protection with the face of Allah, I seek protection with the Messenger of Allah against the evil of whatever He has created, spread and settled.' The Imam said, 'You may seek protection with these letters whenever you like.'"

H 3309, Ch. 49, h 10

A number of our people have narrated from Ahmad ibn Muhammad from 'Uthman ibn 'Isa from Khalid ibn Najih who has said the following:

"Abu 'Abd Allah, *'Alayhi al-Salam*, has said, 'Whenever you are about to sleep in your bed say, "In the name of Allah, I have placed my right side (for Allah) according to the Millah (tradition and culture) of Ibrahim, submitted to the will of Allah and I am not of the pagans."'"

H 3310, Ch. 49, h 11

Muhammad ibn Yahya has narrated from Ahmad ibn Muhammad ibn 'Isa from al-Husayn ibn Sa'Id from al-Nadr ibn Suwayd from al-Qasim ibn Sulayman from Jarrah al-Mada'Ini from abu 'Abd Allah, *'Alayhi al-Salam*, who has said the following:

"When one of you wakes up during the night and says, 'Allah is free of defects, the Lord of the prophets, the Holy Being of the Messengers and the Lord of the suppressed people ('A'immah from the family of the Holy Prophet) all praise belongs to Allah, Who gives life to the dead and He has power over all things,'

Allah, the Most Majestic, the Most Holy, will say, "My servant has spoken the truth and has thanked Me.'"

H 3311, Ch. 49, h 12
Ali ibn Ibrahim has narrated from his father from Hammad ibn 'Isa from Hariz from Zurara from abu Ja'far, *'Alayhi al-Salam*, who has said the following:
"During the night if you wake up say, 'All praise belongs to Allah, who has returned my spirit to me so I can thank Him and worship Him.' When you hear the voice of a rooster then say, 'O the Faultless, the Holy, Lord of the angels and the Spirit, Your mercy comes before Your anger and no one deserves to be worshipped except You alone. I have committed evil deeds and has wronged myself, please forgive me. No one can forgive sins except You.' When you stand up look to the horizons and say, 'O Lord, the dark night is not hidden from You nor is the skies with constellations or the well-stretched earth, or the darknesses one over the other, or the wavy seas or the traveler at night of Your creatures; You know the secret glances of the eyes and what the chests hide. The stars have disappeared, the eyes have gone to sleep and You are the Living the Guardian, slumber cannot overtake You nor sleep. My Lord is free of defects, the Lord of the worlds, and the Holy Being of the messengers; all praise belongs to Allah, Lord of the worlds.'"

H 3312, Ch. 49, h 13
Abu Ali al-Ash'ari has narrated from Muhammad ibn 'Abd al-Jabbar and Muhammad ibn Isma'Il from al-Fadl ibn Shadhan all from Safwan ibn Yahya from 'Abd al-Rahman ibn al-Hajjaj who has said the following:
"When abu 'Abd Allah, *'Alayhi al-Salam*, toward the end of night was to wake up he would raise his voice so people of the house could hear him, saying, 'O Lord, support me against the horror of the Day of Judgment, expand for me the congestion of the grave, grant me the best of what is before death and grant me what is best thereafter.'"

H 3313, Ch. 49, h 14
Ali ibn Ibrahim has narrated from his father from ibn abu 'Umayr from certain individuals of his people in a marfu' manner from abu 'Abd Allah, *'Alayhi al-Salam*, who has said the following:
"When you are about to sleep say, 'O Lord, if You holdback my soul from returning to my body, have mercy on it and if You will allow it to return, please protect it.'"

H 3314, Ch. 49, h 15
Muhammad ibn Yahya has narrated from Ahmad ibn Muhammad ibn 'Isa from Muhammad ibn Khalid and al-Husayn ibn Sa'Id all from al-Nadr ibn Suwayd from Yahya al-Halabi from abu 'Usamah who has said the following:
"I heard abu 'Abd Allah, *'Alayhi al-Salam*, saying, 'Whoever recites Chapter 112 of the Holy Quran one hundred times at the time of going to sleep his deeds of the past fifty years will be forgiven.' Yahya has said that I asked Sama'a about it and he said that abu Basir narrated to him saying, 'I heard abu 'Abd Allah, *'Alayhi al-Salam*, saying the same thing and said to me, "O abu Muhammad, if you try it you will find it firmly established.'""

H 3315, Ch. 49, h 16

A number of our people have narrated from Sahl ibn Ziyad and Ahmad ibn Muhammad all from Ja'far ibn Muhammad al-Ash'ari from ibn al-Qaddah from abu 'Abd Allah, *'Alayhi al-Salam*, who has said the following:

"When the Messenger of Allah were about to go to his bed he would say, 'O Lord, in Your name I live and in Your name I will die,' and when he would wake up he would say, 'All praise belongs to Allah, Who has given me life after causing me to die and before Him is the resurrection.' Abu 'Abd Allah, *'Alayhi al-Salam*, has said, 'Whoever recites verse 255 of Chapter two before going to sleep three times, verses 18,19 of Chapter three, verse 54 of Chapter 7 and verses 53-54 of Chapter 41 two devils will be assigned to protect him against the rebellious devils whether they like or dislike it, and with them from Allah there will be thirty angels who praise Allah, the Most Majestic, the Most Holy, glorify Him, testify that no one deserves to be worshipped except Allah, say that Allah is greater than can be described, plead before Allah for forgiveness for him until that servant (of Allah) wakes up and he will receive all the reward for it (whatever the angels have said).'"

H 3316, Ch. 49, h 17

Ahmad ibn Muhammad al-Kufi has narrated from Hamdan al-Qalanisi from Muhammad ibn al-Walid from Aban from 'Amir ibn 'Ubayd Allah ibn Judha'a from abu 'Abd Allah, *'Alayhi al-Salam*, who has said the following:

"Whoever recites verse 110 of Chapter 18 he will wake up at the hour he wants to wake up."

H 3317, Ch. 49, h 18

Ali ibn Ibrahim has narrated from his father from al-Nawfali from al-Sakuni from abu 'Abd Allah, *'Alayhi al-Salam*, who has said the following:

"The Holy Prophet has said, 'Whoever likes to wake up at night, at the time of going to sleep should say, "(In the name of Allah) O Lord, do not allow me to ignore Your anger, do not allow me to forget speaking of You, do not make me of the careless ones, so I will wake up at such and such hour," Allah, the Most Majestic, the Most Holy, will assign an angel to wake him up at that time.'"

Chapter 50 - Prayer When Leaving One's Home

H 3318, Ch. 50, h 1

Ali ibn Ibrahim has narrated from his father from ibn abu 'Umayr from abu Ayyub al-Khazzaz from abu Hamza who has said the following:

"Once I saw abu 'Abd Allah, *'Alayhi al-Salam*, moving his lips when he wanted to go out of his house while standing at the door. I said, 'I saw you at the door moving your lips when coming out, did you say something?' The Imam said, 'Yes, when a man is leaving his home he should say, "Allah is greater than can be described, [three times], by the help of Allah I come out and by the help of Allah I enter and in Allah I place my trust, [three times]. O Lord, open to me this with goodness and finish it with goodness, protect me against the evil of every moving thing on earth that You keep in Your control. My Lord is on the right path," he will continue to be under the protection of Allah, the Most Majestic, the Most Holy, until He brings him back to the place where he was before.'"

Muhammad ibn Yahya has narrated from Ahmad ibn Muhammad ibn 'Isa from Ali ibn al-Hakam from abu Ayyub from abu Hamza has narrated a similar Hadith.

H 3319, Ch. 50, h 2

Muhammad ibn Yahya has narrated from Ahmad ibn Muhammad ibn 'Isa from Ali ibn al-Hakam from Malik ibn 'Atiyyah from abu Hamza al-Thumali who has said the following:

"Once I went to see Ali ibn al-Husayn, *'Alayhi al-Salam*, and met him at the door when he was coming out saying, 'In the name of Allah, I believe in Allah, and I place my trust in Allah,' he then said, 'O abu Hamza, when a servant (of Allah) comes out of his door a Satan stands on his way, when he says, "In the name of Allah," two angels will say, 'That is enough for you,' when he says, "I believe in Allah," they will say, 'You have found guidance,' when he says, "I place my trust in Allah," they will say, 'You are protected.' Satan then moves away and say to others, 'What can we do to one who is guided, sufficed and protected?' The narrator has said that then the Imam said, 'O Lord, my dignity is in Your hand today,' then he said, 'O abu Hamza, if you leave the people alone they will not leave you alone, if you reject them they will not reject you.' I then asked, 'What should I do then?' The Imam said, 'Give them of your honor just to receive help on the day when you will need help very badly.'"

H 3320, Ch. 50, h 3

A number of our people have narrated from Ahmad ibn Muhammad from 'Uthman ibn 'Isa from abu Hamza who has said the following:

"Once I asked permission to see abu Ja'far, *'Alayhi al-Salam*, and he came out while his lips were moving. I then asked him about it and he said, 'Did you, O al-Thumali, notice it?' I said, 'Yes, may Allah keep my soul in service for your cause, I did.' The Imam said, 'By Allah, I spoke the words that no one before had ever spoken, but that Allah had sufficed him in things important to him of worldly matters or of hereafter.' I (the narrator) then said, 'Please tell me about it.' The Imam said, 'Whoever when coming out of his house says, "In the name of Allah, enough for me is Allah, I place my trust in Allah. O Lord, I ask You to grant me all good in my affairs. I seek protection with You against the humiliation in this world and of torment in the next life," Allah will suffice him in all that is important to him of worldly or of hereafter.'"

H 3321, Ch. 50, h 4

It is narrated from him (narrator of the Hadith above) from Ali ibn al-Hakam from 'Asim ibn Hamid from abu Basir from abu Ja'far, *'Alayhi al-Salam*, who has said the following:

"Whoever says, when coming out of his door, 'I seek protection with that by which the angels of Allah seek protection, against the evil of this new day which when it is its sunset it will not come back, I seek protection against the evil of my soul and the evil of the others, I seek protection against Satan and those who are against the friends of Allah, I seek protection against the evil of Jinn, human beings, the beast and the reptiles and against the evil of involvement in all of the unlawful matters and I place myself under the protection of Allah against all evil,' Allah will forgive him, accept his repentance, suffice him in what is important to him. He will be safeguarded against evil and protected from misfortunes."

H 3322, Ch. 50, h 5

Ali ibn Ibrahim has narrated from his father from ibn Mahbub from Mu'awiyah ibn 'Ammar from abu 'Abd Allah, *'Alayhi al-Salam*, who has said the following:

"When leaving out of your house say, 'In the name of Allah, I place my trust in Allah, and there are no means and no power without Allah. O Lord, I beg You for the best of that for which I have come out and I seek protection against the evil of that for which I have come out. O Lord, expand for me from Your generosity, complete for me Your bounties, apply me in Your obedience, grant me interested in what is with You and cause me to die in Your religion and the religion of Your Messenger, *'Alayhi al-Salam*.'"

H 3323, Ch. 50, h 6

A number of our people have narrated from Ahmad ibn Muhammad from Muhammad ibn Ali from 'Abd al-Rahman ibn abu Hashim from abu Khadijah who has said the following:

"Abu 'Abd Allah, *'Alayhi al-Salam*, when coming out of his house would say, 'O Lord, with Your help I have come out, to You I am submitted, in You I believe, and in You I place my trust. O Lord, make this day a blessing for me, grant me success, victory, support, cleanliness, guidance, its blessings, and divert away from me its evil, and the evil of that which is in it. In the name of Allah, with the help of Allah, Allah is greater than can be described; all praise belongs to Allah, Lord of the worlds. O Lord, I have come out, make my exit a blessing and benefit me thereby.' The narrator has said that on entering his house also he would say this."

H 3324, Ch. 50, h 7

Muhammad ibn Yahya has narrated from Ahmad ibn Muhammad from Muhammad ibn Sinan from al-Rida, *'Alayhi al-Salam*, who has said the following:

"My father when coming out of his house would say, '(I begin) in the name of Allah, the Beneficent, the Merciful. I have come out by means and power of Allah and not by my own means and power, but, O Lord, by Your power and means, in search for sustenance from You, so grant me sustenance in good health.'"

H 3325, Ch. 50, h 8

Ali ibn Ibrahim has narrated from his father from ibn abu 'Umayr from al-Hassan ibn 'Atiyyah from 'Umar ibn Yazid who has said the following:

"Abu 'Abd Allah, *'Alayhi al-Salam*, has said, 'If one recites Chapter 112 of the Holy Quran when coming out of his house, ten times, he will remain in the protection of Allah, the Most Majestic, the Most Holy, and in His custody until he returns home.'"

H 3326, Ch. 50, h 9

A number of our people have narrated from Ahmad ibn Muhammad from Musa ibn al-Qasim from Sabbah al-Hadhdha' who has said the following:

"Abu al-Hassan, *'Alayhi al-Salam*, has said, 'When you like to travel, stand at the door of your house and recite Chapter one of the Holy Quran to your front, right and left and Chapter 112 of the Holy Quran to your front, right and left, Chapter 114 of the Holy Quran and Chapter 113 to your front, right and left, then say, "O Lord, protect me and protect that which is with me, grant me safety and that which is with me, help me reach my destination and that which is with me in a good arrival.'"

"The Imam then asked, 'Have you ever thought that a man is protected but not that which is with him, a man is safe but not that which is with him and a man arrives his destination but not that which is with him?'"

H 3327, Ch. 50, h 10
Al-Humayd ibn Ziyad has narrated from al-Hassan ibn Muhammad from more than one person from Aban from abu Hamza who has said the following:

"Abu Ja'far, *'Alayhi al-Salam*, when coming out of the house would say, 'In the name of Allah, I have come out, in Allah I have place my trust, and there are no means and no power without Allah.'"

H 3328, Ch. 50, h 11
A number of our people have narrated from Sahl ibn Ziyad from Musa ibn al-Qasim from Sabbah al-Hadhdha' from abu al-Hassan, *'Alayhi al-Salam*, who has said the following:

"O Sabbah, if any of you likes to go on a journey he should stand at the door of his house facing the direction of his journey and recite Chapter one of the Holy Quran to his front, right and left, Chapters 114 and 113 to his front, right and left, Chapter 112 to his front, right and left, and verse 255 of Chapter two to his front, right and left, then say, 'O Lord, protect me and that which is with me, keep me safe and that which is with me, help me and that which is with me arrive my destination in a good and beautiful manner.' Allah will grant him protection, safety, good and beautiful arrival to him and that which is with him. Have you ever thought that a man is protected, is safe, arrives well but not that which is with him?'"

H 3329, Ch. 50, h 12
Muhammad ibn Yahya has narrated from Ahmad ibn Muhammad from ibn Faddal from al-Hassan ibn al-Jahm from abu al-Hassan, *'Alayhi al-Salam*, who has said the following:

"When you come out of your house for a journey or arrive home say, 'In the name of Allah, I believe in Allah, I place my trust in Allah, as Allah wills. There are no means and no power without Allah. Devils are on his way but they move away; the angels strike their faces and say, "You have no way to him. He has spoken of the name of Allah, has belief in Him, placed his trust in Him and has said, 'What Allah wills happens. There are no means and no power without Allah.'"

Chapter 51 - Supplications Before Prayer (Daily Prayers)

H 3330, Ch. 51, h 1
Muhammad ibn Yahya has narrated from Ahmad ibn Muhammad ibn 'Isa from Ali ibn al-Nu'Man from certain individuals of his people from abu 'Abd Allah, *'Alayhi al-Salam*, who has said the following:

"Amir al-Mu'minin, Ali ibn abu Talib, *'Alayhi al-Salam*, has said, 'Whoever just before beginning the prayer says the following will be with Muhammad and the family of Muhammad, *'Alayhim al-Salam*: 'O Lord, I am turning to You through Muhammad and his family, *'Alayhim al-Salam*. I assign them as the lead for me before my prayer and seek nearness through them to You, grant me respect through them in this world and in the next life and of those close (to You). You have obliged me for making me know them, conclude for me with obedience to them, knowing them well, and under their guardianship; it is the salvation and end it for me in this (belief), You have power over all things.' Then complete the prayer and say, 'O Lord, place me with Muhammad and the family of Muhammad, *'Alayhim al-Salam*, in good health and in suffering, place me with Muhammad and the family of Muhammad, *'Alayhim al-Salam*, in every dwelling and place of return. O Lord, help me to live in the way of life of Muhammad and the family of Muhammad, *'Alayhim al-Salam*, and die like the death of Muhammad and the family of Muhammad, *'Alayhim al-Salam*, place me with them in all habitations and do not separate me from them. You have power over all things.'"

H 3331, Ch. 51, h 2
A number of our people have narrated from Ahmad ibn Muhammad ibn Khalid from certain individuals of our people in a marfu' manner from the Imam, *'Alayhi al-Salam*, who has said the following:

"Say before beginning the prayer, 'O Lord, I give the lead to Muhammad Your Prophet for the help I need and turn to You through him for my request, grant me respect through him (and his Ahl al-Bayt) in this world and in the next and to be of the people close (to You), O Lord, deem my prayer through them acceptable, my sins forgiven and my call for help through them answered, O the Beneficent, the Merciful.'"

H 3332, Ch. 51, h 3
It is narrated from him (narrator of the Hadith above) from his father from 'Abd Allah ibn al-Qasim from Safwan al-Jammal who has said the following:

"I observed abu 'Abd Allah, *'Alayhi al-Salam*, facing the Qiblah (direction of Ka'bah) before saying Takbir (Allah is greater than can be described) saying, 'O Lord, do not cause me to lose hope in Your favors and to despair me of Your kindness, or become careless about Your displeasure; no one except the losing people become careless toward the displeasure of Allah.' I then said, 'May Allah keep my soul in service for your cause, I have not heard this from anyone before.' The Imam said, 'Of the greatest major sins before Allah is to lose hope of the favors of Allah, despair of the mercy of Allah and to become careless about the displeasure of Allah.'"

Chapter 52 - Supplications After the Prayer (Daily Prayers)

H 3333, Ch. 52, h 1
Muhammad ibn Yahya has narrated from Ahmad ibn Muhammad ibn 'Isa from abu 'Abd Allah al-Barqi from 'Isa ibn 'Abd Allah al-Qummi from abu 'Abd Allah, *'Alayhi al-Salam*, who has said the following:

"Amir al-Mu'minin, Ali ibn abu Talib, *'Alayhi al-Salam*, after completing the prayer at noon time would say, 'O Lord, I seek nearness to You through Your generosity and magnanimity, I seek nearness to You through Muhammad, Your servant, and Your messenger, I seek nearness to You through Your favorite angels, Your messenger prophets and Your Own Self. O Lord, You are Self-sufficient and do not need me and I need You. You are wealthy and I am poor, correct my slips (mistakes) and cover up my sins, provide me help this day, do not punish me for the evil that You know of me, but pardon me and Your munificence may encompass me.' The Imam said, 'Then he would prostrate and say, "O You Who deserves people's observing piety before Him, O You Who grants forgiveness, O Virtuous, and O Merciful, You are more kind to me than my father and mother and all the creatures, accept my plea in providing me help, answering my supplication and prayer, grant me favor for my call while You have already removed so many misfortunes from me."'

H 3334, Ch. 52, h 2

Ali ibn Ibrahim has narrated from his father and Muhammad ibn Isma'll have narrated from al-Fadl ibn Shadhan all from ibn abu 'Umayr from Ibrahim ibn 'Abd al-Hamid from al-Sabbah ibn Sayabah from abu 'Abd Allah, *'Alayhi al-Salam*, who has said the following:

"Whoever, after Maghrib prayer, says three times, 'All praise belongs to Allah, Who does as He wills and does not do what others will,' will receive a great deal of good."

H 3335, Ch. 52, h 3

A number of our people have narrated from Ahmad ibn Muhammad ibn Khalid from his father in a marfu' manner has said the following:

"The Imam, *'Alayhi al-Salam*, after 'Isha' prayer would say, 'O Lord, in Your hand are the measures of the night and day, the measures of this and the next world, the measures of death and life, the measures of the sun and moon, support and betrayal, and the measures of wealth and poverty. O Lord, grant me blessings in the matters of my religion, worldly life, my body, my family and children. O Lord, keep away from me the evil of Arabs, non-Arabs, Jinns and human beings. Make my return to everlasting good and permanent bounties.'"

H 3336, Ch. 52, h 4

It is narrated from him (narrator of the Hadith above) from certain individuals of his people from in a marfu' manner from the Imam, *'Alayhi al-Salam*, who has said the following:

"Whoever after every prayer, holds his beard in his right hand and says, 'O the Owner of glory and magnanimity, have mercy upon me against fire,' three times, with the left hand raised and the palms up to the sky and says, 'Grant me safety from the painful torment,' three times, then removes his hand from his beard and raises it with palms up to the sky and says, 'O Majestic, O Magnanimous, O Beneficent, O Merciful,' then changes the position of his hands and turns his palms up to the sky and says, 'Grant me safety against painful torment,' three times, 'Grant al-Salat (favors) upon Muhammad and his family, the angels and the spirit,' his sins are covered for him, is pleased with, plea for forgiveness for him is continued up to the time of his death, by all the creatures except the two heavy populations of Jinn and humankind. He after completing the testimonies of belief (tashahhud) raising his hands says, 'O Lord, grant me forgiveness, a decisive and ascertained forgiveness that does not leave any of sins that I have committed and that I will never commit any unlawful act thereafter. Grant me good health so that thereafter I will never face any suffering, grant me guidance so that thereafter I will never stray, benefit me O Lord by what You have instructed me with, turn it in my favor and not against me, grant me enough for sustenance and help me to remain content with it. O Lord, accept my repentance, O Allah, O Allah, O Allah, O Beneficent, O Beneficent, O Beneficent, O Merciful, O Merciful, O Merciful, grant me mercy against the roaring fire, extend for me sustenance from Your vast provisions, grant me guidance in disputed matters, in the matters of the truth by Your permission, protect me against Satan, the condemned to stoning, convey to Muhammad and the family of Muhammad, *'Alayhi al-Salam*, a great deal of my greetings of peace, guide me with Your guidance, grant me wealth from Your wealth, allow me to be one of Your sincere friends and grant al-Salat (favors) upon Muhammad and his family, Amin.'

"The Imam said, 'Whoever says this after each prayer Allah will return his spirit to him in his grave and he will be alive receiving sustenance, pampered and happy to the Day of Judgment.'"

H 3337, Ch. 52, h 5

It is narrated from him (narrator of the Hadith above) from certain individuals of his people from in a marfu' manner from the Imam, *'Alayhi al-Salam*, who has said the following:

"Say after the morning prayer, 'O Lord, to You belongs all praise, the eternal praise, with Your eternity, to You belongs all praise, the praise that does end before Your consent, to You belongs all praise, the timeless praise except as Your wish, to You belongs all praise, a praise whose speaker's reward could be no other thing but Your approval, O Lord, to You belongs all praise, to You is the complaint and You are the supporter, O Lord, to You belongs all praise, as You deserve it, all praise belongs to Allah with all of His praiseworthy attributes for all of His bounties until praising reaches such a degree that my Lord loves and is pleased with.' After the morning prayer and before speaking to anyone say, 'All praise belongs to Allah, to the fill of the balance, to the limits of consent, to the weight of the Throne, may I glorfy Allah, Who is free of all defects, to the fill of the balance, to the limits of assent and the weight of the Throne,' four times, then say, 'O Lord, I plead before You like a lowly servant to grant al-Salat (favors) upon Muhammad and his family, forgive our sins, grant our wishes in this world and in the hereafter with ease and good health.'"

H 3338, Ch. 52, h 6

A number of our people have narrated from Sahl ibn Ziyad from certain individuals of his people from Muhammad ibn al-Faraj who has said the following:

"Once abu Ja'far ibn al-Rida, *'Alayhi al-Salam*, wrote to me and instructed me with this supplication saying, 'Whoever recites it after the morning prayer, his wish will come true with ease and Allah will suffice him: "(I begin) in the name of Allah and with Allah. O Lord, grant al-Salat (favors) upon Muhammad and his family. I plead before Allah to keep my affairs in trust with Him, Allah knows well (His) servants. 'Allah protected him (the believer among the people of Pharoah) against the evil of what they had planned against him. . . .'(40:44,45) 'No one deserves to be worshiped except You, You are free of all defects. I have been unjust to myself.' (21:87) 'We answered his prayer and saved him from sorrow and thus, We save the believing people.'(21:88) '. . . Allah is sufficient for us and He is the best representative.' (3:173) 'They returned with the bounties of Allah and additional favors without being touched by evil. . . .' (3:174), it is as

Allah wills, there are no means and no power without Allah, the Most High, the Most Great.

"It is as Allah wills, not as people will. It is as Allah wills even though people may dislike it. Sufficient for me is the Lord instead of those cherished, sufficient for me is the Creator instead of the creatures, sufficient for me is the provider of sustenance instead of the recipients of sustenance, the One Who has always been sufficient for me from the time I existed, sufficient for me is Allah besides Whom no one deserves to be worshipped, before Him I place my trust and He is the Lord of the great Throne.'

"The Imam said, 'When you complete an obligatory prayer say, 'I have accepted the fact that Allah is my Lord, Muhammad is the Holy Prophet, Islam is the religion, the Holy Quran is the Book and so and so . . . (mention your 'A'immah) are my 'A'immah. O Lord, protect Your friend, (whom You have granted Divine Authority) so and so . . . (mention the twelfth Imam) from all directions, front, back, right, left, above and below, grant him a long life and make him the one who will rise with Divine Authority to support Your religion, show him what he loves and is the delight to his eyes, in his own person, his descendents, his family, belongings, his followers and his enemies. Show them (his enemies) what frightens them and show him in them what he loves and be the delight to his eyes, grant the cure for our suffering chests (hearts) and the chests of the believing people.'

"The Imam said, 'The Holy Prophet after completing a prayer would say, "O Lord, forgive me for what I have done and what I will do, what I have hidden, and what I have done in public and forgive my excesses against my own self and that about which You know better than I do. O Lord You are the One Who can move things forward or backwards with Your knowledge of the unseen and through Your power over all creatures. I pray to grant me life as long as it is in my best interest and cause me to die when it is in my best intrest. I plead before You to grant me a sense of concern about You in private and in public, to say the words of the truth in anger or happiness and to economize in poverty and in wealth. I plead before You for bounties that will not vanish and such delight of the eyes that will not discontinue. I plead before You to make me be happy with (Your) determination, with the blessing of death after life, the comfort of life after death, the pleasure of the look at Your face (things that lead to You), the excitement of seeing You, meeting You without being harmed or suffer harmfulness or the misfortune of straying. O Lord, beautify us with the beauty of belief and help us to be guided guides. O Lord, grant us guidance in the matters of those whom You have guided. O Lord, I plead before You for determination in understanding, steadfastness in the affairs, and good understanding. I plead before You for the opportunity to thank You for Your bounties, Your granting good health and yielding to Your right. I plead before You O Lord, to grant me a peaceful heart, and a truthful tongue. I beg You for forgiveness for that which You know. I seek protection with You against the evil of that which You know; You know and we do not know. You have the knowledge of the unseen."'"

H 3339, Ch. 52, h 7

Ali ibn Ibrahim has narrated from his father from ibn abu 'Umayr from Hammad ibn 'Uthman from Sayf ibn 'Amirah who has said the following:

"I heard abu 'Abd Allah, *'Alayhi al-Salam*, saying, 'Jibril (Gabriel) came to Joseph in prison and said to him, "Joseph, after every prayer say, 'O Lord, grant me relief, a way out (of difficulties), and sustenance from the sources I expect and from those I do not expect.'"

H 3340, Ch. 52, h 8

Muhammad ibn Yahya has narrated from Ahmad ibn Muhammad ibn 'Isa from Muhammad ibn 'Abd al-'Aziz from Bakr ibn Muhammad from those whom he has mentioned (in his book) from abu 'Abd Allah, *'Alayhi al-Salam*, who has said the following:

"Whoever says these words with every obligatory prayer will receive protection for his own soul, his home, his belongings and children: 'I seek refuge for myself, belongings, children, family, home and everything of me with Allah, the One and only Self-sufficient Who has not given birth to anyone nor is born from anyone and there is no one like Him. 'I seek refuge [for myself, belongings, children and all that is of me] with the Lord of the opening dawn from the evil of that which He has created, . . .' recite to the end of Chapter 113 of the Holy Quran, Chapter 114, and verse 255 of Chapter 2.'"

H 3341, Ch. 52, h 9

Ali ibn Ibrahim has narrated from his father from ibn abu 'Umayr from Mu'awiyah ibn 'Ammar who has said the following:

"Whoever, after every obligatory prayer says: 'O the One who does as He wills and does not do as others will,' three times, and pleads (before Allah) for his wishes they will be granted.'"

H 3342, Ch. 52, h 10

Al-Husayn ibn Muhammad has narrated from Ahmad ibn Ishaq from Su'Dan from Sa'Id ibn Yasar who has said the following:

"Abu 'Abd Allah, *'Alayhi al-Salam*, has said, 'When you complete your Maghrib (sunset) prayer wipe your hand over your forehead and say, "(I begin) with the name of Allah, besides whom no one deserves to be worshipped, Who knows the unseen and seen, the Beneficent, the Merciful. O Lord, remove from me the sorrow, anxiety, and sadness,' three times.'"

H 3343, Ch. 52, h 11

Ali ibn Ibrahim has narrated from his father from ibn abu 'Umayr from Muhammad al-Ju'Fi from his father who has said the following:

"I often complained about my eyes and once I mentioned it to abu 'Abd Allah, *'Alayhi al-Salam*, and he said, 'Should I teach you a supplication that will be for the good of your worldly life and hereafter and a cure for your eye?' I said, 'Yes, please do so.' The Imam said after Maghrib (sunset) prayer say, 'O Lord, I plead before You through the rights of Muhammad and the family of Muhammad, *'Alayhi al-Salam*, with You to give light to my eyes, understanding in my religion, certainty in my heart, sincerity in my deeds, safety to my soul, increase in my sustenance and gratefulness to You as long as You will keep me (living).'"

H 3344, Ch. 52, h 12

Ali ibn Ibrahim has narrated from his father from m Mahziyar who has that narrated to h Imams abu Ja'far al-Shami saying that narrated to him a man in al-Sham (Damascus) called Hilqamu ibn abu Hilqamu who said the following:

"Once I went in the presence of abu Ibrahim, *'Alayhi al-Salam*. I said, 'May Allah keep my soul in service for your cause, instruct me with a supplication of universal form for this world and hereafter but very short one.' The Imam said, 'After the morning-prayer until sunrise say, "Glory belongs to Allah, the Great and I praise Him. I plead before Allah for forgiveness and I beg of His generosity.'

"Hilqamu has said, 'I (financially) was the worst off person in my family. I received an inheritance from a man whom I did not think was related to me and I had no knowledge, but today I am the most comfortable person among my people and this is only because of what my master, the virtuous servant (of Allah) instructed me with.'"

Chapter 53 - Supplications for Sustenance

H 3345, Ch. 53, h 1

Muhammad ibn Yahya has narrated from Ahmad ibn Muhammad ibn 'Isa from Muhammad ibn Khalid and al-Husayn ibn Sa'Id all from al-Qasim ibn 'Urwah from abu Jamilah from Mu'awiyah ibn 'Ammar who has said the following:

"Once I asked abu 'Abd Allah, *'Alayhi al-Salam*, to instruct me with a supplication for sustenance and he taught me one. I had not found anything else as attracting sustenance as this. The Imam said, 'Say O Lord, grant me out of Your vast magnanimity, lawful and pure sustenance, that is vast, lawful, pure and sufficient for this world and the hereafter in large quantities, pleasant in nutrition with out toiling or being obliged by any of Your creatures except for its being the extra from Your vast generosity; You have said, ". . . ask Allah from His munificence. . . ." (4: 32), from Your munificence I ask sustenance and from Your charity I beg and from Your wealthy hand I plead to receive help.'"

H 3346, Ch. 53, h 2

Ali ibn Ibrahim has narrated from his father from ibn abu 'Umayr from ibn Faddal from Yunus Fadl ibn Shadhan abu Basir who has said the following:

"Once I said to abu 'Abd Allah, *'Alayhi al-Salam*, 'Sustenance has been delayed.' He became angry and then told me to say, 'O Lord, You have undertaken to provide me sustenance and the sustenance of every walking being, O the best to beg from, O the best provider, O the best to plead to, O the best hope, do for me so and so' . . . mention your wish in place of ellipsis.'"

H 3347, Ch. 53, h 3

Ali ibn Ibrahim has narrated from his father from ibn abu 'Umayr from Isma'Il ibn 'Abd al-Khaliq who has said the following:

"Once one of the companions of the Holy Prophet delayed and when he came, the Messenger of Allah asked, 'What caused you to delay?' He replied, 'Illness and poverty.' He then said, 'Should I teach you a supplication with which Allah will remove illness and poverty from you?' He said, 'Yes, O the Messenger of Allah, please do so.' The Messenger of Allah told him to say, 'There are no means and no power without Allah, the Most High, the Most Great, I place my trust before the living One Who does not die, all praise belongs to Allah Who has not taken anyone as His companion or a child, Who has no partner in His kingdom, and there has never been any supporter for Him against humiliation, and speak of His greatness a great deal.'

"The narrator has said that very shortly thereafter the man came to the Holy Prophet saying, 'O Messenger of Allah, He has removed from me illness and poverty.'"

H 3348, Ch. 53, h 4

Ali ibn Ibrahim has narrated from his father from Hammad ibn 'Isa from Ibrahim ibn 'Umar al-Yamani from Zayd al-Shahham from abu Ja'far, *'Alayhi al-Salam*, who has said the following:

"When pleading for sustenance in the obligatory prayer during prostration say, 'O the best to plead to, O the best provider, grant me and my family sustenance from Your vast munificence; You are the Great, the Generous.'"

H 3349, Ch. 53, h 5

Muhammad ibn Yahya has narrated from Ahmad ibn Muhammad ibn 'Isa from al-Husayn ibn Sa'Id from Muhammad ibn Khalid from al-Qasim ibn 'Urwah from abu Jamilah from abu Basir who has said the following:

"Once I complained to abu 'Abd Allah, *'Alayhi al-Salam*, for (lack of) help and asked him to instruct me with a supplication to plead for sustenance and he instructed me with a supplication and thereafter I did not grow to be needy again. The Imam told me to, after the night prayer while in prostration say, 'O the best to call for help and the best to plead to, O provider of vastest charity, O the best hope, grant me sustenance vastly from Your sustenance and find the means of sustenance for me, You have power over all things.'"

H 3350, Ch. 53, h 6

Muhammad ibn Yahya has narrated from Ahmad ibn Muhammad ibn 'Isa from Ahmad ibn Muhammad ibn abu Dawud from abu Hamza from abu Ja'far, *'Alayhi al-Salam*, who has said the following:

"Once a man came to the Holy Prophet and said, 'O Messenger of Allah, I am a person with a family, indebted and my condition has turned into difficulty. Instruct me with a supplication with which I can pray to Allah, the Most Majestic, the Most Holy, so He will grant me sustenance to pay my debts and help my family.' The Messenger of Allah said, 'O servant of Allah, complete a Wuzu properly, then make a two Rak'at prayer performing complete Ruku' and prostration then say, "O the Exalted one, O the only One, O Munificent (eternal), I have turned to You through Muhammad your Prophet, the Prophet of blessings. O Muhammad, O Messenger of Allah, I ask through you from Allah, your Lord and my Lord and the Lord of all things, to grant al-Salat (favors) upon Muhammad and his family, and beg You for a noble relief from Your relief, an easy felicity, a vast sustenance, to place together my chaotic conditions, pay my debts and help my family.'"

H 3351, Ch. 53, h 7

Muhammad ibn Yahya has narrated from Ahmad ibn Muhammad from ibn abu 'Umayr from Aban from abu Sa'Id al-Makari and others from abu 'Abd Allah, *'Alayhi al-Salam*, who has said the following:

"The Messenger of Allah had taught this supplication: 'O Provider to the needy, O Sympathizer with the destitute, O Guardian of the believing people, O Possessor of strong power, grant al-Salat (favors) upon Muhammad and his family, grant me sustenance, good health and suffice me in that which concerns me.'"

H 3352, Ch. 53, h 8

Muhammad ibn Yahya has narrated from Ahmad ibn Muhammad from Mu'ammar ibn Khallad who has said the following:

"I heard abu al-Hassan, *'Alayhi al-Salam*, saying, 'Once abu Ja'far, *'Alayhi al-Salam*, looked upon a man who was saying, "O Lord, I plead before You for lawful sustenance." Abu Ja'far, *'Alayhi al-Salam*, said to him, 'You are asking the sustenance of the prophets, say, "O Lord, I plead before You for lawful sustenance from You that is vast and pure.""

H 3353, Ch. 53, h 9

A number of our people have narrated from Ahmad ibn Muhammad ibn Khalid from Ahmad ibn Muhammad ibn abu Nasr who has said the following:

"Once I said to al-Rida, *'Alayhi al-Salam*, 'May Allah keep my soul in service for your cause. Pray to Allah, the Most Majestic, the Most Holy, to grant me lawful sustenance.' The Imam said, 'Do you know what lawful sustenance is?' I said, 'That which we earn and is pure.' The Imam said that Ali ibn al-Husayn, *'Alayhi al-Salam*, would say, 'Lawful sustenance is the sustenance of the chosen ones.' The Imam then instructed me to say, 'I plead before You for Your vast sustenance.'"

H 3354, Ch. 53, h 10

It is narrated from him (narrator of the Hadith above) from certain individuals of his people from Mufaddal ibn Mazid from abu 'Abd Allah, *'Alayhi al-Salam*, who has said the following:

"Say, 'O Lord, expand my sustenance, grant me a long life, make me of those through whom you provide support for Your religion and do not replace me by the others.'"

H 3355, Ch. 53, h 11

It is narrated from him (narrator of the Hadith above) from abu Ibrahim, *'Alayhi al-Salam*, who, about prayer for sustenance, has said the following:

"O Allah, O Allah, O Allah, I plead before You through those whose right before You is great. Grant al-Salat (favors) upon Muhammad and his family, confer upon me to act according to what You have instructed me of the knowledge of Your right and expand for me the constraint in Your sustenance.'"

H 3356, Ch. 53, h 12

A number of our people have narrated from Sahl ibn Ziyad from Muhammad ibn 'Abd al-Hamid al-'Attar from Yunus ibn Ya'qub from abu Basir who has said the following:

"Once I said to abu 'Abd Allah, *'Alayhi al-Salam*, 'Our sustenance has been delayed.' The Imam was angered and told me to say, 'O Lord, You have undertaken to provide me sustenance, and to all walking beings, O the best to call for help, O the best to plead with, O the best of charity providers, O the best of hope bestow upon me such and such, . . . mention your wish in place of 'such and such'.'"

H 3357, Ch. 53, h 13

Abu Basir has narrated from abu 'Abd Allah, *'Alayhi al-Salam*, who has said the following:

"Ali ibn al-Husayn, *'Alayhi al-Salam*, would pray and plead before Allah for help with this supplication: 'O Lord, I plead before You for good means of living with which I may gain power for all of my needs and continue my life to the next life, but not so affluently with which I may rebel, or such constraints that make me miserable. Expand for me Your lawful sustenance, and increase for me Your generous favor, a delightful bounty, and a charity for me without being obliged. Do not cause me to be held back from paying thanks for Your bounties due to abundance of the same, its attractive beauty and its plentifulness, nor such constraint that toiling for it would reduce my deeds, and its worries fill up my chest (mind). Bestow upon me, O Lord, self-sufficiency from Your evil creatures and a means with which I can gain Your pleasure. I seek protection with You O Lord, against the evil of this world and the evil that is therein, do not make the world a prison for me, or departing it a sorrow. Take me out of its trials and tribulations, while You are happy with me, and my deeds accepted, to the house of life, the dwelling of the virtuous people. Replace for me the vanishing worldly bounties with the bounties of the eternal house. O Lord, I seek protection with You against its constraints, shaky conditions, the attacks of its devils, rulers, its troubles and against the rebelliousness of those who rebel against me in this world. O Lord, plan against those who plot against me, decide against those who transgress against me, turn of no effect that edge of which one may have established against me, divert away from me the flame of the blazing fire that is fueled against me, suffice me the plots of the evil planners, holding back away from me the spies of the unbelievers. Suffice me to cope with the worries for whom I am worried, repulse away from me the evils of the envious ones and grant me protection against such evils with calm and dress me up with Your formidable coat of arms, hide me in Your protective shelter, correct my condition, justify my words by my deeds, bestow upon me blessings in my family and belongings.'"

Chapter 54 - Supplications for Debts

H 3358, Ch. 54, h 1

A number of our people have narrated from Ahmad ibn Muhammad and Sahl ibn Ziyad all from ibn Mahbub from Jamil ibn Darraj from Walid ibn Sabih who has said the following:

"Once I complain to abu 'Abd Allah, *'Alayhi al-Salam*, about debts people owed to me.' The Imam told me to say, 'O Lord, provide an opportunity of Your opportunities in which it will be possible for my borrowers to pay and for me to receive payment, You have power over all things.'"

H 3359, Ch. 54, h 2

Al-Husayn ibn Muhammad al-Ash'ari has narrated from Mu'alla ibn Muhammad from al-Hassan ibn Ali al-Washsha' from Hammad ibn 'Uthman from abu 'Abd Allah, *'Alayhi al-Salam*, who has said the following:

"Once a man came to the Holy Prophet and said, 'O Prophet of Allah, debts and insinuation of the chest (mind) have overcome me.' The Holy Prophet told him to say, 'I place my trust in Allah, the Living, Who does not die, all praise belongs to Allah, Who has not taken any companions, or children, Who has no partner in His kingdom or supporter against defeat, and you must say that Allah is greater than can be described.'

"The Imam said that he thereafter passed by the Holy Prophet who asked him how he was doing. He replied, 'I continued practicing what you had preached, O the Messenger of Allah, Allah enabled me to pay my debts and removed the insinuation from my chest.'"

H 3360, Ch. 54, h 3

Muhammad ibn Yahya has narrated from Ahmad ibn Muhammad from Muhammad ibn Sinan from Muskan from abu Hamza al-Thumali from abu 'Abd Allah, *'Alayhi al-Salam*, who has said the following:

"Once a man came to the Holy Prophet and said, 'O Messenger of Allah, I face a strong insinuation in my chest (mind) and I am a man with a family, indebted and needy.' The Messenger of Allah told him to repeat these words: 'I place my trust in the Living One, Who does not die, all praise belongs to Allah, Who has not taken any companion, or children, Who has no partner in His Kingdom, and no guardian against defeat and you must say that He is greater than can be described.' Shortly thereafter he came and said, 'Allah has removed the insinuation from my chest, enabled me to pay my debts and has increased my sustenance.'"

H 3361, Ch. 54, h 4

Ali ibn Ibrahim has narrated from his father from 'Abd Allah ibn al-Mughirah from Musa ibn Bakr who has said the following:

"Abu Ibrahim, *'Alayhi al-Salam*, had written the following for me on a piece of paper: 'O Lord, return to all of such of Your creatures whose usurped belongings may exist with me, in small or large amounts, with ease and good health and for whatever of such items that my ability, body, certainty, my soul and belongings are not sufficient, enough and able, pay and fulfill them on my behalf from the abundance with You, through Your generosity. Do not leave on me anything (debts) that You will pay off from my good deeds, O the Most Beneficent, of the beneficent ones. I testify that no one deserves to be worshipped except Allah, Who has no partner, and I testify that Muhammad is His servant and messenger that religion is as He has sanctioned that Islam is as He has described that the book is as He has revealed, that the word is as He has spoken, that Allah is the clear Truth. Allah has mentioned Muhammad and his family with words of goodness and has greeted Muhammad and his family with the greeting of peace.'"

Chapter 55 - Supplication for Pain, Worries, Sadness and Fear

H 3362, Ch. 55, h 1

Muhammad ibn Yahya has narrated from Ahmad ibn Muhammad from Muhammad ibn Isma'Il ibn Bazi' from abu Isma'Il al-Sarraj from ibn Muskan from abu Hamza who has said the following:

"O abu Hamza, if you will face something that frightens you, go to a corner of your home, face the Qiblah and perform two Rak'at (a prayer consisting of two times bowing on one's knees) prayer then say, 'O the most sharp-sighted of the on-lookers, O the most kind of hearing of the hearers, O the quickest to judge and O the most Beneficent of the benefactors,' seventy times, each time ask for your wish.'"

H 3363, Ch. 55, h 2

A number of our people have narrated from Sahl ibn Ziyad from 'Abd al-Rahman ibn abu Najran from 'Asim ibn Hamid from Thabit from Asma' who has said the following:

"The Messenger of Allah has said, 'Whoever suffers from sorrow, pain, misfortune or poverty should say, "Allah is My Lord and I do not associate any partner with Him, I place my trust in the Living One who does not die.'"

H 3364, Ch. 55, h 3

Ali ibn Ibrahim has narrated from his father from ibn abu 'Umayr from Hisham ibn Salim from abu 'Abd Allah, *'Alayhi al-Salam*, who has said the following:

"If one suffers from a misfortune, a hardship, or something causes him pain he should uncover his knees, and elbows and touch the ground with his chest then plead before Allah for help, in a prostrating position.'"

H 3365, Ch. 55, h 4

Ali ibn Ibrahim has narrated from his father from ibn Mahbub from al-Hassan ibn 'Ammar al-Dahhan from Misma' from abu 'Abd Allah, *'Alayhi al-Salam*, who has said the following:

"When Joseph's brothers threw him in the well, Jibril (Gabriel) came to him and asked, 'O young man, what are you doing here?' He replied, 'My brothers have thrown me in the well.' Jibril (Gabriel) asked, 'Would you like to get out of the well?' He said, 'That is up to Allah, the Most Majestic, the Most Holy, if He wills, He will take me out.' Jibril (Gabriel) said, 'Allah, the Most High, says you should plead before Him for help with this supplication so He takes you out of the well.' He then asked, 'What is that supplication?' Jibril (Gabriel) told him to say, 'O Lord, I plead before You, acknowledging that all praise belongs to You, no one deserves to be worshipped except You, Who confers favors, the Inventor of the heavens and earth, Possessor of glory and magnanimity, grant al-Salat (favors) upon Muhammad and his family, find a way out of the condition in which I am.' The Imam said, 'What happened to Joseph thereafter is what Allah has mentioned in His book, the Holy Quran.'" (See Chapter 12 of the Holy Quran)

H 3366, Ch. 55, h 5

Muhammad ibn Yahya has narrated from Ahmad ibn Muhammad from Muhammad ibn Isma'Il from abu Isma'Il al-Sarraj from Mu'awiyah ibn 'Ammar from abu 'Abd Allah, *'Alayhi al-Salam*, who has said the following:

"The supplication of abu 'Abd Allah, *'Alayhi al-Salam*, against Dawud ibn Ali when he murdered Mu'alla ibn Khunays and seized the property of abu 'Abd

455

Allah, *'Alayhi al-Salam*, was this supplication: 'O Lord, I plead before You through Your light that does not extinguish, through Your determination that is not hidden, through Your majesty that never ends, through Your bounties that are beyond enumeration and through Your authority with which You prevented the Pharaoh from harming Moses.'"

H 3367, Ch. 55, h 6
Ali ibn Ibrahim has narrated from his father from certain individuals of his people from Isma'Il ibn Jabir from abu 'Abd Allah, *'Alayhi al-Salam*, who has said the following:

"When you are concerned about something, take a shower and perform two Rak'at (a prayer consisting of two times bowing down on one's knees) prayer and say, 'O the One who clears up concerns, removes sorrow, O the Beneficent for this world and the next and the Merciful for both, change my concern to happiness, remove my sorrow, O Allah, the One and only Self-sufficient, who is not born from anyone nor has given birth to anyone, the like of whom there is no one, protect me, cleanse me and remove my misfortune,' then read verse 255 of Chapter 2, Chapter 114 and 113 of the Holy Quran."

H 3368, Ch. 55, h 7
A number of our people have narrated from Ahmad ibn Muhammad from 'Uthman ibn 'Isa from Sama'a from abu 'Abd Allah, *'Alayhi al-Salam*, who has said the following:

"When you are afraid of something say, 'O Lord, no one is an alternative for You and You are the alternative for everyone of Your creatures, suffice me in such and such matters.'"

"In another Hadith the Imam, *'Alayhi al-Salam*, has instructed to say this, 'O the One who suffices in everything and nothing is sufficient for Him in the heavens and earth, suffice me in what is important to me of worldly and the hereafter and bestow al-Salat (favors) upon Muhammad and his family.'

"Abu 'Abd Allah, *'Alayhi al-Salam*, has also said, 'If anyone feels apprehensive in the presence of a ruler, he should say, "By the help of Allah, I seek conquest, by the power of Allah I will achieve success and through Muhammad, *'Alayhi al-Salam*, I turn to (Allah). O Lord, ease up his difficult attitude for me, and soften for me his hardheartedness; You delete what You will, and establish. With You there is the original book." Also say, 'Allah is sufficient for me, no one deserves to be worshipped except Allah and I place my trust in Allah. He is the Lord of the Great Throne, through the means of Allah and His power I seek (from Allah) to prevent their means and power (from harming me), I seek prevention by the Lord, who opens up the dawn, against the evil of what He has created, there are no means and no power without Allah.'"

H 3369, Ch. 55, h 8
It is narrated from him (narrator of the Hadith above) from A number of our people have narrated in a marfu' manner from abu 'Abd Allah, *'Alayhi al-Salam*, who has said the following:

"Of the supplications of my father, *'Alayhi al-Salam*, in an event was this: 'O Lord, grant al-Salat (favors) upon Muhammad and his family, forgive me, have mercy upon me, purify my deeds, make my return easy, guide my heart, bestow upon me security against my fear, good health during all of my life, establish firmly basic proofs of my belief, forgive my sins, whiten my face, safeguard me in my religion, accept with ease my request, expand my sustenance; I am weak, overlook my evil deeds with the virtue before You, do not cause me pain in myself, or my good friends, grant me an opportunity of Your opportunities with which You will take away all such matters with which You have placed me in trial and in return for it (trials) confer upon me with the best of Your habits with me. My power has become weak, my patience is thinning out, my hope in Your creatures is lost, no hope is left except You and I have placed my trust before You. Your power over me, O Lord, to have mercy upon me and bestow upon me good health is just like Your power over me to punish and afflict me with misfortunes. O Lord, speaking of Your kindness comforts me; the hope in Your reward strengthens me. I have never been without Your bounties from the time You created me. You are my Lord, my master, my source of help, my refuge, my protector, my defender, my benevolent, and the undertaker of my sustenance. In Your determinations and decisions whatever is about me, O my Lord, my master, in whatever way You are to determine or decide or finalize make it to be a quick relief for me from all of my sufferings, and good health for me; I do not find anyone to remove it from me except You and no one to rely on except You. O Possessor of glory and magnanimity be with the best of my hopes in You and my wishes, have mercy upon me as I plead, upon my desperation, upon the weakness of my foundation (body), and oblige me with such kindness and all supplicants to You, O the Most Beneficent of the benefactors, and bestow al-Salat (favors) upon Muhammad and his family.'"

H 3370, Ch. 55, h 9

A number of our people have narrated from Sahl ibn Ziyad from Ali ibn Asbat from Isma'Il ibn Yasar from certain individuals who narrated to him and who has said the following:

"When something causes you sadness, say in your last Sajdah (prostration); 'O Jibril (Gabriel), O Muhammad, O Jibril (Gabriel), O Muhammad, *'Alayhi al-Salam*, repeat these words, suffice me in the condition I am; you both are sufficient for me, protect me by the permission of Allah; you both are protectors.'"

H 3371, Ch. 55, h 10

Ali ibn Ibrahim has narrated from his father from ibn abu 'Umayr from Muhammad ibn 'A'Yun from Bashir ibn Muslimah from abu 'Abd Allah, *'Alayhi al-Salam*, who has said the following:

"Ali ibn al-Husayn, *'Alayhi al-Salam*, would say, 'Even if all human beings and Jinns will gather together against me I will not be concerned at all after saying these words: "In the name of Allah, with Allah, from Allah, to Allah, in the way of Allah, and upon the religion of the Messenger of Allah, O Lord, to You I have submitted my soul, to You I have turned my face, from You I have found support for my shelter, and in Your hands I have placed my affairs. O Lord, protect me by the protection of belief from all directions: front, back, right, left, above, below me and before me and defend me with Your means and power; there is no means and no power without You.'"

Muhammad ibn Yahya has narrated from Ahmad ibn Muhammad ibn 'Isa from ibn abu 'Umayr a similar Hadith.

H 3372, Ch. 55, h 11

It is narrated from him (narrator of the Hadith above) from his father from ibn abu 'Umayr from certain individuals of our people from who has said the following:

"Abu 'Abd Allah, *'Alayhi al-Salam*, has said, 'A man once asked me, "What did you say when you met abu Ja'far (Mansur al-'Abbasi, ruler) at Rabadha?" The Imam said that I told him what I said was this: 'O Lord, You are sufficient for everything and there is no alternative for You, suffice me with whatever You will, as You will, whenever and wherever You will.'"

H 3373, Ch. 55, h 12

Muhammad ibn Yahya has narrated from Ahmad ibn Muhammad from al-Hassan ibn Ali from Ali ibn Maysir who has said the following:

"When abu 'Abd Allah, *'Alayhi al-Salam*, went to meet Mansur al-'Abbasi. He (Mansur) told his slave to stand ready and as soon as abu 'Abd Allah, *'Alayhi al-Salam*, enters cut off his neck. When abu 'Abd Allah, *'Alayhi al-Salam*, entered he looked at Mansur and said something to himself that he did not know what it was then he said out loud, 'O the One who is sufficient for all of His creatures, and no one is sufficient for Him, suffice me against the evil of 'Abd Allah ibn Ali.' Mansur turned to be as such that he could not see his slave and his slave could not see him. Mansur then said, 'O Ja'far ibn Muhammad (it seems) we have caused you so much fatigue in this hot day, you may go back.' Abu 'Abd Allah, *'Alayhi al-Salam*, then left his office. Mansur asked his slave, 'What stopped you from carrying my order?' He said, 'By Allah I could not see him, something came as a barrier between him and I.' Abu Ja'far, Mansur said to him, 'If you ever tell this to anyone I will kill you.'"

H 3374, Ch. 55, h 13

It is narrated from him (narrator of the Hadith above) from Ahmad ibn Muhammad from 'Umar ibn 'Abd al-'Aziz from Ahmad ibn abu Dawud from 'Abd Allah ibn 'Abd al-Rahman from abu Ja'far, *'Alayhi al-Salam*, who has said the following:

"The Imam said to me, 'Should I instruct you with a supplication so you can pray? We are a family that whenever something causes us pain or fear a ruler for something we cannot cope with, we pray to Allah with this supplication.' I said, 'Yes, may Allah keep my soul and the souls of my parents in service for your cause, O descendent of the Messenger of Allah.' The Imam told me to say, 'O the One who existed before everything, O the Giver of being to everything, O the Eternal Being after everything, grant al-Salat (favors) upon Muhammad and his family, and confer upon me such and such of my wishes and needs.'"

H 3375, Ch. 55, h 14

A number of our people have narrated from Sahl ibn Ziyad and Muhammad ibn Yahya from Ahmad ibn Muhammad all from Ali ibn Mahziyar who has said the following:

"Muhammad ibn Hamza al-Ghanawi once wrote to me to ask abu Ja'far, *'Alayhi al-Salam*, to instruct him with a supplication that helps make his wish for relief come true. The Imam wrote back to me, 'About the request of Muhammad ibn Hamza who wants to be instructed with a supplication that helps make his wish for relief come true, tell him to hold to this: "O the One who suffices for everything and nothing suffices for Him, suffice me in what concerns me in my condition," I hope this will suffice him in his condition of sadness, by the will of

Allah, the Most High.' I then informed him of the supplication and shortly thereafter he was released from prison.'"

H 3376, Ch. 55, h 15

Ali ibn Ibrahim has narrated from his father from certain individuals of his people from ibn abu Hamza who has said the following:

"I heard Ali ibn al-Husayn saying to his son, 'My son, if anyone of you faces a misfortune, or an incident, he should complete a Wudu and perform two or four Rak'at (a prayer consisting of four times bowing down on one's knees) prayer and then say at the end, "O the One who is the right one to complain to, O the One who hears all the whispers, observes every group, knows all secrets, and O the One who removes misfortunes as He wills, O friend of Ibrahim, O the party of special conversation with Moses, O the One who has chosen Muhammad, *'Alayhi al-Salam*, I plead before You like one whose poverty has become intense, his patience has run thin, his power has weakened, like the pleading of a drowning person who is alien and helpless and cannot find anyone to save him from his suffering except You, O the Beneficent, the Merciful.' Whoever pleads before Allah with this supplication Allah will remove his hardship, if Allah so wills.'"

H 3377, Ch. 55, h 16

Ali ibn Ibrahim has narrated from his father from ibn abu 'Umayr from son of brother of Sa'ld from Sa'ld ibn Yasar who has said the following:

"Once I said to abu 'Abd Allah, *'Alayhi al-Salam*, that I suffer from sadness. The Imam instructed me to say very often, 'Allah, Allah, my Lord, I do not believe in anything as His partner,' if the insinuation and evil thoughts reduce then say, 'O Lord, I am Your servant, son of Your servant and the son of Your female servant, my forehead is in Your control, Your judgment about me is just, Your determination about me is effective. O Lord, I plead before You through every name that is Your name that You have revealed in Your book, or have taught it to any of Your creatures, or has kept in the unseen knowledge with You, to bestow al-Salat (favors) upon Muhammad and his family, make the Holy Quran the light for my eyes, the spring for my heart, removal of my sadness, and banishment of my anxiety. Allah, Allah, my Lord, I do not believe in anything as His partner.'"

H 3378, Ch. 55, h 17

Abu Ali al-Ash'ari has narrated from Muhammad ibn 'Abd al-Jabbar from Safwan from al-'Ala' ibn Razin from Muhammad ibn Muslim from abu Ja'far, *'Alayhi al-Salam*, who has said the following:

"In the night of the attack of the confederate army against the Muslims this was the supplication of the Holy Prophet: 'O the One to whom people in distress cry for help, O the One who answers the plea for help of the helpless people, O the One who removes my concern and anxiety, remove from me my anxiety, concern and trouble; You know my condition and the condition of my companions, suffice me the fear from my enemies.'"

H 3379, Ch. 55, h 18

A number of our people have narrated from Sahl ibn Ziyad from Ali ibn Asbat from Ibrahim ibn Israel from al-Rida, *'Alayhi al-Salam*, who has said the following:

"Once in the neck of one of our female servant, a scrofula appeared, and someone came to me and said, O Ali, tell her to say, 'O Compassionate, O Merciful, O

Lord, O my Master,' repeatedly. The Imam said, 'She did as she was instructed and Allah, the Most Majestic, the Most Holy, removed the disease.' He (Imam) said that this is the supplication with which Ja'far ibn Sulayman had prayed, (his troubles were removed).'"

H 3380, Ch. 55, h 19

Muhammad ibn Yahya has narrated from Ahmad ibn Muhammad from al-Husayn who has said the following:

"Once I asked abu al-Hassan, *'Alayhi al-Salam*, to instruct me with a supplication while I was behind him. The Imam said, 'O Lord, I plead before You, through Your magnanimous face, Your great name, Your majesty beyond reach, through Your power beyond control, to facilitate for me such and such.' The narrator has said that the Imam wrote for me a note in his own handwriting, 'O the One Who is High, thus, has subdued (all things), the unseen Who has knowledge (of all things), O the One who owns (all things), thus, has measured (all things), O the One who gives life to the dead and has power over all things, grant al-Salat (favors) upon Muhammad and his family, and provide me such and such needs." Then the Imam said, 'O the One beside whom no one deserves to be worshipped, grant me favors.' He wrote for me in another note instructing me to say, 'O Lord, defend me by Your means and power. O Lord, I plead before You this day, this month, in this year for Your blessings and if any trouble, misfortune or punishment that may take place therein, keep them away from me and my children by Your means and power; You have power over all things. O Lord, I seek protection with You against the loss of bounties, change in good health, sudden misfortune, and the evil of the past record of deeds. O Lord, I seek protection with You against the evil of my soul, the evil of every walking creature that You control by their forehead You have power over all things. Allah's knowledge encompasses all things and has enumerated all things.'"

H 3381, Ch. 55, h 20

Muhammad ibn Yahya has narrated from Ahmad ibn Muhammad ibn Khalid from 'Umar ibn Yazid who has said the following:

"O the Living, O the Guardian, O the One besides Whom no one deserves to be worshipped, I cry to You for help through Your mercy, suffice me whatever concerns me and do not leave me to myself." One should say it one hundred times in prostrating position.

H 3382, Ch. 55, h 21

A number of our people have narrated from Ahmad ibn Muhammad from certain individuals of his people from Ibrahim ibn Hanan from Ali ibn Surah from Sama'a who has said the following:

"O Sama'a, whenever you have a request before Allah, the Most Majestic, the Most Holy, say this: 'O Lord, I plead before You through, Muhammad and Ali, *'Alayhim al-Salam*, due to their special position and respect before You, for that position and respect, bestow al-Salat (favors) upon Muhammad and his family, and make my such and such wish come true.' On the Day of Judgment, all of the angels of special position before Allah, the messenger prophets, and the believing people who had gone through the test of their faith will stand needy before these two people, Muhammad and Ali, *'Alayhim al-Salam*, on that Day.'"

H 3383, Ch. 55, h 22

Ali ibn Muhammad has narrated from Ibrahim ibn Ishaq al-Ahmar from abu al-Qasim al-Kufi from Muhammad ibn Isma'll from Mu'awiyah ibn 'Ammar and al-'Ala' ibn Sayabah and Zarif ibn Nasih who has said the following:

"When abu Dawaniq (Mansur, one of 'Abbasi rulers) summoned abu 'Abd Allah, *'Alayhi al-Salam*, he raised his hand to the sky and said, 'O Lord, You protected the two boys (mentioned in the Holy Quran in the story of Moses and Khidr) for the goodness and virtue of their father, protect me for the goodness and virtue of my ancestors, Muhammad, Ali, al-Hassan, al-Husayn, Ali ibn al-Husayn, and Muhammad ibn Ali, *'Alayhim al-Salam*. O Lord, with Your help I pray that he be repelled against his throat, I seek protection in You against his evil.' Then he told the camel man to leave for the journey. When Rabi' met him at the door of abu Dawaniq, he said, 'O abu 'Abd Allah, *'Alayhi al-Salam*, his inside is intensely full against you. I have heard him saying, "By Allah I will not leave any of their palm trees without being uprooted, properties without being looted and descendents without being arrested as captives." The narrator has said that the Imam then said something quietly moving his lips. When he entered in the office of abu Dawaniq he offered the greeting of peace and sat down. Abu Dawaniq responded to his greeting and said, 'By Allah I have intended not to leave any of your palm trees without being uprooted, and any property without being seized.' Abu 'Abd Allah, *'Alayhi al-Salam*, then said, 'O Amir al-Mu'Minin, Allah placed Ayyub under the trial and he exercised patience, Dawud was given to him and he thanked. It was determined for Joseph who was forgiven. You are from that lineage and that lineage's behaviors are similar.' Abu Dawaniq said, 'You have spoken the truth. I forgive you.' The Imam said, 'O Amir al-Mu'Minin, whoever so far has spilled the blood of anyone from our family Allah has taken away the power from him.' Abu Dawaniq became angry and excited. The Imam said, 'Hold on O Amir al-Mu'Minin, this power once was with family of abu Sufyan. When they murdered al-Husayn, *'Alayhi al-Salam*, Allah took away the power from them and the family of Marwan inherited it. When Hisham murdered Zayd, Allah took it away from him and Marwan ibn Muhammad inherited it. When Marwan murdered Ibrahim, Allah took away the power from him and gave it to you.' Abu Dawaniq then said, 'You have spoken the truth. Tell me what do you need?' The Imam said, 'I need permission to leave.' Abu Dawaniq said, 'It is in your own hands whenever you like.' The Imam then left and Rabi' said, 'He has ordered ten thousand dirham for you.' The Imam said, 'I do not need it.' He said, 'You are making him (Abu Dawaniq) angry, take it and then give it to charity.'"

H 3384, Ch. 55, h 23

Ali ibn Ibrahim has narrated from his father from ibn abu 'Umayr from Muhammad ibn 'A'Yun from Qays ibn Salmah from abu 'Abd Allah, *'Alayhi al-Salam*, who has said the following:

"Ali ibn al-Husayn would say, 'After saying these words, I will not be concerned at all even if all men and Jinn gather together against me: "In the name of Allah, with (assistance of) Allah, to Allah, in the way of Allah, and upon the religion of the Messenger of Allah, O Allah, grant al-Salat (favors) upon Muhammad and his family, O Allah, to You I have submitted my soul, to You I have turned my face, it is You whom I have sought for backup and in Your hands I have left my affairs, O Lord, protect me with the protection of belief from all directions, the front, back, right, left, above below and before me. Defend me by Your means and power; there are no means and no power without Allah.'"

Chapter 56 - Supplications for Healing Ailments and Diseases

H 3385, Ch. 56, h 1

Muhammad ibn Yahya has narrated from Ahmad ibn Muhammad ibn 'Isa from 'Abd al-Rahman ibn abu Najran and ibn Faddal from certain individuals of our people from abu 'Abd Allah, 'Alayhi al-Salam, who has said the following:

"For an ailment the Imam, 'Alayhi al-Salam, would say, 'O Lord, You have criticized certain nations saying, "(Muhammad), tell them, 'Seek help from those whom you consider equal to Allah. They are not able to remove or change your hardships'" (17:56) O the One besides whom no one is able to provide me relief or divert the hardships away from me, confer al-Salat (favors) upon Muhammad and his family, grant me relief and divert the suffering from me to those who worship things other than You.'"

H 3386, Ch. 56, h 2

Ahmad ibn Muhammad has narrated from 'Abd al-'Aziz ibn al-Muhtadi from Yunus ibn 'Abd al-Rahman from Dawud ibn Razin who has said the following:

"I fell severely ill in Madiana and abu 'Abd Allah, 'Alayhi al-Salam, had found out about it. He wrote to me, 'Your ailment has come to our notice and you should buy one Sa'a (about 3 kg) of wheat, lie down on your back, pour it on your chest, as is done and say, "O Lord, I plead before You through Your name with which when a helpless person pleads before You, You remove his hardship, establish him on earth, and appoint him as Your deputy among Your creatures, bestow al-Salat (favors) upon Muhammad and his family, grant me good health and recovery from my ailment." Then sit straight, collect the wheat around you and say what you just said and distribute it among the destitute a handful for each one and say what you just said (above supplication).'

"Dawud has said, 'I followed his instruction and it was like I was freed from a rope with which I was tied up. Many people tried it and benefited thereby.'"

H 3387, Ch. 56, h 3

Ali ibn Ibrahim has narrated from his father from ibn abu 'Umayr from al-Husayn ibn Nu'aym from abu 'Abd Allah, 'Alayhi al-Salam, who has said the following:

"Once one of the sons of Imam, 'Alayhi al-Salam, complained from an ailment and he told him to say, 'O Lord, cure me with Your treatment, provide me medication from Your medicine and relieve me from Your misfortune; I am Your servant, son of Your servant.'"

H 3388, Ch. 56, h 4

Muhammad ibn Yahya has narrated from Ahmad ibn Muhammad from Ali ibn al-Hakam from Malik ibn 'Atiyyah from Yunus ibn 'Ammar who has said the following:

"Once I said to abu 'Abd Allah, 'Alayhi al-Salam, may Allah keep my soul in service for your cause, about this thing that has appeared on my face, people say that Allah, the Most Majestic, the Most Holy, does not allow it to cause suffering to one about whom He cares.' The Imam said, 'No, that is not so. The fingers of the believing person among the people of Pharaoh were such that bones were visible and he would speak to people extending his hand forward: 'O people, follow the messengers.' (36:20) The Imam then said, 'When it is the beginning of the last third of the night, make Wuzu and stand up for prayer that you (usually) perform. In the last Sajdah (prostration) of the first two Rak'at say, 'O the Most High, O the Most Great, O the Beneficent, O the Merciful, O the Hearer of the pleas for help, O the Conferrer of the good, grant al-Salat (favors) upon Muhammad and his family, facilitate for me of the good of this and the next world that much which You would deem proper, divert away from me the evil of this and the next world that much that You deem proper and relieve me from this pain; - mention it by its name - it has caused me anguish and sadness,' and be persistent in your pleading and prayer.'

"The narrator has said that before his reaching al-Kufa Allah had totally relieved him from that disease.'" (See also Hadith 30 Ch. 103)

H 3389, Ch. 56, h 5

Ali ibn Ibrahim has narrated from his father and A number of our people have narrated from Ahmad ibn Muhammad Drust ibn abu Mansur Muhammad ibn Isma'Il all from Hanan ibn Sadir from his father from abu Ja'far, *'Alayhi al-Salam*, who has said the following:

"Whenever you see a man afflicted with a misfortune, say, 'All praise belongs to Allah, Who has kept me safe from that with which you suffer, that He has given me preference over you and over many creatures,' but be sure not to make him hear what you said.'"

H 3390, Ch. 56, h 6

Muhammad ibn Yahya has narrated from certain individuals of his people from Muhammad ibn 'Isa from Dawud ibn Razin from abu 'Abd Allah, *'Alayhi al-Salam*, who has said the following:

"Place your hand over the painful part and say three times: Allah, Allah, my Lord in all truth, I do not believe in anything as His partner, O Lord, You are (the help) for this and all the great troubles, provide me relief from this pain.'"

H 3391, Ch. 56, h 7

It is narrated from him (narrator of the Hadith above) from Muhammad ibn 'Isa from Dawud from Mufaddal from abu 'Abd Allah, *'Alayhi al-Salam*, who has said the following:

"For pains say, 'In the name of Allah, and with (the help of) Allah, how much is of the bounties of Allah in a painful or painless vein of a thankful or unthankful servant (of Allah).' After an obligatory prayer hold your beard in your hand and say, 'O Lord, relieve me from my pain with an immediate good health and remove hardships from me, say it three times and try it to happen with tears coming from your eyes and a feeling of weeping.'"

H 3392, Ch. 56, h 8

Ali ibn Ibrahim has narrated from his father from ibn abu 'Umayr from Ibrahim ibn 'Abd al-Hamid from a man who has said the following:

"Once I went in the presence of abu 'Abd Allah, *'Alayhi al-Salam*, and complained to him from a pain that I suffered. The Imam instructed me to say, 'In the name of Allah, wipe your hand on the painful area and say, "I seek protection through the power of Allah, I seek protection through the glory of Allah, I seek protection through the greatness of Allah, I seek protection through the community of Allah, I seek protection through the Messenger of Allah, I seek protection through the names of Allah, against the evil of that which I avoid and from the evil of that from which I fear for myself,'" - seven times. I (the narrator) followed the instruction and Allah, the Most Majestic, the Most Holy, removed the pain from me.'"

H 3393, Ch. 56, h 9

Muhammad ibn Yahya has narrated from Ahmad ibn Muhammad ibn 'Isa from al-Washsha' from 'Abd Allah ibn Sinan from 'Awn who has said the following:

"(The Imam) said, 'Wipe with your hand the painful area, then say, 'In the name of Allah, with (the help of) Allah, and through Muhammad the Messenger of Allah, there are no means and no power without Allah, the Most High, the Most Great, O Lord, remove and wipe away from me that which I feel,' then wipe the painful area with your right hand three times.'"

H 3394, Ch. 56, h 10

It is narrated from him (narrator of the Hadith above) from Ahmad ibn Muhammad from Ahmad ibn Muhammad ibn abu Nasr from Muhammad son of brother of Gharam from 'Abd Allah ibn Sinan from abu 'Abd Allah, 'Alayhi al-Salam, who has said the following:

"Place your hand over the painful area then say, 'In the name of Allah, with (the help of) Allah, and through Muhammad the Messenger of Allah, there are no means and no power without Allah, O Lord, wipe away from me that which I feel,' and wipe the area three times."

H 3395, Ch. 56, h 11

Ali ibn Ibrahim has narrated from his father from 'Amr ibn 'Uthman from Ali ibn 'Isa from his uncle who has said the following:

"I asked him (the Imam) to teach me a supplication when I suffer from pain. He said during Sajdah (prostration) say, 'O Allah, O the Beneficent, O the Merciful, O Lord of lords, O Lord of gods (things worshipped), O the King of kings, O Master of masters, cure me with Your treatment from all ailments and diseases; I am Your servant who moves back and forth in Your control.'"

H 3396, Ch. 56, h 12

Muhammad ibn Yahya from Ahmad ibn Muhammad ibn 'Isa from ibn abu Najran from Hammad ibn 'Isa from Hariz from Zurara from one of the two Imams, 'Alayhi al-Salam, who has said the following:

"When you visit a patient say, 'I seek protection for you from Allah, the Great Lord of the great Throne against the evil of every swelling vein and the evil of the heat of fire,' seven times.'"

H 3397, Ch. 56, h 13

It is narrated from him (narrator of the Hadith above) from Ahmad ibn Muhammad ibn 'Isa from Ahmad ibn Muhammad ibn abu Nasr from Aban ibn 'Uthman from al-Thumali from abu Ja'far, 'Alayhi al-Salam, who has said the following:

"Whenever one has complains of pain, he should say, 'In the name of Allah, with (the help of) Allah, and through Muhammad the Messenger of Allah, I seek protection with the majesty of Allah and I seek protection with the power of Allah over everything that He wills, against what I feel.'"

H 3398, Ch. 56, h 14

Muhammad ibn Yahya has narrated from Ahmad ibn Muhammad ibn 'Isa from al-Hassan ibn Ali from Hisham al-Jawaliqi from abu 'Abd Allah, *'Alayhi al-Salam*, who has said the following:

"O the One who sends cures, and removes pain, send upon me a cure for that from which I suffer."

H 3399, Ch. 56, h 15

Muhammad ibn Yahya has narrated from Musa ibn al-Hassan from Muhammad ibn 'Isa from abu Ishaq Sahih al-Sha'Ir from Husayn al-Khurasani who was a baker and has said that he once complained before abu 'Abd Allah, *'Alayhi al-Salam*, from pain and the Imam said the following:

"After prayer place your hand on the area for your prostration and say, 'In the name of Allah, Muhammad the Messenger of Allah, cure me O Healer; there is no cure except Your cure that leaves no ailment without being removed, the cure for all pain and ailments.'"

H 3400, Ch. 56, h 16

Ali ibn Ibrahim has narrated from his father from certain individuals of his people from abu Hamza from abu Ja'far, *'Alayhi al-Salam*, who has said the following:

"Once, Amir al-Mu'minin, Ali ibn abu Talib, *'Alayhi al-Salam*, became ill. The Messenger of Allah visited him and said, 'Say, O Lord, I plead before You for a quick recovery, (the ability to have) patience with misfortune from You and coming out of it into Your favors and mercy."

H 3401, Ch. 56, h 17

Ali ibn Ibrahim has narrated from his father from Harun ibn Muslim from Mas'adah ibn Sadaqa from abu 'Abd Allah, *'Alayhi al-Salam*, who has said the following:

"The Holy Prophet would seek cure with this supplication. He would place his hand over the painful area and say, 'O pain, calm down by the serenity of Allah, silence by the dignity of Allah, be barred by the barrier of Allah, quiet down by the calm of Allah, I protect you O human being by that with which Allah, the Most Majestic, the Most Holy, has protected His Throne, His angels on the day of the shaking and quake.' You should say it seven times or no less than three times."

H 3402, Ch. 56, h 18

Muhammad ibn Yahya has narrated from Ahmad ibn Muhammad ibn 'Isa from 'Amr ibn al-Mubarak from 'Awn ibn Sa'd Mawla al-Ja'fari from Mu'awiyah ibn 'Ammar from abu 'Abd Allah, *'Alayhi al-Salam*, who has said the following:

"Place your hand over the painful area and say, 'O Lord, I plead before You through the Holy Quran that the trusted Spirit brought (to Your Messenger) and it is before You in the original Book, high and full of wisdom, provide me cures with Your treatment, medication with Your medicine and good health from ailment You have caused, - say it three times,' then say, 'O Lord, grant al-Salat (favors) upon Muhammad and his family.'"

H 3403, Ch. 56, h 19

Ahmad ibn Muhammad has narrated from al-'Awfi from Ali ibn al-Husayn from Muhammad ibn 'Abd Allah ibn Zurara from Muhammad ibn al-Fudayl from abu Hamza who has said the following:

"Once my knee became painful and I complain before abu Ja'far, *'Alayhi al-Salam*, and he instructed me to say after prayer, 'O the Most Generous of the givers, O the Best of those pleaded for help, O the Most Merciful of the merciful ones, be kind to my weakness, lack of strength and grant me recovery from my pain.' I (the narrator) followed the instruction and recovered thereafter."

Chapter 57 - (Supplication for) Fortification and Protection

H 3404, Ch. 57, h 1

Humayd ibn Ziyad has narrated from al-Hassan ibn Muhammad from more than one person from Aban from ibn al-Mundhir who has said the following:

"Once I mentioned fear before abu 'Abd Allah, *'Alayhi al-Salam*, and he said, 'I should tell you something that after saying it you will not be frightened during the day or night, say, "In the name of Allah, with (the help of) Allah, I place my trust before Allah; whoever places his trust before Allah, He is suffices him and Allah completes his affairs. Allah has assigned a measure for everything. O Lord, place me under Your protection, in Your neighborhood, include me in Your amnesty and under Your protection.' I (the narrator) heard the case of a man who had practiced this for thirty years. He did not say it one night and a scorpion bit him.'"

H 3405, Ch. 57, h 2

Ali ibn Ibrahim has narrated from his father from Muhsin ibn Ahmad from Yunus ibn Ya'qub from abu Basir from abu 'Abd Allah, *'Alayhi al-Salam*, who has said the following:

"For protection say, 'I seek protection with the majesty of Allah, I seek protection with the power of Allah, I seek protection with glory of Allah, I seek protection with the greatness of Allah, I seek protection with the pardoning of Allah, I seek protection with the forgiveness of Allah, I seek protection with the mercy of Allah, I seek protection with the authority of Allah, Who has power over all things, I seek protection with the generosity of Allah, I seek protection with the community of Allah against the evil of all tyrants and hatemongers and all the condemned devils, all near and far, weak and strong, all poisonous beasts, fear, plague, the evil of all small and large animals, during the night or day, the evil of sinful Arabs and non-Arabs and the evil of the sinful Jinn and man.'"

H 3406, Ch. 57, h 3

Ali ibn Ibrahim has narrated from his father from certain individuals of his people from al-Qaddah from abu 'Abd Allah, *'Alayhi al-Salam*, who has said the following:

"Amir al-Mu'minin, Ali ibn abu Talib, *'Alayhi al-Salam*, has said, 'The Holy Prophet read the following for the protection of al-Hassan and al-Husayn, *'Alayhim al-Salam*, 'I seek protection for both of you with the perfect words of Allah, with all of His beautiful, universal names against the evil of the poisonous ones, that which causes worry, all the evil eyes, and the envious ones when they exercise their envy.' The Holy Prophet then turned to us saying, 'This is how Ibrahim sought protection for Isma'il and Ishaq.'"

H 3407, Ch. 57, h 4

Muhammad ibn Yahya has narrated from Ahmad ibn Muhammad ibn Bukayr from Sulayman al-Ja'fari who has said the following:

"I heard abu al-Hassan saying, 'In the evening when you see the sun about to go down and disappear then say, "In the name of Allah, with (the help of) Allah, all praise belongs to Allah, Who has not taken any companion, or children, Who has no partner in His kingdom or a supporter against weakness, and He is greater than can be described, all praise belongs to Allah Who describes (things) and Himself cannot be described, Who knows all things but Himself cannot be known. He knows the stealth glance of the eyes and whatever the chests hide. I seek protection with His honorable face, and with His great names against the evil of whatever He has spread and has populated, the evil of the things beneath the earth, the evil of what is apparent and that which is hidden, the evil of what I mentioned or did not mention, all praise belongs to Allah Lord of the worlds."

"The Imam mentioned that this is protection against all the beasts, and all devils condemned to stoning and all the biting and stinging animals. One who reads this supplication should have no fear from thieves or the devils.'

"I (the narrator) then said to him, 'I hunt beasts and at night I sleep in ruined places and I feel afraid.' He said on entering them say, 'In the name of Allah, I enter and step your right foot first but when coming out step with your left foot first and mention the name of Allah you will not see any frightening thing.'"

H 3408, Ch. 57, h 5
Muhammad ibn Yahya has narrated from Ahmad ibn Muhammad ibn 'Isa from Ali ibn al-Hakam from Qutaybah al-'A'Sha' who has said the following:
"Abu 'Abd Allah, *'Alayhi al-Salam*, instructed me with this supplication: 'In the name of Allah, the glorious, I seek protection for so and so with (the help of) Allah, the Most Great, against all small living things (vermin, insect, germs, viruses and so forth), the venomous things, evil eyes, plague, the evil of Jinn and human beings of Arabs and non-Arabs, against their sorcery, transgression and against their spell, with reading verse 255 of Chapter 2 and in the second time reading the above supplication say, "In the name of Allah, I seek protection for so and so, with (the help of) Allah, the Glorious One . . . to the end of the above supplication.'"

H 3409, Ch. 57, h 6
Ali ibn Ibrahim has narrated from his father from ibn abu 'Umayr from Ishaq ibn 'Ammar who has said the following:
"Once I said to abu 'Abd Allah, *'Alayhi al-Salam*, 'May Allah keep my soul in service for your cause, I am afraid of scorpions. The Imam said, 'Look at the little bear (Ursa Minor) and of the three stars next to the middle one of them there is a small star. Arabs call it al-Suha'. We call it Aslama, look at it gazing every night and say, 'O Lord of Aslama, confer al-Salat (favors) upon Muhammad and his family, hasten their happiness and grant us safety and protection.' Ishaq has said that he did not miss it except once at which time a scorpion stung bit him.'"

H 3410, Ch. 57, h 7
Ahmad ibn Muhammad has narrated from Ali ibn al-Hassan from al-'Abbas ibn 'Amir from Muhammad abu Jamilah from Sa'D al-Iskaf who has said the following:
"I heard the Imam, *'Alayhi al-Salam*, saying, 'Whoever says these words I guarantee that scorpions and small vermin will not harm him, 'I seek protection through such words of Allah that no virtuous or wicked person is able to bypass,

I seek protection thereby against the evil of whatever He has spread and settled (on earth), against the evil of all walking things on earth under His control. My Lord has the straight path.'"

H 3411, Ch. 57, h 8
Muhammad ibn Yahya has narrated from Ahmad ibn Muhammad from Ali ibn al-Hakam from Ali ibn abu Hamza from abu al-Hassan, *'Alayhi al-Salam,* who has said the following:
"During certain expeditions people complained before the Messenger of Allah against fleas that irritated them. He (the Messenger of Allah) said, 'When going into your bed say, "O black jumping thing that does not stop by the barrier or door I ask you by the original Book, do not irritate me and my companions until the night passes and morning comes with whatever it will bring along.'" The narrator has said, 'As we know the last part of this Hadith has the following expression: 'Until morning comes back when it is the time to come back.'"

H 3412, Ch. 57, h 9
Ali ibn has narrated from ibn Jumhur from his father from Muhammad ibn Sinan from 'Abd Allah ibn Sinan from abu 'Abd Allah, *'Alayhi al-Salam,* who has said the following:
"Amir al-Mu'minin, Ali ibn abu Talib, *'Alayhi al-Salam,* has said, 'If you come face to face with a beast say, 'I seek protection with the Lord of Daniel and the well against the evil of all powerful lions."

Note: Daniel was thrown in a well with wild beasts but they did not harm him.

H 3413, Ch. 57, h 10
Muhammad ibn Ja'far abu al-'Abbas has narrated from Muhammad ibn 'Isa from Salih ibn Sa'id from Ibrahim ibn Muhammad ibn Harun who wrote to abu Ja'iar, *'Alayhi al-Salam,* asking for a supplication for protection of children against bothering gasses:
"The Imam wrote in his own hand writing the following supplications for protection and Salih thought that the Imam had sent them to Ibrahim: 'Allah is greater than can be described, Allah is greater than can be described, Allah is greater than can be described. I testify that no one deserves to be worshipped except Allah. I testify that Muhammad is the Messenger of Allah. Allah is greater than can be described. Allah is greater than can be described. No one deserves to be worshipped except Allah. No one is my Lord, except Allah, to Him belongs the kingdom, all praise belongs to Him and He has no partner. Allah is free of all defects. As Allah willed it was, whatever He did not will did not come into being. O Lord, the Possessor of glory and magnanimity, Lord of Moses, Jesus and Ibrahim who fulfilled his duty, Lord of Ibrahim, Isma'il, Ishaq, Ya'qub and the tribes, no one deserves to be worshipped except You. I glorify You by means of Your signs that You have shown, by means of Your greatness, and by means of the facts with which the prophets pleaded before You for help that You are Lord of the people, that You were before everything and that You will be after everything, I plead before You through Your name with which You hold the skies from falling on earth except by Your permission, through Your perfect words with which You bring the dead to life, grant protection to Your servant so and so against the evil of whatever comes down from the sky and whatever goes up into

the sky, whatever comes out of the earth and whatever enters into it, peace be with the messengers, all praise belongs to Allah, Lord of the worlds.'

"He also wrote in his own handwriting, 'In the name of Allah, with (the help of) Allah, to Allah, and as Allah wills, I seek protection (from Allah) for him with the majesty of Allah, with the might of Allah, with the power of Allah, with the possession of Allah, this writing is cure from Allah for so and so, son of male and female, two servants of Allah, O Allah, bestow al-Salat (favors) upon Muhammad and his family.'"

H 3414, Ch. 57, h 11
A number of our people have narrated from Ahmad ibn Muhammad ibn Khalid from Muhammad ibn Ali from Ali ibn Muhammad from 'Abd Allah ibn Yahya al-Kahili who has said the following:

"Abu 'Abd Allah, *'Alayhi al-Salam*, has said, 'Whenever you may come face to face with a wild beast, read verse 255 of Chapter 2 of the Holy Quran to its face and say, "I swear you by the oath of Allah, the oath of Muhammad, *'Alayhi al-Salam*, the oath of Solomon son of David, the oath of Amir al-Mu'Mini, Ali ibn abu Talib and 'A'immah, the clean ones (of all sins), after the Holy Prophet." The beast will turn away from you by the will of Allah.' I (the narrator) went out and a wild beast came face to face with me. I then swore it and said to it to turn and move out of the way without harming me. I looked at the beast, who had bent his head down, with the tail between the two legs and turned away.'"

H 3415, Ch. 57, h 12
It is narrated from him (narrator of the Hadith above) from Ja'far ibn Muhammad from Yunus from certain individuals of our people from abu al-Jarud from abu 'Abd Allah, *'Alayhi al-Salam*, who has said the following:

"Whoever, after an obligatory prayer, says, 'Under the trust of Allah, the Great, the Most Glorious, I place myself, family, children and all those whose affairs concern me, under the trust of Allah, whose Greatness is awesome, frightful and unapproachable, I place myself, family, children and all those whose affairs concern me,' he will be guarded under the wing of Jibril (Gabriel), his person, family and belongings will be protected.'"

H 3416, Ch. 57, h 13
It is narrated from him (narrator of the Hadith above) in a marfu' manner from the Imam, *'Alayhi al-Salam*, who has said the following:

"If one sleeps alone in a house he should read verse 255 of Chapter 2 of the Holy Quran and say, 'O Lord, calm down my anxiety, change my concern into peace and assist me in my loneliness.'"

H 3417, Ch. 57, h 14
Abu Ali al-Ash'ari has narrated from Muhammad ibn Salim from Ahmad ibn al-Nadr from 'Amr ibn Shimr from Yazid ibn Murrah from Bukayr who has said the following:

"I heard Amir al-Mu'minin, Ali ibn abu Talib, *'Alayhi al-Salam*, saying, 'The Messenger of Allah once said to me, "O Ali I should instruct you with the words that you should say in a troublesome condition or a misfortune: '(I begin) in the name of Allah, the Beneficent, the Merciful. There are no means and no power without Allah, the Most High, the Most Great,' Allah, the Most Majestic, the Most

Holy, will divert away from you through these words, many kinds of misfortune as He wills.'"

Chapter 58 - Supplication Before the Recitation of the Holy Quran

H 3418a, Ch. 58, h 1

In a mursal manner it is narrated that abu 'Abd Allah, *'Alayhi al-Salam*, would read this supplication before reciting from the book of Allah, the Most Majestic, the Most Holy:

"O Lord, our Cherisher, all praise belongs to You, You surpass all things in power and strong authority, all praise belongs to You, You are the Most High with majesty and pride, above the heavens and the great Throne, O Lord, all praise belongs to You, You are Self-sufficient with Your knowledge and every knowledgeable one stands in need for Your knowledge, O Lord, all praise belongs to You, O the One who sends down miracles and signs and the great reminder. O Lord, all praise belongs to You for Your instructing us with wisdom and the great, clear Quran, O Lord, You instructed us before we had any interest in learning it, You appropriated it for us before our having any interest in its benefits. O Lord, this was a favor from You, an act of extra generosity, kindness and mercy to us without our being able or have the resources or power (for such achievement). O Lord, make its reading and memorization of its verses, belief in its unclear verses, acting upon its clear verses beloved to us and a means for its interpretations, guidance in its application and insight in its light.

"O Lord, You have revealed it as a cure for Your friends, misfortune for Your enemies, blindness for those who disobey You, and a light for those who obey You. O Lord, make it a shield for us against Your punishment, protection against Your anger, a barrier against disobeying You, safety against Your displeasure, guide to obey You, a light, for the day we meet You, to see Your creatures, pass Your bridge, and find guidance to Your paradise.

"O Lord, we seek protection with You against facing misfortune to apply it (the Holy Quran), blindness in practicing its guidance, transgressing against its rules, going above the limit or falling short in its rights. O Lord, carry on for us its weight, make due for us its rewards, grant the opportunity to thank for it, make us to look after and care for it.

"O Lord, make us to follow its lawful rules and avoid violating its rules for unlawful things, apply its laws and pay its dues. O Lord, make its recitation sweet to us, give us energy to recite it at night, respect in reading it with clarity, ability to benefit from it in the nights and on both sides of the day.

"O Lord, satisfy us with shorter sleep, wake us up in the hour of the night from the rest of those who rest (sleep), wake us up from sleep, in the time in which prayer is accepted and supplications are heard. O Lord, make our hearts intelligent in its wonderful facts that do not end, delighted in repeated reading to learn a lesson from the review of the reading, and clearly benefit to understand it. O Lord, we seek protection with You against the remaining of its meaning out of our hearts, leaving it (ignored) when we sleep and throwing it behind our backs. We seek protection with You against our hardheartedness toward Your advice for us in it.

"O Lord, benefit us from the signs You have mentioned in it, remind us of the examples You have presented in it, expiate our sins with its interpretation, increase the reward with it (the Holy Quran) the good deeds, raise our degrees with it, and reward in the positions and avail us with it good news after death. O Lord, make it a supply to provide us strength in the waiting area in Your presence (for judgment), a clear path to walk toward You, beneficial knowledge to benefit from, in thanking for Your bounties, a true humility to glorify Your names; You have admitted it as evidence against us that abolishes our excuses, You have made it such a bounty for which we can never pay enough thanks.

"O Lord, make it a friend for us to keep us away from slipping (mistakes), a guide to show us the virtuous deeds, a helping guide to protect us from deviating, a support for us against the other religions until we reach our best hopes. O Lord, make it our intercessor on the day we will meet You, a weapon for the day of progress, testimony for the Day of Judgment, a light for the dark day, when there will be no earth and no sky, the day when every worker will find the result of his work. O Lord, make it for us a quenching source on the day of thirst, success on the day of receiving rewards and (a shield) against the hot fire in which there is a lack of kindness to those heated up therein with its blazing heat. O Lord, grant us privilege with the position of the martyr, living of the people of salvation, and friendship of the prophets; You hear the pleading for help.'"

Chapter 59 - Supplication for Memorizing the Holy Quran

H 3418b, Ch. 59, h 1

A number of our people have narrated from Ahmad ibn Muhammad ibn Khalid from those whom he has mentioned (in his book) from 'Abd Allah ibn Sinan from Aban ibn Taghlib from abu 'Abd Allah, *'Alayhi al-Salam*, who has said the following:

"Abu 'Abd Allah, *'Alayhi al-Salam*, has, when pleading for help to memorize the Holy Quran, said that one should say, 'O Lord, I plead before You and Your servants have never pleaded before anyone who could be like You. I plead before You through Muhammad, Your prophet, and messenger, Ibrahim, Your friend and chosen one, Moses, the party to Your conversation and whisper, Jesus, Your word and spirit, I plead before You through the books of Ibrahim, the Torah of Moses, Zabur of Dawud, Injil of Jesus, the Holy Quran of Muhammad, *'Alayhi al-Salam*, and through every inspiration and revelation that You have made, determinations that You have approved, the right that You fulfilled, those whom You have made rich, the straying that You have guided, the beggars to whom You have given charity, I plead before You through Your name that You place on the night to become dark, through Your name that You place on the day to become bright, through Your name that You place on earth to settle, in the heavens to hold as pillars and in the mountains to stand firm. I plead before You through Your name with which You spread the sustenance, through Your name with which You bring the dead to life, I plead before You through the bond of majesty of Your Throne, the limits of Your mercy and kindness from Your book, I plead before You to bestow al-Salat (favors) upon Muhammad and his family, to confer upon me memorization of the Holy Quran and varieties of knowledge, to establish it firmly in my heart, my hearing, and my sight and mix it with my flesh, blood, bone marrow and make me benefit thereby in my nights and days, through Your kindness and power; there are no means and no power without You, O the Living, the Guardian.'"

In another Hadith additionally it is said, "I plead before You, through Your name with which Your servants whose prayer is accepted prayed and Your prophets, then You forgave them and showed them kindness. I plead before You with everyone of Your names that You have revealed in Your books, with Your name with which Your Throne stood up in place, with Your one name, the only, the single and the sole one, the Most High that fills up all corners, the purifying, the pure, the blessing, the Holy, the Living, the Guardian, the light of the heavens and earth, the Beneficent, the Merciful, the Great, the Most High, and Your revealed book with the truth, Your perfect words, Your full light, with Your greatness and strength."

In another Hadith the Messenger of Allah has said, 'Whoever wants Allah to make him a container (proper follower of the guidance) of the Holy Quran and knowledge should write this supplication in a clean pot with white honey then wash it with rain water before reaching the earth and drink it for three days before breakfast, it will help him memorize the Holy Quran by the will of Allah.'"

H 3419, Ch. 59, h 2
It is narrated from him (narrator of the Hadith above) from his father from Hammad ibn 'Isa in a marfu' manner from Amir al-Mu'minin, Ali ibn abu Talib, *'Alayhi al-Salam*, who has said the following:
"The Messenger of Allah has said, 'I like to instruct you with a supplication to help you not to forget the Holy Quran when you say, "O Lord, favor me to avoid, for ever, disobeying You, as long as You will keep me alive, favor me from being burdened with that which does not concern me, grant me beautiful appearance in that which pleases You from me, hold my heart on memorizing Your book as You have taught me. Confer upon me the opportunity to read the way it will please You with me. O Lord, give light with Your book to my eyes, open thereby my chest, enlightened with it my heart, free up with it my tongue, make my body work for it and strengthen me thereby, there is no helper in this task except You, no one deserves to be worshipped except Allah.'"

Certain individuals of our people have narrated it from Walid ibn Sabih from Hafs al-'A'war from abu 'Abd Allah, *'Alayhi al-Salam*."

Chapter 60 - Concise Supplications for Worldly Needs and the Hereafter

H 3420, Ch. 60, h 1

A number of our people have narrated from Ahmad ibn Muhammad ibn 'Isa from Isma'Il ibn Sahl from 'Abd Allah ibn Jundab from his father from abu 'Abd Allah, *'Alayhi al-Salam*, who has said the following:

"Say, 'O Lord, make me fear You as if I see You and help me to be pious before You, do not make me miserable because of my energy to disobey You, chose me for Your determination, bless me with Your measure so I will not love the delay of that which You have hastened and the quickening of what You have delayed. Make me self reliant, benefit me from my hearing, and eyes and make them inherent in me, support me against those who have done injustice to me, and show me Your power in it, O Lord, and make it a delight to my eyes.'"

H 3421, Ch. 60, h 2

Abu Ali al-Ash'ari has narrated from Muhammad ibn 'Abd al-Jabbar from Safwan ibn Yahya from abu Sulayman al-Jassas from Ibrahim ibn Maymun who has said the following:

"I heard abu 'Abd Allah, *'Alayhi al-Salam*, saying, 'O Lord, assist me in the horror of the Day of Judgment, take me out of this world safely, pair me up with the beings having intensely white and deep black eyes (hur al-'Ayn) suffice me my needs, the needs of my dependents and the needs of people and include me in Your kindness among Your virtuous servants.'"

H 3422, Ch. 60, h 3

Ali ibn Ibrahim has narrated from his father from Hammad ibn 'Isa from Hariz from Zurara from abu Ja'far, *'Alayhi al-Salam*, who has said the following:

"O Lord, I plead to receive from You (my share of) all good which Your knowledge encompasses, I seek protection with You against all evil which is encompassed by Your knowledge, O Lord, I plead before You for good health from You in all of my affairs, I seek protection with You against losses in this world and the torment of the next life."

H 3423, Ch. 60, h 4

Muhammad ibn Yahya has narrated from Ahmad ibn Muhammad ibn 'Isa and A number of our people have narrated from Sahl ibn Ziyad all from Ali ibn Ziyad has said that Ali ibn Basir once wrote to the Imam asking him to write for him a supplication at the bottom of the page of his own letter with instructions, a supplication that would keep him safe from sins and with comprehensive benefits in this world and in the hereafter. The Imam, *'Alayhi al-Salam*, wrote to me in his own handwriting:

"(I begin) in the name of Allah, the Beneficent, the Merciful, O the One who manifests the good things, hides the bad ones, does not rip apart the covering from me (my privacy), O magnanimous in pardoning, O the One who overlooks faults with grace, whose forgiveness is vast, whose hands are wide open with kindness, who is the companion of every whisperer, the end receiver of complaints, who honorably pardons, the great provider of favors, the initiator of bounties before a recipient would deserve it, O Lord, O Master, O Guardian, O Rescuer, grant al-Salat (favors) upon Muhammad and his family, and I plead before You not to place me in the fire.'"

H 3424, Ch. 60, h 5

Muhammad ibn Yahya has narrated from Ahmad ibn Muhammad ibn 'Isa from abu 'Abd Allah al-Barqi and abu Talib from Bakr ibn Muhammad from abu 'Abd Allah, *'Alayhi al-Salam*, who has said the following:

"O Lord, You are my trustee in every distressful condition, You are my hope in all suffering, You are for me in all of my problems, (You are) my trustee and my resources. How many were the distressful conditions wherein the heart weakened, patience ran thin, people near left out and the enemies rejoiced all matters were exhausted? You assisted me in the matters that I had brought before You and complained about them to You, turning away from everyone besides You and You changed it into happiness, removed the hardships and sufficed it (in its removal). You are the patron of all blessings, the provider of all help, the end of all interests, all praise belongs to You a great deal and thanks to You in addition."

H 3425, Ch. 60, h 6

It is narrated from him (narrator of the Hadith above) from Ahmad ibn Muhammad ibn from Ali ibn al-Hakam from Aban from 'Isa ibn 'Abd Allah al-Qummi from abu 'Abd Allah, *'Alayhi al-Salam*, who has said the following:

"Say, 'O Lord, I plead before You through Your Glory, Beauty and Magnanimity to provide me such and such help,' one should mention one's wishes."

H 3426, Ch. 60, h 7

It is narrated from him (narrator of the Hadith above) from ibn Mahbub from al-Fadl ibn Yunus who has said the following:

"Abu al-Hassan, *'Alayhi al-Salam*, once said to me, 'Say very often, "O Lord, do not place me among those whose belief is temporary and do not take me out of shortcomings." I (the narrator) then asked, 'I know who the people of temporary belief are, but what is the meaning of, 'Do not take me out of shortcomings?' The Imam said, 'In every good deed you may perform just for the sake of Allah, the Most Majestic, the Most Holy, you should feel within yourself as falling far short; all people in their deeds between them and Allah, the Most Majestic, the Most Holy, fall far short from perfect.'"

H 3427, Ch. 60, h 8

It is narrated from him (narrator of the Hadith above) from ibn Mahbub from Aban from 'Abd al-Rahman ibn 'A'Yun who has said the following:

"Abu Ja'far, *'Alayhi al-Salam*, has said, 'Allah, the Most Majestic, the Most Holy, forgave a man from the village by two words with which he pleaded before Allah. He said, O Lord, if You punish me, it is because I deserve it and if You forgive me it is worthy of You (Your greatness) and (for this) Allah granted him forgiveness.'"

H 3428, Ch. 60, h 9

It is narrated from him (narrator of the Hadith above) from Yahya ibn al-Mubarak from Ibrahim ibn abu al-'Ala'-Balad, from his uncle from al-Rida, *'Alayhi al-Salam*, who has said the following:

"O the One who guided me to His Ownself and humbled my heart due to its affirming His existence, I plead before You for peace and belief in this world and in the hereafter."

H 3429, Ch. 60, h 10

Ali ibn Ibrahim has narrated from his father from ibn abu 'Umayr from Muhammad ibn abu Hamza from his father who has said the following:

"Once I saw Ali ibn al-Husayn, *'Alayhi al-Salam*, praying in the vicinity of al-Ka'bah in the night. He prolonged in standing so much so that he would lean on his right leg once and then on the left leg. Then I heard him saying with a crying voice, 'O my Master, will You punish me while there is Your love in my heart? If You will do so You will be placing me together with the people with whom, just for Your sake, I had been enemies all along.'"

H 3430, Ch. 60, h 11

Muhammad ibn Yahya has narrated from Ahmad ibn Muhammad from 'Umar ibn 'Abd al-'Aziz from certain individuals of our people from Dawud al-Raqqi who has said the following:

"I would listen to abu 'Abd Allah, *'Alayhi al-Salam*, praying and what he insisted upon most when pleading before Allah was "throught right and virtue" of the five Holy personalities: the Messenger of Allah, Amir al-Mu'minin, Ali ibn abu Talib, Fatimah al-Zahra, al-Hassan and al-Husayn, *'Alayhim al-Salam*.

(For example saying, 'O Lord, throught Muhammad and so and so grant me this and that.')

H 3431, Ch. 60, h 12

It is narrated from him (narrator of the Hadith above) from Ahmad ibn Muhammad from Ali ibn al-Hakam from Ayyub from Ibrahim al-Karkhi who has said the following:

"Abu 'Abd Allah, *'Alayhi al-Salam*, had instructed us with this supplication to read on Fridays: 'O Lord, I have relied on Your help in my needs and I have arrived before You on the day of my poverty and destitution. Today I rely on Your forgiveness more than on my deeds; Your mercy is more vast than my sins. Take all of my needs in Your hands; You have power over all of them. They cause no burden for You and I am desperately needy. I have never received any good from anyone except You and no one has ever diverted any evil from me except You. I do not have any hope in anyone for my worldly or the affairs of the hereafter except from You, nor do I have any hope in anyone for my day of desperation when people leave me in the hole (the grave) dug for me and I am being left to You, O Lord, with my poverty.'"

H 3432, Ch. 60, h 13

Ali ibn Ibrahim has narrated from his father from ibn abu 'Umayr from al-Husayn ibn 'Atiyyah from Zayd ibn al-Sa'Igh who has said the following:

"Once I said to abu 'Abd Allah, *'Alayhi al-Salam*, 'Please, pray to Allah for us.' The Imam said, 'O Lord, give them truthfulness in their words (Hadith), safe keeping of their trust and punctuality for prayer, O Lord, they are the most deserving, among Your creatures, of Your favors, O Lord, grant them favors.'"

H 3433, Ch. 60, h 14

A number of our people have narrated from Sahl ibn Ziyad and Ali ibn Ibrahim has narrated from his father from ibn Mahbub from abu Hamza from Ali ibn al-Husayn, *'Alayhi al-Salam*, who has said the following:

"Amir al-Mu'minin, Ali ibn abu Talib, *'Alayhi al-Salam*, would say, 'O Lord, oblige me with the ability to place my trust in You and leave my affairs in Your hands, agree with Your measures, submit to Your command so that I do not love the hastening of what You have delayed or the delay of what You have hastened, O Lord of the worlds.'"

H 3434, Ch. 60, h 15

Muhammad ibn Yahya has narrated from Ahmad ibn Muhammad from Muhammad ibn Sinan from Sujaym from ibn abu Muhammad ibn Ya'Fur who has said the following:

"I heard abu 'Abd Allah, *'Alayhi al-Salam*, saying, his hands raised to the sky, 'O Lord, do not ever leave me to myself, not even for a blinking of an eye, no less or more than that,' and immediately with this tears flowed down on both sides of his beard. He then turned to me and said, 'O ibn Ya'fur, Allah, the Most Majestic, the Most Holy, left Yunus son of Mathew to his own self for less than a blinking of an eye and that sin came to take place.' I then asked, 'May Allah keep you well, did he reach disbelief in it?' The Imam said, 'No, but dying in such a condition is destruction.'"

H 3435, Ch. 60, h 16

A number of our people have narrated from Ahmad ibn Muhammad ibn Khalid in a marfu' manner has narrated the following:

"Once Jibril (Gabriel) came to the Holy Prophet and said, 'Your Lord says to you, "When you like to worship Me a day or night a true worshipping, raise your hands to Me and say, 'O Lord, all praise belongs to You, the eternal praise with Your eternity, all praise belongs to You, a great unending deal of praise except by Your knowledge, all praise belongs to You, beyond the limits of all limits except by Your wish and will, all praise belongs to You, a great deal of praise for whose speaker nothing is enough reward except Your happiness, all praise belongs to You, all praise, all favors, all pride, all beauty, all the light, all the majesty, all the might, all greatness, all the world, all the hereafter, all the night, all the day, all the creatures and all good is in Your hand and to You all matters return, its apparent and hidden.

"O Lord, all praise belongs to You, the praise for ever, Your trial is well done, Your tribute is glorious, Your bounties are delightful, Your determination is just, Your gifts are generous, Your rewards are handsome and You are the Lord of those on earth and the Lord of those in the heavens. O Lord, all praise belongs to You, a praise in the mighty seven, all praise belongs to You, in the well-stretched earth, all praise belongs to You, to the capability of the servants, all praise belongs to You, to the fill of the lands, all praise belongs to You in the mountains firmly standing, all praise belongs to You in the night when it becomes dark, all praise belongs to You in the day when it is bright, all praise belongs to You, in the hereafter and in the one before, all praise belongs to You, in the, al-Mathani (name of Chapter One of the Holy Quran) and the great Quran. I testify that Allah is free of all defects, I speak of His praise and all of the earth is in His control. On the Day of Judgment the heavens will be folded by His right hand. I testify that You are pure of all defects, our Lord, the Most High, the Most Blessed, the Most Holy, You have created all things by Your power, subdued all things by Your majesty,

You are high above all things by Your highness, You are dominant over all things by Your power, You have invented all things by Your wisdom and knowledge, You have commissioned the messengers with Your books and guided the virtuous people by Your permission, supported the believing people with Your victory, You reign the creatures by Your authority, no one deserves to be worshipped except You alone and You have no partner. We do not worship anyone other than You, we do not ask for help from anyone other than You and we do not incline to anyone other than toward You, You are the One before Whom we complain, the end of our hope, our Lord and our owner.'"

H 3436, Ch. 60, h 17

Ali ibn Ibrahim has narrated from his father from ibn abu 'Umayr from Mu'awiyah ibn 'Ammar who has said the following:

"Once abu 'Abd Allah, *'Alayhi al-Salam*, on his own initiation said to me, 'O Mu'awiyah, bear in mind that a man once came to Amir al-Mu'minin, Ali ibn abu Talib, *'Alayhi al-Salam*, complaining of the delay for the answer to his prayer. Amir al-Mu'minin, Ali ibn abu Talib, *'Alayhi al-Salam*, asked, "Why do you not pray with the quick for acceptance supplication (prayer quickly accepted)?" The man then said, 'Please tell me what that supplication is?' The Imam told him to say, 'O Lord, I plead before You through Your great name, the greatest one, the glorious one, the magnanimous one, the one treasured and hidden, the light of the truth, and the clear authority in the argument. It is a light with light, a light from a light, a light in a light, a light over a light, a light above all lights, a light that illuminates all darkness, crumbles down all hardships, all condemned devils and every hardheaded tyrant. (It is such) a light that the earth cannot hold and the sky cannot not withstand. With it every frightened person feels secure, every magician's magic will turn invalid, and the transgression of every transgressor, the envy of every envier will turn ineffective. Due to its greatness the ocean splits open, the ships sail in safety when the angel speak with it, the waves will have no way to it and that is Your greatest of great, glorious of glorious name, the great light with which You have named Yourself and with it You have established Your power over Your Throne. I turn to You through Muhammad and his family and I plead before You to grant al-Salat (favors) upon Muhammad and his family, to provide me help in such and such of my needs. (One then should mention his wishes)'"

H 3437, Ch. 60, h 18

A number of our people have narrated from Ahmad ibn Muhammad ibn Khalid from his father from Khalaf ibn Hammad from 'Amr ibn abu al-Miqdam who has said the following:

"Abu 'Abd Allah, *'Alayhi al-Salam*, dictated this supplication to me and it is of universal benefit for this and the hereafter. Say after thanking and praising Allah:

"O Lord, You are Allah, no one deserves to be worshipped except You, the Forbearing, the Magnanimous, You are Allah, no one deserves to be worshipped except You, the Majestic, the Wise, You are Allah, no one deserves to be worshipped except You, the One and only, the Conqueror, You are Allah, no one deserves to be worshipped except You, the King, the Compeller, You are Allah, no one deserves to be worshipped except You, the Merciful, the Forgiver, You are Allah, no one deserves to be worshipped except You, Whose retribution is most intense, You are Allah, no one deserves to be worshipped except You, the Great, the Most High, You are Allah, no one deserves to be worshipped except You, The Hearer, the Seeing, You are Allah, no one deserves to be worshipped except You, the Defender, the Most Powerful, You are Allah, no one deserves to be worshipped except You, the Lenient, the Appreciator, You are Allah, no one deserves to be worshipped except You, the Praiseworthy, the Glorious, You are Allah, no one deserves to be worshipped except You, the Forgiving, the Loving, You are Allah, no one deserves to be worshipped except You, the Compassionate, the Obliging, You are Allah, no one deserves to be worshipped except You, the Forbearing, the recompensing, You are Allah, no one deserves to be worshipped except You, the Generous, the Exalted, You are Allah, no one deserves to be worshipped except You, the One, the Only, You are Allah, no one deserves to be worshipped except You, the Unseen, the Ever Present, You are Allah, no one deserves to be worshipped except You, the Apparent and Hidden, You are Allah, no one deserves to be worshipped except You, Who has the knowledge of all things. Your light is complete. You guide, You extend Your hand and give, O our Lord, Your face is the Most Honorable face, Your direction is the best direction, Your gift is the best gift and the most pleasant. When You, our Lord, are obeyed You appreciate, when You are disobeyed You forgive whoever You will, You answer the helpless and remove evil, accept repentance, and ignore sins. Your gifts cannot be matched and Your bounties cannot be counted. The words of praising people cannot reach (the limits of) Your praise.

"O Lord, grant al-Salat (favors) upon Muhammad and his family, grant them happiness quicker, grant them joy, comfort and delight. Make me feel the test of their happiness; destroy their enemies, among the Jinn and human beings. Confer upon us goodness in this world and in the hereafter and protect us against the fire, make us of those who will suffer no fear and sadness and make me of those who exercise patience and place their trust in their Lord, keep me steadfast with the solid word in this life and in the hereafter, bestow upon me blessings in life and in death, on the Day of Judgment, resurrection, reckoning, the balance and in the horrors of the Day of Judgment, keep me safe on the bridge, help me pass over it, grant me beneficial knowledge, true certainty, piety, restraint from worldly things, fear of You and concern that make me reach Your success, will not take me away from You, make me loveable and not hated, receiving support, not betrayed, and grant me all the good of this and the hereafter that I know or that which I do not know, protect me against all evil in its entirety, that which I know and that which I do not know.'"

H 3438, Ch. 60, h 19

A number of our people have narrated from Ahmad ibn Muhammad ibn Khalid from his father from Fadalah ibn Ayyub from Mu'awiyah ibn 'Ammar who has said the following:

"Once I said to abu 'Abd Allah, *'Alayhi al-Salam*, 'Will you instruct me with a special supplication?' The Imam said, 'Yes, I will do so, say, "O the One, the Glorious, the Only, O self-sufficient, Who has not given birth to anyone and is not born from anyone and Who has no partner, O Majestic, O Magnanimous, O

Compassionate, O Obliging, O Hearer of supplications, O the Most Generous of those who are asked for help, O the Best of those who give, O Allah, O Allah, O Allah, You have said, 'Noah pleaded before Us for help and We are the best to answer.'

"Abu 'Abd Allah, *'Alayhi al-Salam*, then said, 'The Messenger of Allah would say, "Yes, indeed, You are the best Who answers, the best to be called for help, and the best to plead with, I plead before You through the light of Your face, through Your majesty, Your power, Your might, I plead before You through Your kingdom, through Your formidable coats of arm and Your community, the members of Your community all of them, through Muhammad, *'Alayhi al-Salam*, and the successors after Muhammad to grant al-Salat (favors) upon Muhammad and his family and provide me help in such and such matters." (One should mention one's wishes).'"

H 3439, Ch. 60, h 20

It is narrated from him (narrator of the Hadith above) from certain individuals of his people from Husayn ibn 'Ammarah from Husayn ibn abu Sa'id al-Makari and Jahm ibn abu Jahmah from abu Ja'far - a man from al-Kufa who was know by his being father of someone - who has said the following:

"Once I asked abu 'Abd Allah, *'Alayhi al-Salam*, to instruct me with a supplication with which I can pray to Allah. The Imam agreed and told me to say, 'O the One who is my hope in all that is good, O the One whose anger is not feared (in certain cases) in every mistake, O the One who grants a great deal for very little, O the One who gives to whoever asks Him for help out of compassion and kindness, O the One who gives to those who do not even ask for help and do not even know Him, grant al-Salat (favors) upon Muhammad and his family, bestow upon me for my plea all the good of the world and the hereafter; what You have given me already is not just a little and increase for me from Your vast generosity, O the Magnanimous One.'"

H 3440, Ch. 60, h 21

It is narrated from him (narrator of the Hadith above) in a marfu' manner from abu Ja'far, *'Alayhi al-Salam*, who instructed his brother 'Abd Allah ibn Ali with following supplication:

"O Lord, raise the degree of my knowledge upwards, do not allow any enemy or envier to become covetous of me, protect me standing, sitting, awake or sleeping. O Lord, forgive me, favor me, guide me to Your straight path, save me from the heat of hell, shake off of me my liabilities and sins and make me of the best of best of the world."

H 3441, Ch. 60, h 22

Muhammad ibn Yahya has narrated from Ahmad ibn Muhammad from al-Husayn ibn Sa'ld from 'Uthman ibn 'Isa and Harun ibn Kharijah who has said the following:

"I heard abu 'Abd Allah, *'Alayhi al-Salam*, saying, '(O Allah) grant mercy upon me in the matters for which I do not have the ability to remain patient.'"

H 3442, Ch. 60, h 23

It is narrated from him (narrator of the Hadith above) from Ahmad ibn Muhammad from al-Husayn ibn Sa'Id from al-Nadr ibn Suwayd from ibn Sinan from Hafs from Muhammad ibn Muslim who has said the following:

"I asked him to instruct me with a supplication. He asked, 'Why do you not pray with the supplication of pleading before Allah for help?' I (the narrator) then asked, 'What is the supplication of pleading before Allah for help?' The Imam said say, 'O Lord, the Lord of the seven heavens and all that is in between, the Lord of the great Throne, Lord of Jibril (Gabriel), Michael and Israfeil, Lord of the great Quran, and Lord of Muhammad, the last of the prophets, I plead before You through that with which You keep the heavens, with which You keep the earth, with which You disperse the gatherings and place together what is scattered, with which You provide sustenance to the living, with which You keep the counts of sands, the weight of the mountains and the measurement of the oceans.' Then ask Allah's al-Salat (favor) for Muhammad and his family and ask for help and insist pleading before Allah for help.'"

H 3443, Ch. 60, h 24

Ali ibn Ibrahim has narrated from his father from al-Hassan ibn Ali from Karram from ibn abu Ya'fur from abu 'Abd Allah, *'Alayhi al-Salam*, who has said the following:

"O Lord, fill my heart with love for You, concern about You, affirmation of and belief in Your existence, fear from You and longing toward You, O Glorious, O Magnanimous. O Lord, make me love meeting You, and such meeting to be good, mercy, and full of blessings, join me with the virtuous and do not leave me behind with the wicked ones. Join me with the virtuous of the past and those to come, lead me on the path of virtuous ones, assist me against my soul by that with which You assist the virtuous ones against their souls, do not turn me in the evil from which You want to rescue me, O Lord of the worlds. I plead before You for a belief free of timing before meeting You, with which You will keep me living, cause me to die, and raise me up with it when You will resurrect me. Free my heart from showing off, desire for popularity, and doubt in Your religion.

"O Lord, give me victory in Your religion, energy to worship, understanding of Your creatures, support me twice with Your kindness (in this life and hereafter), brighten my face with Your light, make me interested in what is with You, cause me to die in Your way and in Your religion, the religion of Your Messenger.

"O Lord, I seek protection against laziness, old age, cowardice, stinginess, carelessness, hardheartedness, weakness, and destitution. I seek protection with You, O Lord against a soul that does not become satisfied, the heart that does not become humble, the supplication that is not heard, and the prayer (formal) that does not yield any benefit. I seek protection with You for myself, my family, and my children against condemned Satan.

"O Lord, no one can protect me against You, I do not find any place to hide from You, do not humiliate me and do not throw me in perdition and in torment. I plead before You to keep me to remain steadfast in Your religion, affirm Your book, and follow Your messenger.

"O Lord, speak of me with Your mercy and do not speak of me with my sins, accept from me (my good deeds), increase for me from Your generosity; I am interested toward You. O Lord, make my reward for speaking and sitting to be Your happiness with me, make my deeds and supplication purely for You, make my reward paradise through Your mercy, place me together with all I pleaded for before You and increase for me through Your favor; I am greatly interested toward You. O Lord, the stars have disappeared, eyes have gone to sleep, You are living and guarding, the dark night cannot disappear from You nor the starry skies or the well-stretched earth, the choppy ocean, or the darkness upon darkness. You send mercy upon whomever You will among Your creatures; You know the secret glance of the eyes and what the hearts conceal. I testify to what You have testified for yourself, to what Your angels have testified, and people of knowledge have testified that no one deserves to be worshipped except You, the Majestic, the Wise. Whoever does not testify to what You have testified for yourself, Your angels have testified, and people of knowledge have testified, then write my testimony in place of their testimony. O Lord, You are the Peace, and from You is peace. I plead before You, O the Owner of glory and magnanimity to set my neck free of the fire.'"

H 3444, Ch. 60, h 25

Ali ibn Ibrahim has narrated from his father from ibn Mahbub from Muhammad ibn Yahya al-Khath'ami from abu 'Abd Allah, *'Alayhi al-Salam*, who has said the following:

"Once abu Dharr came to the Messenger of Allah while Jibril (Gabriel) was, in the form of Dihyah al-Kalbi (one of the companions of the Holy Prophet), in a private meeting with the Messenger of Allah. When he saw them he turned away from them and did not want to disrupt their conversation. Jibril (Gabriel) said, 'O Muhammad this was abu Dharr passed by us and did not offer us the greeting of peace, had he done so we would have responded to his greeting. O Muhammad, he has a supplication with which he prays, and is well-known among the inhabitants of the heaven. When I will ascend ask him about it.'

"When Jibril (Gabriel) left, abu Dharr came to the Holy Prophet and the Messenger of Allah said to him, 'O abu Dharr what stopped you from offering us the greeting of peace when you passed by?' He said, 'O Messenger of Allah I thought the person with you was Dihyah al-Kalbi in a private meeting for something of your affairs.' The Messenger of Allah said, 'That was Jibril (Gabriel), O abu Dharr and he said, "Had he (abu Dharr) offered us the greeting of peace we would have responded to his greeting." When abu Dharr learned that it was Jibril (Gabriel) he, Allah knows well, how deeply he regretted his not offering the greeting. The Messenger of Allah asked, 'What is the supplication with which you pray? Jibril (Gabriel) has informed me that you have a prayer whereby you implore and it is well-known in heaven' He said, 'Yes, O Messenger of Allah, I say, "O Lord, I plead before You for peace and belief in You, affirmation of Your prophet, well-being and safety from all misfortunes, to be thankful for the well-being and safety and free of want from the people.'"

H 3445, Ch. 60, h 26

Ali has narrated from his father from ibn Mahbub from Hisham ibn Salim from abu Hamza who has said the following:

"I acquired this supplication from abu Ja'far, Muhammad ibn Ali, *'Alayhi al-Salam*. Abu Ja'far, *'Alayhi al-Salam*, would call it al-Jami' (comprehensive supplication):

"In the name of Allah, the Beneficent, the Merciful, I testify that no one deserves to be worshipped except Allah alone, Who has no partner and I testify that Muhammad is His servant and messenger. I believe in Allah, in all of His messengers, in all that He has revealed to all the messengers, that the promise of Allah is true, meeting Him is true, Allah has spoken the truth, and the messengers have preached.

"All praise belongs to Allah, Lord of the worlds, all glory belongs to Allah whenever anyone glorifies Allah, the way Allah loves to be glorified, all praise belongs to Allah whenever anyone praises Allah in the way Allah loves to be praised, no one deserves to be worshipped except Allah whenever anyone expresses this declaration and testimony as Allah loves to be spoken of as such, Allah is greater than can be described, whenever anyone speaks of Allah as such and as Allah loves to be spoken of as such.

"O Lord, I plead before You for the opening of virtue and good and its end, its pleasures and benefits, its blessings and what I know of as well as what I do not know of and my memory has fallen short to keep them.

"O Lord, plan for me the means of knowing it (good and virtue), open for me its doors, cover me with the blessings of Your kindness, oblige me with protection against slipping away from Your religion, cleanse my heart from doubt, do not allow the immediate issue of living of this life divert my attention away from the rewards of the next life, engage my heart in saving what You will not accept my ignorance of it. Humble my tongue for all virtuous deeds, cleanse my heart from showing off, do not allow it (showing off) running in my joints, but making my deeds stand pure.

"O Lord, I seek protection with You against the evil of all kinds of indecency, the apparent and the hidden, its carelessness and all of whatever the condemned Satan wants to involve me in, whatever a hostile ruler wants from me, which Your knowledge encompass and You have the power to divert away from me.

"Lord I seek protection with You against the encounters of Jinns and human beings, their anger, evil altercations, evil plots, sinful exposures of the Jinn and human beings that may cause me to slip away from my religion, may ruin my hereafter, harm me in my living or an incident of misfortune from them that I may not have the power to deal with, or patience to bear. Do not cause me to suffer such things, O Lord, and its hardships that may prevent me from speaking of You and divert me away from Your worship. You are the protector, the defender, and the savior from all such things. I plead before You O Lord, for comfort in my living as long as You will allow me to live, a living with which I will be able to obey You and earn Your happiness with me, and move thereby to the house of life tomorrow. Do not provide me a sustenance that may cause me to transgress, do not afflict me with a poverty that gives me misery due to constraint, grant me a share good enough for my hereafter, a living that is vast, pleasing, and delightful in my worldly life. Do not make the world a prison for me, or departing it a sorrowful to me, provide me protection against its trials and tribulations. Make my deeds in it acceptable, and my efforts appreciated.

"O Lord, whoever intends evil against me, plan against him similarly, whoever plots against me, plan against him and protect me the concern of that which has causes me concern, plot against whoever plots against me; You are the best devisor, cause blindness to the eyes of the unbelievers, oppressors, rebellious ones and enviers against me.

"O Lord, send upon me comfort and calm from You and dress me up with Your protective coat of arms, save me with Your safe guarding cover, beautify me with Your well-being, good and beneficial health. Make my words and deeds true. Grant me blessings in my children, my family and my property.

"O Lord, forgive me for whatever I have done before, whatever I will do, whatever I neglected, did intentionally, out of laziness, openly or secretly. O the Most Merciful of all merciful ones.'"

H 3446, Ch. 60, h 27
Abu Ali al-Ash'ari has narrated from Muhammad ibn 'Abd al-Jabbar from Safwan ibn Yahya from al-'Ala' ibn Razin from Muhammad ibn Muslim from abu Ja'far, *'Alayhi al-Salam*, who has said the following:
"Say, 'O Lord, increase my sustenance, prolong my life, forgive my sins and make me of those whom You employ to support Your religion and do not replace me by others.'"

H 3447, Ch. 60, h 28
Muhammad ibn Yahya has narrated from Ahmad ibn Muhammad from Muhammad ibn Sinan from Ya'qub ibn Shu'ayb from abu 'Abd Allah, *'Alayhi al-Salam*, who has said the following:
"O the One who appreciates the very little and pardons a great deal, who is forgiving and merciful, forgive my sins, the pleasures of which are gone and the consequences have remained."

H 3448, Ch. 60, h 29
Through the same chain of narrators it is narrated from Ya'qub ibn Shu'ayb from abu 'Abd Allah, *'Alayhi al-Salam*, who has said the following:
"O light, O Holy, O the First of the beings in the beginning, O the Last of the beings of the later times, O the Beneficent, O the Merciful, forgive my such sins that change the bounties, forgive my such sins that bring in misfortunes, forgive my such sins that crush the protections, forgive my such sins that send down evil conditions, forgive my such sins that assist the enemy, forgive my such sins that hasten destruction, forgive my such sins that cut off hope, forgive my such sins that darken the space, forgive my such sins that remove the cover and grace,

forgive my such sins that repulse the prayer and forgive my such sins that turn away the rain from the sky."

H 3449, Ch. 60, h 30
It is narrated from him (narrator of the Hadith above) from Muhammad ibn Sinan from Ya'qub ibn Shu'ayb from abu 'Abd Allah, *'Alayhi al-Salam*, who has said the following:
"Say, 'O my asset in my pain and suffering, O my companion in my severe hardships, O my benefactor, and O my abundant rain fall whenever I may desire.'

"The Imam said that of the supplications of Amir al-Mu'minin, Ali ibn abu Talib, *'Alayhi al-Salam*, is the following: 'O Lord, You have written down the consequences, know the news, have information about the secrets, You have taken over the place between us and (our) hearts, thus, secrets are public to You and the hearts have over flown (with desire to come to you). Your command upon a thing, whenever You will, is only Your saying, 'Be,' it then comes into existence, say through Your kindness to Your obedience to enter in all and every part of my parts and do not depart from me until I will meet You, and say through Your kindness to disobedience to You to move out of all and every part of my parts and do not ever approach me thereafter until I will meet You, provide me sustenance in this world but make me live with a reduced amount and do not isolate me whenever I desire it, (sustenance) O the Beneficent one.'"

H 3450, Ch. 60, h 31
Ali ibn Ibrahim has narrated from his father from ibn Mahbub from al-'Ala' ibn Razin from 'Abd al-Rahman ibn Sayabah who has said the following:
"Once abu 'Abd Allah, *'Alayhi al-Salam*, gave me this supplication: 'All praise belongs to Allah, the Owner, and worthy of praise, the end and the location of all praise. Those who believe in His Oneness have achieved purity, those who worship Him have found guidance, those who obey Him have triumphed and those who have sought His protection have found security. O Lord, O possessor of generosity and glory, beautiful praise and thanks, I plead before You like one who has humbled himself before You with his neck, rubbed his nose on the ground before You, as well as his face, humiliated his soul before You, whose tears have flooded for fear from You, and have continued flowing, who has confessed to his sins before You, his blunders have disgraced him before You, his crimes have made him shunned in Your presence, his power has weakened before You, his resources have diminished, his means of trickery are cut off, all falsehood has disappeared from him, his sins have forced him to lowly positions before You, and to humble himself before You, and to beg You for help. I plead before You like the plea of one who is more desirous in pleading before You than the one pleading as above, who prays before You like him and begs for help more intensely than him.

"O Lord, favor the destitution of my expression, humility of my position, my seat and humility before You with my neck. O Lord, I plead before You for guidance against straying, understanding against blindness and intelligence against transgression. O Lord, I plead before You to help me praise You the most in comfort, bear beautiful patience in hardships, the best thanks to You whenever it is the occasion to thank and submission in the doubtful conditions. I plead before You for power to obey You, weakness in disobedience, for the ability to flee to You from You, and to seek nearness to You, so that, O Lord, I seek Your happiness, give preference to doing what makes You happy with me even though it may anger the people, while I seek Your satisfaction.

"O Lord, who can I hope if You do not have kindness for me, or who cares for me if You keep me far away, or whose forgiveness benefits me, if You punish me, or whose gifts should I hope for if You deprive me of Your gifts, or who can have honor for me in his hands if You degrade me, whose degrading of me can harm me if You honor me.

"O Lord, how bad are my deeds, how obnoxious are my acts, how brutal is my heart, how lengthy are my (worldly) yearnings, how short is my life that has made it so daring to disobey my creator!

"O Lord, how good is Your trial for me, how manifest are Your bounties upon me! Your bounties upon me have become so much that I cannot even count them. My thanks to You for the preferences that You have given to me, in the joy for the bounties, is so little that I have subjected myself to punishment. I have forgotten speaking of You, have indulged in ignorance after knowledge, crossed over from justice to transgression, from virtuous deeds to sin and to fleeing for fear and sorrow. How small and little are my virtuous deeds compared to my numerous sins, how many and great are my sins compared to the small size of my structure, and weak limbs!

"O Lord, how lengthy are my (worldly) hopes in my short life, how short is my life in my lengthy hopes, how hideous is my inside and my outside! O Lord, I have no ground if argued, no excuse to find excuses, no gratitude if I would be tried or if I am favored unless You assist me to be grateful for the favor You have done to me.

"O Lord, how light will be my balance tomorrow if You will not make it weigh heavy! How reckless is my tongue if You do not keep it in place! How black is my face if You do not whiten it! O Lord, how would I deal with my sins of the past that have crushed my limbs! O Lord, how can I seek worldly desires and weep for failing to achieve them but do not weep while my regrets for disobedience have intensified and my transgression has gone to the extremities! O Lord, the worldly motives prompted me and I quickly responded, and relied upon them willingly. The motives for the gains of the hereafter prompted me but I lingered and delayed to respond and to move faster to them like the fast moving to the worldly motives, its worthless vanities, smashed up beyond use materials and its fast disappearing mirage.

"O Lord, You have frightened and encouraged me and have argued against me to prove me a slave and have sufficed me in my sustenance, but I felt secure from

Your warning and lagged behind in acting upon Your encouragement, did not trust Your guarantee, and took Your argument lightly.

"O Lord, change my feeling of security from Your warning in this world into fear, my procrastination into zeal and zest and my taking Your argumentation against me lightly into serious concern and anxiety and then make me to be happy with the share of sustenance that You have assigned for me, O Magnanimous, O Magnanimous, I plead before You through Your great name so You be happy (with me) when You are angry, I beg for relief in pain and suffering, light in darkness, and understanding in the confusion of tribulation.

"O Lord, make my shield against sins formidable, my position in paradise high, my deeds all accepted, my virtuous deeds to come in multiples and pure. I seek protection with You against all misfortune, the apparent and hidden, against overeating and overdrinking, against the evil of what I know and that which I do not know. I seek protection with You against my buying ignorance at the cost of knowledge, harshness at the cost of forbearing, injustice at the cost of justice, cutting off good relations with relatives at the cost of maintaining good relations with relatives, intolerance at the cost of exercising patience, straying at the cost of guidance and disbelief at the cost of belief.'"

Ibn Mahbub has narrated from Jamil ibn Salih that he has narrated that Ali ibn Salih had a similar supplication and at the end he has added, "Amin, O Lord, of the worlds."

H 3451, Ch. 60, h 32
Ibn Mahbub has said that Nuh ibn Yaqdan has narrated from abu 'Abd Allah, *'Alayhi al-Salam*, who has said the following:
"Say this prayer, 'O Lord, I plead before You for Your favor that cannot be achieved except with Your happiness, for (Your help to) come out of all disobedience that cannot happen without Your approval, for (Your help to) enter into all that makes You happy, for safety from all dangers, for departure from all major sins that have happened from me, willingly or have slipped out mistakenly, or have passed in my mind due to satanic induction.

"I plead before You to place fear in me that can keep me within the limits of Your approval, shatter away from me all lustful evil thoughts that have passed in my desires, that have made my opinion slip away to crossover Your lawful limits. I plead before You, O Lord, to take the best that You know, and ignore all the evil that You find or mistakes that I had no knowledge of or did have the knowledge thereof.

"I plead before You for increased sustenance, restraining to suffice with basic needs, coming out of confusing conditions with clearly stated instructions, correctness in evidence, truth in all circumstances, yielding to justice for people against or for my soul, dealing humbly in yielding to justice in all circumstances of anger and contentment, avoiding small or greater degrees of transgression in my words or deeds, completion of Your bounties in all things, and thankfulness to You for it so You are content with happiness.

"I plead before You for guidance in all the good choices wherein choices exist and are easy to achieve not that which is hard to achieve. O Magnanimous, O Magnanimous, O Magnanimous, open for me the door to the fact in which there is well being (of the body and spirit) and relief, open for me its door and ease it off to leave. If You may determine for any of Your creatures to overpower me then hold and seize him by his hearing, his eyes, tongue, and hand, seize him from his right, left, behind, front and before him and prevent him from reaching me with evil. Your neighbor is well protected, glorious is the praise of Your face, and no one deserves to be worshipped except You. You are my Lord, and I am Your slave and servant. O Lord, You are my hope in all pains, You are my hope in all hardships, in all troubles that befall me, on You I depend and You are my resources. How many are the pains that weaken the heart, diminish in it the means, bring rejoice for the enemy, and exhaust the resources. I present them before You, complain to You against it, come to You of all things so You provide me relief and suffice me against it (such pains), thus, You are my benefactor of all the bounties with me, the appropriator of all of my needs, and the end of all of my desires. All praise belongs to You a great deal and (I am) thankful to You in addition.'"

H 3452, Ch. 60, h 33

Ali ibn Ibrahim has narrated from his father from ibn abu 'Umayr from Mansur ibn Yunus from abu Basir from abu 'Abd Allah, *'Alayhi al-Salam*, who has said the following:
"Say, 'O Lord, I plead before You, to grant me such words as those of repenting people and their deeds, the light of the prophets and their truthfulness, salvation of the fighters for Your cause and their rewards, thankfulness of the chosen ones and their good advice, actions of those who speak of You and their certainty, belief of the scholars and their deep understanding, worship of the concerned people and their humility, the judgment of the experts in the law (Shari'a) and their discipline, worries of the pious people and their interest (in religion), the affirmation of the believing people and their trusting (Allah) and the hope of the virtuous people and their good deeds.

"O Lord, I plead before You grant me a reward as that granted to those who thank (You), the position of those very near to (You) and the friendship of the prophets. O Lord, I plead before You to grant me a fear like that of the people who act for Your sake, the acts of those who fear You, the humility of those who worship You, the certainty of those who place their trust in You and the trust of the believing people with You. O Lord, You know my needs without being taught, and You are capable of helping without being burdened. You are the One Whom no pleading person can overcome verbally, or anyone can find faults with or anyone can exhaust His praise. O Lord, You are as You say and above what we say. O Lord, provide me immediate relief, great rewards, and beautiful covering. O Lord, You know that in doing injustice to myself and transgressing against it I did not take anyone as Your opposition, partner, companion, or a child.

"O the One whom pleading cannot confuse, nothing can preoccupy in listening to one from listening to the other, seeing one from seeing the other and the insistence of insisting people cannot tire Him. I plead before You to provide me relief in this hour from the sources I except or from that which I do not expect; You bring to life the bones that have turned to ashes; You have power over all things. O the One to whom my thanks had been very little but He has not deprived me, my sins were monstrous but He has not disgraced me, He found me in sins but did not encounter me. He created me for what He has created me but I have acted against what He has created me for. What a great owner are You O my Master! What a despicable slave am I! You have found me, You are the best of finders O Lord! What a despicable thing am I to look for! It is Your slave, the son of Your slave and the son of Your female slave before You to deal with as You will. O Lord, the voices have silenced, movements have calmed down, every loving one has sought privacy with his beloved, and I have sought privacy with You. You are the beloved to me, make the privacy that I have sought with You my freedom from the fire. O the One above whom there is no person of knowledge more praiseworthy. O the One below whom there is no creature barred to reach Him. O the First before all things, O the Last after all things. O the One who has no elements, O the One for whom there is no end for annihilation, O the One of perfect attributes, O the most lenient of providers, O the One who communicates with all languages and is spoken to as well, O the One whose forgiveness had been there from long before, whose hold is stern, whose kingdom is solid, I plead before You through Your name with which You faced Moses, O Allah, O the Beneficent, O the Merciful, O the One, no one deserves to be worshipped except You. O Lord, You are Selfsufficient, I plead before You to bestow al-Salat (favors) upon Muhammad and his family and admit me in paradise."

H 3453, Ch. 60, h 34
Muhammad ibn Yahya has narrated from Ahmad ibn Muhammad from Muhammad ibn al-Walid from Yunus who has said the following:

"Once I asked al-Rida, *'Alayhi al-Salam*, to instruct me with a concise supplication. The Imam instructed me to say, 'O the One who has guided me to His Own self and has humbled my heart with its affirmation of His existence, I plead before You for peace and belief.'"

H 3454, Ch. 60, h 35
Ali ibn abu Hamza has narrated from certain individuals of his people from abu 'Abd Allah, *'Alayhi al-Salam*, who has said the following:

"Once a man came to Amir al-Mu'minin, Ali ibn abu Talib, *'Alayhi al-Salam*, and said, 'O Amir al-Mu'minin, I inherited a property but did not give even one dirham in obedience to Allah, the Most Majestic, the Most Holy. I thereafter made an earning and did not spend anything in obedience to Allah. Instruct me with a supplication that can replace for me things of the past, and what I have done be forgiven as well as what I may do.' The narrator has said that the Imam told him, 'Say.' The man asked, 'What should I say, O Amir al-Mu'minin?'

"The Imam said, 'Say as I say, "O my light in all darkness, O my comfort in all dreadful conditions, O my hope in all painful matters, O my trust in every hardship, O my guide in all straying conditions, You are my guide, when all guidance of guides is cut off but Your guidance remains. Whoever You guide does not stray off the right path. You granted me favors and made it delightful, You provided me sustenance in abundance, You fed me and made my food best, You bestowed upon me and made it the best gift without my deserving it by means of my deeds but initiated from You due to Your magnanimity and generosity. I found strength from Your magnanimity to disobey You, I gained power from Your sustenance but I disappointed You, I ruined my life in what You disliked, my daring against You, my committing what You had forbidden, my entering in things You prohibited, did not prevent You from turning to me with Your generosity, Your forbearance did not hold You back from doing favors to me even if I returned to sin and disobedience to You, You always turn back with generosity and bounty but I always sin. How magnanimous You are to those who confess before You to their sins!

"How majestic You are to those who humble themselves before You! Before Your magnanimity I confess my sins and for Your majesty I humble myself before You. It now is all up to You what You will do to me in Your magnanimity and with my confessing my sins before You for Your majesty and my begging respectfully, I plead before You to deal with me the way it is worthy of You not according to what I deserve.'"

This is the end of the Book of prayer/supplication. It is followed by the Book of the Excellence of the Holy Quran of the Book al-Kafi. All praise belongs to Allah alone and Allah has granted blessings upon Muhammad and his family.

In the Name of Allah, the Beneficient, the Merciful

Part Three:
Book of the Excellence of the Holy Quran

Chapter 1

H 3455, Ch. 1, h 1

Ali ibn Muhammad has narrated from al-'Abbas from h n Fadl ibn Shadhan 'Abd al-Rahman from Sufyan al-Hariri from his father from Sa'd al-Khaffaf from abu Ja'far, *'Alayhi al-Salam*, who has said the following:

"O Sa'd, learn the Holy Quran; on the Day of Judgment the Holy Quran will come in the best form that people may have ever seen. People will be present in one hundred thousand and twenty rows: the followers of Prophet Muhammad will form eighty thousand rows. The other forty thousand rows will consist of the followers of the other prophets. The Holy Quran will come to the rows of the Muslims in the form of a well-shaped man, offer them the greeting of peace and they look to him and say to each other, 'No one deserves to be worshipped except Allah, the forbearing the magnanimous, this man is one of the Muslims whom we know from his picture and qualities, however, he has been striving about the Holy Quran much harder than we, thus, he has been given this beauty, grace and light which we have not received.

"He (the Quran in the form of a person) passes toward the row of the martyrs who look at him and say, 'No one deserves to be worshipped except Allah, the Lord, the Merciful. We know from the signs and qualities he is a martyr, however, he has been of the martyrs at sea, thus, he has received this beauty and grace that is not given to us.' The Imam said, 'Then it will pass toward the martyr at sea and the martyrs at sea look at him with astonishment and say, "He is of the martyrs at sea; we know him from his signs and qualities, however, on the island where he suffered must have been much more dangerous than the island where we suffered, thus, he has received this beauty, grace and light.'

"Then he approaches the rows of the prophets and messengers in the form of a messenger prophet. The prophets and messengers look at him and their astonishment increase. They will say, 'No one deserves to be worshipped except Allah, the Most Forbearing, the Magnanimous, this is a messenger prophet; we know him from his picture and qualities, however, he has been much more virtuous.' The Imam said, 'They will come to the Messenger of Allah and ask him, "O Muhammad, who is this?" He then will ask, 'Do you not know him?' They will say, 'We do not know him, however, Allah has not been angry with him.' The Messenger of Allah will say to them, 'This is the authority of Allah over His creatures. He offers them greeting of peace and passes thereby to the rows of the angels in the form of a special angel. The angels will look at him and their astonishment increases, his status will seem very great to them. They will say our Lord is Most High, Most Holy. This servant is of the angels. We know him from his picture and qualities, however, he has been more close and special to Allah, the Most Majestic, the Most Holy, thus, he is dressed up with this much light and beauty that we have not received.' Then he will come before Allah, the Most Majestic, the Most Blessed, the Most High, and will bow down below the Throne.

"Allah, the Most Blessed, the Most High, will speak to the Holy Quran saying, 'My true spoken words and authority on earth, look up and ask for your wishes. Your wishes shall be granted and your intercession shall be accepted. How did you find my servants?'

"The Holy Quran will then say, 'My Lord, certain ones among them kept me safely protected and did not lose anything from me but others among them lost me and disrespected me and called me lies even though I was Your authority to all of Your creatures.' Allah, the Most Majestic, the Most Holy, then will say, 'I swear by My Majesty, Greatness and Highness that I shall give the best reward on this day because of you and shall punish severely because of you.'

"The Imam then continued saying, 'The Holy Quran will raise his head in another shape.' I (the narrator) asked the Imam, 'O abu Ja'far in what shape it will return?' The Imam said, 'It will come in the shape of a changed man, slim and tired looking. People in the gathering will see him. Then he will come forward to one of our followers who knew it and would argue with it against the people, opposed to 'A'immah. The Holy Quran will ask him, 'Do you know me'? The man will look it (the Holy Quran) and say, 'O servant of Allah, I do not know you.' The Holy Quran then will return in his former shape with which it existed among people, and will ask, 'Do you still not know me'? He will say, 'Yes, I do know you.' It will say, 'I am the Holy Quran for which you kept the whole night awake and faced suffering in your life, hearing disappointing words from people when you spoke from me. Obviously every merchant enjoys the benefit of his trade. Today I am behind you with full support. The Holy Quran will then proceed with him to the Throne of the Lord of Majesty, the Most Blessed, the Most High, and the Quran then will say, 'Lord, this servant of You was very close to me and very careful about me. He would love others because of me and hate others just because of me.'

"Allah, the Most Majestic, the Most Holy, will then say, 'Allow my servant enter paradise and allow him be dressed and crowned and then let him come back to see his friend, the Quran.' When that servant of Allah will be well rewarded he will then come back to see his friend the Holy Quran, Allah, the Most High will ask the Holy Quran, 'Are you happy with Our rewards given to your friend?' the Holy Quran will say, 'Lord, I consider it is not enough and I request that he should receive more of all the good things. Allah then will say, 'I swear by My Majesty, Honor and Highness, I shall reward him and others like him with five things and more: I shall give them eternal youth, good health free from illness, wealth free from poverty, happiness free from sadness and life free from death.'

"The Imam then read this verse: 'They will not experience any death other than that which they have already been through.' (44:56)

"I (the narrator) then said to abu Ja'far, *'Alayhi al-Salam*, 'May Allah keep my soul in service for your cause, does the Holy Quran speak?' The Imam smiled and said, 'May Allah grant favors upon our weak Shi'a (followers), they are people of submission.' Then he said, 'Yes, O Sa'D, prayer speaks. It has a form and shape. It commands and prohibits.' Sa'D then said, 'It changed my color and I said, "I will not be able to speak of this among people." Abu Ja'far, *'Alayhi al-Salam*, said, 'Are people anything else besides our Shi'a (followers)? Those who do not know the right of the prayer, they have denied our rights.' The Imam then said, 'O Sa'd do you want, I will make you hear the words of the Holy Quran?' I said, 'Yes, may Allah grant you favors.' The Imam said, 'Prayer prohibits indecency and unlawful matters and speaking of Allah is greater,' "prohibition" is speaking, (stopping people from going to) "indecency and unlawful matters" (that) are (nothing else but certain) men. We are the Dhikr of Allah, speaking of Allah, and we are greater.'" (The Holy Quran prohibits people from following certain people called indecency and unlawful matters)

H 3456, Ch. 1, h 2
Ali ibn Ibrahim has narrated from his father al-Nawfali from al-Sakuni from abu 'Abd Allah, *'Alayhi al-Salam*, who has said the following:
"The Messenger of Allah has said, 'O people, you live in peacetime during a fast moving journey. You have seen night, day, sun and moon turn every new into old, every far near, and bring the time of every promise near at hand. Prepare the means for a long journey.' The Imam said, 'Miqdad ibn Aswad then stood up and asked, "O Messenger of Allah, what is the 'peace time'?" The Messenger of Allah said, "It is the time to complete (the task) and cut off (from this world). When mischief confuses you like a dark night you must hold to the Holy Quran; it is an intercessor (an associate whose association is beneficial) whose intercession will be accepted and a solicitor whose words are believed. Whoever gives it the lead it will take him to paradise. Whoever leaves it behind (it) will then drive him to the fire. It is a guide that shows the best path. It is the book that contains details and explanations, and accomplishments. It is a criterion and not a useless thing. It has face and hidden meanings. Its face meaning is law and its hidden meaning is knowledge. Its face meaning is unique and its hidden meaning is deep. It has stars and upon its stars there are stars. Its wonders do not end and its rare facts do not become old. In it there is the torch of guidance, and the lighthouses of wisdom. It serves as proof of veracity of knowledge (for one who wants to verfy the truth of his Knowledge) and who has come to know the attribute, permit him brighten his eyes to reach the attribute. It saves from destruction, and protects against danger. Thinking is life for the heart of an intelligent person, just as in darkness one finds the way with help from light. Thus, your freedom (from worldly attractions) must be the best and your delays the shortest.'"

H 3457, Ch. 1, h 3
Ali ibn Ibrahim has narrated from his father from 'Abd Allah ibn al-Mughirah from Sama'a ibn Mehran who has said the following:

"Abu 'Abd, *'Alayhi al-Salam*, has said, the Majestic, the Almighty, has revealed to you His book. It is truthful and virtuous. In it there is news about you, the news of those before you, the news about those after you, the news about the heaven and earth and if one brings you such news, you are astonished.'"

H 3458, Ch. 1, h 4

Muhammad ibn Yahya has narrated from Ahmad ibn Muhammad ibn 'Isa from Muhammad ibn Sinan from abu al-Jarud who has said the following:

"Abu Ja'far, *'Alayhi al-Salam*, has said that the Messenger of Allah has said, 'I will be the first to arrive before the Majestic, the Almighty on the Day of Judgment, His book and my family, then my followers whom I will ask about what they have done to the book of Allah and my family.'"

H 3459, Ch. 1, h 5

Muhammad ibn Yahya has narrated from Ahmad ibn Muhammad ibn Yahya from Talhah ibn Zayd from abu 'Abd Allah, *'Alayhi al-Salam*, who has said the following:

"In this Quran is the lighthouse of guidance and torches for dankness. One must brighten his eyes and open them in such light; thinking is life for the seeing eyes just as light helps one walking in the dark."

H 3460, Ch. 1, h 6

Ali ibn Ibrahim has narrated from his father from Muhammad ibn 'Isa from Yunus from abu Jamilah who has said the following:

"Abu 'Abd Allah, *'Alayhi al-Salam*, has said, 'It is in the will of Amir al-Mu'minin, Ali ibn abu Talib, *'Alayhi al-Salam*, to his companions, "You must know that the Holy Quran is guidance during the day and light in the dark night against the existing hardships and poverty.'"

H 3461, Ch. 1, h 7

Ali has narrated from his father from al-Nawfali from al-Sakuni from abu 'Abd Allah, *'Alayhi al-Salam*, who has said the following:

"Once a man complained to the Holy Prophet for having pain in his chest and he, *'Alayhi al-Salam*, said, 'Seek a cure from the Holy Quran; Allah, the Most Majestic, the Most Holy, says, "It is a cure for that which is in the chest (the heart).'"

H 3462, Ch. 1, h 8

Abu Ali al-Ash'ari has narrated from certain individuals of his people from al-Khashshab in a marfu' manner from the Imam, *'Alayhi al-Salam*, who has said the following:

"Abu 'Abd Allah, *'Alayhi al-Salam*, has said, 'I swear by Allah, Khilafat (leadership after the Holy Prophet) will never return to the family of abu Bakr and 'Umar. It will never return to descendents of 'Umayyah, and never to the children of Talhah and al-Zubayr. It is because they abandoned the Holy Quran, cancelled the noble traditions, and suspended the laws. The Messenger of Allah has said, "The Holy Quran is guidance against straying, clarification against blindness, stability against wavering, light against darkness, brightness in incidents, protection against destruction, intelligence against temptation, clear statement against mischief, and completion (of aim) in the world to the hereafter. In it there is your perfect religion. Whoever deviates from the Holy Quran is headed to the fire.'"

H 3463, Ch. 1, h 9

Hamid has narrated from al-Hassan ibn m h from Wuhayb ibn Hafs from abu Basir who has said the following:

"I heard abu 'Abd Allah, *'Alayhi al-Salam*, saying, 'The Holy Quran forbids and commands, it commands (people to go) to paradise and prohibits (people from going) to the fire.'"

H 3464, Ch. 1, h 10

Ali ibn Ibrahim has narrated from his father from Salih ibn al-Sindy from Ja'far from his father ibn Bashir from Sa'd al-'Iskaf who has said the following:

"The Messenger of Allah has said, 'The longer chapters of the Holy Quran were given to me as alternative to Torah, the chapters of one hundred verses in place of Injil, al-Mathani (Chapter 1) in place of al-Zabbur, in addition I was favored with sixty eight detailed chapters. It is dominant over other books, Torah was for Moses, Injil for Jesus and al-Zabur for David.'"

H 3465, Ch. 1, h 11

Abu Ali al-Ash'ari has narrated from Muhammad ibn Salim from Ahmad ibn al-Nadr from 'Amr ibn Shimr from Jabir from abu Ja'far, *'Alayhi al-Salam*, who has said the following:

"On the Day of Judgment the Holy Quran will come in the best shape and form. He will pass by the Muslims who will say, 'This man is from us.' He will pass toward the prophets who will say that he is of us, then he will pass toward the special angels who will say that he is one of us until he is before the Lord of Majesty, the Most Majestic, the Most Holy, and will say, 'O Lord, so and so son of so and so suffered from thirst, spent the night in vigil in the world so and so son of so and so did not suffer thirst and did not spend his night in vigil (for worship).' Allah, the Most Blessed, the Most High, will say, 'Admit them in paradise.' He will stand up and they will also rise and follow him. The believing people will be told, 'Read and climb.' The Imam said that the believing people will read and climb until they will reach their position that is for them and occupy their places.'"

H 3466, Ch. 1, h 12

Ali ibn Ibrahim has narrated from his father and A number of our people have narrated have narrated from Ahmad ibn Muhammad and Sahl ibn Ziyad all from ibn Mahbub from Malik ibn 'Atiyyah from Yunus ibn 'Ammar who has said the following:

"Abu 'Abd Allah, *'Alayhi al-Salam*, has said, 'On the Day of Judgment there will be three books of records: the book of the record of the good deeds, the book of the record of the bounties and the book of the record of the evil deeds. The records of the good deeds and the bounties will be compared and (in a particular case) the record of the bounties overwhelm all the good deeds and the record of the evil deeds will remain for the son of Adam's accountability, however, the Holy Quran will come forward in the best form and say, "O Lord, this believing servant would tire himself in reciting me and spend long hours during the night reading from me. During his Tahajjud (special prayer at night) his eyes would flood with tears, O Lord, make him happy as he would make me happy." The Imam said that the Most

Majestic, the Almighty, will say, 'My servant, open your right hand. He fills it up with contentment of Allah, the Most Majestic, the Almighty, his left hand with the favor of Allah and then it will be said to him, 'This is paradise and it is permissible for you. Read (from the Holy Quran) and climb up.' On reading a verse he will climb one degree (in happiness).'"

H 3467, Ch. 1, h 13

Ali ibn Ibrahim has narrated from his father and Ali ibn Muhammad al-Qasani all have narrated from al-Qasim ibn Muhammad from Sulayman ibn Dawud from Sufyan ibn 'Uyayna from al-Zuhri who has said the following:

"Ali ibn al-Husayn, *'Alayhi al-Salam*, has said, 'Having the Holy Quran with me I will have no fear or anxiety, even if everyone between the East and West may all die.' On reading verse four of Chapter 1, "The owner (of the kingdom) on the Day of Judgment," repeatedly he seemed as if he were about to die.'"

H 3468, Ch. 1, h 14

Ali ibn Ibrahim has narrated from his father ibn abu 'Umayr from Ibrahim ibn 'Abd al-Hamid from Ishaq ibn Ghalib who has said the following:

"Abu 'Abd Allah, *'Alayhi al-Salam*, has said, 'When Allah, the Most Majestic, the Most Holy, will gather together all the people of the past and later generation, a person the like of whom in beauty has never been seen will appear. The believing people will look at him (the Holy Quran) and say, 'This is one of us, the best that we have ever seen. He will come to them and pass them. The martyrs will look at him, and he will pass them until the last one among them and they will say, 'This is the Holy Quran.' He will pass all of them toward the messengers who will say, 'This is the Holy Quran,' he will pass them toward the angels who will say, 'This is the Holy Quran,' and he will pass them until he will approach the right side of the Throne and stand up at that point. The Almighty will say, 'I swear by my Majesty and Glory, and High status, this day I will honor those who had honored him and bring low those who had disregarded him.'"

Chapter 2 - The Excellence of the Carriers of the Holy Quran

H 3469, Ch. 2, h 1

Ali ibn Ibrahim has narrated from his father from al-Hassan ibn abu al-Husayn al-Farsi from Sulayman ibn Ja'far from his father al-Ja'fari from al-Sakuni from abu 'Abd Allah, *'Alayhi al-Salam*, who has said the following:

"The Messenger of Allah has said, 'People of the Holy Quran are of the highest degree among men, except the prophets and the messengers of Allah, thus, you should not consider them weak in the matters of their rights; with Allah, the Most Majestic, the Almighty, they have a special status.'"

H 3470, Ch. 2, h 2

A number of our people have narrated from Ahmad ibn Muhammad from Sahl ibn Ziyad all from ibn Mahbub from Jamil ibn Salih from al-Fudayl ibn Yasar from abu 'Abd Allah, *'Alayhi al-Salam*, who has said the following:

"One who has memorized the Holy Quran and follows its laws will be with the honorable angels who carry Allah's messages."

H 3471, Ch. 2, h 3

Through the same chain of narrators it is narrated from abu 'Abd Allah, *'Alayhi al-Salam*, who has said the following:

"The Messenger of Allah has said, 'Learn the Holy Quran; on the Day of Judgment it will come to his friends in the form of a most beautiful young person of pale complexion and will speak to his friend saying, "I am the Quran for which you kept awake so often and endured thirst during the heat of midday, dried up your mouth and let your tears flow. I will be with you whenever you will go. Every trader is after his trade. Today I look after the trade of everyone who had a deal with me. Honor will come to you from Allah, the Most Majestic, the Most Holy, as good news for you. The man will receive a crown and peace will be placed on his right hand and eternal life in paradise in his left hand and he will be dressed with two dresses of paradise, then he will be told, 'Read and climb.' For each verse that he will read he will climb up one degree and his parents, if they are of the believers, will each receive two dresses of paradise and they will be told that this is for your teaching the Holy Quran to your child.'"

H 3472, Ch. 2, h 4

Ibn Mahbub has narrated from Malik ibn 'Atiyyah from Minhal al-Qassab from abu 'Abd Allah, *'Alayhi al-Salam*, who has said the following:

"If a young believing person reads the Holy Quran, it mixes with his flesh and blood. Allah, the Most Majestic, the Most Holy, will include him among the honorable and virtuous carriers of the message of Allah and on the Day of Judgment the Holy Quran will be his supporter. The Holy Quran will say, 'O Lord, every worker has received the reward for his deeds except my worker. Provide him the most honorable reward.' Allah will then dress him with two dresses of paradise and crown him with the crown of honor and then ask the Holy Quran, 'Did We make you happy?' The Holy Quran will say, 'Lord, I wished for him better than this.' Allah will then give peace in his right hand, eternity in his left hand and will say to him read from the Holy Quran one verse and go one degree higher. Then the Holy Quran is asked again, 'Did we reward him good and make you happy?' The Holy Quran will say, 'Yes, Lord.'

"The Imam said, 'If one reads the Holy Quran very often and faces difficulties to memorize it due to weaker memory, Allah will give him twice as much reward.'"

H 3473, Ch. 2, h 5

Abu Ali al-Ash'ari has narrated from al-Hassan ibn Ali ibn Yusuf from ibn Thabit from 'Amr ibn Jami' from abu 'Abd Allah, *'Alayhi al-Salam*, who has said the following:

"The Messenger of Allah has said, 'The one expected to be the most humble in private and in public is the carrier of the Holy Quran, the one expected the most to perform prayer and fast in private and in public is the carrier of the Holy Quran. Then he called out loud, "O carrier of the Holy Quran, beautify with the Holy Quran for the sake of Allah, Allah will beautify you with it, do not beautify with it for the sake of people; Allah for this will cause you to be shunned. Whoever completes the Holy Quran, it is as if he has saved prophet-hood between his two sides, only divine revelation does not come to him. Whoever collects the Holy Quran has gained handsomely, thus, he toward one who behaves toward him ignorantly, does behave as such, with one who behaves toward him with anger, he does not do as such, and with one who behaves toward him irritably, he does not do so, however, he pardons, ignores, forgives, bears patiently out of respect for the Holy Quran. If one who has received the Holy Quran thinks that what others have received is better than what he has received, he has given significance to what Allah is has made worthless and has considered as worthless what Allah has given greatness.'"

H 3474, Ch. 2, h 6

Abu Ali al-Ash'ari has narrated from al-Hassan ibn Ali ibn 'Abd Allah from 'Ubays ibn Hisham who has said that Salih ibn al-Qammat has narrated from Aban ibn Taghlib has narrated from abu 'Abd Allah, *'Alayhi al-Salam*, who has said the following:

"People are of four kinds. I (the narrator) then asked, 'May Allah keep my soul in service for your cause, who are they?' The Imam said, 'A man who has received belief but not the Holy Quran, a man who has received the Holy Quran but not belief, a man who has received both belief and the Holy Quran and a man who has received none of then.' I (the narrator) then said, 'May Allah keep my soul in service for your cause, explain it to me.' The Imam said, 'The one who has received belief but not the Holy Quran is like a fruit that is sweet but has no aroma, the one who has received the Holy Quran but not belief is like pears that has a sweet fragrance but tastes bitter. The one who has received both the Holy Quran and belief is like citrus that tastes sweet and has a sweet fragrance. The one who has received neither the Holy Quran nor belief is like Hanzal (a bitter tasting fruit of a plant that tastes bitter and smells bitter).'"

H 3475, Ch. 2, h 7

Ali ibn Ibrahim has narrated from his father and Ali ibn Muhammad al-Qasani all have narrated from al-Qasim ibn Muhammad from Sulayman ibn Dawud from Sufyan ibn 'Uyayna from al-Zuhri who has said the following:

"Once I asked Ali ibn al-Husayn, *'Alayhi al-Salam*, 'What deed is more virtuous?' He said, 'Al-Hall al-Murtahal.' I then asked, 'What is al-Hall al-Murtahal?' The Imam said, 'It is one who opens the Holy Quran and completes reading, whenever he begins he arrives at the end of the Holy Quran.' The Imam said that the Messenger of Allah has said, 'If one who has received the Holy Quran would think that what others have received is better than what he has received, he has considered something very great as insignificant, and something insignificant as very great.'"

H 3476, Ch. 2, h 8

Muhammad ibn Yahya has narrated from Ahmad ibn Muhammad from Sulayman ibn Rashid from his father from Mu'awiyah ibn 'Ammar who has said the following:

"Abu 'Abd Allah, *'Alayhi al-Salam*, once said to me, 'If anyone reads the Holy Quran, he is wealthy and there is no poverty thereafter, otherwise, he will never be wealthy.'"

H 3477, Ch. 2, h 9

Abu Ali al-Ash'ari has narrated from Muhammad ibn 'Abd al-Jabbar from ibn abu Najran from abu Jamilah from Jabir from abu Ja'far, *'Alayhi al-Salam*, who has said the following:

"The Messenger of Allah has said, 'O community of the readers of the Holy Quran be pious before Allah, the Most Majestic, the Most Holy, in the matters of the responsibility that He has placed upon you toward His book. I will be questioned and you will be questioned. I will be questioned about the preaching of the message and you will be questioned about your responsibility toward the book of Allah and my Sunnah (the laws).'"

H 3478, Ch. 2, h 10

Ali ibn Ibrahim has narrated from his father from al-Qasim ibn Muhammad from Sulayman ibn Dawud al-Minqari from Hafs who has said the following:

"I heard Musa ibn Ja'far, *'Alayhi al-Salam*, asking a man, 'Do you like to live forever in this world'? The man said, 'Yes, I do so.' The Imam asked, 'Why would you do so?' The man said, 'So that I can read Chapter 112 of the Holy Quran.' The Imam, *'Alayhi al-Salam*, remained calm for a while and after an hour said, 'O Hafs, if any of our Shi'a (followers) do not do good in reading the Holy Quran, in his grave he will receive instruction to read so that Allah will raise him with his proper status; the positions and degrees in paradise are proportionate to the verses of the Holy Quran. One will be told to read and climb. He then reads and climbs up.' Hafs has said, 'I never saw anyone more afraid for himself than Musa ibn Ja'far, *'Alayhi al-Salam*, or more hopeful in all people. His reading was full of sadness. When reading the Holy Quran he seemed like addressing (speaking to) a human being.'"

H 3479, Ch. 2, h 11

Ali has narrated from his father from al-Nawfali from al-Sakuni from abu 'Abd Allah, *'Alayhi al-Salam*, who has said the following:

"The Messenger of Allah has said, 'The carriers of the Holy Quran will be the most knowledgeable people of paradise, the assiduously working people will be the leaders in paradise and the messengers will be the masters of the people of paradise.'"

Chapter 3 - Those Who Learn the Holy Quran with Difficulties

H 3480, Ch. 3, h 1

A number of our people have narrated from Ahmad ibn Muhammad and Sahl ibn Ziyad all from ibn Mahbub from Jamil ibn Salih from al-Fudayl ibn Yasar who has said the following:

"I heard abu 'Abd Allah, *'Alayhi al-Salam*, saying, 'Those who face difficulty memorizing the Holy Quran due to lesser ability of memorization will be rewarded twofold.'"

H 3481, Ch. 3, h 2

Ali ibn Ibrahim has narrated from his father from ibn abu 'Umayr from Mansur ibn Yunus from al-Sabbah ibn Sayabah who has said the following:

"I heard abu 'Abd Allah, *'Alayhi al-Salam*, saying, 'One for whom memorizing the Holy Quran is difficult, his reward is twofold and those for whom it is easy, they are with the pioneers (the earliest Muslims).'"

H 3482, Ch. 3, h 3

Ali ibn Ibrahim has narrated from his father from Ahmad ibn Muhammad from Sulaym al-Farra' from a man from abu 'Abd Allah, *'Alayhi al-Salam,* who has said the following:

"Abu 'Abd Allah, *'Alayhi al-Salam,* has said, 'It is worthwhile for a Muslim to learn the Holy Quran before his death or should be in the process of learning.'"

Chapter 4 - One Who Memorizes the Holy Quran Then Forgets

H 3483, Ch. 4, h 1

A number of our people have narrated from Ahmad ibn Muhammad an Abu Ali al-Ash'ari from Muhammad ibn 'Abd al-Jabbar all from ibn Faddal from abu Ishaq, Th'labah ibn Maymun from Ya'qub al-Ahmar who has said the following:

"Once I said to abu Abdullah, *'Alayhi al-Salam,* 'May Allah keep my soul in service for your cause, I had learned the Holy Quran but now it is gone (forgotten). Pray to Allah, the Most Majestic, the Most Holy, so I learn it again?' The narrator has said that the Imam seemed shocked and said, 'May Allah and all of us help you learn the Holy Quran again and we are about ten people.' The Imam then said, 'If one knows one chapter of the Holy Quran and then leaves it alone, on the Day of Judgment that chapter will come to him in the best form and will greet him. The man will ask, 'Who are you?' It will say, 'I am chapter so and so of the Holy Quran. If you had not left me alone, I would have taken you with me to this high rank.' The Imam then said, 'You must hold fast to the Holy Quran.'"

H 3484, Ch. 4, h 2

Ali ibn Ibrahim has narrated from his father from ibn abu 'Umayr from abu al-Maghra' from abu Basir who has said the following:

"Abu 'Abd Allah, *'Alayhi al-Salam,* has said, 'If one forgets a chapter from the Holy Quran it will appear to him in the best form and high position in paradise. When he will see it he will say how beautiful you are! I wish you were mine.' It will ask, 'Do you not know me? I am chapter so and so, had you not forgotten me I would have raised you to this.'"

H 3485, Ch. 4, h 3

Ibn abu 'Umayr has narrated from Ibrahim ibn 'Abd al-Hamid from Ya'qub al-Ahmar who has said the following:

"Once I said to abu 'Abd Allah, *'Alayhi al-Salam,* 'I am indebted a great deal and due to worries I am about to forget the Holy Quran.' The Imam, *'Alayhi al-Salam,* said, 'The Holy Quran, the Holy Quran! On the Day of Judgment the chapter and the verse of the Holy Quran will come and say, 'Had you not forgotten me I would have taken you today to such and such high ranks in paradise.'"

H 3486, Ch. 4, h 4

Hamid ibn Ziyad has narrated from al-Hassan ibn Muhammad ibn Sama'a and a number of our people have narrated from Ahmad ibn Muhammad all from Muhsin ibn Ahmad from Aban ibn 'Uthman from ibn abu Ya'qub who has said the following:

"I heard abu 'Abd Allah, *'Alayhi al-Salam,* saying, 'If a man knows a chapter then forgets it or just leaves it and will enter paradise, it will appear above him in the best form and ask, "Do you know me?" He will say, 'No, I do not know you.' It will say, "I am chapter so and so, you did not follow me and left me. I swear by

Allah, had you acted upon my instructions I would have raised you to this degree, pointing with his hand to the above.'"

H 3487, Ch. 4, h 5

Abu Ali al-Ash'ari has narrated from al-Hassan ibn Ali ibn 'Abd Allah from al-'Abbas ibn 'Amir from al-Hajjaj al-Khashshab from abu Kahmas al-Haythami ibn 'Ubayd who has said the following:

"Once I asked abu 'Abd Allah, *'Alayhi al-Salam*, about a man who reads the Holy Quran and then forgets and I repeated it before him three times asking, 'Is it an offense on his part?' The Imam said, 'No.'"

H 3488, Ch. 4, h 6

Muhammad ibn Yahya has narrated from Ahmad ibn Muhammad ibn 'Isa from Muhammad ibn Khalid and al-Husayn ibn Sa'id all from al-Nadr ibn Suwayd from Yahya al-Halabi from 'Abd Allah ibn Muskan from Ya'qub al-Ahmar who has said the following:

"Once I said to abu 'Abd Allah, *'Alayhi al-Salam*, 'May Allah keep my soul in service for your cause, I am facing such problems and difficulties that I forget so many good things even some of the Holy Quran.' The Imam was shocked upon my mentioning the Holy Quran and said, 'If a man forgets a chapter of the Holy Quran, on the Day of Judgment that chapter will appear to him with a certain rank and offers him the greeting of peace. The man will ask, 'Who are you?' The chapter of the Holy Quran will say, 'I am chapter so and so of the Holy Quran which you forgot, and I wish you had not forgotten me; today I could have taken you to such and such high ranks. He will point to a certain rank.' The Imam then said, 'You must hold fast to the Holy Quran and learn it. Certain people learn the Holy Quran so that others call him a very good reader of the Holy Quran. Others learn the Holy Quran so that people praise him for his vocal attractiveness in reciting the Holy Quran. There is nothing good in all of this. Certain people learn the Holy Quran and at night they stand upon their feet with the Holy Quran as well as during the day and they are not concerned whether others know this about them or not.'"

Chapter 5 - Reciting the Holy Quran

H 3489, Ch. 5, h 1

Ali has narrated from his father from Hammad from Hariz from abu 'Abd Allah, *'Alayhi al-Salam*, who has said the following:

"The Holy Quran is a covenant of Allah with His creatures. A Muslim must look at his covenant and read fifty verses every day."

H 3490, Ch. 5, h 2

Ali ibn Ibrahim has narrated from his father and Ali ibn Muhammad all from al-Qasim ibn Muhammad from Sulayman ibn Dawud from Hafs ibn Ghiyath from al-Zuhri who has said the following:

"I heard Ali ibn al-Husayn, *'Alayhi al-Salam*, saying, 'Verses of the Holy Quran are treasures, whenever a treasure is opened you should look into it.'"

Chapter 6 - The Houses Wherein the Holy Quran is Read

H 3491, Ch. 6, h 1
A number of our people have narrated from Ahmad ibn Muhammad from Ali ibn al-Hakam from al-Fudayl ibn 'Uthman from Layth ibn abu Sulaym in a marfu' manner from the Holy Prophet who has said the following:

"Light up your homes by means of reading the Holy Quran and do not turn them into graves as the Jews and Christians had done. They pray in churches and synagogues and leave their homes of no use. If reading of the Holy Quran is more often in a house, goodness increases therein, its inhabitants receive expanded sustenance and it will shine to the inhabitants of the heaven just as stars shine for the people of this world (earth).'"

H 3492, Ch. 6, h 2
Muhammad ibn Yahya has narrated from Ahmad ibn Muhammad ibn 'Isa from Muhammad ibn Khalid and al-Husayn ibn Sa'id all from al-Nadr ibn Suwayd from Yahya ibn 'Imran al-Halabi from 'Abd al-'Ala' Mawla 'Ale (family) S'am from abu 'Abd Allah, *'Alayhi al-Salam*, who has said the following:

"A house wherein a Muslim reads the Holy Quran is looked upon by the inhabitants of heavens, just as the inhabitants of earth like to look at a shining star in the skies.'"

H 3493, Ch. 6, h 3
Muhammad ibn Ahmad and A number of our people have narrated from have narrated from Sahl ibn Ziyad all from Ja'far ibn Muhammad ibn 'Ubayd Allah from ibn al-Qaddah from abu 'Abd Allah, *'Alayhi al-Salam*, who has said the following:

"Amir al-Mu'minin, Ali ibn abu Talib, *'Alayhi al-Salam*, has said, 'A house wherein the Holy Quran is read, Allah, the Most Majestic, the Most Holy, is spoken of, blessings therein increase, the angels come down therein and Satan keeps away from it. It shines to the inhabitants of the heaven just as stars shine to the people of the earth. A house where the Holy Quran is not read, and Allah, the Most Majestic, the Most Holy, is not spoken of, its blessings reduce, angels leave it and devils crowd therein.'"

Chapter 7 - The Reward for Reading the Holy Quran

H 3494, Ch. 7, h 1
A number of our people have narrated from Ahmad ibn Muhammad, Sahl ibn Ziyad and Ali ibn Ibrahim has narrated from his father all from ibn Mahbub from 'Abd Allah ibn Sinan from Mu'adh ibn Muslim from 'Abd Allah ibn Sulayman from abu Ja'far, *'Alayhi al-Salam*, who has said the following:

"If one reads the Holy Quran in prayer standing Allah will write down for him the reward for one hundred good deeds for each letter. If one reads the Holy Quran in prayer sitting Allah will write down for him the reward for fifty good deeds for each letter and if one reads without being in prayer, Allah will write for him the reward for ten good deeds for each letter.'"

Ibn Mahbub has said, "I have heard this Hadith from Mu'adh the way ibn Sinan has narrated."

H 3495, Ch. 7, h 2

Ibn Mahbub has narrated from Jamil ibn Salih from al-Fudayl ibn Yasar from abu 'Abd Allah, *'Alayhi al-Salam*, who has said the following:

"Why should any thing prevent a business man working in the market place from reading one chapter from the Holy Quran before going to sleep when he is home? For the reading of each verse the reward for ten good deeds will be written down for him and ten of his evil deeds will be deleted."

H 3496, Ch. 7, h 3

Muhammad ibn Yahya has narrated from Ahmad ibn Muhammad ibn 'Isa from Ali ibn al-Hakam or others Sayf 'Umayrah from a man from Jabir from Musafir from Bashir ibn Ghalib al-Asadi from al-Husayn ibn Ali, *'Alayhi al-Salam*, who has said the following:

"Al-Husayn ibn Ali, *'Alayhi al-Salam*, has said, 'Whoever reads from the Holy Quran in his prayer in a standing position, Allah, the Most Majestic, the Most Holy, writes down for him the reward for one hundred good deeds for each letter and if one reads from the Holy Quran without being in prayer, Allah writes down for him the reward for ten good deeds for each letter, and if one listens to the reading of the Holy Quran, Allah writes down for him the reward for one good deed for each letter.

"If one completes reading the whole Quran at night, the angels pray for him until morning, and if he completes during the day the angels pray for him until night and his prayers are accepted. This is better for him than all that is between the heaven and earth.' I (the narrator) then said, 'This is for one who reads the Holy Quran. What is for one who does not read?' The Imam said, 'O brother from bnu Asad, Allah is generous, glorious and magnanimous if one reads whatever he can, Allah will reward him.'"

H 3497, Ch. 7, h 4

Muhammad ibn Yahya from Muhammad ibn al-Husayn from al-Nadr ibn Suwayd from Khalid ibn Mad al-Qalanisi from abu Hamza al-Thumali from abu Ja'far, *'Alayhi al-Salam*, who has said the following:

"If one, while in Makkah, reads the Holy Quran beginning on a Friday and completes reading the next Friday or within less or more time ending on Friday the reward for it will be written like the reward for a reading commencing from the first ever Friday in the world to the last Friday that there will ever be. The same will be the reward for reading in other days."

H 3498, Ch. 7, h 5

Muhammad ibn Yahya has narrated from Ahmad ibn Muhammad ibn 'Isa from Muhammad ibn Khalid and al-Husayn ibn Sa'id all from al-Nadr ibn Suwayd from Yahya al-Halabi from Muhammad ibn Marwan from Sa'D ibn Tarif from abu Ja'far, *'Alayhi al-Salam*, who has said the following:

"The Messenger of Allah has said, 'One who reads ten verses from the Holy Quran in a night he is not written of the neglectful people. If one reads fifty verses, he is written of those who speak of Allah. If one reads one hundred verses, he is written of the pleading people before Allah. If one reads two hundred verses, he is written of those who express humility before Allah. If one reads three hundred verses he is written of the successful ones. If one reads five hundred verses, he is written of those striving for the cause of Allah. If one reads one thousand verses one Qintar of Tibr, gold will be his reward. A Qintar is equal to fifteen thousand Mithqal of gold. A Mithqal is equal to twenty four Qirat and the smallest Qirat is of the size of the mountain of 'Uhud and the largest equals to the size of space between earth and the sky.'"

H 3499, Ch. 7, h 6

Abu Ali al-Ash'ari has narrated from Muhammad ibn 'Abd al-Jabbar and Muhammad ibn Yahya from Ahmad ibn Muhammad all from Ali ibn Hadid from Mansur from Muhammad ibn Bashir - who has narrated such Hadith from abu 'Abd Allah, *'Alayhi al-Salam*, also from Ali ibn al-Husayn, *'Alayhi al-Salam*, who has said the following:

"If one listens to the reading of one letter from the book of Allah, the Most Majestic, the Most Holy, without reading, Allah writes for him the reward for one good deed, deletes one of his evil deeds and raises for him one degree. If one reads looking but without audible voice Allah writes for him the reward for one good deed for each letter, deletes one of his evil deeds and raises him one degree. If one learns one clear letter Allah writes for him the reward for ten good deeds, deletes his ten evil deeds and raises him ten degrees. The Imam said, 'I do not say, 'for every verse.' I say for every letter. 'B', 'T' and so forth are letters.' The Imam said, 'If one reads one clear letter in prayer in a sitting position Allah writes for him the reward for fifty good deeds, deletes fifty of his evil deeds and raises for him fifty degrees. If one reads one letter in prayer standing, Allah, for each letter, writes for him the reward for one hundred good deeds, deletes one hundred of his evil deeds and raises him one hundred degrees. If one completes reading the Holy Quran, for him there is an accepted prayer, sooner or later.'

"I (the narrator) then said to the Imam, 'May Allah keep my soul in service for your cause, is it completing the whole of it'? The Imam said, 'Yes, it is completing the whole of the Holy Quran.'"

H 3500, Ch. 7, h 7

Mansur has narrated from abu 'Abd Allah, *'Alayhi al-Salam*, the following:

"I heard abu 'Abd Allah, *'Alayhi al-Salam*, saying, 'The Messenger of Allah has said, "Complete reading of the Holy Quran is reading to the extent that you know.'"

Chapter 8 - Reading the Holy Quran from a Copy

H 3501, Ch. 8, h 1

A number of our people have narrated from Ahmad ibn Muhammad from Ya'qub ibn Yazid in a marfu' manner from abu 'Abd Allah, *'Alayhi al-Salam*, who has said the following:

"If one reads the Holy Quran from a copy, he benefits from his eyesight, and his parents receive relief even if they are unbelievers."

H 3502, Ch. 8, h 2

It is narrated from him (narrator of the Hadith above) from Ali ibn al-Husayn from al-Hassan al-Darir from Hammad ibn 'Isa from abu 'Abd Allah, *'Alayhi al-Salam*, who has said the following:

"Abu 'Abd Allah, *'Alayhi al-Salam*, has said, 'I love the presence of a copy of the Holy Quran in a house; Allah, the Most Majestic, the Most Holy, thereby wards off devils.'"

H 3503, Ch. 8, h 3

A number of our people have narrated from Sahl ibn Ziyad from ibn Faddal from those whom he has mentioned (in his book) from abu 'Abd Allah, *'Alayhi al-Salam*, who has said the following:

"Three things will complain before Allah, the Most Majestic, the Most Holy: A Mosque where no one of the neighborhood performs prayer, a scholar among the ignorant people and the copy of the Holy Quran on which dust has accumulated and no one reads it."

H 3504, Ch. 8, h 4

Ali ibn Muhammad has narrated from ibn Jumhur from Muhammad ibn 'Umar ibn Mas'adah from al-Hassan ibn Rashid from his grandfather from abu 'Abd Allah, *'Alayhi al-Salam*, who has said the following:

"Reading of the Holy Quran from a copy relieves suffering punishment of one's parents even if they are unbelievers."

H 3505, Ch. 8, h 5

A number of our people have narrated from Sahl ibn Ziyad from Yahya ibn al-Mubarak from 'Abd Allah ibn Jabalah from Mu'awiyah ibn Wahab from Ishaq ibn 'Ammar who has said the following:

"Once I said to abu 'Abd Allah, *'Alayhi al-Salam*, 'May Allah keep my soul in service for your cause, I memorize the Holy Quran by heart and read from my memory, is that more virtuous or looking on a copy of the Holy Quran?' The narrator has said that the Imam said to me, 'It is better to look in a copy. Have you not heard that looking at a copy of the Holy Quran is an act of worship?'"

Chapter 9 - Reading the Holy Quran with Elocution and Attractive Tone of Voice

H 3506, Ch. 9, h 1

Ali ibn Ibrahim has narrated from his father from Ali ibn Ma'bad from Wasil ibn Sulayman who has said the following:

"Once I asked abu 'Abd Allah, *'Alayhi al-Salam*, about the words of Allah, the Most Majestic, the Most Holy, 'Read the Holy Quran in a distinct elocution (tartil). . . .' (73:4) The Imam said, 'Amir al-Mu'minin, Ali ibn abu Talib, *'Alayhi al-Salam*, has said, "It is to pronounce clearly and distinctively. Do not rush it like poems or scatter like pebbles but shake up your hard hearts thereby instead of your rushing to finish the chapter.'"

H 3507, Ch. 9, h 2

Ali ibn Ibrahim has narrated from his father from ibn abu 'Umayr from those whom he has mentioned (in his book) from abu 'Abd Allah who has said the following:

"The Holy Quran has come down with sadness, thus, you should read it with sadness."

H 3508, Ch. 9, h 3

Ali ibn Muhammad has narrated from Ibrahim al-Ahmar from 'Abd Allah ibn Hammad from 'Abd Allah ibn Sinan from abu 'Abd Allah, *'Alayhi al-Salam*, who has said the following:

"Read the Holy Quran with Arabic accent and voice. You must not read it with the accent of the sinful people who commit major sins. After me there will come people who will read the Holy Quran like singing, lamentations and in the monkish manner, which does not pass even their throats toward their hearts that are upside down and so are the hearts of those who like them."

H 3509, Ch. 9, h 4

A number of our people have narrated from Sahl ibn Ziyad from Muhammad ibn Hassan ibn Shammun who has that narrated to him Ali ibn Muhammad al-Nawfali from abu al-Hassan, *'Alayhi al-Salam,* who has said the following:

"Once accents and voices were mentioned before abu al-Hassan, *'Alayhi al-Salam,* and he said, 'Once Ali ibn al-Husayn, *'Alayhi al-Salam,* was reading and someone passing by suffered a shock due to the beauty of his voice. If the Imam were to manifest such reading people could not bear its beauty.' I (the narrator) then said, 'The Messenger of Allah during his prayer would not raise his voice in reading the Holy Quran.' The Imam said, 'The Messenger of Allah would make people behind him do only what they could tolerate.'"

H 3510, Ch. 9, h 5

Ali ibn Ibrahim has narrated from his father from ibn abu 'Umayr from Sulaym al-Farra' from those whom he has mentioned (in his book) from abu 'Abd Allah, *'Alayhi al-Salam,* who has said the following:

"Abu 'Abd Allah, *'Alayhi al-Salam,* has said, 'Read the Holy Quran with clarity; it is Arabic.'"

H 3511, Ch. 9, h 6

Ali ibn Ibrahim has narrated from his father from Ali ibn Ma'bad from 'Abd Allah ibn al-Qasim from 'Abd Allah ibn Sinan from abu 'Abd Allah, *'Alayhi al-Salam,* who has said the following:

"Allah, the Most Majestic, the Most Holy, sent revelation to Moses son of 'Imran, peace be upon him, 'Whenever you stand before me, do so like a humble and poor person, whenever you read the Torah, read it with sad voice.'"

H 3512, Ch. 9, h 7

It is narrated from him (narrator of the Hadith above) from Ali ibn Ma'bad from 'Abd Allah ibn al-Qasim from 'Abd Allah ibn Sinan from abu 'Abd Allah, *'Alayhi al-Salam,* who has said the following:

"The Messenger of Allah has said, 'What my followers have received is no less than three things: Beauty, attractive voice and memorization.'"

H 3513, Ch. 9, h 8

It is narrated from him (narrator of the Hadith above) from Ali ibn Ma'bad from Yunus from 'Abd Allah ibn Muskan from abu Basir from abu 'Abd Allah, *'Alayhi al-Salam,* who has said the following:

"The Holy Prophet has said, 'The most beautiful thing in beauty is beautiful hair and the attractive tone of voice.'"

H 3514, Ch. 9, h 9

It is narrated from him (narrator of the Hadith above) from Ali Ma'bad from 'Abd Allah ibn al-Qasim from 'Abd Allah ibn Sinan from abu 'Abd Allah, *'Alayhi al-Salam,* who has said the following:

"The Holy Prophet has said, 'For everything there is an ornament, the ornament of (reading) the Holy Quran is attractive tone of voice.'"

H 3515, Ch. 9, h 10

A number of our people have narrated from Sahl ibn Ziyad from Musa ibn 'Umar al-Sayqal from Muhammad ibn 'Isa from al-Sakuni from Ali ibn Isma'il al-Maythami from a man from abu 'Abd Allah, *'Alayhi al-Salam,* who has said the following:

"Allah, the Most Majestic, the Most Holy, never sent a messenger who did not have attractive voice."

H 3516, Ch. 9, h 11

Sahl ibn Ziyad has narrated from al-Hajjal from Ali ibn 'Aqabah from a man from abu 'Abd Allah, *'Alayhi al-Salam*, who has said the following:

"Ali ibn al-Husayn, *'Alayhi al-Salam*, was the best among the people for his attractive voice in reading the Holy Quran. The water carrier would stop in front of his door to listen to his reading and abu Ja'far, *'Alayhi al-Salam*, was the best among the people for his attractive voice."

H 3517, Ch. 9, h 12

Hamid ibn Ziyad has narrated from al-Hassan ibn Muhammad al-Asadi from Ahmad ibn al-Hassan al-Maythami from Aban ibn 'Uthman from Muhammad ibn al-Fudayl who has said the following:

"Abu 'Abd Allah, *'Alayhi al-Salam*, has said, 'It is undesirable (makruh) to read Chapter 112 in one breath.'"

H 3518, Ch. 9, h 13

Ali ibn Ibrahim has narrated from his father from ibn Mahbub from Ali ibn abu Hamza from abu Basir who has said the following:

"Once I said to abu Ja'far, *'Alayhi al-Salam*, 'When I read the Holy Quran, I raise my voice. Satan comes and says, "You are only showing this off to people and your family."' The Imam said, 'O abu Muhammad, read in a middle of the way reading, so your family may hear. Give turns to your voice in reading the Holy Quran; Allah, the Most Majestic, the Most Holy, loves an attractive voice in which there is fluctuations and oscillations.'"

Chapter 10 - People Fainting (Reading the Holy Quran)

H 3519, Ch. 10, h 1

A number of our people have narrated from Sahl ibn Ziyad from Ya'qub ibn Ishaq al-Dabbiy from abu 'Imran al-Armani from 'Abd Allah ibn al-Hakam from Jabir who has said the following:

"Once I said to abu Ja'far, *'Alayhi al-Salam*, 'There are people when remembering something from the Holy Quran or is mentioned before them they suffer a shock to the extent that even if their hands or legs are cut they do not realize.' The Imam said, 'Glory belongs to Allah. That is from Satan. That is not how believing people are described. It is only softening, tender feelings, a few tears and anxiety.'"

Abu Ali al-Ash'ari has narrated from Hassan from abu 'Imran al-Armani from 'Abd Allah ibn al-Hakam from Jabir from abu Ja'far, *'Alayhi al-Salam*, a similar Hadith.

Chapter 11 - Within What Period of Time the Holy Quran Should Be Read and Completed?

H 3520, Ch. 11, h 1

Ali ibn Ibrahim has narrated from his father from Hammad from al-Husayn ibn al-Mukhtar from Muhammad ibn 'Abd Allah who has said the following:

"Once I asked abu 'Abd Allah, *'Alayhi al-Salam*, 'Can I read the Holy Quran in one night?' The Imam said, 'I do not like your reading it in less than a month's time.'"

H 3521, Ch. 11, h 2

A number of our people have narrated from Sahl ibn Ziyad from certain individuals of his people from Ali ibn Hamza who has said the following:

"Once I went in the presence of abu 'Abd Allah, *'Alayhi al-Salam*, and abu Basir said to the Imam, 'May Allah keep my soul in service for your cause, can I read the Holy Quran in one night in the month of Ramadan?' The Imam said, 'No.' He then asked, 'Can I read it in two nights?' The Imam said, 'No.' He then asked, 'Can I read it in three nights?' The Imam said, 'Haa' pointing with his hand meaning, "yes, you can." The Imam then said, 'O abu Muhammad, for the month of Ramadan there is respect and rights which is unlike the other months. Among the companions of Muhammad, *'Alayhi al-Salam*, there were those who would read the Holy Quran in one month or less. The Holy Quran is not read in a big rush. It should be read with proper elocution and distinct pronunciations. When you come across a verse that speaks of paradise you should pause and ask Allah, the Most Majestic, the Most Holy, to give it to you and when you come across a verse that speaks of the fire, pause and seek protection with Allah against it.'"

H 3522, Ch. 11, h 3

Muhammad ibn Yahya has narrated from Muhammad ibn al-Husayn from Ali ibn al-Nu'Man from Ya'qub ibn Shu'ayb from Husayn ibn Khalid who has said the following:

"Once I asked abu 'Abd Allah, *'Alayhi al-Salam*, 'In how many days should one complete reading the Holy Quran?' The Imam said, 'You may read it in five or seven days. I, however, have a copy of the Holy Quran that is divided into fourteen parts.'"

H 3523, Ch. 11, h 4

A number of our people have narrated from Ahmad ibn Muhammad ibn Khalid from Yahya ibn Ibrahim ibn abu al-Balad from his father from Ali ibn al-Mughirah who has said the following:

"Once I asked abu al-Hassan, *'Alayhi al-Salam*, 'My father once asked your grandfather about reading all of the Holy Quran in one night.' '(Do you mean it to happen) every night?' Your grandfather inquired. 'Yes, in the month of Ramadan.' My father replied. Your grandfather asked him, 'In the month of Ramadan?' My father said, 'Yes, in the month of Ramadan if I could.' My father would read the Holy Quran forty times in the whole month of Ramadan. After my father I would read the Holy Quran sometimes more and sometimes less than he did, as I would get a chance within my work, activities and laziness. On 'id day (after the month of Ramadan) I would assign the reward for reading the Holy Quran once for the Holy prophet, one for Imam Ali, one for Al-Sayyidah Fatimah and one for each Imam until yourself and I assigned the reward for reciting the Holy Quran once for you from the time I am doing this. Will there be anything for me in this? The Imam said, 'On the Day of Judgment, you will be with them.' 'Allah is greater than can be described, this much for me!' I exclaimed. The Imam, *'Alayhi al-Salam*, said three times, 'Yes.'"

H 3524, Ch. 11, h 5

Muhammad ibn Yahya has narrated from Ahmad ibn Muhammad from Ali ibn al-Hakam from Ali ibn abu Hamza who has said the following:

"Once, abu Basir asked abu 'Abd Allah, *'Alayhi al-Salam*, when I was also present, 'May Allah keep my soul in service for your cause, can I read the Holy Quran in one night?' The Imam said, 'No.' He then asked, 'Can I read it in two nights?' The Imam said, 'No,' until he reached six nights, the Imam, *'Alayhi al-Salam*, made a hand gesture saying 'Ha'a,' (a hint for approval). Then the Imam, *'Alayhi al-Salam*, said, 'O abu Muhammad, note that among the companions of Muhammad, *'Alayhi al-Salam*, before you, there were those who would read the Holy Quran once in a month or less. The Holy Quran is not read in a big rush but it is read with proper elocution and distinct pronunciation. When you come across a verse that speaks of the fire you pause and ask Allah for protection.' Abu Basir then asked, 'Can I read the Holy Quran in the month of Ramadan once every night?' The Imam said, 'No.' He then asked, 'Can I read it in two nights?' The Imam said, 'No.' He then asked, 'Can I read it in three nights?' The Imam said, 'Ha'a,' with a hand gesture for approval saying, 'Yes, the month of Ramadan is not like the other months. It has its rights and respect. Increase in prayer as much as you can.'"

Chapter 12 - The Holy Quran Will be Raised as it Was Sent Down

H 3525, Ch. 12, h 1

Ali ibn Ibrahim has narrated from his father from al-Nawfali from al-Sakuni from abu 'Abd Allah, *'Alayhi al-Salam*, who has said the following:

"The Holy Prophet has said, 'A non-Arab of my followers reads the Holy Quran in his non-Arabic language, but the angels raise it in Arabic.'"

H 3526, Ch. 12, h 2

A number of our people have narrated from Sahl ibn Ziyad from Muhammad ibn Sulayman from certain individuals of his people from who has said the following:

"Once I said to abu al-Hassan, *'Alayhi al-Salam*, 'May Allah keep my soul in service for your cause, we hear certain verses of the Holy Quran that we do not have with us as we hear them and we cannot read as good as we receive from you. Are we committing sins in this matter?' The Imam said, 'No, you are not committing any sins, read as you have learned. The one to teach you will come soon.'"

Chapter 13 - The Excellence of the Holy Quran

H 3527, Ch. 13, h 1

Muhammad ibn Yahya has narrated from Ahmad ibn Muhammad ibn 'Isa from Badr from Muhammad ibn Marwan from abu Ja'far, *'Alayhi al-Salam*, who has said the following:

"Whoever reads Chapter 112 of the Holy Quran once receives blessings. Whoever reads it twice, he and his family receive blessings. Whoever reads it three times, he, his family and his neighbors receive blessings. Whoever reads it twelve times, Allah will build for him twelve palaces in paradise and the keepers will say, 'We should go and see the palaces of our brother so and so.' Whoever reads it one hundred times his sins of twenty-five years will be forgiven, except murders and properties. Whoever reads it four hundred times will receive a reward equal to that for four hundred martyrs, each of whom martyred after the destruction of his horse. Whoever reads it one thousand times in one day and night will not die before seeing his place in paradise or is shown for him (to a third party).'"

H 3528, Ch. 13, h 2

Hamid ibn Ziyad has narrated from al-Husayn ibn Muhammad from Ahmad ibn al-Hassan al-Maythami from Ya'qub ibn Shu'ayb from abu 'Abd Allah, '*Alayhi al-Salam*, who has said the following:

"When Allah, the Most Majestic, the Most Holy, commanded certain verses of the Holy Quran to descend to earth, they clung to the Throne asking, 'O Lord, why are You sending us to people of sins and evil deeds.' Allah, the Most Majestic, the Most Holy, inspired them to descend saying, 'I swear by My Majesty and Glory that any Shi'a (followers) of Ahl al-Bayt (family of Muhammad, '*Alayhim al-Salam*), who reads you after an obligatory prayer every day I will look at him with My hidden eyes (special favor) everyday seventy times and in every look fulfill his seventy wishes and accept him with whatever sins he may have. The verses are Chapter One of the Holy Quran, verses 18-19 and 26-27 of Chapter 3 and verse 255 of Chapter 2 of the Holy Quran.'"

H 3529, Ch. 13, h 3

Abu Ali al-Ash'ari has narrated from Muhammad ibn Hassan from Isma'il ibn Mehran from al-Hassan ibn Ali ibn abu Hamza from Muhammad ibn Sukayn from 'Amr ibn Shimr from Jabir who has said the following:

"I heard abu Ja'far, '*Alayhi al-Salam*, saying, 'Whoever reads all the chapters that begin with the word, 'Sabbaha, or Yusabbihu' before going to sleep will not die before seeing the twelfth Imam, and when he dies, he will be in the neighborhood of Muhammad, '*Alayhi al-Salam*.'"

H 3530, Ch. 13, h 4

Muhammad ibn Yahya has narrated from Muhammad ibn al-Husayn from Ali ibn al-Nu'Man from 'Abd Allah ibn Talhah from Ja'far, '*Alayhi al-Salam*, who has said the following:

"The Messenger of Allah has said, 'Whoever reads Chapter 112 of the Holy Quran before going to sleep one hundred times, Allah forgives fifty years of his sins.'"

H 3531, Ch. 13, h 5

Hamid ibn Ziyad has narrated from al-Khashshab from ibn Baqqah from Mu'adh from 'Amr ibn Jami' in a marfu' manner from Ali ibn al-Husayn, '*Alayhi al-Salam*, who has said the following:

"The Messenger of Allah has said, 'Whoever reads four verses from the beginning of Chapter 2 of the Holy Quran, verse 255- 257 and three verses from the end of this Chapter, he will not experience anything in his own self or property that he dislikes, Satan will not approach him and he will not forget the Holy Quran.'"

H 3532, Ch. 13, h 6

Muhammad ibn Yahya has narrated from Ahmad ibn Muhammad from ibn Mahbub from Sayf ibn 'Umayrah from a man from abu Ja'far, '*Alayhi al-Salam*, who has said the following:

"Whoever reads Chapter 97 of the Holy Quran aloud, he is considered as one unsheathing his sword in the way of Allah, whoever reads it silently he is considered as one who has been soaked with his own blood in the way of Allah and whoever reads it ten times, about one thousand of his sins will be forgiven."

H 3533, Ch. 13, h 7

Abu Ali al-Ash'ari has narrated from Muhammad ibn 'Abd al-Jabbar from Safwan ibn Yahya from Ya'qub ibn Shu'ayb from abu 'Abd Allah, *'Alayhi al-Salam*, who has said the following:

"My father, *'Alayhi al-Salam*, would say, 'Chapter 112 of the Holy Quran is one third and Chapter 109 is one forth of the Holy Quran.'"

H 3534, Ch. 13, h 8

A number of our people have narrated from Ahmad ibn Muhammad from al-Hassan ibn Ali from al-Hassan ibn al-Jahm from Ibrahim ibn Mihzam from a man who had heard abu al-Hassan, *'Alayhi al-Salam*, saying the following:

"Whoever reads verse 255 of Chapter 2 at the time of going to bed he will not fear paralysis, by the will of Allah, and whoever reads it after every obligatory prayer, poisonous things will not harm him.' The Imam said, 'Whoever forwards Chapter 112 between himself and a tyrant, Allah, the Most Majestic, will prevent the tyrant from harming him. He reads it to all directions: his front, back, right and left. When he does so, Allah, the Most Majestic, the Most Holy, provides him good dealings from the tyrant and protects him against his evil.' The Imam said, 'When you fear something read one hundred verses from the Holy Quran as you like and then say three times, "O Lord, remove the misfortune from me.""

H 3535, Ch. 13, h 9

Muhammad ibn Yahya has narrated from Ahmad ibn Muhammad from al-Hassan ibn Ali from Ishaq ibn 'Ammar from abu 'Abd Allah, *'Alayhi al-Salam*, who has said the following:

"Whoever reads one hundred verses of the Holy Quran in prayer in the night, Allah, the Most Majestic, the Most Holy, will write down for him the reward for one night's worshipping. Whoever reads two hundred verses without being in prayer, the Holy Quran, on the Day of Judgment, will not argue against him. Whoever reads five hundred verses in one day and night, Allah, the Most Majestic, the Most Holy, writes down for him in the protected tablet one Qintar of good deeds. One Qintar is one thousand two hundred 'Awqiyah, which is greater than the mountain of 'Uhud.'"

H 3536, Ch. 13, h 10

Abu Ali al-Ash'ari has narrated from Muhammad ibn Hassan from Isma'il ibn Mehran from al-Hassan ibn Ali ibn abu Hamza from Mansur ibn Hazim from abu 'Abd Allah, *'Alayhi al-Salam*, who has said the following:

"If one does not read Chapter 112 in twenty-four hours in any of the five prayers it will be said to him, 'O servant (of Allah) you are not one of those who perform prayer.'"

H 3537, Ch. 13, h 11

Through the same chain of narrators it is narrated from al-Hassan ibn Sayf ibn 'Umayrah from abu Bakr al-Hadrmi from abu 'Abd Allah, *'Alayhi al-Salam*, who has said the following:

"Whoever believes in Allah and in the life to come should not ignore reading Chapter 112 (al-'Ikhlas) of the Holy Quran after an obligatory prayer. Whoever does so (reads it), Allah will collect for him the good of this and the next life, forgive him, his parents and their children."

H 3538, Ch. 13, h 12

It is narrated from him (narrator of the Hadith above) from al-Hassan ibn Ali ibn abu Hamza in a marfu' manner from abu 'Abd Allah, *'Alayhi al-Salam*, who has said the following:

"Chapter six (al-An'am) was revealed all in one piece escorted by seventy thousand angels until it came down upon Muhammad, *'Alayhi al-Salam*. You must maintain its greatness and respect it. The name of Allah, the Most Majestic, the Most Holy, is mentioned therein at seventy places. Had people known what is in reading it, they would not have ignored it."

H 3539, Ch. 13, h 13

Ali ibn Ibrahim has narrated from his father from al-Nawfali from al-Sakuni from abu 'Abd Allah, *'Alayhi al-Salam*, who has said the following:

"The Holy Prophet performed prayer for Sa'd ibn Mu'adh and said, 'A delegate of seventy thousand angels was there, among them Jibril (Gabriel) was also there. They all performed prayer for him (the dead body of Sa'd ibn Mu'adh) and I said, 'O Jibril (Gabriel), what is it that made him deserve your prayers?' He said, 'It was his reading Chapter 112 (al-'Ikhlas) standing, sitting, riding, walking, coming and going.'"

H 3540, Ch. 13, h 14

A number of our people have narrated from Sahl ibn Ziyad from Ja'far ibn Muhammad ibn Bashir from 'Ubayd Allah ibn al-Dihqan from Drust from abu 'Abd Allah, *'Alayhi al-Salam*, who has said the following:

"The Messenger of Allah has said, 'Whoever read al-Hakum al-Takathur Chapter 102 of the Holy Quran at bedtime will be safe from the mischief of the grave.'"

H 3541, Ch. 13, h 15

Muhammad ibn Yahya has narrated from Ahmad ibn Muhammad ibn 'Isa from Muhammad ibn Isma'il ibn Bazi' from 'Abd Allah ibn al-Fald al-Nawfali in a marfu' manner from an Imam, *'Alayhi al-Salam*, who has said the following:

"Whenever I read al-Hamd (Chapter One of the Holy Quran) for pain, seventy times, it was relieved."

H 3542, Ch. 13, h 16

Ali ibn Ibrahim has narrated from his father from ibn abu 'Umayr from Mu'awiyah ibn 'Ammar from abu 'Abd Allah, *'Alayhi al-Salam*, who has said the following:

"If you read al-Hamd (Chapter One of the Holy Quran) seventy times over a dead body and it comes back to life, do not be astonished."

H 3543, Ch. 13, h 17

It is narrated from him (narrator of the Hadith above) from Ahmad ibn Bakr from Salih from Sulayman al-Ja'fari who has said the following:

"I heard abu al-Hassan, *'Alayhi al-Salam*, saying, 'If a child maintains reading every night Chapters 113, 114 three times each and Chapter 112 one hundred times or, if he cannot do it, fifty times Allah, the Most Majestic, the Most Holy, diverts all health problems of childhood and dehydration, stomach disorder and blood pressure all the time, as long as he maintains such readings until his old age. If he would maintain it or is made to maintain it, he will remain safe until the time Allah, the Most Majestic, the Most Holy, will take his soul away.'"

H 3544, Ch. 13, h 18

Ali ibn Ibrahim has narrated from his father from ibn abu 'Umayr from al-Husayn ibn Ahmad al-Minqari who has said the following:

"I heard abu Ibrahim, *'Alayhi al-Salam*, saying, 'If one considers one verse of the Holy Quran sufficient (for his protection) from East to West, it is enough [with certainty].'"

H 3545, Ch. 13, h 19

Al-Husayn ibn Muhammad has narrated from Ahmad ibn Ishaq and Ali ibn Ibrahim has narrated from his father all from Bakar ibn Muhammad al-Azdi from a man from abu 'Abd Allah, *'Alayhi al-Salam*, who about supplications for protection has said the following:

"Find a new pot made of clay and fill it with water then read Chapter 97 of the Holy Quran on it thirty times, then hang it from something, use it for drink and wuzu and add water if so desired (if Allah wills)."

H 3546, Ch. 13, h 20

A number of our people have narrated from Sahl ibn Ziyad from Idris al-Harithi from Muhammad ibn Sinan from Mufaddal ibn 'Umar who has said the following:

"Abu 'Abd Allah, *'Alayhi al-Salam*, said, 'O Mufaddal, protect yourself from all people with this: '(I begin) in the name of Allah, the Beneficent, the Merciful', and with Chapter 112 by reading toward each directions: right, left, front, back, above and below. When you enter in the presence of a tyranical ruler read it three times when looking at him, count it with your left hand and continue reading until you leave his presence.'"

H 3547, Ch. 13, h 21

Muhammad ibn Yahya has narrated from 'Abd Allah ibn Ja'far from al-Sayyari from Muhammad ibn Bakr from abu al-Jarud from al-Asbagh ibn Nubatah from Amir al-Mu'minin, Ali ibn abu Talib, *'Alayhi al-Salam*, who has said the following:

"I swear by the One who sent Muhammad, *'Alayhi al-Salam*, with the truth and honored his family, all supplications for protection is in the Holy Quran. In the Holy Quran there is protection against fire, theft, straying of animals from the owner, lost items, or runaway persons. Whoever wants to know, ask me. The narrator has said that a man then stood up and said, 'Instruct me in something against fire and drowning' The Imam said, 'Read this verse: "The (true) Guardian is certainly Allah Who has revealed the Book and is the Guardian of the righteous ones." (7:196) and 'They have not paid due respect to Allah. The whole earth will be gripped in His hands on the Day of Judgment and the heavens will be just like a scroll in His right hand. Allah is by far more Glorious and High to be considered equal to their idols.' (39:67) Whoever reads them will be safe from burns and drowning. [The man read them and fire broke out in the homes of his neighbors. His house was in the middle but remained unaffected]. Then another man stood up and said, 'O Amir al-Mu'Minin, *'Alayhi al-Salam*, my horse is unyielding and I am afraid of it.' The Imam said, 'Read in his right ear: ". . . all that is in the heavens and the earth have submitted themselves to His will, either by their own free will or by force? To Allah all things do return." (3:83) [He read the above verse and his horse became subservient]. Another man stood up and said, 'O Amir al-Mu'Minin, my land is filled with wild beasts. They overwhelm my house to get their prey.' The Imam said, 'Read: "A Messenger from your own people has come

513

to you. Your destruction and suffering is extremely distressful to him. He really cares about you and is very compassionate and merciful to the believers.'" (9:128)

(Muhammad), if they turn away from you, say, 'Allah is sufficient (support) for me. No one deserves to be worshipped except Allah. In Him I trust and He is the Owner of the Great Throne.' (9:129) [This man also was saved from the beasts after reading the Quranic reading].

"Thereafter another man stood up and said, 'O Amir al-Mu'Minin, in my stomach there is yellow water. Is there any cure for it?' The Imam said yes, without dirham and dinar, 'Write verse 255 of Chapter 2 of the Holy Quran on your stomach, then wash and drink it to save it in your stomach, you will be cured by the will of Allah, the Most Majestic, the Most Holy.' [This man also followed the instruction and was cured]. Another man stood up and asked about his straying animal. The Imam said, 'Read Chapter 36 in two Rak'at (a prayer consisting of two times bowing down on one's knees) prayer and say, "O guide of the straying, return my straying animal to me.' [This man also followed the instruction and his animal was returned]. Another man stood up and said, 'O Amir al-Mu'minin, tell me about a runaway.' The Imam said, 'Read: "Or they (the deeds of the unbelievers) are like the darkness of a deep, stormy sea with layers of giant waves, covered by dark clouds. It is darkness upon darkness whereby even if one stretches out his hands, he cannot see them. One can have no light unless Allah gives him light."' (24:40) [He followed the instruction and his runaway person was found]. Thereafter another man stood up and said, 'O Amir al-Mu'minin, tell me about theft. Every night they steal my things.' The Imam said, 'When going to bed read, "(Muhammad), tell them, 'It is all the same whether you call Him Allah or the Beneficent. All the good names belong to Him. (Muhammad), do not be very loud or slow in your prayer. Choose a moderate way of praying.' (17:110) Say, 'It is only Allah who deserves all praise. . . .' (17:111) Amir al-Mu'minin, Ali ibn abu Talib, 'Alayhi al-Salam, has said, 'If one is in an uninhabited land at night the angels will guard him and devils move away from him upon his reading this: 'Your Lord is Allah Who established His dominion over the Throne (of the realm) after having created the heavens and the earth in six days. He made the night darken the day, which it pursues at a (considerable) speed and He made the sun and the moon submissive to His command. Is it not He who creates and governs all things? Blessed is Allah, the Cherisher of the Universe.' (7:54) The narrator has said that a man traveled and stayed at a ruined town without reading the above verse of the Holy Quran, Satan overwhelmed him and was holding his face. His (Satan's) friend told him to wait. It made the man wake up and read the above verse of the Holy Quran. Satan then said to his friend, 'May Allah humiliate you, now stay here to guard him till morning.' In the morning he came to Amir al-Mu'minin, Ali ibn abu Talib, 'Alayhi al-Salam, and informed him of the incident saying, 'In your words I found cure and truth.' After sunrise he went to the place and he found a bunch of the hairs of the devil on the ground.'"

H 3548, Ch. 13, h 22

Muhammad ibn Yahya has narrated from Ahmad ibn Muhammad from Muhammad ibn Sinan from Salmah ibn Muhriz who has said the following:

"I heard abu Ja'far, *'Alayhi al-Salam*, saying, 'If al-Hamd, (the first Chapter of the Holy Quran) would not cure one, nothing else could cure one.'"

H 3549, Ch. 13, h 23

A number of our people have narrated from Sahl ibn Ziyad from Isma'il ibn Mehran from Safwan ibn Yahya from 'Abd Allah ibn Sinan from abu 'Abd Allah, *'Alayhi al-Salam*, who has said the following:

"Whoever at the time of going to bed reads Chapter 109 of the Holy Quran, Allah, the Most Majestic, the Most Holy, will write down for him immunity from polytheism."

H 3550, Ch. 13, h 24

Ali ibn Ibrahim has narrated from his father from Ali ibn Ma'bad from his father from those whom he has mentioned (in his book) from abu 'Abd Allah, *'Alayhi al-Salam*, who has said the following:

"Do not be dismayed in reading Chapter 99 of the Holy Quran. If one reads it in the optional prayers, Allah, the Most Majestic, the Most Holy, protects him, all the time, against earthquakes and will not die thereby or by lightening and of worldly calamities until the time of his death. When he dies a noble angel comes to him from his Lord, sits near his head and says to the angel of death, 'Be kind to the friend of Allah. It is he who very often spoke of me and read this Chapter.' The Chapter will also say similar words. The angel of death will then say, 'My Lord has commanded me to listen to Him, obey Him and will not take his spirit out without His commanding me to do so. When He commands me, then I take his spirit out.' The angel of death remains with him until he commands to take his spirit out. When the curtains are moved aside and he sees his places in paradise, his spirit comes out very gently as the gentlest treatment. Thereafter his spirit is escorted to paradise by seventy thousand angels rushing him to paradise."

Chapter 14 - The Rare Ahadith

H 3551, Ch. 14, h 1

A number of our people have narrated from Ahmad ibn Muhammad ibn Khalid from Isma'il ibn Mehran from 'Ubays ibn Hisham from those whom he has mentioned (in his book) from abu Ja'far, *'Alayhi al-Salam*, who has said the following:

"The readers of the Holy Quran are of three kinds: There is a man who has learned the Holy Quran and has taken it as a piece of merchandise to attract the rulers thereby and dominate the people. There is a man who has learned the Holy Quran, preserved its letters, but has lost its laws. He has kept its letters without change. (I wish) Allah would not increase the number of people like him as the carrier of the Holy Quran.

"There is a man who has applied the medicine of the Holy Quran to the wounds of his heart, it keeps him vigilant during the night, he endures thirst during the day, stands up in mosques and leaves his bed for its (the Holy Quran) sake. Through such people Allah, the Most Majestic, the Almighty, defends the land against the enemies, and through them he sends down rain from the sky. By Allah, such ones among the readers of the Holy Quran are like alchemy in rarity and value."

H 3552, Ch. 14, h 2

A number of our people have narrated from Sahl ibn Ziyad and Ali ibn Ibrahim has narrated from his father all from ibn Mahbub from abu Hamza from abu Yahya from al-Asbagh ibn Nubatah who has said the following:

"I heard Amir al-Mu'minin, Ali ibn abu Talib, 'Alayhi al-Salam, saying, 'The Holy Quran came in three parts: One third about us (Ahl al-Bayt) and about our enemies, one third about traditions and axioms and one third about obligations and laws.'"

H 3553, Ch. 14, h 3

A number of our people have narrated from Ahmad ibn Muhammad ibn Muhammad from al-Hajjal from Ali ibn 'Aqabah from Dawud ibn Farqad from those whom he has mentioned (in his book) from abu 'Abd Allah, 'Alayhi al-Salam, who has said the following:

"The Holy Quran came in four parts: One fourth is about lawful matters, one fourth about unlawful matters, one fourth about traditions and laws and one fourth about the news of what was before you and what will be after you and ways to settle your disputes."

H 3554, Ch. 14, h 4

Abu Ali al-Ash'ari has narrated from Muhammad ibn 'Abd al-Jabbar from Safwan from Ishaq ibn 'Ammar from abu Basir from abu Ja'far, 'Alayhi al-Salam, who has said the following:

"The Holy Quran came in four parts: One fourth is about us (Ahl al-Bayt) one fourth about our enemies, one about traditions and axioms and one fourth about obligations and laws."

H 3555, Ch. 14, h 5

A number of our people have narrated from Ahmad ibn Muhammad and Sahl ibn Ziyad from Mansur ibn al-'Abbas from Muhammad ibn al-Hassan al-Sarriy from abu 'Abd Allah, 'Alayhi al-Salam, who has said the following:

"The first thing that was revealed to the Messenger of Allah was, '(I begin) in the name of Allah, the Beneficent, the Merciful. Read in the name of your Lord . . .' (Chapter 96) and the last thing was, 'When support comes from Allah. . . .'" (Chapter 110)

H 3556, Ch. 14, h 6

Ali ibn Ibrahim has narrated from his father and Muhammad ibn al-Qasim from Muhammad ibn Sulayman from Dawud from Hafs ibn Ghiyath who has said the following:

"Once I asked abu 'Abd Allah, 'Alayhi al-Salam, about the words of Allah, the Most Majestic, the Most Holy, 'The month of Ramadan is the month in which the Quran was revealed, . . .' (2:185) but there were twenty years between its first and last (words).' Abu 'Abd Allah, 'Alayhi al-Salam, said, 'The Holy Quran was revealed in one piece in the month of Ramadan to Bayt al-Ma'mur, then it was revealed in twenty years.' The Imam said, 'The Holy Prophet has said, "The books of Ibrahim were revealed in the first night of Ramadan, Torah was revealed on the sixth day of Ramadan, Injil was revealed after thirteen nights of the month of Ramadan had passed, al-Zabur was revealed after twenty six days were passed from the month of Ramadan and the Holy Quran was revealed after twenty-three days had passed from the month of Ramadan.'"

H 3557, Ch. 14, h 7

A number of our people have narrated from Sahl ibn Ziyad from Muhammad ibn 'Isa from certain individuals of his people from abu 'Abd Allah, *'Alayhi al-Salam*, who has said the following:

"Abu 'Abd Allah, *'Alayhi al-Salam*, has said, 'The Holy Quran is not to be used for omens or prophecy.'"

H 3558, Ch. 14, h 8

Ali ibn Ibrahim has narrated from his father from Safwan from Muskan from Muhammad ibn al-Warraq who has said the following:

"Once I showed to abu 'Abd Allah, *'Alayhi al-Salam*, a copy of the Holy Quran decorated with writings of gold in a stamp form and at the end of chapters there were writings with gold. He did not criticize anything in it except the writing of the Holy Quran with gold saying, 'I do not like the writing of the Holy Quran in anything except black ink, just as it was written the first time.'"

H 3559, Ch. 14, h 9

A number of our people have narrated from Ahmad ibn Muhammad from Muhammad ibn 'Isa from Yasin al-Darir from Hariz from Zurara from abu Ja'far, *'Alayhi al-Salam*, who has said the following:

"In the last third of the month of Ramadan, you may take a copy of the Holy Quran, open it, place before you and say, 'O Lord, I plead before You through Your revealed book and through what is in it and in it there is Your greatest, the magnificent name and Your beautiful names, what is feared and what is hoped for, to make me of those whom You have freed from the fire' and then ask for help for whatever you like or need help."

H 3560, Ch. 14, h 10

Abu Ali al-Ash'ari has narrated from Muhammad ibn Salim from Ahmad ibn al-Nadr from 'Amr ibn Shimr from Jabir from abu Ja'far, *'Alayhi al-Salam*, who has said the following:

"Abu Ja'far, *'Alayhi al-Salam*, has said, 'For everything there is a spring. The spring for the Holy Quran is the month of Ramadan.'"

H 3561, Ch. 14, h 11

Ali ibn Ibrahim has narrated from his father from ibn Sinan or others from those whom he has mentioned (in his book) who has said the following:

"Once I asked abu 'Abd Allah, *'Alayhi al-Salam*, whether al-Quran and al-Furqan are two different things or one thing? The Imam said, 'Al-Quran is the name of the whole book and al-Furqan is that much that is clearly understood and is necessary to act accordingly thereby.'"

H 3562, Ch. 14, h 12

Al-Husayn ibn Muhammad has narrated from Ali ibn Muhammad from al-Washsha' from Jamil ibn Darraj from Muhammad ibn Muslim from Zurara from abu Ja'far, *'Alayhi al-Salam*, who has said the following:

"The Holy Quran is one. It has come from One, however, the differences come from the narrators."

H 3563, Ch. 14, h 13

Ali ibn Ibrahim has narrated from his father from ibn abu 'Umayr from 'Umar ibn 'Udhaynah from al-Fudayl ibn Yasar who has said the following:

"Once, I said to abu 'Abd Allah, *'Alayhi al-Salam*, 'People say that the Holy Quran was revealed upon seven letters.' The Imam said, 'They, the enemies of Allah, lie. It was revealed upon one letter from One source.'"

H 3564, Ch. 14, h 14

Muhammad ibn Yahya has narrated from 'Abd Allah ibn Muhammad from Ali ibn al-Hakam from 'Abd Allah ibn Bukayr from abu 'Abd Allah, *'Alayhi al-Salam*, who has said the following:

"The Holy Quran was revealed in a manner like, 'I speak to you, but it is the neighbor who must listen.'"

It is narrated, in another Hadith, from abu 'Abd Allah, *'Alayhi al-Salam*, who has said the following:

"The meaning of 'I speak to you, but it is the neighbor who must listen', is that whenever Allah, the Most Majestic, the Most Holy, has addressed His prophet in critical expressions they, in fact, are addressed to others and not the Holy Prophet such as: 'Had We not strengthened your faith you might have relied on them some how,' (17:74) is addressed to others (not the Holy Prophet).'"

H 3565, Ch. 14, h 15

A number of our people have narrated from Sahl ibn Ziyad from Ali ibn al-Hakam from 'Abd Allah ibn Jundab from Sufyan ibn al-Samt who has said the following:

"Once I asked abu 'Abd Allah, *'Alayhi al-Salam*, 'How was the Holy Quran revealed?' The Imam said, 'Read as you are instructed.'"

H 3566, Ch. 14, h 16

Ali ibn Muhammad has narrated from certain individuals of his people from Ahmad ibn Muhammad ibn abu Nasr who has said the following:

"Once, abu al-Hassan, *'Alayhi al-Salam*, gave me a copy of the Holy Quran saying, 'Do not look at it.' I opened and read in it (Chapter 98) 'The unbelievers were not . . .' and I found therein the names of seventy people from Quraysh with their names and the names of their fathers.' The narrator has said that the Imam, *'Alayhi al-Salam*, sent a message to me, 'Send the copy back to me.'"

H 3567, Ch. 14, h 17

Muhammad ibn Yahya has narrated from Ahmad ibn Muhammad from Husayn ibn Sa'id from al-Nadr ibn Suwayd from al-Qasim ibn Sulayman from abu 'Abd Allah, *'Alayhi al-Salam*, who has said the following:

"Abu 'Abd Allah, *'Alayhi al-Salam*, has said, 'Once my father said to me, "Whoever mixes up the Holy Quran becomes an unbeliever."'"

H 3568, Ch. 14, h 18

It is narrated from him (narrator of the Hadith above) from al-Husayn ibn al-Nadr from al-Qasim ibn Sulayman from abu Maryam al-Ansari from Jabir who has said the following:

"I heard abu Ja'far, *'Alayhi al-Salam*, saying, 'A copy of the Holy Quran had fallen in the sea, when they found it all the writing was gone except: '. . . is it not the case that all things end up in the presence of Allah. . . .'" (42:53)

H 3569, Ch. 14, h 19

Al-Husayn ibn Muhammad has narrated from Mu'alla ibn Muhammad from al-Washsha' from Aban from Maymun al-Qaddah who has said the following:

"Once abu Ja'far, *'Alayhi al-Salam*, said to me, 'Read.' I then asked, 'What should I read?' The Imam said, 'Read from Chapter 9.' I (the narrator) tried to find it but he said, 'Read from Yunus (which is Chapter 10).' I (the narrator) then read: 'The righteous will receive good rewards for their deeds and more. Their faces will suffer no disgrace or ignominy. . . .' (10:26) The Imam said, 'The Messenger of Allah has said, "It is astonishing to me, why should I not grow old much quicker when I read the Holy Quran."'"

H 3570, Ch. 14, h 20

Ali ibn Muhammad has narrated from Salih ibn abu Hammad from al-Hajjal from those whom he has mentioned (in his book) who has said the following:

"Once I asked one of the two Imam, *'Alayhi al-Salam*, about the words of Allah, the Most Majestic, the Most Holy: 'It has been revealed in plain Arabic.' (26:195) The Imam said, 'It (the Holy Quran) explains the languages but the languages do not explain it.'"

H 3571, Ch. 14, h 21

Ahmad ibn Muhammad has narrated from Muhammad ibn Ahmad al-Nahdi from Muhammad ibn al-Walid from Aban from 'Amir ibn 'Abd Allah ibn Jadha'h from abu 'Abd Allah, *'Alayhi al-Salam*, who has said the following:

"Whoever reads the last verse of al-Kahf (Chapter 18) can wake up at night at the hour that he intends to wake up."

H 3572, Ch. 14, h 22

Abu Ali al-Ash'ari and others have narrated from al-Hassan ibn Ali al-Kufi from 'Uthman ibn 'Isa from Sa'id ibn Yasar who has said the following:

"Once, I said to abu 'Abd Allah, *'Alayhi al-Salam*, 'Your Mawla, Sulaym says that of the Holy Quran with him there is only Yasin, Chapter 36. At night he wakes up and completes reading of the Holy Quran whatever is available with him, can he repeat it reading?' The Imam said, 'Yes, he can do so.'"

H 3573, Ch. 14, h 23

Muhammad ibn Yahya has narrated from Muhammad ibn al-Husayn from 'Abd al-Rahman ibn abu Hashim from Salim ibn Salamah who has said the following:

"Once, a man read before abu 'Abd Allah, *'Alayhi al-Salam*, certain letters from the Holy Quran, while I was present, which were not like those that people read. Abu 'Abd Allah, *'Alayhi al-Salam*, said, 'Stop this reading. Read as people read until the one who will establish Divine Authority on earth will come. When he will come, the book of Allah, the Most Majestic, the Most Holy, will be read upon its limits. He then brought the copy of the Holy Quran that Ali, *'Alayhi al-Salam*, had written and said, 'Ali, *'Alayhi al-Salam*, brought this to people when he completed writing down the Holy Quran in one copy and said to them, "This is the book of Allah, the Most Majestic, the Most Holy, as Allah had revealed upon Muhammad, *'Alayhi al-Salam*, and I have written it in one copy from two tablets." They said, 'With us there is the comprehensive copy of the Holy Quran. We do not need it.' He then said, 'By Allah you will never see this from today on. It was necessary for me to tell you after I completed writing it down so you can read.'"

H 3574, Ch. 14, h 24

Ali ibn Ibrahim has narrated from his father from Safwan from Sa'id ibn 'Abd Allah al-A'Raj who has said the following:

"Once I asked abu 'Abd Allah, *'Alayhi al-Salam*, about a man who reads the Holy Quran but then he forgets, he reads again and forgets. Is it an offense? The Imam said, 'No, it is not an offense.'"

H 3575, Ch. 14, h 25

Ali has narrated from his father from al-Nadr ibn Suwayd from al-Qasim ibn Sulayman from abu 'Abd Allah, *'Alayhi al-Salam*, who has said the following:

"My father has said, 'Whoever mixes one part of the Holy Quran with the other part he turns into an unbeliever.'"

H 3576, Ch. 14, h 26

A number of our people have narrated from Sahl ibn Ziyad and Muhammad ibn Yahya from Ahmad ibn Muhammad ibn 'Isa all from ibn Mahbub from Jamil from Sadir from abu Ja'far, *'Alayhi al-Salam*, who has said the following:

"Surah al-Mulk (Chapter 67) is a protector. It protects against the torment of the grave. It (Surah al-Mulk) is written in the Torah. Whoever reads it at night has done a great good deed and with it he will not be written of the neglectful ones. I read it in Ruku' position while, sitting after 'Isha' prayer. My father would read it every day and night. When the person who reads it will be placed in the grave the interrogating angels (Na'kir and Nakir) will enter his grave from the direction of his feet. His feet will say, 'You cannot enter from our side. This servant (of Allah) would stand on us and read Surah al-Mulk every day and night.' When they try to enter his grave from the middle section his middle section will say, 'You cannot enter from my side of the grave. This servant (of Allah) had placed Surah al-Mulk inside of me.' When they try to enter from the side of his face his tongue will say, 'You cannot enter from my side. This servant (of Allah) would read with me Surah al-Mulk every day and night.'"

H 3577, Ch. 14, h 27

Muhammad ibn Yahya has narrated from Ahmad ibn Muhammad from Ali ibn al-Hakam from 'Abd Allah ibn Farqad and al-Mu'alla ibn Khunays who have said the following:

"Once we were in the presence of abu 'Abd Allah, *'Alayhi al-Salam*, and with us Rabi'ah al-Ra'y was also present. We spoke of the excellence of the Holy Quran. Abu 'Abd Allah, *'Alayhi al-Salam*, said, 'If ibn Mas'ud does not read the Holy Quran the way we read, he is straying.' Rabi'ah then said, '(Is it) straying?' The Imam said, 'Yes, (it is) straying.' Abu 'Abd Allah, *'Alayhi al-Salam*, then said, 'We read the Holy Quran as my father did.'"

H 3578, Ch. 14, h 28

Ali ibn al-Hakam has narrated from Hisham ibn Salim from abu 'Abd Allah, *'Alayhi al-Salam*, who has said the following:

"Abu 'Abd Allah, *'Alayhi al-Salam*, has said, 'The Holy Quran that Jibril (Gabriel) brought to Muhammad, *'Alayhi al-Salam*, had seventeen thousand verses.'"

Note: According to commentators, the word 'Teen' (Arabic 'een') in seventeen' is an edition by the scribes. Seven thousand verses is perhaps a rounded up figure, which is not very far from reality.

This is the end of the Book of the Excellence of the Holy Quran of the Book al-Kafi. It is followed by the Book of Social Manners. All praise belongs to Allah alone and Allah has granted blessings upon Muhammad and his family.

In the Name of Allah, the Beneficient, the Merciful

Part Four:
The Book of Social Manners

Chapter 1 - The Necessary Part of Social Manners

H 3579, Ch. 1, h 1

A number of our people have narrated from Ahmad ibn Muhammad from Ali ibn Hadid from Murazim who has said the following:

"Abu 'Abd Allah, *'Alayhi al-Salam*, has said, 'You must pray in the Mosques, maintain good neighborly relations with people, present your testimony, and attend funeral processions. You need people. There is no one who does not need people in his life. People need each other.'"

H 3580, Ch. 1, h 2

Muhammad ibn Isma'il has narrated from al-Fadl ibn Shadhan and Abu Ali al-Ash'ari from Muhammad ibn 'Abd al-Jabbar from Safwan ibn Yahya from Mu'awiyah ibn Wahab who has said the following:

"Once I asked abu 'Abd Allah, *'Alayhi al-Salam*, 'What is the proper way to deal with ourselves, our people, our associates and the people in general?' The Imam said, 'You must return their trust, present your testimony for and against them, visit them during their illness and attend their funerals.'"

H 3581, Ch. 1, h 3

Muhammad ibn Yahya has narrated from Ahmad ibn Muhammad from al-Husayn ibn Sa'id and Muhammad ibn Khalid all from al-Qasim ibn Muhammad from Habib al-Khath'ami who has said the following:

"I heard abu 'Abd Allah, *'Alayhi al-Salam*, saying, 'You must maintain restraint from worldly attractions (sins), maintain persistence in work, attend funerals, and visit people during their illness. You should attend the Mosque with your own people, and love for people what you love for yourselves. Would it not be embarrassing for one of you to see that a neighbor recognizes your rights but you do not recognize the rights of your neighbor?'"

H 3582, Ch. 1, h 4

Muhammad ibn Yahya has narrated from Ahmad ibn Muhammad from Ali ibn al-Hakam from Mu'awiyah ibn Wahab who has said the following:

"Once I asked the Imam, *'Alayhi al-Salam*, 'What is the proper way to deal with ourselves and our people, our associates of the people who do not believe as we do?' The Imam said, 'Look to your 'A'immah (plural of Imam) whom you follow and do what they do. By Allah, they, ('A'immah) visit their sick people, attend their funerals, present their testimony for and against them and return their trust.'"

H 3583, Ch. 1, h 5

Abu Ali al-Ash'ari has narrated from Muhammad ibn 'Abd al-Jabbar from Safwan ibn Yahya from abu 'Usamah Zayd al-Shahham who has said the following:

"Once abu 'Abd Allah, *'Alayhi al-Salam*, said to me, 'Convey greetings of peace from me to all that you will see of those who obey me and uphold my words. Tell them that I enjoin upon you to be pious before Allah, the Most Majestic, the Most Holy, to restraint yourselves from the worldly attractions (sins) in the matters of your religion, to work hard, to maintain truthfulness in your words, keep your trust, perform long prostrations, and to maintain good neighborly relations. This is what Muhammad, *'Alayhi al-Salam*, has brought (from Allah). Return the trust to those who have entrusted you, whether they are virtuous people or evildoers. The Messenger of Allah would command to return the needle and swing thread. Maintain good relations with the people of your tribe, attend their funerals, visit their sick people, and fulfill your obligations toward them. If one of you maintains restraint in the worldly attractions (sins) in the matters of his religion, is truthful in his words, keeps his trust, has acquired proper moral discipline to behave toward people, it will be said about him, 'This is a Ja'fari (follower of Ja'far ibn Muhammad, *'Alayhi al-Salam*)', and this will bring me joy and delight and they will say, 'This is the discipline of Ja'far.' If otherwise, its misfortune and disgrace will trouble me and they will say, 'This is the behavior of Ja'far.'

'By Allah my father spoke to me about a man who lived with a Shi'a (followers) of Ali, *'Alayhi al-Salam*, tribe whose beauty was in his keeping his trust, fulfilling his obligations, and his being the most truthful in his words. With him they would keep their important documents and valuables. If one were to ask people of the tribe about him, they would ask, "Who is like him? He is the most trusted one in safekeeping of valuables and the most truthful in his words.""""

Chapter 2 - Proper Social Relations

H 3584, Ch. 2, h 1

Ali ibn Ibrahim has narrated from his father from Hammad from Hariz from Muhammad ibn Muslim who has said the following:

"Whoever you associate with, if you can maintain an upper hand (in your dealings with him) do so (be more beneficial)."

H 3585, Ch. 2, h 2

A number of our people have narrated from Ahmad ibn Muhammad ibn Khalid from Isma'il ibn Mehran from Muhammad ibn Hafs from abu al-Rabi' al-Shami who has said the following:

"Once I went in the presence of abu 'Abd Allah, *'Alayhi al-Salam*, and the house was full of people. There were people from Khurasan, from al-Sham and from various horizons and I could not find a place to sit. Abu 'Abd Allah, *'Alayhi al-Salam*, sat in his place and he was leaning against a pillow. He said, 'O Shi'a (followers) of the family of Muhammad, *'Alayhi al-Salam*, bear in mind that one who is not able to control his soul when angry is not from us, and so also is one who does not better his association with his associates, show proper behavior with those who exercise proper behavior, befriend those who befriend him, provide protection to those who protect him, observe proper table manners with those who share with him the table. O Shi'a (followers) of the family of Muhammad, *'Alayhi al-Salam*, be pious before Allah to the best of your abilities. There are no means and no power without Allah.'"

H 3586, Ch. 2, h 3

Ali ibn Ibrahim has narrated from his father from ibn abu 'Umayr from those whom he has mentioned (in his book) from abu 'Abd Allah, *'Alayhi al-Salam*, who has said the following:

"About the words of Allah, the Most Majestic, the Most Holy, 'We believe you to be a righteous person,' (12:36) the Imam said, 'He would make room for others in a gathering, lend money to the needy and assist the weak.'"

H 3587, Ch. 2, h 4

Muhammad ibn Yahya has narrated from Ahmad ibn Muhammad from Muhammad ibn Sinan from 'Ala' ibn al-Fudayl from abu 'Abd Allah, *'Alayhi al-Salam*, who has said the following:

"Abu Ja'far, *'Alayhi al-Salam*, would say, 'Show respect for your friends and dignify them. Do not be aggressive to each other, do not harm or envy each other. Beware of stinginess and be sincere and righteous servants of Allah.'"

H 3588, Ch. 2, h 5

Muhammad ibn Yahya has narrated from Ahmad ibn Muhammad ibn 'Isa from al-Hajjal from Dawud ibn abu Yazid and Tha'Labah and Ali ibn 'Aqabah from certain individuals who narrated to him from one of the two Imam, *'Alayhi al-Salam*, who has said the following:

"Restraint from associating people brings in their animosity."

Chapter 3 - People Whose Friendship and Association is Necessary

H 3589, Ch. 3, h 1

A number of our people have narrated from Ahmad ibn Muhammad from Husayn ibn al-Hassan from Muhammad ibn Sinan from 'Ammar ibn Musa from abu 'Abd Allah, *'Alayhi al-Salam*, who has said the following:

"Amir al-Mu'minin, Ali ibn abu Talib, *'Alayhi al-Salam*, has said, 'It is not against you to associate with a person of reason even though you may not appreciate his generosity but you can benefit from his reason. However, you must avoid his immoral manners. Do not ignore the association of a magnanimous person, even though you may not benefit from his reason but you can benefit from his magnanimity by the help of your own reason. Flee, very far away from a power-hungry, irrational person.'"

H 3590, Ch. 3, h 2

It is narrated from him (narrator of the Hadith above) from 'Abd al-Rahman ibn abu Najran from Muhammad ibn al-Salt from Aban from abu al-'Udays who has said the following:

"O Salih, follow the one who makes you cry while providing good advice and do not follow the one who makes you laugh but is cheating. You will all return to Allah and will find out."

H 3591, Ch. 3, h 3

It is narrated from him (narrator of the Hadith above) from Muhammad ibn Ali from Musa ibn Yasar al-Qattan from al-Mas'udi from Dawud from Thabit ibn abu Sakhrah from abu al-Za'li who has said the following:

"Amir al-Mu'minin, Ali ibn abu Talib, *'Alayhi al-Salam*, has said that the Messenger of Allah has said, 'Consider who you talk to (make friendship). Everyone after death will find the forms of his associates in the presence of Allah; these forms follow the worldly origins. A good form is from a good origin and an evil form is from an evil origin. At the time of his death everyone observes me in my person.'"

H 3592, Ch. 3, h 4

Ali ibn Ibrahim has narrated from his father from ibn abu 'Umayr from certain individuals from al-Halab from 'Abd Allah ibn Muskan from a man from people of al-Jabal whose name is not mentioned and who has said the following:

"You should maintain good relations with your old associates and friends, be cautious about a new one who does not have any protection, responsibility, or commitment and always avoid (caution) the one whom you trust the most."

H 3593, Ch. 3, h 5

A number of our people have narrated from Ahmad ibn Muhammad in a marfu' manner from abu 'Abd Allah, *'Alayhi al-Salam*, who has said the following:

"To me, the most beloved of my brethren (friends) is the one who most points out my defects to me."

H 3594, Ch. 3, h 6

A number of our people have narrated from Ahmad ibn Muhammad from Muhammad ibn al-Hassan from 'Ubayd Allah al-Dehqan from Ahmad ibn 'A'idh from 'Ubayd Allah al-Halabi from abu 'Abd Allah, *'Alayhi al-Salam*, who has said the following:

"There can be no friendship without its rules. You may call one a friend only when he follows such rules and those who do not follow such rules cannot be called a friend. First of all a friend must be the same inside and outside. Secondly, he must consider your beauty his own beauty and your flaw as his flaw. Thirdly that he does not change because of high position and wealth. Fourth, that he does not hold back from you what is within his capabilities. Fifth, with the above, he does not leave you out in unfortunate circumstances."

Chapter 4 - Those Whose Association and Friendship is Undesirable

H 3595, Ch. 4, h 1

A number of our people have narrated from Ahmad ibn Muhammad ibn Khalid from 'Amr Aban ibn 'Uthman 'Uthman from Muhammad ibn Salim al-Kindy from those whom he has mentioned (in his book) from abu 'Abd Allah, *'Alayhi al-Salam*, who has said the following:

"When Amir al-Mu'minin, Ali ibn abu Talib, *'Alayhi al-Salam*, were to take his place on the pulpit he would say, 'A Muslim, must avoid friendship with three kinds of people: A bold-faced indecent, an idiot and a liar. A bold-faced-indecent person attempts to make his acts seem attractive to you and loves that you behave like he does. He does not assist you in your religious matters and the matters of the hereafter. Closeness to him is injustice, hardheartedness, and his coming and going is disgrace for you.

'An idiotic person does not indicate anything good for you, nor is there any hope in him to remove any bit of evil from you even if he may try his best. Perhaps he may want to benefit you, instead he only harms you. His death is better than his living, his silence is better than his speaking, and his being at a distance is better than his being nearby.

'The liar is one with whom you can never have a happy life. He carries your words out and others' words in to you. Whenever he may run out of words he then mixes them with others so much so that even when speaking the truth is not believed and he causes differences among people with animosity to sow envy in the hearts. You must be pious before Allah, the Most Majestic, the Most Holy, and look after your own souls.'"

H 3596, Ch. 4, h 2

In the Hadith of 'Abd al-'Ala' from abu 'Abd Allah, *'Alayhi al-Salam*, it is said that Amir al-Mu'minin, Ali ibn abu Talib, *'Alayhi al-Salam*, said:

"It is not proper for a Muslim man to become a friend of an indecent person; he tries to make his deeds seem attractive to him and loves that one to behave like him (indecent). He does not assist him in his religious matters or the matters of the hereafter. The coming and going of an indecent person is a disgrace to one."

H 3597, Ch. 4, h 3

A number of our people have narrated from Ahmad ibn Muhammad from 'Uthman ibn 'Isa from Muhammad ibn Yusuf from Maysir from abu 'Abd Allah, *'Alayhi al-Salam*, who has said the following:

"It is not proper for a Muslim man to become friends with an indecent, an idiot and a liar."

H 3598, Ch. 4, h 4

A number of our people have narrated from Sahl ibn Ziyad from Ali ibn Asbat from certain individuals of his people from abu al-Hassan, *'Alayhi al-Salam*, who has said the following:

"Jesus, son of Mary has said, 'An evil companion commits injustice and an evil friend brings destruction. Consider who to become friends with.'"

H 3599, Ch. 4, h 5

Muhammad ibn Yahya has narrated from Ahmad ibn Muhammad and Muhammad ibn al-Husayn from Muhammad ibn Sinan from 'Ammar ibn Musa who has said the following:

"Abu 'Abd Allah, *'Alayhi al-Salam*, once said to me, 'O 'Ammar, if you like bounties bring you delight, kindness becomes complete, and the affairs of life well-organized you then should not associate with the slaves and the lowly persons. If you trust them, they betray you, if they speak, they lie to you. If you may suffer a misfortune, they leave you out. If they promise you, they disregard it.'"

H 3600, Ch. 4, h 6

He has also said, 'I heard abu 'Abd Allah, *'Alayhi al-Salam*, saying:

"The virtuous ones' love of other virtuous ones is a rewarding deed for them. Indecent ones loving the virtuous ones is a credit for the virtuous ones. Indecent ones' hating the virtuous ones beautifies the virtuous ones. Virtuous one's hating the indecent ones is a loss to the indecent ones."

H 3601, Ch. 4, h 7

A number of our people have narrated from Sahl ibn Ziyad and Ali ibn Ibrahim has narrated from his father all from 'Amr ibn 'Uthman from Muhammad ibn 'Adhafir from certain individuals of their people from Muhammad ibn Muslim and abu Hamza from abu 'Abd Allah and his father, *'Alayhi al-Salam*, who has said the following:

"My father, Ali ibn al-Husayn, *'Alayhi al-Salam*, once said to me, 'My son, look for five kinds of people. Do not befriend them, speak to or accompany them on a road.' I then asked, 'O father, who are they? Define them for me.' He said, 'Never befriend a liar; he is like a mirage. He shows what is far very near and what is near, in fact, very far. Never befriend a sinful person; he may sell you for a meal or even less. Never befriend a stingy person; he betrays you in the matter of his property at a time when you need help urgently. Never befriend an idiotic person; he may intend to benefit you, instead he causes you injuries. Never befriend one who has failed to maintain good relations with relatives; I have found him condemned in the book of Allah, the Most Majestic, the Most Holy, in three places. Allah, the Most Majestic, the Most Holy, has said:

"If you ignore the commands of Allah, would you then also spread evil in the land and sever the ties of kinship? (47:22) Allah has condemned these people and made them deaf, dumb, and blind." (47:23)

'Allah, the Most Majestic, the Most Holy, has said, "Those who disregard their covenant with Allah after He has taken such a pledge from them, who sever the proper relations that Allah has commanded them to establish, and those who spread evil in the land will have Allah's condemnation instead of reward and will face the most terrible end." (13:25)

'Allah, the Most Majestic, the Most Holy, has said, ". . . who break their established covenant with Him and the relations He has commanded to be kept and who spread evil in the land. These are the ones who lose a great deal."'" (2:27)

H 3602, Ch. 4, h 8
A number of our people have narrated from Ahmad ibn Muhammad from Musa ibn al-Qasim who has said the following:
"I heard al-Muharibi narrate from abu 'Abd Allah, *'Alayhi al-Salam*, from his ancestors, *'Alayhi al-Salam*, who has said, 'The Messenger of Allah has said, "Association with three kinds of people deadens the heart (reason): association with the lowly, speaking to women and sitting with the wealthy."'"

H 3603, Ch. 4, h 9
Ali ibn Ibrahim has narrated from his father from certain individuals of his people from Ibrahim ibn abu al-Balad from those whom he has mentioned (in his book) who has said the following:
"Luqman (mentioned in Chapter 31 of the Holy Quran), peace be upon him, said to his son, 'Do not become very close (to people), lest you become the farthest from them (frequent involvement may cause friction and disturbance) and do not keep very far in total isolation and oblivion. Every moving thing loves its kind and the sons of Adam love their kind. Do not spread your goods when there is demand. Just as there is no friendship between the wolf and the sheep so also there is no friendship between a virtuous person and an evildoer. Whoever moves close to asphalt and tar, it will smear him out so also is association with an evildoer whose manners may spread to his associates. Whoever likes to dispute will be abused. Whoever enters places of evil activities will be accused (of evil doing).

Whoever associates with an evildoer will not remain safe. Whoever does not control his tongue will regret.'"

H 3604, Ch. 4, h 10

Abu Ali al-Ash'ari has narrated from Muhammad ibn 'Abd al-Jabbar from ibn abu Najran from 'Umar ibn Yazid from abu 'Abd Allah, *'Alayhi al-Salam*, who has said the following:

"Do not befriend blasphemers and do not associate with them; people may consider you as one of them. The Messenger of Allah has said, 'A man follows the religion of his friend and associates.'"

H 3605, Ch. 4, h 11

Abu Ali al-Ash'ari has narrated from Muhammad ibn 'Abd al-Jabbar from al-Hajjal from Ali ibn Ya'qub al-Hashimi from Harun ibn Muslim from 'Ubayd ibn Zurara who has said the following:

"Abu 'Abd Allah, *'Alayhi al-Salam*, has said, 'Never befriend an idiotic person; the more delightful you may become from his side the closer it will get to your misfortune.'"

Chapter 5 - Finding Love and Affection Among People

H 3606, Ch. 5, h 1

Muhammad ibn Yahya has narrated from Ahmad ibn Muhammad and Ali ibn Ibrahim has narrated from his father all from ibn Mahbub from Hisham ibn Salim from abu Basir from abu Ja'far, *'Alayhi al-Salam*, who has said the following:

"Once an Arab man came to the Holy Prophet and said, 'Instruct me with good advice.' Of the good advice to him was: 'Love people, they will love you.'"

H 3607, Ch. 5, h 2

A number of our people have narrated from Ahmad ibn Muhammad ibn Khalid from 'Uthman ibn 'Isa from Sama'a from abu 'Abd Allah, *'Alayhi al-Salam*, who has said the following:

"Dealing with people in a graceful manner is one third of (the power) reason."

H 3608, Ch. 5, h 3

Ali ibn Ibrahim has narrated from his father from al-Nawfali from al-Sakuni from abu 'Abd Allah, *'Alayhi al-Salam*, who has said the following:

"The Messenger of Allah has said, 'Three things purify a Muslim's love for his brother (in belief): meeting him in a cheerful manner, preparing for him a seat if he wants to sit down in a gathering, and calling him by his names that he loves most.'"

H 3609, Ch. 5, h 4

Through the same chain of narrators it is narrated from abu 'Abd Allah, *'Alayhi al-Salam*, who has said the following:

"The Messenger of Allah has said, 'Showing that one loves people is half (the power) of reason.'"

H 3610, Ch. 5, h 5

A number of our people have narrated from Sahl ibn Ziyad from Ali ibn Hassan from Musa ibn Bakr from abu al-Hassan, *'Alayhi al-Salam*, who has said the following:

"Showing that one loves people is one half (the power) of reason."

H 3611, Ch. 5, h 6

Muhammad ibn Yahya has narrated from Ahmad ibn Muhammad ibn 'Isa from Muhammad ibn Sinan from Hudhayfah ibn Mansur who has said the following:

"I heard abu 'Abd Allah, *'Alayhi al-Salam*, saying, 'Whoever holds his hands off the people has held back only one hand, however, they will hold many hands off of him.'"

H 3612, Ch. 5, h 7

A number of our people have narrated from Ahmad ibn Muhammad ibn Khalid from certain individuals of his people from Salih ibn 'Aqabah from Sulayman ibn Ziyad al-Tamimi from abu 'Abd Allah, *'Alayhi al-Salam*, who has said the following:

"Al-Hassan ibn Ali, *'Alayhi al-Salam*, has said, 'A person close to another person is one whom love has brought so close even though his lineage is far remote. A person far away is one whom love has distanced a part even though his lineage is near and close. There is nothing so close to another thing than the hands to the body, but when it becomes disloyal it is cut off and when it is cut off the body's blood is held back from flowing out.'"

Chapter 6 - One's Telling His Brother of His Love

H 3613, Ch. 6, h 1

A number of our people have narrated from Ahmad ibn Muhammad ibn Khalid from his father from Muhammad ibn 'Umar (ibn 'Udhaynah) from his father from Nasr ibn Qabus who has said the following:

"Abu 'Abd Allah, *'Alayhi al-Salam*, once said to me, 'If you love one of your brothers (in belief), tell him about it; Ibrahim said, "O Lord, show me how do You bring the dead back to life?" The Lord asked, "Do you not believe it?" He said, "Yes, I firmly believe, but it is to comfort my heart . . ."'" (2:260)

H 3614, Ch. 6, h 2

Ahmad ibn Khalid and Muhammad ibn Yahya have narrated from Ahmad ibn Muhammad ibn 'Isa all from Ali ibn al-Hakam from Hisham ibn Salim from abu 'Abd Allah, *'Alayhi al-Salam*, who has said the following:

"When you love a man, tell him about it; it strengthens your love for one another."

Chapter 7 - Offering the Greeting of Peace

H 3615, Ch. 7, h 1

Ali ibn Ibrahim has narrated from his father from al-Nawfali from al-Sakuni from abu 'Abd Allah, *'Alayhi al-Salam*, who has said the following:

"The Messenger of Allah has said, 'Offering the greeting of peace is voluntary, but answering it is obligatory.'"

H 3616, Ch. 7, h 2

Through the same chain of narrators it is narrated from abu 'Abd Allah, *'Alayhi al-Salam*, who has said the following:

"If one begins speaking before offering the greeting of peace, do not speak to him."

H 3617, Ch. 7, h 3

Through the same chain of narrators it is narrated from abu 'Abd Allah, *'Alayhi al-Salam*, who has said the following:

"The Messenger of Allah has said, 'A person who is closer to Allah and His Messenger is the one who initiates the offering of the greeting of peace.'"

H 3618, Ch. 7, h 4

A number of our people have narrated from Sahl ibn Ziyad from 'Abd al-Rahman ibn abu Najran from 'Asim ibn Hamid from Muhammad ibn Muslim from abu Ja'far, *'Alayhi al-Salam*, who has said the following:

"Salman, May Allah grant him favors, would say, 'Offer the greeting of peace from Allah openly; the unjust do not receive the greeting of peace from Allah.'"

H 3619, Ch. 7, h 5

A number of our people have narrated from Ahmad ibn Muhammad from ibn Faddal from Tha'Labah' ibn Maymun from Muhammad ibn Qays from abu Ja'far, *'Alayhi al-Salam*, who has said the following:

"Allah, the Most Majestic, the Most Holy, loves offering the greeting of peace openly, loud and clearly."

H 3620, Ch. 7, h 6

It is narrated from him (narrator of the Hadith above) from ibn Faddal from Mu'awiyah ibn Wahab from abu 'Abd Allah, *'Alayhi al-Salam*, who has said the following:

"Allah, the Most Majestic, the Most Holy, has said, 'Really stingy is one who is stingy in offering the greeting of peace.'"

H 3621, Ch. 7, h 7

A number of our people have narrated from Sahl ibn Ziyad from Ja'far ibn Muhammad al-Ash'ari from ibn al- Qaddah from abu 'Abd Allah, *'Alayhi al-Salam*, who has said the following:

"When anyone of you offers the greeting of peace he should say it loud and clear so he will not complain that no one answered his greeting of peace. He may have offered, but no one may have heard it and when any one of you answers the greeting he should say it loud and clear so that the one offering it will not say, 'I offered them the greeting of peace but no one answered.'

"The Imam then said, 'Amir al-Mu'minin, Ali ibn abu Talib, *'Alayhi al-Salam*, has said, 'If you do not become angry you will not be made angry, offer the greeting of peace loud and openly, speak nicely, perform prayer at night when people are sleeping and you will enter paradise in peace.' Then he read the words of Allah, the Most Majestic, the Most Holy: '. . . the Peace, the Protector, the Watchful Guardian. . . .'" (59:23)

H 3622, Ch. 7, h 8

Muhammad ibn Yahya has narrated from Ahmad ibn Muhammad ibn 'Isa from ibn Mahbub from 'Abd Allah ibn Sinan from abu 'Abd Allah, *'Alayhi al-Salam*, who has said the following:

"The initiator of the offering of the greeting of peace is closer to Allah and His Messenger."

H 3623, Ch. 7, h 9

A number of our people have narrated from Ahmad ibn Muhammad ibn Khalid from Ali ibn al-Hakam from Aban from al-Hassan ibn al-Mundhir who has said the following:

"I heard abu 'Abd Allah, 'Alayhi al-Salam, saying, 'If one offering the greeting of peace says, "(I offer) you to be in peace," it is equal to ten good deeds. Saying, '(I offer) you to be in peace, and May Allah grant you favors,' is equal to twenty good deeds. Saying, '(I offer) you to be in peace, and May Allah grant you favors and blessings,' is equal to thirty good deeds.'"

H 3624, Ch. 7, h 10

Ali ibn Ibrahim has narrated from his father from Salih ibn al-Sindi from Ja'far ibn Bashir from Mansur ibn Hazim from abu 'Abd Allah, 'Alayhi al-Salam, who has said the following:

"In three cases the 'greeting' is answered in a plural case even if there is only one person: for one's sneezing, it is said, 'May Allah grant you (plural) favor.' when a man offers the 'greeting of peace' saying, '(I offer you to) be in peace', the answer is '(I offer you to) be in peace,' and when a man pleads before Allah for good health for another man, he should say, 'May Allah grant you (plural) good health, even if there is only one person; there are others with him (the guarding angels).'"

H 3625, Ch. 7, h 11

Muhammad ibn Yahya has narrated from Muhammad ibn al-Husayn in a marfu' manner from an Imam who has said the following:

"Abu 'Abd Allah, 'Alayhi al-Salam, would say, 'Three kinds of people do not offer greetings: one walking in funeral procession, one walking to attend Friday prayer and in the bathing places.'"

H 3626, Ch. 7, h 12

A number of our people have narrated from Ahmad ibn Muhammad from 'Uthman ibn 'Isa from Harun ibn Kharijah from abu 'Abd Allah, 'Alayhi al-Salam, who has said the following:

"It is of humility to offer the greeting of peace to whomever you meet."

H 3627, Ch. 7, h 13

Ahmad ibn Muhammad has narrated from ibn Mahbub from Jamil from abu 'Ubaydah al-Hadhdha' from abu Ja'far, 'Alayhi al-Salam, who has said the following:

"Once Amir al-Mu'minin, Ali ibn abu Talib, 'Alayhi al-Salam, passed by a people and offered them the greeting of peace and they answered, '(We offer) you peace, May Allah grant you favors, blessings, forgiveness and His pleasure.' Amir al-Mu'Minin, 'Alayhi al-Salam, said to them, 'Do not say to us more than what the angels said to Ibrahim. They said, 'May Allah grant you favors and blessings, O the people of the house' (of the Holy Prophet).'"

H 3628, Ch. 7, h 14

Muhammad ibn Yahya has narrated from Ahmad ibn Muhammad from ibn Mahbub from Ali ibn Ri'ab from abu 'Abd Allah, 'Alayhi al-Salam, who has said the following:

"The completion of greetings of peace for one at home is to shake hands and for one on a journey it is to hold him in one's arms."

H 3629, Ch. 7, h 15

Ali ibn Ibrahim has narrated from his father from al-Nawfali from al-Sakuni from abu 'Abd Allah, 'Alayhi al-Salam, who has said the following:

"Amir al-Mu'minin, Ali ibn abu Talib, *'Alayhi al-Salam*, has said, 'It is undesirable for a man to say, "May Allah keep you living," then remain silent without offering the greeting of peace thereafter.'"

Chapter 8 - The One Who Must Offer the Greeting of Peace

H 3630, Ch. 8, h 1

Muhammad ibn Yahya has narrated from Ahmad ibn Muhammad from al-Husayn ibn Sa'id from al-Nadr ibn Suwayd from al-Qasim ibn Sulayman from Jarrah al-Mad'ini from abu 'Abd Allah, *'Alayhi al-Salam*, who has said the following:

"The younger ones offer greetings of peace to the elders, passing by those who are stationary and fewer people to those of a greater number."

H 3631, Ch. 8, h 2

Ali ibn Ibrahim has narrated from his father from Salih ibn al-Sindi from Ja'far ibn Bashir from 'Anbasah ibn Mus'ab from abu 'Abd Allah, *'Alayhi al-Salam*, who has said the following:

"Those fewer in number initiate greetings of peace to those of a greater number, one riding to the one walking, people riding mules to those riding donkeys and those riding horses offer greeting of peace to those riding on mules."

H 3632, Ch. 8, h 3

A number of our people have narrated from Sahl ibn Ziyad from Ali ibn Asbat from ibn Bukayr from certain individuals of his people who has said the following:

"I heard abu 'Abd Allah, *'Alayhi al-Salam*, saying, 'A person riding should offer greetings of peace to the one walking, the one walking to the one stationary and sitting. On meeting a group the one in smaller numbers offers the greeting of peace to that in greater numbers and one person offers greetings of peace to a group.'"

H 3633, Ch. 8, h 4

Sahl ibn Ziyad has narrated from Ja'far ibn Muhammad al-Ash'ari from ibn al-Qaddah from abu 'Abd Allah, *'Alayhi al-Salam*, who has said the following:

"A person riding should offer greetings of peace to the one walking on foot and the one standing should offer greetings of peace to the one sitting."

H 3634, Ch. 8, h 5

Muhammad ibn Yahya has narrated from Ahmad ibn Muhammad from 'Umar ibn 'Abd al-'Aziz from Jamil from abu 'Abd Allah, *'Alayhi al-Salam*, who has said the following:

"If two groups attend the same meeting, the group entering last should offer greetings of peace to those who have entered first."

Chapter 9 - Offer or Answer of Greetings of Peace by One Person From a Group is Sufficient

H 3635, Ch. 9, h 1

A number of our people have narrated from Sahl ibn Ziyad from Ali ibn Asbat from ibn Bukayr from certain individuals of his people from abu 'Abd Allah, *'Alayhi al-Salam*, who has said the following:

"If one person from a group passing by another group offers the greeting of peace it is sufficient for all and so also is for an answer if only one person from the stationary group responds."

H 3636, Ch. 9, h 2

Muhammad ibn Yahya has narrated from Ahmad ibn Muhammad from ibn Mahbub from 'Abd al-Rahman ibn al-Hajjaj who has said the following from the Imam:

"If one person offers the greeting of peace for a whole group it is considered enough and sufficient."

H 3637, Ch. 9, h 3

Muhammad ibn Yahya has narrated from Ahmad ibn Muhammad from Muhammad ibn Yahya from Ghiyath ibn Ibrahim from abu 'Abd Allah, *'Alayhi al-Salam*, who has said the following from the Imam:

"If one person from a group offers the greeting of peace it is sufficient for all and so also is for an answer if only one person from the stationary group responds."

Chapter 10 - Offering Greeting of Peace to Women

H 3638, Ch. 10, h 1

Ali ibn Ibrahim has narrated from his father from Hammad ibn 'Isa from Rib'i ibn 'Abd Allah from abu 'Abd Allah, *'Alayhi al-Salam*, who has said the following:

"The Messenger of Allah would offer greeting of peace to women and they would respond to him. Amir al-Mu'minin, Ali ibn abu Talib, *'Alayhi al-Salam*, would offer greeting of peace to women but he disliked offering it to the young women. He would say, 'I fear their voice may attract me and a feeling may cause me more harm than the reward for offering the greeting of peace.'"

Chapter 11 - Greeting of Peace and Non-Muslims

H 3639, Ch. 11, h 1

Ali ibn Ibrahim has narrated from his father from ibn abu 'Umayr from ibn 'Udhaynah from Zurara from abu Ja'far, *'Alayhi al-Salam*, who has said the following:

"Once, a Jewish person went in the presence of the Messenger of Allah while 'A'ishah was with him. The Jewish person said, 'Sam 'Alaykum instead of 'Salamun 'Alaykum.' The Messenger of Allah said, 'Alaykum.' Then another Jewish person came and said the same thing as the one before and the Messenger of Allah responded just as before. Then a third Jewish person came. He also said what the other two had said before and the Messenger of Allah responded just as that to the other two before. 'A'ishah became angry and said, 'Alaykum al-Sam (wrath and condemnation) O Jewish group, brethren of monkeys and swine.' The Messenger of Allah said to her, 'O 'A'ishah, if name-calling were to appear with a shape and form it would have a very evil shape. Wherever gentleness is placed it beautifies it and removing it is only to make it despised.'

"'A'ishah then asked, 'O the Messenger of Allah, did you not hear their words: 'al-Sam 'Alaykum?' The Messenger of Allah said, 'I heard them but did you not note what I said? I said, ''Alaykum'. Whenever a Muslim offers you the greeting of peace say, 'Salamun 'Alaykum,' but when a non-Muslim says something in their manners, just say, 'Alaykum', meaning the same to you.'"

H 3640, Ch. 11, h 2

Muhammad ibn Yahya has narrated from Ahmad ibn Muhammad ibn 'Isa from Muhammad ibn Yahya from Ghiyath ibn Ibrahim from abu 'Abd Allah, *'Alayhi al-Salam*, who has said the following:

"Amir al-Mu'minin, Ali ibn abu Talib, *'Alayhi al-Salam*, has said, 'Do not initiate the offering of the greeting of peace to people of the Book, but if they offered just say, "wa 'Alaykum"'

H 3641, Ch. 11, h 3

A number of our people have narrated from Ahmad ibn Muhammad ibn Khalid from 'Uthman ibn 'Isa from Sama'a who has said the following:

"Once I asked abu 'Abd Allah, *'Alayhi al-Salam*, about Jewish, Christians and pagans' greetings to one sitting, how should he respond? The Imam said, 'He will say, ''Alaykum'''

H 3642, Ch. 11, h 4

Muhammad ibn Yahya has narrated from Ahmad ibn Muhammad from ibn Faddal from ibn Bukayr from Barid ibn Mu'awiyah from Muhammad ibn Muslim from abu 'Abd Allah, *'Alayhi al-Salam*, who has said the following:

"When a Jew, Christian or a pagan greets you with peace just say, ''Alayka' meaning, 'the same to you.'''

H 3643, Ch. 11, h 5

Abu Ali al-Ash'ari has narrated from Muhammad ibn Salim from Ahmad ibn Muhammad ibn abu Nasr from 'Amr ibn Shimr from Jabir from abu Ja'far, *'Alayhi al-Salam*, who has said the following:

"Once abu Jahl along with a people from Quraysh went to abu Talib and said, 'Your cousin has offended us and has harmed our idols, call him and command him to stop bothering our gods and we will stop bothering his Lord.'

"The Imam said, 'Abu Talib sent for the Messenger of Allah. He was called and he came. He did not see in the house but pagans and he said, '(I offer) greetings of peace to those who follow guidance.' He sat down and abu Talib informed him of what the people had said. The Messenger of Allah asked, 'What if I instruct them with a word of goodness that will be better for them than this and with which they can rule the Arabs and subdue their stiff necks?' Abu Jahl then asked, 'What is that word?' The Messenger of Allah advised him to say, 'No one deserves to be worshipped except Allah.' They placed their fingers in their ears and fled saying, 'We have not heard anything like this in other religions. This is only something falsely invented.' Allah, the Most High, then sent this: 'Sad. I swear by the Quran, which is full of reminders of Allah (that you are a Messenger) (38:1). In fact, the unbelievers are the ones who are boastful and quarrelsome (38:2). How many ancient generations did We destroy? (On facing Our torment) they cried out for help, but it was too late for them to escape.' (38:3)

'It seems strange to the pagans that a man from their own people should come to them as a prophet. The unbelievers have said, 'He is only a lying magician' (38:4). They ask, 'Has he condemned all other gods but One? This is certainly strange.' (38:5)

'A group of the pagans walked out of a meeting with the Prophet and told the others, 'Let us walk away. Be steadfast in the worship of your gods. This man wants to dominate you (38:6). We have heard nothing like this in the latest religion. This is only his own false invention.'" (38:7)

H 3644, Ch. 11, h 6

Muhammad ibn Yahya has narrated from 'Abd Allah ibn Muhammad from Ali ibn al-Hakam from Aban ibn 'Uthman from Zurara from abu 'Abd Allah, *'Alayhi al-Salam*, who has said the following:

"In response to a Jew or Christian You should say, 'Salam', meaning peace be upon us or whoever deserves it."

H 3645, Ch. 11, h 7

Ali ibn Ibrahim has narrated from his father from ibn abu 'Umayr from 'Abd al-Rahman ibn al-Hajjaj who has said the following:

"Once I asked abu al-Hassan Musa, *'Alayhi al-Salam*, 'If I needed to visit a Christian physician, can I offer the greeting of peace and pray for him?' The Imam said, 'Yes, but your prayer will not benefit him.'"

H 3646, Ch. 11, h 8

Muhammad ibn Yahya has narrated from Ahmad ibn Muhammad ibn 'Isa from ibn Mahbub from 'Abd al-Rahman ibn al-Hajjaj who has said the following:

"Once I asked abu al-Hassan Musa, *'Alayhi al-Salam*, 'If I needed to visit a Christian physician, can I offer him the greeting of peace and pray for him?' The Imam said, 'Yes, but your prayer will not benefit him.'"

H 3647, Ch. 11, h 9

A number of our people have narrated from Ahmad ibn Muhammad ibn Khalid from Muhammad ibn 'Isa ibn 'Ubayd from Muhammad ibn 'Arafah from abu al-Hassan al-Rida, *'Alayhi al-Salam*, who has said the following:

"It was asked from abu 'Abd Allah, *'Alayhi al-Salam*, 'How do I pray for a Jew or a Christian?' He had said, 'Say, "May Allah grant you blessing in this world."'"

H 3648, Ch. 11, h 10

Hamid ibn Ziyad has narrated from al-Hassan ibn Muhammad from Wahab ibn Hafs from abu Basir from one of the two Imam, *'Alayhi al-Salam*, who has said the following:

"About shaking hands with a Jew or a Christian he had said, 'Shake hands with them from behind clothes and if you shook their hand without clothes then you must wash your hands.'"

H 3649, Ch. 11, h 11

Abu Ali al-Ash'ari has narrated from al-Hassan ibn Ali al-Kufi from al-'Abbas ibn 'Amir from Ali ibn Mu'ammar from Khalid al-Qalanisi who has said the following:

"Once I asked abu 'Abd Allah, *'Alayhi al-Salam*, 'What should I do if I meet a tax paying non-Muslim and he shakes my hand?' The Imam said, 'Wipe it with soil or against a wall.' I asked, 'What about one who is abusive of 'A'immah?' The Imam said, 'Wash it (your hand).'"

H 3650, Ch. 11, h 12

Abu Ali al-Ash'ari has narrated from Muhammad ibn 'Abd al-Jabbar from Safwan from al-'Ala' ibn Razin from Muhammad ibn Muslim from abu Ja'far, *'Alayhi al-Salam*, who has said the following:

"About a man who had shaken hand with Majusi (Zoroastrian), the Imam said, 'He must wash it but he does not need to perform wuzu again.'"

Chapter 12 - Correspondence with Non-Muslim Taxpayers

H 3651, Ch. 12, h 1

Ahmad ibn Muhammad al-Kufi has narrated from Ali ibn al-Husayn ibn Ali ibn Asbat from his uncle, Ya'qub ibn Salim from abu Basir who has said the following:

"Abu 'Abd Allah, *'Alayhi al-Salam*, was asked about the case of a man who needs help from a Majusi (Zoroastrian) or a Jew, a Christian or that he is a farm employee of the influential people of his land and writes to him for an important need, should he begin by offering greetings of peace to the chief in writing, knowing that he does it for help? The Imam said, 'Do not start with his name, however, you may offer him greetings of peace in your letter. The Messenger of Allah would write to Kisra and Qaysar.'"

H 3652, Ch. 12, h 2

Ali ibn Ibrahim has narrated from his father from Isma'il ibn Marrar from Yunus from 'Abd Allah ibn Sinan from abu 'Abd Allah, *'Alayhi al-Salam*, who has said the following:

"The Imam was asked about the case of a man who writes to a chief officer of Majus and begins with the name of the chief before his own name. The Imam said, 'It is permissible if it is for seeking favors.'"

Chapter 13 - Overlooking

H 3653, Ch. 13, h 1

A number of our people have narrated from Ahmad ibn Muhammad ibn Muhammad from 'Abd Allah ibn Muhammad al-Hajjal from Tha'Labah ibn Maymun from those whom he has mentioned (in his book) from abu 'Abd Allah, *'Alayhi al-Salam*, who has said the following:

"Once in the presence of abu 'Abd Allah, *'Alayhi al-Salam*, there were people speaking to him. One man mentioned the name of another man and he began to criticize him and complained against him. Abu 'Abd Allah, *'Alayhi al-Salam*, asked, 'Where from can you have a perfect brother? Who is among man, free and pure of faults and flaws?'"

H 3654, Ch. 13, h 2

Muhammad ibn Yahya has narrated from Ahmad ibn Muhammad ibn 'Isa from Ali ibn al-Hakam and Muhammad ibn Sinan from, Ali ibn abu Hamza from abu Basir who has said the following:

"Abu 'Abd Allah, *'Alayhi al-Salam*, has said, 'Do not be a spy against people; you will remain without friends.'"

Chapter 14 - Rare AHadith

H 3655, Ch. 14, h 1

Muhammad ibn Yahya has narrated from Ahmad ibn Muhammad ibn 'Isa from Muhammad ibn Sinan from al-'Ala' ibn al-Fudayl and Hammad ibn 'Uthman who has said the following:

"I heard abu 'Abd Allah, *'Alayhi al-Salam*, saying, 'Look in your heart, if it dislikes your friend, one of you has done something (wrong).'"

H 3656, Ch. 14, h 2

A number of our people have narrated from Ahmad ibn Muhammad ibn Khalid from Isma'il ibn Mehran from al-Hassan ibn Yusuf from Zakariya ibn m h from Salih ibn al-Hakam who has said the following:

"I heard a man asking abu 'Abd Allah, *'Alayhi al-Salam*, 'A man says he loves me. How can I know if he really loves me?' The Imam said, 'Test your own heart. If you love him, he also loves you.'"

H 3657, Ch. 14, h 3

Abu Bakr al-Habbal has narrated from Muhammad ibn 'Isa al-Qattan al-Mada'ini who has said that I heard my father saying, 'Mas'adah ibn al-Yasa' who has said the following:

"Once I said to abu Ja'far, *'Alayhi al-Salam*, 'By Allah, I love you.' Abu Ja'far, *'Alayhi al-Salam*, looked down for a short while then he raised his head and said, 'O abu Bishr you have spoken the truth. Ask your heart about what my heart has of your love. My heart has informed me about what your heart has for me.'"

H 3658, Ch. 14, h 4

A number of our people have narrated from Sahl ibn Ziyad from Ali ibn Asbat from al-Hassan ibn al-Jahm who has said the following:

"Once I said to abu al-Hassan, *'Alayhi al-Salam*, 'Do not forget me in your prayers.' The Imam asked, 'How do you know I forget you?' I (the narrator) then thought in my soul and said to myself that he (Imam) prays for his Shi'a (followers) and I am a Shi'a. I then said to the Imam, 'I know, you do not forget me in your prayers.' The Imam asked, 'How did you find out?' I said, 'You pray for your Shi'a and I am your Shi'a.' The Imam asked, 'Did you find out by any means other than that?' I said, 'No.' The Imam said, 'If you like to know what I have for you, see what you have for me in your heart.'"

H 3659, Ch. 14, h 5

Ali ibn Ibrahim has narrated from his father from al-Al-Nadr ibn Suwayd from al-Qasim ibn Sulayman from Jarrah al-Mada'ini from abu 'Abd Allah, *'Alayhi al-Salam*, who has said the following:

"See your heart. If it dislikes your friend then notice that one of you have done something newly wrong.'"

Chapter 15 - Response to Sneezing

H 3660, Ch. 15, h 1

Muhammad ibn Yahya has narrated from Ahmad ibn Muhammad ibn 'Isa from al-Husayn ibn Sa'id from al-Nadr ibn Suwayd from al-Qasim ibn Sulayman from Jarrah al-Mad'ini who has said the following:

"Abu 'Abd Allah, *'Alayhi al-Salam*, has said, 'Of the rights of a Muslim on his brother (in belief) is that on meeting him he should offer him the greeting of peace, visit him when he is ill, look after his interests in his absence and respond to his sneezing. On sneezing one should say: "All praise belongs to Allah, Lord of the worlds, who has no partner." In response to sneezing one should say, "May Allah grant you favors." The sneezing person should reply back by saying, "May Allah guide you, and look after your concerns." Of such rights is to accept his invitation and attend his funeral.'"

H 3661, Ch. 15, h 2

Ali ibn Ibrahim has narrated from his father from Harun ibn Muslim from Mas'adah ibn Sadaqah from abu 'Abd Allah, *'Alayhi al-Salam*, who has said the following:

"The Messenger of Allah has said, 'You should respond to one's sneezing even if he is behind the island. In another Hadith it is said, 'Even if it (response) is from behind the ocean.'"

H 3662, Ch. 15, h 3

Al-Husayn ibn Muhammad has narrated from Mu'Alla ibn Muhammad from al-Hassan ibn Ali from Muthanna from Ishaq ibn Yazid and Mu'ammar ibn abu Ziyad ibn Ri'ab who have said the following:

"Once we were in the presence of abu 'Abd Allah, *'Alayhi al-Salam*, when a man sneezed and no one from the group responded until he (the Imam) initiated saying: 'Glory belongs to Allah, why did no one respond? It is of the rights of a Muslim upon the Muslim to visit him when he is ill, accept his invitation, attend his funeral and respond to his sneezing.'"

H 3663, Ch. 15, h 4

Muhammad ibn Yahya has narrated from Ahmad ibn Muhammad ibn 'Isa from Safwan ibn Yahya who has said the following:

"Once I was in the presence of al-Rida, *'Alayhi al-Salam*, and he sneezed. I said, 'May Allah grant you al-Salat (favors).' He sneezed again, and said, 'May Allah grant you favors.' He sneezed again and I said, 'May Allah grant you favors.' I then said, 'May Allah keep my soul in service for your cause, if one like you (Imam) would sneeze should we say what we say to each other like: "May Allah grant you mercy? Or should we say what I just said, '(May Allah grant you al-Salat?'" The Imam said, 'Yes, do you not say, "O Lord, grant al-Salat upon Muhammad and the Ahl al-Bayt, family of Muhammad?"' I said, 'Yes, we do.' The Imam said, 'Do you not say, "(O Lord,) be merciful to Muhammad and the Ahl al-Bayt, family of Muhammad?"' Then the Imam said, 'Yes, Allah grants al-Salat to him and has been merciful to him. Our saying, "May Allah grant him al-Salat is a blessing for us and a way of our seeking nearness to Allah (thereby).'""

H 3664, Ch. 15, h 5

It is narrated from him (narrator of the Hadith above) from Ahmad ibn Muhammad ibn 'Isa from Ahmad ibn Muhammad ibn abu Nasr who has said the following:

"Once I heard al-Rida, *'Alayhi al-Salam*, saying, 'Yawning is from Satan and sneezing is from Allah.'"

H 3665, Ch. 15, h 6

Ali ibn Muhammad has narrated from Salih ibn abu Hammad who has said the following:

"Once I asked the scholar about sneezing and the reason for praising Allah thereafter. The Imam said, 'From Allah there are bounties in His servant, in his good health for his body and soundness of his limbs. The servant forgets remembering Allah, the Most Majestic, the Most Holy, for such bounties. When he forgets Allah commands the air to pass through his body and come out of his nose. He then praises Allah for it and his praising at such time is thanking that he had forgotten.'"

H 3666, Ch. 15, h 7

A number of our people have narrated from Ahmad ibn Muhammad ibn Khalid from Faddal from Ja'far ibn Yunus from Dawud ibn al-Hosayn who has said the following:

"Once we were in the presence of abu 'Abd Allah, *'Alayhi al-Salam*. I counted that the people present were fourteen. Abu 'Abd Allah, *'Alayhi al-Salam*, sneezed and no one from the people said anything. Abu 'Abd Allah, *'Alayhi al-Salam*, then asked, 'You did not respond. Why did you not respond? It is of the rights of a believing person on the other believing person to visit him in his illness, attend his funeral, and respond to his sneezing, or he said, yusammithu (response to his sneezing) and when he invites accept his invitation.'"

H 3667, Ch. 15, h 8

Abu Ali al-Ash'ari has narrated from Muhammad ibn Salim from Ahmad ibn al-Nadr from 'Amr ibn Shimr from Jabir who has said the following:

"Abu Ja'far, *'Alayhi al-Salam*, has said, 'Sneezing is a good thing. It benefits the body and reminds one of Allah, the Most Majestic, the Most Holy.' I then said, 'Nearby to us there are people who say, "There is nothing in sneezing for the Messenger of Allah." The Imam said, 'If they are lying, the intercession of Muhammad will not avail them.'"

H 3668, Ch. 15, h 9

Ali ibn Ibrahim has narrated from his father from ibn abu 'Umayr from certain individuals of his people from who has said the following:

"Once a man sneezed in the presence of abu Ja'far, *'Alayhi al-Salam*, and he said, 'All praise belongs to Allah.' Abu Ja'far, *'Alayhi al-Salam*, did not respond and said, 'Our rights are reduced.' Then he said, 'Whenever anyone of you sneezes he should say, "All praise belongs to Allah, Lord of the worlds and Allah has granted al-Salat (favors) upon Muhammad and the Ahl al-Bay (family of Muhammad).'" The narrator has said that the man then said it and abu Ja'far, *'Alayhi al-Salam*, responded.'"

H 3669, Ch. 15, h 10

Ali has narrated from his father from ibn abu 'Umayr from Isma'il al-Basri from al-Fudayl ibn Yasar who has said the following:

"Once I said to abu Ja'far, *'Alayhi al-Salam*, 'People do not like saying, "O Allah grant al-Salat, (favors) upon Muhammad and the Ahl al-Bay (family of Muhammad)," in three conditions: when sneezing, when slaughtering an animal and at the time of having intimate relations with their spouses.' Abu Ja'far, *'Alayhi al-Salam*, said, 'What is wrong with them, woe upon them! It is due to their hypocrisy, may Allah condemn them.'"

H 3670, Ch. 15, h 11

It is narrated from him (narrator of the Hadith above) from ibn abu 'Umayr from Sa'd ibn abu Khalaf who has said the following:

"Whenever abu Ja'far, *'Alayhi al-Salam*, would sneeze in response it was said, 'May Allah be kind to you,' and he would say, 'May Allah grant you forgiveness and be kind to you.' When anyone sneezed in his presence he would say, 'May Allah, the Most Majestic, the Most Holy, grant you forgiveness.'"

H 3671, Ch. 15, h 12

It is narrated from him (narrator of the Hadith above) from his father from al-Nawfali from al-Sakuni from abu 'Abd Allah, *'Alayhi al-Salam*, who has said the following:

"A young boy who had not yet reached puberty once sneezed in the presence of the Holy Prophet and said, 'All praise belongs to Allah.' The Holy Prophet said, 'May Allah place blessings in you.'"

H 3672, Ch. 15, h 13

Muhammad ibn Yahya has narrated from 'Abd Allah ibn Muhammad from Ali ibn al-Hakam from Aban ibn 'Uthman from Muhammad ibn Muslim from abu Ja'far, *'Alayhi al-Salam*, who has said the following:

"When a man sneezes he should say, 'All praise belongs to Allah [Lord of the worlds] who has no partner.' In response one should say, 'May Allah grant you blessings.' If it is repeated then one should say, 'May Allah forgive you and forgive us.' The Messenger of Allah was asked if there was a special verse of the Holy Quran about it or something with a mention of Allah. He said, 'Anything in which there is a mention of Allah is good.'"

H 3673, Ch. 15, h 14

Muhammad ibn Yahya has narrated from Ahmad ibn Muhammad from Muhammad ibn Sinan from al-Husayn ibn Nu'aym from Misma' ibn 'Abd al-Malik who has said the following:

"Once abu 'Abd Allah, *'Alayhi al-Salam*, sneezed and said, 'All praise belongs to Allah, Lord of the worlds,' then he placed his finger over his nose and said, 'Humble is my nose before Allah with complete humility.'"

H 3674, Ch. 15, h 15

Abu Ali al-Ash'ari has narrated from Muhammad ibn Salim from Ahmad ibn al-Nadr from Muhammad ibn Marwan in a marfu' manner from Amir al-Mu'minin, Ali ibn abu Talib, *'Alayhi al-Salam*, who has said the following:

"Amir al-Mu'minin, Ali ibn abu Talib, *'Alayhi al-Salam*, has said, 'Whoever upon sneezing says, "All praise belongs to Allah, Lord of the worlds, in all conditions, will not suffer from pain in his ears and teeth."'"

H 3675, Ch. 15, h 16

Muhammad ibn Yahya has narrated from Ahmad ibn Muhammad and others from ibn Faddal from certain individuals of his people from abu 'Abd Allah, *'Alayhi al-Salam*, who has said the following:

"For a tooth and earache when you hear a person sneeze, you should first say, 'All praise belongs to Allah.'"

H 3676, Ch. 15, h 17

Ali ibn Ibrahim has narrated from his father from Salih ibn al-Sindi from Ja'far ibn Bashir from 'Uthman from abu 'Usamah who has said the following:

"Abu 'Abd Allah, *'Alayhi al-Salam*, has said, 'If one hears a person's sneezing and praises Allah, the Most Majestic, the Most Holy, and asks Allah to grant al-Salat (favors) upon Muhammad and the Ahl al-Bayt (family of Muhammad), he will not suffer from a toothache or eye trouble.' The Imam then said, 'When you hear it (sneezing) respond to it even if there is an ocean between you and the person sneezing.'"

H 3677, Ch. 15, h 18

Abu Ali al-Ash'ari has narrated from certain individuals of his people from ibn abu Najran from certain individuals of our people from abu 'Abd Allah, *'Alayhi al-Salam,* who has said the following:

"Once a Christian man sneezed in the presence of abu 'Abd Allah, *'Alayhi al-Salam,* and the people said, 'May Allah guide you.' Abu 'Abd Allah, *'Alayhi al-Salam,* said, 'Say, "May Allah grant you mercy."' They said, 'He is a Christian.' The Imam said, 'Allah will not guide him until He grants him mercy.'"

H 3678, Ch. 15, h 19

Ali ibn Ibrahim has narrated from his father from Harun ibn Muslim from Mas'adah ibn Sadaqah from abu 'Abd Allah, *'Alayhi al-Salam,* who has said the following:

"The Messenger of Allah has said, 'When a Muslim person sneezes and remains silent for reasons of illness, the angels say for him, "All praise belongs to Allah, Lord of the worlds," if he would say, 'All praise belongs to Allah, Lord of the worlds the angels will say, "May Allah forgive you."''The narrator has said that the Holy Prophet has said, 'Sneezing in a person suffering illness is an indication of good health and bodily comfort.'"

H 3679, Ch. 15, h 20

Muhammad ibn Yahya has narrated from Muhammad ibn Musa from Ya'qub ibn Yazid from 'Uthman ibn 'Isa from 'Abd al-Samad ibn Bash 'Amir from Hudhayfah ibn Mansur from abu 'Abd Allah, *'Alayhi al-Salam,* who has said the following:

"Sneezing is beneficial to all parts of the body if it is not more than three times, if it is more than three times then it is an illness and disease.'"

H 3680, Ch. 15, h 21

Ahmad ibn Muhammad al-Kufi has narrated from Ali ibn al-Hassan from Ali ibn b t from his Uncle, Ya'qub n Salim from abu Bakr al-Hadrami who said the following:

"Once I asked abu 'Abd Allah, *'Alayhi al-Salam,* about the words of Allah, the Most Majestic, the Most Holy, 'The most undesirable voice is the voice of donkeys.' (31:19) The Imam said, 'It is a bad sneezing.'"

H 3681, Ch. 15, h 22

Muhammad ibn Yahya has narrated from Ahmad ibn Muhammad from al-Qasim ibn Yahya from his grandfather al-Hassan ibn Rashid from abu 'Abd Allah, *'Alayhi al-Salam,* who has said the following:

"If one sneezes, places his hand over his nose and says, 'All praise belongs to Allah, Lord of the worlds, (all praise belongs to Allah), a great deal of praise, as He deserves, Allah has granted al-Salat (favors) and peace upon Muhammad, His Holy Prophet, and the Ahl al-Bay (family of Muhammad), a small flying thing, smaller than a grasshopper and larger than a fly, will come out of his left nostril until it reaches beneath the Throne and asks for him forgiveness from Allah to the Day of Judgment.'"

H 3682, Ch. 15, h 23

Muhammad ibn Yahya has narrated from Ahmad ibn Muhammad from certain individuals of his people from a man of 'Ammah (non-Shi'a) who has said the following:

"I would sit in the meeting place of abu 'Abd Allah, *'Alayhi al-Salam,* I swear by Allah that I had not seen any meeting place nobler than his meeting place. One day he asked me, 'Where from does sneeze come?' I said, 'It comes out of the nose.' He said, 'You have got it wrong.' I then said, 'May Allah keep my soul in service for your cause, from where does it come?' The Imam said, 'It comes from the whole body, just as a reproductive seed comes out of the whole body and its exit is through penis.' The Imam then asked, 'Have you noted that when one sneezes his whole body moves and a person sneezing is safe from death for seven days?'"

H 3683, Ch. 15, h 24

Ali ibn Ibrahim has narrated from his father from al-Nawfali from al-Sakuni from abu 'Abd Allah, *'Alayhi al-Salam*, who has said the following:

"The Messenger of Allah has said, 'Sneezing is a sign of truthfulness.'"

H 3684, Ch. 15, h 25

Ali ibn Ibrahim has narrated from his father from al-Nawfali from al-Sakuni from abu 'Abd Allah, *'Alayhi al-Salam*, who has said the following:

"The Messenger of Allah has said, 'If a man is speaking about something and someone sneezes, this is evidence of the truth.'"

H 3685, Ch. 15, h 26

A number of our people have narrated from Sahl ibn Ziyad from Ja'far ibn Muhammad al-Ash'ari from ibn al-Qaddah from ibn abu 'Umayr from abu 'Abd Allah, *'Alayhi al-Salam*, who has said the following:

"The Messenger of Allah has said, 'Sneezing is verification of the truthfulness of a person's words.'"

H 3686, Ch. 15, h 27

A number of our people have narrated from Ahmad ibn Muhammad from Muhsin ibn Ahmad from Aban ibn 'Uthman from Zurara from abu Ja'far, *'Alayhi al-Salam*, who has said the following:

"If one sneezes three times, the special expressions for this purpose should be said only up to three times and thereafter should be left alone."

Chapter 16 - The Necessity to Honor an Old Muslim

H 3687, Ch. 16, h 1

Muhammad ibn Yahya has narrated from Ahmad ibn Muhammad and Ali ibn Ibrahim has narrated from his father all from ibn Mahbub from 'Abd Allah ibn Sinan who has said the following:

"Abu 'Abd Allah, *'Alayhi al-Salam*, has said, 'It is of honoring Allah, the Most Majestic, the Most Holy, to honor a Muslim man advanced in age.'"

H 3688, Ch. 16, h 2

Ali ibn Ibrahim has narrated from his father from al-Nawfali from al-Sakuni from abu 'Abd Allah, *'Alayhi al-Salam*, who has said the following:

"The Messenger of Allah has said, 'Whoever recognizes the excellence of an old person due to his age and treats him with dignity, Allah will grant him protection against the horror on the Day of Judgment.'"

H 3689, Ch. 16, h 3

Through the same chain of narrators it is narrated from abu 'Abd Allah, *'Alayhi al-Salam*, who has said the following:

"The Messenger of Allah has said, 'Whoever treats an old Muslim person with dignity, Allah, the Most Majestic, the Most Holy, will grant him protection against the horror of the Day of Judgment.'"

H 3690, Ch. 16, h 4

A number of our people have narrated from Ahmad ibn Muhammad ibn Khalid from Muhammad ibn Ali from Muhammad ibn al-Fudayl from Ishaq ibn 'Ammar who has said that he heard abu al-Khattab narrate from abu 'Abd Allah, *'Alayhi al-Salam*, the following:

"There are three kinds of people whose rights are not ignored, except by a hypocrite, well-known in hypocrisy: of such people is an old person in Islam, the carrier of the Holy Quran and the Imam who possesses the noble merit of justice."

H 3691, Ch. 16, h 5

It is narrated from him (narrator of the Hadith above) from abu Nahshal from 'Abd Allah ibn Sinan who has said the following:

"Once abu 'Abd Allah, *'Alayhi al-Salam*, said to me, 'It is respecting Allah, the Most Majestic, the Most Holy, to respect an old believing person. Whoever honors an old believing person has begun (with) honoring Allah. Whoever disrespects an old believing person, Allah will send to him someone who will disrespect him before his death.'"

H 3692, Ch. 16, h 6

Al-Husayn ibn Muhammad has narrated from Ahmad ibn Ishaq from Sa'dan ibn Muslim from abu Basir and others from abu 'Abd Allah, *'Alayhi al-Salam*, who has said the following:

"It is honoring Allah, the Most Majestic, the Most Holy, to honor an old Muslim."

Chapter 17 - Honoring the Honorable

H 3693, Ch. 17, h 1

A number of our people have narrated from Sahl ibn Ziyad from Ja'far ibn Muhammad al-Ash'ari from 'Abd Allah ibn al-Qaddah from abu 'Abd Allah, *'Alayhi al-Salam*, who has said the following:

"Once two men came to Amir al-Mu'minin, Ali ibn abu Talib, *'Alayhi al-Salam*, he prepared one seat for each one. One of them sat on the seat but the other refused. Amir al-Mu'minin, Ali ibn abu Talib, *'Alayhi al-Salam*, said to him, 'Take your seat; no one refuses to appreciate being honored except a donkey.' The Imam then said, 'The Messenger of Allah has said, "When the honorable person of a people comes to you, you must treat him with honor."'"

H 3694, Ch. 17, h 2

Ali ibn Ibrahim has narrated from his father from al-Nawfali from al-Sakuni from abu 'Abd Allah, *'Alayhi al-Salam*, who has said the following:

"The Messenger of Allah has said, 'When a noble and honorable person of a people comes to you, you must treat him with honor.'"

H 3695, Ch. 17, h 3

A number of our people have narrated from Ahmad ibn abu 'Abd Allah from Muhammad ibn 'Isa from 'Abd Allah al-'Alawi from his father from his grandfather who has said the following:

"Amir al-Mu'minin, Ali ibn abu Talib, *'Alayhi al-Salam*, has said, 'When 'Adi ibn Hatim came to the Holy Prophet, he brought him ('Adi) to his house. In his house there was nothing to use as a seat except a sack (storage for dates) and a pillow made of animal skin. With such items the Messenger of Allah prepared a seat for 'Adi ibn Hatim.'"

Chapter 18 - The Right of a Newcomer

H 3696, Ch. 18, h 1

Ali ibn Ibrahim has narrated from his father from al-Nawfali from al-Sakuni from abu 'Abd Allah, *'Alayhi al-Salam,* who has said the following:

"The Messenger of Allah has said, 'It is of the rights of a newcomer on the people of the house to gently escort him when entering and leaving.' The Imam said that the Messenger of Allah has said, 'When anyone enters the house of his brother (in belief), the host then is his commander until he leaves.'"

Chapter 19 - Safe Guarding the Trust of a Meeting

H 3697, Ch. 19, h 1

A number of our people have narrated from Sahl ibn Ziyad and Ahmad ibn Muhammad all from ibn Mahbub from 'Abd Allah ibn Sinan from ibn abu 'Awf who has said the following:

"I heard abu 'Abd Allah, *'Alayhi al-Salam,* saying, 'Meetings are trusts (in the hands of the attendants).'"

H 3698, Ch. 19, h 2

Ali ibn Ibrahim has narrated from his father from ibn abu 'Umayr from Hammad ibn 'Uthman from Zurara from abu Ja'far, *'Alayhi al-Salam,* who has said the following:

"The Messenger of Allah has said, 'Meetings are a trust (that attendants must not violate)."

H 3699, Ch. 19, h 3

A number of our people have narrated from Ahmad ibn Muhammad ibn Khalid from 'Uthman ibn 'Isa from those whom he has mentioned (in his book) from abu 'Abd Allah, *'Alayhi al-Salam,* who has said the following:

"The meetings are trusts. No one must make public anything that one's companion does not want to be made public unless it is with his permission, or he is trusted and does it only for his good."

Chapter 20 - Private Conversations

H 3700, Ch. 20, h 1

Muhammad ibn Yahya has narrated from Ahmad ibn Muhammad ibn 'Isa from al-Hassan ibn Mahbub from Malik ibn 'Atiyyah from abu Basir from abu 'Abd Allah, *'Alayhi al-Salam,* who has said the following:

"Out of three people, two of them should not hold a private conversation because it saddens and hurts the feelings of the third."

H 3701, Ch. 20, h 2

A number of our people have narrated from Ahmad ibn abu 'Abd Allah from Muhammad ibn Ali from Yunus ibn Ya'qub from abu al-Hassan, the first, *'Alayhi al-Salam,* who has said the following:

"Out of three people in one house, two of them should not hold a private conversation because it saddens the third."

H 3702, Ch. 20, h 3

Ali ibn Ibrahim has narrated from his father from al-Nawfali from al-Sakuni from abu 'Abd Allah, *'Alayhi al-Salam*, who has said the following:

"The Messenger of Allah has said, 'To one who disturbs the conversation of his Muslim brother it is like scratching his face.'"

Chapter 21 - Manner of Sitting

H 3703, Ch. 21, h 1

A number of our people have narrated from Ahmad ibn Muhammad ibn Khalid from al-Nawfali from 'Abd al-'Azim ibn 'Abd Allah ibn al-Hassan al-'Alawi in a marfu' manner from the Imam who has said the following:

"The Holy Prophet would sit with three postures: al-Qurfusa'. In this posture both knees are up and one holds them with both arms and hands around them, folding both legs backwards so one can sit on them and one leg folded and the other spread over the folded one. He was never seen sitting with legs squared."

H 3704, Ch. 21, h 2

Ali ibn Ibrahim has narrated from his father from ibn abu 'Umayr from those whom he has mentioned (in his book) from abu Hamza al-Thumali who has said the following:

"I saw Ali ibn al-Husayn, *'Alayhi al-Salam*, when sitting place one foot over his thigh. I said, 'People dislike this sitting posture and say, "It is the sitting posture of the Lord."' The Imam said, 'I sit this way to relieve myself of tiredness. The Lord does not tire and slumber or sleep cannot overcome Him.'"

H 3705, Ch. 21, h 3

Ali has narrated from his father from ibn abu 'Umayr from Muhammad ibn Murazim from abu Sulayman al-Zahid from abu 'Abd Allah, *'Alayhi al-Salam*, who has said the following:

"Whoever feels content with a seat without formalities in a gathering, Allah, the Most Majestic, the Most Holy, and His angels continue doing and asking favors for him until he leaves the gathering."

H 3706, Ch. 21, h 4

Ali ibn Ibrahim has narrated from his father from certain individuals of his people from Talhah ibn Zayd from abu 'Abd Allah, *'Alayhi al-Salam*, who has said the following:

"The Messenger of Allah most of the time would sit facing the direction of Qiblah (Ka'bah)."

H 3707, Ch. 21, h 5

Abu Ali al-Ash'ari has narrated from Mu'Alla ibn Muhammad from al-Washsha' from Hammad ibn 'Uthman who has said the following:

"Once abu 'Abd Allah, *'Alayhi al-Salam*, was sitting with his right foot on his left thigh. A man said, 'May Allah keep my soul in service for your cause, this sitting posture is not desirable.' The Imam said, 'It is not so. That is a thing the Jews say that when Allah, the Most Majestic, the Most Holy, finished creating the heavens and earth and took His place on the Throne, He sat in this posture to rest and relax. Allah, the Most Majestic, the Most Holy, revealed 255 of Chapter 2 of the Holy Quran, "Allah exists. No one deserves to be worshipped except Allah, the Everlasting and the Guardian of life. Drowsiness or sleep does not seize him. . .

."' (2:255) Abu 'Abd Allah, *'Alayhi al-Salam*, continued to remain in that sitting posture.'"

H 3708, Ch. 21, h 6
A number of our people have narrated from Ahmad ibn Muhammad ibn Khalid from his father from 'Abd Allah ibn al-Mughirah from those whom he has mentioned (in his book) from abu 'Abd Allah, *'Alayhi al-Salam*, who has said the following:

"When the Messenger of Allah was to enter a house he would sit at the nearest place to the entrance."

H 3709, Ch. 21, h 7
Muhammad ibn Yahya has narrated from Ahmad ibn Muhammad ibn 'Isa from Muhammad ibn Yahya from Talhah ibn Zayd from abu 'Abd Allah, *'Alayhi al-Salam*, who has said the following:

"Amir al-Mu'minin, Ali ibn abu Talib, *'Alayhi al-Salam*, would say, 'The market place of the Muslims is like their Mosque, the one who first takes a place stays there until night.' The narrator has said that he (the Imam) would not charge any rent for the shops.'"

H 3710, Ch. 21, h 8
Ali ibn Ibrahim has narrated from his father from al-Nawfali from al-Sakuni from abu 'Abd Allah, *'Alayhi al-Salam*, who has said the following:

"The Messenger of Allah has said, 'In a gathering during summer the distance between two people should be an elbow's length (about eighteen inches) so that no difficulty is caused to any of them.'"

H 3711, Ch. 21, h 9
Ali has narrated from his father from ibn abu 'Umayr from Hammad ibn 'Uthman who has said the following:

"Once, I saw abu 'Abd Allah, *'Alayhi al-Salam*, sitting in his house near the door facing the Ka'bah."

Chapter 22 - Sitting in a Leaning or Folded Posture in the Mosque

H 3712, Ch. 22, h 1
Ali ibn Ibrahim has narrated from his father from al-Nawfali from al-Sakuni from abu 'Abd Allah, *'Alayhi al-Salam*, who has said the following:

"The Messenger of Allah has said, 'Sitting in the Mosque in a leaning posture is the monkish practice of the Arabs. The gathering place of believing people is the Mosque, and their monastery is their home.'"

H 3713, Ch. 22, h 2
It is narrated from him (narrator of the Hadith above) from his father from al-Nawfali from al-Sakuni from abu 'Abd Allah, *'Alayhi al-Salam*, who has said the following:

"The Messenger of Allah has said, 'Sitting in the Mosque in al-'Ihtiba' posture (knees folded with thighs against the belly by a piece of cloth or by one's arms) is the wall of Arabs.'"

H 3714, Ch. 22, h 3

Muhammad ibn Isma'il has narrated from al-Fadl ibn Shadhan and Ali ibn Ibrahim has narrated from his father all from ibn abu 'Umayr from Ibrahim ibn 'Abd al-Hamid from abu al-Hassan, *'Alayhi al-Salam*, who has said the following:

"The Messenger of Allah has said, 'Sitting in the Mosque in al-'Ihtiba' posture, (knees folded with thighs against the belly by a piece of cloth or by one's arms) is the wall of Arabs.'"

H 3715, Ch. 22, h 4

A number of our people have narrated from Ahmad ibn Muhammad ibn Khalid from 'Uthman ibn 'Isa from Sama'a who has said the following:

"Once I asked abu 'Abd Allah, *'Alayhi al-Salam*, about a man who uses one piece of cloth for al-'Ihtiba'. The Imam said, 'If it covers his private parts then it is not an offense.'"

H 3716, Ch. 22, h 5

It is narrated from him (narrator of the Hadith above) from Muhammad ibn Ali from Ali ibn Asbat from certain individuals of our people from abu 'Abd Allah, *'Alayhi al-Salam*, who has said the following:

"It is not permissible for a man to perform al-'Ihtiba' across the Ka'bah."

Chapter 23 - Funny Stories and Laughing

H 3717, Ch. 23, h 1

Muhammad ibn Yahya has narrated from Ahmad ibn Muhammad ibn 'Isa from Mu'ammar ibn Khallad who has said the following:

"Once I asked abu al-Hassan, *'Alayhi al-Salam*, 'May Allah keep my soul in service for your cause, can a man be with a people who speak and laugh at funny stories?' The Imam said, 'It is not an offense if there is not that.' I (the narrator) then thought 'that' was his signal to indecent acts. The Imam then said, 'Arabs would come to the Messenger of Allah and bring him gifts and then say, "Pay us for our gifts." The Messenger of Allah would laugh. When he felt sad he would say, "What happened to the Arab man? I wish he comes by."'"

H 3718, Ch. 23, h 2

A number of our people have narrated from Ahmad ibn Muhammad ibn Khalid from Sharif ibn Sabiq from al-Fadl ibn abu Qarrah from abu 'Abd Allah, *'Alayhi al-Salam*, who has said the following:

"Every believing person knows how to tell funny stories. I asked, 'What is al-Da'abah?' The Imam said, 'It is funny stories.'"

H 3719, Ch. 23, h 3

It is narrated from him (narrator of the Hadith above) from Muhammad ibn Ali from Yahya ibn Sallam from Yusuf ibn Ya'qub from Salih ibn 'Aqabah from Yunus al-Shaybani who has said the following:

"Abu 'Abd Allah, *'Alayhi al-Salam*, has said, 'How is your telling funny stories for each other?' I said, 'It is very little.' The Imam said, 'Do not do so. Telling funny stories is of delightful moral discipline. You can bring joy to your brother (in belief). The Messenger of Allah would tell funny stories to bring cheerfulness feelings to a man.'"

H 3720, Ch. 23, h 4

Salih ibn 'Aqabah has narrated from 'Abd Allah ibn Muhammad al-Ju'fi who has said the following:

"I heard abu Ja'far, *'Alayhi al-Salam*, saying, 'Allah, the Most Majestic, the Most Holy, loves a funny storyteller in a group free of abusive matters.'"

H 3721, Ch. 23, h 5

A number of our people have narrated from Sahl ibn Ziyad from Ali ibn Asbat from al-Hassan ibn Kulayb from abu 'Abd Allah, *'Alayhi al-Salam*, who has said the following:

"The laughing of a believing person is smiling."

H 3722, Ch. 23, h 6

Ali ibn Ibrahim has narrated from his father from ibn abu 'Umayr from Mansur from Hariz from abu 'Abd Allah, *'Alayhi al-Salam*, who has said the following:

"Much laughing deadens the heart. He has also said, 'Much laughing melts one's religion just as water melts salt.'"

H 3723, Ch. 23, h 7

Ali ibn Ibrahim has narrated from his father from al-Nawfali from al-Sakuni from abu 'Abd Allah, *'Alayhi al-Salam*, who has said the following:

"Abu 'Abd Allah, *'Alayhi al-Salam*, has said, 'It is ignorance to laugh without astonishment.' The narrator has said that the Imam would say, 'In laughing do not allow your teeth to become visible, when you have committed disgraceful deeds. One who has committed evil deeds should not feel secure about what kinds of misfortune the night may bring.'"

H 3724, Ch. 23, h 8

Ali ibn Ibrahim has narrated from his father from ibn abu 'Umayr from Hafs ibn al-Bakhtari who has said the following:

"Abu 'Abd Allah, *'Alayhi al-Salam*, has said, 'Beware of jokes; it takes away the dignity of one's face.'"

H 3725, Ch. 23, h 9

It is narrated from him (narrator of the Hadith above) from ibn abu 'Umayr from those whom he has mentioned (in his book) from abu 'Abd Allah, *'Alayhi al-Salam*, who has said the following:

"If you love a person, do not play jokes on him and do not argue with him."

H 3726, Ch. 23, h 10

It is narrated from him (narrator of the Hadith above) from his father from ibn abu 'Umayr from Hammad from al-Halabi from abu 'Abd Allah, *'Alayhi al-Salam*, who has said the following:

"Laughing loud is from Satan."

H 3727, Ch. 23, h 11

Hamid ibn Ziyad has narrated from al-Hassan ibn Muhammad al-Kindi from Ahmad ibn al-Hassan al-Maythami from 'Anbasah al-'Abid who has said the following:

"I heard abu 'Abd Allah, *'Alayhi al-Salam*, saying, 'Much laughing eliminates the dignity of one's face.'"

H 3728, Ch. 23, h 12

A number of our people have narrated from Sahl ibn Ziyad from Ja'far ibn Muhammad al-Ash'ari from ibn al-Qaddah from abu 'Abd Allah, *'Alayhi al-Salam*, who has said the following:

"Amir al-Mu'minin, Ali ibn abu Talib, *'Alayhi al-Salam*, has said, 'Beware of joking; it attracts hatred and hostility and it is a minor form of name-calling.'"

H 3729, Ch. 23, h 13

Muhammad ibn Yahya has narrated from 'Abd Allah ibn Muhammad from Ali ibn al-Hakam from Aban ibn 'Uthman from Khalid ibn Tahman from abu Ja'far, *'Alayhi al-Salam*, who has said the following:

"If you have laughed loudly, say, 'O Lord, please, do not hate me.'"

H 3730, Ch. 23, h 14

Muhammad ibn Yahya has narrated from Ahmad ibn Muhammad ibn 'Isa from al-Hajjal from Dawud ibn Farqad and Ali ibn 'Aqabah and Tha'Labah in a marfu' manner from abu 'Abd Allah, *'Alayhi al-Salam*, and abu Ja'far, *'Alayhi al-Salam*, or one of them who has said the following:

"Much joking eliminates the dignity of one's face and much laughing hurls belief far away."

H 3731, Ch. 23, h 15

Hamid ibn Ziyad has narrated from al-Hassan ibn Muhammad from Ahmad ibn al-Hassan al-Maythami from 'Anbasah al-'Abid who has said that I heard abu 'Abd Allah, *'Alayhi al-Salam*, say the following:

"Joking is a minor form of name-calling."

H 3732, Ch. 23, h 16

A number of our people have narrated from Ahmad ibn Muhammad ibn Khalid from 'Uthman ibn 'Isa from ibn Muskan from Muhammad ibn Marwan from abu 'Abd Allah, *'Alayhi al-Salam*, who has said the following:

"Beware of joking; it eliminates the dignity of one's face and his respect."

H 3733, Ch. 23, h 17

Muhammad ibn Yahya has narrated from Ahmad ibn Muhammad from al-Barqi from abu al-'Abbas from 'Ammar ibn Marwan who has said the following:

"Abu 'Abd Allah, *'Alayhi al-Salam*, has said, 'Do not quarrel; it eliminates your brilliance and do not play jokes; people grow rude and daring against you."

H 3734, Ch. 23, h 18

Ali ibn Ibrahim has narrated from his father from Salih ibn al-Sindi from abu Ja'far ibn Bashir from 'Ammar ibn Marwan from abu 'Abd Allah, *'Alayhi al-Salam*, who has said the following:

"Do not play jokes; rudeness will be used against you."

H 3735, Ch. 23, h 19

A number of our people have narrated from Ahmad ibn Muhammad from ibn Mahbub from Sa'd ibn abu Khalaf from abu al-Hassan, *'Alayhi al-Salam*, who has said the following:

"The Imam said in his will to one of his sons or that he said, 'My father said to one of his sons: "Beware of playing jokes; it eliminates the light of your belief, and decreases your manhood.'"

H 3736, Ch. 23, h 20

It is narrated from him (narrator of the Hadith above) from ibn Faddal from al-Hassan ibn al-Jahm from Ibrahim ibn Mehzam from those whom he has mentioned (in his book) from abu al-Hassan, the first, *'Alayhi al-Salam*, who has said the following:

"Yahya (John) ibn Zakariya would weep and would not laugh. Jesus, son of Mary would laugh and weep. What Jesus did was better than what Yahya would do."

Chapter 24 - Rights of Neighbors

H 3737, Ch. 24, h 1

Ali ibn Ibrahim has narrated from his father from ibn abu 'Umayr and Muhammad ibn Yahya from al-Husayn ibn Ishaq from Ali ibn Mahziyar from Ali ibn Faddal from Fadalah ibn Ayyub all from Mu'awiyah ibn 'Ammar from 'Amr ibn 'Akramah who has said the following:

"Once I went in the presence of abu 'Abd Allah, *'Alayhi al-Salam*, and said to him, 'My neighbor causes me suffering.' The Imam said, 'Be kind to him.' I said, 'I wish Allah will not grant him any kindness.' The Imam turned away from me and I did not like to leave him and I said, 'He does this and that to me and keeps causing me to suffer.' The Imam said, 'Had you come openly against him could you defend your self sufficiently?' I said, 'Yes, I could certainly have the upper hand.' The Imam said, 'This is one of those who envy people for what Allah has granted them through His generosity. If he finds one enjoying bounties, he then turns his anguish against that person's family, and if he did not have family, he turns against his servants, and if he did not have any servant he then remains sleepless for the whole night and spends the day in anguish and anger.

'Once a man from Ansar (people of Madinah) came to the Messenger of Allah and said, "I have purchased a house in the neighborhood of such and such tribe. The nearest neighbor is as such that not only do I not have any hope for receiving any good from him, I do not feel safe from him also." The Imam said that the Messenger of Allah commanded Ali, *'Alayhi al-Salam*, Salman, abu Dharr and, I forgot the other one, I think he mentioned Miqdad, to announce in the Mosque at the top of their voices, "One from whose hands his neighbors are not safe has no belief and faith." They announced it three times. He then pointed out that each forty house in front back, right and left are neighbors.'"

H 3738, Ch. 24, h 2

Muhammad ibn Yahya has narrated from Ahmad ibn Muhammad ibn 'Isa from Muhammad ibn Yahya from Talhah ibn Zayd from abu 'Abd Allah from his father, *'Alayhi al-Salam*, who has said the following:

"I have read in the book of Ali, *'Alayhi al-Salam*, that the Messenger of Allah wrote (and got it signed) for the people of Ansar and Muhajirin and people related to them from Yathrib: 'The neighbor is like one's soul that cannot be harmed or made to sin. The respect for the neighbor is like the respect for one's mother.' This is the Hadith in brief.'"

H 3739, Ch. 24, h 3

A number of our people have narrated from Ahmad ibn Muhammad ibn Khalid from Isma'il ibn Mehran from Ibrahim ibn abu Raja' from abu 'Abd Allah, *'Alayhi al-Salam*, who has said the following:

"Maintaining good neighborly relations increases one's sustenance."

H 3740, Ch. 24, h 4

A number of our people have narrated from Sahl ibn Ziyad from Ali ibn Asbat from h is uncle Ya'qub ibn Salim from Ishaq ibn 'Ammar who has said the following:

"I heard abu 'Abd Allah, *'Alayhi al-Salam*, saying, 'When Benjamin also was taken away from Jacob, he pleaded before Allah for help, saying, "Have mercy on me. You have taken away my eyesight and my son." Allah, the Most Blessed, the Most High, sent him inspiration, "Even if I will cause them to die I will give them life again for you so you will live with them, however, remember the sheep that you slaughtered, you and so and so used it for food and so and so in your neighborhood was fasting but he receive nothing from it.""

H 3741, Ch. 24, h 5
In another Hadith it is said that Jacob thereafter would announce around his home up to a distance of three miles every morning, "Whoever needs food, come to the house of Jacob" and in the evening also would announce, 'Whoever needs dinner come to the house of Jacob.'"

H 3742, Ch. 24, h 6
Ali ibn Ibrahim has narrated from his father from ibn abu 'Umayr from Ishaq ibn 'Ammar ibn 'Abd al-'Aziz from Zurara from abu 'Abd Allah, 'Alayhi al-Salam, who has said the following:

"Once Fatimah, 'Alayha al-Salam, came to the Messenger of Allah and complained about certain matters. The Messenger of Allah gave her a tablet to read. It was written on the tablet: 'Whoever believes in Allah and the Day of Judgment must not cause suffering to his neighbor. Whoever believes in Allah and the Day of Judgment must treat his guest with honor. Whoever believes in Allah and the Day of Judgment must speak of good or remain silent.'"

H 3743, Ch. 24, h 7
A number of our people have narrated from Ahmad ibn Muhammad ibn Khalid ffrom his father from Sa'dan from abu Mas'ud who has said the following:

"Abu 'Abd Allah, 'Alayhi al-Salam, once said to me, 'Maintaining good neighborly relations increases one's life span and the development of the country.'"

H 3744, Ch. 24, h 8
It is narrated from him (narrator of the Hadith above) from al-Nahiki from Ibrahim ibn 'Abd al-Hamid from al-Hakam al-Khayyat who has said the following:

"Abu 'Abd Allah, 'Alayhi al-Salam, has said, 'Maintaining good neighborly relations increases the development of the country and one's life span.'"

H 3745, Ch. 24, h 9
It is narrated from him (narrator of the Hadith above) from certain individuals of his people from Salih ibn Hamza from al-Hassan ibn 'Abd Allah from 'Abd Salih, 'Alayhi al-Salam, who has said the following:

"Not to cause suffering to neighbors is not a good neighborly relation, however, to be a good neighbor and to exercise patience in suffering (caused by the neighbors) is a good neighborly relations."

H 3746, Ch. 24, h 10
Abu Ali al-Ash'ari has narrated from al-Hassan ibn Ali al-Kufi from 'Uthman bays ibn Hisham from Mu'awiyah ibn 'Ammar from abu 'Abd Allah, 'Alayhi al-Salam, who has said the following:

"The Messenger of Allah has said, 'Maintaining good neighborly relations develops the country and extends one's lifespan."

H 3747, Ch. 24, h 11

A number of our people have narrated from Ahmad ibn Muhammad from Muhammad ibn 'Abd Allah from Isma'il ibn Mehran from Muhammad ibn Hafs from abu al-Rabi' al-Shami who has said the following:

"Abu 'Abd Allah, *'Alayhi al-Salam*, once speaking to the people who had filled up his house said, 'You must take notice that those who fail to maintain good relations with their neighbors are not of our people and followers.'"

H 3748, Ch. 24, h 12

It is narrated from him (narrator of the Hadith above) from Muhammad ibn Ali from Muhammad ibn al-Fudayl from abu Hamza who has said the following:

"I heard abu 'Abd Allah, *'Alayhi al-Salam*, saying, 'A believing person is one whose neighbors are safe from his bawa'iq, I then asked, 'What is bawa'iq,' The Imam said, 'His injustice and transgressions.'"

H 3749, Ch. 24, h 13

Abu Ali al-Ash'ari has narrated from Muhammad ibn 'Abd al-Jabbar from Muhammad b n Isma'il from Hanan ibn Sadir from his father from abu Ja'far, *'Alayhi al-Salam*, who has said the following:

"Once a man came to the Holy Prophet and complained against his neighbor. The Messenger of Allah said to him, 'Bear patience.' The man came the second time. The Holy Prophet said, 'Bear patience.' The man came the third time. The Holy Prophet said to him, 'On Friday when people go to the Mosque take your belongings out and place them on the road so that all who go to the Mosque see them. If they asked you tell them your story. He did as he was told to do. His neighbor came and asked him to return his belongings home saying, 'Allah will be against me in your favor if I will not stop doing what I would do before.'"

H 3750, Ch. 24, h 14

It is narrated from him (narrator of the Hadith above) from Muhammad ibn 'Abd al-Jabbar from Muhammad ibn Isma'il from 'Abd Allah ibn 'Uthman from abu al-Hassan al-Bajali from 'Ubayd Allah al-Wasafi from abu Ja'far, *'Alayhi al-Salam*, who has said the following:

"The Messenger of Allah has said, 'One who spends the night with his stomach full while his neighbor is hungry does not believe in me. Any (people of the town) who sleep at night with their stomachs full while among them are hungry people, to such people, on the Day of Judgment, Allah will not look with kindness.'"

H 3751, Ch. 24, h 15

A number of our people have narrated from Ahmad ibn Muhammad from ibn Faddal from abu Jamilah from Sa'd ibn Tarif from abu Ja'far, *'Alayhi al-Salam*, who has said the following:

"Of the back-breaking misfortunes, one is a bad neighbor who hides all good things about his neighbor and publicizes all the bad things about him."

H 3752, Ch. 24, h 16

It is narrated from him (narrator of the Hadith above) from Muhammad ibn Ali from Muhammad ibn al-Fudayl from Ishaq ibn 'Ammar from abu 'Abd Allah, *'Alayhi al-Salam*, who has said the following:

"The Messenger of Allah has said, 'I seek protection with Allah against a bad neighbor of a residence. The neighbor whose eye sees you and whose heart is against you. When he observes a good thing it disappoints him and if he sees a bad thing he becomes happy.'"

Chapter 25 - Boundaries of Neighborhood

H 3753, Ch. 25, h 1

Ali ibn Ibrahim has narrated from his father from ibn abu 'Umayr from Mu'awiyah ibn 'Ammar from 'Amr ibn 'Akramah from abu 'Abd Allah, *'Alayhi al-Salam*, who has said the following:

"The Messenger of Allah has said, 'Every forty houses from the front, back, right and left are neighbors.'"

H 3754, Ch. 25, h 2

It is narrated from him (narrator of the Hadith above) from his father from ibn abu 'Umayr from Jamil ibn Darraj from abu Ja'far, *'Alayhi al-Salam*, who has said the following:

"The limits of a neighborhood are forty houses on all sides, front, back, right and left."

Chapter 26 - Good Companionship and the Rights of a Travel Mate

H 3755, Ch. 26, h 1

Muhammad ibn Yahya has narrated from Ahmad ibn Muhammad from Muhammad ibn Sinan from 'Ammar ibn Marwan who has said the following:

"Once Abu 'Abd Allah, *'Alayhi al-Salam*, advised me, 'You must remain pious before Allah, keep your trust, speak the truth, maintain good companionship relations and there is no power without Allah.'"

H 3756, Ch. 26, h 2

Ali ibn Ibrahim has narrated from his father from Hammad from Hariz from Muhammad ibn Muslim from abu Ja'far who has said the following:

"If in your association with people you can maintain the upper hand (be more beneficial), you should do so."

H 3757, Ch. 26, h 3

Ali ibn Ibrahim has narrated from his father from al-Nawfali from al-Sakuni from abu 'Abd Allah, *'Alayhi al-Salam*, who has said the following:

"The Messenger of Allah has said, 'Of the two companions, the one who is more kind to his companion is more beloved to Allah, the Most Majestic, the Most Holy.'"

H 3758, Ch. 26, h 4

A number of our people have narrated from Ahmad ibn abu 'Abd Allah from Ya'qub ibn Yazid from A number of our people have narrated from abu 'Abd Allah, *'Alayhi al-Salam*, who has said the following:

"The Messenger of Allah has said, 'It is of the rights of a traveler on his companions to look after him for three days if he falls ill.'"

H 3759, Ch. 26, h 5

Ali ibn Ibrahim has narrated from his father from Harun ibn Muslim from Mas'adah ibn Sadaqah from abu 'Abd Allah, *'Alayhi al-Salam*, who has said the following:

"Once, Amir al-Mu'minin, Ali ibn abu Talib, *'Alayhi al-Salam*, accompanied a taxpaying non-Muslim. The taxpaying non-Muslim asked, 'Where you want to go, O servant of Allah?' Amir al-Mu'Minin, *'Alayhi al-Salam*, said, 'I want to go to al-Kufah.' The taxpayer's road changed. Amir al-Mu'Minin, *'Alayhi al-Salam*, kept walking along with him. He asked, 'Did you not say that you wanted to go to al-Kufah? He said, 'Yes, that is true.' The non-Muslim taxpayer said, 'You have missed the road to al-Kufah.' The Imam said, 'Yes, I know that.' The non-Muslim asked, 'Why are you then coming with me when you know the road?' Amir al-Mu'Minin, *'Alayhi al-Salam*, said, 'This is to observe a part of the companionship rights, that is, escorting one gently on their departing each other. This is what our Holy Prophet has instructed us with.' The non-Muslim asked, 'Has he said that?' The Imam said, 'Yes, that is what he has said.' The non-Muslim said, 'It is true that whoever followed him did so because of his noble deeds. I testify that I have accepted your religion. The non-Muslim came back along with Amir al-Mu'Minin, *'Alayhi al-Salam*, and when he recognized him, he became a Muslim.'"

Chapter 27 - Correspondence

H 3760, Ch. 27, h 1
A number of our people have narrated from Ahmad ibn Muhammad from Sahl ibn Ziyad all from ibn Mahbub from those whom he has mentioned (in his book) from abu 'Abd Allah, *'Alayhi al-Salam*, who has said the following:

"To maintain contact with friends in the town is by visiting, on a journey and out of town by correspondence."

H 3761, Ch. 27, h 2
Ibn Mahbub has narrated from 'Abd Allah ibn Sinan from abu 'Abd Allah, *'Alayhi al-Salam*, who has said the following:

"It is necessary to reply a letter just as it is necessary to answer a greeting of peace. The initiator of a greeting of peace is closer to Allah and His messenger."

Chapter 28 - The Rare Ahadith

H 3762, Ch. 28, h 1
Muhammad ibn Yahya has narrated from Ahmad ibn Muhammad from al-Washsha' from Jamil ibn Darraj from abu 'Abd Allah, *'Alayhi al-Salam*, who has said the following:

"The Messenger of Allah would look to every one of his companions in equal proportions of time. He would look to this and then to that person. The Messenger of Allah was never seen stretching his legs in a gathering of his companions. When he would shake hands, with a person, the Messenger of Allah would not pull back his hand before the other man. When they noticed it thereafter a man shaking hands with him would pull his hand away quickly."

H 3763, Ch. 28, h 2
Muhammad ibn Yahya has narrated from Ahmad ibn Muhammad from Mu'ammar ibn Khallad from abu al-Hassan, *'Alayhi al-Salam*, who has said the following:

"When a man is present, call him by his Kunyah (father of so and so) and in his absence call him by his name."

H 3764, Ch. 28, h 3

Ali ibn Ibrahim has narrated from his father from al-Nawfali from al-Sakuni from abu 'Abd Allah, *'Alayhi al-Salam*, who has said the following:

"The Messenger of Allah has said, 'Whoever loves his Muslim brother should ask what his name, the name of his father, his tribe and family is. It is of necessary rights and truthful brotherhood (friendship) to ask such questions; otherwise, it is a foolish recognition.'"

H 3765, Ch. 28, h 4

A number of our people have narrated from Ahmad ibn Muhammad ibn Khalid from Ya'qub ibn Yazid from Ali ibn Ja'far from 'Abd al-Malik ibn Qudamah from his father from Ali ibn al-Husayn, *'Alayhi al-Salam*, who has said the following:

"The Messenger of Allah one day said to the people in his meeting, 'Do you know what is (of one's) weakness?' They said, 'Allah and the Messenger of Allah know better.' He then said, 'There are three kinds of weaknesses: First, a friend prepares food for another friend but fails to keep his promise and does not come for food. Second, one of you meets a man and wants to know who he is but fails to acquire such information and he departs the man. Third, is about women, one becomes close to his wife and depletes his energy before she is satisfied.' 'Abd Allah ibn 'Amr al-'As asked, 'What should he do, O the Messenger of Allah?' He said, 'He should hold back until it comes from both of them in concert.'"

"In another Hadith it is said that the Messenger of Allah has said, 'The weakest of all is one who meets a man and is attracted to him but does not ask his name, his relationships or where he lives.'"

H 3766, Ch. 28, h 5

It is narrated from him (narrator of the Hadith above) from 'Uthman ibn 'Isa from Sama'a who has said the following:

"I heard abu al-Hassan Musa saying, 'Keep your decorum intact between yourself and your brother (friend) and preserve it; removal is the elimination of bashfulness.'"

H 3767, Ch. 28, h 6

Muhammad ibn Yahya has narrated from Ahmad ibn Muhammad from Ali ibn Isma'il from 'Abd Allah ibn Wasil from 'Abd Allah ibn Sinan who has said the following:

"Abu 'Abd Allah, *'Alayhi al-Salam*, has said, 'Do not trust your brother (friend) in totality; a sudden fall of attachment is never repairable.'"

H 3768, Ch. 28, h 7

Muhammad ibn Yahya has narrated from Ahmad ibn Muhammad from 'Umar ibn 'Abd al-'Aziz from Mu'Alla ibn Khanis and 'Uthman ibn Sulayman al-Nakhkhas from Mufaddal ibn 'Umar and Yunus ibn Zabyan who have said the following:

"Abu 'Abd Allah, *'Alayhi al-Salam*, has said, 'Try your brothers (friends) in two things that if not found then keep away from them, keep away, keep away from them. The two qualities are the preservation of their prayers on time and kindness to their brethren in good and bad times.'"

Chapter 29

H 3769, Ch. 29, h 1

Allah Ahmad ibn Muhammad from 'Umar ibn 'Abd al-'Aziz from Jamil ibn Darraj who has said the following:

"Abu 'Abd Allah, *'Alayhi al-Salam*, has said, 'Do not ignore the expression, "(I begin) in the name of Allah, the Beneficent, the Merciful," even if it is followed by a poem.'"

H 3770, Ch. 29, h 2

A number of our people have narrated from Ahmad ibn Muhammad ibn Khalid from Muhammad ibn Ali from al-Hassan ibn Ali from Yusuf ibn 'Abd al-Salam from Sayf ibn Harun Mawla Ale (family) Ju'dah who has said the following:

"Abu 'Abd Allah, *'Alayhi al-Salam*, has said, 'Write "(I begin) in the name of Allah, the Beneficent, the Merciful," with the best of your handwriting. Do not extend the letter 'B' more than the letter 'S'.'"

[Note: this may apply to kufi handwriting only].

H 3771, Ch. 29, h 3

It is narrated from him (narrator of the Hadith above) from Ali ibn al-Hakam from al-Hassan ibn al-Sari from abu 'Abd Allah, *'Alayhi al-Salam*, who has said the following:

"Do not write, '(I begin) in the name of Allah, the Beneficent, the Merciful,' 'for so and so' (in a letter), but it is not an offense to write at the back of the letter, 'for so and so'.'"

H 3772, Ch. 29, h 4

It is narrated from him (narrator of the Hadith above) from Muhammad ibn Ali from al-Nadr ibn Shu'ayb from Aban ibn 'Uthman from al-Hassan ibn al-Sari from abu 'Abd Allah, *'Alayhi al-Salam*, who has said the following:

"Do not write in the letter: 'For abu so and so' but write 'To abu so and so'. In the address area one should write, 'For abu so and so'."

H 3773, Ch. 29, h 5

It is narrated from him (narrator of the Hadith above) from 'Uthman ibn 'Isa from Sama'a who has said the following:

"Once I asked abu 'Abd Allah, *'Alayhi al-Salam*, about a man who initiates writing to another man. The Imam said, 'It is not an offense. It is an excellent act when a man initiates honoring his brother (in belief).'"

H 3774, Ch. 29, h 6

It is narrated from him (narrator of the Hadith above) from Ali ibn al-Hakam from Aban ibn al-Ahmar from Hadid ibn Hakim from abu 'Abd Allah, *'Alayhi al-Salam*, who has said the following:

"It is not an offense for a man to begin with the name of his friend in a letter instead of his own name."

H 3775, Ch. 29, h 7

Ali ibn Ibrahim has narrated from his father from ibn abu 'Umayr from Murazim ibn Hakim who has said the following:

"Abu 'Abd Allah, *'Alayhi al-Salam*, ordered to write a letter about an issue. The letter was written and was shown to him and there was no exception in it. The

Imam said, 'How can you expect that this may be completed without exception (that is, if Allah so wills)? Look into it and write down exceptions whenever needed.'"

H 3776, Ch. 29, h 8
It is narrated from him (narrator of the Hadith above) from Ahmad ibn Muhammad ibn abu Nasr who has said the following:

"Abu al-Hassan al-Rida, *'Alayhi al-Salam*, would dry up the ink on a newlywritten letter by means of placing soil on it and would say that doing so is not an offense."

H 3777, Ch. 29, h 9
Ali ibn Ibrahim has narrated from his father from ibn abu 'Umayr from Ali ibn 'Atiyyah who has said the following:

"He had seen a soiled letter of abu al-Hassan al-Rida, *'Alayhi al-Salam*."

Chapter 30 - Prohibition of Burning Papers with Writings on Them

H 3778, Ch. 30, h 1
Muhammad ibn Yahya has narrated from Ahmad ibn Muhammad from Ali ibn al-Hakam from 'Abd al-Malik ibn 'Utbah who has said the following:

"Once I asked abu al-Hassan, *'Alayhi al-Salam*, about the papers that accumulate if they can be burned in which names of Allah may also be found. The Imam said, 'No, they must not be burned instead, first they should be washed with water.'"

H 3779, Ch. 30, h 2
It is narrated from him (narrator of the Hadith above) from al-Washsha'from 'Abd Allah ibn Sinan who has said the following:

"I heard abu 'Abd Allah, *'Alayhi al-Salam*, saying, 'Do not burn the papers, but wipe or wash them away and then you may burn them.'"

H 3780, Ch. 30, h 3
Ali ibn Ibrahim has narrated from his father from ibn abu 'Umayr from Hammad ibn 'Uthman from Zurara who has said the following:

"Once abu 'Abd Allah, *'Alayhi al-Salam*, was asked about a name of the names of Allah that a man tries to delete with his saliva. The Imam said, 'It should be deleted with the cleanest thing that you can find.'"

H 3781, Ch. 30, h 4
Ali has narrated from his father from al-Nawfali from al-Sakuni from abu 'Abd Allah, *'Alayhi al-Salam*, who has said the following:

"The Messenger of Allah has said, 'You may delete (writing of) the book of Allah, the Most High and words mentioning Him with the cleanest thing that you can find.' He prohibited the burning of the book of Allah and to delete it with a pen.'"

H 3782, Ch. 30, h 5
Ali has narrated from his father from ibn abu 'Umayr from Muhammad ibn Ishaq ibn 'Ammar from abu al-Hassan Musa, *'Alayhi al-Salam*, who has said the following:

"The Imam, *'Alayhi al-Salam*, was asked about the surfaces on which a mention of Allah, the Most Majestic, the Most Holy, is written. The Imam said, 'Wash it clean.'"

This is the end of the Book of Social Manners. All praise belongs to Allah and all favors. Allah has granted favors upon Muhammad and the Ale (family) of Muhammad, the clean and pure ones.

www.ingramcontent.com/pod-product-compliance
Lightning Source LLC
Chambersburg PA
CBHW062353090426
42740CB00010B/1264